D1360951

CRIMINOLOGY

SECOND EDITION

CRIMINOLOGY

SECOND EDITION

PIERS BEIRNE
University of Southern Maine

JAMES MESSERSCHMIDT
University of Southern Maine

HARCOURT BRACE COLLEGE PUBLISHERS

Fort Worth   Philadelphia   San Diego   New York   Orlando   Austin   San Antonio
Toronto   Montreal   London   Sydney   Tokyo

Vice President, Publisher	TED BUCHHOLZ
Executive Editor	CHRISTOPHER P. KLEIN
Assistant Editor	LINDA WILEY
Project Editor	ELIZABETH C. ALVAREZ
Production Manager	DEBRA JENKIN
Art Director	BURL SLOAN
Cover Inset Image	© REED KAESTNER/ZEPHYR PICTURES

ISBN: 0-15-501926-0

Library of Congress Catalog Card Number: 94-77147

Address for Editorial Correspondence: Harcourt Brace College Publishers, 301 Commerce Street, Suite 3700, Fort Worth, TX 76102.

Address for Orders: Harcourt Brace & Company, 6277 Sea Harbor Drive, Orlando, FL 32887-6777. 1-800-782-4479, or 1-800-433-0001 (in Florida).

Printed in the United States of America

4   5   6   7   8   9   0   1   2   3   090   10   9   8   7   6   5   4   3   2   1

For Erik, Jan, Simon, and Ulla

PREFACE TO THE SECOND EDITION

Never did we expect that the demand for *Criminology* would justify a second edition so soon after publication of the first! In this new edition, we have tinkered with the original organization of chapters so that the structure of the book has an added coherence and a tighter feel to it. Where necessary, we have revised certain sections of the book, in some cases adding material, in others, subtracting. New and up-to-date empirical data are presented throughout the book, and we discuss types of crime not previously addressed, including hate crimes, homosexual partner battering, crimes against animals, and collective embezzlement.

The aim of *Criminology* is to introduce the basic aspects of modern criminology to undergraduate students. This is no easy task in such a diverse discipline as criminology. All textbook authors have to make a number of hard choices. This book very much reflects our teaching experience in the undergraduate criminology program at the University of Southern Maine, where our course in criminology both surveys the major areas of the discipline and also provides an introduction to more specialized, upper-level courses in criminology. We have attempted to strike a balance between depth of analysis and breadth of coverage and to make the book comprehensive in its coverage of the sociological aspects of criminology. While we aim to survey all the major aspects of the field, we especially emphasize the importance of historical, feminist, and comparative perspectives on crime.

This book is divided into three parts. **Part One (Chapters 1–3)** focuses on two surprisingly difficult questions: What is crime? How can we measure crime? Chapter 1 outlines the two major ways in which popular discourse about crime is articulated—through the mass media and through the pronouncements of the moral entrepreneurs of social problems—and it summarizes the key elements of crime as a legal category. The chapter stresses the importance of sociological definitions of crime and introduces the three key sociological concepts of criminology: crime, criminal law, and criminalization. Chapter 2 outlines the major sources of crime data. These include both official crime data (the F.B.I.'s *Uniform Crime Reports*, the *National Crime Victimization Survey*, and records of various federal agencies) and unofficial crime data (self-report studies, participant observation, biographies, and comparative and historical data). We stress here that crime data can never represent criminal behavior objectively, because there are inherent biases in the way that all data are conceived and constructed. Data do not speak for themselves! How crime data are explained, therefore, depends both on criminologists' concepts of crime and on the assumptions underlying their theories of crime. The importance of this point will become clear as the contents of the book unfold. In Chapter 3, we offer a critical sociological perspective on the relationship between crime and structured social inequality. We examine the influence on patterns of crime and victimization in the United States of four major forms of social inequality: class, gender, race, and age.

Part Two (Chapters 4–9) provides an introduction to various types of crime. Typologies of crime can be constructed in an infinite variety of ways. We have chosen a sociological typology that combines (1) those crimes usually defined in the legal codes and (2) those outside the criminal law that have received much attention in the sociological literature. Because crime is found in every social institution, the chapters in Part Two offer a comprehensive understanding of the nature, extent, types, and costs of crime not only in the street, but also in the family, the workplace, and the state. In these chapters, we rely heavily on research done in the United States, but we also include material from other countries, such as Canada and Britain.

Part Three (Chapters 10–16) is a systematic guide to modern criminological theory. Theories about crime can be violently misunderstood by wrenching them from the context of the era in which they were conceived; the seven chapters in Part Three, therefore, unfold chronologically, with respect both to the contents of each chapter and to the position of each chapter in relation to the other six. We believe that all theories, including those popular today, should at first be understood historically. One virtue of this belief is the humbling discovery that our understanding of crime has advanced only very little beyond that of theorists of a century ago, such as Émile Durkheim, Adolphe Quetelet, and Karl Marx. In describing each theory, we try to show why it arose when it did, what theories it modified or supplanted, how it was understood and criticized by its competitors, and how it contributes to our understanding of crime today.

Finally, in Chapter 16 we try to show how the understanding of crime in the United States can be significantly enhanced by extending our examination to crime in other societies. We outline the key concepts and sources of data in comparative criminology and assess the merits of various cross-national generalizations about crime and crime rates.

No textbook in the social sciences has the license to assume that its contents are objective. Textbooks differ in their descriptions of theories and in the importance, or lack thereof, that they attribute to them. Textbook authors must decide which theories should be included and which ignored. This textbook suffers from similar biases, so you should be aware of our rough perception of them. The contents of Chapters 10–16 were chosen only after we wrestled with two key questions. Is a given theory a fossilized museum-piece with little theoretical relevance to our understanding of crime and criminology today? If so, it will not be found here. Does the theory contribute to the development of sociological criminology? If it does, we have tried to include it here.

We have avoided the conventional division in criminology textbooks between "crime" and "corrections" by altogether omitting the usual lengthy descriptions of the criminal justice system. Our focus in this book is not criminal justice but crime, and we have tried to discuss the complexity of the latter in the depth we believe it warrants. Accordingly, various aspects of social control (criminalization, labeling, police practices, comparative penal policies, and so on) naturally press their claims for attention, and we explore them here especially when they affect the links between crime and structured social inequality.

Chapter Previews and Chapter Reviews

Each chapter begins with a **chapter preview** of the main themes that follow. Included in the preview is a list of **key terms** that you should be especially aware of as you read through the chapter. These terms are highlighted in the text and then immediately followed by a definition to help you understand them more easily. At the end of each chapter, a **chapter review** outlines the major points that have been discussed.

Questions for Class Discussion and Recommended Readings

Each chapter review is followed by several **questions for classroom discussion**. These are followed by an annotated list of **recommended readings** that will be helpful for essays or term papers.

References and Glossary

After the main text, there is a comprehensive, alphabetical list of **references** cited in the book. In the body of the text, you will find the references cited in the following way: (Smith, 1989:21). This example begins with the last name of the author ("Smith"), then gives the year the material was published or written ("1989"), and ends with the page number of the citation ("21"). We also make extensive use of "*ibid.*" when we refer to the same work cited in the immediately preceding citation. In the **glossary** students will find brief definitions of all of the key terms used in the book.

A Note on Chauvinist Language

In writing this textbook, we have been especially sensitive to chauvinist language, which creates the impression that one particular group—gender, race, country, species, and so on—is superior to another. For example, we do not use "he," "his," or "him" when referring to people in general, because these terms effectively exclude women. Similarly, we do not refer to the United States as "America," because the latter term should properly be reserved to signify the entire Western hemisphere—North, Central, and South America.

Acknowledgments

A book such as this inevitably incurs many debts. First and foremost, we thank our students, many of whom forced us to clarify our ideas and who provided us with critical (at times, very critical!) comments during our classroom presentations of the material in the book. We especially want to thank Michele I. Hartford, Kathleen Shibles, and Debbie Beal.

Several of our colleagues at the University of Southern Maine have been generous with their time, but we are especially indebted to Barbara Perry. Thanks, too, to Jill Kendall and Rosy Miller, without whose help, in a great variety of ways, this book would never have been completed so smoothly. The University of Southern Maine's College of Arts and Sciences has also been very generous with the two indispensable commodities of time and financial assistance.

Many colleagues and friends at other institutions were kind enough to read portions of the manuscript. Their comments have undoubtedly turned it into a far better book than it otherwise would have been. In this regard, we are indebted to Tom Bernard (Pennsylvania State University), Alan Block (Pennsylvania State University), Bill Chambliss (George Washington University), Meda Chesney-Lind (University of Hawaii, Manoa), Albert Cohen (University of Connecticut), Nanette Davis (Portland State University), Travis E. Eaton (Northeast Louisiana State University), Colin Goff (University of Winnipeg), Casey Groves (University of Wisconsin, Green Bay), Stuart Henry (Eastern Michigan University), Eileen Leonard (Vassar College), Dale M. Lindekugel (Eastern Washington University), Eleanor Miller (University of Wisconsin, Milwaukee), Patricia Murphy (SUNY Geneseo), John C. Quicker (California State University-Dominguez Hills), Donald J. Shoemaker (Virginia Polytechnic Institute and State University), and Steve Spitzer (Suffolk University). Needless to say, we blame them entirely for any errors in this book! For additional help with certain aspects of the book, we wish to acknowledge the generosity of Stephan Bunker (Maine Uniform Crime Reporting Program), Jean-Ri Cojuc (University of Southern Maine), Paul Cromwell (University of Texas of the Permian Basin), Drew Humphries (Rutgers University), Ciaran McCullagh (University College, Cork), and Paul Knepper (Northern Kentucky University).

This book could not have been written without the constant support of the staff of the Interlibrary Loan Services at U.S.M.'s Luther Bonney Library; James Brady, Cassandra Fitzherbert, and Kathryn Gatchall have our heartfelt thanks for their unfailing understanding and good humor. We were also always made to feel welcome by the staff of the Hawthorne-Longfellow Library at Bowdoin College.

Finally, for their great enthusiasm and their sensitivity, we wish to thank the staff at Harcourt Brace, especially Chris Klein, Linda Wiley, Beth Alvarez, Jeff Beckham, Burl Sloan, and Debra Jenkin.

BRIEF TABLE OF CONTENTS

TABLE OF CONTENTS

PART ONE

INTRODUCTION

CHAPTER 1

WHAT IS CRIME?

Preview

Chapter 1 introduces:

☞ the distorted images of crime projected by the mass media.
☞ the difference between viewing crime as a social problem and understanding it as a sociological problem.
☞ the legalistic definition of crime.
☞ various sociological definitions of crime, including crime as a violation of conduct norms, crime as social harm or analogous social injury, crime as a violation of human rights, and crime as a form of deviance.
☞ three of the key concepts of criminology: "crime," "criminal law," and "criminalization."

Key Terms

analogous social injury	deviance
conduct norm	human rights
crime	social problem
criminalization	sociological problem
criminal justice system	the state
criminal law	

1.1 ——————   IMAGES OF CRIME

The focus of this book is crime. What is crime? How much crime is there? How can we explain it? Even before reading this book, you probably have a variety of opinions about the causes of crime, its harmful effects, and how best to control it. Crime is a topic about which all of us tend to hold very strong opinions. But you will learn here that crime is a very difficult phenomenon to explain. Nowhere in this book will you be offered any neat and tidy answers. There are none!

Whatever the depth of your opinions about crime, you live in an era that views it as one of the leading social problems facing society today. Many members of society have become genuinely fearful of crime. On TV, in everyday conversation, and in our worst nightmares, our fears are constantly fueled by images of crime, especially violent crime.

Crime as a Social Problem

Twenty-five years ago the National Commission on the Causes and Prevention of Violence made the following bleak predictions about the quality of life in large cities in the near future (1970:38–39):

> High-rise apartment buildings and residential compounds protected by private guards and security devices will be fortified cells for upper-middle and high-income populations living at prime locations in the city.
>
> Suburban neighborhoods, geographically far removed from the central city, will be protected mainly by economic homogeneity and by distance from population groups with the highest propensities to commit crimes.
>
> Lacking a sharp change in federal and state policies, ownership of guns will be almost universal in the suburbs, homes will be fortified by an array of devices from window grills to electronic surveillance equipment, armed citizen volunteers in cars will supplement inadequate police patrols in neighborhoods closer to the central city, and extreme left-wing and right-wing groups will have tremendous armories of weapons that could be brought into play without any provocation.
>
> High-speed, patrolled expressways will be sanitized corridors connecting safe areas, and private automobiles, taxicabs, and commercial vehicles will be equipped routinely with unbreakable glass, light armor, and other security features. Inside garages or valet parking will be available at safe buildings in or near the central city. Armed guards will "ride shotgun" on all forms of public transportation.
>
> Streets and residential neighborhoods in the central city will be unsafe in differing degrees, and the ghetto slum neighborhoods will be places of terror with widespread crime, perhaps entirely out of police control during nighttime hours. Armed guards will protect all public facilities such as schools, libraries, and playgrounds in these areas.

In 1970 the National Commission on the Causes and Prevention of Violence predicted that before very long most private homes in the United States would be protected by an array of security devices. Current trends support the prediction.

> Between the unsafe, deteriorating central city on the one hand and the network of safe, prosperous areas and sanitized corridors on the other, there will be, not unnaturally, intensifying hatred and deepening division. Violence will increase further, and the defensive response of the affluent will become still more elaborate.

Because of our great fear of crime the Commission warned that we are in danger of closeting ourselves in anti-crime fortresses. To a certain extent the Commission's terrifying images of life in large U.S. cities have not been contradicted, at least not in the minds of the public or, as we will soon see, in the messages conveyed by the media.

To many of us it seems that we live in a society whose obsession with crime reaches into almost every corner of our public and private lives. Presidential candidates campaign on the promise of restoring "law and order" to the nation's streets. Presidential elections are sometimes decided in favor of the candidate with a "hard-line" approach to the detection and punishment of criminals. But there is a widespread feeling that crime and violence are rapidly spinning out of control, and are quite unaffected by police intervention. Neighborhood Crime Watch programs and vigilante groups like the Guardian Angels have surfaced across the country. Opinion polls show that the public believes crime is one of the most important problems facing this country today (such as Gallup, 1993:57), and that the greatest problem facing the nation's public schools is not an absence of academic excellence but a lack of student discipline. Research consistently shows that the relatively powerless sections of the community—such as the elderly, females, and blacks—experience the greatest fear of crime and suffer the greatest psychological trauma from its effects (such as Ortega and Myles, 1987; Lagrange and Ferraro, 1989; Smith and Hill, 1991; and see Chapter 4.2).

Moreover, it is almost certainly true that the rate of violent crime in the U.S. is now higher than that of any other technologically developed nation in the world (see Chapter 16). According to journalist Jane Gross (1989:A1):

> In the roughest neighborhoods of cities besieged by the drug trade, where buildings are pocked with bullet holes and the streets ring with gunfire, hospitals have become urban MASH units, with paramedics and doctors treating wounds once seen only on the battlefield.

Physicians across the country, including Dr. Garen Wintemute (a University of California professor and a former medical director of a refugee camp in Cambodia), have described the increasing prevalence in the United States of exploded organs and pulverized bones, the flood of internal bleeding and bodies riddled from high-velocity, rapid-fire assault rifles like the AK-47 (*ibid.*).

It is no exaggeration that since the early 1960s crime has become one of the leading social problems in the United States today. But what are "social problems"? How are they defined as social problems, by whom, and for what reasons?

We must stress that there is no *objective* set of social conditions whose harmful effects necessarily make them social problems. As Herbert Blumer writes, a social problem must be understood "primarily in terms of how it is defined and conceived in society" (1971:300). What is regarded as a social problem thus varies over time—child abuse, for example, has only quite recently been seen as a full-blown problem (see Chapter 4.2). Whether something is regarded as a social problem also varies with the person or group looking at it. For example, some people regard social inequality as a social problem; others see it as a virtue that encourages competition and economic responsibility. Some regard the use of animals in laboratory experiments as a necessary step in the elimination of disease among humans; others see this as unjustified abuse.

Whether any given circumstances are defined as a social problem depends on the activities of numerous "moral entrepreneurs," including the pressure tactics of private interest groups (for instance, the American Medical Association [AMA], trade unions, Mothers Against Drunk Driving [MADD], and so on) and the professional utterances of public officials (such as politicians, judges, and police and correctional officers). Nowadays, the ability to convey concern to the public about some problem occurs largely through the mass media (TV in particular, but also newspapers, advertising, movies, videos, and so on). The mass media is the most influential mechanism for creating public agreement that a certain social condition is a social problem. Observe some of its images of crime.

The mass media routinely produce stereotypical images of crime for popular consumption, such as this scene from the television series "NYPD Blue."

Crime in the Mass Media

Each of us already possesses a considerable stock of information about crime. We know, for example, that some areas of cities are safer than others. We know that it is dangerous to leave infants unattended, front doors unbolted, cars unlocked, bicycles unchained. We routinely process such knowledge, and we take defensive action accordingly.

We know, or at least we think we know, what sorts of people are likely to commit a crime. Each of us has an image of the "typical" criminal—a sick, degenerate, violent person who preys on human decency and society. But crime is an extraordinarily difficult phenomenon to explain given that our obsession with it is seldom based on rational reflection. Far from it. In modern societies like the United States, everyday images of crime tend to be filtered through the self-interested, and often unfocused, lenses of the mass media.

Reflect for a moment on some of the typical images of crime routinely conveyed to us by the mass media. The media feature two predominant images of crime: *the amount of crime* and *the most common types of crime*.

Crime consumes an enormous chunk of dramatic and informational space in the media. According to media researcher Doris Graber (1980:26), 33 percent of the total TV program time in the United States is devoted to crime or law-enforcement shows, with a concentration at prime-time viewing. Among the most popular prime-time crime TV shows in the 1990s are "NYPD Blue," "In the Heat of the Night," "Law and Order," "Civil Wars," "The Commish,"

"Picket Fences," and "Missing Persons." Many topical TV shows (such as "L.A. Law") also regularly concern crime, as do such documentaries as "Unsolved Mysteries," "Face to Face with Connie Chung," "48 Hours," "60 Minutes," and "20/20." New "reality-based" shows—some featuring talk-show interaction among police officers or even audience participation—include "Cops," "Rescue 911," "Stories of the Highway Patrol," and "America's Most Wanted." In addition to the content of TV shows, our images of the amount of crime are also conveniently prepackaged for us by TV news and by newspapers. A high percentage of stories in the evening and late-night local news programs concerns crime, as do their lead items. Indeed, it has been found that crime and justice topics occupy 20 percent of local television offerings, 13 percent of national television news content, and 25 percent of all newspaper news space (Ericson, Baranek, and Chan, 1987:45; Surette, 1992: 62–64).

It is important to recognize that the media are preoccupied with *violent* crime rather than other forms of crime. Nearly all the prime-time crime shows mentioned previously, for example, exclusively address violent crime. According to a violence index used by researcher George Gerbner for the years 1967 to 1987, approximately 80 percent of all TV programs contained violence (Liebert and Sprafkin, 1988:116–119). In addition, at least 90 percent of children's cartoon shows contain violence (*ibid.*). Although the definition of violence in Gerbner's index may seem overly broad to some (it includes violence in humorous situations, for example), the fact remains that violence—however defined—is the staple of the crime-related TV diet. In the news, as well, there is a strong bias toward coverage of murder, sexual crimes, and other forms of violence, often coupled with drug abuse (Sheley and Ashkins, 1981; Humphries, 1981; Ericson *et al.*, 1987:45; Ericson *et al.*, 1989).

Moreover, the mass media episodically channel viewer attention toward particular sorts of immoral or criminal behavior (Jenkins, 1988; and see Barak, 1988). Examples of "moral panics" aided by the media include the white slavers of the Progressive Era, "sex-fiends" in the 1940s, communists in the 1950s, serial murderers during the 1980s (see Chapter 2.1), and the everpresent "druggie." As Philip Jenkins (1988:1) warns:

> If we relied solely on the evidence of the mass media, we might well believe that every few years, a particular form of immoral or criminal behavior becomes so dangerous as almost to threaten the foundations of society. . . . These panics are important in their own right for what they reveal about social concerns and prejudices—often based on xenophobia and anti-immigrant prejudice.

At this point, let us comment briefly on the typical images of crime conveyed by the mass media:

First, the enormous volume of crime-related items in the media wrongly creates the image of a society with an enormous amount of violent crime. For the moment we must leave entirely open the question of "how much" crime there is in the United States, yet it must be stressed that the volume of crime in the media (in

TV shows and news items) bears scant relation to what is reported in official crime data, such as the FBI's *Uniform Crime Reports* (see Chapter 2.1). Graber (1980:39) found in *The Chicago Tribune*, for example, that although murder constitutes only 0.2 percent of all crimes recorded by the police, it comprises 26.2 percent of all newspaper entries about crime.

Second, the media have created the misleading impression that crime rates consistently increased during the last decade. From the 1940s to the present, the percentage of total TV program time devoted to crime-related shows has persistently increased; thus, the prime-time seasons between 1984 and 1988 had the most new or continuing crime- and justice-related shows in television history (Kania and Tanham, 1987:8). However, according to official crime data, the violent crime rate *fell* sharply in the 1980s (Bureau of Justice Statistics, 1989:13; and see Chapter 2.1).

Third, the media distort the incidence of nonviolent crime. Thus, whereas nonviolent crimes like theft comprise 47 percent of all crimes reported to the police, such crimes constitute only 4 percent of all crime items in newspapers (Graber, *ibid.*; and see Chapter 2.1).

We should not be too surprised that the mass media's images of crime are almost never objective. After all, the mass media depend for their existence on reporting—or creating—the apparently unusual. When social life is routine and orderly, there is little news. Media executives know full well that nothing sells like violence. To maximize its audience, the media feature unusual events rather than representative events; it emphasizes the sensational rather than the mundane. As criminologist Jock Young (1971:35) concludes about the powerful effect the mass media have on perpetuating stereotypes of criminals:

> The type of information which the mass media portray is that which is "newsworthy." They select events which are *atypical*, present them in a *stereotypical* fashion and contrast them against a backcloth of normality which is *overtypical*.

The media thus provide various distorted, prepackaged images of crime. Such images do not, of course, allow us to learn much about the true nature of crime. To accomplish this we must obtain a clearer idea of what crime actually is. In other words, we need a working definition of "crime."

1.2 ———— DEFINITIONS OF CRIME

The question "What is crime?" is a surprisingly difficult one to answer. Consider, for example, the events discussed in Robert Ritchie's (1986) book *Captain Kidd and the War Against the Pirates.*

During the 1690s the soon-to-be infamous Captain William Kidd had operated in the Caribbean as a rather obscure Scottish pirate from New York City. In 1695 he obtained a commission as a privateer, which allowed him to engage essentially in the same piratical activities, but this time with the economic support and moral blessings of the King and of some of the most powerful families in England. The purpose of Kidd's commission was to sail to the Indian Ocean and put an end to the practices of pirates from the North American colonies who were plundering British East India Company ships. For attacking and capturing one or more pirate ships, and bringing some pirates to trial, a handsome profit would be earned by all the backers of the scheme, including Kidd and the King himself. However, for doing roughly what he was commissioned to do, Kidd did not earn the fame and fortune to which he believed he was legally entitled. In 1701, in London, Kidd was tried on charges of murder and multiple conspiracies, convicted after a farcical trial, sentenced to death by hanging, and—after a false start when the hangman's rope broke and the unfortunate Kidd lay stunned on the ground—he was duly executed. During his trial and during his execution—a dramatic time when convicts were expected to repent their sins, beg the indulgence of the Lord, and warn the many onlookers not to tread in their sinful footsteps—Kidd continually protested his innocence.

Why Kidd the pirate believed that he was innocent of murder and piracy is a matter of great interest. William Kidd had been caught in the complicated and rapidly changing web of maritime trade and British imperialism of the late 17th century. Although there was little evidence that he had engaged in (illegal) piracy rather than (legal) privateering—and therefore no proper reason existed for British authorities to prosecute him—Kidd's activities in the Red Sea (against the French and against the Dutch East India Company) ensnared him "in a larger movement that would find him a convenient symbol for a much broader problem" (*ibid.*:128). Even though Kidd was never very successful either as a pirate or as a privateer, the problem in which he found himself the unwitting victim is easy to grasp: he was squeezed by the coincidence of two forces. On the one hand were the thriving British companies, such as the East India Company, that needed order and regularity on the high seas for the profitable expansion of their commerce. On the other hand were the administrative and military apparatuses of the British state that, after tremendous expansion as a result of various European wars, could not tolerate maverick and unpredictable challenges to their power. Privateering, or legalized piracy, was therefore doomed. Kidd's activities as a privateer commissioned by royalty and by the rich were suddenly transformed in meaning and re-termed "piracy."

This story offers a good example of how difficult it is to pinpoint the precise nature of crime. Clearly, Kidd's actions were defined as piracy rather than national heroics largely because of the changing fortunes of British imperialism. It is also clear that there was nothing in the nature of Kidd's actions that was inherently criminal. What, then, is crime?

As a historical phenomenon, the concept of crime is of fairly recent origin. Prior to the 18th century, both in western Europe (Spector, 1981) and in colonial North America (Chapin, 1983), for example, most offenses typically were—when not handled privately—the province either of canon law (religious law) or of civil law (especially the law of torts). Moreover, what constitutes crime varies from one culture to another. Indeed, anthropologists have been unable

Captain Kidd—pirate or victim?

to find any behavior that is universally defined as crime (see Chapter 16.3). Although all known societies have a concept of murder, for example, few societies define the act of murder in exactly the same way. Given such variation, it follows that it is nearly impossible for criminologists to agree on a precise definition of crime, or even an act seemingly as simple to define as murder. Many sociologists and historians suggest that because even what counts as crime changes over time within the same culture, there is nothing in the nature of any behavior that makes it inherently criminal (see Chapter 14.3). How, then, should crime be defined?

Serious debate among criminologists about the proper definition of crime can be traced to the publication of a report initiated by New York's Bureau of Social Hygiene in 1933 (Michael and Adler, 1933). In this report, written by lawyer Jerome Michael and philosopher Mortimer Adler, it was stressed that great confusion will arise unless criminologists can agree on a precise definition of crime. Only if crime is defined clearly and precisely will it be possible to distinguish criminal behavior from noncriminal behavior.

> [t]he most precise and least ambiguous definition of crime is that which defines it as behavior which is prohibited by the criminal code. . . . It follows that a criminal is a person who has behaved in some way prohibited by the criminal law. (*ibid.*:2–3)

Following Michael and Adler's argument, Paul Tappan claimed that "crime is an intentional act in violation of the criminal law (statutory and case law), committed without defense or excuse, and penalized by the state as a felony or misdemeanor" (Tappan, 1947:100). In this view, therefore, crime is a *legalistic* category of behavior. Let us examine some of the major aspects of the legalistic definition of crime.

Crime as a Legal Category

The preceding legalistic definition of crime contains several elements whose formal origins can be traced to the English common law ("customary" law) of the twelfth century. First and foremost, a crime must be forbidden by *criminal law*. So, too, criminal law must provide punishment for a crime—a basic principle expressed in the English common law doctrine *nullum crimen sine lege, nulla poena sine lege* (no crime without law, no punishment without law). The formal purpose of criminal law is to protect members of the public from the wrongdoing of others. Rules of criminal law can be found either in statutory law (enacted by legislatures) or in common law (enacted from judicial decisions and based on a principle known as *stare decisis*). Criminal law is distinguished from civil law—such as tort law and contract law—which deals with private wrongs. Whereas a violation of civil law leaves a defendant open to civil suit, a violation of criminal law potentially places a defendant at the point of entry in the criminal justice system (see Figure 1-1).

The criminal law categorizes crime in two ways. First, crimes are either *mala in se* or *mala prohibita*. This old and somewhat artificial distinction ostensibly

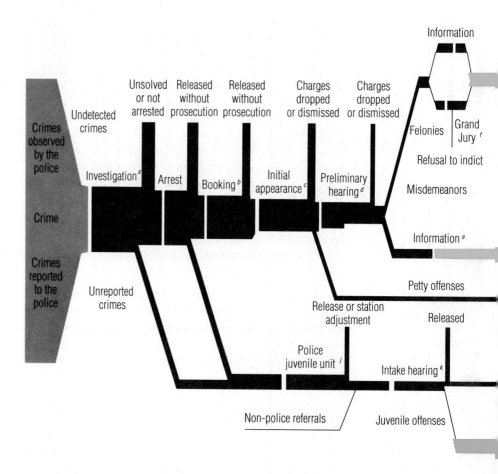

Police   **Prosecution**   **Courts**

Crimes observed by the police

Crime

Crimes reported to the police

Undetected crimes

Unsolved or not arrested

Released without prosecution

Released without prosecution

Charges dropped or dismissed

Charges dropped or dismissed

Information

Felonies   Grand Jury ʳ

Refusal to indict

Misdemeanors

Information ᵉ

Petty offenses

Released

Investigation ᵃ   Arrest   Booking ᵇ   Initial appearance ᶜ   Preliminary hearing ᵈ

Unreported crimes

Release or station adjustment

Police juvenile unit ʲ   Intake hearing ᵏ

Non-police referrals   Juvenile offenses

ᵃ May continue until trial.

ᵇ Administrative record of arrest. First step at which temporary release on bail may be available.

ᶜ Before magistrate, commissioner, or justice of peace. Formal notice of charge, advice of rights. Bail set. Summary trials for petty offenses usually conducted here without further processing.

ᵈ Preliminary testing of evidence against defendant. Charge may be reduced. No separate preliminary hearing for misdemeanors in some systems.

ᵉ Charge filed by prosecutor on basis of information submitted by police or citizens. Alternative to grand jury indictment: often used in felonies, almost always in misdemeanors.

FIGURE   **The Criminal Justice System**
1-1   *Source: U.S. Government Printing Office.*

Corrections

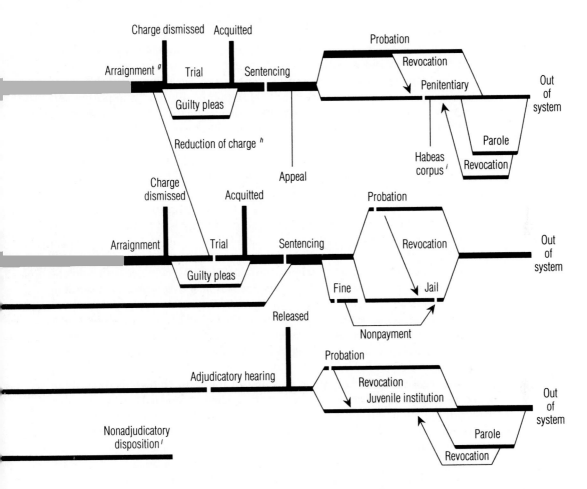

^rReviews whether government evidence sufficient to justify trial. Some states have no grand jury system: others seldom use it.

^gAppearance for plea: defendant elects trial by judge or jury (if available): counsel for indigent usually appointed here in felonies. Often not at all in other cases.

^hCharge may be reduced at any time prior to trial in return for plea of guilty or for other reasons.

ⁱChallenge on constitutional grounds to legality of detention. May be sought at any point in process.

^jPolice often hold informal hearings, dismiss or adjust many cases without further processing.

^kProbation officer decides desirability of further court action.

^lWelfare agency, social services, counseling, medical care, etc., for cases where adjudicatory handling not needed.

refers to the differences between "acts that are evil in themselves" (*mala in se*) and "acts that are prohibited" (*mala prohibita*). Lawyers take this distinction to mean that crimes *mala in se* are acts so inherently evil that they are universally considered evil, whereas crimes *mala prohibita* are acts prohibited by statute, the list of which changes as society evolves. Second, the criminal law distinguishes between felonies and misdemeanors. Although these two categories of crime are often separated by procedural differences, the most important difference between them is that felonies are punishable either by death or by imprisonment in a state penitentiary for a term of not less than one year, while misdemeanors are punishable either by fine or by a term in a local jail of less than one year.

A second element of a crime is that it must contain a voluntary illegal *act or omission* (known as the *actus reus*, some examples of which are given in Chapter 2 [Figure 2-1]). Negatively, this means that no one can be prosecuted for bad or evil thoughts, although words (such as incitement to riot) can sometimes constitute a criminal act. In addition, failure to act (*omission*) can be criminal in circumstances where there is a legal duty to act. Examples of crimes by omission are leaving the scene of a traffic accident and failure to file an annual tax return with the Internal Revenue Service.

To entail culpability for a crime, a criminal act must coincide with a defendant's mental state, variously known as *criminal intent* or *mens rea*. According to the American Law Institute's *Model Penal Code* (§ 2.02), one is not guilty of an offense unless one acted with *purpose* to do the forbidden act, or with *knowledge* of the nature of the act, or with *recklessness* or *negligence*. In some cases intent can be "transferred" as, for example, when A intends to shoot B, but misses and kills C.

To legal scholars the precise meaning of the term "intent" is often quite elusive. For example, certain categories of individuals are judged legally incapable of forming intent: juveniles under the age of 14 and those certified as insane or severely retarded. Moreover, in cases of *strict liability* intent is not a necessary requirement of guilt. Examples of strict liability offenses include *felony murder* (a murder committed during a serious felony like rape or arson) and *statutory rape* (sexual intercourse with a juvenile, which usually means under 16 years of age).

An act or omission is not a crime if a defendant has a *justification* for doing it or if he or she lacks the *criminal responsibility* required by the element of *mens rea*.

The defense of justification can be raised in three instances: duress, necessity, and duty. The defense of *duress* is typically limited to homicides. Thus, a killing may be justified if an individual reasonably believes that he or she is about to be killed or seriously harmed by another. The defense of *necessity* is available to defendants who are somehow threatened by natural circumstances over which they have no control, but can be used only when there is no other "reasonable" course of action available. For example, one would not be guilty of vandalism if, trapped inside a burning department store, one smashed a window in order to escape. The defense of *duty* is typically raised by public authorities such as police officers. Many killings by police officers in the line of duty are therefore termed "justifiable homicides." This defense is also available in the United States to teachers who use "reasonable" discipline in schools.

Finally, an act or omission may not be a crime if one lacks the necessary criminal responsibility. An individual may lack criminal responsibility—a condition that negates *mens rea*—in several ways, including the controversial pleas of *entrapment* and *insanity*. The defense of entrapment is intended to discourage the state from creating a crime where none would otherwise have existed. According to the *Model Penal Code* (§ 2.13), entrapment occurs when police methods entice an average law-abiding citizen to commit a crime. The defense of insanity differs from all other defenses in that, in most jurisdictions, if the plea is successful, the defendant is neither acquitted nor released but found "not guilty by reason of insanity." In some states, since the 1980s, defendants may be found "guilty but mentally ill," in which case they are confined to mental institutions until "cured," at which point they must finish their sentences in prison. This verdict almost always results in commitment of defendants to mental institutions, often for a longer period than if they had been found guilty of the crime charged. In the United States the majority of states base the legal criteria of insanity on the definition contained in the *Model Penal Code* (§ 4.01):

> (1) A person is not responsible for criminal conduct if at the time of such conduct, as a result of mental disease or defect, he lacks substantial capacity to appreciate the criminality (wrongfulness) of his conduct, or to conform his conduct to the requirements of law. (2) The terms "mental disease or defect" do not include an abnormality manifested only by repeated criminal or otherwise antisocial conduct.

A key element of the legalistic definition of crime—*mens rea*—is based on the assumption that crime is behavior engaged in by individuals who are capable of exercising free will. As you progress through Part Two (Types of Crime) and Part Three (Criminological Theory) of this book, you will learn that such an assumption cannot be used to explain crime. Rather than looking to free will as the "cause" of crime, we will suggest that the starting point of explanation is that individuals' actions are, in varying degrees, determined by their position in society.

Sociological Definitions of Crime

The complex social realities of crime cannot be grasped either by the simple images of crime manufactured by the media and by the moral entrepreneurs of social problems or by the definition of crime as a legal category. The purpose of criminology is to chip away at stereotypical or value-laden images of crime, and then to examine what remains. The academic discipline of criminology has a lengthy intellectual history. As we outline in Chapter 10, the origins of modern criminology can be traced to the rise of the classical (1760–1820) and the positivist (1820–1890) schools of thought, both of which flourish today. The term "criminology" derives from the Latin word *crimen*, meaning "judgment," "accusation," or "offense." Though the word "criminologist" appeared in Britain in the 1850s, "criminology" was first used to define the academic study of crime by the Italian sociologist Baron Raffaele Garofalo in 1885 (Beirne, 1993:233–238). Establishing itself as a respectable academic discipline in the United States during the Progressive Era (1890–1915), criminology has since become a specialized area within sociology.

We now explore four sociological definitions of crime used by criminologists: (1) crime as a violation of conduct norms, (2) crime as a social harm, (3) crime as a violation of human rights, and (4) crime as a form of deviance.

Crime as a Violation of Conduct Norms   In his short yet influential book *Culture Conflict and Crime*, Thorsten Sellin complained that "[c]riminology as traditionally conceived is a bastard science grown out of public preoccupation with a plague" (1938:3). Sellin correctly believed that it was unscientific for criminologists to base their studies on what the public happened to regard as a "plague" or, as we have already described such concerns, as a social problem. In studying the causes of phenomena, Sellin pointed out, scientists should study objective facts as they occur in their natural states rather than as they are seen by the subjective concerns of the public, the government, powerful social groups, and the criminal law. Sellin was especially concerned that criminologists should not accept Michael and Adler's argument that the basic unit of study should be the behavior prohibited by the rules of criminal law. As Sellin (*ibid.*:23) stated:

> The unqualified acceptance of the legal definitions of the basic units or elements of criminological inquiry violates a fundamental criterion of science. The scientist must have freedom to define his own terms, based on the intrinsic character of his material and designating properties in that material which are assumed to be universal.

Sellin contended that the basic units of criminological research should be "conduct norms." Modern societies contain a great number of conflicting groups. From the point of view of the group of which one is a member, for every person there are *normal* (right) and *abnormal* (wrong) forms of conduct—the norm depending on the social values of the group that formulates it. Such norms are the rules that govern appropriate behavior. Sellin insisted that there are different types of conduct norms, including custom, tradition, ethics, religion, and rules of criminal law. Conduct norms are found "wherever social groups are found, namely, universally. They are not the creation of any *one* normative group; they are not confined within political boundaries; they are not necessarily embodied in law" (*ibid.*:30). Sellin therefore concluded that a scientific criminology should focus on the violation of all forms of conduct norm and on the study of *abnormal conduct* in general. For Sellin, crime is but one form of conduct norm, distinguished from others by the fact that it violates the conduct norms specifically defined by the criminal law.

Sellin's rejection of the legalistic definition of crime and his advice about the proper subject matter of criminology are extremely important. Clearly, criminologists would be foolish to limit their studies simply to what the criminal law happens to forbid. Imagine, for example, how difficult it would be to study trends in the crime of marijuana use in a state where pot was constantly criminalized and decriminalized according to the whims of legislative and public opinion.

Sellin's advice has yet to exert much influence within criminology. Criminologists would simply be overwhelmed by the scope of their subject matter if they studied violations of *all* forms of conduct norm. However, Sellin's recommendation moves us to ask a question of immense relevance to all criminological research: Why are violations of one particular form of conduct regarded as crime and not others?

Crime as a Social Harm or an Analogous Social Injury   A direct outgrowth of the debate between the concepts of crime respectively held by Michael and Adler and by Sellin is the important position articulated by Edwin Sutherland (1949) in his book *White Collar Crime*. Sutherland was angry that many white-collar offenses were processed as civil violations rather than as crimes. He argued that (*ibid.*:46)

> The essential characteristic of crime is that it is behavior which is prohibited by the State as an injury to the State and against which the State may react, at least as a last resort, by punishment. The two abstract criteria generally regarded by legal scholars as necessary elements in a definition of crime are legal description of an act as socially harmful and legal provision of a penalty for the act.

To Sutherland it is clearly unfair that white-collar offenders—for example, those found in civil suits to have violated regulatory laws such as the Sherman Antitrust Act or to have engaged in deceptive advertising—are not stigmatized as criminals. For Sutherland, the behavior of white-collar offenders meets the two characteristics of his definition of crime: their behavior is socially harmful and they are punished for it (by fines). Because white-collar "offenses" are in fact "crimes" (however such behavior is defined by the state), Sutherland argues they should be studied by criminologists. Sutherland's perspective on white-collar offenses has exercised great influence in criminology, as is discussed later in this book (Chapters 7 and 12.4). At this point, however, we should stress that Sutherland's perspective is not *opposed* to the legalistic definition of crime. Rather, he suggests that criminologists should use an *expanded* definition of crime based on behavior prohibited either by criminal law or by regulatory law.

Whereas Sutherland argues that any *illegalities* that cause social harm should be criminalized, some radical criminologists (such as Reiman, 1984; Michalowski, 1985) urge that *any behavior* should be criminalized if it causes social harm or "analogous social injury." For Michalowski, the concept of *analogous social injury* refers to "legally permissible acts or sets of conditions whose consequences are similar to those of illegal acts" (1985:317). This extension of Sutherland's position has far-reaching implications. Under this view, "crimes" might include any violent or untimely death; illness or disease; deprivation of adequate food, clothing, shelter, or medical care; and reduction or elimination of the opportunity for individuals to participate effectively in the political decision-making processes that affect their lives (*ibid.*:318). Consider the following examples of events that are not regarded as crimes by the U.S. legal system:

▲— Cigarette smoking caused 417,000 deaths (20 percent of all deaths) in the United States in 1990, and smoking-related fires claimed another 1,362 lives. The total financial cost of these deaths was $68 billion, including direct health care costs (Office of Technology Assessment, U.S. Congress, 1993).

▲— Each year in the U.S. more than 200,000 Americans are injured or killed owing to negligence by doctors (Jesilow, Pontell, and Geis 1993:19, citing a Ralph Nader-affiliated study).

▲— Each year in the U.S. approximately 6,000 workers are killed in job-related accidents, as many as 100,000 die because of exposure to dangerous substances, at least 10 million suffer injuries at work (at least 3 million of which are serious), and 390,000 workers contract new cases of job-related diseases (see Chapter 7.2).

Given the definition of crime as "analogous social injury," it seems fair to conclude that such facts justify *criminal* prosecution of an undetermined number of tobacco manufacturers and distributors, surgeons, and industrial employers. Sociologically, expanded definitions of crime that include both "social harm" and "analogous social injury" are therefore a marked corrective to the biased values underlying the legalistic definition of crime. In passing, however, it should be noted that these expanded definitions leave themselves open to the plausible objection that what counts as social harm or as analogous social injury is as value-laden a category as is criminal law.

Crime as a Violation of Human Rights   In response to the biased values enshrined in criminal law (see especially Chapters 11.3, 14.4), some criminologists have suggested that crime should be defined as any behavior that violates an individual's "human rights." In this view, all people have certain natural and inalienable rights (to life, liberty, happiness, and so on) that derive simply from their status as human beings. Violations of these rights, the argument continues, provide criminology with a more objective unit of analysis than does the legalistic definition of crime.

The most passionate plea that crime be defined in terms of human rights has been made by Herman and Julia Schwendinger (1975). The Schwendingers argue that the definition of crime according to the "historically determined rights of individuals" is a valuable humanistic approach to the problem of crime. For the Schwendingers there are two divisions of human rights: those personal rights that are absolutely essential to life (such as the right to good health) and

Demonstrating against racism and social injury.

those essential to a dignified human existence (for instance, freedom of move-ment, free speech, a good education, employment, the right to unionize, a certain standard of housing, and so on). In addition, the Schwendingers argue that anything that causes a "social injury" should also be considered a crime. Examples of social injury include imperialism, sexism, racism, and poverty. The Schwen-dingers have even suggested that some governments should be considered crimi-nal if they do nothing to alleviate poverty (*ibid.*:137):

> Isn't it time to raise serious questions about the assumptions underly-ing the definition of the field of criminology, when a man who steals a paltry sum can be called a criminal while agents of the State can, with impunity, legally reward men who destroy food so that price levels can be maintained whilst a sizable portion of the population suffers from mal-nutrition?

The Schwendingers' argument emphasizes the fact that criminology is an inherently political activity. We inevitably make political choices when we decide what we identify as "crime." Should we study the crimes of the poor and powerless, as have most criminologists until quite recently? Whose side are we on in the struggle between the powerful and the powerless? Is it important that we be "objective" in our studies? Can we ever be objective?

The suggestion that violations of human rights be the basis of criminology is an admirable one, not least because it brings to the fore such important questions as these. Moreover, the concept of human rights—as a category of social injury that varies neither across cultures nor over time—seems to offer criminology a broader and more objective definition of crime than does the concept of crime as a legal category. Specifically, it opens up for analysis the obvious fact that legal categories themselves might sometimes be "criminal": laws that forbid freedom of speech, that limit opposition to political parties, and so on.

However, for criminology a major problem with the human rights approach is that, like the content of criminal law, what constitutes a "right" does in fact vary considerably. In some societies, such as the United States, human rights tend to be defined in *individualistic* terms. Individual-based rights tend to refer to the right of individuals to *do* certain things. Yet in other societies, such as several in Western Europe, in Canada, and elsewhere, rights tend to be defined in more *social* terms: the right to employment, and to minimum standards of housing, health, and education (Los, 1983). Given these differences, it is difficult indeed to agree on which violations of what rights should constitute crime.

Moreover, the emphasis by criminologists on *human* rights tends to obscure the fact that the rights of *animals* to a natural and peaceable existence are frequently violated by humans. Since the middle of the 19th century, and even earlier, some animal rights have been recognized and secured both in state anticruelty laws and in federal legislation. Laws currently in force include the Animal Welfare Act (1966, as amended), the Endangered Species Act (1969), the Marine Mammal Protection Act (1972), and the Improved Standards for Laboratory Animals Act (1985). But quite apart from the legal and/or illegal atrocities routinely committed against them in factory farms, rodeos, circuses, zoos, and in commercial laboratories, animals are abused by humans both in domestic households and in their "wild" or natural habitats. Violations of animal rights, we believe, are crimes that also must be investigated by criminologists.

Crime as a Form of Deviance   In the early 1960s, during a period of widespread social unrest, the study of crime was indelibly influenced by sociological theories of deviance. *Deviance* may be defined as any social behavior or social characteristic that departs from the conventional norms and standards of a community or society and for which the deviant is sanctioned. Examples of deviant social behavior include witchcraft, bank robbery, picking one's nose in public, mental illness, homosexuality, stuttering, sadomasochism, and murder. Examples of deviant social characteristics are extremes of height and weight, aggressiveness, laziness, and beauty.

Several aspects of deviance shed light on the study of crime. Even from the preceding short list it is clear, first, that the variety of deviant practices and deviant social characteristics is in principle infinite. What constitutes deviance varies from era to era and from society to society. Homosexuality, for example, was often regarded in classical Greece as a conforming social practice rather than as deviance. Moreover, within the same society at a point in time, the perception of deviance varies by class, gender, race, and age. Second, deviance is commonplace. Each of us has committed a deviant act at one time or another. Some of us commit many deviant acts in the course of a single day! Third, all deviant behavior is potentially subject to sanction. Deviant behavior can be subject to positive sanctions (such as winning a Nobel prize for the discovery of penicillin) or to negative sanctions (social censure for picking one's nose in public). Fourth, the norms and standards violated by deviant acts are quite diverse. They can originate in religion, political belief, etiquette, fashion, and criminal law. Of course, not all deviant acts are criminal acts (and vice versa).

The deviance perspective implies that there is nothing in the nature of any act that identifies it as deviant. Rather, deviance is in the eye of the beholder. This implication raises several important sociological questions for the study of crime. Although we explore these questions in greater depth later (Chapter 14.3), certain of them are worth mentioning here.

1. Why is certain behavior regarded as deviant?

2. Who defines such behavior as deviant, how, and why?

3. What are the consequences for an individual whose deviant behavior is subject to sanction?

4. Why are some deviant practices defined as criminal but not others?

Toward an Eclectic Definition of Crime

This book views crime as a "sociological problem," and surveys the various sociological approaches to crime that we term "criminology." To focus on crime as a *sociological problem* is to explain how patterns of crime arise from the interplay of political, economic, social, and ideological structures in society. In other words, we devote scant attention to explanations of crime that ignore the importance of such factors and that reduce its causes to the level of the individual. In pure form, examples of such "reductionism" are found, for example, in those biological explanations of crime that emphasize the links between criminality and the physical constitution of the individual, and in psychological explanations that focus on the links between crime and such conditions as "defective character," "loose morals," and so on. This book, then, purposefully focuses on the sociological questions uppermost in modern criminology.

The chief task of criminology is to understand crime as a sociological problem. Yet, we have seen already that criminologists disagree about the best sociological definition of crime. This disagreement partly stems, we believe, from a mistaken search for a universal definition of crime that can be applied to all cultures, places, and times.

We hold to no fixed or dogmatic position concerning the definition of crime. Sometimes we agree with the way in which criminal law defines crime; at other times we simply question its adequacy. Occasionally we prefer and use other definitions of crime. For example, in Chapter 4.1–4.2 we point out that many women are victimized every year by the act of forcible rape defined by criminal law; but we also acknowledge that the traditional criminal law definition of rape ("sexual intercourse obtained through the threat or actual use of physical violence") ignores acts that could be defined as rape, such as forms of nonphysical sexual coercion—for example, the male (either heterosexual or homosexual) who informs his economically dependent mate: "If you don't 'put out,' I'll leave you." In Chapter 7.2 we go considerably beyond the legalistic definition of crime (including both criminal law and regulatory law), arguing that corporate crime is any illegal and/or socially injurious act of intent or indifference that occurs for the purpose of furthering corporate goals, and that physically and/or economically abuses individuals in the United States or abroad. Finally, our definition of political crime (see Chapter 9) is somewhat broader than the legalistic definition, in that it includes not only crimes committed *against* the state but also crimes committed *by* the state. In the latter we include both domestic political crimes (unlawful or unethical acts by state officials and state agencies where victimization occurs inside the United States) and international political crimes (violations of domestic and international law by state officials and agencies whose victimization occurs outside the United States).

1.3 ———— CRIME, CRIMINAL LAW, AND CRIMINALIZATION

At this point we would do well to ask why it is that crime is usually defined, for most nonsociological purposes, as behavior that violates criminal law. Another way of putting this question is: Why is it that criminal law usually defines what behavior is criminal? As soon as we ask (dangerously circular!) questions such as these, we should realize that criminology cannot be confined to the study of criminal behavior, because the concept of "criminal *behavior*" depends for its meaning on the concept of "criminal *law*."

A few introductory words are appropriate here about the role of criminal law in the process of criminalization (and see Chapters 11.2, 11.3, 14.4, 15.3).

State, Law, and Social Control

Sociologically, the ideas and institutions of law vary greatly from one culture to another. Negatively, this means that law is not necessarily what some lawmakers or zealots claim that it is. Law is not an earthly expression of the will of God; it may not represent the interests of "the people," and it has no necessary connection with justice. Law is above all else a social phenomenon created by members of society under specific historical conditions. Law has not always existed in the past; it might not exist in the future.

The great bulk of research in sociology and anthropology reveals that law originated with the emergence of social inequality and, specifically, that it accompanied the transition from stateless societies to state societies. Law has not always existed because not all human societies have been characterized by social inequality. Indeed, until approximately 10,000 years ago, hunting and gathering societies were the dominant form of social organization, and these societies had very egalitarian social, economic, and political relations. In these small-scale societies (about 50 members), property was communally owned, there were no social classes, and there was no organized state or societal ruler. Even in horticultural societies, which emerged after hunting and gathering societies, social relations were highly egalitarian, significant differences in wealth and power did not occur, and their leaders typically had no coercive powers over others (O'Kelly and Carney, 1986:37). Neither in hunting and gathering nor in horticultural societies did a state exist, and a common morality was maintained by the authority of custom rather than the rule of law (Diamond, 1973). Within these stateless societies, offenses and conflicts were managed informally in a variety of nonlegal ways such as self-help, avoidance, negotiation, settlement by a third party, and toleration (Black, 1989:74–77; and see Durkheim's analysis in Chapter 11.2).

Not until the development of agricultural societies did class inequalities become prevalent, wherein economic productivity was expanded by new techniques such as the plow, fertilization, and irrigation. Increased productivity permitted new life-styles that were not devoted solely to economic survival and subsistence. In some agricultural societies—such as in Greece by the fourth century B.C.—class relations developed in which slaves did most of the productive labor and slave owners dominated and appropriated the economic surplus. In others—such as those of medieval Europe—the majority of the population were peasants, whereas the monarch, the nobles, and the church owned most of the land, which they obtained through military might and conquest. In both slave and feudal agricultural societies, a particular class controlled and appropriated the economic surplus, creating significant social inequalities.

An important feature of agricultural societies was the rise of states and legal systems. The *state* may be defined as the central political institution of a given society. Its major apparatuses are the government (legislature and executive), the legal system, the military, and a variety of public bureaucracies for the collection of taxes, management of public health, maintenance of law and order, and so on. The legal system is both a state apparatus and, through its constitutional and administrative branches, the chief mechanism for defining the sphere of state activities.

Rules of law have a variety of sources, such as superstition, divine oracles, religion, prophecy, charismatic leadership, court cases, and legislatures. According to the great German sociologist Max Weber (1924, I:34):

> An order will be called *law* if it is externally guaranteed by the probability that physical or psychological coercion will be applied by a *staff* of people in order to bring about compliance or avenge violation.

Law is thus distinguished from other rules of behavior—habit, convention, tradition, custom—by its coercive nature and by professional enforcement of its codes. Law's coercive nature can be expressed in shame, ridicule, censure, ostracism, imprisonment, torture, terror, and death. Law's "staff," to use Weber's term, can be composed of witches and wizards, kings and queens, popes and

TABLE 1-1   **Four Styles of Social Control**

	PENAL	COMPENSATORY	THERAPEUTIC	CONCILIATORY
Standard	Prohibition	Obligation	Normality	Harmony
Problem	Guilt	Debt	Need	Conflict
Initiation of case	Group	Victim	Deviant	Disputants
Identity of deviant	Offender	Debtor	Victim	Disputant
Solution	Punishment	Payment	Help	Resolution

Source: Black (1976), p. 5.

rabbis, village elders, chiefs, prophets, military warlords, federal judges, and state legislators, among others.

As a social phenomenon, law is a state form of *social control*. As such, its object is to manufacture conformity and to suppress what the state defines as deviance. In his book *The Behavior of Law*, Donald Black (1976:4–6) suggests there are four basic styles of law, each corresponding to a broader style of social control: penal, compensatory, therapeutic, and conciliatory (see Table 1-1). Each style defines deviant behavior in its own way, with its own logic, methods, and language. Black (1976:2; and see Hembroff, 1987) defines law as *governmental* social control. In the penal style of social control, the "problem" is to establish "guilt" when an "offender" has violated a "prohibition," and its solution is "punishment." Black argues that the quantity and the style of law (including penal law) in a given society both vary inversely with certain factors, such as the power of other forms of social control and their levels of social inequality. When other forms of social control (such as, family ties, religion, and so on) are weak, for example, the power and the extent of law will be relatively strong (*ibid.*:6–7, 107–111). Moreover, following the lengthy "conflict" tradition in the sociology and the anthropology of law (see Chapter 14.4). Black argues that law varies directly with social inequality. That is, the societies with the most law are those with the most social inequality (see Chapters 6.1, 11.2, 11.3, 14.4).

Many criminologists argue that nowhere is the relationship between social inequality and crime more evident than in the process of "criminalization." We turn now to this important concept.

Law and Criminalization

The term "criminalization" refers to the process whereby criminal law is selectively applied to social behavior. This threefold process involves (1) the enactment of legislation that outlaws certain types of behavior, (2) the surveillance and the policing of that behavior, and (3) if detected, its punishment. The study of the process of criminalization is therefore an indispensable part of the study of crime, and examples of that process are frequently given in this book.

As we conclude this introductory chapter, we note that the broad nature of the criminalization process in Western industrialized societies is now the subject of heated debate among criminologists (Lowman, Menzies, and Palys, 1987;

Ratner and McMullan, 1987; Cohen, 1988; Edwards, 1988). Argument rages over three wide-ranging questions. First, how did the criminalization process contribute to the rise of western industrialized societies when they first emerged during the 17th century? Second, is criminalization today a neutral process or does it *generally* serve the interests of the powerful? Third, does criminalization contribute to the maintenance of specific forms of contemporary *social* inequality (by class, gender, race, and age)? Each question is addressed in due course, the answers falling at or in between two extremes. One extreme claims that since its inception on a large scale (during the 18th century), the criminalization process has on the whole contributed to the rise of modern society in rational and humane ways. The other extreme suggests that criminalization has operated, in more or less subtle ways, as an instrument to defend the interests of powerful new social classes (for example, the capitalist class) and to undermine the interests of the powerless.

Our general view of criminalization, and thus also of criminal law itself, is that it tends to reflect the interests of the powerful. We will therefore often look at the ways in which the criminalization process maintains unequal social relationships between the powerful and the powerless—especially in the areas of class, gender, race, and age. Nevertheless, we do not view this tendency dogmatically. Sometimes criminalization is a direct product of power struggles, reflecting the political strengths of specific power groups. At other times it is only marginally connected to power struggles. At still others it appears to transcend power struggles altogether.

REVIEW

Chapter 1 introduced the different images of crime found in the discourse of social-problem movements, of mass media, and of sociology. The major task of the chapter was to learn about the three key sociological concepts of criminology: crime, criminal law, and criminalization.

Images of Crime

1. It is no exaggeration to say that since the early 1960s crime has become one of the leading social problems in the United States. But there is no objective set of social conditions whose perceived harmful effects necessarily make them social problems. What is regarded as a social problem varies over time and across cultures. What is defined as a social problem depends on numerous factors, including the activities of moral entrepreneurs.

2. Mass media have become the single most influential mechanism for organizing public sentiment so that a certain social condition is perceived as a social problem.

3. Mass media routinely provide distorted information about the amount of crime, the most common types of crime, and who typically commits crimes.

Definitions of Crime

1. The legalistic definition of crime distinguishes between crime *mala in se* and *mala prohibita* and between felonies and misdemeanors. To constitute a crime, according to this definition, behavior must be prohibited by law, must be voluntary, and must coincide with a defendant's mental state. An act or omission is not a crime if a defendant is justified in doing (or omitting) it or if a defendant lacks the criminal responsibility required by *mens rea*.

2. This book views crime as a "sociological problem," and surveys the various sociological approaches to crime that we term "criminology." To focus on crime as a *sociological problem* is to explain how patterns of crime arise from the interplay of political, economic, social, and ideological structures in society.

3. The question "What is crime?" is extremely difficult to answer because there is little agreement about the defining sociological characteristics of crime. Criminologists have labored with a variety of sociological definitions of crime, including crime as a violation of conduct norms, crime as a social harm and analogous social injury, crime as a violation of human rights, and crime as deviance.

4. This book uses an eclectic definition of crime.

Crime, Criminal Law, and Criminalization

1. The term "criminalization" refers to the process whereby criminal law is selectively applied to social behavior. The sociological study of criminal law is therefore an integral part of criminology. Specifically, the criminalization process involves the enactment of legislation that outlaws certain types of behavior and provides for surveillance and policing of that behavior, and, if detected, punishment.

2. Not all societies have had law. Most research shows that law originated with the emergence of social inequality and that it accompanied the transition from stateless to state societies.

3. The distinguishing features of law are its coercive nature, its reliance on a professional staff, and its use as a state form of social control.

4. The general view of the criminalization process in this book, and thus also of criminal law, is that it tends to reflect the interests of the powerful (in terms of class, gender, race, and age). However, there is no substitute for careful historical and empirical analysis.

QUESTIONS FOR CLASS DISCUSSION

1. Consider the facts in the following short story about cannibalism among a group of cave (speluncean) explorers caught in a life-threatening situation in the Commonwealth of "Newgarth." The story is adapted from a fictitious law case created by legal philosopher Lon Fuller (1949, excerpted in Schur, 1968:19–20). Although *The Case of the Speluncean Explorers* is fictitious, it is probably based on an actual case of cannibalism at sea in 1884, and the bizarre trial that resulted from it in England (Simpson, 1984).

☞ The Case of the Speluncean Explorers

[F]ive members of an amateur cave-exploring society were trapped inside a deep and isolated cave following a landslide. After some time, through the efforts of relatives and the cave-exploring society, rescuers located the cave only to encounter repeated obstacles to removing the trapped men. At great monetary expense and the cost of ten rescuers' lives (in a subsequent landslide), the rescue operation finally succeeded thirty-two days after the men entered the cave. On the twentieth day, communication between the rescuers and the trapped explorers had been established, when it was discovered that the latter had with them in the cave a radio transmitter-receiver. At that time, the trapped men asked for medical advice as to whether they could live without food (there was none in the cave) for the time engineers had determined would be required to rescue them. A physicians' committee at the rescue site stated that they could not. When the trapped men later inquired if they could survive by consuming the flesh of one of their number, the reply ("reluctant") was in the affirmative. But the explorers could get no guidance at all (from the physicians or from any clergyman or judge) when they went on to ask about the advisability of casting lots to determine who should be killed and eaten.

When the men were finally released, the rescuers learned that on the twenty-third day one of them, Whetmore, had been killed and eaten by the other four. Although originally it had been Whetmore's idea (at first resisted by his companions) that such an act might be necessary for survival, and also that a casting of lots would be the fairest means of selection, just before the dice were cast, Whetmore changed his mind. His companions disallowed this sudden switch, however, and cast the dice for him, after obtaining his agreement that this procedure was fair; he lost and was put to death and eaten by the others.

After they had recuperated, the four survivors were charged with Whetmore's murder.

Having read the facts in *The Case of the Speluncean Explorers*, you should also know that Newgarth law commands that "Whoever shall willfully take the life of another shall be punished by death." In this case the defendants were charged with the crime of murder, convicted, and sentenced to death.

Assume the defendants appealed the verdict and the sentence in *The Case of the Speluncean Explorers*, and that you are a member of the appeals court. How would you decide the appeal? Are the defendants guilty of murder? What defense is available to them, if any? If their conviction in the lower court is upheld, would you recommend executive clemency (a pardon)?

2. According to the Centers for Disease Control, tobacco is responsible for more than 434,000 deaths annually in the United States (*Associated Press*, 10.10.93). This is more than the annual number of deaths caused by alcohol, heroin, crack, automobile and airplane accidents, murder, suicide and AIDS combined. Do you think that tobacco manufacturers should be prosecuted for homicide?

3. There is some evidence that criminals portrayed in mass media tend to be more middle-aged, more affluent, more glamorous, and more often white than their representation in official crime data suggests (Garofalo, 1981; Surette, 1992:63–64). How would you interpret such evidence?

RECOMMENDED READINGS

Chambliss, William and Robert Seidman (1982). *Law, Order, & Power*. Reading, MA: Addison-Wesley. A sociological analysis of law that uses materials from anthropology and history to understand the working of legal doctrine and legal institutions.

Cohen, Stanley (1988). "The Object of Criminology: Reflections on the New Criminalization." Pp. 235–276 in Stanley Cohen, *Against Criminology*. New Brunswick, NJ: Transaction Books. Discusses the sources and forms of the expanded process of criminalization in the last decade.

Michalowski, Raymond J. (1985). *Order, Law, and Crime*. New York: Random House. Chapters 3–4 discuss how the powerful in premodern societies create social order and cope with trouble.

Schwendinger, Herman and Julia Schwendinger (1975). "Defenders of Order or Guardians of Human Rights?" Pp. 113–138 in Ian Taylor, Paul Walton, and Jock Young (eds.), *Critical Criminology*. London: Routledge & Kegan Paul. A guide to the respective limitations of the several definitions of crime.

Surette, Ray. (1992). *Media, Crime and Criminal Justice*. Pacific Grove, CA: Brooks/Cole. A lucid and comprehensive text on numerous aspects of media, crime, and criminal justice.

CHAPTER 2

THE MEASUREMENT OF CRIME

2.1   **Caution: Data Do Not Speak for Themselves!**

2.2   **Official Crime Data**
        Police Data: *Uniform Crime Reports*
        Victimization Data: *National Crime Victimization Survey*
        Federal Agencies and Corporate Crime

2.3   **Unofficial Crime Data**
        Self-Report Data
        Biographical Data
        Participant Observation
        Comparative and Historical Data

2.4   **Assessment**

Preview

Chapter 2 introduces:

☞ the major sources of official crime data.
☞ the major sources of unofficial crime data.
☞ the idea that crime data do not have a factual, objective existence
   independent of concepts about crime.

Key Terms

concept	statistics
crime rate	theories
methodology	unofficial crime data
official crime data	victimization surveys
positivism	

Chapter 2 outlines the major sources of crime data; precisely what such data tell us about specific types of crime is analyzed in later chapters (especially Chapters 4-9).

Criminologists usually distinguish between "official crime data" and "unofficial crime data." **Official crime data** are the data collected by the government and its official agencies (the "state"), such as the Federal Bureau of Investigation and the Department of Justice. **Unofficial crime data** are the nongovernmental data usually collected by private or independent agencies and researchers. Thus, the sources and the types of unofficial crime data are quite varied. In distinguishing between official and unofficial sources of crime data, we do not imply that one data source is in principle necessarily better than another—although in practice this is often true. Rather, official and unofficial crime data typically measure different aspects of crime.

The majority of crime data is presented in the form of statistics. Interestingly, the term "statistics" derives from the 17th-century English term "state-istics," which referred to state data about births, marriages, and deaths. **Statistics** can be defined as "a set of techniques for the reduction of quantitative data (that is, a series of numbers) to a [limited] number of more convenient and easily communicated descriptive terms" (Levin and Fox, 1988:15); it is also "a set of decision-making techniques which aid researchers in drawing inferences from samples to populations and, hence, in testing hypotheses" (ibid.:17). Because contemporary statistical data are so extensively used for social purposes, we tend to be lulled into thinking that they represent objective facts. However, neither "statistics" nor "data" nor "facts" can ever be entirely free of the biases inherent in the means with which they are conceived and constructed. The implications of this critical point will soon become obvious.

2.1 _____ CAUTION: DATA DO NOT SPEAK FOR THEMSELVES!

In the following pages we describe the major sources of data for studying crime today. But before we describe these data we must discuss how they are influenced by concepts and theories.

In the early 19th century, when official crime data were first systematically recorded, "positivist" criminologists like Adophe Quetelet believed that crime can be observed directly by using the procedures of the natural sciences (see Chapter 10.2). In this view, crime—like rocks, plants, and insects—exists in a natural state quite independently of the concepts and the theories of the criminologist. Positivist criminology is based on the idea that the collection of data about human beings follows the same scientific procedures as the collection of data in the natural sciences. This view, however, greatly distorts the process of scientific investigation. Why this is so can be understood by an analogy with astronomy.

Suppose that two astronomers are examining the surface of the moon through a telescope. Suppose also that one of the astronomers is peering into her telescope in the year 1500 (in essence, pre-Copernicus) and the other in the year 1900 (namely, post-Copernicus). Now ask yourself whether the two astronomers would see the same thing. It can be argued that both astronomers would see the same image projected by the moon: a roundish, bright, yellowish object in the sky. But beyond the optico-chemical level of sensory perception, would our two astronomers really "see" the same image? The answer is probably "no." The astronomers would see (or interpret) lunar data in terms of (1) their respective concepts of "the moon," of "optics," and so on, and of (2) their theories of planetary motion. The lunar image seen by the 15th century astronomer differs remarkably from that seen by our modern-day astronomer. The former, for example, would see a roundish, bright, yellowish object *that moves in orbit around the earth.* The latter, relying on modern theories of astronomy, would see a roundish, bright, yellowish object *that has a certain alignment with the earth and the sun.* Astronomers' perceptions of lunar images, in other words, are structured by their respective astronomical concepts and theories.

This example demonstrates that data are not objective facts that exist independently of the concepts and of the theories of those who observe them. Data do not speak for themselves!

Let us apply this heavenly insight to the world of crime. When we study crime it would be a great mistake to believe that we can simply observe, measure, and collect the "facts and nothing but the facts" about crime. We do not—indeed cannot—collect facts about crime through direct observation. What constitutes a fact about crime depends on our concepts and theories of crime. Crime data, like all other data, are structured by concepts and theories. What counts as crime data is therefore very much open to debate. If you refer back to Chapter 1.2, you will recall that the recognition of certain behavioral data (such as killing someone) as crime depends on whichever *concept* of crime is accepted as authoritative. Using the legalistic concept of crime, for example, murder is limited to those killings that are contrary to rules of criminal law. Thus, legally, if a police officer kills someone the killing is not murder if it is reasonable under the circumstances and if it occurs in the lawful execution of police duties. Using another concept of crime, such as human rights (concepts of which are themselves quite variable), yields very different crime data. Thus, to some proponents of human rights (but not to those who favor the legalistic concept of crime), murder might also include negligent surgery, many worker deaths caused by employer neglect of safety conditions, cigarette-induced deaths resulting from the commercial activities of tobacco companies, and the like (see generally Reiman, 1979:44–94). Similarly, the criminologist Ian Taylor (1983:91) disagrees with

> the widespread view of homicide as a highly "factual" offense, thought to be evidenced by the existence of a corpse. Homicide is thought amongst experts to have a very high degree of "reportability" (in that very few homicides are thought to be unobserved or unpunished). On both counts, there is room for skepticism. . . . There are good reasons for questioning the meaning of coroners' reports in cases of nonnatural death, and there

are increasingly strong reasons for questioning whether the deaths that occur among the terminally ill, or amongst old people in care, especially in institutional settings, are absolutely unaided. Perhaps most routinely of all, there is good evidence to suggest that many more of the deaths occurring in road traffic "accidents" involving criminal negligence should be appearing in homicide statistics at present.

2.2 ———— OFFICIAL CRIME DATA

Publication of national crime statistics was pioneered in France in 1827 (see Chapter 10.2), but not until a century later, in 1927, was a committee on Uniform Crime Records established in the United States. Three years later, in 1930—after some bureaucratic wrangling between the Federal Bureau of Investigation (FBI) and the Bureau of the Census—the FBI began to publish its *Uniform Crime Reports* (Sherman, Christensen, and Henderson, 1982). In January 1930, 400 cities representing 20 million inhabitants in 43 states began to participate in the *Uniform Crime Reports* (or *UCR*) program.

The *UCR* has been published each year since 1930 under congressional mandate, and is popularly regarded as the most reliable set of crime data in the United States. Our immediate task is to examine what the *UCR* measures, and then to assess how reliable the data actually are.

Police Data: *Uniform Crime Reports*

The *UCR* is compiled each year in Washington, D.C., by FBI statisticians. The FBI receives data from crime reports submitted voluntarily by more than 16,000 state, country, and city law enforcement agencies. In 1992 these agencies had jurisdiction over 242 million U.S. inhabitants, or 97 percent of the total population as established by the Bureau of the Census. The coverage is 90 percent in cities outside metropolitan areas, and 86 percent in rural areas.

The meaning of much *UCR* data hinges on a distinction drawn by the FBI between "Index Crimes" and "Non-Index Crimes." The *UCR* provides diverse statistical information about eight Index ("Part I") Crimes, but much scantier information about 21 Non-Index ("Part II") Crimes. The FBI regards Index Crimes as the most serious crimes: murder and nonnegligent manslaughter, forcible rape, robbery, aggravated assault, burglary, larceny-theft, motor vehicle theft, and arson (see Figure 2-1 for definitions of these offenses). Non-Index Crimes—apparently regarded by the FBI as less serious crimes—include assault (except aggravated assault); forgery and counterfeiting; fraud; embezzlement; buying, receiving, and possessing stolen property; carrying and possessing weapons; prostitution and commercialized vice; sex offenses (except forcible rape and prostitution); drug abuse violations; gambling, offenses against family and children; driving under the influence; liquor law offenses; drunkenness; disorderly conduct; vagrancy; all other offenses (except traffic); suspicion; curfew and loitering law violations; and runaways. In addition to the FBI's view that Index

FIGURE 2-1 *Uniform Crime Reports*—Index (Part I) Crime Definitions

▲— **Murder and Nonnegligent Manslaughter:**   the willful (nonnegligent) killing of one human being by another.

▲— **Forcible Rape:**   the carnal knowledge of a female forcibly and against her will. (Attempts are included, but statutory rape [without force] and other sex offenses are not.)

▲— **Robbery:**   the taking or attempting to take anything of value from the care, custody, or control of a person or persons by force or by threat of force or violence and/or by putting the victim in fear.

▲— **Aggravated assault:**   the unlawful attack by one person upon another for the purpose of inflicting severe or aggravated bodily injury. (This type of assault is usually accompanied by the use of a weapon, and it includes attempts.)

▲— **Burglary:**   the unlawful entry of a structure to commit a felony or theft. (Three subdivisions include forcible entry, unlawful entry where no force is used, and attempted forcible entry.)

▲— **Larceny-theft:**   the unlawful taking, carrying, leading, or riding away of property from the possession or constructive possession of another. (Included are shoplifting, pocket-picking, purse-snatching, thefts from motor vehicles, thefts of motor vehicle parts and accessories, bicycle thefts, and so forth, in which no force, violence, or fraud occurs.)

▲— **Motor Vehicle Theft:**   the theft or attempted theft of a motor vehicle. (Included are the stealing of automobiles, trucks, buses, motorcycles, motorscooters, and snowmobiles.)

▲— **Arson:**   any willful burning or malicious burning or attempt to burn, with or without intent to defraud, a dwelling house, public building, motor vehicle or aircraft, personal property of another. . . . (Excluded are fires of suspicious or unknown origin.)

Source: Federal Bureau of Investigation, 1993, adapted from pp. 13–53.

Crimes are more serious than Non-Index Crimes (a subject to which we return in a moment), *UCR* crime data are also distinguished by their source. Data about Index Crimes derive from information that comes to the attention of police departments, which in turn usually derives from *reports* of crime to the police by members of the public. For Non-Index Crimes data are limited to cases involving actual police arrests.

The *UCR* primarily focuses on crime trends of the eight Index Crimes. In this regard the *UCR* tabulates:

1.   the number of offenses

2.   the offense rate per 100,000 population

3.   whether the offense rate was greater or lesser than the previous year

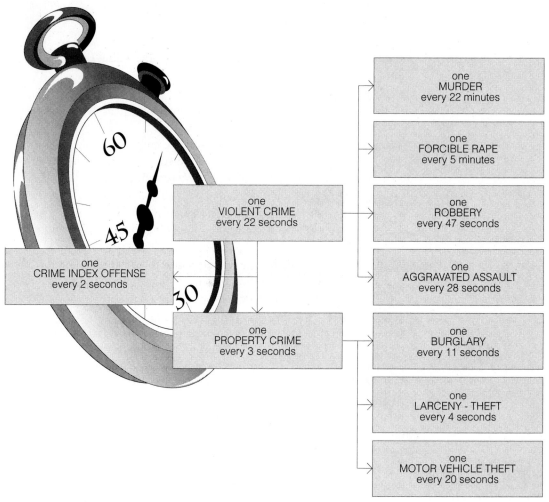

one
CRIME INDEX OFFENSE
every 2 seconds

one
VIOLENT CRIME
every 22 seconds

one
PROPERTY CRIME
every 3 seconds

one
MURDER
every 22 minutes

one
FORCIBLE RAPE
every 5 minutes

one
ROBBERY
every 47 seconds

one
AGGRAVATED ASSAULT
every 28 seconds

one
BURGLARY
every 11 seconds

one
LARCENY - THEFT
every 4 seconds

one
MOTOR VEHICLE THEFT
every 20 seconds

FIGURE   Relative Frequency of Index Crimes
2-2   *Source: Federal Bureau of Investigation, 1993, p. 4.*

4. the offense rate by region (for example, South, North, Northeast, Midwest)

5. the "nature" of the offense (age, gender, and race of offenders and victims)

6. the arrest (or clearance) rates for the offense

The *UCR* displays the relative frequency of the Index Crimes (see Figure 2-2); changes in the number and in the rate of Index Crimes (see Figure 2-3); the composition of each Index Crime in the Index Crime rate (see Figure 2-4); and the respective crime rates of the four regions, individual states, and cities and towns of varying size. In addition, the *UCR* provides data about arrest trends

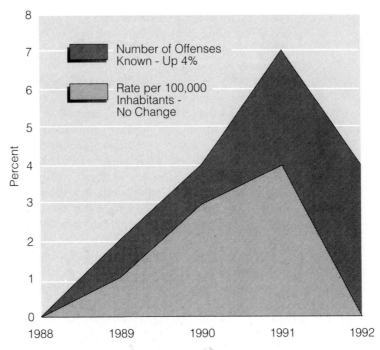

FIGURE Crime Index Total, 1988–1992
2-3   *Source: Federal Bureau of Investigation, 1993, p. 7.*

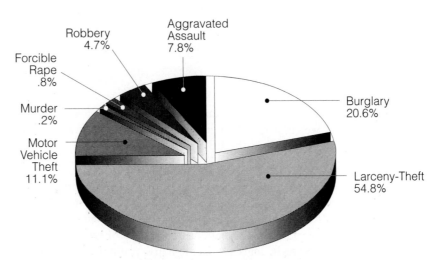

FIGURE Composition of *Uniform Crime Reports* Crime Index, 1992
2-4   *Source: Federal Bureau of Investigation, 1993, p. 8.*

by state, city, suburban and rural areas; and about police employment, by region, state, cities, suburban and rural counties, and universities and colleges.

Because we frequently refer to the concept of "crime rates," it is important to know exactly what is meant by a *crime rate*. To understand this concept, let us talk in terms of "percentages" and "rates." A percentage is simply a proportion (or "rate"), a number per 100 ("*centum*" is Latin for "100").

A basic reason for using percentages is that they give us a feel for proportion. This "feel" is actually an implicit comparison with other known proportions. For instance, how are we to interpret the results of a survey reporting that 2,000 persons in California and 500 persons in Maine are afraid of crime? Does this mean that persons in California are four times more fearful of crime than persons in Maine? To answer the latter question requires a common scale—a proportion or rate of those surveyed. Percentage (per 100 scale) is the most commonly used scale to establish the rate of people in both states who report they are afraid of crime. Generally, the lower the rate, the larger the base figure. Thus, 90 percent is easily translated to 9 of 10. But when we want to know something such as the prevalence of crime relative to the population, the rate is extremely low.

The foregoing can be illustrated by studying a concrete example of a homicide rate. In Table 2-1 we are given the number of homicides and also the homicide rates per 100,000 U.S. inhabitants reported in the *UCR* for 1991 and 1992. Consider first the number and the rate of homicides in 1992, when the population in the United States was estimated to be 255,483,870. Given that the number of homicides in 1992 was 23,760, the homicide rate per 100,000 population was 9.3. This crime rate is calculated as follows:

$$\frac{23,760}{255,483,870} \times 100,000 = 9.3$$

Moreover, if the homicide rate in 1992 was 9.3 and in 1991 was 9.8, then there was a decline of 0.5 homicides per 100,000 inhabitants. Thus, the homicide rate in 1992 was 5.1 percent less than the rate in 1991 or

$$\frac{0.5}{9.8} \times 100 = 5.1$$

Before examining the actual reliability of the crime data provided by the *UCR*, we emphasize how important the *UCR* program is as a source of crime data. In the words of the FBI (*UCR*, 1993:1) itself:

> While the Program's primary objective is to generate a reliable set of criminal statistics for use in law enforcement administration, operation, and management, its data have over the years become one of the country's leading social indicators. The American public looks to *UCR* for information on fluctuations in the level of crime, while criminologists, sociologists, legislators, municipal planners, the press, and other students of criminal justice use the statistics for varied research and planning purposes.

TABLE 2-1	**Homicide Rate Trend, 1991–1992**	

YEAR	NUMBER OF OFFENSES	RATE PER 100,000 INHABITANTS
1991	24,703	9.8
1992	23,760	9.3
Percent change	−3.8	−5.1

Source: Federal Bureau of Investigation, 1993, p. 13.

Assessment of the *Uniform Crime Reports*

Criminologists often debate the question of how well the *UCR* measures the crime rate in the U.S. Answers to this question tend to be twofold. First, it is claimed that although the *UCR* does a commendable job of measuring the crime rate, it could do even better with more sophisticated, or more sensitive methodological techniques. We term this sort of claim a "methodological" criticism. *Methodology* involves the techniques of measurement used to collect and manipulate empirical data. Two examples of methodological techniques are opinion polls and statistical analyses. Second, it is claimed that because of various conceptual biases in its methodological techniques, the *UCR* does not and cannot ever do a respectable job of measuring the crime rate. We term this sort of claim a "conceptual" criticism. A *concept* involves an idea that describes a property of an empirical datum or a relation among empirical data. It is usually a smaller part of a theory that is used to generate hypotheses. The "United States" is an example of a concept; some of the properties of the concept of the United States include "sovereignty," "50 states," "part of North America," and so on.

There are numerous methodological criticisms of the *UCR*. Consider five of the most important:

1. There is an unknown, but probably massive, amount of crime that goes unreported to the police and, therefore, never shows up in the *UCR*. This component is often termed the "dark figure" of crime. Methodologically, as we shall see, this figure can perhaps be reduced with the use of victimization surveys and self-report studies.

2. Because participation in the *UCR* program is voluntary, not all police departments send crime reports to the FBI. Consequently, the FBI attempts to estimate crime rates in such jurisdictions. It is, of course, extremely difficult to assess the accuracy of their estimates.

3. The *UCR* does not include federal crimes (such as blackmail), an omission that tends to underestimate the crime rate.

4. In any single criminal event, only the most serious crime reported to the police is included in the *UCR*. For example, if an armed man breaks into a person's home (burglary or criminal trespass), forces a woman inside to engage in sexual intercourse with him (rape), kills her (murder), and

escapes with some of her belongings (robbery), only the murder is reflected in the *UCR*. Arguably, this understates the volume of crime.

5. The *UCR*'s "Crime Index Total" actually misrepresents the crime rate in any given year. It is an FBI composite figure for public and media consumption arrived at by combining the totals of each of the eight Index Crimes in any given year. The Crime Index Total misleads because no attempt is made to distinguish offenses by severity. Thus, if in any given year the actual number of the other six offenses had remained the same (as well as population size), with an accompanying decrease of 3,000 larcenies and an increase of 3,000 homicides, the Crime Index Total would show the "crime rate" had remained constant. Yet it is somewhat disingenuous to claim that a constant crime rate could be one in which a decrease in the number of larcenies (many of which involve theft of $50 or less) somehow cancels out an identical increase in the number of homicides. Clearly, larceny and homicide should not carry the same weight.

In addition to methodological criticisms of the *UCR*, there are three major conceptual criticisms of its status as a document that claims to measure the crime rate. Perhaps the first and most obvious conceptual criticism is that the *UCR* records only *legally defined* categories of crime (see Chapter 1.2). It must be stressed that *UCR* categories of crime are *not* scientific or objective categories—they reflect the biases enshrined in the rules of criminal law and the values of legislatures and the judicial system. Given one's personal viewpoints, *UCR*'s biases may seem either good or bad, or indifferent. But biases they are.

The ramifications of such biases are examined in greater detail in Section 2.3 of this chapter. Of this point, however, consider a simple example of *UCR* vulnerability to this sort of criticism. If *you* believe crime is less a violation of law than it is a breach of human rights, for example, then the *UCR* does not and cannot measure what constitutes "crime." Whether or not they are defined as such in criminal law, if sexism and racism are crimes, the *UCR*—which counts neither of these as crimes—does a poor job of measuring crime.

A second conceptual criticism of the *UCR* is that the composition of the Crime Index imparts a distorted image of the seriousness of crime. Recall that the Index includes murder, rape, robbery, aggravated assault, burglary, larceny, motor vehicle theft, and arson (see Figure 2-1 for definitions of these offenses). The FBI apparently includes these eight crimes in the Index because they occur in large numbers and because the public regards them as the most serious crimes. But these two reasons are rather flimsy. There is considerable agreement that murder, rape, robbery, aggravated assault, and arson are very serious crimes and that they should be recorded as serious crimes in the Index. Yet why are all burglaries, larcenies, and motor vehicle thefts sufficiently serious to warrant inclusion in the Index? How is it that the theft of a bicycle (a larceny) is recorded as a serious crime but child abuse is not? Moreover, with the exception of larceny, the crimes recorded in the greatest numbers (for instance, fraud, drug abuse violations, driving under the influence) are actually Non-Index crimes.

The FBI is also frequently accused of omitting a variety of serious crimes from the Index. With the exception of arson, all Index crimes are typically committed by members of relatively powerless sections of society. The white-collar, corporate, and political crimes of the more powerful sections of society—which in the last decade the public increasingly views as serious crimes—are Non-Index offenses to which the FBI gives relatively little attention. Why the FBI omits these latter crimes from the Index is a matter of broad speculation, including:

1. its incompetence
2. its insensitivity to the plight of the powerless
3. its political bias in favor of the powerful (see Chapter 9.2)
4. its recognition of the fact that crimes typically or exclusively committed by the powerful are difficult to detect, often covered up, and seldom reported to the police (see Chapter 7.2)

The third conceptual criticism of the *UCR* takes several forms. However, most of these cluster around an intriguing question: Does the *UCR* actually measure criminal behavior (whether defined in terms of legal categories or human rights) or, instead, the bureaucratic activities of official agencies such as the police and the FBI? (Kitsuse and Cicourel, 1963; Erikson, 1966; Cicourel, 1968; but see Hindess, 1973.)

There are countless factors that influence how official crime statistics are socially constructed. Consider only the situation of the police. Quite apart from a change in "actual" criminal behavior, official crime statistics can be altered by changes in police reporting procedures, by improved or faster technological assistance, by changes in relations between the police and the citizenry, by crusades against particular crimes, by an increase in the ratio of police officers to population, and even by simple manipulation of crime reports. On this last point, we emphasize that all police agencies are faced with two contradictory pressures in the representation of their activities to the FBI, to the media, and to the public:

1. It is in their best interests to ensure that officially recorded crime rates are low (tending to show they are doing their job of fighting crime).
2. It is in their best interests to ensure that officially recorded crime rates are high (allowing them to ask for higher budgets and more personnel).

All police departments operate at some point between these two pressures.

Some time ago, sociologists John Kitsuse and Aaron Cicourel (1963) suggested that criminologists should be concerned chiefly with how crime rates are constructed by official agencies. Rather than searching for some mythical "crime rate" independent of how it is socially constructed, criminologists should examine instead the bureaucratic practices of agencies that record crime. The starting point of criminology, their argument implies, is understanding the behavior of those who define, classify, and record certain behavior as "crime" (see Chapter 14.3).

To appreciate Kitsuse and Cicourel's argument, consider how it applies to our understanding of the process by which "criminal behavior" enters the *UCR*. For a crime report to enter as a datum in the *UCR*, at least five events must occur:

1. Someone must perceive an event or behavior as a crime.

2. The crime somehow must come to the attention of the police, either through the police actually observing it (very rare) or through a report from a victim, through a confession, or through detective work.

3. The police must agree that a crime has occurred.

4. The police must code the crime on the proper *UCR* form and the form must be submitted to the FBI.

5. The FBI must include the crime in the *UCR*.

Yet each of these events is subject to enormous social interpretation and negotiation. The "facts" in these events, in other words, do not speak for themselves; each event is socially constructed.

A dramatic example of how crime rates may reflect official activity more than criminal behavior itself is provided by Philip Jenkins' (1988) controversial research on serial murders. Jenkins was initially puzzled by the substantial and well-publicized increase in the serial murder rate that apparently occurred between 1983 and 1985. According to Jenkins, it was the mass media that first presented the volume of serial murders in the United States as an "epidemic" unknown in other societies. The cause of the epidemic was often seen to be the growth of the pornography industry, whose sexually explicit materials tend to arouse the aggressive nature of certain sick individuals who had been abused as children. Harrowing TV interviews with convicted serial killers—Ted Bundy, Edmund Kemper, Henry Lee Lucas—added fuel to media fires. Jenkins (*ibid.*:1) quotes a Justice Department claim "that as many as 4,000 Americans a year, half of them under the age of 18, are murdered" by serial killers.

Jenkins suggests that, although serial murder may well represent a growing and heinous menace to society, the mass media and Justice Department officials have grossly inflated their estimates of total annual serial murders. According to Jenkins' analysis—in what amounts to the best and most complete identification of serial killers in the United States this century—serial killers account for no more than 350–400 murders each year. How, then, is it possible to distort and exaggerate *UCR* homicide data? What motives prompt such distortions?

Jenkins describes the bureaucratic *UCR* process that makes homicide data especially susceptible to manipulation. Whenever a murder is committed, the police department of jurisdiction involved is required to complete a lengthy *UCR* report and submit it to the FBI; the deadline for submission is the first five days of the month after the crime is reported. As Jenkins continues (*ibid.*:4), the police must also

> submit a supplementary homicide report, addressing topics like character-istics of the victim and offender; weapon; relationship of victim to of-fender; circumstances surrounding death; and so on. "Offenders" can be single, multiple or unknown. At this early stage, the police might well know neither the offender, a motive, nor the exact circumstances of the death. All these would thus be recorded as unknown.
>
> Weeks or months later, the situation might well change, and the correct procedure would be for the department to submit a new report to amend the first. Here though there is enormous room for cutting corners. The death has been notified, and whether a further correction is submitted depends on many factors. A conscientious officer in a profes-sional department with an efficient record system would very probably notify the reporting center that the murder was no longer "unsolved" or "motiveless" especially in an area where murder was a rare crime. Other officers in other departments might well feel that they have more import-ant things to do than to submit a revised version of a form they have already completed. This would in fact represent a third form on a sin-gle case.
>
> The chance of follow-up information being supplied will depend on a number of factors: the frequency of murder in the community; the importance given to record-keeping by a particular chief or supervisor; the organizational structure of the department (for instance, whether records and data are the responsibility of a full-time unit or of an individ-ual); and the professional standards of the department. The vast majority of departments are likely to record the simple fact of a murder being committed; only some will provide the results of subsequent investiga-tions, though these are crucial to developing any kind of national statistical profile of American homicide.

The result of this bureaucratic process is that for many cases of homicide, even though an offender and a motive were subsequently discovered, the FBI will have only a "motiveless/offender unknown" entry in their records. In 1966 the *UCR* recorded 11,000 murders in the U.S., and of these, 644 (5.9 percent) were "motiveless." In 1982 there were 23,000 murders, with 4,118 (17.8 percent) "motiveless." By 1984 the "motiveless" category had risen to 22 percent (Jenkins, 1988:4). As Jenkins describes it, there has been an alarming tendency on the part of the media and the U.S. Department of Justice to assume that all or most "motiveless" murders are the work of serial killers.

Why would the Justice Department continue with this fabrication? Jenkins admits that he opposes the idea of a conspiracy whereby the Justice Department is seen as responsible for creating the illusion of an epidemic of serial murders. Nevertheless, he claims, the serial murder "epidemic" served certain organiza-tional goals of the Justice Department. Although some FBI officials placed the number of serial murders at several hundred rather than several thousand, the orthodoxy of the latter figure was never properly contradicted by the FBI. Why not? According to Jenkins (*ibid.*:5), the serial murder "epidemic"

> became a justification for a new center for the study of violent crime at the FBI Academy in Quantico, VA, with a new Violent Criminal Apprehension Program (VICAP). In the previous two years, attempts to expand FBI databanks had met serious challenges, both from civil libertarians and from local law enforcement agencies. Similar opposition might well have been expected to the new federal interest in violent criminals.
>
> In practice, the serial killer panic helped to justify the new proposals, and the creation of a National Center for the Analysis of Violent Crime (NCAVC) was announced by President Reagan in June 1984, with an explicit focus on "repeat killers." . . . Early NCAVC publicity emphasized how frequently serial murderers "transcend jurisdictional boundaries," while serial murderers were characteristically "highly transient criminals." . . . However, it was mentioned that in the future, the new databank would expand its attention—to "rape, child molestation, arson and bombing." . . . Serial murder thus provided a wedge for an expansion of the federal role in law enforcement intelligence.

Jenkins' account of this transformation of "unsolved" homicide data into data about serial murders is a *dramatic* example of the way in which crime data are socially constructed. Equally as interesting, and perhaps even more compelling, is knowledge of the ways in which crime data are *routinely* constructed by the public and the police. Consider the findings of Donald Black's (1970) well-known study of members of the public (complainants) who report crimes to the police.

Whether or not police agree that a crime has occurred and, if so, whether they formally record it as a crime, are outcomes preceded by complicated processes of social interpretation and negotiation. Black (1970) investigated these processes in his study of routine police work in predominantly blue-collar residential areas of Boston, Chicago, and Washington, D.C. He reported that after a victim or an observer of a crime has reported (namely, as a complainant) the crime to the police, there are five conditions that influence whether or not a crime is actually accepted and formally recorded as a crime by the police.

The Legal Seriousness of the Crime   The police are more likely to write a crime report if the crime is a felony rather than a misdemeanor. In Black's study, 72 percent of felonies were written up as reports, but only 53 percent of misdemeanors. "It remains noteworthy," writes Black, "that the police officially disregard one-fourth of the felonies they handle in encounters with complainants" (1970:738).

The Complainant's Preferences   When called to the scene of a crime the police are extremely dependent on a complainant's definition of the situation. Does the complainant want the police to take official action? Does the complainant want the matter settled informally and outside official channels? Is the complainant indifferent as to further action? Black found that the police almost always agree with a complainant's preference for informal action. In situations where a complainant wishes official police action, the police complied in 84 percent of felony situations and 64 percent of misdemeanor situations.

The Relational Distance   How seriously the police regard a complainant depends partly on the relational distance between the victim and the alleged offender. The social relationship between a crime victim and an offender can be of three types: (1) fellow family members; (2) friends, neighbors, or acquaintances, and (3) strangers. Black found that when a complainant expresses a preference for official action, the police are least likely to comply in type (1), more likely in type (2), and most likely in type (3). Black also found that relational distance is often more important than the legal seriousness of the crime: "The police are more likely to give official recognition to a misdemeanor involving strangers . . . than to a felony involving friends, neighbors, or acquaintances" (*ibid.*:740).

The Complainant's Deference   Suspects rather than complainants are likely to be antagonistic toward the police. Not surprisingly, Black found that the more deference or respect shown police by a complainant, in both felony and misdemeanor situations, the more likely they are to file an official crime report. As Black puts it: "official crime rates and the justice done through police detection of criminal offenders, therefore, reflect the politeness of victims" (*ibid.*:744).

The Complainant's Status   Do the police discriminate in favor of complainants of high social status? In attempting to answer this question, Black considered status along two dimensions: class and race. For class, Black found the police tend to discriminate in favor of white-collar complainants in felony situations. In other words, the higher a complainant's social status, the more likely is it the police will respond to his (Black did not examine "her") complaint that a crime has been committed. For race, however, he found it almost impossible to arrive at a solid conclusion about discrimination. This is because most crime is intra-racial (for instance, whites tend to commit crimes against whites, blacks against blacks, Hispanics against Hispanics, and so on). Suppose, for example, that the police tend to respond more often to a white complainant than to a black complainant. It is difficult to know whether this response is discriminatory because, given that whites tend to commit crimes against whites more often than against minorities, in favoring a white complainant the police would also be more likely to be pursuing a white offender. Similarly, if the police are less likely to respond to a black complainant, they are more likely to be discriminating in favor of a black offender.

In summary, in this section we have outlined the first source of official crime data—the *UCR*. We have described both the most important data contained in the *UCR* and also their methodological and conceptual limitations. We have shown that police crime reports do not simply "enter" the *UCR* as objective data. Whether crime reports appear in the *UCR* and, if so, how they appear, depend crucially on decisions of omission or commission by the public, the police, and the FBI. We note that at least some of the methodological criticisms of the *UCR* might disappear with the FBI's introduction of a variety of changes planned to take effect gradually from the mid-1990s onwards (FBI, 1992). The redesigned *UCR* will provide "incident-based" data on both victim and offender characteristics and will be termed the *National Incident-Based Reporting System* (*NIBRS*).

The *NIBRS* will collect data on each crime incident and arrest within 22 offense categories comprising 46 "Group A" offenses; 11 "Group B" categories will have only arrest data reported. "Group A" categories include arson; assault; bribery; burglary/breaking and entering; counterfeiting/forgery; destruction/ damage/vandalism of property; drug/narcotic offenses; embezzlement; extortion/blackmail; fraud; gambling; homicide; kidnapping/abduction; larceny; motor vehicle theft; pornography/obscene material; prostitution; robbery; forcible sex offenses; nonforcible sex offenses; stolen property offenses; and weapon law violations. "Group B" categories include bad checks; curfew/loitering/vagrancy violations; disorderly conduct; DUI; drunkenness; nonviolent family offenses; liquor law violations; "Peeping Tom" offenses; runaway; trespass; and all other offenses.

We turn now to a second source of official crime data—the victimization surveys of the *National Crime Victimization Survey*.

Victimization Data: *National Crime Victimization Survey*

We have seen that the unreported "dark figure" of crime represents a large question mark in the statistical data of the *UCR*. We have implied that the actual size of the dark figure is unknowable, and that there is no good reason to suppose either that it is constant from year to year or that it has a fixed ratio with reported crime. Moreover, because the volume of crime reported in the *UCR* depends as much on police activity as it does on the actual amount of criminal activity, in principle the size of the dark figure of crime is infinite. Simply, there is as much officially recorded crime as the criminal law defines, as the public reports, and as the police accept.

During the last two decades, criminologists in the U.S. and abroad (see Chapter 16.2) have increasingly turned to "victimization surveys" to understand more about the volume and the rate of crime. *Victimization surveys* examine representative samples of a general population in an attempt to discern what crimes have been experienced in a given period. Although smaller victimization surveys occasionally have been conducted by individual researchers, a victimization survey of a large national sample of U.S. households has been conducted

Number of victimizations

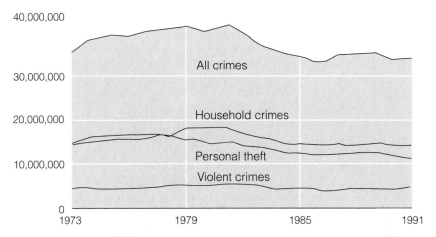

Victimization Trends for 1973–1991
2-5   *Source: Bureau of Justice Statistics,* Highlights from 20 Years of Surveying Crime Victims, *(Washington, D.C.:*
U.S. Department of Justice, 1993), p. 7.

by the Bureau of Justice Statistics each year since 1972. This is the *National Crime Victimization Survey.*

The *National Crime Victimization Survey* (NCVS) is based on a representative sample of about 42,000 households, the entire sample being interviewed twice each year (on a rotational basis) for three years. In person and by computer-assisted telephones, interviewers ask the sample's 83,000 household residents aged 12 and over for a history of the crimes committed against them in the previous year. One of the intended advantages of the *NCVS* over the *UCR* is its ability to discover information about crimes not reported to the police. The crimes examined by the *NCVS* include rape, robbery, assault, robbery or assault resulting in personal injury, personal theft, burglary, household larceny, and motor vehicle theft.

The *NCVS* surveys are designed not as a substitute for the *UCR* program but as a complement to it. Indeed, direct comparisons of data in the *NCVS* and in the *UCR* are of dubious value because the sources from which they derive are quite different. Whereas crime rates in the *UCR* derive from reports of *incidents* of crime to the police, crime rates in the *NCVS* derive from reports of *victimizations* to survey interviewers. In other words, *NCVS* data are based on individuals actually victimized; *UCR* data are based on criminal acts. Because their sources of data differ, the *UCR* and the *NCVS* tend to tell us rather different things about crime.

Certain of the principal findings (Bureau of Justice Statistics, 1988a, 1988b, 1988c; 1993; and see Figure 2-5 and Figure 2-6) of the *NCVS* reflect:

▲— Only 38 percent of all *NCVS* crimes are reported to the police. Just under half of all violent crimes, two-fifths of all household crimes, and

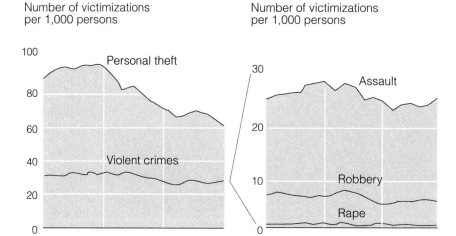

FIGURE 2-6   **Trends in Victimization Rates of Personal Crimes for 1973–1991**

Source: Bureau of Justice Statistics, Criminal Victimization, 1991 *(1993), Report NCJ-136947.*

slightly more than one-fourth of all crimes of personal theft are reported to the police.

▲— From 1973 to 1991, the level of crime overall has decreased since its peak year in 1981.

▲— Motor vehicle theft is the crime most often reported to the police (70 percent), and personal larceny (theft of purse, wallet, or cash) without contact the least often (25 percent).

▲— More than two in five black males will be victimized by a violent crime three or more times in their lifetime. About 50 percent of blacks and 40 percent of whites will suffer a completed violent crime in their lifetime.

▲— Based on 1973–1992 rates, nearly one in 12 females will be a victim of a completed or an attempted rape. The estimated rate for black females is one in nine.

▲— The percentage of households touched by crime since 1975 has declined more for whites than for blacks. Hispanic households were more vulnerable to crime than non-Hispanic households in 1991, especially for robbery, burglary, household theft, and motor vehicle theft.

▲— In 1991, 12.1 percent of the population in the West was victimized, 9.1 percent in the Midwest, 9.0 percent in the South, and 6.9 percent in the Northeast.

Assessment of the *National Crime Victimization Survey*

The *NCVS* originally was devised to yield a better idea of the size of the dark figure of crime unreported in the *UCR*. In this it has been reasonably successful:

NCVS data document that a massive amount of crime goes unreported to the police. Additionally, despite consistent increases in the rates of *UCR* Index Crimes during the 1980s, *NCVS* data reveal that victimization rates remained remarkably stable during the same period, with fluctuations (both up and down) from one year to the next limited to below 2 percent. However, this somewhat comforting finding points to the unfortunate fact that increases in *UCR* Index Crime rates may be due less to changes in criminal activity than to changes in public willingness to report crimes to the police.

The *NCVS* surveys are not without their limitations, however. Richard Sparks (1981; and see Biderman *et al.*, 1967) points to three methodological problems in the *NCVS*:

Underreporting to Interviewers   Although victimization surveys always reveal more crime than that recorded in police-based documents such as the *UCR*, the *NCVS* also understates the crime rate. Because many crimes are often somewhat insignificant to their victims, they tend to be forgotten; the tendency to forget increases as the time between the crime and an *NCVS* interview increases.

Response Biases   Because "being a survey respondent" is a rather middle-class game, the rate of underreporting is distributed unevenly throughout the class structure. Irrespective of actual victimization, whites are more likely than blacks to report having been victimized, and so are college graduates in relation to those with less education.

Time-in-Sample Bias   *NCVS* respondents are supposed to be interviewed every six months for a total of seven interviews. As interviewee participation in the *NCVS* increases, their reported victimization rates decrease consistently. This decrease may arise because, having been made more aware of victimization simply by exposure to interviewer questions, respondents take increasing precautions against victimization. But the reported victimization rates of often-interviewed participants also might fall because respondents are less cooperative (essentially, less candid) in later interviews.

In light of such problems, the Bureau of Justice Statistics has proposed several important changes to the *NCVS*, scheduled for full implementation in the mid-to-late 1990s (Bureau of Justice Statistics, 1988:2–3; 1989). These changes include a new strategy for improving the accuracy of victimization-incident recall, for expanding the scope of crimes covered (including vandalism), and for dealing with changing victimization rates over a longer period of time (a longitudinal design) so as to permit analysis of such issues as (*ibid.*):

▲— whether crime victimization is a factor in the geographic mobility of respondents

▲— long-term health and economic consequences of victimization

▲— victim contacts with the criminal justice system over an extended period of time

▲— victims who experience one-time, periodic, or relatively continuous victimization, together with such factors as the type of crime and victim (or offender characteristics) that vary across these different temporal patterns

▲— the degree to which respondents in one year also account for victimizations in other years.

Federal Agencies and Corporate Crime

We emphasize that neither the *UCR* nor the *NCVS* contains data about crimes committed by corporations in the United States. Although we discuss corporate crime at some length later in this book (Chapter 7.2), it is worth mentioning here that various federal agencies and regulatory bodies are an important source of official data about corporate crime. In addition, some data about transnational corporate crime are contained in the reports and activities of a variety of international agencies, such as the World Health Organization (see Chapter 16).

Although there is no national clearinghouse for corporate crime data, we have a good idea of the range of sources available by referring to the institutional origins of some of the many official documents used by Marshall Clinard and Peter Yeager (1980) in their pathbreaking book *Corporate Crime:* for financial violations, the Securities and Exchange Commission; for environmental violations, the Environmental Protection Agency; for labor violations, the Equal Employment Opportunity Commission, the Occupational Safety and Health Administration, the National Labor Relations Board, and the Wage and Hour Division of the Department of Labor; for manufacturing violations, the Consumer Product Safety Commission, the National Highway Traffic Safety Administration, and the Food and Drug Administration; for unfair trade practices, the Federal Trade Commission; and for administrative violations, U.S. federal courts.

Corporate violations become known to these agencies in many ways, including: (1) consumer complaints, (2) government investigations, (3) congressional committees, and (4) complaints made by corporate competitors (*ibid.*:81). However, it is important to realize that the extent of corporate misconduct not reported in the documents of federal agencies is enormous (Chapter 7.2). Such data thus suffer from some of the same problems encountered by police data.

2.3 —————— UNOFFICIAL CRIME DATA

In addition to the three sources of official crime data just described, there are several unofficial (that is, nongovernmental) sources of crime data: self-reports, biographies, participant observation, and comparative and historical data. We shall refer often to these data sources.

Self-Report Data

Given that the volume of crime is always underestimated by official crime statistics such as the police-based *UCR* and the victim-based *NCVS*, criminologists have long felt that a more complete picture of criminal activity can be had by using offender-based data. One means with which criminologists have sought to obtain offender-based data is the self-report questionnaire. In self-report studies researchers distribute questionnaires to respondents and ask them to admit—anonymously—whether they have committed certain offenses and, if so, how often. An example of questionnaire items from the National Youth Survey is given in Figure 2-7.

The first use of a self-report questionnaire was by Austin Porterfield (1946) in his study of delinquency among male and female Texas college students. Porterfield found no significant difference between the delinquent involvement of the students and a group of youth who had been processed by the juvenile court. At the same time, however, he discovered that the differential in court appearances between the two groups grew out of the powerlessness of the court children—overwhelmingly of low socioeconomic status—and the social disruption of their families.

Since Porterfield's pioneering research numerous self-report studies have shown that police-based data seriously underestimate the criminal activity of certain segments of the population. Thus, whereas police-based data show that those who commit crimes in the United States are disproportionately young, male, and black, self-report findings have typically found far less differences among offenders, and especially so in terms of their social class (Weis, 1976; Tittle, Villemez, and Smith, 1978).

For example, among the findings of his self-report study of middle-class delinquency, Joseph Weis (1976) found that "[t]he often-cited 1:6 ratio of male to female arrestees is twice as large as the mean ratio of 1:2.56 self-reported participants in delinquent behavior." However, Weis also discovered large gender differences in the prevalence (the proportion of a given population that commits crime), incidence (the rate at which a given criminal population commits crime), and seriousness of delinquent involvement: young males are more often involved than are young females in the most serious offenses.

In recent years, however, criminologists have begun to revise the image of criminal activity generated by self-report studies. Critics of self-report research point out that self-report studies have a number of important methodological defects (Elliott and Ageton, 1980:96). First, the self-report technique is vulnerable to exaggeration by respondents. It has been found that young males, especially, often exaggerate the extent of their delinquency (even on anonymous questionnaires). Second, some respondents do not remember their delinquent involvements, especially for more trivial offenses. Third, until quite recently most of the items on self-report questionnaires concerned relatively minor offenses. Fourth, in many self-report studies the respondents have not been drawn from a representative sample of the population but from a group easily accessible to

FIGURE 2-7   **Self-Reported Delinquency and Drug-Use Items as Employed in the National Youth Survey**

How many times in the last year have you:

1. purposely damaged or destroyed property belonging to your *parents* or other family *members?*
2. purposely damaged or destroyed property belonging to a *school?*
3. stolen (or tried to steal) a *motor vehicle*, such as a car or motorcycle?
4. stolen (or tried to steal) something worth more than $50?
5. knowingly bought, sold, or held stolen goods (or tried to do any of these)?
6. thrown objects (such as rocks, snowballs, or bottles) at cars or people?
7. carried a hidden weapon other than a plain pocketknife?
8. attacked someone with the intent to seriously hurt or kill him or her?
9. been involved in gang fights?
10. cheated on school tests?
11. been loud, rowdy, or unruly in a public place (disorderly conduct)?
12. had (or tried to have) sexual relations with someone against his or her will?
13. avoided paying for such things as movies, bus or subway rides, and food?
14. been drunk in a public place?
15. failed to return extra change a cashier gave you by mistake?
16. made obscene telephone calls, such as calling someone and saying dirty things?

How often in the last year have you used:

17. alcoholic beverages (beer, wine, hard liquor)?
18. marijuana/hashish (grass, pot, hash)?
19. hallucinogens (LSD, mescaline, peyote, acid)?
20. amphetamines (uppers, speed, whites)?
21. barbiturates (downers, reds)?
22. heroin (horse, smack)?
23. cocaine (coke)?

Source: Elliott and Ageton (1980), pp. 108–109, amended.

the researcher (such as, high school or college students). Each problem casts doubt on precisely what self-report studies try to do—present a balanced picture of delinquent involvement.

Certain problems of self-report research have been explicitly addressed in a study by Delbert Elliott and Suzanne Ageton (1983), who examined the delinquency of 2,375 youths ages 11–17 drawn from the National Youth Survey. The methodology of their study was far more sensitive than were previous studies to the problems of measuring crime through self-report studies. Among Elliott and Ageton's (*ibid.*:165) findings are that:

> Middle-class youth (both sexes) are less likely to be involved in serious offenses than are working- or lower-class youth. Further, even when they are involved in serious crimes, middle-class youth commit fewer offenses than do working- and lower-class youth. There are substantial class differences in both the prevalence and incidence of serious crime.
>
> When the focus is shifted from serious offenses to delinquent acts in general, there are few significant class differences in the proportions of youth reporting one or more delinquent acts. The frequency at which delinquent acts are committed does vary by class for males, however. Middle-class males commit substantially fewer delinquent acts each year than do working- and lower-class males. Females of all classes have relatively low rates of offending compared to working- and lower-class males, but there is no consistent pattern of class differences in female incidence rates.

Assuming that Elliott and Ageton's findings from self-report data are correct, how we interpret their findings is a matter of considerable debate (as we see throughout this book). It is one thing to show empirically that males, blacks, and members of the lower class tend to commit serious crimes more often than do females, whites, and members of the middle and upper classes. But it is quite another matter to explain why this is so.

Biographical Data

Another source of data about criminal activity is the personal account of their activities given criminologists by criminals. This data source was popularized in the 1920s and 1930s by investigations conducted by the Chicago School of Criminology. Chicago criminologists encouraged researchers to mix with the people they were studying (see Chapter 12.2). Well-known biographies in the literature of criminology include:

▲— Edwin Sutherland's (1937) *The Professional Thief* (see Chapter 12.4), based on the recollections of Broadway Jones, alias "Chic Conwell," a professional thief, ex-drug addict, and ex-convict from Philadelphia who worked for 20 years as a pimp, pickpocket, shoplifter, and confidence man.

▲— Carl Klockars' (1974) *The Professional Fence* (see Chapter 5.2), based on "Vincent Swaggis' " story of his life as a fence (one who receives and sells stolen goods), which discusses the methods he used to obtain stolen goods for as little money as possible as well as the elaborate rationalizations he developed to justify his career as a fence.

▲— William Chambliss' (King and Chambliss, 1984) *Boxman* (see Chapter 4.2), which is an account of "Harry King's" career as a "boxman" (safe cracker), his philosophy of life, and his lavish consumerism.

▲— Darrell Steffensmeier's (1986) *The Fence* (see Chapter 5.2), based on "Sam Goodman's" life as a fence who uses his antique shop as a front to deal in stolen merchandise, and who discusses the relationships among fences, thieves, customers, and criminal justice personnel, and the skills required to perform fencing activities.

▲— Laurie Taylor's (1984) *In the Underworld*, written after Taylor was introduced to the London underworld by John McVicar, an infamous gangster of the 1960s who (while in prison) graduated with a degree in sociology from the Open University.

▲— Stuart Hills' (Hills and Santiago, 1992) *Tragic Magic* records the escapades of recovering addict Ron Santiago, a 42-year-old black male of Cuban ancestry. Set in New York, this is a harrowing and engrossing story of robberies, burglaries, drugs, and prison.

Although one must be extremely cautious in generalizing from the experiences of one criminal to an entire segment of society, biographies of criminals can be a fertile source for further investigations. Each of the preceding studies adds relevant information to our stock of knowledge about the social world of the professional criminal.

Participant Observation

Participant observation, a form of field research, focuses on observing people in their natural settings and doing so as unobtrusively as possible. It is especially useful for observing the behavior of people (such as members of criminal syndicates, Hells' Angels, and nudist colonies) who, for one reason or another, do not usually allow known outsiders to participate in their social world. Ideally, participant observation depends on the subjects of study being unaware that the observer is in fact an observer. Among the many participant observation studies in the literature of criminology and the sociology of deviance are:

▲— William Foote Whyte's (1943) *Streetcorner Society*. Seeking to "build a sociology based on observed interpersonal events" (*ibid.*:358), Whyte lived for three years in "Cornerville," where he ate, drank, played, and talked intimately with members of a slum neighborhood. He concluded that the "slum" community of street-corner boys was highly organized, a fact invisible to conventional outsiders who could see only its disorganized and aimless life-styles.

▲__ Ned Polsky's (1967) *Hustlers, Beats, and Others*. Polsky exposed the techniques of poolroom hustling by engaging in participant observation as a hustler's opponent, a hustler's backer, and as a hustler himself.

▲__ Laud Humphrey's (1970) *Tearoom Trade*. Humphrey's account of impersonal homosexual encounters in public facilities was the result of field research, during the course of which he gained entry into the subculture by posing as a lookout.

▲__ Jason Ditton's (1977) *Part-Time Crime* (and see Chapter 7.1), in which the English criminologist Ditton went undercover as a dispatch operative, observing the routine "fiddles" to which sales operatives in Wellbread's Bakery were prone.

▲__ Jack Douglas and Paul Rasmussen's (1977) *The Nude Beach*, in which Douglas and Rasmussen observed the complicated interaction among bathers on a nude beach in La Jolla, California.

▲__ Marc Reisner's (1991) *Game Wars* takes us inside the underworld of Cajun alligator poachers and ivory importers, focusing on the dangerous investigations of undercover U.S. Fish and Wildlife game warden Dave Hall.

Each study is a classic example of how to gather data by the method of participant observation. Each study produced data available only to participants. However, the actual practice of participant observation is plagued with difficult questions. Some of the questions concern ethics—where is the dividing line between the appropriate gathering of data about human subjects and invading their right to privacy? Thus, both Humphrey's (1970) observation of gay men in homosexual encounters and Douglas and Rasmussen's (1977) research on nudists have been accused of being unethical. Other questions concern danger—what happens if the researcher is detected by the subjects? Still others concern objectivity—how can one study something objectively if one is a part of what one studies?

Because field research is rarely either detached observation on the one hand, or embroiled participation on the other, participation often becomes a question of "how much?" To fully immerse oneself in the situation is to risk altering the events one observes and perhaps even losing sight of one's role as a researcher. But field researchers argue that these risks are small compared to the benefits to be gained from being a participant. A stranger to a situation may easily take a word, a sigh or other gesture, or a relationship for something wholly different from what it means to a participant (Singleton, Straits, Straits, and McAllister, 1988, p. 302).

Comparative and Historical Data

The great French sociologist Émile Durkheim (1895:157) once remarked that "comparative sociology is not a special branch of sociology, it is sociology itself." So it is, too, with criminology. Comparative criminology, whose promise and whose pitfalls are documented in Chapter 16, is a frequently ignored, relatively undeveloped, yet crucial dimension of criminology. Its focus is cross-cultural or historical investigation of crime. It allows us to compare crime rates in the United States—as well as their causes and the effectiveness of government policies toward them—with those in other cultures, places, and times. Does the United States have a higher homicide rate, for example, than Japan, Canada, or England? If so, why?

Typically, comparative data are used to compare crime in two or more countries at one point in time. Comparative data about crime, like other crime data, have both official and unofficial sources. Official crime data derive from the activities and reports of national governments and government agencies. These data can be found in the reports of such international agencies as the United Nations, the World Health Organization, and the International Police Organization (Interpol). Some researchers are even beginning to compare the findings of victimization surveys conducted in different countries. Unofficial crime data derive from the reports and findings of such private organizations as Amnesty International and, potentially, from the use of self-report, participant observation, and biographical data in a comparative context. However, for comparative purposes, these data are quite difficult to interpret (see Chapter 16.2).

Other types of comparative study can be based on historical data. The diverse sources of historical data include official statistics (on crime, prison populations, health, and so on), court records, books, newspapers, journals, pamphlets, plays, and oral histories. Historical data help us examine the past in order to understand how we have arrived at the present; ideally, they allow us to make generalizations about crime that stand outside the peculiarities of any given era. Historical studies of crime are therefore implicitly comparative. Douglas Hay's (1975) study of crime and criminal law in 18th-century England, for example, revealed that in societies where the criminal justice system is based on terror—in this case, execution for the most petty of offenses—a national police force might be quite unnecessary. Occasionally, historical studies of crime are also cross-cultural. A good example of a study that is both historical and cross-cultural is *The Politics of Crime and Conflict* by Ted Robert Gurr, Peter Grabosky, and Roger Hula (1977). Their study revealed that the relationship between public policies and crime rates in Calcutta, London, Stockholm, and Sydney during a 150-year period was in many ways strikingly similar, despite the enormous social, economic, and political differences among these disparate cities.

2.4 ———— ASSESSMENT

In this chapter we have described the major sources of data for studying crime today. But we must stress that crime data can *never* represent criminal behavior in a neutral or unbiased way—data do not speak for themselves! The particular crime rate identified and measured by official crime data, for example, very much depends on the legalistic concepts that guide the process of measurement. We do not, of course, mean by this that criminologists intentionally distort data to suit their own purposes. Rather, we mean that data are identified and defined by concepts, and that criminologists naturally differ in the concepts of crime they hold appropriate for the study of crime.

This is an important point, for as you read the contents of this book, you will learn that how criminologists *explain* (interpret) crime data depends both on their concepts of crime and on the assumptions underlying their *theories* of crime. Theories are sets of assumptions, mediated by concepts, that guide the interpretation of data. Theories try to explain both regularities and irregularities in data. In exactly the same way that what constitutes crime data depends on any given concept of crime so, too, how we explain crime data depends, to a certain extent, on the assumptions of our theories.

REVIEW

Chapter 2 outlined the major sources of data available to criminologists. Official crime data are published by the state and by state agencies. In the United States such publications include the *Uniform Crime Reports* (*UCR*), the *National Crime Victimization Survey* (*NCVS*), and diverse federal records of corporate crime. Unofficial crime data include self-report data, biographical data, participant observation, and comparative and historical data. In this chapter you learned, however, that crime data can *never* represent criminal behavior in a neutral or unbiased way. We now review the major points of the chapter.

Caution: Data Do Not Speak for Themselves!

1. Data are not objective facts that exist independently of the concepts and theories of those who observe them. Such data can never represent criminal behavior in a neutral or unbiased way.

2. Data are identified and defined by concepts about whose appropriateness criminologists naturally differ. In exactly the same way that what constitutes crime data depends on any given concept of crime, so, too, how we explain crime data depends, to a certain extent, on the assumptions of our theories.

Official Crime Data

1. The *UCR* distinguishes between eight Index Crimes (Part I) and 21 Non-Index Crimes (Part II). Data about Index Crimes derive from reports to the police, and data about Non-Index Crimes, from police arrests.

2. The *UCR* annually tabulates data about the number and rate of crimes; crime trends by year and region; the age, sex, and race of offenders and victims; and offense clearance rates.

3. Criticisms of the *UCR* are either methodological or conceptual. Among the latter is the limitation that the *UCR* records only legally defined categories of crime. Ultimately, however, we cannot be sure whether the *UCR* measures criminal behavior or the bureaucratic activities of official agencies. Whether or not police officers accept a crime report depends on the legal seriousness of the crime, the complainant's preferences, the relational distance between victim and offender, and the complainant's deference and social status.

4. The *NCVS* victimization surveys (based on reports of victimizations) were designed to complement the *UCR*, but comparisons between them are of dubious value.

5. The *NCVS* indicates that only 37 percent of all crimes are reported to the police, that females and black males are among the most victimized groups in the population, and that nearly one-third of all households annually suffer some form of victimization.

6. Difficulties with *NCVS* data include underreporting to interviewers, response biases, and time-in-sample bias.

7. Neither the *UCR* nor the *NCVS* contains any data about corporate crime; however, various federal agencies and regulatory bodies are important sources of such data.

Unofficial Crime Data

1. Self-report data are offender-based data obtained from questionnaires. These data have tended to show that middle-class youth commit as much crime as working-class youth, but that there are large gender differences in the prevalence, incidence, and seriousness of delinquent involvement. Critics of self-report studies argue that the data suffer from young male exaggerations, from biases due to failure to recall delinquency, and from a concentration on the relatively minor offenses committed by juveniles.

2. Biographical data are accounts of personal activities given by criminals to criminologists. Biographies can be a fertile source for further investigation, but are notoriously resistant to generalization.

3. Participant observation is a form of field research whose goal is to observe people as unobtrusively as possible in their natural settings. Its actual practice is plagued with difficult questions, including the problem of deciding where the dividing line lies between the appropriate gathering of data about human subjects and invasion of their right to privacy.

4. Comparative and historical data are closely related. Comparative data chiefly derive from the activities and reports of national governments and such international agencies as the UN, the WHO, and Interpol. Such data typically are used to compare crime in two or more countries at one point in time. Historical data derive from a great diversity of sources.

Such data permit us to generalize about crime in a manner outside the peculiarities of any given era; occasionally the generalizations are also cross-cultural.

QUESTIONS FOR CLASS DISCUSSION

1. Which do the *Uniform Crime Reports* measure: activities of offenders or activities of the police?
2. Do victimization surveys help us understand the true extent of the dark figure of crime?
3. Can crime data ever represent objective facts?

RECOMMENDED READINGS

Hindess, Barry (1973). *The Use of Official Statistics in Sociology*. London: Macmillan. A critique of the view that official statistics are incapable of measuring an objective reality. Hindess especially takes issue with the arguments of Cicourel and Kitsuse on which we have somewhat relied in this chapter.

Irvine, John, Ian Miles, and Jeff Evans (1981) (eds.). *Demystifying Social Statistics*. London: Pluto Press. A collection of 22 essays that analyzes how statistical data are socially constructed.

Keat, Russell and John Urry (1975). *Social Theory as Science*. London: Routledge & Kegan Paul. This book demonstrates, as a reviewer (Philip Abrams) suggests on the dust jacket, just why sociology offends those whose work requires the maintenance of authority, whether the authority is that of office or of positivist science.

Sparks, Richard F. (1981). "Surveys of Victimization—An Optimistic Assessment." *Crime and Justice: An Annual Review of Research*, 3:1–60. A detailed assessment of both the potential and pitfalls of victimization surveys.

CHAPTER 3

INEQUALITY, CRIME, AND VICTIMIZATION

Preview

Chapter 3 introduces:

☞ social inequality and its relation to crime.
☞ how social position both permits and prevents criminal opportunity.
☞ patterns of crime and victimization in the United States.

Key Terms

age   race
class   social inequality
gender   social position

A s emphasized in Chapters 1 and 2, crime is a **sociological problem.** To understand the varieties of crime, then, it is essential to establish their sociological context—how crime is shaped by the social factors of society. Accordingly, in Chapter 3 we discuss considerable sociological research necessary to grasp the patterns of crime in U.S. society.

Chief among the social factors underlying crime is structured social inequality. All industrialized societies are marked by social inequalities. Critical aspects of life—such as economic benefits, life chances, social privileges, and political power—are intimately connected to the historically developed social inequalities that structure society. Inequality is a sociological question, a product of human history.

In contemporary U.S. society, there are four major forms of inequality that influence crime: class, gender, race, and age. These inequalities create different life experiences for people depending upon their class, gender, race, and age characteristics, and they also shape patterns of crime and victimization. In other words, criminal opportunities and victimization are intimately related to **social position** in the class, gender, race, and age hierarchies of society. Social position thus refers to one's individual location in society based on the social characteristics of class, gender, race, and age.

Some scholars, especially psychologists, attempt to explain why one individual commits crime and another individual in the same social position does not. Although an intriguing question, our focus here lies in explaining sociological **patterns** of crime. Why do members of one class disproportionately commit a certain type of crime? Why do men commit more crimes than women? To answer such questions we must analyze those inequalities in social structures that shape our lives. Social position—in terms of class, gender, race, and age—influences, limits, and structures human behavior, whether that behavior is legal or illegal, harmful or safe. Social position permits and precludes criminal opportunities. The patterns of crime therefore reflect the broader inequalities embedded in society.

In the real world, social inequalities are actually interrelated. But in this chapter, for analytical purposes, we discuss class, gender, race, and age separately. As participating members of society, each of us has simultaneously a class, gender, race, and age social position. All four positions interact to structure society and its accompanying patterns of crime and victimization. Unfortunately, in an introductory textbook it is impossible to provide a complete picture of the relationship between social inequality and crime. Thus, our discussion is limited to an examination of why and how general patterns of crime and victimization occur in the United States.

3.1 _____ CLASS AND CRIME

In the United States there exists sharp class divisions and inequalities that structure the patterns of crime and victimization. Although class position is associated with level of income, occupation, and education, it is determined chiefly by the way in which the production system of a society is organized. Historically, societies have organized production in different ways, and this in turn creates different types of social classes. Class, then, becomes an important sociological concept for understanding patterns of crime. We define a *social class* as a group of people who share the same position in the same production system. Class structures both economic relationships and inequalities, and also the *type* and *seriousness* of crime.

Patterns of Crime and Victimization

The *Uniform Crime Reports* does not rank the crime rates of different social classes. However, John Braithwaite (1981:38) reviewed a significant number of studies employing official statistics to generate data on the relationship between class and crime, and concluded they all "showed lower-class juveniles to have substantially higher offense rates than middle-class juveniles. Among adults, all . . . studies found lower-class people to have higher crime rates." Moreover, Braithwaite's (1979a:62) earlier review of nearly 300 studies based on official statistics *and* self-reports concluded that:

1. Lower-class adults commit those types of crime handled by the police (conventional crimes) at a higher rate than do middle-class adults.

2. Adults living in lower-class areas commit those types of crime handled by the police at a higher rate than do adults living in middle-class areas.

3. Lower-class juveniles commit crime at a higher rate than do middle-class juveniles.

4. Juveniles living in lower-class areas commit crime at a higher rate than do juveniles living in middle-class areas.

Regarding specific-offense types, self-report studies over the last 10 years indicate that class differences exist for both serious property crime and interpersonal crimes of violence (Currie, 1985; Box, 1983; Elliott and Huizinga, 1983; Thornberry and Farnworth, 1983). A delinquency study by Elliott and Huizinga (*ibid.*) is of particular importance because it analyzed both the percentage of a social class committing certain offenses at a specific time (prevalence) and the frequency with which these class members commit crimes (incidence). For status offenses and general delinquency, class differentials in prevalence were practically nonexistent. Elliott and Huizinga did, however, find significant class differentials for youth in the serious conventional crimes: middle-class youth were far less likely to report committing such crimes than were lower- and working-class youth. Regarding incidence, the same pattern held: both male and female middle-class youth were much less likely than were other youth to report committing serious crimes.

As emphasized in Chapters 1 and 2, conventional crimes are only one aspect of the entire range of crimes. Unfortunately, criminological studies of class and crime have concentrated on class differences in conventional crimes, ignoring white-collar and political crimes. Although poor and working-class people may commit the more serious conventional crimes handled by the police, members of the professional-managerial class (traditionally seen as the middle class) have greater opportunities to commit white-collar and political crimes. In fact, when we consider this class/crime link, it is clear the vast bulk of avoidable harm and economic loss originates from the professional-managerial class. Consequently, the *type* and *seriousness* of crime are associated with social class position: conventional crimes tend to be committed more often by the poor and working classes; white-collar and political crimes tend to be committed more often by the professional-managerial class.

The *National Crime Victimization Survey* provides information on victimization and aids in the formulation of conclusions about the *intra-* and *interclass* nature of conventional crimes. As Table 3-1 shows, for rape, robbery, assault, and personal larceny with contact, the lower the family income the greater the chance of victimization. The most frequent victims of such crimes are those with an annual family income of less than $10,000. We can conclude that such crimes as rape, robbery, assault, and personal larceny with contact tend to be *intraclass:* both the *offenders* and the *victims* are usually members of the same class.

However, for personal larceny without contact, Table 3-1 shows there are high rates of both intra- and interclass victimization. In other words, the highest and the lowest family income groups report the most victimization.

Table 3-2 shows victimization rates for the category termed "household crimes" (burglary, household larceny, and motor vehicle theft). Each household crime shows a different pattern: burglary victimization declines with annual family income; household larceny victimization remains relatively stable throughout all incomes; and motor vehicle theft increases with annual family income.

With the exception of personal larceny without contact and motor vehicle theft, conventional crime victimization is therefore an intraclass phenomenon. In other words, the poor tend to victimize the poor, but are *also* more susceptible to syndicated, corporate, and political crime victimization. Consequently, the poor face crime from all directions. John Lea and Jock Young (1984:73) provide an excellent example of this tragedy:

> A typical scenario is a modern housing estate which has a high rate of burglary, street robbery and interpersonal violence. But this community also has a higher rate of police attacks than other places. . . . The faulty construction of the houses is such that there is a constant problem of heat loss and dampness—all adding to the tenants' bills and a direct result of a fraudulent deal between certain councillors and the building contractors ten years ago. . . . The factory down the road pollutes the atmosphere way above the safety limits; the machines on which many of the tenants work are not adequately guarded.

With this information in mind, we consider theory and research on class and crime.

TABLE 3-1   Personal crimes, 1991: Victimization rates for persons age 12 and over, by type of crime and annual family income of victims

TYPE OF CRIME	RATE PER 1,000 PERSONS AGE 12 AND OVER						
	LESS THAN $7,500	$7,500– $9,999	$10,000– $14,999	$15,000– $24,999	$25,000– $29,999	$30,000– $49,999	$50,000 OR MORE
All personal crimes	121.5	102.9	103.4	88.3	88.8	85.4	85.7
Crimes of violence	59.4	42.1	43.1	30.9	31.9	25.0	19.9
Completed	25.2	20.3	18.6	11.2	11.7	8.4	5.4
Attempted	34.2	21.8	24.5	19.7	20.2	16.6	14.5
Rape	1.8	0.0*	1.7	1.0	0.3*	0.8	0.4*
Robbery	9.6	7.9	7.6	5.0	6.0	3.7	3.3
Completed	5.7	6.2	6.4	3.5	3.0	2.3	1.8
With injury	2.4	2.6*	3.0	1.0	1.1*	0.5*	0.7*
From serious assault	1.3*	1.1*	1.4	0.5*	0.7*	0.3*	0.2*
From minor assault	1.1*	1.5*	1.6	0.5*	0.4*	0.1*	0.5*
Without injury	3.3	3.7	3.5	2.5	2.0	1.8	1.1
Attempted	3.9	1.7*	1.1*	1.6	3.0	1.5	1.5
With injury	2.2	0.5*	0.2*	0.5*	0.2*	0.3*	0.8
From serious assault	1.0*	0.5*	0.1*	0.1*	0.2*	0.3*	0.4*
From minor assault	1.2*	0.0*	0.1*	0.4*	0.0*	0.0*	0.3*
Without injury	1.7	1.1*	0.9*	1.1	2.8	1.2	0.7*
Assault	48.0	34.2	33.9	24.8	25.6	20.5	16.2
Aggravated	19.6	9.5	9.8	7.5	8.3	6.3	3.9
Completed with injury	8.3	4.8	3.9	2.6	2.3	2.2	1.2
Attempted with weapon	11.3	4.8	5.9	4.8	5.9	4.1	2.7
Simple	28.4	24.7	24.1	17.4	17.3	14.2	12.3
Completed with injury	10.3	9.3	7.8	4.9	6.1	3.5	2.2
Attempted without weapon	18.1	15.3	16.3	12.4	11.1	10.7	10.1
Crimes of theft	62.1	60.8	60.2	57.4	56.9	60.4	65.8
Completed	58.5	56.4	55.4	54.1	52.8	56.9	61.3
Attempted	3.6	4.4	4.8	3.3	4.1	3.5	4.5
Personal larceny with contact	3.5	2.8*	2.7	2.5	1.5*	1.6	2.1
Purse snatching	1.0*	0.7*	0.9*	0.6*	0.6*	0.5*	0.8
Pocket picking	2.5	2.2*	1.8	1.9	0.9*	1.1	1.2
Personal larceny without contact	58.6	57.9	57.5	54.9	55.4	58.8	63.7
Completed	55.3	53.6	52.7	51.8	51.5	55.4	59.4
Less than $50	21.3	19.6	20.1	23.6	20.4	21.5	20.6
$50 or more	30.2	31.5	28.3	26.7	29.3	31.9	37.0
Amount not available	3.7	2.4*	4.2	1.4	1.9	2.1	1.8
Attempted	3.3	4.4	4.8	3.1	3.9	3.4	4.4
Population age 12 and over	18,430,370	7,865,690	19,024,060	34,134,110	14,318,880	47,190,800	35,611,150

Note: Detail may not add to total shown because of rounding.
Excludes data on persons whose family income level was not ascertained.
*Estimate is based on about 10 or fewer sample cases.

Source: Department of Justice, 1992, p. 33.

TABLE 3-2 Household Crimes, 1991: Victimization rates by type of crime and annual family income

TYPE OF CRIME	RATE PER 1,000 HOUSEHOLDS						
	LESS THAN $7,500	$7,500– $9,999	$10,000– $14,999	$15,000– $24,999	$25,000– $29,999	$30,000– $49,999	$50,000 OR MORE
Household crimes	**186.7**	**173.6**	**175.5**	**168.2**	**136.2**	**155.2**	**148.9**
Completed	159.8	140.7	149.3	142.7	116.3	132.1	127.8
Attempted	26.9	33.0	26.3	25.6	19.9	23.0	21.0
Burglary	80.8	68.9	65.1	49.4	44.5	43.8	41.4
Completed	61.6	48.1	48.9	39.0	37.8	33.1	34.9
Forcible entry	22.6	22.9	20.6	16.9	13.0	16.7	11.9
Unlawful entry without force	39.0	25.3	28.3	22.1	24.8	16.4	23.0
Attempted forcible entry	19.2	20.7	16.2	10.4	6.7	10.7	6.6
Household larceny	95.5	85.5	91.5	96.5	75.8	87.2	79.8
Completed	90.8	78.5	87.8	89.4	69.3	82.7	75.4
Less than $50	41.0	35.4	33.6	41.2	26.8	35.8	28.5
$50 or more	44.4	39.9	48.9	43.7	40.1	43.0	43.4
Amount not available	5.4	3.2*	5.2	4.5	2.3*	3.9	3.6
Attempted	4.7	7.0	3.7	7.1	6.6	4.5	4.4
Motor vehicle theft	10.4	19.3	19.0	22.4	15.9	24.2	27.6
Completed	7.4	14.0	12.6	14.2	9.2	16.3	17.5
Attempted	3.1	5.3*	6.4	8.1	6.6	7.8	10.1
Total number of households	11,446,200	4,459,670	9,834,890	16,509,010	6,536,300	20,022,920	14,174,160

Note: Detail may not add to total shown due to rounding.
Excludes data on families whose income level was not ascertained.
*Estimate is based on about 10 or fewer sample cases.

Source: Department of Justice, 1992, p. 46.

Class and Varieties of Crime

Class inequalities have not always been the norm in human societies. Through societal evolution from gathering-hunting to industrialized capitalist societies, the class structure has changed. In industrial-capitalist societies such as the United States (which evolved over the last 200 years), class and economic inequalities persist. As outlined earlier, class position is determined by societal organization of production. In industrialized capitalist societies—based on private ownership of the means of production (such as land, tools, factories, money, and so on)—a market of landless but "free" laborers is prevalent. These laborers (working class) sell their labor to the owners of the means of production (capitalist class) in order to survive. Thus, in the United States a four-class hierarchy has developed, based on a group's relationship to the production process and productive property. As depicted in Figure 3-1, at the top of the hierarchy is the *capitalist class*—those who own the major means of production. This ownership allows members of this class to have leisurely and expensive life-styles. The capitalist class consists of approximately 1.5 to 2 percent of the population; some well-known members are the Du Ponts, Kennedys, Mellons, and Rockefellers. Immediately below the capitalist class is the *professional-managerial class*—those who do not own the means of production but who manage it for the owners. This class consists of approximately 15 percent of the population, and is made

FIGURE 3-1   The Class Hierarchy

up of such social positions as highly paid corporate and financial executives who make the critical investment and economic decisions of their corporations. Also in this class are U.S. Representatives and Senators as well as highly paid professors, doctors, lawyers, and judges. The vast majority of people in the United States (close to 70 percent) are members of the *working class*—those who work for a wage and do not control any portion of the means of production. Finally, at the bottom of the hierarchy are the *poor* (13.5 percent)—those who are unemployed or who work for a wage that keeps them below the poverty line.

These unequal class relationships help explain the class patterns of crime and victimization. Regarding conventional crimes handled by the police, research shows that economic conditions associated with the poor and working classes— in particular, unemployment, income inequality, and quality of job—play a significant role in their perpetuation. Notwithstanding the inconsistencies in research on the relationship between unemployment and conventional crime, the majority of studies report a link between the two. M. Harvey Brenner's (1976) pioneering work in the 1970s, for instance, found that when the unemployment rate increased 1 percentage point, there was a corresponding 4-percent increase in homicides and a 6-percent increase in robberies. In the 1980s, research again uncovered a link between unemployment and conventional crime. James Defronzo's (1983:128) study of 39 U.S. metropolitan areas found that "unemployment rates had statistically significant positive effects on rape, burglary, and larceny." Thornberry and Christensen (1984) investigated the employment history of 1,000 boys born in 1945 and related this to the boys' involvement in conventional criminality. They concluded that "unemployment has significant instantaneous effects on crime" (*ibid.*:408). In other words, crime seems to follow the onset of unemployment. Finally, Cook and Zarkin (1985) investigated the business cycle and its relationship to conventional crime from 1933 to 1980. They concluded that "an increase in the unemployment rate from, say, 7 percent to 8 percent will result in a 2.3 percent increase in the robbery rate and a 1.6

Sociological research has found a correlation between unemployment and conventional crime.

percent increase in the burglary rate" (*ibid.*:126). Consequently, when large numbers of people are unemployed, there appears to be an increase in the conventional crime rate.

Given a correlation between unemployment and conventional crime, we cannot forget that other characteristics—such as gender and age—play an equally significant role in the patterning of conventional crime. Indeed, as noted later in this chapter, both the elderly and women have high unemployment rates yet do not commit conventional crimes at the rate, for instance, that young males do. Consequently, gender and age mediate the unemployment/crime association.

In addition to unemployment, income inequality significantly affects conventional crime. Braithwaite's (1979:216) study of 193 U.S. metropolitan areas found "strong and consistent support for the hypothesis that cities in which there is a wide income gap between poor and average-income families have high rates for all types of crime." Jacobs (1981) studied property crimes and income inequality in some 200 cities and established a strong relationship between economic inequality and the crimes of burglary and larceny. Jacobs' study is important because it helps us understand why high rates of property-crime victimization occur in higher income groups. As Jacobs (*ibid.*:22–23) points out:

> When there are large differences in resources in a metropolitan area, those with little to lose and much to gain will find that potential victims with more to steal are located only a limited distance away. . . . The less successful can readily observe the fruits of affluence in unequal metropolitan areas. It follows that in a society where there is a great cultural

emphasis placed on economic success, pronounced differences in resources seem to result in more property crimes.

In other words, relative class deprivation and inequality seem conducive to higher rates of conventional property crime. This notion of relative deprivation helps explain the high personal larceny without contact and motor vehicle theft victimization rates for high income groups.

Other research demonstrates that income inequality directly affects both the rate of property crimes (Carrol and Jackson, 1983) and the rate of violent crimes (Blau and Blau, 1982). Blau and Blau's (*ibid.*) study found that in the 125 largest metropolitan areas, high rates of interpersonal violence largely result from economic inequalities. Income inequalities in cities promote interpersonal violence because "in a society founded on the principle 'that all men are created equal,' economic inequalities rooted in ascribed positions violate the spirit of democracy and are likely to create alienation, despair and conflict" (*ibid.*:26). Other studies make similar conclusions about violent crime. For instance, Stack and Kanavy (1983:71–72) investigated the relationship between economic conditions and rape, reporting strong support "for an economic theory of crime based on unemployment as well as income inequality. Both variables exert positive, independent effects on rape."

Finally, the quality of occupation available seems to be highly associated with conventional crime. When jobs are low paying, unstable, and menial and offer little opportunity for advancement, conventional property crime becomes significantly more attractive. In his important book *Confronting Crime*, Elliot Currie (1985) reviews the literature on the relationship between the secondary labor market and conventional crime and concludes that not only unemployment and income inequality affect the conventional crime rate, but that another consistent influence is

the *quality* of work—its stability, its level of pay, its capacity to give the worker a sense of dignity and participation, the esteem of peers and community. In our society these fundamental needs are virtually impossible to satisfy without a job—but they are all too often difficult even *with* a job, and nearly impossible in many of the kinds of jobs available in America today, especially to the disadvantaged young.

In a class society, those at the bottom are more likely to experience such economic conditions as unemployment, lower relative incomes, and the degradation and alienation associated with low-paying jobs. Consequently, they are also more likely to turn to conventional crime.

These unequal economic conditions are also associated with crimes of the *hidden economy*—those economic transactions that are unreported and often illegal. For instance, babysitting for a friend is a *legal* part of the hidden economy. Illegal transactions of the hidden economy consist of conventional property crimes—from robbery to fencing—but also such crimes as illegal drug distribution, gambling, prostitution, and employee theft. The hidden economy entails

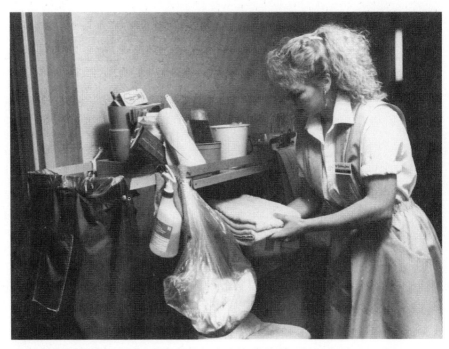

The quality of work available in lower- and working-class communities is a consistent influence on the conventional crime rate.

large numbers of people participating in economic activity—working, buying, selling—outside the view and control of the state (Mattera, 1985:1). Employee theft and the amateur trade in stolen goods are examples of activities within this hidden economy. Moreover, as Stuart Henry (1987:144) and others suggest: "Modern capitalist industrial society encourages such economies by creating structural inequalities based on class." When the legitimate labor market offers few attractive alternatives, illicit work—selling drugs, running numbers rackets, engaging in prostitution, and organizing criminal syndicates—becomes relatively inviting. For example, some poor and working-class women elect prostitution not only for economic survival but also for the independence it offers. Eleanor Miller (1986:140) reported in her work on deviant street networks that prostitutes, in their own way, have a degree of independence, excitement, and autonomy that similarly qualified persons in the world of legal work rarely enjoy. As noted, most jobs available to the poor and working class are routine, confining, and seriously alienating. One prostitute put it this way: "You don't have certain hours you have to work. You can go to work when you want, leave when you want . . . you don't have a boss hanging over you, you're independent" (James, 1982:302).

However, conventional crimes of the hidden economy are not found solely on the street. Indeed, most crime occurs in the workplace. As Box (1987:34) shows, economic conditions such as inflation can affect the working class by pushing people into higher tax brackets and reducing the overall purchasing power of their remaining income. The result is that those who experience reduced standards of living and are not prepared to endure it sometimes turn to tax evasion, embezzlement, fraud, and other forms of occupational crime and off-the-books income.

However, occupational crimes cannot be explained solely by economic deprivation. Closer examination of crimes such as employee theft reveals that the *internal* structure of the workplace is equally important. Hollinger and Clark's (1983:86) study of employee theft in three different industries concluded that this crime "is best understood within the social context of the work environment that includes perceived job dissatisfaction as a principal component." Dissatisfaction includes not only job quality, as discussed, but also such issues as *perceived inequality.* Many workers, when belittled by employers and thus reminded of the inequality in the workplace, turn to employee theft to "get back" at the boss or company. Altheide *et al.* (1978:103) provide an example:

> After a clean-up boy was lectured on the correct way to mop floors, the boy took several books to show the manager he was not to be belittled. Now the books were not made known to the manager, but were shown to friends with a story of how he showed the manager. . . . These types of thefts also occurred when the employees felt they had been screwed out of something. For instance, one employee took a shirt from men's wear because he didn't get time and a half for working a Sunday.

It is the unequal relationships within the workplace, and workers' resentment of that inequality, that often trigger employee theft. Moreover, according to Henry (1987:145, 146), employers often tolerate a certain amount of employee theft as a "hidden arm of control"; workplace thefts thus simply become "cheap symbolic concessions" to overall class inequality.

Thus far we have explored crimes largely associated with the poor and working classes, and how social position permits and precludes opportunities for committing conventional crimes. However, with the development of large corporations, financial institutions, and the state, a corresponding consolidation of a professional-managerial class has emerged. Members of this class can of course commit conventional crimes, but their structural position also provides the opportunity to engage in corporate and political crimes. The remainder of this section is devoted to a brief discussion of each.

Within corporate management today there exists an inner circle comprising the leading corporate executives of major corporations (Useem, 1984: 59–75). These executives are members of the same clubs and business associations, attend similar universities, and generally hold conservative political views. Moreover, they all have a similar corporate motive—profit making—which serves both their individual corporations and this segment of the professional-managerial class.

Corporations in a capitalist economy endure only if they make a profit; yet profit making is not simply a matter of individual corporate greed. Rather, the pressure to make profits is created and enforced by the competitive structure of capitalism as an economic system. Corporations that do not continually reinvest their capital are likely to be "eaten up" by those that do. This pressure for profits drives many corporate executives to engage in corporate crime. As Stuart Hills (1987:190) argues in his book *Corporate Violence:*

> In a capitalist economy, profit-seeking firms must often compete in an uncertain and unpredictable environment. Competitive market pressures, fluctuating sales, increasing costs for safety and health measures, consumer and environmental concerns, governmental regulations, and other constraints may limit the ability of the business firm to achieve its profit goals through legitimate opportunities. Thus, some corporations may evade and violate the law or engage in practices that many Americans would consider unethical, endangering the well-being of workers, consumers, and citizens.

In other words, in the pursuit of profit, corporate executives must overcome several obstacles to succeed at profit making, such as minimizing costs and creating demand. Corporate executives can increase profits by keeping down costs. The lower the cost to the corporation for labor, tools, machinery, and so on, the higher the profits. Many corporate executives secure profits by minimizing costs of worker, consumer, and environmental safety. The pressure to minimize costs helps create the conditions for corporate crimes (such as unsafe working conditions, unsafe products, environmental pollution, subminimum wages) and transnational corporate crimes (such as dumping unsafe products and moving unsafe working conditions to more favorable environments).

A corporation has difficulty making a profit if it fails to sell what it produces. Thus, in addition to minimizing costs, corporate executives must create a demand for their product. This necessity is conducive to corporate deception in marketing, especially when demand for the product is erratic and variable. Corporate executives thus may conquer this obstacle by engaging in such corporate crimes as consumer fraud, false advertising, and other deceptive practices (Messerschmidt, 1986:115–116; Box, 1983:36).

In sum, then, although every corporation is not criminal, in a profit-driven society corporations are inherently criminogenic because of the intrinsic aspects of profit-making and the obstacles a corporation must overcome to achieve its primary goal. Because of such corporate priorities, incentives exist that make corporate crime the logical outcome. In fact, sociological studies show that when corporate profits decline, corporate crime occurs more often (Clinard and Yeager, 1981:129; Box, 1987:98–102; Simpson, 1986, 1987). Thus, corporate executives, their structural position in the professional-managerial class, and the necessity of profit-making help us understand corporate crime.

This constant requirement for profit-making is also related to corporate association with criminal syndicates (traditionally known as "organized crime"). Profits from the illegal sale and distribution of goods and services often are laundered in large financial institutions, providing profits for both the syndicate and these corporations. There is, then, a close relationship between the hidden economy and the formal economy. Through labor racketeering, criminal syndicates also serve corporate interests by providing a means of preventing unionization and for controlling labor organizing, which helps minimize costs. In short, the symbiotic relationship between criminal syndicates and legitimate businesses serves both interests by helping them achieve their common goal of profit-making.

Members of the professional-managerial class serving in the political arena can use their position for personal ends. For instance, politicians can gain financially by engaging in a variety of corrupt practices, such as bribery and the misuse of state funds. Political crimes for personal economic gain provide another example of how class position patterns the type of crime.

Finally, the state operates in certain ways to serve the economic interests of corporations. Although the managers of the state have historically come from the capitalist and professional-managerial classes, the state is not simply an *instrument* of any class. In a capitalist economy the state operates to protect and support a corporate-dominated economy that chiefly serves the needs of the capitalist class. As noted in Chapter 1.3, the state came into being with the development of social classes in agricultural societies; since then the economically dominant class has usually been the most politically powerful class. However, this does not mean the state operates in a monolithic manner. Rather, state actions result from political conflicts among classes and also within the capitalist class (Beirne, 1979). Nevertheless, these conflicts are embedded in an overall state policy of maintaining a viable capitalist economy. As Parenti (1983:4) points out, the very organization of the state reflects its close involvement with the economy:

> Thus one finds the departments of Commerce, Labor, Agriculture, Interior, Transportation, and Treasury, and the Federal Trade Commission, the National Labor Relations Board, the Interstate Commerce Commission, the Federal Communications Commission, and the Securities and Exchange Commission all involved in regulating economic activity. Most of the committees in Congress can be identified according to their economic functions.

Inasmuch as the major corporations (Fortune 500) dominate the U.S. economy, the state has a particular interest in their viability. This intimate relationship between the state and the economy often leads to political crime. For example, those who manage the state are interested in bolstering a healthy capitalist economy, not only for generating state revenues but also for their continued political futures. Consequently, state managers take actions that facilitate corporate investment.

Corporations base their foreign investment decisions on such things as cost of labor and raw materials, size of market, and political climate (stability) of the society receiving the capital. Is the working class under control? Will the state raise taxes? Does the state support business freedom? If the answers to such questions are negative, it is unlikely that corporations will invest. Consequently,

U.S. foreign policy has supported practices that permit the greatest opportunity for corporations to invest in other countries. Revolutionary movements in Africa and Central and Latin America, for example, that challenge the status quo also threaten corporate profits. The result is that the U.S. government has supported reactionary and oppressive regimes to quell such movements—as in Iran under the Shah and in Chile under Pinochet—and the CIA and National Security Council have moved to overthrow democratically elected governments. In other words, the state sometimes engages in international political crimes because of its inherent need to protect and maintain a capitalist economy.

The preceding discussion has provided selected examples of the relationship between types and seriousness of crime with class inequality and social position. Class position and inequality, however, provide only a partial understanding of how the patterns of crime and victimization occur in the United States. We now turn to a second, although equally important, sociological factor—gender inequality and crime.

3.2 ——— GENDER AND CRIME

Sex and *gender* are not synonymous. Sex refers to the biological and physiological differences between men and women. Gender refers to historically and culturally developed patterns of behavior and relationships between males and females. Gender relations have developed sociologically into unequal relationships between males and females. This inequality has profound consequences for patterns of crime and victimization. In fact, gender is probably the best predictor of crime and victimization.

Patterns of Crime and Victimization

Arrest data, self-report studies, and victimization surveys help us form a picture of which gender commits the greatest number of conventional crimes and what *types* of conventional crimes are associated most often with each gender. Consider arrest data. According to the *Uniform Crime Reports* (*UCR*), males clearly outnumber females in terms of arrest numbers. Men comprise the overwhelming majority of those arrested for the eight major felonies. Indeed, in every case except larceny, men account for 86 percent or more of the arrests. The most significant crimes committed by females, according to the arrest data, are larceny (32 percent), forgery and counterfeiting (35 percent), fraud (42 percent), embezzlement (39 percent), and prostitution and commercialized vice (65 percent) (FBI, 1993:234).

Considerable research has employed self-report studies to generate data on gender and crime. Although we cannot discuss all aspects of this work here, Douglas Smith and Christy Visher (1980:693) have reduced the majority of this research (44 studies) to a single data base from which they determined the magnitude of the relationship between gender and crime. Smith and Visher concluded that the findings of the self-report studies were remarkably similar to arrest data. Thus, males reported much more involvement in conventional crimes, especially in serious felonies. Moreover, in number and type, the female contribution to conventional crimes was found to be quite similar to the arrest data. However, Smith and Visher (*ibid.*:698) established that the arrest data underreport women's involvement in nonserious property crimes such as shoplifting and fraud, particularly for female youth. In other words, according to self-report studies, adult involvement in conventional crimes seems more male dominated than is youth crime, especially for property crimes. Subsequent studies have reached similar conclusions (Feyerherm, 1981; Figueira-McDonough *et al.*, 1981; Hindelang, 1981).

Regarding victimization surveys, Hindelang (1979:143) examined *National Crime Victimization Survey* data from 1972 to 1976 to determine how far they agreed with *UCR* arrest data on gender. Hindelang (*ibid.*:152) concluded:

> In general it appears that even at the earliest stage in the offending process for which data are available, the conclusions we can draw about sex and involvement in crime from victimization survey data are essentially the same as those derived from arrest data for the same types of crimes.

Thus, arrest, self-report, and victimization data all suggest that both male adults and youth commit more conventional crimes and more serious types of conventional crimes than do female adults and youth. When women commit conventional crimes, they are primarily less serious offenses against property. In other words: "the profile of the typical female offender is much the same as it was 20 years ago—a minor property offender" (Morris, 1987:69). Women are most likely to commit larceny, fraud, and embezzlement (Messerschmidt, 1986:79–81). Males disproportionately commit interpersonal crimes of violence and property crimes, especially the more serious ones. Moreover, males have a virtual monopoly on the commission of syndicated, corporate, and political crime (*ibid.*:99–129; Box, 1983:169; Steffensmeier, 1983). Thus, males commit the greatest number of crimes and the most serious types of them.

As Table 3-3 shows, males also have the highest rate of victimization for both interpersonal crimes of violence (except rape) and personal property crimes. Both men and women are more often victimized by theft than by violence, and the most common form of victimization is personal larceny without contact. Consequently, the highest victimization rate is *intragender:* males victimizing males. Nevertheless, there is substantial *intergender* victimization: males violating women—such as rape and violence against women in the family.

Gender and Varieties of Crime

The patterns of crime and victimization previously identified reflect broader social inequalities between men and women. Unequal relations between men and women have resulted in men controlling the institutional structures of

TABLE 3-3   Personal crimes, 1991: Victimization rates for persons age 12 and over, by type of crime and gender of victims

TYPE OF CRIME	RATE PER 1,000 PERSONS AGE 12 OR OLDER		
	BOTH SEXES	MALE	FEMALE
All personal crimes	**92.3**	**105.1**	**80.4**
Crimes of violence	31.3	40.3	22.9
Completed	11.9	14.7	9.3
Attempted	19.4	25.6	13.5
Rape	0.8	0.2*	1.4
Completed	0.3	0.0*	0.6
Attempted	0.5	0.2*	0.8
Robbery	5.6	7.8	3.5
Completed	3.7	4.9	2.5
With injury	1.3	1.7	0.8
From serious assault	0.6	1.1	0.2*
From minor assault	0.6	0.6	0.6
Without injury	2.4	3.2	1.7
Attempted	1.9	2.9	1.0
With injury	0.6	0.9	0.4
From serious assault	0.3	0.5	0.1*
From minor assault	0.3	0.3	0.3
Without injury	1.3	2.0	0.6
Assault	24.9	32.4	17.9
Aggravated	7.8	11.5	4.4
Completed with injury	2.9	4.3	1.6
Attempted with weapon	4.9	7.2	2.9
Simple	17.0	20.9	13.4
Completed with injury	5.0	5.4	4.6
Attempted without weapon	12.0	15.5	8.8
Crimes of theft	**61.0**	**64.8**	**57.5**
Completed	56.9	60.5	53.6
Attempted	4.1	4.3	3.9
Personal larceny with contact	2.3	2.1	2.6
Purse snatching	0.7	0.1*	1.2
Pocket picking	1.7	2.0	1.4
Personal larceny without contact	58.7	62.7	54.9
Completed	54.7	58.5	51.3
Less than $50	21.2	20.9	21.6
$50 or more	30.7	35.2	26.6
Amount not available	2.7	2.4	3.1
Attempted	4.0	4.3	3.6
Population age 12 and over	205,344,910	98,929,210	106,415,700

Note: Detail may not add to total shown because of rounding.
*Estimate is based on about 10 or fewer sample cases.

Source: Department of Justice, 1992, p. 22.

society and, therefore, controlling women, too. In 1983, "women form[ed] 52 percent of the world's population, perform two-thirds of the world's labor, receive one-tenth of the world's wages, and own less than one-hundredth of its property" (Burstyn, 1983b:55). Moreover, women make up less than 5 percent of the world's top governmental, church, and military officials (*ibid.*).

Patterns of crime and victimization in contemporary U.S. society reflect these unequal gender relations. We consider first how these gender relations are structured, and then relate that structure theoretically to the empirical evidence on gender and crime.

As industrialization has developed, women have been drawn out of the home and into the labor market in increasing numbers. More women today work in the labor market than ever before. For example, in 1970, 32 percent of all women 16 years and older were in the labor force; by 1991 this figure had risen to 57 percent (*Statistical Abstract of the U.S.*, 1992:381). Yet, as women enter the labor market they are segregated into certain "feminine" occupations. Approximately two-thirds of women working in the labor market are employed in service, retail, and clerical jobs (Sidel, 1987:61). These occupations are among the lowest paid positions in the labor market and provide little opportunity for advancement (*ibid.*). Women make up 96 percent of nurses; 98 percent of pre-kindergarten and kindergarten teachers; 84 percent of cashiers; 98 percent of secretaries, stenographers, and typists; 90 percent of clerks; 91 percent of bank tellers; 97 percent of child-care workers; and 88 percent of waiters and waitresses. At the other end of the job hierarchy, only 6 percent of engineers are women, 7 percent of dentists, 16 percent of physicians, and 16 percent of lawyers and judges (*Statistical Abstract of the U.S.*, 1992:392–393).

Women's position in this unequal, gendered labor market helps explain their patterns of crime. For example, as women experience economic pressure from increasing inflation and low pay, they are more likely to engage in crimes such as embezzlement. Moreover, the gender division of labor identified previously determines the type of embezzlement women are most likely to commit. Although women make up slightly more than one-third of all embezzlers, they are primarily petty embezzlers. Seventy percent of those who embezzle more than $1,000 are males; 81 percent of those embezzling between $1 and $150 are women (Messerschmidt, 1986:88). The gendered nature of embezzlement relates to women's subordinate position in the gender division of labor. As is clear from the foregoing evidence, the occupations in which women are employed today are not positions that handle large quantities of money. Kathleen Daly (1989:781) reports in her research on gender and white-collar crime that, with regard to bank embezzlement, because women are more likely to be bank tellers and men bank officers, "women are more likely than men to take cash from the till, and men are more likely to manipulate documents."

In addition, women's motivation to engage in embezzlement seems to differ from that of men. Males embezzle because they experience a nonshareable financial problem they bring on themselves, such as gambling losses or "spending

Women sometimes embezzle—from institutions such as banks—to help solve unexpected financial problems arising in the family.

money foolishly," tending to rationalize their illegal behavior as simply "borrow-ing" (Cressey, 1971:80–105). Women embezzle because of unexpected financial problems and the impact these problems have on others. As Dorothy Zietz (1981:80) documents in her research on embezzlement, women embezzlers

> consciously sacrifice their positions of trust in an effort to meet responsi-bilities associated with the role of wife and mother. Their behavior seemed to have a Joan of Arc quality, a willingness to be burned at the stake to obtain for a loved one the medical care needed or some service essential to his welfare.

In other words, women tend to embezzle because their social positions are—even though they work outside the home—predominantly those of homemakers and caretakers. Rather than viewing their embezzlement as borrowing, the women in Zietz's study felt that any conduct—even embezzlement—was justified when it seemed the only solution to a problem affecting the welfare of a marriage or the potential loss of a child or lover (*ibid.*:80–81). Daly's (1989:777) study also records that family need is one of the most frequent reasons women give for engaging in embezzlement.

Women's position in the gender division of labor also helps explain their involvement in other property crimes, such as larceny and fraud. The literature on the *feminization of poverty* indicates that "the fastest growing population living in poverty today is made up of women and children" (Sidel, 1987:25). The increasing impoverization of women is caused by such factors as (1) the rising divorce rates and attendant rapid development of female-headed households; (2) the gender division of labor, which continues to discriminate against women; (3) the lack of adequate child care, and (4) a welfare system that maintains its recipients below the poverty line (*ibid.*:15). In 1985, 34 percent of all female-headed households with children under 18 years lived below the poverty line. In terms of race, 51 percent of African American and 53 percent of Hispanic female-headed households were below the poverty line (Andersen, 1988:130). Not surprisingly, most female offenders are either unemployed or working in low-paying, menial types of jobs (Miller, 1986). Research confirms this relationship between the feminization of poverty and women's property crimes. For instance, Steven Box and Chris Hale (1983:199) report:

> As women become economically worse off, largely through unemployment and inadequate compensatory levels of welfare benefits, so they are less able and willing to resist the temptations to engage in property offenses as a way of helping solve their financial difficulties.

Four years later, after reviewing close to 50 studies on economic conditions and crime, Box (1987:43) concluded that "the most plausible reason" for women's increasing involvement in property crimes "is that more women have become economically marginalized." Gender inequality, interacting with class inequality, structures women's social position and, therefore, female crime in U.S. society as well.

Finally, considerable support for the links among gender inequality, social position, and crime is provided by Miller's (1986) research on deviant street networks and the social context of female hustling in property crimes and prostitution. Miller (*ibid.*:172) argues that gender inequality in the marketplace has left "women and the households they often head in greater need over the last two decades than in the immediately preceding period." This helps explain, Miller concludes, women's increasing involvement in street networks. But gender inequality also helps structure the division of labor *within* street networks themselves. As Miller (*ibid.*:37) points out, the controlling members of the street networks are men whose

> major source of continuous income derives from the hustling activity of women who turn their earnings over to them in exchange for affection, an allowance, the status of their company, and some measure of protection. . . . These men form loose alliances to control the women who work for them, to promote their own hustling endeavors, and to socialize.

As in society as a whole, gender inequalities are prevalent in street networks wherein men tend to dominate and control their activities. Gender inequality determines who fills which positions—even inside street networks—and thus structures the opportunities for crime.

Although segregation into the "pink-collar ghetto" (Howe, 1977) structures women's conventional criminality, women are largely absent from the major professions. Given that more women have become corporate managers in recent years, women managers are still systematically segregated into such lower-status managerial positions as personnel, research, affirmative action, and equal employment (Hymowitz and Schellhardt, 1986:1). These jobs do not lead to decision-making positions within the corporation. Rather, they are recommending bodies, where "*women do the work* to find out what is needed—make recommendations, and then *men decide* what is to be done with regard to these recommendations" (Sokoloff, 1980:243). In other words, the gender division of labor within the corporate managerial structure effectively segregates women from, but places men in, positions of power where corporate crimes are contrived. This process has been referred to as the *old-boy network*, a sponsorship system that recruits junior male executives into the upper ranks of the managerial divisions of the corporation (Messerschmidt, 1993). It appears this old-boy network remains quite strong as a mechanism for maintaining the unequal corporate gender division of labor (Hymowitz and Schellhardt, 1986:1–5). Consequently, corporate crime is a male-dominated activity. In the sample referred to earlier, Daly (1989:776) found that men committed 98 percent of Securities and Exchange Commission violations, 99.5 percent of antitrust violations, and 95 percent of bribery violations. She also identified a clear gender difference in white-collar crime motivation: women's white-collar crimes are more often motivated from a need to make personal and familial ends meet while men's are more frequently associated with a need to make business ends meet (*ibid.*:786–787). Thus, the respective occupational crimes of males and females reflect different social positions in the gender division of labor.

In the political arena, the gender division of labor likewise guarantees that political crime is dominated by men. There has never been a female president or vice president; only nine women have served in presidential administrations; and in the "Year of the Woman" in U.S. politics, only 48 of the 435 representatives in Congress and 6 of the 100 senators in 1993 were women (Messerschmidt, 1993:155). Thus, women constitute more than 50 percent of the U.S. population yet hold less than 10 percent of the seats in Congress. This absence of women from top governmental positions also results from an old-boy network. The gender division of labor within mainstream political parties—the Democratic and Republican parties in the United States—makes it extremely difficult for women either to reach positions of party responsibility or to be supported as candidates by parties. As Varda Burstyn (1983:73–74) shows, the major positions in mainstream political parties

> go to the people who control the funds and make political policy and alliances, people who are almost always men freed from much of the organizational nitty-gritty by the women's support work. . . . Thus in

the mixed gatherings of party life where political policy, strategy, and selection of candidates is formally decided, the men predominate and dominate.

The result is that men fill the ranks of those positions that are the chief source of political crime.

An old-boy network also functions in criminal syndicates and street gangs. Steffensmeier (1983) shows that women are excluded or underrepresented in criminal syndicates and, if present, are allocated less-valued roles. Criminal syndicates are masculine dominated because of what Steffensmeier (*ibid.*:1012–1016) terms "homosocial reproduction," "sex-typing," and the "task environment of crime." Homosocial reproduction refers to the ways in which those in powerful positions fill positions with men like themselves. Because men dominate (control and populate) criminal syndicates, they prefer to work, associate, and do business with other men. This homosocial reproduction works in tandem with sex-typing. According to Steffensmeier, males in criminal syndicates stereotype women and criminal work in certain ways that effectively discriminate against women. Males in criminal syndicates, for example, see their work as (1) too hard, heavy, and dangerous for women and (2) too degrading and cheapening for women, leading to a loss of women's dignity. Steffensmeier (*ibid.*:1013) adds that men view "women as not as *capable*, or not as skilled, or not as stable; and believe that, while women *take orders* from men, men do not take orders from any woman." Finally, the task environment of crime means that to survive in the world of crime, a criminal syndicate must deal with the threat of arrest and imprisonment as well as threats from other criminal groups. Consequently, because both *secrecy* and *violence* are inextricable aspects of criminal syndicates, they recruit people the leaders feel certain can help satisfy these needs. As Steffensmeier (*ibid.*:1014) states:

> A premium is placed on attributes such as trust and reliability and on physical characteristics such as strength and "muscle"—the capacity for force or violence. These characteristics have not been the prerogative of females. Furthermore, there is an almost inexhaustible pool of males to fill openings in crime groups; there are few empty places left for females.

These three factors identified by Steffensmeier show that the structure of criminal syndicates tends to reflect the broader gender inequalities of society.

All this does not mean, of course, that women are never involved in important roles within professional and syndicated crime. Clearly, in the past (Block, 1977, 1980) and today (Carlen, 1988) some women have been involved in such criminal activities. The important point is that these activities are highly dominated by men, a phenomenon socially determined by gender relations in the broader society.

Not surprisingly, males also dominate street gangs. Within a culture based on gender inequality, parents tend to control the spare time of young females more closely than that of males, leaving males freer to explore the outside world and to come into contact with one another (Hagan *et al.*, 1979). Young male criminality is therefore much more likely than is female criminality to be collective in nature (Messerschmidt, 1986:63). And as Box (1983:182) points out, women are seen by male gang members as emotional, unreliable, illogical, and untrustworthy—"not the type of person you want along on an armed robbery." Thus, the old-boy network also infiltrates street gangs. When women are members of street gangs, they usually inhabit powerless positions and are pushed to the periphery of social activity. As Anne Campbell (1984:242–243) reports in her book *Girls in the Gang:*

> Females must accept the range of roles within the gang that might be available to them in society at large. The traditional structure of the nuclear family is firmly duplicated in the gang. In straight society the central, pivotal figure is the male. His status in the world of societal and material success is the critical factor, while the woman supports, nurtures, and sustains him. The gang parodies this state of affairs, without even the economic infrastructure to sustain it, for the male rarely works and often it is the female who receives a more stable income through welfare. Nevertheless, the males constitute the true gang! Gang feuds are begun and continued by males; females take part as a token of their allegiance to the men.

Finally, interpersonal violence against women is also closely associated with gender inequalities. Although some rapists actually may be psychopathic, research indicates that the vast majority are not emotionally disturbed. For example, comparisons of males convicted of rape with control groups of males not convicted indicate that the two groups are "indistinguishable in both their sexual behavior and other characteristics" (Morris, 1987:178). Moreover, most assumptions about rape held by the public—such as rape is impossible, women want to be raped, "no" means "yes," and rape is a sexual act—have been disproven by research (see *ibid.*: 166–178 for a review). Most criminologists therefore view rape as the result of the structural subordination of women in contemporary society.

The United States actually has been described as a rape-prone society. In her research of 186 tribal societies, social anthropologist Peggy Sanday (1981) found that high rape rates occur in societies that are dominated by males and that feature male violence. Rape-prone societies, then, are those in which males dominate politically, economically, and ideologically, and that glorify male violence. Rape-free societies, Sanday found, are marked by relative gender equality, the belief that the sexes are complementary, and a low level of interpersonal violence overall. Thus, Sanday's work helps us understand why the United States can be considered a rape-prone society. Not only is U.S. society dominated politically, economically, and ideologically by males, but it also glorifies male violence in the street, in sports, and in the state, and so on.

Most rapists are motivated by hatred, anger, power, and dominance (Groth and Birnbaum, 1979; Holmstrom and Burgess, 1980). Indeed, what enables rape—from date rape to rape involving overt use of physical violence—is the assertion of dominance (Morris, 1987:178). As Messerschmidt (1986:135) has put it:

> The rapist uses sex as a violent attack on the integrity of the woman as a person. In a rape, what is normally understood as an act of affection becomes an act of hate. This act destroys the woman's integrity by denying the victim her own will to engage, or not to engage, in sexuality as she pleases. By prohibiting this freedom, the rapist creates conditions of dominance and subordination.

Rape reflects the dominance/subordination relationships in patriarchal culture. Rape is the most extreme example of the exploitation of women as devalued objects (Schur, 1984:30–34).

The crime of rape also illustrates the relationship between social position and victimization. Although all women are vulnerable to rape, certain social characteristics—such as class and age—increase the possibility of victimization. According to victimization surveys, the vast majority of women victimized by rape are teenage females living in lower-class communities (Messerschmidt, 1986:137). Consequently, a woman's social position—based on such characteristics as age and class—increases or decreases her risk of victimization.

Like rape, violence by men in the family (wife rape, wife battering, and incestuous assault) reflects gender power and inequality. The structure of the traditional nuclear family encourages the husband/father to view "his" wife and children as under his control. Violence in the family is intimately linked to our cultural expectation that males are authority figures within monogamous relationships (Dobash and Dobash, 1979). Some men therefore feel they have the right to dominate and control their wives, and wife battering serves to ensure continued compliance with their commands. If a wife questions such authority in any way, a violent husband turns to force simply to "get his way" (*ibid.*). Susan Schechter (1982:219, 222) points out:

> Battering is one tool that enforces husbands' authority over wives or simply reminds women that this authority exists. . . . A man beats to remind a woman that the relationship will proceed in the way he wants or that ultimately he holds the power.

Women's subordinate social position reinforces masculine dominance and violence in the family. If a wife is unemployed or works in a low-paying job, as is all-too-typical nowadays, it is easier for a husband to control her. In this type of society a husband usually has the economic power and the wife is dependent, often even if she works outside the home. Such conditions make it very difficult for her to leave a violent relationship, especially if she has children.

Economic dependency and powerlessness in the family also affect the likelihood of wife rape. Because of this unequal economic familial relationship, wife rape may not be physically violent in nature. A husband can obtain access to "his" wife's body, if she is unwilling to "oblige" him, by threatening a beating or loss of affection or economically supportive relationship (Box, 1983:124). The wife may thus conclude that unwanted sexual intercourse is not as harmful as the alternative—economic poverty and distress. This situation is exacerbated for women with children and/or without skills.

Similarly, incestuous assault results from the powerlessness of children (especially young girls) in the family and their economic and emotional dependence. Children are essentially a captive population economically and emotionally dependent upon parents. Particularly at young ages, children do what is necessary to maintain a supportive relationship with their parents, even to the extent of keeping incestuous assault secret. Consequently, this dependency and powerlessness makes incestuous assault highly exploitative and nonconsensual. As Edwin Schur (1988:172–173) points out:

> The matter of consent underscores the central role of dependency in the sexual victimization of children. One cannot consent when one is not mature enough to do so. But equally significant is the fact that one cannot consent freely when one is in a position of great dependency.

In other words, to understand incestuous assault it is essential to understand power within the family. Incestuous assault primarily entails a father as perpetrator and his daughter as victim (see Chapter 4.2). The power and authority claimed by the father structures the offender/victim relationship in incestuous assault. Believing that women's role is to serve the needs of men—including sexual needs—the male authority figure uses his power to assault his daughter incestuously. As Morris (1987:188) states, this crime is "a product of patriarchal family relations. Like wife assault and rape, it tends to occur when traditional beliefs about the roles of man and woman, husband and wife, father and daughter are taken to extremes."

Our discussion points to the fact that analysis of gender inequality adds considerably to our understanding of the patterns of crime and victimization in U.S. society. As with class position, gender position structures the opportunities for engaging in crime and the possibilities of being victimized by crime. In addition to class and gender, racial inequality also structures patterns of crime and victimization.

3.3 _____ RACE AND CRIME

Genetic differences in skin color assume social significance when used to justify unequal treatment of one race by another. Race relations, like class and gender relations, have developed into unequal relations in which one race (white) uses skin color to legitimate domination and control of other races. Simultaneously, this inequality has important consequences for the patterns of crime and victimization in the United States.

Although whites continue to dominate several racial and ethnic groups in the United States—such as Native Americans, Asians, Mexican Americans, and

African Americans—we focus on the inequality between whites and African Americans and the relationship of that inequality to crime and victimization. We concentrate on these two groups because, unfortunately, criminologists generally have ignored other racial and ethnic groups and, therefore, there are insufficient data with which to make comparisons. We begin with a discussion of racial patterns of crime and victimization, and then turn to a discussion of race and varieties of crime.

Patterns of Crime and Victimization

The *UCR* indicates that whites account for approximately 75 percent of all arrests and African Americans 25 percent. However, racial disparities become evident when we take population into account. African Americans constitute only 12.7 percent of the U.S. population (*Current Population Reports*, 1988:47), yet account for almost 50 percent of violent crime arrests and for over 30 percent of property crime arrests (FBI, 1988:182). Moreover, abundant sociological studies using official data have shown that African Americans are overrepresented as offenders (Hindelang *et al.*, 1979:999).

Although arrest data show striking differences in rates for adults, self-report studies show that African American and white youth report similar involvement in youth crime. For example, Huizinga and Elliott (1987:215) reported in their national study that "there are few if any substantial and consistent differences between the delinquency involvement of different racial groups."

When specific offenses are analyzed, however, it appears that African American adults and youth report more involvement in the most serious conventional crimes, especially crimes of interpersonal violence. For example, Hindelang *et al.* (1979:1000–1001) found that "blacks and whites differ in *serious* delinquent behavior but are more similar in less serious forms of delinquent behavior." In other words, they found that racial differences increase with the severity of the crime. Similarly, Elliott and Ageton (1980:106) found that with

> respect to offenses against persons, the black/white differential is indeed greater for serious (as compared with nonserious) offenses. However, with respect to property offenses this is not the case.

Moreover, Hindelang's (1981:464–469) analysis of victim data—in which victims report such characteristics of offenders as race, approximate age, and so on—showed that African American male youth were more often reported as offenders in crimes of interpersonal violence and property crimes committed against a person such as robbery.

Thus, the higher *arrest* rate for African Americans is probably the result of *both* the criminal justice system's selection bias (see Chapter 2.1) and a greater involvement of African Americans in conventional crimes. Criminologists have known for quite some time that when individuals of different social classes and races come into contact with the criminal justice system *for the same crime,* young lower-class minority males are more likely to be arrested, prosecuted, convicted,

For the same crime, young, lower working-class, racial minority males are more likely than other males to be arrested, prosecuted, convicted, and sentenced to prison for longer terms.

and sentenced to prison for longer terms (Reiman, 1984). Nevertheless, to argue that the higher arrest rate for African Americans is *solely* the result of a racist criminal justice system and that in reality the crime rate for all racial groups is otherwise the same, is "tantamount to the suggestion that the black community does not in reality suffer any additional ill-effects from racial discrimination" (Lea and Young, 1984:111). Because of racial inequality in U.S. society, African Americans indeed suffer considerable discriminatory and oppressive conditions that whites do not. It is this disadvantageous social position that most likely results in a higher crime rate by African Americans than otherwise would be expected for their population size.

African Americans are also more often the victims of violent crime. As Table 3-4 shows, African Americans are victimized at a greater rate for all personal crimes, but, in particular, for robbery and assault, whereas whites are more likely to be the victims of theft. Moreover, as Table 3-5 shows, African Americans are victimized at a higher rate than whites for all household property crimes in

TABLE 3-4   Personal crimes, 1991: Victimization rates for persons age 12 and older, by type of crime and race of victims

TYPE OF CRIME	RATE PER 1,000 PERSONS AGE 12 AND OVER		
	WHITE	BLACK	OTHER
All personal crimes	**90.9**	**105.6**	**80.2**
Crimes of violence	29.6	44.4	28.1
Completed	10.7	21.0	10.9
Attempted	18.9	23.4	17.3
Rape	0.9	0.6*	0.3*
Robbery	4.4	13.5	7.4
Completed	2.8	9.1	6.4
With injury	1.0	2.8	0.9*
From serious assault	0.5	1.7	0.3*
From minor assault	0.5	1.1	0.6*
Without injury	1.8	6.3	5.5
Attempted	1.6	4.3	1.0*
With injury	0.5	1.4	0.0*
From serious assault	0.2	1.1	0.0*
From minor assault	0.3	0.4*	0.0*
Without injury	1.1	2.9	1.0*
Assault	24.3	30.4	20.5
Aggravated	7.4	11.1	8.2
Completed with injury	2.6	5.5	1.4*
Attempted with weapon	4.8	5.6	6.8
Simple	16.9	19.3	12.3
Completed with injury	4.9	6.2	3.1*
Attempted without weapon	12.0	13.1	9.2
Crimes of theft	**61.4**	**61.1**	**52.0**
Completed	57.3	56.8	47.0
Attempted	4.0	4.3	5.0
Personal larceny with contact	2.0	4.6	3.5*
Purse snatching	0.6	1.2	1.0*
Pocket picking	1.4	3.4	2.5*
Personal larceny without contact	59.4	56.5	48.5
Completed	55.5	52.2	43.5
Less than $50	21.7	19.3	17.7
$50 or more	31.1	30.0	23.5
Amount not available	2.8	2.8	2.3*
Attempted	3.9	4.3	5.0
Population age 12 and over	174,476,630	24,137,310	6,730,960

Note: Detail may not add to total shown because of rounding.
*Estimate is based on about 10 or fewer sample cases.

Source: Department of Justice, 1992, p. 24.

particular, for both personal larceny with and without contact. Thus, we can conclude that conventional crimes—especially crimes of interpersonal violence and household property crimes—are *intraracial.* Nevertheless, there seems to be an increasing rate of *interracial* violence directed by whites *against* African Americans. (See Chapter 4.1.)

**TABLE
3-5**   Household crimes, 1991: Victimization rates by type of crime and race of head
of household

TYPE OF CRIME	RATE PER 1,000 HOUSEHOLDS			
	ALL RACES	WHITE	BLACK	OTHER
Household crimes	**162.9**	**156.6**	**207.6**	**170.7**
Completed	138.1	133.3	172.8	140.0
Attempted	24.8	23.3	34.8	30.7
Burglary	53.1	50.2	74.5	51.9
Completed	41.4	39.5	55.1	42.1
Forcible entry	17.2	15.1	32.8	17.1
Unlawful entry without force	24.1	24.4	22.3	25.0
Attempted forcible entry	11.7	10.7	19.4	9.8*
Household larceny	88.0	87.0	96.2	85.1
Completed	82.7	81.6	92.0	79.8
Less than $50	34.7	35.2	32.6	26.5
$50 or more	43.6	42.3	51.3	49.2
Amount not available	4.5	4.0	8.1	4.1*
Attempted	5.3	5.4	4.3	5.3*
Motor vehicle theft	21.8	19.4	36.9	33.7
Completed	13.9	12.2	25.8	18.1
Attempted	7.9	7.2	11.1	15.7
Total number of households	96,839,300	82,952,520	11,283,680	2,603,100

Note: Detail may not add to total shown due to rounding.
*Estimate is based on about 10 or fewer sample cases.

Source: Department of Justice, 1992, p. 22.

Conventional crimes are only one aspect of criminality and, unfortunately, criminologists have concentrated their analysis of race and crime only on racial differences in rates of conventional crimes. However, whites clearly dominate in corporate and political positions where corporate and political crimes are committed (Staples, 1987:6). Therefore, although conventional crimes may be committed more often by African Americans than whites, the more harmful and economically damaging white-collar and political crimes are disproportionately committed by whites.

Race and Varieties of Crime

As we point out in our discussion of "hate crimes" (Chapter 4.1), African Americans are among the most frequent victims of interracial violence. However, they are also the primary victims of conventional crime. Discrimination continues to augment the disadvantages African Americans already suffer, creating conditions for high rates of intraracial crime. Obstacles experienced by the white working class are greater for African Americans because of racial discrimination. For example, the differences between African American and white family income have changed little since 1960 when African American family income was only 55.4 percent of white family income: by the late 1980s it had increased to only

55.7 (Joe, 1987:289). Other economic differences between African Americans and whites include the following (*ibid.*:289–292):

▲— Less than 4 percent of white families have incomes under $5,000; 15 percent of African American families have incomes under $5,000.

▲— Seventeen percent of white families, but only 6 percent of African American families, have income over $50,000.

▲— The median net worth of white households is $39,140; for African Americans it is $3,400.

▲— Thirty percent of all African American households have either a zero or negative net worth because their liabilities exceed their assets.

▲— Forty-six and a half percent of all African American children under 18 are officially poor; 16.7 percent of all white children are poor.

▲— Fifty-nine percent of all African American families with children, and 20 percent of all white families with children, are headed by women.

▲— Fifty-two percent of African American female-headed households are poverty stricken, and the median income for African American female-headed households has fallen 8 percent since 1968.

Mindful of the foregoing information, the relationship between unemployment and crime discussed in the class and crime section above is especially helpful in understanding the high crime rates of African American male and female youth. Research has consistently shown that the overrepresentation of African American adults and youth in conventional crime statistics is the result of racial economic inequality (Green, 1970; Loftin and Hill, 1974; Calvin, 1981; Elliott and Huizinga, 1983). Indeed, the 1954 official unemployment rates of African American (13.4 percent) and white (14.0 percent) 16–17-year-olds were almost identical (Duster, 1987:305). By 1981, however, 40.1 percent of African American 16–17-year-olds and 19.9 percent of white 16–17-year-olds were officially unemployed. By 1984 the African American and white youth official unemployment rates for these ages had increased to 50.5 percent and 22.0 percent, respectively (Department of Labor, 1988:517–538). In other words, although the unemployment rate for *all* youth has worsened, increasing economic inequality between white and African American youth has occurred since the mid-1950s.

The high rates of property crimes committed by African American youth has thus stemmed from their deteriorating economic situation. Other research supports this argument. Good and Pirog-Good (1987:122) analyzed the relationship among employment, property crime, and African American youth, finding "a vicious circle for blacks in which lower employability increases their criminality which further lowers their employability." As African American employment increases, it "subsequently lowers their criminality, having the effect of further enhancing their employability" (*ibid.*:123). Similarly, Phillips and Votey (1987) used data of the National Longitudinal Survey of Young Americans to examine a variety of relationships, including the impact of legitimate labor market activity on participation in property crime. Their findings confirmed the hypothesis that "black and white differences in criminal participation . . . reflect differences in economic opportunity" (*ibid.*:129). Finally, an extensive study of the relationship among labor market conditions, inner-city African American youth, and crime reported similar results. For African American youth

> crime serves an economic function by providing many with a substantial income source. . . . A fundamental influence on criminal behavior is the role of economic factors, such as labor market status. Respondents who were in school or employed were much less likely to engage in crime. . . . Respondents who were not employed or in school were much more strongly driven by economic incentives to commit crime (Viscusi, 1986:343).

Viscusi also found a relationship between crime and quality of job, especially the low paying jobs available to African American youth. As Viscusi (*ibid.*:343) states: "If youth can make more money from crime than from labor market earnings, they will be more likely to engage in crime."

One increasingly profitable crime is selling drugs. However, though dealing drugs may be financially rewarding, it has a dangerous negative side (Moore, 1988:53):

> To many poor black kids living in a run-down housing project, the thriving drug business looks a lot more accessible and promising than school or a traditional job, despite the obvious down side: violence, murder and possibly their own death.

Those involved in the drug trade clearly are more likely to be both the perpetrators and the victims of violence. Yet violence, as we have seen earlier, is related to such structural conditions as income inequality. Although most studies on this topic have concentrated on class and crime, a study by Blau and Blau (1982) related income inequality to race. As noted, in their study of the 125 largest metropolitan areas in the United States, Blau and Blau (*ibid.*:121) found that the greater the gap between incomes in a metropolitan area, the higher the rate of criminal violence. When they controlled for class, Blau and Blau found that socioeconomic inequality between African Americans and whites has a positive and direct effect on criminal violence. In other words, inequalities rooted in ascribed racial positions create alienation and despair and have a profound impact on the generation of criminal violence. This helps us understand the high violent crime rates of *both* African American females and African American males.

Self-report studies consistently show that African American females have higher rates of violent crimes—such as homicide and assault—than do white females (Ageton, 1983; Lewis, 1981; Cernkovich and Giordano, 1979). However, Freda Adler (1975:138–139) has argued that for all crimes, African American female criminality "parallels the criminality of black males more closely than the criminality of white women does that of white men" and that it "exceeds that of white females by a much greater margin than black males over white

Socioeconomic inequality between blacks and whites has a direct effect on criminal violence.

males." Several criminologists have challenged Adler's propositions. Using victim survey data, Young (1980:32) reported that neither of Adler's propositions could be supported. More recently, Laub and McDermott (1985:89–91) also used victim data to test Adler's two propositions. For the first, they found that the conventional crime ratio of African American males/females was smaller than the ratio of white males/white females—but only for *violent* crimes, not property crimes. In their words: "In the assaultive crimes but not the theft crimes, it is true that black females are closer to black males than white females are to white males" (*ibid.*:89). Moreover, when Laub and McDermott analyzed total personal crimes, they established that the African American male/female ratio was *larger* than the white male/female ratio. Regarding Adler's second proposition, Laub and McDermott likewise found that for assaultive crimes the ratio of African American females/white females was greater than the ratio of African American males/white males—but for property crimes the African American female/white female ratio was *smaller* than the African American male/white male ratio. After examining total personal crimes, Laub and McDermott similarly reported that the ratio for African American females/white females was smaller than the ratio for African American males/white males. These findings should not be surprising, as they lend support to Blau and Blau's (1982) thesis that criminal violence is associated with racial inequality. Indeed, as Currie (1985:153) adds after reviewing the literature on homicide and race:

> Homicide is the leading cause of death for blacks of both sexes between the ages of fifteen and twenty-four: 39 percent of black men

and 25 percent of black women who die at these early ages are murdered. At this age, homicide death rates are five times higher for blacks than whites among men and four times higher for women.

Thus, although the African American female violent crime rate is high (but not higher than the white male rate), within the African American community the vast majority of criminal violence is committed *by* African American men *against* African American men. For African American men aged 15–44, homicide is the leading cause of death, and African American men are eight times as likely to die by murder than are white males (*ibid.*:154).

In summary, racial inequality structures substantial conventional crime, both interracial and intraracial. Interracial violence results from extreme racist beliefs in a racially segregated and unequal society. Crime by African Americans is the product of their positions in class and racial hierarchies, which are, of course, mediated by gender.

As argued earlier, combined class, gender, and racial inequality also determines who can engage in white-collar and political crimes. Only 5.7 percent of executive, administrative, and managerial positions and 6.7 percent of professional positions are held by African Americans (*Statistical Abstract of the U.S.*, 1992:392). Moreover, there has never been an African American president or vice president, and not more than 10 percent of House or Senate members are currently African American. Thus, racial inequality determines that whites much more often hold those positions in which the most serious and harmful crimes—white-collar and political crimes—occur. Racial inequality—as with class and gender inequality—governs social position in society and, therefore, criminal opportunities.

3.4 _____ AGE AND CRIME

Economic benefits, social privileges, and political power are based not only on class, gender, and race but also on age. Even such basic rights as sexual activity, voting, and drinking alcohol are conferred by age. Thus, age inequality and age discrimination exist in U.S. society, being most pronounced for youth but also affecting the elderly. Unequal generational divisions between young and old are prevalent, and social behavior—including crime—is linked to the aging process. One's position in the age hierarchy permits or precludes opportunity for engaging in crime. Consider the patterns of crime and victimization based on age.

Patterns of Crime and Victimization

According to arrest data in the *UCR* (FBI, 1993:227), participation in conventional crime rises with age, peaks in the teenage and early adulthood years, and then declines. Two important age patterns for conventional property and violent crimes emerge. Property crime arrest rates peak between the ages of 13 and 17, and then decline rather quickly. For violent crimes the rate peaks at around the ages of 18 and 19, and declines much more slowly with age.

Some have questioned arrest data on age. For example, because youth tend to commit conventional crimes in groups, this allegedly makes them more visible to the police and thus more likely to be arrested. Youth are also, according to some, less skilled than are adults in committing crime and, therefore, more likely to be arrested. It may be, then, that arrest statistics on age are biased, thus explaining the overrepresentation of youth in *UCR* data. However, self-report studies report very similar age patterns for conventional crimes and empirical examination of such possible biases (using both self-report and victimization surveys) "suggests that the biases do not account for the relation between age and crime" (Hirschi and Gottfredson, 1983:552). We conclude therefore that arrest data are reliable evidence of age distribution of conventional crime.

Tables 3-6 and 3-7 show victimization rates for conventional crimes by age. For crimes of violence and property, young persons aged 12–24 have the highest rates of victimization. For victims over the age of 24, both violent and property crime rates decline with age, so that those aged 65 years and older have the lowest victimization rates for both violent and property crimes. Moreover, as Table 3-7 shows, household crime victimization rates are highest for the youngest heads of household and decline with age. For conventional crimes, then, the highest victimization rates are *intra-age*.

Age and Varieties of Crime

We begin with a discussion of age differences. David Greenberg (1977) shows that during transition from childhood to adolescence, links to parents decrease (yet economic dependence remains) while receptivity to peers and peer evaluation increases. Being popular and connected with the "right" groups becomes critically important for most youth. The partial disengagement of youth from family and heightened closeness to peers, combined with advertising directed toward the teenage market, have created the conditions for youthful involvement in pleasure-seeking, consumption-oriented social lives. Indeed, participation in this teenage social life requires money for buying the "right stuff": clothing, cosmetics, cigarettes, alcoholic beverages, narcotics, recorded music, transistor radios, gasoline for cars and motorcycles, tickets to films and concerts, and meals in restaurants. However, because teenage labor force participation has declined drastically, youth are finding it more and more difficult economically to support their participation in teen life. Thus, the high rates of property crimes for youth ages 12–19 is, for Greenberg (*ibid*.:197), "a response to the disjunction between the desire to participate in social activities with peers and the absence of legitimate sources of funds needed to finance this participation." Because of teenage social position, youth property crimes increasingly serve as an alternative to work.

When youth leave high school—and when their social position changes

TABLE 3-6 Personal crimes, 1991: Victimization rates for persons age 12 and over, by type of crime and age of victims

TYPE OF CRIME	RATE PER 1,000 PERSONS IN EACH AGE GROUP						
	12–15	16–19	20–24	25–34	35–49	50–64	65 AND OVER
All personal crimes	163.9	185.1	189.4	106.3	75.5	45.0	23.2
Crimes of violence	62.7	91.1	74.6	34.9	20.0	9.6	3.8
Completed	23.6	32.4	27.9	15.3	6.9	3.3	1.6
Attempted	39.1	58.7	46.7	19.6	13.1	6.3	2.2
Rape	1.1*	3.5	1.7	1.0	0.6	0.2*	0.0*
Robbery	10.0	8.3	13.9	7.2	4.0	1.8	1.9
Completed	5.9	4.9	8.7	5.4	2.6	1.4	1.1
With injury	1.5*	2.6	3.1	1.8	0.9	0.3*	0.3*
From serious assault	0.3*	1.0*	2.3	0.9	0.5*	0.1*	0.3*
From minor assault	1.2*	1.6*	0.8*	0.9	0.5*	0.2*	0.0*
Without injury	4.4	2.4	5.6	3.6	1.6	1.1	0.8*
Attempted	4.1	3.4	5.2	1.8	1.5	0.5*	0.8*
With injury	1.3*	0.9*	1.5	0.5*	0.7	0.1*	0.1*
From serious assault	0.4*	0.3*	0.8*	0.3*	0.5*	0.0*	0.0*
From minor assault	0.9*	0.6*	0.8*	0.2*	0.3*	0.1*	0.1*
Without injury	2.8	2.5	3.7	1.3	0.7	0.4*	0.7*
Assault	51.6	79.2	59.0	26.6	15.4	7.6	1.8
Aggravated	12.9	25.5	23.0	8.3	3.9	2.4	0.9
Completed with injury	5.5	7.8	8.9	3.4	1.5	0.5*	0.3*
Attempted with weapon	7.5	17.6	14.1	4.9	2.4	1.9	0.6*
Simple	38.7	53.8	36.0	18.3	11.4	5.2	0.9
Completed with injury	12.0	17.7	9.3	6.1	2.7	1.4	0.2*
Attempted without weapon	26.7	36.0	26.7	12.2	8.7	3.7	0.7*
Crimes of theft	101.2	94.1	114.8	71.4	55.6	35.4	19.5
Completed	98.8	89.0	105.0	65.5	51.8	32.8	18.8
Attempted	2.4	5.1	9.8	5.9	3.8	2.6	0.6*
Personal larceny with contact	2.5	3.1	3.5	2.8	1.5	1.8	2.6
Purse snatching	0.2*	0.7*	0.5*	0.8	0.5	0.8	0.9
Pocket picking	2.4	2.4	3.0	2.0	1.0	1.0	1.8
Personal larceny without contact	98.7	90.9	111.3	68.7	54.0	33.6	16.8
Completed	96.3	86.0	101.5	62.9	50.4	31.2	16.3
Less than $50	63.4	38.8	29.4	22.5	17.4	10.3	6.6
$50 or more	29.3	43.2	67.8	37.3	30.8	18.2	8.3
Amount not available	3.6	4.0	4.3	3.1	2.3	2.7	1.4
Attempted	2.4	5.0	9.8	5.8	3.6	2.4	0.5*
Population in each age group	13,783,200	13,364,290	17,989,660	42,829,550	53,833,490	33,103,780	30,440,910

Note: Detail may not add to total shown because of rounding.
*Estimate is based on about 10 or fewer sample cases.

Source: Department of Justice, 1992, p. 23.

TABLE 3-7   Household crimes, 1991: Victimization rates by type of crime and age of head of household

TYPE OF CRIME	RATE PER 1,000 HOUSEHOLDS				
	12–19	20–34	35–49	50–64	65 AND OVER
Household crimes	**445.6**	**213.2**	**184.5**	**137.6**	**80.1**
Completed	404.0	179.1	154.7	117.8	70.3
Attempted	41.5	34.1	29.8	19.8	9.8
Burglary	193.6	72.8	58.8	39.4	27.0
Completed	171.1	55.4	45.2	31.5	22.1
Forcible entry	45.7	25.3	18.7	13.3	7.5
Unlawful entry without force	125.4	30.1	26.5	18.3	14.6
Attempted forcible entry	22.5*	17.4	13.6	7.8	4.9
Household larceny	206.4	114.0	100.0	75.0	45.2
Completed	198.2	106.6	93.7	70.9	43.1
Less than $50	77.3	42.7	36.8	31.1	23.2
$50 or more	118.7	59.3	51.9	35.6	16.1
Amount not available	2.1*	4.6	5.0	4.3	3.9
Attempted	8.2*	7.5	6.3	4.0	2.0
Motor vehicle theft	45.5	26.4	25.8	23.2	8.0
Completed	34.7	17.1	15.8	15.3	5.1
Attempted	10.8*	9.3	9.9	7.9	2.9
Total number of households	833,060	25,916,390	30,234,390	19,226,400	20,629,030

Note: Detail may not add to total shown due to rounding.
*Estimate is based on about 10 or fewer sample cases.

Source: Department of Justice, 1992, p. 45.

accordingly—peer evaluation decreases, and opportunities for becoming financially self-sufficient expand. This reduces teenage motivation to engage in property crimes, and their involvement in property crimes drops off rapidly at post-high school ages. As Greenberg (1983:33) states in the language of anomie and control theory:

> Employment, leaving school, military enlistment, and marriage eliminate major sources of criminogenic frustration, and at the same time supply informal social control.

Greenberg also attempts to explain the high rates of interpersonal violence in the 16–24 age group. As discussed earlier in this chapter, interpersonal crimes of violence are committed primarily by males. Traditional gender roles call for males to work outside the home and support a family. However, lower- and working-class males have less of a chance than other males of fulfilling these roles. This, Greenberg (1977:207) reasons, generates a masculine status anxiety in which such men

> may attempt to alleviate their anxiety by exaggerating those traditionally male traits that *can* be expressed. Attempts to dominate women (including rape) and patterns of interpersonal violence can be seen in these terms.

In other words, crime can . . . provide a sense of potency that is expected and desired but not achieved in other spheres of life.

Greenberg points out that arrest rates for interpersonal crimes of violence peak in the immediate post-high school age brackets when primarily lower- and working-class males—who do not attend college—anticipate or actively seek full-time work. He argues that masculine status anxiety not only helps us understand age variations in interpersonal crimes of violence, but class, gender, and race as well. Greenberg concludes that the variable relationship between age and crime depends on historical, cultural, and economic factors. Patterns of crime in the United States therefore reflect the particularly developed age segregation and the social position of youth.

Not everyone agrees that age is an important factor in explaining patterns of crime. Hirschi and Gottfredson (1983:552), for example, agree that the age distribution of crime depicted in the *UCR* is accurate and that it "represents one of the brute facts of criminology." But whereas Greenberg argues that the age distribution of crime varies with social conditions, Hirschi and Gottfredson contend that the age distribution of crime is *invariant* across all social and cultural conditions. For them the shape and form of the age distribution remains "virtually unchanged" from time to time and place to place (*ibid.*:554–562). Criminological theory and research therefore need not consider age as an important variable in explaining crime.

Greenberg (1985) has countered this argument with considerable historical and cross-cultural evidence. Greenberg (*ibid.*:12) shows that today there is less adult crime relative to juvenile crime in the United States than there used to be. Similarly, in analyzing other societies—both industrial and preindustrial—a shift toward younger ages in criminality is clearly noticeable once industrialization occurs. For example, in contemporary Norway, the age distribution of crime is similar to the United States. Yet as criminologist Nils Christie (cited in *ibid.*:12) points out:

> Police statistics for 1870 showed no peak for teenagers. They did not exist at that time. A hundred years ago, the peak was somewhere in the middle twenties and with a *slow decrease* in criminal activity among the older groups (emphasis added).

For the Banyoro and Basoga (two preindustrialized Bantu-speaking peoples of Uganda), the peak age of homicide is 35, and rarely are homicides committed by teenagers (*ibid.*:13). Consequently, Greenberg's theory of the age distribution of conventional crime remains the most sound, and empirical research supports his conclusions (Cohen and Land, 1987). In particular, Steffensmeier *et al.* (1989) examined arrest data on age in the United States for three time periods: 1940, 1960, and 1980. They found that considerable change in the age of offending occurred from 1940 to 1980. As Steffensmeier *et al.* (*ibid.*:803) state: The "most significant change has been the progressive concentration of offending among the young; this suggests increasing discontinuity in the transition from adolescence to adulthood in modern times."

However, although Greenberg's theory is intriguing, it implies that age is the single most important variable for explaining crime. Indeed, Greenberg (*ibid.*:212) suggests that youth have developed into their own social class, which would seem to reduce the importance of other social divisions and characteristics:

> In modern capitalist societies, children of all classes share, for a limited period, a common relationship to the means of production (namely exclusion) which is distinct from that of most adults, and they respond to their common structural position in fairly similar ways.

Yet age is not a simple or homogeneous category; it is divided not only by class but also by gender and race. Research suggests that distinct youth subcultures—based on such categories as race and class—develop within a broader youth culture (Brake, 1980; Hall *et al.*, 1978; Mungham and Pearson, 1976; Hall and Jefferson, 1976), that these youth subcultures differ from one another, and that they can become hostile and antagonistic toward each other (Willis, 1978; Schwendinger and Schwendinger, 1985). Mungham and Pearson (*ibid.*:7) go so far as to argue that working-class, skinhead subcultures developed in reaction to the middle-class hippy subculture of the 1960s and early 1970s. The result was a distinct *style* that is "both a caricature and a reassertion of solid male working-class toughness." As we will discuss in Chapter 4.1, however, skinhead subcultures also represent racist hatred. Greenberg's theory downplays this subcultural differentiation and conflict. Although age structures patterns of crime and victimization, it is not a uniform entity.

Herman and Julia Schwendinger (1985) consider the foregoing in their book *Adolescent Subcultures and Delinquency*, wherein they show that there are different, yet cohesive, adolescent subcultures and that competition and conflict often prevail among them. Struggling for status and recognition in a broader youth culture, young people organize into such specific groups as *socialites* (professional-managerial class), *intermediaries* (working class), and *street-corner youth* (the poor). The Schwendingers (*ibid.*:181–182) found that almost all youth engage in some form of delinquency, yet the seriousness and frequency of youth crime "moves upward from the domain of socialite groups through the intermediary types and peaks within the domain of the street corner groups."

It is not only the segregation and subordination of youth in society as a whole—and its accompanying adolescent subcultures—that generates specific patterns of crime, however, but also their subordination within specific institutions. Unequal relationships between parents and children can set the stage for generational conflict and at least three types of crime: child physical abuse, incestuous assault, and youth crime. Child abuse results from power relations across generations and the accompanying ideology that children should at all times be subordinate to parents. A thin line separates authoritarian, punitive, and harsh forms of discipline, on the one hand, and child abuse on the other; indeed, they seem to coexist. And it is increasingly evident that these violent and abusive generational relationships breed subsequent crime by the victims of child abuse. After reviewing considerable evidence on this topic, Elliot Currie (1985:203) concludes:

> That violent homes breed violent children has been driven home over and over again by recent studies. To be sure, not every abused child becomes delinquent or aggressive; and tracing clear and unequivocal links between abuse and later violence is a complicated and difficult problem for researchers. But the evidence is much too strong to ignore.

A recent study by Cathy Spatz Widom (1989) supports such a conclusion. Widom (*ibid.*:254–260) compared a large sample of substantiated and validated cases of child abuse and neglect with a control group of individuals with no official record of either abuse or neglect. While the intergenerational transmission of violence is not inevitable, the results of the study indicate that childhood victimization in the home has "demonstrable long-term consequences for adult criminal behavior" (*ibid.*:265). Abused and neglected individuals were found to have higher rates of adult crime than those of the control group as well as a larger number of arrests. Abused and neglected individuals were also found to be arrested more often for specific violent crimes than were members of the control group. And although females generally commit fewer crimes than males, "abused females were more likely than control females to have an arrest as an adult." (*ibid.*:265. See also Rivera and Widom, 1990).

Similarly, research reveals a strong relationship between incestuous assault and future delinquency. As we will detail in Chapter 4.2, the vast majority of victims of incestuous assault (both girls and boys) report severe forms of trauma, leading many to run away from home. Girls on the street report high rates of physical abuse and incestuous assault (Chesney-Lind, 1989:22). Running away from incestuous assault and a violent home, these young women and men turn to crime to survive. As Meda Chesney-Lind (*ibid.*:23) points out after reviewing the literature on young women, once on the street they begin

> engaging in prostitution and other forms of petty property crime. They also begin what becomes a lifetime problem with drugs. As adults, the women continue in these activities since they possess truncated educational backgrounds and virtually no marketable occupational skills.

Consequently, the powerlessness of children in the home and the extreme results of that subordination—child physical abuse, incestuous assault, and neglect—contribute to crime both quantitatively and qualitatively. Moreover, this finding demonstrates the important ties among social position, victimization, and subsequent crime.

Although the social position of youth presents young people with opportunities for committing certain crimes, it also precludes them from committing others. Systematically denied access to the labor market, youth are effectively segregated from positions where workplace-related crimes—such as embezzlement and corporate crimes—as well as political crimes occur. For corporate and

Child abuse tends to increase an abused person's chances of being involved in conventional crime.

political crimes, the ages 30–55 clearly dominate, as these are the prime ages of employment and, therefore, the most powerful age group in society. Thus, as Steffensmeier *et al.* (1989:827) point out: In "contrast to the age curves for ordinary crimes, which tend to be sharply peaked, it may be that the age curves for *lucrative* criminality not only peak much later but tend not to decline with age."

As stated earlier, the elderly are also increasingly segregated and subordinated in the United States. Not surprisingly, more criminologists have become interested in the topic "crime and the elderly" (Goetting, 1983; Willbanks and Kim, 1984; Newman, Newman, and Gewirtz, 1984; McCarthy and Langworthy, 1988). An important article by Cullen, Wozniak, and Frank (1985:155) concluded that the majority (78 percent) of elderly arrests are for larceny, which is almost six times higher than the next highest category, aggravated assault. Elderly males and females seem to commit larceny in equal proportions (Feinberg, 1984). Moreover, the elderly tend to steal household and personal necessities of low value—such as toothpaste, cigarettes, and tools (Curran, 1984). It should be noted, however, that although larceny seems to be the most frequent crime committed by the elderly, they are much less likely to commit larceny than any other age group (Klemke, 1992:43–44).

TABLE 3-8   **Labor Force Participation Rates, by Gender and Age: 1960, 1970, 1980, 1986, 1991**

	1960	1970	1980	1986	1991
Male					
20–24	88.1	83.3	85.9	85.8	83.4
25–34	97.5	96.4	95.2	94.6	93.7
35–44	97.7	96.9	95.5	94.8	94.2
45–54	95.7	94.3	91.2	91.0	90.5
55–64	86.8	83.0	72.1	67.3	66.9
65 and over	33.1	26.8	19.0	16.0	15.8
Female					
20–24	46.1	57.7	68.9	72.4	70.4
25–34	36.0	45.0	65.5	71.6	73.3
35–44	43.4	51.1	65.5	73.1	76.6
45–54	49.8	54.4	59.9	65.9	72.0
55–64	37.2	43.0	41.3	42.3	45.3
65 and over	10.8	9.7	8.1	7.4	8.6

Source: Statistical Abstract of the U.S., 1992, p. 381.

As would be expected from our earlier analysis, elderly property crime rates are correlated with adverse economic conditions. In fact, those above the age of 55, and especially 65, have an economic situation similar to that of youth. Table 3-8 shows that the labor force participation rate for people 55 and older has decreased since 1960: for males aged 55–64 it fell from 86.8 in 1960 to 66.9 in 1991, for ages 65 and over it fell from 33.1 to 15.8. Although the female labor force participation rate increased for those aged 55–64 (from 37.2 to 45.3), for those 65 and over it dropped from 10.8 in 1960 to 8.6 in 1991. This decreasing labor force participation rate may help explain the high rate of larceny by people over 65. Bachand and Chressauthis (1988:101) recently investigated the relationships among inflation, unemployment, labor force participation rates, and elderly crime. They concluded that as each of these economic factors worsens, so, too, does the property crime rate of the elderly.

REVIEW

This chapter discussed considerable empirical research to help explain the patterns of crime and victimization in U.S. society. Of primary importance is the structured inequality that exists in U.S. society. Class, gender, race, and age hierarchies determine social position and thus criminal opportunities.

Class and Crime

1. Arrest data, self-report studies, and victimization surveys all show that conventional crimes by adults and youth are disproportionately concentrated in the lower and working classes.

2. White-collar and political crimes are disproportionately committed by members of the professional-managerial class.

3. Victimization data show that all conventional crimes—except personal larceny without contact and motor vehicle theft—are likely to be intra-class.

4. Unemployment, income inequality, and job quality are associated both with conventional crimes and with nonoccupational crimes of the hidden economy.

5. Economic conditions—such as inflation and job quality—as well as perceived inequality within the workplace itself are conducive to occupational crimes such as employee theft.

6. Corporate crimes are caused chiefly by the desire of corporate executives to overcome obstacles to profit making.

7. Because of their position within the state, politicians have opportunities to gain financially by engaging in a variety of corrupt practices.

8. The close association between the state and the economy creates conditions for systematic state crime—such as international political crimes.

Gender and Crime

1. Arrest data, self-report studies, and victimization surveys show that male adults and youth are the chief perpetrators of all forms of conventional crime.

2. Males have a virtual monopoly on the commission of syndicated, corporate, and political crimes.

3. When females commit crime, they engage mostly in petty forms of theft like shoplifting, fraud, and minor embezzlement and in prostitution.

4. Victimization data on conventional crimes suggest that males victimize other males, except for crimes of rape and violence in the family.

5. Women's subordinate position in the gender division of labor structures the type of embezzlement women commit.

6. The feminization of poverty is associated with female fraud, shoplifting, and other forms of petty theft.

7. Males dominate in syndicated, corporate, and political crimes because of their power systematically to exclude women from positions where these crimes originate.

8. Male violence toward women derives from gender inequality, the structural subordination of women, and the power and dominance accorded men in U.S. society.

Race and Crime

1. Data on race and crime suggest that African American adults and youth commit a disproportionate amount of conventional crimes—especially interpersonal crimes of violence.

2. Whites clearly dominate the more harmful and economically damaging white-collar and political crimes.

3. Victimization data show that conventional crimes are intraracial in nature (such as, African Americans typically victimize African Americans and whites typically victimize whites).

4. Because racial oppression multiplies African Americans' disadvantages, they experience a disproportionate number of economic and social obstacles.

5. Overrepresentation of African American adults and youth in conventional crime statistics—both property crimes and interpersonal crimes of violence—is the result of racial economic inequality.

6. The racial hierarchy results in white domination of the positions where white-collar and political crimes occur.

Age and Crime

1. Conventional crime arrest rates vary with age. Property crimes peak between 15 and 17 years of age and decline rapidly with age; violent crimes peak around 18 and 19 years of age and decline much more slowly.

2. Victimization rates for conventional crimes show that young persons aged 12–24 have the highest rates of conventional crime victimization.

3. The high rate of property crime for youth results from their desire to participate in youth social activities and from a lack of adequate funds to pay for them.

4. Not all criminologists agree that age is an important factor in crime.

5. Power and inequality within the family can create social positions leading to the victimization of youth. This victimization has implications for future involvement in crime.

6. White-collar and political crimes are committed by the most powerful age group, 30–55 years.

7. Elderly crime consists mostly of petty forms of theft, such as shoplifting, and is caused by their decreasing participation in the labor market.

QUESTIONS FOR CLASS DISCUSSION

1. Choose several crimes. Then explain how social position permits and prevents opportunities for their commission.

2. Discuss how the interaction of class, gender, race, and age affects criminal opportunities. Cite several examples.

3. How does our discussion of the varieties of crime differ from those offered by the media?

RECOMMENDED READINGS

Box, Steven (1987). *Recession, Crime and Punishment*. London: Macmillan. This book provides a review and discussion of North American and British research on the impact of unemployment and income inequality on crime.

Chesney-Lind, Meda and Randall G. Shelden (1992). *Girls, Delinquency, and Juvenile Justice*. Belmont, CA: Wadsworth. An excellent discussion of the relation among gender, crime by girls, and the juvenile justice system.

Cullen, Francis, John Woziak and James Frank (1985). "The Rise of the Elderly Offender: Will a 'New' Criminal Be Invented?" *Crime and Social Justice* 23:151–165. This article successfully challenges the assumption that the elderly are now engaging in conventional crime at an unprecedented rate.

Greenberg, David (1977). "Delinquency and the Age Structure of Society." *Contemporary Crises* 1(2):189–224. The most important theoretical essay on youth crime during the 1970s and 1980s.

Hall, Stuart *et al.* (1978). *Policing the Crisis: Mugging, the State and Law and Order*. London: Macmillan. The final chapter is a fruitful inquiry into the relationships among race, class, and conventional crime.

Messerschmidt, James W. (1993). *Masculinities and Crime: Critique and Reconceptualization of Theory*. Lanham, MD: Rowman and Littlefield. This book examines how crime can be a resource in the social construction of masculinity.

Schur, Edwin (1988). *The Americanization of Sex*. Philadelphia: Temple University Press. This book contains a useful discussion of *coercive sexuality*—rape, wife beating, incestuous assault, and sexual harassment.

PART TWO

TYPES OF CRIME

CHAPTER 4

INTERPERSONAL VIOLENCE

4.1 Murder, Assault, and Rape
Murder and Assault
Hate Crimes
Rape

4.2 Interpersonal Violence in the Family
Heterosexual Wife Rape and Battering
Homosexual Partner Battering
Child Abuse, Incestuous Assault, and Neglect

4.3 Sexual Harassment
What Is Sexual Harassment?
Sexual Harassment at Work

Preview

Chapter 4 introduces:

☞ the different types of interpersonal violence.
☞ the nature and extent of interpersonal violence.
☞ the varying definitions of interpersonal violence.

Key Terms

aggravated assault	manslaughter
battering	murder
child abuse	rape
child neglect	sexual harassment
hate crime	social coercion
incestuous assault	victim precipitation
interpersonal coercion	wife rape

*I*nterpersonal crimes of violence have profoundly affected the way most of us live. Forty percent of the U.S. population state in surveys that they fear being home alone, fear being by themselves in the center of the city, and fear specific acts, such as murder, assault, and rape (Pollock and Rosenblat, 1984:34). Fear of crime simply becomes for many citizens fear of the streets as well as fear of being home alone, and clearly alters our life-style.

Moreover, we are particularly afraid of strangers. In 1967 the President's Commission on Law Enforcement and the Administration of Justice reported that "the fear of crimes of violence is not a simple fear of injury or death or even of all crimes of violence, but at bottom, a fear of strangers" (President's Commission, 1967:52). There is no reason to believe this has changed. Many of us assume that most violent crimes are committed on the streets by strangers. We fear most of all the random, unprovoked attack on the street by a stranger.

Much of this fear, however, is (as noted in Chapter 1.1) caused by the mass media, for it is here that most people develop their comprehension of where and by whom violent crime is committed. Magazines, newspapers, and television focus on dramatic, violent crimes like murder; "prime-time criminals," usually strangers to their victims, commit their crimes on the street. A distorted view of crime is thus encouraged.

Indeed, most conventional crime is not violent. There are many more crimes against property than crimes of interpersonal violence. Moreover, and as we learn in this chapter, crimes of interpersonal violence occur most frequently indoors and, therefore, are more or less invisible to the public; the perpetrators and victims—although sometimes strangers—are usually relatives, friends, and acquaintances. This is not to say, however, that crimes of interpersonal violence in the United States are not a substantial problem. We as citizens are rightly concerned about a major social cancer: the United States—according to the best available evidence—has a higher level of interpersonal violence than any other industrialized country (Currie, 1985).

With this in mind, we turn now to a discussion of certain specific acts of interpersonal violence. We discuss the nature, extent, and types of three categories of interpersonal violence: (1) murder, assault, and rape; (2) violence in the family; and (3) sexual harassment. These crimes are also referred to by many criminologists as "one-on-one" or "person-to-person" crimes because one individual inflicts violence on another. Interpersonal violence therefore differs from other types of violence—such as corporate violence—that not only inflict more harm on larger numbers of people, but also do not entail direct face-to-face interactions. Corporate violence is discussed in Chapter 7.2.

4.1   MURDER, ASSAULT, AND RAPE

When we commonly think of violent crimes, usually what comes to mind are the crimes of murder, assault, and for women in particular, rape. In this section we look at the nature, extent, and types of these three forms of interpersonal violence. We begin with a combined discussion of murder and assault and then cover the crime of rape.

Murder and Assault

Murder is defined as "the willful (nonnegligent) killing of one human being by another" (FBI, 1993:7). Individuals also can be charged by the state with *manslaughter* for killing another person through gross negligence. The difference between murder and manslaughter is based on intent, or what is referred to as *mens rea* (a guilty mind is present in the offender)—the conscious intent of the offender is to kill. In murder, malice is always present, although the degree of murder is based on the level of premeditation (essentially, plotting the murder in advance). Manslaughter is divided into two types, voluntary and involuntary. Voluntary manslaughter occurs when there is sudden passion arising from an immediate adequate cause. If the victim does not die but sustains serious injury, the crime is defined by the state as assault. Involuntary manslaughter results when one individual unintentionally kills another through recklessness or gross negligence, such as might happen during an automobile accident.

There are approximately 20,000 murders every year in the United States. The most comprehensive source for determining the number of murders is the *Uniform Crime Reports (UCR)*. Obviously, it is impossible to conduct victimization surveys on murder. Although it is difficult to conceal a killing from official investigation, a number of murders may be ignored, overlooked, or disregarded; coroners may err in ruling an accidental death as a murder; and some bodies simply may be hidden. Thus, while we must rely on police data as our source for determining the nature and extent of murder in the United States, this evidence must be viewed with skepticism.

In 1992 there were 23,760 murders in the United States. This means that approximately 9 of every 100,000 people were victims of murder (FBI, 1993:13). Although murder is the most serious form of interpersonal violence, fortunately it occurs the least often. In 1992 murder accounted for only 1 percent of those violent crimes identified by the FBI—murder, assault, rape, and robbery (*ibid.* 13). (We identify robbery as a property crime and discuss it in Chapter 5.1.)

Murder also occurs primarily in big cities. Wolfgang (1968:246) studied crime in relation to city population and concluded that "the larger the city category, the higher the crime rate for all 'serious' crime combined." Moreover, studies over several decades have consistently shown a close relationship between city size and murder rates. That is, the larger the city the higher the murder rate (Boggs, 1966; Glaser, 1970; McLennan, 1970; Harries, 1974; Clinard, 1974). This is true today as well (FBI, 1988:10).

Although murder rates are related to city size, this does not mean that *city population growth* increases the murder rate. In fact, some longitudinal studies have reported consistent declines in murder rates when population has increased (Powell, 1966; Ferdinand, 1967; Lane, 1979). Archer and Gartner (1984:98–117) investigated this paradox, attempting to answer the question: Why do large cities currently have higher homicide rates than small cities if there is no evidence of increasing rates as a city grows? Looking cross-culturally, they determined from their study that today's larger cities have always had higher murder rates than the national murder rate. Archer and Gartner (*ibid.*:116) conclude:

> This analysis showed that city rates have consistently exceeded national rates, even when the cities were much smaller in absolute terms. The determinant of a city's homicide rate is therefore not the absolute size of the city but its size *relative* to its contemporary society. We believe that this interpretation explains why homicide rates do not necessarily increase as a city grows. Large cities have always had relatively high homicide rates because they have always been more urban than their national environments.

Thus, high murder rates are related to city size but not to city growth.

The *typical* killing—whether in large cities or small—results from disagreements between individuals who know each other. According to the *Uniform Crime Reports* (FBI, 1993:17) for 1992, in 39 percent of murders the relationship between offender and victim was unknown. However, 47 percent involved family members, friends, neighbors, and acquaintances, and 14 percent involved strangers (*ibid.*:17). Moreover, the largest percentage of murders in 1992 involved arguments over romantic triangles, property and money, and other issues. The typical murder, then, involves family, friends, and acquaintances, who are for a variety of reasons involved in an argument—usually over a trivial matter—that eventually leads to a killing. Consequently, according to *UCR* data we have more to fear from those to whom we are close than from strangers.

Marc Riedel and Margaret Zahn (1985) reached the same conclusion in a very thorough analysis of FBI murder data for the 1980s. Riedel and Zahn used "Supplementary Homicide Reports"—monthly law-enforcement reports containing detailed data on victims, offenders, and circumstances of the murders for that month—to investigate the nature and extent of murder over an 11-year period. From these data, the authors identified three major types of murder: *family* (victim and offender were members of the same family), *acquaintance* (victim and offender were known to each other but not members of the same family), and *stranger* (victim and offender were total strangers). Riedel and Zahn (*ibid.*:10) found that of those murders in which the victim-offender relationship was known, between 57 and 62 percent were either family or acquaintance murders, and that 13 to 14 percent could be classified as stranger murders.

It is therefore not surprising to find that the typical murder is also related to routine social activities among family, friends, and acquaintances. Murder is most likely to occur during times when routine activities are more concentrated around the home. For example, murder occurs most often during summer vacations (July and August) and Christmas holiday seasons, which are traditionally a time when family members, neighbors, and friends are together (FBI 1993:15). Moreover, as Messner and Tardiff (1985:258–260) reported in their research on murder, weekend murders are more likely to occur at home, amongst family members, and during the early evening hours, very likely reflecting "the

A publicized example of "family murder": the father of Marvin Gaye Jr. at his arraignment for the murder of his son.

tendency for persons to be at home during the dinner hours and then go out in the hours immediately following."

Although the typical murder discussed thus far is characteristic of the largest proportion of murders, there are other types. For example, *professional murder* takes place when one individual kills another for personal profit. An unwritten "contract" is arranged, usually over the telephone, between people who have never met personally. The victim, or "hit," is normally unknown to the killer, as this makes it easier for the killer to "deny the victim" (Levi, 1981:52). Moreover, by conceptualizing the killing as a "business" or as "just a job," professional murderers can deny wrongfulness and thus justify their behavior even further (*ibid.*:53).

Another type of murder, *serial murder*, occurs when an individual kills a number of people over a period of time. There are two types of serial murderers. First, there are those killers who murder within the general area of their residence. An example of this type of serial murderer is John Wayne Gacy, who in 1979 murdered 33 young boys in or near his home and then buried them in the crawl space of his home, the attic, inside the walls, and under the patio and driveway. Second, there are murderers who kill outside the proximity of their own residences. Examples of this type are Theodore Bundy, who was found guilty of killing over 20 women in Washington, Utah, and Colorado, and Henry Lee Lucas, who *admitted* killing 365 people in 25 states. According to some researchers, at least 142 of Lucas' killings have been verified (Holmes and DeBurger, 1985:30–31).

There is controversy over the annual number of serial murder victims in the United States. Basing their conclusion on law-enforcement data and "the probable proportion of missing children who have fallen prey to these predators," Holmes and DeBurger (1988:19) estimate that between 3,500 and 5,000 persons are victims of serial murderers each year. As noted in Chapter 2.2, however, Philip Jenkins' (1988) investigation of FBI serial murder data reveals at most 350–400 murders associated with serial killers.

Finally, a *mass murder* is committed when an individual kills a number of people at once, rather than singly over time. Obviously, mass murder can occur in other ways—such as by the state—but the context here is the *interpersonal* manner in which mass murder may occur. Thus, an example of a mass murder is a husband/father who kills his wife and children. Serial and mass murders are the rarest types of murder, yet attract—as we all know—the most media attention.

The most common weapon used to commit murder in the United States is a firearm. In 1992 approximately 70 percent of all murders were committed with a firearm, 55 percent with a handgun (FBI, 1993:17). Riedel and Zahn (1985:45–51) found the handgun to be the weapon of choice in all three major types of murder—family, acquaintance, and stranger. Many people argue that because of the relationship between firearms and murder, firearms (especially handguns) should be controlled rigidly by the state. Others, in particular members of the National Rifle Association (NRA), argue that "Guns do not kill, people do."

Though the debate over firearm ownership and murder is likely to continue for some time, sociologists and criminologists have generated some interesting information that sheds light on the subject. First, firearm ownership varies by region, which correlates with the regional murder rates. The South has both the highest murder rate and the highest rate of firearm ownership. The Northeast, on the other hand, has the lowest murder rate and the lowest rate of firearm ownership (FBI, 1993:8; Newton and Zimring, 1969; Erskine, 1972; Wright and Marston, 1975). Second, the chance of dying from a firearm wound is much higher than from assault with a knife, club, or fist. In fact, assaults with firearms are two to six times more likely to result in death than assaults with knives

Serial murderer Jeffrey Dahmer.

(Wright, Rossi, and Daly, 1983:18, 198). Wright, Rossi, and Daly (*ibid.*:18) note, however, that this "*might* imply that guns are intrinsically more lethal (in which case their restriction might lower the homicide rate)," but it might also imply "that people who are intent on bringing death to their victim preferentially choose firearms as the means (in which case firearm restrictions would not lower the homicide rate)." Nevertheless, some criminologists have shown that increases in murder are correlated with increases in firearm ownership (Fisher, 1976; Farley, 1980). Third, because of easy availability of firearms, more accidental deaths and injuries occur. Approximately 30,000 deaths and 900,000 injuries occur each year because of criminal, accidental, and suicidal uses of firearms (Wright, Rossi, and Daly, 1983:16).

All of this does not mean that firearms *cause* murder. However, it is obvious that households with firearms present are more likely—during a family argument, for instance—to experience a firearm death than are households without firearms. Moreover, because approximately 83 percent of the population report feeling safer at home if they possess a firearm, it is not surprising to find that (*ibid.*:229, 25–45, 311; Walker, 1989:181):

▲— at least 50 percent of all U.S. households possess a firearm

▲— about one household in four owns a handgun

▲— approximately 120 million–160 million firearms are in private hands in the United States

▲— at least one city (Kennesaw, Georgia) has an ordinance requiring *every* household to have a firearm

Thus, although there is scant evidence to suggest that firearm ownership deters crime (Green, 1987), by assuming it does and then purchasing guns, households actually become less, rather than more, safe and secure.

In 1958 criminologist Marvin Wolfgang coined the term "victim-precipitated murder," applying it to those murders in which "the victim is a direct, positive precipitator in the crime" (Wolfgang, 1958:252). In victim-precipitated murder, the victim is the first to display and use a deadly weapon or to strike a blow and, therefore, "the first to commence the interplay of resort to physical violence" (*ibid.*:252). For example, such a murder may involve two people having an argument during which the victim threatens the offender with a knife. Responding, the offender pulls out a gun and fires a fatal bullet. In approximately one of every four murders, the victim precipitates the killing (*ibid.*:254; Mulvihill, Tumin, and Curtis, 1969:226).

A number of criminologists have questioned the victim-precipitation thesis, suggesting that the interaction between offender and victim actually involves challenges and provocations by *both* participants to the killing. In his research, David Luckenbill (1977) finds that murder results from an "intense interchange" between offender, victim, and sometimes an audience, and parallels a "character contest" wherein both offender and victim attempt to maintain "face" at the other's expense. This interchange between offender and victim takes place as follows:

1. The victim makes what the offender perceives as an offensive move, gesture, or remark.

2. The offender then retaliates with a verbal or physical challenge.

3. The victim then retaliates, creating a "working" agreement that commits both parties to a violent resolution of the conflict.

4. The battle eventually results in the death of the victim.

In 63 percent of Luckenbill's cases such an exchange between offender and victim took place (*ibid.*:179). Richard Felson and Henry Steadman (1983) reported similar results, concluding that the typical murder involves both offender and victim contributing to the violent conflict.

Although Luckenbill's theory is intriguing, it is questionable whether it is applicable to all forms of murder. Obviously, it is little help in understanding professional, serial, and mass murder. Moreover, Nancy Jurik and Peter Greg-ware (1992) have shown that for female-perpetrated murder, the idea of a character contest does not seem to hold in many cases, such as murder resulting from child abuse and killing in self-defense (to avoid wife beating). Thus, Lucken-bill's theory may help us understand *some* male offender/male victim murder, but is inadequate when applied to typical female offender/male victim murders. As Jurik and Gregware (*ibid.*:196) show, while Luckenbill emphasizes a character contest, their data on women "suggest the salience of strategic, life-saving dimen-sions and an imposed—rather than consensual—characterization of the violence in these homicides."

Aggravated assault is "an unlawful attack by one person upon another for the purpose of inflicting severe or aggravated bodily injury" (FBI, 1988:21). Aggravated assault is usually accompanied by the use of a weapon or by other means likely to produce death or great bodily harm.

Assault and murder are closely related crimes. In fact, much of what has already been discussed regarding murder can also be applied to aggravated assault. However, there are some differences between the two crimes. The first and most obvious difference is that an assault does not result in an actual death. Although the typical assault and murder are similar in most major respects, it is the existence of a dead body that creates the major difference between them. If a killing does not occur, the crime is some type of assault.

A second difference is that there are more assaults in the United States than murders. In 1992 there were 1.2 million reported aggravated assaults, resulting in a rate of approximately 442 per 100,000 individuals (FBI, 1993:31). This rate is more than 40 times the murder rate. However, in its *National Crime Victimization Survey (NCVS)*, the Department of Justice found that only 57 percent of the victims of aggravated assault reported the crime to the police (Department of Justice, 1992:11). Consequently, aggravated assault occurs much more often than the *UCR* data indicate. Indeed, the *NCVS* estimated that over 5 million assaults occurred in 1992 (*ibid.*:11).

Finally, according to the *NCVS* (Department of Justice, 1992:53), assaults—unlike murder—involve strangers (54 percent of the time) more often than relatives, friends, and acquaintances. However, victims may be less likely to report assaults by people they know. Thus, it could well be that regarding the victim/offender relationship, aggravated assault is similar to murder.

Hate Crimes

A pervasive fact of life in Western industrialized societies is "hate crimes," or violence perpetrated on people because of their race, ethnicity, or sexual orientation. Recent studies of hate crimes reveal that they are significantly more widespread than earlier believed. For example, a study of antigay and lesbian violence in eight U.S. cities—Boston, New York, Atlanta, St. Louis, Denver, Dallas, Los Angeles, and Seattle—found that among those surveyed (Berrill, 1992:20):

▲— 19 percent reported having been punched, hit, kicked, or beaten at least once in their lives because of their sexual orientation.

▲— 44 percent had been threatened with physical violence.

▲— 94 percent experienced some type of victimization—such as verbal abuse, physical assault, vandalized property, or being spat upon, chased, or pelted with objects.

▲— More than two-thirds (68 percent) of those threatened with violence and nearly half (47 percent) of those assaulted reported multiple victimizations.

Moreover, despite the many positive changes resulting from the civil rights movement, racism persists in the U.S., expressing its extreme form in racist attacks on African Americans and other racial and ethnic minorities. During the 1970s there were increasing reports of racial violence against African Americans by white youth. In 1980, the Subcommittee on Crime of the U.S. House of Representatives investigated this violence. In its report, *Increasing Violence Against Minorities*, the Subcommittee found anti-African American attacks both by individuals (primarily young white males) and by groups such as the Ku Klux Klan. The report concluded that there "is abundant evidence of a marked increase in the incidence of criminal violence directed against minority groups" (U.S. House of Representatives, 1980:2). The media reported some of this violence, such as the attack by Klan members on civil rights marchers in Cumming, Georgia, and the beating of several African American youth—and the eventual death of one after being hit by a car—by young white males in Howard Beach, New York. Both these cases occurred in the late 1980s. Examples of violent incidents that did not receive media attention in the 1980s include (Marable, 1983:233–234):

▲— the lynching of a 19-year-old African American youth in Mobile, Alabama.

▲— the tortured body of an African American man floating in a river in Cleveland, Mississippi (his genitals had been cut off and the coroner reported finding his penis in his stomach).

▲— the lynching of a 45-year-old African American man in Tallahatchie County, Mississippi.

▲— the lynching of a 32-year-old African American man who had been badly beaten in the head and face (his hands were tied behind him and he had been shot point-blank in the head).

Moreover, a number of *skinhead* gangs have sprung up around the country. Skinheads hold extremely conservative and neo-Nazi views and they routinely target racial and ethnic minorities and homosexuals for violent attacks. Indeed, Mark Hamm's (1993) important study *American Skinheads: The Criminology and Control of Hate Crime* reports that the defining characteristics of skinhead ideology are racism, homophobia, and anti-semitism.

"Skinhead" gangs hold white supremacist views and routinely target people of color for violent attacks.

Hate crimes differ from other forms of interpersonal violence in three important ways: they are more vicious, extremely brutal, and frequently perpetrated at random on total strangers (commonly a single victim) by multiple offenders (usually groups of white working-class male teenagers) (Levin and McDevitt, 1993:11–20). An example is the killing of Mulugeta Seraw (Hamm, 1993:3–4). In the early morning hours of November 13, 1988, Seraw (an Ethiopian immigrant) was saying goodnight to a few of his friends in Portland, Oregon. Suddenly, three young white males—all members of the East Side White Pride skinhead gang—approached Seraw and his Ethiopian friends carrying baseball bats. When the assault was finished, Seraw's skull was fractured in two places, killing him. Hamm (*ibid.*:4) describes what the police found in the three-room apartment of two of the skinheads:

> In the first room, they discovered a collection of baseball bats and clubs. In the second, they found racist propaganda published by a South- ern California organization known as the White Aryan Resistance

(W.A.R.). And in the third room, they found a small library on the rise and fall of Nazi Germany.

Evidence also shows that hate crimes are increasingly reported to the police (Knickerbocker, 1990:6). This increase may not represent an actual increase in the number of hate crimes but, rather, victims may feel more secure now in reporting the crime. However, Levin and McDevitt (1993:34) argue that this increase is most likely the result in the U.S. of a "growing *culture of hate*: from humor and music to religion and politics, a person's group affiliation—the fact that he or she *differs from people in the in-group*—is being used more and more to provide a basis for dehumanizing and insulting that person." Although this "culture of hate" does not actually cause hate crimes, in a social context of growing unemployment and hard economic times, coupled with an influx of recent immigrants from Eastern Europe, Asia, Africa, and Latin America, as well as a visible gay/lesbian rights movement, a culture of hate provides "support and encouragement to those who seek to express their personal version of bigotry in some form of criminal behavior" (*ibid.*:42–43).

Rape

Rape, as traditionally defined in the criminal law (FBI, 1993:23), is "the carnal knowledge of a female forcibly and against her will." By concentrating on "against her will," the criminal law makes it imperative that the threat or actual use of physical violence by the offender be present to constitute proof that the victim did not consent. Consequently, this traditional definition of rape actually means, in practice, sexual intercourse obtained by the threat or actual use of physical violence. Hence, the criminal law labels rape "forcible rape."

In 1992 there were 109,062 reported forcible rapes, representing a rate of 43 per 100,000 (FBI, 1993:23). This rate constituted 6 percent of those violent crimes identified by the FBI (murder, assault, rape, and robbery). However, once again we must view the police data with caution, inasmuch as the majority of rapes are not reported to the police (Bureau of Justice Statistics). Indeed, Diana Russell (1984:96) found that only between 9 and 10 percent of rapes and attempted rapes were reported to the police. This is due, as Edwin Schur (1984:151) states, to "the trauma the rape victim experiences, the shame she often is made to feel, and also her likely perception that getting involved with the criminal justice system would itself be traumatic and possibly futile." Moreover, because there is considerable evidence that women have a far greater chance of being raped by someone they know, rather than by a stranger, this clearly affects the victim's decision to report the crime. Women who have been raped by someone they know—husband, friend, or acquaintance—are the least likely to report the crime. A study of victimization data over a 10-year period found that almost 60 percent of stranger rapes, but only 45 percent of nonstranger rapes, were reported to the police (Bureau of Justice Statistics, 1985:3). Other research shows that if the circumstances of the rape involve a violent attack by a stranger, the victim is more likely to report it to the police (Russell, 1984:96–97). Indeed, if the woman did not experience a high level of force, was not threatened with a dangerous weapon, and was not seriously injured, she is less likely to view herself as a rape victim and therefore less likely to report it to the police (Williams, 1984:464). Women raped by someone they know are less likely to report the crime to the police because they may feel (1) embarrassed, (2) that they should have been able to prevent the rape, (3) that they want to protect the assailant, or (4) that they will not be believed (Bureau of Justice Statistics, 1985:2). Also, the police do not take seriously a substantial proportion of rape complaints, and only slightly more than one-half of reported rapes are ever cleared (Clark and Lewis, 1977; Sanders, 1980; Box, 1983). In 1992 the FBI reported that 52 percent of reported rapes were cleared by an arrest (FBI, 1993:207).

Consequently, for all the preceding reasons, the number of rapes in U.S. society is much larger than statistics in the *Uniform Crime Reports* indicate. Indeed, sociologist Allan Griswold Johnson (1980) analyzed victimization surveys to determine the likelihood that a 12-year-old female in 1980 would be a victim of forcible rape during the remainder of her life. Johnson (*ibid.*:145) concluded that "20–30 percent of girls now twelve years old will suffer a violent sexual attack during the remainder of their lives." Moreover, a study of 930 women in San Francisco concluded that there is a 26-percent chance that a woman in that city will be the victim of a completed forcible rape sometime in her life, and a 46-percent probability that she will become a victim of either completed or attempted forcible rape (Russell, 1984:51). Clearly, a great number of women are the victims of forcible rape (as defined by the criminal law) every year.

However, many feminists have argued that the traditional criminal law definition of forcible rape is inadequate, for it recognizes only one type of force—sexual intercourse obtained through the threat or actual use of physical violence. Some feminists argue that this definition does not provide for rape resulting from intimidation or pressure other than the threat or actual use of physical force. For example, a rape omitted from this traditional definition involves a woman who is coerced *economically*—"If you don't 'put out' you'll be fired"—where her overt genuine consent is absent (Box, 1983:122–127). Thus, an expanded definition of rape has been proposed that includes "sexual access gained by any means where the female's overt *genuine* consent is absent" (*ibid.*:125). This particular expanded definition of rape is both similar to and different from the traditional definition. It is similar in that absence of consent must exist; its difference lies in the emphasis on physical and economic coercion. As Shere Hite (1976:296) agrees:

> Anyone who is economically and legally dependent on another person, as women traditionally have been and in the majority of cases still are, is put in a vulnerable and precarious position when that person expects or demands sex or affection. . . . The fact that she does not feel

free *not* to please him . . . reveals the presence of an element of fear and intimidation.

Moreover, some feminists have pointed out that the traditional definition of rape does not include *all* rapes that occur through the threat or actual use of physical violence. These feminists note that in many states today the violent forcible rape of a wife is simply not considered rape. In other words, married women raped by their husbands are excluded from the law. Consequently, if we use the above expanded definition of rape, we see that rape occurs even more frequently in the United States than most people recognize.

Not everyone agrees with this expanded definition of rape, however. Some argue that an important distinction should be made between those who are coerced physically and those who may be coerced in other ways. For example, David Finkelhor and Kersti Yllö (1985:84–98) argue that although labeling as rape sexual assault obtained through economic force highlights how oppressive and coercive sex is under certain circumstances, it simultaneously expands, and therefore dilutes, the meaning of the word "rape." Moreover, they argue it is extremely difficult to determine when force or coercion is being used in a relationship. For these two reasons, then, Finkelhor and Yllö contend that the term "rape" should be used only for situations of actual or threatened physical force. This does not mean that other kinds of force are not employed. Indeed, Finkelhor and Yllö (*ibid.*:89–90) hold that

> a woman whose husband tells her he is going to humiliate her publicly if she won't perform some sexual act, for instance, may be making a more fearsome and devastating threat than a man who threatens only to push himself on his wife. We would be prepared to call this type of coercion forced sex, but not rape.

Thus, Finkelhor and Yllö propose that there are two types of *sexual coercion* in the United States, but that sexual coercion, although frightening and traumatic, is clearly not, and should not be considered, rape. They distinguish "social coercion" from "interpersonal coercion." Social coercion occurs, for example, when women feel they should have sex with their husbands because it is their wifely "duty." Many women feel they cannot say no because they are married, or because he pays the bills, or because of religious authority. Thus, there exist *social* pressures on women to have sex with their husbands even if they do not want to do so. Interpersonal coercion, Finkelhor and Yllö's second type of sexual coercion, occurs when a woman has sex with her husband or an employer in the face of nonviolent threats. For example, a wife may have sex with her husband "to keep peace in the house," or a female employee may have sex with her boss to gain a promotion or just simply to keep a job.

Whether we agree with Finkelhor and Yllö or the expanded definition of rape, the important point to understand is that sexual coercion can, and in fact does, occur in other ways than through the threat or actual use of physical violence.

By reason of the pervasive nature of sexual assault, many women today have a realistic fear of rape. More specifically, women 35 years and younger fear rape more than any other violent or property offense (Warr, 1985). As Warr (*ibid.*:242) concluded in his study of the fear of rape among women: "It is beyond question that rape is currently a central fear in the lives of a large proportion of women" (*ibid.*:242). Thus, because of the existence of rape and the fear that attends it, women are, as criminologist Dorie Klein (1982:211) argues, essentially "under house arrest, their activities constrained by what is dismissed as a brutal fact of life."

Paralleling murder, rape is more likely to be committed by someone the victim knows. Women are more likely to be raped by an acquaintance or a date than by a stranger and more than two-thirds of women are raped by someone they know (Russell, 1984:61).

The preceding evidence is concerned only with *forcible rape*, where the threat or actual use of physical violence occurs. As we have seen, forcible rape is perpetrated by strangers and nonstrangers alike, most frequently by the latter. Forcible rape ranges from assaults, where little if any physical harm is inflicted, to the fusion of sexuality and aggression, resulting in violent beatings and even mutilation of body parts (Medea and Thompson, 1974; Brownmiller, 1975; Groth and Birnbaum, 1979).

In response to argument for an expanded definition of rape, rape literature has established at least three possible types of rape in addition to physically violent forcible rape (it should be added that attempts to reframe rape conceptually have had little impact on legal definitions, except in the category of wife rape). The first two have been discussed already, "social coercion" and "interpersonal coercion." A third argument has been made that rape occurs through *seduction* arising out of an acceptable intimate situation, but where the victim decides not "to go as far" as sexual intercourse. For example, Steven Box (1983:128) argues that the male

> for a variety of reasons, but mainly a mixture of self-defined sexual urge and the need to dominate adversaries, pursues and pressurises, cajoles and bullies, and ultimately "persuades." Physical force is rarely used because it is rarely needed. . . . The offender . . . seeks to pursue his own pleasure, hoping and maybe believing that in doing so he will give pleasure to his "reluctant" and "coy" partner. He firmly believes in his own masculinity and the right of men to harry and hound their prey, but within the "gentlemanly" rules of the "seduction game."

What Box is, of course, arguing is that "date rape" need not occur through the threatened or actual use of physical violence. The victim, in a seductive situation, may feel "guilty" at not letting her partner have what he wants. She may decide to continue the relationship on "his terms" or may simply become exhausted and "unable to resist, at which point she may well say to herself 'so what,' although afterwards, when her energy returns, she may well regret her passivity and submissiveness" (*ibid.*:128).

Some sociologists and criminologists argue that date rapes are simply "victim-precipitated rapes." According to Menachem Amir (1971:266), writing in the early 1970s, "victim-precipitated rape" occurred in

> those rape situations in which the victim actually, or so it was deemed, agreed to sexual relations but retracted before the actual act or did not react strongly enough when the suggestion was made by the offender(s). The term applies also to cases in risky situations marred with sexuality, especially when she uses what could be interpreted as indecency of language and gestures, or constitutes what could be taken as an invitation to sexual relations.

Amir (1967:493; 1971:266) believed that victims of rape are sometimes a "complementary partner" to their own victimization and he concluded that about 19 percent of the rapes in his Philadelphia study were victim-precipitated.

Following Amir, in a study of victim-precipitation and violent crime, Lynn Curtis (1974:600) defined victim-precipitated rape as "an episode ending in forced intercourse when a female first agreed to sexual relations, or clearly invited them verbally and through gestures, but then retracted before the act." Curtis found that only 4 percent of the rapes in his survey were victim-precipitated.

One year later, Nelson and Amir (1975) analyzed the "hitchhiker victim of rape." They found that between 1968 and 1970 in Berkeley, California, women hitchhikers comprised 20 percent of reported rapes. From this, Nelson and Amir (*ibid.*:62) concluded that hitchhike rape is simply victim-precipitated rape and, therefore, "if there were no hitchhiking females a reduction in the total number of rapes in Berkeley would occur."

A number of feminists have responded to the idea of "victim-precipitated rape," arguing that a male bias is clearly revealed in this theorizing—the male criminologists simply identifying with the rapist (Griffin, 1971; Medea and Thompson, 1974; Greer, 1975; Russell, 1975; Brownmiller, 1975; Clark and Lewis, 1977; Box, 1983; Schwendinger and Schwendinger, 1983). As Julia and Herman Schwendinger (1983:66) point out:

> The concept of victim precipitation can be criticized because its defining elements are exactly the same as those chosen by male supremacists, who insist that a victim's right to refuse sex can be ignored because the rapist has the right to force sexual intercourse when she is considered responsible for arousing him sexually.

According to feminists, then, the "victim-precipitated rape theorists" fail to acknowledge the victim's rights, in particular, the right to change her mind whenever she pleases. Feminists see this as collusion—this is exactly what the rapist has done, namely, refused to recognize the victim's right to change her mind. The Schwendingers (1983:66) argue that the victim-precipitation theory of rape simply takes the rapist's judgments and rationalizations at face value—"She was asking for it" or "She did not resist strongly enough" or "She changed her mind too late"—and transforms them into a causal explanation of rape. Moreover, by shifting blame for the rape from offender to victim, these theorists divert attention from the rapist as well as from the broader macrosociological factors forming the context in which rape occurs (Box, 1983:135). Thus, although the idea of victim-precipitation may be relevant to the crime of murder, it is clearly wrong to apply the concept to rape. As Box (*ibid.*:135) asks: "By what stretch of the imagination do rape victims initiate the sexual assault? Do they actually start to assault sexually the persons who subsequently assault them sexually?"

Others have even gone further than the preceding criticisms, arguing that the idea of victim-precipitated rape is based on the pervasive myth in our society that men have a special and overwhelming "urge" or "drive" toward heterosexual intercourse. According to this myth, men have virtually an uncontrollable sexual need that, once "sparked," must find instant satisfaction, regardless of the consequences. Thus, if a woman awakens this sexual desire by engaging in provocative behavior, it is argued, the male cannot be held responsible for his behavior because the "urge" will be too strong for him to control. However, and as feminist criminologist Carol Smart (1976:95) responds, the

> basic fallacy of the male sex-drive myth lies in the belief that rape is a spontaneous act (an immediate response to desire) and that it is a purely sexual act engaged in for the purpose of sexual satisfaction.

Rapists do not randomly and spontaneously assault their victims. Even Amir (1971:142) found that approximately 82 percent of rapes in his sample were either partially or entirely planned. Most rapists spend time looking for women in locations most likely to be immune from surveillance, such as inside a home, an apartment, or a motor vehicle. Thus, rape is not an explosive act, the result of sudden and uncontrollable sexual desire. It also seems doubtful that rape is used solely to gain sexual satisfaction, especially when we consider the violence associated with this crime. Most rapists are indeed violent. Once again, Amir (*ibid.*:155) found that in 85 percent of his cases violence was used: beatings occurred in 45 percent, choking in 11.5 percent, and roughness in 28.5 percent. Sexual humiliation occurred in 26.8 percent of the cases: repeated intercourse was the most common form, occurring in 42.8 percent, and fellatio the next most common at approximately 35 percent (*ibid.*:159). More recent studies have confirmed that over two-thirds of rapists engage in some degree of violence and a little less than one-half use some type of weapon (Bart and O'Brien, 1985:27–28). Thus, as Smart (1976:96) concludes:

> Unless we can accept that sexual need and desire are only to be fulfilled when accompanied by alarming degrees of violence and sexual degradation, it must be the case that rape is an act of extreme hostility and not a purely sexual act.

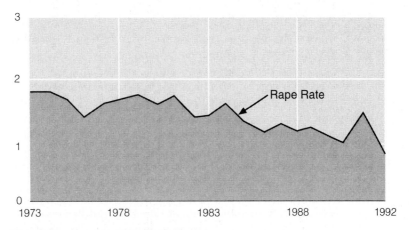

FIGURE   **Rape Rate over the Past 20 Years**
4-1   **(Number of rapes per 1,000 females age 12 or over)**
Source: Bureau of Justice Statistics, 1993, p. 9.

Rape is an act of violent sexual domination intended to devalue and humiliate women. It is not an expression of the sexual desire for women.

According to the FBI, the rate of reported rape continues to rise. Since 1988 the number of rape offenses reported to the police has risen by 18 percent (FBI, 1993:25). Yet, as discussed earlier, these figures may not represent an actual increase in the number of completed rapes. It may simply be that rape victims today—because of the availability of rape crisis centers and the increased public knowledge about rape, both of which are largely due to the efforts of the women's movement—feel more secure in reporting the crime, even if they are raped by someone they know. Indeed, victimization data (as revealed in Figure 4-1) show that from 1973 to 1992, rape victimization has probably remained quite stable or actually decreased.

Regardless of whether or not rape is increasing, rape victims share a common aftershock that indicates a pattern of reaction to the assault. Rape victims are initially shocked, angry, and unwilling to believe something such as this could happen to them. Moreover, their general routine is disrupted, as they experience an alteration in sleeping, eating, and relationships. They also feel helpless and guilty, have difficulty doing simple tasks, and experience restlessness, uncontrollable mood changes, and fear (Holmstrom and Burgess, 1983:20–33).

Rape victims experience suffering and pain for years. A study comparing victims and nonvictims of rape at one month, six months, and a year after the rape, indicated that even after one year the rape victims were more anxious, fearful, suspicious, and confused than their nonvictim counterparts (Kilpatrick et al., 1981). Moreover, rape victims must contend with the reactions of others to the rape. Raped women are often treated wrongfully by relatives and friends. For example, Daniel Silverman and Sharon L. McCombie (1980:175) report that lovers and husbands of rape victims, because they often cannot escape the thought that their lover or wife was "tainted" by the rapist, feel physical disgust when they approach their "unclean" lover or wife sexually. In short, the world of rape victims is permanently changed.

In the 1970s, rape crisis centers were set up (primarily by feminists) as places where rape victims could go for help immediately after the rape as well as for post-rape counseling. The best of these centers offered 24-hour hotlines, short- and long-term counseling, training programs for police officers, community education programs on rape prevention, and substantial numbers of hospital staff and volunteers (Shuchman, 1981:29). By 1980, however—because it became increasingly difficult to obtain funding—approximately one-third of all the centers that existed in the mid-1970s had closed and many existing centers were able to offer only the hotline (*ibid.*:28–29). Consequently, at present many women experiencing the aftershock of rape have nowhere to go for help.

In the traditional definition of rape, the victims of forcible rape are always female. However, there are cases of males being forcibly raped by both males and females. When women are arrested for forcible rape, they are usually an accomplice to a man, assisting him in raping a female. This was just the case with Susanne Perrin of Oakland, California, who was forced by her husband— through repeated episodes of rape and battering—to hunt down other potential victims (Russell, 1982:280–282). However, there are also cases of women raping men without being an accomplice to a man. These types of rape are extremely uncommon and statistically insignificant (Groth and Birnbaum, 1979:185–188).

Male rape of another male is also rare, except in prison. In prison a male's chance of being a rape victim increases. It has been estimated that in U.S. prisons approximately one of every five male inmates has been raped. And the combination of continued budget cuts, longer sentences, overcrowding, and understaffing will most likely increase its incidence (Cahill, 1985:32). Rape as an act of violent sexual domination intended to devalue and humiliate the victim is a widespread practice in male prisons. Young men in U.S. prisons must seek protection from stronger, older, and more powerful inmates, and many of them become sexual slaves to their "protectors." Others are forced into prostitution and traded for such prison commodities as cigarettes (*ibid.*). As Anthony Scacco (1982:vii) concludes in his work on rape in male prisons:

> In today's world the judge who sentences a young person to reform school or prison passes male rape on him as surely as the sentence. Every inmate has a very short time, once inside, to pick a "wolf" (a tough protector) or face gang rape, becoming the "girl" of the institution, or death.

Rape in male prisons is thus more than a power dynamic among men. As Don Sabo (1992:6) recently argued:

> In the muscled, violent, and tattooed world of prison rape, woman is symbolically ever-present. The prison phrase "make a woman out of you" means that you will be raped. Rape-based relationships between prisoners

Rape crisis centers provide important advice and counseling to rape victims. Continued funding for these centers is crucial if they are to remain open.

are often described as relations between "men" and "women" and in effect conceptualized as "master" and "slave."

In other words, the social dynamics of prison rape are extremely instructive in understanding the rape of women in the larger society.

Moreover, it is quite unlikely that a male will be the victim of a rape unless he is incarcerated and, even then, once he has reached adulthood he is virtually safe from any form of sexual assault (Groth and Birnbaum, 1979:119).

4.2   INTERPERSONAL VIOLENCE IN THE FAMILY

The family is, on the one hand, a "haven in a heartless world," a place where love and security prevail. It is also, on the other hand, a site of conflict among its members. Unfortunately, for many this conflict turns into violence. Although considerable violence occurs among family members (as we have seen), violent crimes like murder, assault, and rape are not specific to the family and may occur outside its boundaries. In this section we focus on those types of interpersonal violence that occur only within the family setting. An accurate measure of interpersonal violence specific to the family is difficult to establish, but sociologists estimate that the problem is widespread for families throughout Western industrialized societies (Dobash and Dobash, 1979; Straus, Gelles, and Steinmetz, 1980). We discuss five types of interpersonal violence specific to the family—wife rape, battering, child abuse, incestuous assault, and neglect.

Heterosexual Wife Rape and Battering

"It is within marriage," write sociologists Dobash and Dobash (1979:75), "that a woman is most likely to be slapped and shoved about, severely assaulted, killed or raped." In fact, a growing number of sociologists and criminologists are recognizing that wife rape is more common than rape by dates, acquaintances, and strangers (Gelles, 1977; Hunt, 1979; Russell, 1982). In the section above on rape we showed—using Russell's study—that when rape and attempted rape are *combined*, acquaintance and date rape are the most prevalent types. Russell (1984:62) went on to argue that *any* woman could be raped by an acquaintance, friend, date (assuming the woman had one), relative, authority figure, or stranger. However, wife rape is different in the sense that *only* women who have ever been married can actually be raped by a husband or ex-husband. Thus, Russell (*ibid.*:61–62) calculated rape and attempted rape based upon the percentage of women who had ever been married—rather than as a percentage of the entire sample—and found that "the prevalence of wife rape increases from 8 percent to 12 percent. This percentage places rape and attempted rape by husbands second only to rape and attempted rape by acquaintances" (*ibid.*:62). When Russell looked only at *completed* rapes (rather than the combination of completed and attempted rapes), she found that more women had been victimized by their husbands than by any other type of perpetrator. Although only 3 percent of the women in her sample were the victim of a completed rape by a stranger, 5 percent were the victim of a completed rape by a lover or ex-lover and 8 percent were the victim of a completed rape by a husband or ex-husband. One could therefore conclude from Russell's data that the more intimate the relationship between the victim and the offender, the greater the chance that the rape attempt will be completed.

In a more recent study, Finkelhor and Yllö (1985) surveyed 323 Boston-area women to determine how widespread wife rape is there. Finkelhor and Yllö (*ibid.*:6–7) found that 10 percent of these women had experienced a rape by a husband or ex-husband, whereas only 3 percent had been raped by a stranger. In addition, another 10 percent of the women had been raped by a date. Finkelhor and Yllö (*ibid.*:7) conclude that "sexual assaults by intimates, including husbands, are by far the most common type of rape."

Moreover, the victims of wife rape report not only that the rape by their husbands was frightening and brutal, but that it involved humiliation, degradation, and hatred. In addition, they experienced physical injuries and for years suffered psychological trauma. The following are selected examples of wife rape that Finkelhor and Yllö (*ibid.*:18) found in their research:

▲— One woman was jumped in the dark by her husband and raped in the anus while slumped over a woodpile.

▲— One woman had a six-centimeter gash ripped in her vagina by a husband who was trying to "pull her vagina out."

▲— One woman was gang raped by her husband and a friend after they surprised her alone in a vacant apartment.

▲— One woman was raped at knifepoint by her estranged partner.

▲— One woman was forced to have sex the day after returning from gynecological surgery, causing her to hemorrhage and obliging her to return to the hospital.

▲— One woman was forced to have sex with her estranged husband in order for her to see her baby, whom he had kidnapped.

For most victims of wife rape, sexual assault is a common occurrence rather than an isolated episode in their marriage. Finkelhor and Yllö (*ibid.*:23) found that 50 percent of the women in their study had been assaulted 20 times or more. Other studies show that between 70 and 80 percent of victims of wife rape have been victimized more than once (Russell, 1982).

Women are not only assaulted by their current husband, many are victimized by their ex-husbands. In the Russell (1982:237) study, 15 percent, or one in every seven, was raped by an ex-husband. The Finkelhor and Yllö (1985:205) study similarly found that 25 percent of the women had been raped by an ex-husband.

There also seems to be a close relationship between wife rape and wife beating. Some form of interpersonal violence occurs in approximately 50 percent of all intimate relationships, with women by far the most abused (Klein, 1979:20). We have more to say about wife beating shortly; the importance of wife beating to our discussion here is that it often occurs together with wife rape. Studies indicate that between 30 and 60 percent of all wife beating involves some form of sexual abuse (Prescott and Letko, 1977:18; Walker, 1979:112). In Russell's (1982:91) study, 36 percent of the women interviewed experienced some combination of beating and rape: 9 percent were primarily the victim of wife rape, but were beaten also; for 22 percent of the wives, the frequency of rape and beating was approximately equal; 5 percent were primarily the victim of wife beating, but were also raped. In the Finkelhor and Yllö (1985:23) study, 50 percent of the wife rape victims were battered. Moreover, battered women seem the most vulnerable of all wife rape victims to repeated rapes. As Finkelhor and Yllö (*ibid.*:23–24) found:

> Twice as many battered women suffered chronic rapes (twenty times or more) as the other raped women. In addition to being punching bags, the battered women were also, as one woman put it, "masturbating machines."

Thus, the wife batterer is more likely to be simultaneously the wife rapist.

However, this does not mean that the sexual assault of a wife cannot occur without violence—the threat or actual use of physical force. On the contrary, sexual intercourse can be coercive in other ways ("social coercion" and/or "interpersonal coercion") as the following examples illustrate (Hite, 1976:236):

> In my relationship I am forced to give sex because of the marriage vows. My husband has on occasion threatened to withhold money or favors—that is, permission of some sort or another—if I do not have sex with him. So I fake it. What the hell. When the kids are older I just might lay my cards on the table.

> I really felt I was earning my room and board in bed for years, and if I wanted anything my husband was more likely to give it to me after sex. Now that I am self-supporting I don't have to play that game any more. What a relief!

It is clear, then, that the sexual assault of a wife is not limited to battered women. It occurs as well in marriages where there is little or no physical violence (Finkelhor and Yllö, 1985:37).

In 1977 Susan Steinmetz (1977–1978:500) argued that the percentage of wives having used physical violence against their husbands often exceeds that of the husbands' violence against their wives. Many scholars criticized Steinmetz for not measuring the outcomes of the violence as well as failing to recognize that women are legally disadvantaged and more vulnerable because they are generally less powerful than men (Pleck *et al.*, 1977–1978; Gelles, 1979). Moreover, most research has demonstrated that wife battering is not only more prevalent but also more damaging than "husband battering" (see Klein, 1979:20 for a review of this research). When women do attack their husbands, it is usually out of desperation and self-defense against a lengthy history of escalating wife rape and/or battering (Browne, 1987). Indeed, when a woman commits murder (1) it usually occurs in her home; (2) men are usually the victim, often a husband or lover; and (3) the victim most likely initiated the violence leading to their death (Jurik and Gregware, 1992:182–185).

Throughout the 17th, 18th, and 19th centuries in western Europe, it was legal for men to beat their wives, as long as the method used, and the extent of the violence, remained within certain limits (Andersen, 1988:170). For example, in 18th-century France the law restricted violence against wives to "blows, thumps, kicks, or punches on the back if they leave no traces." Moreover, the law did not allow for the use of "sharp-edged or crushing instruments" (*ibid.*:170). The phrase "rule of thumb" is derived from English common law, which specified that a man could beat his wife—for disciplinary reasons—as long as he used a stick no thicker than his thumb (*ibid.*). An ordinance, still in effect in Pennsylvania in the 1970s, prohibited a husband from beating his wife after 10:00 in the evening and on Sundays (Martin, 1982:266).

Although ideas on wife battering have changed considerably—it is now socially abhorred and illegal—it still occurs more frequently than most people believe. It is impossible to generate useful statistics on wife battering because the beating most likely has taken place in isolation from the community and most victims are too embarrassed to report the assault to the police, social service agency, or shelter. Therefore, in order to understand the prevalence of wife battering, we must rely on estimates provided by researchers in the field.

Estimates of the amount of wife battering in this country vary. For instance, *Time* (1983:23) magazine reported in 1983 that 6 million women are physically abused each year by their husbands, battery being the "single major cause of injury to women, more significant than auto accidents, rapes, or muggings." Sociological research has been more conservative. In studying more than 2,000 heterosexual couples, Murray Straus (1977–1978:445) found that "in any one year, approximately 1.8 million wives are beaten by their husbands." Prevalence studies indicate that between 25 and 33 percent of heterosexual couples experience wife battering (Renzetti, 1992:18). However, most women battered by their husbands do not report the incident; approximately one in every 10 cases is reported to the police (Davis, 1987:2). Thus, the amount of wife battering is probably higher than the above figures indicate.

Many women are beaten repeatedly over a period of years. This violence does not entail simply slapping, shoving, and pushing, but intensifies into serious injuries to the victim. Women are burned, stabbed, and shot; bones and teeth are fractured; and miscarriages and severe internal injuries occur (Schechter, 1982:16; Dobash and Dobash, 1979:238).

Nevertheless, heterosexual wife battering is not uniformly distributed across society. Walter DeKeseredy and Ronald Hinch (1991:26–28) recently reviewed the research on wife battering and found that:

▲— married women are more likely to be beaten than unmarried women

▲— women aged 18–34 are more likely to be victimized than women of other age groups

▲— low-income men are more likely to assault their wives than males in higher income groups

▲— unemployed men are more likely than both employed and part-time employed men to abuse their wives

We have learned that in many instances battered women are also subjected to another form of abuse, rape. However, many battered women also report being the victims of *verbal abuse*. Lenore Walker (1978:144) found that wife beating and verbal abuse occur simultaneously, concluding that they "cannot be separated." Verbal abuse attacks a woman's dignity and self-worth, and may go on for hours. (Schechter, 1982:17).

As with rape, past scholars have labeled some forms of wife battering "victim-precipitated" or "victim provoked." In one of the earliest articles on the subject of wife battering, Snell, Rosenwald, and Robey (1964) concluded that the wife actually encouraged the husband to beat her. In "The Wifebeaters' Wife,"

Wife battering happens much more frequently than we commonly assume.

women married to a wife batterer are described as aggressive, masculine, and sexually frigid, whereas their husbands are allegedly shy, sexually ineffectual, and "mother's boys." Therefore, in order to compensate, the "castrated male" occasionally beats "his" wife, while the wife allows the beating to occur in order to satisfy her guilt and secret masochism. The following is an example of one of Snell *et al.*'s (*ibid.*:109) cases and their description of it:

> The husband stopped drinking shortly after his wife began treatment, and the violent arguments practically stopped. This improvement, while not lasting, was impressive to him and his wife, and they both felt, for different reasons, that it was due to her treatment. He took it as confirmation that she had been the "cause" of his behavior; she felt that it was because she was learning how to "handle" his behavior. We felt that the initial improvement was due to the venting of the wife's hostility and manipulative behavior out of the marriage, taking pressure off the husband.

The authors conclude that "one cannot hope to understand the offender and his offense without having some understanding of the people with whom he has to deal" (*ibid.*:112). Although research has shown that battered women are more likely to be passive and nonassertive and the battering men the violent and aggressive ones (Walker, 1977–1978, 1979), feminists have viewed articles like the preceding examples as profoundly disturbing. As Susan Schechter (1982:22) responds:

By never condemning the violence, the authors sanction it. The husband's main problem is his weakness, not his assaultiveness. Moreover, the woman not only deserves the violence because of her own aggression and coldness, but also needs and causes it for her psychic well-being. If she only fulfilled her feminine role more adequately and demurely, she would not provoke his rage. One could conclude that if women were sexually "giving" when their husbands were drinking, never said a public word about being beaten, and certainly never called the police for protection, all would be fine. The stories of thousands of battered women who did just that and were beaten even more brutally belie these conclusions.

Articles arguing "victim precipitation" continued into the late 1970s. For example, Faulk (1977:121) argued that the most common type of wife batterer is a "dependent passive husband" who tries "to please and pacify his wife," but finds that she is often "querulous and demanding." The resulting beating is then "an explosion which occurred after a period of trying behavior by the victim. There was often a precipitating act by the victim" (*ibid.*:121). As with the Snell *et al.* article, Faulk adopts, as feminists assert, the husbands' perspective. According to this view: "The husband loses control because of his wife; he has neither the will to resist her 'provocation' nor responsibility for his behavior" (Schechter, 1982:22). Consequently, the reader is persuaded to sympathize with the man and blame the victim for everything. Schechter (*ibid.*:24) concludes her criticism of "victim-precipitated wife battering":

> Common sense tells us that all people who know each other intimately irritate each other: irritation does not cause violence; it is an excuse offered by a man who believes he has the authority and right to beat women. Victim provocation theories leave sexist behavior and ideology unquestioned. They keep us scrutinizing the victim's behavior and, as a result, remove responsibility from the man, the community, and the social structures that maintain male violence.

Contrary to the above, wife battering occurs primarily as a means of demonstrating masculinity and the effect is the social control of the victim (Messerschmidt, 1993).

An important question always asked by students of wife abuse is "Why doesn't she leave?" Several researchers have answered this question, reporting that women stay in a violent relationship for a number of reasons. First, of course, is fear. The wife fears that if she leaves, the husband will find her and injure her even more severely. Many women also fear for the safety of others (such as children), and they fear being without a home and losing the status of "wife" (Stanko, 1985:58). Second, most battered women do not have the material resources to survive. Many are normally full-time homemakers, with few marketable skills, and several children for whom to provide. Finally, women in abusive situations experience a "learned helplessness"; they feel a lack of control over their lives, are guilt-ridden, ashamed, and ultimately blame themselves for the failure of their marriage (Walker, 1977–1978). As a result, many women remain silent and continue in an abusive relationship.

However, because of the existence of shelters today, more and more women are able to leave such situations. There are over 900 women's shelters in the United States offering short-term refuge for women and their children (see Davis, 1988 for an excellent discussion of the different types of shelters for battered women).

Homosexual Partner Battering

Most research on battering concentrates on heterosexual relationships. However, recent studies suggest that battering is not simply inherent to heterosexual monogamy but, rather, occurs in other family forms, such as homosexual relationships.

Like heterosexual wife battering, homosexual partner battering is difficult to document. Therefore, we must rely on estimates. In the only major work on battering in gay male relationships to date, David Island and Patrick Letellier (1991) estimate in *Men Who Beat the Men Who Love Them* that between 350,000 (10 percent) and 650,000 (20 percent) gay men per year are battered in the gay men's community. Similarly, Claire Renzetti (1992:17–19) recently examined studies on battering in lesbian relationships, concluding that this type of battering is comparable to, or possibly higher than, heterosexual wife battering. Thus, we can conclude from recent studies of homosexual partner battering that homosexuals, like heterosexuals, frequently "aggress against their intimate partners in ways that are physically and emotionally abusive and sometimes violent" (*ibid.*:19).

Additionally, the dynamics of homosexual partner battering are similar to heterosexual wife battering. In both types, the effect of the battering is the social control of the victim. Island and Letellier (1991:76–77) conclude for battering in gay male relationships:

> The batterer tends to control and dominate the behavior, speech, decisions, thoughts, general activities, circle of friends, spending patterns, clothing choices, reading materials, and eating habits of the victim. Over time, the perpetrator increases his efforts to widen the circle of control to include more and more of the victim's life.

Similarly, Barbara Hart's (1986:174) examination of battering in lesbian relationships concluded:

> Like male batterers, lesbians who batter seek to achieve, maintain and demonstrate power over their partners in order to maximize the ready accomplishment of their needs and desires. Lesbians batter their lovers because violence is often an effective method to gain power and control over intimates.

Moreover, most victims of homosexual partner battering remain in abusive relationships for similar reasons as heterosexual wife battering victims (Island and Letellier, 1991:93–98; Renzetti, 1992:78–88; Lobel, 1986:19–72). Thus, overall homosexual partner battering is in many ways very similar to heterosexual wife battering.

Child Abuse, Incestuous Assault, and Neglect

Prior to the 1960s, no laws existed that criminalized child abuse—not because there was no child abuse, but because it was not in the interests of medical doctors to "see" it. According to Stephen Pfohl (1984), four factors impeded the recognition of child abuse by the medical profession:

1. Physicians were unaware of the possibilities of an abuse diagnosis.

2. Many physicians were unwilling to believe that parents would abuse their own children.

3. The "norm of confidentiality" created an obstacle for an abuse diagnosis.

4. Physicians were reluctant to become involved with the criminal justice system because it was time consuming and hindered their ability to control the consequences of such a diagnosis.

However, for a specific speciality within medicine—pediatric radiology—these four barriers, Pfohl argues, did not apply. Abusive diagnosis was in fact an ultimate consequence of their mission: pediatric radiologists constantly viewed children's X-rays and thus observed broken bones and other abnormalities. Pediatric radiologists were also removed from direct contact with the patient's family and thus had no need to be fearful of confidentiality. Most importantly, the "discovery" of child abuse provided pediatric radiologists—working in a low-profile speciality—the possibility of greater recognition within the medical community, as well as an opportunity to coalesce with more academic segments of that community, such as psychiatrists. Thus, as Pfohl (*ibid*.:61) points out: "The organizational advantages surrounding the discovery of abuse by pediatric radiology set in motion a process of labeling abuse as deviance and legislating against it." Indeed, in a four-year period beginning in 1962, all 50 states passed laws against child abuse. Consequently, the "discovery" of child abuse "manifestly contributed to the advancement of humanitarian pursuits while covertly rewarding" pediatric radiology with enhanced status (*ibid*.:45).

Since its discovery, public concern about child abuse increased dramatically, so that by the mid-1980s, 90 percent of the U.S. population considered it a serious national problem (Wolfe, 1985:462). Moreover, although more people today seem concerned about child abuse, the media have helped perpetuate the myth that most abuse of children—especially sexual abuse—occurs *outside* the home by day-care workers and child molesters lurking around elementary school playgrounds. However, most physical and sexual abuse of children occurs within the family (Gil, 1970; Pelton, 1981).

This mother and her daughter were both abused by the same man.

Among researchers in the area of child abuse there tends to be agreement that child abuse takes three forms—physical, sexual, and emotional. Thus, when we speak of *child abuse* we refer to those intentional acts of a parent or guardian that result, or are likely to result, in physical, mental, or emotional injury or impairment of a child. *Child neglect* is injury or impairment resulting from a parent or guardian's inattention to a child's basic needs for health, nutrition, shelter, education, supervision, affection, and protection. (Dubowitz, Black, Starr, and Zuravin, 1993; National Center on Child Abuse and Neglect, 1993).

Various researchers have attempted to estimate the extent of child abuse and neglect in the United States. The National Center on Child Abuse and Neglect (1993), basing their data on substantiated *reports* nationwide, estimated that more than 1.5 million children under 18 years of age suffered abuse and/or neglect in 1991; this is a rate of approximately 39 per 1,000 children. Straus and Gelles (1988)—in a nationally representative sample that considered only physical violence against children by a parent (based on whether the child was kicked, bitten, punched, beaten up, burned, or scalded, or was threatened or attacked with a knife or gun)—estimate that approximately 24 per 1,000 children are physically abused each year. Moreover, when Straus and Gelles added "hitting the child with an object" to the above list, they found that approximately 110 per 1,000 children are the victims of *serious* violence by a parent.

Although the physical abuse of children in the United States is extremely high, research indicates that child neglect is more prevalent and its consequences just as serious as physical abuse. As Wolock and Horowitz (1984:534) conclude after a careful review of the literature:

A major contradiction exists between what is known about child maltreatment and how it is defined as a social problem. Although child abuse has been the focus of professional and public attention, child neglect is the more prevalent problem. . . . Nor is neglect necessarily less severe than abuse.

Indeed, at least 12 types of neglect have been documented in the child neglect literature (Dubowitz *et al.*, 1993:16):

▲— refusal or delay to provide physical health care

▲— refusal or delay to provide mental health care

▲— supervisory neglect

▲— custody refusal

▲— custody-related neglect

▲— abandonment/desertion

▲— failure to provide a stable home

▲— neglect of personal hygiene

▲— housing hazards

▲— inadequate housing sanitation

▲— nutritional neglect

▲— educational neglect

Although the basic needs of most children in Western industrialized societies are satisfied, a large number of children experience neglect in some or all of the areas listed above (*ibid.*:16).

Moreover, there are important gender differences regarding abuse and neglect. According to the National Center on Child Abuse and Neglect (1993:29–33), females are more likely to be abused and to suffer injuries due to abuse than are males. Females experience more abuse than do males, whereas males experience more neglect than do females. For both males and females, abuse and neglect increase with age.

Regarding the perpetrators of this crime, we find that although women perform most of the child care in U.S. society, they commit only about 50 percent of the *physical* abuse and neglect of children. In other words, 50 percent of those who physically abuse and neglect children are men, who have on average little responsibility for children (Breines and Gordon, 1983:504).

Sexual abuse in the family is also referred to as *incestuous assault* (Butler, 1979). According to Levi-Strauss (1971), the incest taboo was originally directed toward the prevention of marriage inside the family. The incest taboo attempted, according to this view, to prohibit reproductive mating within the family unit. However, even though this taboo has been successful in preventing marriage and reproductive sexual relations between family members, the best evidence suggests that another type of incest—nonconsensual "sexual relations" between members of the same family other than husband and wife—is hardly rare in U.S. society (Breines and Gordon, 1983:521). It is this latter type of incest—incestuous assault—with which we are concerned here.

Because incestuous assault has been surrounded by extreme secrecy, it is difficult to document the actual amount in the United States. Nevertheless, some researchers have attempted to do this. Judith Herman (1981), in her book *Father-Daughter Incest*, analyzed a number of studies that focused on the prevalence of incest. These studies obtained information from more than 5,000 women from all over the United States, finding that from one-fifth to one-third of the women reported having had some sort of childhood sexual encounter with an adult male. Between 4 and 12 percent of the women interviewed reported a sexual experience with a relative and one woman in every 100 had a sexual experience with her father or stepfather. In *The Secret Trauma*, Diana Russell (1986) found that 16 percent of the 930 women interviewed reported at least one experience of incest before the age of 18 years. Of these women (152), 12 percent had been sexually abused by a relative before their 14th birthday (*ibid.*:60). Thus, incestuous assault is by no means rare.

Most incestuous assault is committed by an adult male (usually the father) with the victim a child (usually the daughter) under the age of 18 (Russell, 1986; Herman, 1981; Butler, 1979). Certain "typical characteristics" of incestuous assault include the following (Chesney-Lind, 1989:21; Herman and Hirschman, 1977:743):

▲— Approximately 70 percent of incestuous assault victims are female.

▲— The majority of victims are either the oldest child or the only daughter, and the assault usually begins between the ages of 6 and 9.

▲— Incestuous assault usually begins earlier for girls than for boys, and victimization of girls lasts longer than for boys.

▲— The assault commonly takes place repeatedly, lasting three years or more.

▲— Sexual contact is normally limited to fondling and masturbation if the victim has not reached puberty, but with older children sexual intercourse is more likely to occur.

As with other sexual assaults, the victim experiences incestuous assault as coercive. At first—because of her young age—the victim is unable to comprehend what is happening. However, as she suffers the assaults over time, she eventually understands that something "different" and wrong is happening to her. She feels guilty and humiliated, and blames herself for the continued assaults (Stanko, 1985:25). Many such victims not only experience fear, anxiety, depression, anger, and difficulties in school, they also run away from home (Chesney-Lind, 1989:21–22). Incestuously assaulted women also reveal that they remain frightened and upset years later (Finkelhor, 1979; Herman, 1981). Moreover, many prostitutes report that their first sexual experience was in the home as a result of an incestuous assault (Stanko, 1985; James, 1982). Prostitutes have informed sociologists that as victims of incestuous assault, they were first bribed by an adult family male (sex for clothes, toys, and affection, for example), only later to be forced into sexual intercourse with him (Chesney-Lind and Rodriquez, 1983). Consequently, they learn that they can obtain commodities by making their bodies available to men.

Finally, father-daughter incestuous assault seems to cause the most trauma. In Russell's (1986:231–232) sample, 54 percent of victims where fathers were the perpetrators reported being extremely upset by the assault(s), compared with 25 percent of victims of all other incest perpetrators combined. The following are some of the factors that may have contributed to this greater trauma (*ibid.*:213–232):

▲— Fathers were more likely to impose vaginal intercourse on their daughters than were other incest perpetrators.

▲— Fathers sexually abused their daughters more frequently than did other incestuous relatives.

▲— Fathers were more likely to use physical force than were other incestuous relatives.

▲— In the vast majority of cases, the father was also the victim's provider.

Most father-daughter incest occurs in families maintaining traditional male-dominant and authoritarian attitudes. The fathers expect sexual, housekeeping, and child-rearing services from their wives. When this "breaks down"—because of physical and mental illness, alcoholism, and drug addiction, or simply because the wife is not "performing well"—they turn to their daughter(s). The incestuous father does not engage in these expectations himself but usually delegates that responsibility to the eldest daughter, while simultaneously perpetrating incestuous assault upon her. As a result, this daughter may gain some power in the family, but her basic experience is "shame and guilt, isolation, and an oppressive disproportionate sense of responsibility for holding the family together, which she accomplishes in part by keeping her secret" (Breines and Gordon, 1983:526).

4.3 _____ Sexual Harassment

In Chapter 6.2 we discuss some of the hazards in the workplace for *both* male and female workers. Primarily for women, however, the danger of *sexual harassment* also exists on the job. Although workplace dangers such as unsafe working conditions are of an impersonal nature, sexual harassment is different, entailing violence perpetrated in a personal manner. Moreover, sexual harassment exists in settings other than the workplace and is committed by others than one's employer. For these reasons we discuss sexual harassment as interpersonal violence, rather than occupational crime.

What Is Sexual Harassment?

Female workers have always been victims of sexual harassment, but it was not until the mid-1970s that sexual harassment was recognized as a social problem (Benson and Thomson, 1982:236). And it was not until 1980 that sexual harassment actually became a crime. The Equal Employment Opportunity Commission of the federal government issued guidelines in 1980 for determining sexual harassment as a violation of Title VII of the U.S. Civil Rights Act. This Act was intended to prohibit discrimination on the basis of gender, and its guidelines apply to federal, state, and local government agencies as well as to private employers with 15 or more employees. The guidelines specify that employers have an "affirmative duty" to prevent and eliminate sexual harassment on the job, and that "unwelcome sexual advances, requests for sexual favors, and other verbal or physical conduct of a sexual nature" are offenses if submission is explicitly or implicitly a condition of the individual's employment. When the submission or rejection affects one's employment, and/or it affects an individual's work performance by creating a working environment that is intimidating, hostile, and offensive, a violation of Title VII has also occurred (Pear, 1980:1, 20). Thus, following this definition, sexual harassment includes not only sexist jokes and innuendos, "accidental" collisions and fondling, and constant ogling and pinches, but attempted and completed forcible rape and "interpersonal coercion."

Sexual Harassment at Work

Myths about sexual harassment—such as that it affects only a few women, that women really "ask for it," and that charges of sexual harassment are commonly false—continue to be perpetuated in U.S. society (Andersen, 1988:133). However, studies of sexual harassment indicate the prevalence of *nonconsenting* interpersonal sexual violence in the workplace. Sociologist Edwin Schur (1984:136–137) summarizes certain studies not based on random samples:

> An upstate New York survey conducted in 1975 by the Working Women United Institute found that of the 155 women questioned, 70 percent reported they had been harassed at least once. In a 1976 *Redbook Magazine* study, with 9,000 readers responding, 88 percent reported having experienced some form of sexual harassment and 92 percent considered the problem serious. A survey of workers at the United Nations, in the same year, disclosed that of the 875 persons polled one-half of the women and 31 percent of the men were either aware of sexual pressures existing within the organization or had directly experienced them.

In 1981 the Merit System's Protection Board conducted a study of sexual harassment among federal employees for the Subcommittee on Investigations of the House Committee on Post Office and Civil Service (Russell, 1984:269–270). The Board found (in their random sample of over 20,000 federal employees)

Admiral Frank Kelso, the Navy's top officer, was involved in the Tailhook sexual harassment scandal.

that 42 percent of all female employees reported being sexually harassed at work. Moreover, most likely because of the national "teach-in" on sexual harassment following the confirmation hearings of Supreme Court Justice Clarence Thomas, the number of sexual harassment complaints filed with the Equal Employment Opportunity Commission jumped from 5,694 cases in 1990 to 10,900 cases in the first eight months of 1993 (Ingrassia, 1993:57). What all these studies reveal is that sexual harassment in the workplace is most likely widespread.

Studies of sexual harassment also indicate that rape and "interpersonal coercion" exist within the workplace. Interpersonal coercion (recalling our earlier discussion in this chapter) involves economic threats made by a male supervisor to the effect that if the female employee or possible employee does not engage in sexual intercourse with him she either will not be hired, retained, or promoted, or else will be fired, demoted, or transferred to a more unpleasant position. If we assume that the female employee or possible employee does not secretly desire sexual intercourse with the male supervisor, such threats can be very coercive. As Box (1983:143) argues, "Economic deprivation is a serious and expensive cost even when set beside unwelcome and undesired coitus." Two women who experienced this type of interpersonal coercion described it in the following way (cited in MacKinnon, 1979:32):

> If I wasn't going to sleep with him, I wasn't going to get my promotion.

> I was fired because I refused to give at the office.

The effects on the victims of these and other types of sexual harassment are severe. The majority of women report emotional stress, such as nervousness, fear, and sleeplessness, as well as interference with their job performance, and many also find it necessary to obtain psychological help (Schur, 1984:139). Moreover, victims of sexual harassment at work report higher rates of absenteeism and low productivity. Sexual harassment not only affects a victim's self-esteem but costs an average Fortune 500 company (24,000 employees or more) $6.7 million a year (Crawford, 1993:17). In addition, for those victims who refuse sexual demands their job is at stake (*ibid.*). Consider what happened to one woman who refused to "give at the office." The supervisor,

> following rejection of his elaborate sexual advances, barraged the woman with unwarranted reprimands about job performance, refused routine supervision or task direction, which made it impossible for her to do her job, and then fired her for poor work performance (MacKinnon, 1979:35).

This threat of job loss or actually being fired for not complying with the sexual demands of a male supervisor seems most prevalent for women in traditional female jobs (Andersen, 1988:134). For women who enter traditionally male occupations, "harassment seems to be a form of retaliation directed against women for threatening male economic and social status. In these settings, harassment expresses men's resentment of the presence of women" (*ibid.*:134).

An example of this indignation and outright hostility occurred at the Tailhook Association convention of top Navy pilots in 1991. According to a report prepared by the Pentagon Inspector General, sexual assaults at the convention "varied from victims being grabbed on the buttocks to victims being groped, pinched and fondled on their breasts, buttocks and genitals. . . . Some victims were bitten by their assailants, others were knocked to the ground and some had their clothing ripped or removed" (cited in Gordon, 1993:1). This violence against women officers, the report concluded, was "not significantly different from those at earlier meetings" and was in fact "widely condoned by the Navy's civilian and military leaders" (*ibid.*:1).

Probably the most notorious feature of the convention was the "gauntlet," in which women who attempted to walk through a hotel hallway were fondled and assaulted by approximately 200 men. In total, 117 naval officers were implicated in one or more incidents of sexual assault and other demeaning practices such as "mooning" (baring one's buttocks at women), "ballwalking" (publicly exposing one's testicles), and "sharking" (biting women on the buttocks). Finally, it should not be surprising to learn that a number of male officers wore T-shirts during the convention with "Women are Property" and "He-man Women's Haters Club" printed on them (Gordon, 1993; Goodman, 1993).

REVIEW

In this chapter we have discussed interpersonal crimes of violence—murder, assault, hate crimes, rape, wife and homosexual partner battering, child abuse, incestuous assault, child neglect, and sexual harassment. These crimes create extensive public concern and fear—and rightly so—inasmuch as the United States has the highest level of violent crime in the industrialized world. However, crimes of interpersonal violence occur most often indoors—not on the streets—and are usually committed by relatives, friends, and acquaintances of the victim.

Murder, Assault, Hate Crimes, and Rape

1. Murder is the most serious form of interpersonal violence; fortunately, it occurs the least often.
2. Murder is primarily a big-city crime and occurs most frequently in the South.
3. There is little evidence suggesting that owning a firearm is the chief cause of murder.
4. In some cases the interaction between offender and victim involves threats and retaliation by both participants to the murder.
5. There are important similarities and differences between murder and aggravated assault.
6. Hate crimes differ from other forms of interpersonal violence in that they are more vicious, excessively brutal, and frequently perpetrated at random on total strangers (commonly a single victim) by multiple offenders.
7. Rape occurs much more often in the United States than most people recognize.
8. Sociologists, criminologists, and feminists are currently debating the appropriate definition of rape.
9. Women fear rape more than any other offense.
10. The idea of victim-precipitated rape is a myth.
11. Most rapists engage in some degree of violence, their victims experiencing both physical injuries and psychological trauma.
12. Although there are a few reported cases of women raping men, males are relatively safe from sexual assault unless they are in prison.

Interpersonal Violence in the Family

1. Women of completed rapes are victimized more by their husbands than by any other type of perpetrator.
2. Victims of wife rape feel humiliated and degraded, and experience psychological trauma for years afterward.

3. Between 30 and 60 percent of battered women are also raped by their husbands.

4. Wife battering is far more prevalent and damaging than husband beating.

5. Wife battering was legally and socially acceptable for centuries.

6. Between 2 and 6 million wives are battered by their husbands each year.

7. Most battered women are also abused verbally by their husbands.

8. The idea of victim-precipitated wife rape and wife battering is a myth.

9. Many women, because of social and economic pressures, feel they cannot leave an abusive relationship.

10. Homosexual battering—in lesbian and gay male relationships—seems to occur at a similar rate as wife battering in heterosexual relationships.

11. The dynamics of battering in lesbian and gay male relationships are similar to those in heterosexual relationships.

12. Most physical and sexual abuse of children occurs inside the family.

13. Child neglect is more prevalent than child physical abuse, and its consequences just as serious.

14. There are important gender differences in child abuse and neglect, especially as children grow older.

15. Men and women each commit 50 percent of the physical abuse and neglect of children.

16. Incestuous assaults are by no means rare in the United States; most are committed by an adult male (usually the father) and the usual victim is a child under 18 (generally a daughter).

17. Incestuously assaulted girls and women find the encounter coercive, and years later many report still being frightened and upset.

18. Father-daughter incest causes the most trauma.

Sexual Harassment

1. Sexual harassment includes behavior ranging from sexist jokes to "interpersonal coercion" and rape.

2. Sexual harassment in the workplace is not uncommon in U.S. society.

3. Sexual harassment causes emotional stress and interferes with job and nonoccupational performance.

4. Sexual harassment not only entails an employer/employee relationship but also occurs in other settings.

5. Sexual harassment varies with the victim's occupation.

QUESTIONS FOR CLASS DISCUSSION

1. The media foster the image that most interpersonal violence occurs in the streets; as we have seen, it mostly takes place indoors. Discuss why you think the media distort the reality of interpersonal violence and why most violence occurs indoors.

2. Is there a "culture of hate" in North America?

3. Compare the legal definition of rape with the expanded definition. Is the legal definition too narrow, or is it satisfactory as it stands?

4. There are clear gender differences for child abuse, incestuous assault, and neglect. Discuss why you think such gender differences exist.

5. We identified two myths of sexual harassment. Can you think of others? Why do you think sexual harassment varies depending upon victim occupation?

RECOMMENDED READINGS

Browne, Angela (1987). *When Battered Women Kill.* New York: The Free Press. This book is a study of the dynamics in heterosexual relationships and how the progression from courtship to death of a wife batterer may result.

Finkelhor, David and Kersti Yllö (1985). *License to Rape: Sexual Abuse of Wives.* New York: Holt, Rinehart and Winston. One of the best studies of wife rape, with valuable suggestions for ending this crime.

Griffin, Susan (1971). "Rape: The All-American Crime." *Ramparts* (September):26–35. A classic discussion of many of the myths surrounding the crime of rape.

Jurik, Nancy and Peter Gregware (1992). "A Method for Murder: The Study of Homicides by Women." *Perspectives on Social Problems* 4:179–201. An excellent study of the gender dynamics involved when women commit murder.

Luckenbill, David F. (1977). "Criminal Homicide as a Situated Transaction." *Social Problems* 25 (December):176–186. Although not the general theory of murder it purports to be, this study provides an important examination of the interaction between victim and offender in a murder situation.

MacKinnon, Catharine A. (1979). *Sexual Harassment of Working Women.* New Haven, CT: Yale University Press. One of the first significant studies of sexual harassment and the legal issues involved.

Russell, Diana E. H. (1984). *Sexual Exploitation.* Beverly Hills, CA: Sage. An examination of the prevalence of rape, incestuous assault, and workplace harassment.

———. (1986). *The Secret Trauma: Incest in the Lives of Girls and Women.* New

York: Basic Books. The best study to date of the phenomenon of incestuous assault.

Schur, Edwin (1984). *Labeling Women Deviant: Gender, Stigma, and Social Control.* New York: Random House. A superb discussion of the evidence and issues surrounding violence in the family.

Wolfgang, Marvin (1958). *Patterns in Criminal Homicide.* Philadelphia: University of Pennsylvania Press. The classic statement on the dynamics and patterns of murder.

Wright, James D., Peter H. Rossi, and Kathleen Daly (1983). *Under the Gun: Weapons, Crime, and Violence in America.* New York: Aldine Publishing Company. An in-depth look at firearm ownership, the control of firearms, and the relationship of these to violent crime.

CHAPTER 5

PROPERTY CRIME

5.1 Stealing and Dealing
Robbery
Burglary
Larceny
Motor Vehicle Theft
Fencing

5.2 Damage and Deception
Arson
Fraud

5.3 The Debate on Professional Property Crime
The Decline of Professional Property Crime
The Changing Nature of Professional Property Crime

Preview

Chapter 5 introduces:

☞ what sociologists mean by property crime.
☞ the different types of property crime.
☞ the difference between amateur and professional property offenders.
☞ the nature, extent, and costs of property crime.

Key Terms

amateur property crime	larceny
arson	motor vehicle theft
automobile theft	professional property crime
burglary	property crime
check fraud	robbery
credit-card fraud	shoplifting
fencing	tax fraud

I*n Chapter 4 we discussed interpersonal crimes of violence. Most crime, however, is not violent, but entails the taking of property. When we compare crimes of interpersonal violence with property crimes identified here, property crimes constitute approximately 90 percent of all crimes reported to the police. Moreover, according to* **National Crime Victimization Survey (NCVS)** *data, property crimes make up more than 90 percent of all victimizations (Department of Justice, 1993:12).*

In addition to being more frequent, property crimes differ from crimes of interpersonal violence in another significant way: offender and victim are, in most cases, strangers. For crimes like burglary, automobile theft, and arson, usually no direct interaction between offender and victim takes place. And in those crimes where interaction does exist—such as check fraud—it is not immediately apparent that a crime has even been committed.

We define property crime as the unlawful damage to, or taking of, the property of another, regardless of whether the threat of or actual use of physical violence occurs. We discuss seven types of property crimes: robbery, burglary, larceny, automobile theft, fencing, arson, and fraud. While discussing each, we examine the similarities and differences between professional and amateur property offenders. Professional and amateur property offenders are similar in that each commits the same type of crime. In other words, there are both professional and amateur robbers, burglars, auto thieves, and so forth; however, professionals and amateurs differ in important ways. Professionals carefully plan and execute their crimes, using sophisticated techniques and skills. They are committed to crime as a life-style, and tend to specialize in one particular form of property crime. Amateurs engage in crime when the opportunity arises, do not extensively plan their theft, do not always think of themselves as criminals, and do not usually specialize in one type of property crime.

5.1 ———— STEALING AND DEALING

Our discussion of property crime begins with what most of us—including criminologists—consider to be the major forms of property theft: robbery, burglary, larceny, motor vehicle theft, and fencing.

Robbery

Robbery is defined as the unlawful taking or attempting to take something of value from another person or persons by using some type of violent force or threat of force. Robbery is a unique crime and ranks among the most feared because it entails both threatened or actual use of violence and also loss of property to the victim. Moreover, robbery—unlike the other property crimes discussed in this chapter—is similar to interpersonal crimes of violence in another way: it involves a direct confrontation between offender and victim.

Robbery also differs in significant ways from interpersonal crimes of violence: robberies are more likely to involve two or more offenders; the majority of robberies are committed by strangers to the victim (in 1992 four out of every five), and robbery offenders are more likely to use weapons (approximately 70 percent of all robberies in 1992) (Department of Justice, 1993:10). Moreover, the primary motive of the robbery offender is not violence, but economic gain. Thus, *sociologically* it is better to designate robbery a property crime and not a crime of violence. In robbery, violence is secondary to the taking of property: violence is a means to obtain a more significant end.

In 1992 there were 672,478 robberies reported to the police, or approximately 264 per 100,000 inhabitants (FBI, 1993:26). However, the *NCVS* (Department of Justice, 1993:10) disclosed that for 1992 slightly over half of all robberies were reported to the police. Consequently, the *NCVS* reported almost twice as many robberies as the police, for a total of 2.2 million (*ibid.*:10). Although we do not have a completely accurate figure for the total robberies in a given year, it is safe to assume that the police are aware of only slightly more than half.

Many U.S. citizens feel that robbery almost always entails violence. When one thinks of robbery, what usually comes to mind is a mugging—someone physically attacked on the street and a purse or wallet stolen. However, only about 1 in 20 robberies involve some degree of violence resulting in an injury to the victim, and only about 8 percent of all victims are treated in the hospital (Department of Justice, 1993:10; Cook, 1986:405).

Nevertheless, the likelihood of violence occurring, and thus of an injury inflicted, is related to the type of robbery. *Strong-arm robbery* (sometimes referred to as unarmed robbery because the offender robs without the use of a weapon) is actually much more dangerous than *armed robbery* (the display of a deadly weapon to carry out the robbery). Approximately twice as many strong-arm robbery victims, compared to armed-robbery victims, are injured (Wright *et al.*, 1983:208). Not only are armed robberies less dangerous than strong-arm robberies, they occur more often and are more likely to be successful (Department of Justice, 1993:10).

Strong-arm robberies are more likely to result in injury because, without the presence of a weapon, the offender does not have any means—other than the threat or actual use of physical violence—of intimidating the victim into complying. Crucial to a successful—and nonviolent—robbery is the ability to induce *terror* in the victim. A weapon can maximize terror while lessening the chance of injury (Walsh, 1986:92–96). Thus, strong-arm robbers must turn to violence in order to create terror and to make the robbery successful. Moreover, in strong-arm robbery situations, it is more likely that the victim will resist. David Luckenbill (1982:815) found, for instance, that in 95 percent of the strong-arm robbery cases he examined, the victims resisted the offender. Victim resistance therefore arguably plays an important role in increasing the amount of violence in strong-arm robbery cases.

In armed-robbery cases, the type of resistance is strongly related to the likelihood of victim injury. According to Zimring and Zuehl (1986:18), for example, armed-robbery victims who *actively* resist through refusal, flight, and physical force are more than 14 times as likely to be killed as are those who resist passively or cooperate with the robber. Passive resistance refers to the victim responding that, for example, she or he has no money. Cooperation occurs when the victim offers no resistance at all. The Zimring and Zuehl study found that although only 8 percent of armed-robbery victims *actively* resist, they account for approximately 55 percent of all victims who are killed (*ibid.*). This finding supports Einstadter's earlier (1969) conclusion that even though unarmed robbery may result in more injuries, when control of the scene by the *armed* robber is lost or compromised (for instance, the victim produces a weapon), the potential for violence is significant. Thus, armed victims increase the potential for violence rather than preventing it.

The victim's response to a robber is affected by the offender's capacity and intent to injure as well as the victim's capacity and ability to avoid injury. If offenders appear capable of inflicting injury and victims consider themselves incapable of resisting, victims usually comply with offender demands. However, if offenders appear incapable of inflicting injury and victims consider themselves capable of resisting, the victims attempt, in most cases, to resist the commands of offenders (Luckenbill, 1982:817).

Consequently, armed robberies are less violent because the weapon serves—as John Conklin (1972) points out in his classic study of robbery—an *instrumental* function for the robber. The weapon does this in four essential ways (*ibid.*:110–112). First, the weapon creates a *buffer zone* between offender and victim, instilling fear in the victim and therefore making it easier for the robber to hold people at a distance and to control them. Second, the weapon provides the means with which to *intimidate* the victim, therefore minimizing the chance of violence and injury. If the display of the weapon does not sufficiently frighten the victim, most robbers, according to Conklin, use such additional methods to accomplish their goal as holding the end of the gun barrel to the victim's head. If the victim continues to resist, the weapon serves a third function—to *make good the threat*—whereby the robber strikes the victim on the side of the head or actually shoots or stabs the victim. Fourth, the weapon *ensures escape* from the scene. The weapon helps to keep victims, witnesses, and the police from hindering a rapid escape. Because what worries robbers most is "being seen and identified, getting caught, getting trapped in crowds and so on," the weapon clearly serves as an important instrument in helping guarantee that none of this occurs (Walsh, 1986:94).

Robbery is similar to murder and assault in that it involves a face-to-face confrontation between offender and victim. In fact, Luckenbill (1981) goes so far as to argue that robbery actually entails a "transaction" between offender and victim. From his research, Luckenbill (*ibid.*:28–41) developed a model of robbery consisting of four stages. Each stage involves important tasks that the offender and victim execute together. In the first stage, the offender—having selected a victim—creates "copresence" with the victim by moving into striking range without causing suspicion. In other words, the robber attempts a "normal appearance" while maintaining an appropriate position for the imminent robbery. After establishing copresence—and after the offender decides and subsequently initiates the robbery—the victim determines in the second stage whether to resist, whereas the offender considers how much force, if any, is required to obtain the desired property. It is this interaction, and acknowledgment by both offender and victim, that creates a *common robbery frame* to which each, Luckenbill argues, most likely adheres. Once a common robbery frame is established, the third stage involves transfer of the property. Although transfer is in most cases under the control of the offender, several obstructions may occur: the victim may not adhere to the robbery frame; outsiders may disrupt the robbery; the offender may not have the knowledge and skill required to complete the transfer. Assuming transfer of the property takes place, the fourth stage involves the offender's escape, such as jumping into a "getaway car" and/or containing the victim in some fashion (such as tying up the victim).

Luckenbill's work is important in that it shows robbery to be more than illegal behavior by an offender: robbery is an interaction involving joint contributions by both offender and victim. However, although robbery involves an interaction to which both offender and victim contribute, it is hardly a simple "transaction" between equal partners as Luckenbill seems to argue. The key point in a robbery scenario is that the interaction is coercive, one party—the offender—exercising a dominant power position over the victim. "Transaction" implies "equality" where equality does not exist.

It is also questionable whether Luckenbill's model is applicable to all robbery types. For instance, does his model help us understand (1) robbery of banks and armored cars, (2) muggings and purse snatchings, and/or (3) robbery during a burglary? In fact, these robbery types constitute the majority of all robberies. Over 50 percent of robberies are committed against persons who as part of their employment are in charge of money and goods (for example, banks and armored cars); 20–25 percent of robberies occur in the open following a sudden attack (such as muggings and purse snatchings); 12–17 percent of robberies occur on private premises (for instance, during a burglary) (Walsh, 1986:82; McClintock and Gibson, 1961:16–17).

Each of the preceding robberies identifies robbery in terms of victim location. However, while this is helpful, it does not tell us much about robbery *offenders*. Robberies that are similar in appearance may be, as Conklin (1972:60–63) notes, "committed by quite different types of offenders." We agree with Conklin (*ibid.*:63–71) and Walsh (1986:56–107) that a typology of robbery should also include offender characteristics. Two robber types selected by scholars for detailed examination, and first discussed in typology form by Conklin, are professionals and opportunists, or amateurs. Both types can be involved in similar robbery scenarios. The recent study by Walsh (1986:81–91) drew this conclusion, successfully combining a typology of incidents—based on victim location—with a typology of professional and opportunist offenders. We now discuss the basic characteristics of these two important types of robbery offenders.

Professional robbers carefully plan and execute their crimes, exhibiting greater skill than other robbery offenders and, usually, operating with accomplices (Conklin, 1972:63). Walsh (1986:74) found that when professionals operate with accomplices, they commonly are people "recommended" to them. The professional commits to robbery as a life-style, engages in sophisticated planning, effects "neutralization of security measures near the target, and investigates, prior to the robbery, all possible escape routes" (Conklin, 1972:64). Thus, professional robbers are considerably more skilled and conduct more extensive planning than other robbers.

Conklin (*ibid.*:64) identified two types of professional robbers. The first commits robbery almost exclusively. The second commits other types of crime but occasionally commits robbery with professional skill. In addition to these "solo professionals," Walsh (1986:154) found two other types of professionals—criminal syndicates that assemble teams of robbers, and independent, small, professional teams of two or three robbers.

Professionals—whether teams or individuals—usually rob persons who, as part of their employment, are in charge of money or goods. However, they do not view themselves as robbing individuals per se but an "amorphous mass—a bank, a supermarket, a loan company" (Einstadter, 1969:80). In other words, professional robbers view themselves as taking from "the company," not from the actual individuals involved. They rarely rob patrons who happen to be at the scene of the robbery, and report that a clerk or teller is less likely to cause a fuss over the robbery because it is "nonpersonal money" being taken (Walsh, 1986:82). As one professional robber put it: "It isn't his money. They're not hurting" (cited in Einstadter, 1969:80).

One of the most lucrative professional robberies occurred in December of 1978 at the Lufthansa cargo terminal, Kennedy Airport. A team of six ski-masked professional robbers broke a chain-link fence, short-circuited the alarm system, tied up 10 people, and made off with possibly as much as $8 million in cash and $1 million in jewelry (Feiden, 1979:37).

The opportunist—or *amateur* robber—is probably the most common type of robber. Opportunists do not commit to robbery on a long-term basis as do professionals. Rather, these amateurs rob infrequently, choosing such easily accessible and vulnerable victims as the elderly, public drunks, taxi drivers, and people walking alone on unlit streets. Opportunists are also involved in other forms of conventional property theft, such as shoplifting (Conklin, 1972:68–71).

When we commonly think of "street crime" or "muggings," it is an opportunistic robbery that we usually contemplate. These haphazard, random, and spur-of-the-moment robberies are often committed in teams or groups by teenage offenders, generally net only small amounts of cash (only one in six nets more than $250), and frequently are accompanied by an assault (Hall *et al.*, 1978:3–28; Cook, 1983:18–19; Cook, 1986:405). In fact, the larger the group, and the stronger the friendship among its members, the greater the chance for violence (Walsh, 1986:100–104).

Four of every five opportunistic robberies are the work of strangers to the victim(s) (Bureau of Justice Statistics, 1993:10). Moreover, opportunists rob their

**TABLE
5-1**   Robbery, Percent Distribution, 1992

[BY POPULATION GROUP]	GROUP I (63 CITIES, 250,000 AND OVER; POPULATION 46,118,000)	GROUP II (126 CITIES, 100,000 TO 249,999; POPULATION 18,792,000)	GROUP III (340 CITIES, 50,000 TO 99,999; POPULATION 23,472,000)	GROUP IV (657 CITIES, 25,000 TO 49,999; POPULATION 22,864,000)	GROUP V (1,528 CITIES, 10,000 TO 24,999; POPULATION 24,185,000)	GROUP VI (6,177 CITIES UNDER 10,000; POPULATION 21,003,000)	COUNTY AGENCIES (3,698 AGENCIES; POPULATION 72,221,000)
TOTAL[1]	100.0	100.0	100.0	100.0	100.0	100.0	100.0
Street/highway	62.8	54.0	49.4	44.5	37.3	26.1	37.0
Commercial house	10.5	12.5	13.9	14.3	14.6	12.8	14.9
Gas or service station	1.8	2.7	3.0	3.7	4.7	3.7	4.3
Convenience store	3.0	7.0	7.5	8.3	10.6	9.9	10.8
Residence	9.6	9.7	9.5	10.1	10.4	9.7	13.8
Bank	1.1	2.2	2.6	2.6	3.2	2.3	2.3
Miscellaneous	11.1	11.9	14.0	16.5	19.2	35.5	16.9

[1]Because of rounding, percentages may not add to totals.

Source: FBI, 1993, p. 29

victims—more than 50 percent of the time—on the street or in some outdoor area near their own home, such as a park, a playground, or a parking lot (*ibid.*:50–51; Cook, 1983:13, 18–19). Opportunistic robberies occur more often in inner districts of the largest cities. As shown in Table 5-1, as size of city population increases, proportion of street/highway robberies reported to police increases. The table also shows that although street robberies increase with city size, other forms of robbery actually decrease with city size. In addition to city size, a study of robbery victims from 1973 to 1984 found that residents of inner cities—as opposed to suburbs and nonmetropolitan areas—suffer the highest robbery rates (Harlow, 1987:3). Consequently, we can safely conclude that most opportunistic robberies occur in the inner districts of our largest cities.

Finally, robbery seems to be increasingly the province of opportunists rather than professionals. This is particularly the case for the crime of *bank robbery*. A government study concluded the following (Bureau of Justice Statistics, 1984:2):

> The majority of bank robberies appear to be unsophisticated and "unprofessional" crimes: 76% of bank robbers used no disguises despite the widespread use by banks of surveillance equipment, 86% never inspected the bank prior to the offense, and 95% had no long-range scheme to avoid apprehension and spend the money without being noticed.

It seems a new type of bank robber has emerged. Haran and Martin (1977:29) found in their study (of 500 convicted bank robbers between 1964 and 1975) that the bank robber of the 1960s was a "pro" with "a certain maturity" and "prestige among his peers," who carefully planned his or her robberies. The robber of the 1970s was unsophisticated, engaged in little planning, and conceived his or her robberies in a very amateurish way. In other words, a new breed of bank robber had arrived in the 1970s (*ibid.*). However, because Haran and Martin based their study on *convicted* bank robbers actually serving time, it could be that the professionals of the 1960s actually became more sophisticated in the 1970s and, therefore, were not caught. Haran and Martin (1984:47) present three reasons why they think this is not the case:

> First, bank robbery is perhaps the most fully reported of any crime known to the police. This is due to the regulations of the Federal Deposit Insurance Corporation, which insures over 95 percent of all banks. The FDIC regulations require the reporting of all bank losses by theft or burglary. This ensures the reporting of bank robberies. Second, according to the FBI, over 80 percent of the bank robbers are identified and arrested. . . . Third, the conviction rate of those arrested for this crime and prosecuted in the Federal courts is exceptionally high, averaging 88.8 percent.

Thus, there is good reason to believe that a new breed of bank robber emerged in the United States in the 1970s and continues into the 1990s.

Burglary

Burglary is defined as unlawful entry of a house, business, or other structure, with the intent to commit a felony. Thus, although robbery entails theft through the threat or actual use of violence, for burglary to occur someone must actually enter a structure unlawfully with the intent to commit a felony. Moreover, burglary—like the other property crimes to be discussed in this chapter—differs from robbery in another critical way: it very seldom involves a direct, face-to-face confrontation between offender and victim.

The FBI categorizes burglary in three ways: forcible entry, unlawful entry without force, and attempted forcible entry. In 1992, 69 percent of all burglaries reported to the police involved forcible entry, 23 percent were unlawful entries without force, and 8 percent were forcible entry attempts (FBI, 1993:39). In the same year there were 2,979,884 burglaries reported to the police, or approximately 1,168 per 100,000 inhabitants (FBI, 1993:38). However, the *NCVS* (Department of Justice, 1993:12) reported that for 1993 only about half of all burglaries were reported to the police. Consequently, the *NCVS* reported almost twice as many burglaries occurring as did the FBI, for a total of 4.8 million (*ibid.*:12). As with robbery, the police probably know about, at most, only 50 percent of all burglaries committed. Some other facts from the *NCVS* on burglary include (*ibid.*:12):

▲— About 4 percent of all households in the United States experienced one or more burglaries in 1992.

▲— Almost three in 10 burglaries result in losses of $500 or more.

▲— The estimated economic loss to victims of household burglaries was $4.2 billion in 1991.

Burglars can also be classified as amateurs and professionals. Amateurs and professionals are similar in that both may burglarize houses and/or businesses and might operate alone or work with others in a team (Walsh, 1986: 3–4). However, they also differ in important ways.

Amateur burglars enter a structure when they "feel the need." Their style of intrusion is extremely unsophisticated—perhaps simply breaking a window or breaking down a door. Because amateurs are more interested in volume of burglaries than in quality, very little planning is involved. Amateur burglars rarely specialize in theft of specific items, but steal a variety of merchandise as opportunities arise: usually accessible goods such as televisions, stereos, VCRs, CD players, silverware, jewelry, and money (Walsh, 1977: 62–63; Walsh, 1986:33). Thus, amateurs are part-time burglars who engage in burglary as "only a small, episodic part of a life of crime in general" (Walsh, 1986:22).

Most amateur burglars engage in theft for personal financial gain. In Bennett and Wright's (1984) study, 46 percent of the burglars interviewed claimed they committed the offense only when they were short of money. Moreover, approximately 50 percent of those burglars who stated a use to which the money would be put maintained that "it was for subsistence or basic everyday needs"; the other 50 percent burglarized to obtain money for entertainment, gambling, drinking, or drugs (*ibid.*:32).

Finally, some amateur burglars are likely to commit "opportunistic" burglaries—that is, discovering a vulnerable and attractive target while involved in other activities (lawful or unlawful) and immediately engaging in the burglary. However, the majority of amateurs first decide to commit a burglary—as stated previously, when they "feel the need"—next search for a suitable target, and then immediately commit the burglary when a promising target is identified (*ibid.*:43–46).

Professional burglars are specialists who employ considerable skill and planning in executing a burglary. They select only targets of substantial value and rarely carry weapons (Walsh, 1977:61). A good example of a professional burglar is Harry King—a boxman (safecracker)—who reported to Chambliss (1984:31–37) all the intrigues and skill required to enter a building successfully, open or "kidnap" a safe, and efficiently escape. King's activities followed closely Sutherland's model of the professional thief outlined in Chapter 12.4. King learned his trade from another professional boxman, working initially as an apprentice. He eventually made his living from burglary, engaging in extensive planning and never feeling the need to carry a weapon during a "caper." Moreover, he kept up with the latest technology applicable to his trade. According to King (*ibid.*:35), it is essential for the professional to be familiar with the latest "burglary tools," such as drills and saws, and to spend time practicing and preparing for future capers.

Another example of a professional burglar is Pete Salerno, who specialized in stealing jewelry (Abadinsky, 1983:13–79). He learned how to burglarize homes from another jewel thief, spending six months as an apprentice. Just as King, Salerno learned that to be a successful professional burglar required careful planning. He would drive around during the day "scouting out big, fancy homes," and gathered information in the library on such matters as where to find "prime real estate" as well as studying about different types of gems (*ibid.*:26). Most of his capers occurred when the victims were at home entertaining guests, and Salerno would steal from $150,000 to $500,000 worth of jewelry (*ibid.*).

Professional burglars also rely on contacts with *tipsters,* or persons who identify possible burglary targets for the burglar. As Neal Shover (1972:546) points out in his examination of professional burglars: "A 'tipster' . . . conveys information to a burglar about certain premises or its occupants which is intended to aid him in burglarizing those premises." In addition to tipsters, professional burglars establish important contacts with police, attorneys, and judges. This liaison with members of the criminal justice system frequently allows professional burglars to "fix" their cases prior to committing the burglaries. King (Chambliss, 1984:84) found it easy to fix cases because "the only people that really profit from theft are the fix, the judge, and the district attorney." The sociological literature indicates that professional burglars commonly rely on "the fix" (Abadinsky, 1983:70–75). As Inciardi (1975:65) points out: "The *fixing* of arrests and pending court appearances is engineered through bribing victims, police, witnesses, bailiffs, court personnel, juries, prosecutors, or judges."

Larceny

In Chapter 7.1 we discuss employee theft—the taking of merchandise and job-related items from one's workplace. Our immediate concern, however, is with nonoccupational theft, or what is commonly referred to as larceny. *Larceny* is the unlawful taking of property from the possession of someone other than one's employer. In 1992, there were 7.9 million larcenies in the United States reported to the police, or approximately 3,103 per 100,000 inhabitants (FBI, 1993:43). The FBI includes a variety of crimes under the larceny designation. As shown in Figure 5-1, this variety ranges from purse snatching to theft of motor vehicle accessories.

The *NCVS* categorizes larceny quite differently than does the FBI, dividing it into "personal larceny with contact" (theft of purse, wallet, or cash without the threat or actual use of physical violence) and "personal larceny without contact" (theft without direct contact from any place other than the victim's home, such as theft of an umbrella from a restaurant, a radio from the beach, or a bicycle from a school yard) (Department of Justice, 1993:13). In 1992, the *NCVS* (*ibid.*:13) reported 484,800 cases of personal larceny with contact and 11,726,030 cases of personal larceny without contact.

New types of larceny are always being made possible by technological change. A recent example—not yet examined by sociologists and criminologists—is cellular phone number theft, which costs cellular carriers an estimated $300 million per year in unauthorized calls (Flanagan and McMenamin, 1992). A common method of stealing a cellular phone number is through "cloning," which involves altering the microchip in another cellular phone so that the phone

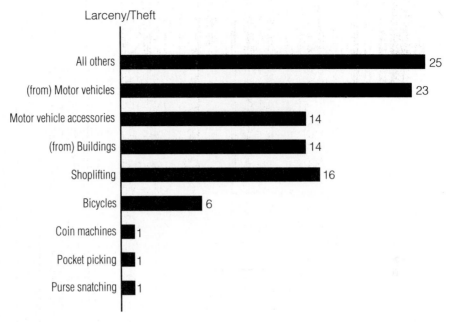

Larceny/Theft

All others	25
(from) Motor vehicles	23
Motor vehicle accessories	14
(from) Buildings	14
Shoplifting	16
Bicycles	6
Coin machines	1
Pocket picking	1
Purse snatching	1

FIGURE   **Larceny Analysis, 1992, in Percentages**
5-1   *Source: FBI, 1993, p. 47.*

number matches the one stolen from an authentic customer. The conversion can be accomplished with a personal computer, and cellular phone numbers are "either purchased from insiders or plucked from the airwaves with a legal device, about the size of a textbook, that can be plugged into a vehicle's cigarette lighter receptacle" (*ibid.*: 189).

One particular type of larceny—shoplifting—has been accorded extraordinary attention by sociologists and criminologists. *Shoplifting*—theft of property from a retail store by "customers"—accounts for approximately 25–30 percent of all business losses (Klemke, 1992:10). Approximately 4 of every 10 individuals shoplift at some time during their lives (Kallis and Vanier, 1985:459); the median theft averages $15 worth of merchandise (Murphy, 1986:27–50). Additional estimates of the cost of shoplifting include (Baumer and Rosenbaum, 1984:18–20; Farrell and Ferrara, 1985:3–6; Ray, 1987:234–239):

▲— Approximately $3–4 billion each year is lost to shoplifting, adding as much as 5 percent to the cost-of-living index.

▲— The loss in taxes to the federal government amounts to almost one-half billion dollars each year.

▲— Approximately one of every 12 shoppers shoplifts.

Obviously, not only businesses suffer losses from shoplifting. As consumers, we are victims too. Businesses simply raise their prices to compensate for their losses; consumers pay for it. *The Washington Post* reported in the 1980s that the

Approximately 40 percent of us shoplift at some time during our lives.

average consumer in Washington, D.C., pays almost $300 dollars a year to reimburse business losses due to shoplifting (Pyatt, 1987:E1).

One of the earliest efforts by a sociologist to study shoplifting is the classic work by Cameron (1964), *The Booster and the Snitch*. Cameron (1964:39–60) divides shoplifters into two types: "boosters," who steal merchandise to sell it, and "snitches," who steal for their own consumption. In other words, the booster is a professional who steals for the purpose of making money; the snitch is an amateur who steals for personal use. According to Cameron, boosters—comprising about 10 percent of shoplifters—possess five characteristics:

1. Boosters work a large number of stores rather than a few large stores.

2. Boosters employ considerable planning and skill to execute their theft.

3. Boosters steal only expensive merchandise and, like professional robbers and burglars, sell it to a professional fence.

4. Boosters often easily "fix" their cases if caught.

5. Boosters employ very sophisticated methods and devices for engaging in shoplifting.

These devices include "booster bloomers," garments especially designed to hold stolen merchandise, and "booster boxes," specifically designed to look like wrapped packages but that actually contain secret openings into which items can be placed quickly and easily (*ibid.*:40–50, 56–58).

The type of professional shoplifter receiving the greatest attention has been the so-called "California Pro," who shoplifts in a wide geographical area and sells large quantities of merchandise to a fence (Baumer and Rosenbaum, 1984:26). In the United States, professional shoplifters tend to operate in rings. One group allegedly has a membership as high as 1,000 and steals as much as $150 million worth of merchandise each year (*ibid.*).

The other 90 percent of shoplifters, according to Cameron, are snitches, or amateurs, who possess the following characteristics:

1. Snitches are "respectable" members of the community.
2. Snitches do not think of themselves as criminals.
3. Snitches have no criminal associations or connections.
4. Snitches steal from a store when the opportunity arises.
5. Snitches do not plan extensively, but enter the store "prepared" to shoplift (equipped with "shopping lists," large handbags, briefcases, shopping bags, and scissors and razor blades for snipping off price tags).

Snitches simply place items in pockets or inside coats, sometimes actually wearing the stolen merchandise under their clothing, or engage in such activities as price-tag switching, whereby they pay less for merchandise (*ibid.*:58–60). Self-report studies indicate that snitching is a fairly common activity in the United States (Baumer and Rosenbaum, 1984:18–19). Again, about 40 percent of shoppers have shoplifted at some time.

Cameron's findings are important because they show shoplifting to be a very frequent crime and one committed not primarily by professionals, "lower-class" people, or a unique criminal element of deranged, psychologically disturbed people. Rather, shoplifting is committed by "normal" and "ordinary" individuals.

Initially, the work of Robin (1963) on patterns of department-store shoplifting and of Won and Yamamoto (1968) on middle-class shoplifting, confirmed the major findings published by Cameron. More recently, Farrell and Ferrara (1985:9–30) and Baumer and Rosenbaum (1984:26–27) also supported Cameron's booster/snitch typology, and Meier's (1983:1499) discussion of professional shoplifters agreed with Cameron. But Meier adds that being a professional shoplifter means that one must acquire adequate training and learn "which items can be fenced, with what percentage of profit, and to whom." Meier (*ibid.*) also points out that snitches are more likely to switch or remove price tags, or simply grab "merchandise and run from the store (most salespeople do not run after thieves)," and that many juveniles engage in considerable planning for their shoplifting escapades.

However, some of Cameron's findings can be questioned. For example, Lloyd Klemke's (1992:71) recent review of shoplifting literature indicates that "significant numbers of boosters who shoplift for resale also shoplift for their own use." Moreover, many snitches do not enter a store prepared to shoplift but, rather, their shoplifting is often a spur-of-the-moment act. One snitch interviewed by Klemke (*ibid.*:72) stated:

> I never went into a store knowing that I was going to shoplift. I would just be walking around and then take something, makeup or candy, never thinking before that I would. Just see it. Didn't really think about it.

Fifty-six percent of Klemke's sample of "college student shoplifters" claimed they did not plan on shoplifting prior to entering the store (*ibid.*:72).

Finally, after a careful review of the literature on shoplifting in the United States, Britain, and Australia, Murphy (1986:58) concluded that instead of shoplifting being a peculiar and strange activity, it is an offense that many people engage in at some time in their life, and that "far from being an offense motivated by personal frustrations of whatever sort," shoplifting is "an everyday activity."

Motor Vehicle Theft

Motor vehicle theft is the unlawful taking or attempting to take a motor vehicle such as an automobile, van, truck, or motorcycle. In 1992 there were 1,610,834 motor vehicle thefts reported to the police, or approximately 632 per 100,000 inhabitants (FBI, 1993:49). The estimated national loss from reported motor vehicle theft was $7.6 billion in 1992 and at the time of the theft the average value per vehicle stolen was $4,713 (*ibid.*: 50).

The *NCVS* (Bureau of Justice Statistics, 1993:14) found that for 1992, 92 percent of completed motor vehicle theft victimizations were reported to the police. Not surprisingly, the *NCVS* reported a figure close to the FBI total: approximately 2 million motor vehicle thefts in 1992 (*ibid.*:14).

Some other facts, from the *NCVS*, about motor vehicle theft (*ibid.*: 14):

▲— When based on the number of vehicles owned, the motor vehicle theft rate for 1992 was about 13 motor vehicle thefts per 1,000 vehicles.

▲— Of all the households in the United States, 2 percent were the victims of one or more motor vehicle thefts in 1992.

▲— The most common place for a motor vehicle theft to occur is in a parking lot or garage.

▲— In 1991, motor vehicle theft resulted in an estimated $8.5 billion in direct losses to victims.

▲— The rate of motor vehicle theft is higher for renters (29 per 1,000) than for homeowners (18 per 1,000).

▲— Motor vehicle theft rates are higher in central cities (37 per 1,000 households) than suburban areas (21 per 1,000) or rural areas (six per 1,000).

Most scholars—as with larceny—have concentrated on one type of motor vehicle theft, automobile theft. Also, as with robbery, burglary, and larceny, sociologists have dichotomized auto thefts into the primary types of amateur and professional. One of the earliest applications of this typology is seen in Jerome Hall's (1952:250–256) well-known book, *Theft, Law and Society*. For

Hall, most auto thieves are amateur *joyriders* who steal automobiles for excitement and to "show off," quickly abandoning the car after a short time. According to Hall, joyriders mostly steal cars with unlocked doors, open windows, keys in the ignition, and sometimes even the motor running. According to *The Washington Post*, recent evidence confirms Hall's conclusion: roughly 30 percent of cars stolen have their keys inside the automobile and 80 percent are left unlocked (Wheeler, 1986:A37).

Professional auto thieves steal automobiles in more indirect and skillful ways. According to Hall, many simply work with repair-shop employees who secure duplicate keys for the professional thief. Others steal cars advertised in newspapers by providing the owner with a "down payment," never to be heard from again. Once an automobile is stolen, many professionals work with, or personally control, a "chop-shop," in which a stolen automobile is stripped of all saleable accessories. These accessories are sold to dealers, repair shops and garages, and professional fences. In 1986 *The Washington Post* reported that being in the "chop-shop business" can be financially rewarding. A $10,000 car can be chopped up and the parts sold for around $40,000 (Wheeler, 1986:A37). Moreover, increasing adult involvement in auto theft, together with increasing thefts of trucks and commercial vehicles and declining recovery rates in the 1980s, led the National Institute of Justice to conclude that auto theft is increasingly becoming the province of professionals (*The New York Times*, 1984:A13).

The most recent sociological discussion of auto theft—by McCaghy, Giordano, and Henson (1977:376–383)—argues that Hall's typology is too simplistic for this crime. According to these sociologists, auto thieves "are a more complex lot" (ibid.:377), and they suggest a typology that includes five categories: (1) joyriding, (2) short-term transportation, (3) long-term transportation, (4) commission of another crime, and (5) profit. We now examine each.

McCaghy *et al.* agree with Hall that joyriding auto theft signifies recreational, nonutilitarian, short-term use of cars. For the joyrider, the primary goal is not simply to obtain transportation, but rather "automobile symbolism is predominant: the car is stolen not for what it does, but for what it means" (*ibid.*:378). The second type—short-term transportation—is similar to joyriding in the sense that it clearly involves short-term use of a stolen automobile. It differs, however, in that the thief's primary interest in the car is its ability to provide transportation from one location to another—from one place in the city to another, or even from one state to another. As with joyriding, many juveniles are involved in short-term auto theft. The third type—long-term transportation—involves thieves who steal the vehicle with the intent of keeping it for long-term personal use. This type of auto thief usually steals automobiles outside his or her state of residence, and upon returning home, if not before, repaints the vehicle. Most long-term auto thieves are adults. Some auto thieves—the fourth type—steal cars to aid them in the commission of another crime, such as robbery, burglary, or larceny. This fourth type represents only a small portion of all auto thieves, even though the scenario is depicted over and over again on prime-time television. Once again, the motivation is utility of the automobile. Finally, the fifth type identified by McCaghy *et al.* is profit, which is somewhat similar to Hall's "professional." However, for McCaghy *et al.*, this fifth type includes a wide variety of individuals whose purpose is not to keep the car, but to resell it, or its parts, for profit. They identify two forms of this type: amateurs and professionals. Amateurs, on the one hand, steal a car to strip it of easily accessible components such as batteries, tires, and a variety of engine parts. They sell these parts to friends, acquaintances, or amateur fences, or they re-equip their own cars using some of the parts. Professionals, on the other hand, are highly organized, reselling expensive stolen cars in the U.S. and internationally. Professionals alter the vehicle registration numbers and falsify registration papers. Many purchase expensive wrecked vehicles and their ownership documents for a very low cost. They steal an identical car (year, make, model), replacing the vehicle identification number plate with that of the wrecked vehicle and also making other minor alterations. Subsequently, the converted vehicle is sold to an "unsuspecting party who registers and retitles the vehicle in his or her name, giving it a legitimate identity virtually impossible to trace to the thief" (*The New York Times*, 1984:A13). McCaghy *et al.* argue that professionals are also involved in the chop-shop business, specializing in the sale of specific parts to fences: hoods, fenders, bumpers, grills, and other hard-to-obtain parts.

Although amateurs and professionals clearly differ in skill and quality of theft, they both consider the automobile a valuable piece of property. Auto theft for profit differs from the other types of auto theft identified by McCaghy *et al.*—joyriding, short- and long-term transportation, and aiding the commission of another crime—because those who commit these latter types consider the automobile either a symbol or a form of transportation.

All of the above examples of auto theft usually occur without direct contact between offender and victim. However, in the 1990s a new type of auto theft began to be discussed in the media—carjacking—in which the auto thief uses direct physical force to steal a car from a driver. In a carjacking, automobiles are stolen from drivers in such places as rest stops, service stations, car washes, red lights, and shopping-mall parking lots. Probably the most well-known carjacking was that of Pamela Basu in 1992. Carjackers confronted her one block from her house—as she waited for a red light—and she was dragged to her death while entangled in the seat belt.

Fencing

Fencing is buying and selling—or dealing in—stolen goods. A fence's sources of goods include not only robbers, burglars, shoplifters, and auto thieves, but also fraudsters (whom we discuss in the next section) and employee thieves (whom we examine in Chapter 7.1). Once a thief successfully steals "the goods" and does not plan to make personal use of them, he or she must dispose of the goods as quickly as possible. Amateurs are more likely than professionals to engage in "self-fencing"—that is, selling the stolen goods to people who do not

Carjacking is a form of motor vehicle theft in which the perpetrator uses direct physical force to steal a car from the driver.

know the goods are stolen or selling them to consumers who are unconcerned with their origin. Many people jump at the opportunity to buy items at a discount; consequently, amateurs find accessible outlets for stolen merchandise in friends, acquaintances, and on the street generally (McIntosh, 1976:257).

Some amateur thieves, however, sell their goods to *amateur fences*. Stuart Henry's (1978; 1976) work on the amateur trade in stolen goods is interesting in this regard. Henry (1976:794) defines amateur fencing as "the activity of regular part-time purchase of genuine quality merchandise (usually, though not necessarily stolen) for the purpose of selling cheaply for the interest of those involved." Most amateur fences *say* they participate in the trade of stolen goods for personal economic gain. Notwithstanding, it seems that amateur fences rarely make money. Henry (*ibid.*:796–797) found this to be the case because amateur fences are unlikely to come into contact with either highly valued articles or large quantities of these items, and when they do, they find it is difficult to resell them. But more importantly, the price charged by the fence is determined by the nature of the relationship between the fence and the buyer. Most stolen goods go from the amateur fence to relatives and friends who "are often given the goods and not even charged cost price," and when friends and relatives are charged, it is rarely more than the fence actually paid for the items (*ibid.*:798). Thus, even though amateur fencing is structured in terms of economic exchange, Henry concludes that, in actuality, the majority of deals are made for the purpose of reaffirming established relationships. Amateur fencing provides the individual fence with "status, prestige and reciprocal social favors" (Walsh and Poole, 1983:89). As Henry (1976:801) states: "the social content of the relations surrounding amateur exchange outweighs the material value of the goods involved." Amateur trade in stolen goods becomes a means of sustaining a network of communal relations among relatives, friends, and acquaintances. Consequently, amateur trade in stolen goods is quite informal and even takes place in people's homes. Henry (1978:18) provides an example: "Whenever Jim, a shoplifter, supplied cheap goods to Freddy, a plumber, there would be a Sunday-morning knock at the door: 'I got some suits: Do you want them?'"

Professional thieves, however, are much more likely to do business with a *professional fence* who buys the stolen merchandise from the thief to resell it at a profit. Several classic studies have examined professional fencing operations in relation to property theft. Within such literature there seems to be consensus that most professional fences have strong ties to the legitimate business community. As Hall (1952:155) wrote in his previously cited book, *Theft, Law and Society*, the professional fence is "an established participant" in the legitimate "economic life of society." Professional fences are "offshoots from legitimate businesses," frequently specialize in a chosen field, and thus are "able to evaluate merchandise expertly and to compete generally on the basis of their special skills" (*ibid.*:157).

Marilyn Walsh (1977:15) reports that the average professional fence in her study was "a 45–55-year-old white, male businessman. As such, he looked strikingly similar to most managers and administrators in wholesale and retail trades." For Walsh (*ibid.*:15) then, the professional fence is "strikingly dissimilar" to the thief and is "demographically a very ordinary man."

Finally, the most recent—and methodologically the most rigorous—study of the professional fence, by Darrell Steffensmeier (1986:20), confirms that the "overwhelming majority of fences . . . are simultaneously proprietors or operators of a legitimate business which provides a cover or front for the fencing." "Sam Goodman," the main character of Steffensmeier's book, is a legitimate and successful businessperson who also—as part of his business—sells stolen merchandise. In Sam's view, it is very difficult for anyone to succeed in business without "chiseling" in some form or fashion; professional fencing is simply his type of chiseling.

The legitimate business identity of the professional fence covers the comings and goings of thieves, making thieves indistinguishable from customers and legitimate delivery persons (Klockars, 1974:88). In short, the evidence on fencing shows, as Henry (1977:133) puts it:

> that it is not the case that one species of actor, the "fence," buys stolen goods, whereas another, the "businessman," buys legitimate ones. Rather it demonstrates that businessmen buy cheap goods in order that they may sell at a profit; a greater or lesser proportion of their purchases may be illicit.

The professional fence is "in the shadow of two worlds" (the subtitle of Steffensmeier's book), providing legitimate and illegitimate goods in the business world while simultaneously buying stolen goods in the criminal world. Professional fencing is in fact indistinguishable from legitimate business activity.

Some scholars feel that the professional fence actually controls the thief, playing the central and primary role of all those involved in property theft. In this view, according to Dermot Walsh and Adrian Poole (1983:88), the professional fence is at the center of a

> "stolen property system," a gigantic distribution circuit which locates, plans, facilitates and executes the acquisition, conversion and redistribution of stolen property and reintegrates it into the legitimate property system.

Marilyn Walsh (1977:175), in her book *The Fence*, argues that because the professional fence specializes in certain types of products, the thief is forced to target those goods preferred by the fence. The influence of the fence over the thief is therefore "quite explicit and directive" and, consequently

> the fence exerts power in contemporary property theft and shapes a thief's criminal career by either limiting or expanding his access to crime partners or to the acquisition of new skills. The fence, then, is the controlling influence over both the thief and his theft activities. As such, the fence of stolen goods emerges as the prime mover in property theft.

A number of other scholars of fencing—in particular McIntosh (1976) and Henry (1977)—take issue with this conclusion. McIntosh reinvestigated several alleged cases throughout history of the professional fence as the "prime mover" in property theft. She concluded that rather than evidencing a professional fence exercising central control over property theft operations, these cases actually revealed that the professional fence simply advances money to thieves and buys goods from them. For McIntosh, although thieves and fences are independent of each other, they simultaneously engage in mutually beneficial market relations. Both the thief and the fence become experts and develop a network of contacts within their own particular market. In short, neither exercises control over the other (*ibid.*:262–263).

Henry (1977) expands on McIntosh's conclusions, arguing that in order for the professional fence to be the "Mr. Big" of property crime, we must assume (1) that thieves are not independent of fences in their criminal activities and (2) that the police are not involved in supporting these operations. Regarding the first assumption, Henry (*ibid.*:126) replies:

> While the thief is supposed to be dependent upon the receiver he is, at the same time, assumed to engage in his theft activity independently of him. But if he is independently motivated to theft, that is, in some

sense *a priori* a "thief," then he will steal irrespective of whether or not receivers exist.

Regarding the second assumption, Henry (*ibid.*:132) argues that because of their respective positions, both the professional fence and the police have access to resources desired by the other. The professional fence can help the police make "good busts" by providing information as to who commits crime as well as where the goods are most likely to be found. The professional fence can also help secure the return of stolen goods and offer the police themselves stolen goods either at a discount price or even free of charge. In return, the police can warn the professional fence of impending investigations and of the dangers of purchasing certain stolen goods, as well as protect the professional fence by quashing investigations that may lead their way. Finally, by patronizing his store, the police provide an essential legitimacy for conducting business. Steffensmeier's (1986:148) study confirms these conclusions, finding that "the police may cultivate fences as suppliers of criminal intelligence in exchange for what may be virtual freedom to buy and sell stolen goods."

Thus, neither the thief nor the fence is the prime mover of property crime. Rather, "stealing and dealing" are simply steps in a loosely structured, yet mutually supportive, *network* of individuals involved in acquiring and distributing stolen property. This network consists of thieves, fences, criminal justice personnel, criminal syndicate figures, goods transporters, and buyers (Steffensmeier, 1986:157–158).

This last category—the buyers—includes upfront store customers, auction patrons, antique dealers, businesses and business people, other fences, police officers and other legal officials, and individuals and groups who make special "orders," such as members of criminal syndicates (*ibid.*:109–115). The police and criminal syndicate categories require a brief discussion. There is an understanding in the world of a professional fence that certain criminal syndicates have the "property rights" to certain types of goods. For Sam (Steffensmeier's fence), whenever he acquired stolen cigarettes and liquor, these immediately went to specific syndicate figures. Moreover, because Sam's business involved antiques, criminal syndicates would send stolen antiques his way. Thus, a reciprocal relationship seems to exist between a professional fence and a criminal syndicate (*ibid.*:97).

There can also be a close relationship between the professional thief and criminal syndicates. Abadinsky (1983:64–65) reports that criminal syndicates provide vital services to thieves, such as information on the police, whom to "connect" with in the case of arrest, information on possible targets, reliable fences, financial assistance, and protection. In return, the professional thief offers the skill and ability required to provide "the goods" criminal syndicates are interested in.

Regarding the police:

> Fences are able to offer various "perks" or payoffs to the police and other legal officials. . . . In return for these perks, the police may be less

zealous in responding to complaints against the fence or may sabotage an ongoing investigation (Steffensmeier, 1986:152).

Most detectives who frequented Sam's shop were simply recipients of Sam's generosity, yet a few were "actively on the take" (*ibid.*:153).

In Klockars' (1974:104) earlier case study of the fence "Vincent Swaggi," it was found that the largest single group of his buyers was in some way connected to the criminal justice system: police officers, detectives, lawyers, judges, customs officials, insurance adjusters, and crime reporters. The relationship between Swaggi and these buyers was quite comfortable and friendly. As Klockars (*ibid.*) points out:

> A joking atmosphere prevails, with "What's hot today, Vince?" as a standard opening from Vincent's law enforcement customers. Although Vincent has heard that question a thousand times he always answers, "Everything," and laughs.

Consequently, both amateur and professional thievery, as well as amateur and professional fencing, must be understood as being embedded in a network of relations with other legitimate and illegitimate people.

5.2 —————— DAMAGE AND DECEPTION

Arson and fraud, although property crimes, are somewhat different from property theft. Rather than the direct theft of money and/or goods, arson involves *damage* to property of another and fraud involves deliberate *deception* of another for personal economic gain.

Arson

Arson is the willful or malicious burning of a house, public building, motor vehicle, aircraft, or other property of another. In 1992 there were 102,009 arson offenses reported to the police, or approximately 48 per 100,000 inhabitants (FBI, 1993:54). The vast majority of arson crimes occur in cities with populations of over 1 million (*ibid.*). In addition, it is not just in big cities, but also in the economically declining inner-city neighborhoods of big cities that the most common arson sites exist (Brady, 1983:4). Arson also causes more injury, death, and property loss than any other crime listed by the FBI as a felony (*ibid.*:1). Moreover, the number of arson incidents has increased steadily, as the following data suggest (*ibid.*:3–4):

▲— From 1951 to 1977 the number of arson incidents increased by over 3,100 percent, from 5,600 incidents to over 177,000.

▲— In 1964 arson caused less than 3 percent of all fire losses; by 1981 arson losses had risen to 30 percent.

▲— Arson accounts for an increasing proportion of all fire deaths—the poverty-ridden and minorities of the inner cities the most victimized.

When we think of arson, what commonly comes to mind is the psychologically deranged pyromaniac we see on prime-time television. Clearly there are cases of individuals who have an "uncontrollable impulse" to start fires, and who engage in this behavior for the excitement and mere "pleasure" of setting fires and watching structures burn; however, their number is indeed small when compared with other types of arsonists (National Institute of Law Enforcement and Criminal Justice, 1980:7–9). Excluding pyromaniacs, four major types of arson have been identified by sociologists, police officials, and firefighters. The types are based on arsonist motives and include: crime concealment, revenge, vandalism, and profit (*ibid.*:9; Boudreau *et al.*, 1977:19–24). We briefly consider each type.

Crime concealment refers to individuals setting fires to destroy evidence—for example, of a burglary, a larceny, or a murder. In such cases individuals employ arson to remove any evidence connecting the perpetrator to the crime or to prevent identification of the victim. In addition, people set fires to destroy records that contain evidence of other crimes, such as frauds and white-collar crimes like embezzlement and corporate crimes (Boudreau *et al.*, 1977:19). According to the National Institute of Law Enforcement and Criminal Justice (NILECJ) (1980:9), approximately 7 percent of all arsons result from crime concealment.

Revenge arsons—which account for approximately 18 percent of all arsons (*ibid.*)—result from quarrels, hatred, and jealousy among lovers, neighbors, employees, family members and relatives, and persons motivated by racist and religious contempt (Boudreau *et al.*, 1977:19). Children sometimes express resentment against siblings who receive greater attention by burning a brother's or sister's bed, and/or may indicate incest victimization by setting afire the bed in which they are victimized. Similarly, women who are the victims of physical and/or sexual abuse in the home may obtain revenge by setting afire the bed— quite possibly with the perpetrator asleep in it—as depicted in the TV movie, "The Burning Bed." An example of arson resulting from religious contempt is the burning of abortion clinics by right-wing fundamentalists. In 1986, for example, an arson fire caused $20,000 damage to an abortion clinic in Toledo, Ohio, only 24 hours after two clinics in Cincinnati were set afire by arsonists and 12 hours after a bomb threat emptied another clinic in Toledo (*The New York Times*, 1986:6).

The third type of arson—vandalism—usually is associated with youths who set fires in schools, automobiles, and vacant buildings. The alleged motive is excitement, because youths "do not have anything exciting to do" (Boudreau *et al.*, 1977:19). Vacant buildings often serve as playgrounds for inner-city youths, some of whom may rationalize that a fire in such a building will not hurt anyone. Watching the building burn, as well as the Fire Department extinguishing it, can be "exciting" to these youth. Thus, most vandalism fires occur shortly after

"Arson-for-profit" results in more property damage and lives lost and injured than other types of arson.

3 p.m., when children are generally dismissed from school (Jacobson, 1985:50). It is estimated that approximately 35 percent of all arson fires are the result of vandals (NILECJ, 1980:9).

Finally, the most costly arson—in terms of property damaged and lives lost and injured—results from profit-making ventures. Forty percent of all arsons may be the result of "arson-for-profit" (*ibid.*). There are several ways individuals can profit from arson: "stop-loss" arson—when businesses on the verge of great financial loss or even financial ruin "sell" the business to an insurance company by setting it ablaze to obtain the coverage proceeds; "property improvement or rehabilitation" arson—where property owners improve a structure or replace deteriorating furnishings from the proceeds of small fire insurance claims; "elimination of competition" arson—where a business eliminates its competition by setting it afire; and "extortion, coercion, and intimidation" arson—where criminal syndicates use the threat of arson to extort money from businesses (Jacobson, 1985:37–45). However, arguably the most lucrative and destructive form of arson-for-profit occurs when individuals purchase a particular property—usually in an economically depressed area of a city—and insure the property for more than its value. By setting the property ablaze, the owner can reap a substantial profit.

Brady's (1983) study of arson concentrated on this latter type of arson-for-profit. His research goes considerably beyond an examination of individuals, connecting arson-for-profit to major banks and criminal syndicates in one particular city, Boston. Brady (*ibid.*:6–9) shows first that there was, in the late 1970s and early 1980s, a pattern to the fires occurring in Boston—arson being demographically concentrated within certain poor Boston neighborhoods, such as Roxbury, North Dorchester, East Boston, and Jamaica Plain. Within these economically depressed areas, arson was more common in buildings owned by absentee landlords than in either owner-occupied tenements or public housing projects. Many of these privately owned buildings had been abandoned, and between 1978 and 1982 more than one-half of Boston's 3,000 arsons occurred in abandoned buildings.

Brady (*ibid.*:10) further shows that these buildings are not abandoned because of a "natural process of neighborhood evolution," but because of "discriminatory mortgage-lending policies of banks which deny credit to certain districts of the inner city in order to invest in more profitable suburban real estate." This latter practice is known as *redlining*, which devastates neighborhoods by forcing small businesses to close because they cannot secure bank loans. Moreover, landlords fail to repair their buildings, eventually abandoning them because property values decline drastically. Brady found that arson is specifically concentrated in these areas.

In addition to the foregoing, Brady (*ibid.*:11–12) presents convincing evidence that, because of redlining, banks actually foreclose on unpaid bank mortgages, resulting in their holding neglected and abandoned buildings. Clearly, this appears to represent a great financial loss for the bank. Not so, as Brady (*ibid.*:11) explains:

> Enter the organized crime racketeers. They offer to buy the "problem buildings," often at a price far greater than true market value, on condition that the bank write out a new mortgage for close to the full purchase price, and sometimes more, to cover the cost of "renovation." Thus, the racketeers acquire large numbers of properties with little investment of their own capital. In some cases they can further increase their "leverage" by arranging second, third or fourth mortgages whose total value far exceeds the original inflated purchase price. Backed by mortgages from a major bank, it is fairly simple to arrange insurance coverage for the buildings at a level well above the total value of the mortgages.

The over-mortgaged and over-insured property is then set fire by criminal syndicate figures or individuals who earn a living as professional "torches." Not only do criminal syndicates gain, but so do banks, as potential losses represented by foreclosure are actually turned into profit because "the new mortgage paid by the insurance company greatly exceeds the old bad debt assumed under foreclosure" (*ibid*).

An excellent example of the comfortable relationship between banks and criminal syndicates is the case of the South Boston Savings Bank (*ibid.*:11–12). From 1970 to 1977 the bank foreclosed on 76 properties, 39 of these suffering 79 fires, or almost two fires per property. In 1978 it was discovered that some of the most notorious Boston arsonists were clients of the bank. Brady (*ibid.*:12) lists these shady figures as follows:

Caroll St. Germaine, convicted arsonist and murderer (over $500,000 to 1978); Russell Tardanico, convicted arsonist (over $730,000 in 16 mortgages to 1982); George Lincoln, confessed "torch" and arsonist who turned "state's witness" in exchange for immunity in a 1978–1979 Boston arson conspiracy trial (over $150,000 in five mortgages in 1978); Nicholas Shaheen, convicted arsonist (over $100,000 in five mortgages to 1978).

Brady's research shows the extent of arson-for-profit and how different types of crime are actually linked together. In the case of arson, banks (corporate crime) are connected to racketeers (criminal syndicates) who in turn are linked to "torches" (property crime). Indeed, we cannot understand the crime of arson— and many other crimes for that matter—without analyzing such connections.

More recently, Jacobson and Kasinitz (1986) have described the conviction of two South Bronx insurance brokers and landlords. The two brokers, Bernard Gold and Eugene Bell, together with several hired "torches" and insurance adjusters, were convicted in 1985 of federal conspiracy charges related to 50 fires in 17 buildings in the South Bronx. Gold and his associates purchased buildings from banks and insurance companies for as little as $2,500, yet insured these buildings through other companies—either based in another state or another country, such as Lloyd's of London—for between $200,000 and $500,000. What this particular case shows, according to Jacobson and Kasinitz (*ibid.*:512), is the relationship between insurance companies and arson, and

> how simple it can be to insure buildings for vastly more than they are worth, and how little attention some insurers pay to the condition of the properties they insure or to the track records of the landlords with whom they do business. Finally, it reminds us that many reputable insurance companies are reluctant to undertake their own investigations of suspicious fires or to help law enforcement agencies pursue criminal charges.

Fraud

In Chapter 7.1 and 7.2 we discuss occupational fraud and corporate financial fraud; here we focus on nonoccupationally related frauds such as check and credit-card fraud and defrauding the government. We begin with an examination of the former.

The crimes thus far analyzed—interpersonal crimes of violence and property crimes such as robbery and burglary—are clearly recognizable as crimes by an offender against a victim. In contrast, *check fraud*—deliberately deceiving someone for personal gain by producing a counterfeit or forged check—has "little in the criminal act or the interaction between the check passer and the person cashing the check to identify it as a crime" (Lemert, 1967:101). In other words, check fraud is not at the time of its commission easily recognizable as a crime. Indeed, this holds true for all forms of fraud discussed in this section; it is not until sometime later that the event is determined to be a crime.

Individuals can even fool themselves by engaging in check fraud without knowing it. For instance, if someone continually writes checks against his or her account at a time when that account does not hold sufficient funds to cover the checks, the checks normally are returned "Nonsufficient Funds" (NSF)— the individual could be prosecuted for fraud. Other forms of check fraud include altering checks, forging someone else's personal checks, producing counterfeit personal and payroll checks, stealing government checks (checks rendering a salary, tax refund, pension, welfare allotment, and/or veteran benefit), and forging a signature.

Two recent cases of check fraud—both reported in *The Washington Post*— help illustrate the different types of this crime. In the first case a Bronx delicatessen owner fraudulently endorsed two-party welfare hotel checks, profiting as much as $1 million. The welfare checks were made payable to both a welfare hotel and to the welfare recipients for the purpose of paying for shelter. In order to prevent recipients from cashing the checks and simply retaining the monies the welfare agency required a hotel endorsement. The delicatessen owner fraudulently endorsed the checks in the name of the hotel, and then deposited the checks in his own bank account. He then returned some cash to the recipients, usually about one-third the face value of each check (Barron, 1987:B3).

The second case concerned a father and son involved in a fraudulent check scheme. The two traveled together around the country in a van, breaking into real-estate firms, automobile dealerships, and other commercial businesses for the purpose of stealing bank payroll checks. The two would "hit up" seven businesses per day, netting $2,000 each day for their efforts. When the two were arrested, they were found with phony identification cards, blank Social Security cards, blank birth certificates, a payroll check-writing machine, and a laminating machine (Yorke, 1987:A18).

It is difficult to know how much check fraud exists in the United States. Our best estimate comes from the Treasury Department in its annual report of investigative activity, indicating that it investigated 116,645 check forgery cases in 1987, closing 109,026 of them (Department of Treasury, 1988:1). However, as with other government statistics, the Treasury Department's official data do not accurately represent the amount of check fraud in the United States. We can conservatively assume that the amount of check fraud is at least two to three times higher than the Treasury Department's figure.

Lemert's (1967:99–134) classic study of "naive" and "systematic" check forgery remains the most extensive examination of check fraud. Naive check forgers are amateurs who commit the crime only when they have an urgent need for money and who are unfamiliar with "criminal techniques" (*ibid.*:102– 105). The naive check forger, Lemert found, ordinarily has completed more years of school than the general population and works in a variety of clerical, skilled, and professional occupations. Lemert also established that a majority of naive check forgers reside in the community in which their crimes are committed.

Systematic check forgers (*ibid.*:109–113) view themselves as forgers, regularly employ a special technique to pass bad checks, and organize their lives around check fraud. Some systematic check forgers view their fraud as a "regular business," but most do not, engaging in it for the alleged "fast and luxurious" life (*ibid.*:110). These forgers give special attention to such details as banking hours and the best places to present checks; yet, according to Lemert, such details serve only as "guides" for the fraud. Moreover, systematic check forgers are less likely than other professional property offenders to use the "fix" because they simply have "too many bad checks outstanding and too many victims to mollify by offering restitution" (*ibid.*111). The systematic check forger is different from other professional property offenders in another way. According to Lemert, check forgery requires neither a high degree of technical skill nor a long learning "apprenticeship"; you simply "learn as you go." However, systematic check forgery does require the ability to impersonate someone else and, therefore, success is based on development of expertise in assuming fictitious roles. Finally, although the systematic check forger tends to be migratory (like other professional property offenders), most tend to work alone, avoiding contact with a network of illegitimate and legitimate people. Lemert (*ibid.*:112–113) found that some systematic check forgers work in "check passing gangs" and a few "contract out" their services, yet the majority operate on a solitary basis. These forgers manufacture or steal checks (usually personal or payroll checks), and then work alone to pass them illegally.

Lemert's discussion of check fraud identified fraudsters as migratory isolates; Tremblay (1986) found fraudsters working together in groups. Tremblay investigated check frauds and credit-card frauds (defined as the unauthorized use of a credit card for personal gain by someone other than the cardholder) related to a "check guarantee program" of a major bank, where all credit cardholders—whether customers of the bank or not—could withdraw $500 a day from any domestic branch by check if they presented their credit card to guarantee the transaction. The bank saw this program as a marketing opportunity, encouraging regular customers to use its resources while simultaneously attracting noncustomers. However, it was precisely at the introduction of this program that a wave of check and credit-card frauds began.

According to Tremblay (*ibid.*:238–241), three major types of fraud occurred as a result of this program: check guarantee fraud, purchase credit-card fraud, and purchase check fraud. The first, check guarantee fraud, occurs when individuals "ride" a stolen credit card—or several cards—by cashing checks (also stolen) in numerous bank branches in the shortest possible time. The term *ride* refers to the total number of banks visited by fraudsters with just one credit card; "the take" is the total amount of cash withdrawals per ride. In this case, an average ride would yield a take of approximately $6,000 whereas particularly successful rides increased the take to as much as $15,000 (*ibid.*:242). The other types of fraud discussed by Tremblay—purchase check and purchase credit-card fraud—simply entailed using stolen checks and credit cards to purchase goods from retail stores.

The overall network of fraud consisted of thieves (people who stole the checks and cards), riders (people who used the checks and cards in banks and stores), and fences (who bought the fraudulently obtained merchandise). Tremblay (*ibid.*) found that this overall scheme could not have operated without:

▲— Access to a stable supply of stolen checks, credit cards, and other identification items, such as stolen drivers' licenses.

▲— Thieves available to obtain the checks, cards, and "identification kits." Men who frequented prostitutes had their wallets stolen by them, who then sold the stolen cards to the fraudsters. Other targets were hospital employees and sports club members, because they remove their clothes during their work and leisure routines.

▲— False bank accounts as a means for obtaining personalized checks, which were then fraudulently used.

▲— Access to a complex fencing network for purchase check and purchase credit-card frauds.

Tremblay's research is important because it challenges the assumption that check fraud—and also credit card fraud—is committed in isolation. Tremblay emphasizes the links between different criminal practices and illicit markets. Indeed, other research indicates that large organized schemes account for one-half the total dollar loss due to credit card fraud (Caminer, 1985:748).

The government is also a potential victim of fraudsters. It is estimated that the federal government loses as much as $70 billion a year to fraud (Chemerinsky, 1981:1482). One reason for such a high figure is that defrauding the government is actually limitless because of the vast number and variety of government programs. To fraudsters, the federal government is a bottomless financial pit. As one federal study pointed out, the "involvement of so much money, and so many people and institutions makes the federal programs vulnerable to fraud" (cited in *ibid.*:1484). For example, according to *The Washington Post*, in one program—Aid to Families with Dependent Children (AFDC)—the government lost $1.1 billion in 1986 because of overpayments or because of payments to ineligible individuals (Rich, 1988:A15). Although some of this loss is due to welfare agency error, the vast majority has been found to result from either client error or fraud (Greenberg *et al.*, 1986:17–18). However, Wolfe and Greenberg (1986:453) reported in their study of welfare fraud a "modest fraud rate of 2 to 4 percent of the combined AFDC and Food Stamps caseload." In other words, 96 to 98 percent of AFDC and Food Stamp recipients do *not* engage in fraud. The small percentage who engage in welfare fraud employ a variety of methods that include (Chemerinsky, 1981:1485–1487):

▲— misrepresenting eligibility for the welfare program

▲— falsifying qualifying information, such as income, birth date, Social Security number, and marital status

▲— creating "ghost eligibles," or fictitious people who are awarded benefits

Income-tax fraud, however, is probably the most prevalent form of defrauding the government. Cheating on one's income tax is made possible in the United States because of:

1. the complexity of the tax codes
2. the seemingly infinite number of deductible expenses
3. the Internal Revenue Service's (IRS) reliance on a system in which taxpayers calculate their own tax bill
4. the small number of returns actually scrutinized by the IRS (Mattera, 1985:9)

Throughout the 1980s individuals seemed increasingly willing to violate income-tax laws. For example, 75 percent of taxpayers audited in 1986 had penalties imposed on them, up from 62 percent in 1980 (Scherschel, 1987:63).

Simon and Witte (1982:7–15) have identified four major forms of tax fraud. The first, "underreported wages of tax filers," refers to income earned in off-the-books activity. An example is working a second job—for which earnings are paid in cash—but filing an income-tax return only for wages earned from the first job. Another example concerns the many workers who arrange with their employer to report only a certain amount of their wages; therefore, the "portion reported allows the individual to qualify for social security, unemployment, and similar benefits, while taxes and social insurance payments are avoided on the unreported portion" (*ibid.*:7). By operating on a cash-for-labor basis, employee *and* employers avoid paying taxes because there is no record of earnings. This operation occurs in the second type of tax fraud as well—"unreported wages for nonfilers" (*ibid.*:9)—wherein people earn wages and salaries in a variety of ways, but file no income-tax return for *any* portion of it. This completely off-the-books employment is not uncommon among restaurant and construction workers, as well as among providers of personal services, such as house painters and appliance repair persons. The third type of tax fraud discussed by Simon and Witte (*ibid.*:10) is "underreported income of the self-employed." Much income earned by the self-employed—from carpenters to small businesses and independent professionals—is underreported to the IRS. In fact, some businesses and professionals have been found to "use double sets of books, fake invoices, deduct fictitious expenses, and conceal assets by placing them in the names of friends, relatives, and shell corporations" (*ibid.*:10). Finally, the fourth type of tax fraud is "income of the self-employed who do not file" (*ibid.*:12). This refers to self-employed individuals—such as carpenters and independent professionals, as well as some small business persons—who file no tax return at all. However, this type of tax fraud is arguably not very prevalent for small businesses, because "fixed business operations give too much exposure to the IRS to make it safe to entirely fail to file tax returns" (*ibid.*). Thus, businesses who cheat more commonly underreport income on their tax return.

Not just citizens living within the U.S. boundaries engage in tax fraud. According to *The Washington Post*, U.S. citizens living abroad cheat on their taxes to as much as $2 *billion* a year, and as many as 60 pecent of them file no income-tax return at all (Rowe, 1986:G1).

5.3 _____   ## THE DEBATE ON PROFESSIONAL PROPERTY CRIME

Throughout this chapter we have discussed professional property offenders in almost every crime examined—from robbery to fraud. In our discussion of robbery, in particular, we cited some evidence suggesting that fewer and fewer professional robberies are occurring, bank robberies in particular becoming more and more the alleged province of opportunists. However, for other property crimes we have presented evidence that professionals continue to prosper. This leads to an important and controversial question: Is the extent of professional property crime diminishing? Some criminologists believe it is; others do not. Consider next some views on this topic.

The Decline of Professional Property Crime

Inciardi (1975:76–82) answers the preceding question in the affirmative, maintaining that professional property crime began to decline in the 1940s. Assuming that a professional criminal behavior system maintained itself for centuries, Inciardi contends that with the emergence of important 20th-century technological advances in the machinery of social control, professional crime began to decline and may now face extinction. Advances in police technology—such as fingerprinting, telecommunications, and vehicle surveillance—increased the probability of detection and apprehension of professional criminals. Moreover, "changes in national and local statutes also proved to be detrimental to the professional criminal," as did rigid enforcement of drug laws, resulting "in long-term incarcerations for many" (*ibid.*:81). Finally, according to Inciardi (*ibid.*), "changes within the bureaucratic structure of many police and court systems made the fixing of cases more difficult."

Thus, the combined effect of these factors has reduced the number of professional property offenders and has weakened the overall stability of the "profession," making it increasingly difficult for new recruits to emerge. For Inciardi (*ibid.*:82), then, professional property crime "will continue to atrophy until its more unique qualities become only references within the history of crime."

The Changing Nature of Professional Property Crime

Others, however, have different opinions about professional property crime. Staats (1977:61–62), for example, argues that changes in opportunities may alter professional criminal activities. Like legitimate behavior, criminal behavior responds to available opportunities and social conditions; therefore, rather than simply declining in prevalence, professional criminal activity may be responding to the supply and demand for illegal goods and services and new developments in technology. Staats uses the examples of safecracking and fraud to make his point. He argues that safecracking has declined because of increased police surveillance, technological advances in safe design, and an increase in credit transactions. Because of these developments, safecracking is not only more difficult to perform and complete successfully, it is also less profitable than it was. Nevertheless, because cash transactions are decreasing, we can anticipate, Staats argues, professional property offenders moving more and more into check and credit-card fraud. Consequently, for Staats, professional property crime most likely responds to changing social conditions, rather than simply declining.

Similarly, Chambliss (1984:142–151) argues that sociologists "every few years" invariably assert that "like the cowboy and the hangman," the professional property offender is about to become extinct. Yet, Chambliss (*ibid.*:143) points out, professional property offenders keep turning up, and

> new types of theft are developed. New ways of opening safes emerge. When banks transfer their money to Brinks Armored Car Service then the thieves work out ways of robbing the armored cars. . . . The overwhelming evidence is that professional theft is no more dead today than it ever has been. There have always been a small cadre of devotees who consider themselves professional thieves, who plan their capers carefully, and who develop their craft through apprenticeship and with planning.

Thus, for Chambliss as with Staats, it is the rapidly changing nature of professional property crime that leads people to assume it is vanishing.

In addition, Chambliss (*ibid.*:143) points out that professional property offenders serve a useful service to society, and as long as this service remains, so will professional property crime. First, according to Chambliss, professional property offenders provide a service to the legal order. Chambliss opposes Inciardi's argument that the police have developed an adversarial posture toward professional crime and that this is one reason for its alleged decline. Chambliss argues that professional property offenders actually help the police perform their duties more efficiently and less strenuously than they otherwise could. Such professional thieves provide the police and prosecution with information about and admit to crimes that would otherwise go unresolved. Consequently, they help the police to improve clearance records. In return, the professional property offender receives a "license to steal." For Chambliss, a symbiotic relationship exists between professional property offenders and the actors in the legal system.

Professional property offenders, Chambliss argues, are also valuable to other groups—to insurance companies that sell theft insurance and to safe manufacturers that sell safes. Echoing some earlier remarks by Karl Marx, Chambliss (*ibid.*:146) goes on to point out that the professional thief

> makes jobs not only for people who make the safes he opens but for insurance companies. He makes jobs for lawyers, policemen, social workers, judges, prosecuting attorneys and, not the least of all, professors who

write books about thieves, students who study them (and thereby stay a little longer from the already overly populated labor market), book publishers, book salesmen. Indeed, an entire industry thrives on the work of the thieves. And the thief contributes to technological advance: safes are made safer, locks are made more secure, innovations occur in the handling of money (notice the armored car and the entire industry that has grown up around this), ingenious devices are invented for the protection of stores, factories and homes.

Finally, Chambliss (*ibid*.:148–149) argues that professional property offenders help to maintain the established social order. They do this by hindering lower-class youth from overthrowing the economic and political relations within society. Instead, lower-class youth find a place in capitalist social relations, "and their place is likely to be one for which the model of the thief is a useful vision" (*ibid*.:149). If such youth have the ability and luck, they become professional property offenders; otherwise they resort to petty criminality and/or drug addiction. As Chambliss (*ibid*.:149) concludes, the vision of the professional property offender for the lower-class youth is "like the vision of the president of a corporation," because it provides a "useful image in the makeup of the world of the growing child, and it helps to maintain at least acquiescence if not outright support for things as they presently exist."

REVIEW

This chapter examined seven different types of property crimes: robbery, burglary, larceny, motor vehicle theft, fencing, arson, and fraud. These property crimes are different from crimes of interpersonal violence in certain ways:

1. They occur much more frequently.

2. Offender and victim are usually strangers.

3. In many cases no direct interaction occurs between offender and victim.

4. In some cases—like most frauds—it is not immediately apparent that a crime has been committed.

Stealing and Dealing

1. Robbery is a unique property crime involving direct interaction between offender and victim. It also entails both the threatened or actual use of physical violence and property loss to the victim.

2. Because robbery differs from crimes of interpersonal violence in significant sociological ways, we label it a property crime.

3. Strong-arm robbery is considerably more dangerous than armed robbery.

4. Robbery involves an interaction between offender and victim.

5. Robbery can be classified both in terms of incidents and offenders. The two major types of robbery offenders are professionals and opportunists.

6. Burglars can be classified as professionals and amateurs.

7. One type of larceny—shoplifting—has received the most attention by sociologists.

8. Forty percent of people have shoplifted at some time, creating tremendous economic loss to society.

9. There are two major types of shoplifters, boosters (professionals) and snitches (amateurs).

10. Most sociologists who studied motor vehicle theft have concentrated on automobile theft.

11. Individuals steal automobiles for joyriding, short- and long-term transportation, commission of another crime, and for profit.

12. Fencing is the buying and selling of stolen goods, and is conducted by both amateurs and professionals.

13. The majority of amateur fences sell their goods to relatives, friends, and acquaintances—not for purposes of economic gain, but to enhance established relationships.

14. Most professional fences have strong ties to the legitimate business community and are part of a loosely structured, yet mutually supportive, network of individuals involved in acquiring and distributing stolen property.

15. This network consists of thieves, fences, criminal justice personnel, criminal syndicates, goods transporters, and buyers.

Damage and Deception

1. Arson causes more injury, death, and property loss than any other of the *UCR Index* offenses.

2. There are four major types of arson: crime concealment, revenge, vandalism, and profit.

3. The most costly type of arson—in terms of property damage and lives lost and injured—results from profit-making ventures.

4. Check fraud can consist of drawing checks on insufficient funds in a checking account, forging someone else's personal check, producing counterfeit personal and payroll checks, altering payroll checks, and stealing government checks and forging a signature.

5. Two major types of check fraud are naive forgers (amateurs) and systematic forgers (professionals).

6. Systematic forgers differ from other professional property offenders in significant ways.

7. Check and credit-card fraudsters may work alone or in groups.

8. Federal welfare programs and the Internal Revenue Service are the victims of substantial fraud.

Professional Property Crime

1. Sociologists disagree on whether professional property crime is diminishing.

2. Some criminologists argue that professional property crime began to decline in the 1940s and all evidence suggests a demise of this "profession."

3. Other criminologists argue that social conditions and technological developments alter the opportunities for, not necessarily the amount of, professional criminal activities.

QUESTIONS FOR CLASS DISCUSSION

1. Identify and discuss how property crimes differ from crimes of interpersonal violence.

2. This textbook argues that robbery is a property crime. Examine that assessment of this crime and present an argument for or against its conclusion.

3. What is the fencing network?

4. Is professional property crime increasing, decreasing, or simply changing? Explain your answer in detail.

RECOMMENDED READINGS

Brady, James (1983). "Arson, Urban Economy, and Organized Crime: The Case of Boston," *Social Problems* 31:1–27. This article is a well-researched and shocking account of arson-for-profit in the city of Boston.

Cameron, Mary Owen (1964). *The Booster and the Snitch*. New York: Free Press. The classic study of shoplifting, which still holds much relevance today.

Conklin, John (1972). *Robbery and the Criminal Justice System*. New York: Lippin-cott. The first major and now classic work on the crime of robbery.

Henry, Stuart (1976). "The Other Side of the Fence," *Sociological Review* 24:793–806. This article is a thorough analysis and thought-provoking discussion of the amateur fence.

King, Harry and William J. Chambliss (1984). *Harry King: A Professional Thief's Journey*. New York: John Wiley and Sons. This book gives an eye-opening account of the professional burglar and an important commentary on the future of professional property crime.

Klemke, Lloyd W. (1992) *The Sociology of Shoplifting: Boosters and Snitches Today.* Westport, CN: Praeger. An update on shoplifting data and the application of criminological theories to that data.

Lemert, Edwin M. (1967). *Human Deviance, Social Problems, and Social Control.* Englewood Cliffs, NJ: Prentice-Hall. Contains Lemert's classic study of naive and systematic check forgery.

Mattera, Philip (1985). *Off the Books.* New York: St. Martin's. This book discusses off-the-books activity and the emergence of the underground economy.

McCaghy, Charles H., Peggy C. Giordano, and Trudy Knicely Henson (1977). "Auto Theft: Offender and Offense Characteristics," *Criminology* 15:367–385. Though somewhat outdated, this article remains a credible examination of automobile theft.

Staats, Gregory R. (1977). "Changing Conceptualizations of Professional Criminals: Implications for Criminology Theory," *Criminology* 15:49–65. A review of the changing conceptions—at least since Sutherland—of sociologists concerning professional crime.

Steffensmeier, Darrell J. (1986). *The Fence: In the Shadow of Two Worlds.* Totowa, NJ: Rowman and Littlefield. The most rigorous account of fencing operations ever published.

CHAPTER 6

PUBLIC-ORDER CRIME

Preview

Chapter 6 introduces:

☞ what sociologists mean by public-order crimes.
☞ the different types of public-order crimes.
☞ the nature and extent of public-order crimes.
☞ different perspectives on whether public-order crimes are harmful and victimize individuals and/or society.

Key Terms

abortion	lottery
complaintless crimes	pari-mutuel betting
decriminalization	prostitution
legalization	victimless crimes

In *Chapter 4 we discussed crimes of interpersonal violence and in Chapter 5 we examined property crime. Both of these types of crime encompass an **offender** and a **victim,** and it is relatively easy to ascertain that **harm** has occurred. In public-order crime—such as gambling, drug abuse, abortion, prostitution, and pornography—it is unclear whether an offender or a victim even exists, or whether a harm has occurred. In fact, it is debatable whether such activity should be identified as crimes.*

*Some criminologists argue that **victimization** is a critical element of these activities. They point, for instance, to prostitutes as the harmed victims of prostitution, women as the harmed victims of pornography, and drug addicts as the harmed victims of illegal drug use. As Victoria Swigert (1984:97) suggests, "Whether or not such persons consent, their lives are reduced; hence, they are the victims of these activities."*

*Ten years earlier than Swigert, Edwin Schur (1974:6) argued that to **outsiders** a harm may seem to have occurred, yet to **insiders** (or participants) no harm was perpetrated and, therefore, no offender or victim exists. Indeed, as Schur (ibid.) explains, these are for him "victimless crimes":*

> Victimless crimes are created when we attempt to ban through criminal legislation the exchange between willing partners of strongly desired goods and services. The "offense" in such a situation, then, consists of a consensual transaction—one person gives or sells another person something he or she wants.

*Realizing that those directly involved in public-order crimes do not feel harmed or victimized and, therefore, do not **report** such behavior to the police, Schur (1984:183) eventually termed these behaviors "complaintless crimes."*

Others do not see victimization of individuals as the important issue, arguing that the purpose of public-order laws is to legitimate a certain version of morality. Once again, Swigert (1984:97) articulates this position:

> Shared morals and ethics bind individuals to one another. Without these bonds, society would disintegrate. A legally enforced morality, therefore, is a necessary cost of human association.

*According to this position, the purpose of public-order laws is to maintain a public **moral** order. Those who violate these laws, it is asserted, simply harm the overall social order. This position, however, fails to acknowledge that the state selectively enforces a certain type of morality. Put differently, only certain types of behavior are deemed immoral and, therefore, criminalized by the state. For example, the state "sweeps" up streetwalkers while allowing "call girls" to conduct their trade. Thus, one type of prostitution is considered immoral; another type is not.*

In this chapter we discuss a variety of issues regarding how public-order "crimes" selectively enforce morality, and different arguments concerning harm and victimization. Although the number of public-order crimes is vast, we limit ourselves to examine five: gambling, drug use/abuse, abortion, prostitution, and pornography.

6.1 _____ GAMBLING

Gambling is a classic public-order crime. We analyze a variety of issues surrounding gambling, with particular attention directed at the appropriateness/inappropriateness of the victimless crime concept.

In Chapter 8.2 we discuss *illegal* gambling and its relationship to criminal syndicates; our concern here is legal or *commercial* gambling, which takes such forms as state-regulated lotteries, casinos, and horse racing.

Perspectives on Gambling

Gambling has existed in a variety of forms throughout U.S. history. Nevertheless, individuals and groups have consistently voiced opposition to gambling. Some label it immoral behavior, arguing that gambling debases individual responsibility by contributing to an ideology that holds it acceptable to obtain something without working for it. Gambling allegedly undermines the ethic that "hard work for honest pay" is the appropriate route to success. For example, one religious group in the United States opposes gambling on three grounds (cited in Bell, 1976:178):

> (1) It nourishes a desire for gain without a labor of production. (2) It nourishes a desire for excitement as an escape from the realities of life, a similar motive to that of the drug addict or alcoholic. (3) It nourishes an unwholesome competitive spirit. . . . Gambling is antisocial and economically indefensible. It is pleasure obtained at the expense of another. It seeks to take for self that which belongs to another, without labor or compensation.

This view of gambling as an immoral and corruptible practice has been voiced since the 1700s. As Thomas Jefferson (cited in Rosecrance, 1988:18) once stated: "Gaming corrupts our disposition and teaches us a habit of hostility against all mankind."

Others have, not surprisingly, disagreed with the preceding views. Those who argue that gambling is moral behavior declare that positive values are promoted by gambling (such as "the competitive spirit") and that gambling is really no different from other games and forms of play (Smith and Abt, 1984:122–132). Still others argue that outlawing gambling actually creates other social problems, such as criminal syndicates, and all the "immoral" difficulties associated with it. Libertarians assert we all have the right to engage in any activity as long as that activity does not infringe on the rights of others. Inasmuch as gambling is seen by gamblers as a harmless consensual moral activity, they argue that gambling should be made available to everyone.

Still others have argued that a critical issue is ignored in that debate. Bedau (1974:100), for example, points to the fact that the state "allows persons to gamble with their money, so long as they spend it on risky ventures (the stock market)," but that, at the same time, the state "prohibits them if they wish to

TABLE 6-1 States with Legalized Gambling as of 1988

STATE OR DISTRICT	BINGO	HORSE RACING	LOTTERIES	DOG RACING	JAI ALAI	SPORTS BETTING	OFFTRACK BETTING	CASINOS
Alabama	x	x	. . .	x	. . .	. . .	. . .	. . .
Alaska	x	. . .	. . .	. . .	. . .	. . .	. . .	. . .
Arizona	x	x	x	x				
Arkansas	. . .	x	. . .	x	. . .	. . .	. . .	. . .
California	x	x	x	. . .	. . .	. . .	. . .	. . .
Colorado	x	x	x	x	. . .	. . .	. . .	. . .
Connecticut	x	x	x	x	x	. . .	x	. . .
Delaware	x	x	x	. . .	. . .	. . .	. . .	. . .
Florida	x	x	x	x	x	. . .	. . .	. . .
Georgia	x	. . .	. . .	. . .	. . .	. . .	. . .	. . .
Hawaii	. . .	. . .	. . .	. . .	. . .	. . .	. . .	. . .
Idaho	. . .	x	x	. . .	. . .	. . .	. . .	. . .
Illinois	x	x	x	. . .	. . .	. . .	. . .	. . .
Indiana	. . .	. . .	. . .	. . .	. . .	. . .	. . .	. . .
Iowa	x	x	x	x	. . .	. . .	. . .	. . .
Kansas	x	. . .	x	. . .	. . .	. . .	. . .	. . .
Kentucky	. . .	x	. . .	. . .	. . .	. . .	. . .	. . .
Louisiana	x	x	. . .	. . .	. . .	. . .	. . .	. . .
Maine	x	x	x	. . .	. . .	. . .	. . .	. . .
Maryland	x	x	x	. . .	. . .	. . .	. . .	. . .
Massachusetts	x	x	x	x	. . .	. . .	. . .	. . .
Michigan	x	x	x	. . .	. . .	. . .	. . .	. . .
Minnesota	x	x	. . .	. . .	. . .	. . .	. . .	. . .
Mississippi	. . .	. . .	. . .	. . .	. . .	. . .	. . .	. . .
Missouri	x	x	x	. . .	. . .	. . .	. . .	. . .
Montana	x	x	x	. . .	. . .	. . .	. . .	. . .
Nebraska	x	x	. . .	. . .	. . .	. . .	. . .	. . .
Nevada	x	x	. . .	x	x	x	x	x
New Hampshire	x	x	x	x	. . .	. . .	. . .	. . .
New Jersey	x	x	x	. . .	. . .	. . .	. . .	x
New Mexico	x	x	. . .	. . .	. . .	. . .	. . .	. . .
New York	x	x	x	. . .	. . .	. . .	x	. . .
North Carolina	x	. . .	. . .	. . .	. . .	. . .	. . .	. . .
North Dakota	x	. . .	. . .	. . .	. . .	. . .	. . .	x*
Ohio	x	x	x	. . .	. . .	. . .	. . .	. . .
Oklahoma	x	x	. . .	. . . /	. . .	. . .	. . .	. . .
Oregon	x	x	x	x	. . .	. . .	. . .	. . .
Pennsylvania	x	x	x	. . .	. . .	. . .	. . .	. . .
Rhode Island	x	x	x	x	x	. . .	. . .	. . .
South Carolina	x	. . .	. . .	. . .	. . .	. . .	. . .	. . .
South Dakota	x	x	x	x	. . .	. . .	. . .	. . .
Tennessee	x	x	. . .	. . .	. . .	. . .	. . .	. . .
Texas	x	. . .	. . .	. . .	. . .	. . .	. . .	. . .
Utah	. . .	. . .	. . .	. . .	. . .	. . .	. . .	. . .
Vermont	x	x	x	x	. . .	. . .	. . .	. . .
Virginia	x	. . .	x	. . .	. . .	. . .	. . .	. . .

continued

**TABLE
6-1**   **States with Legalized Gambling as of 1988** *continued*

STATE OR DISTRICT	BINGO	HORSE RACING	LOTTERIES	DOG RACING	JAI ALAI	SPORTS BETTING	OFFTRACK BETTING	CASINOS
Washington	x	x	x	. . .	. . .	. . .	. . .	. . .
West Virginia	x	x	x	x	. . .	. . .	. . .	. . .
Wisconsin	x	x	x	. . .	. . .	. . .	. . .	. . .
Wyoming	x	x	. . .	. . .	. . .	. . .	. . .	. . .
District of Columbia	x	. . .	x	. . .	. . .	. . .	. . .	. . .

*North Dakota allows low-stakes casino betting (maximum bets $2), with proceeds going to charity.

Source: Rosecrance, 1988, pp. 4–5.

spend it on others (the numbers pool)." What Bedau identifies here is the clear and contradictory nature of the enforcement of morality by the state. Thus, those who assert that gambling is immoral, yet also view risky ventures in the stock market as moral, are arguing on shaky ground.

Lotteries, Casinos, and Pari-Mutuel Betting

Today, gambling seems to enjoy wide acceptance in the U.S. Table 6-1 lists the states that have legalized gambling. As of 1988, 46 states allowed some type of legal gambling and only four states—Hawaii, Indiana, Mississippi, and Utah—outlawed all forms of gambling. Approximately 60 percent of the population gamble in one form or another every year, and this figure is most likely increasing (Eadington and Frey, 1984:9). Moreover, in excess of $208 billion was wagered in 1988, over 85 percent attributable to state lotteries, casinos, and pari-mutuel betting (*Business Week*, 1989:114). We now consider each of these types of legal gambling.

A *lottery* is "a game in which chances to share in the distribution of prizes are determined by lot, or drawing" (Abt *et al.*, 1985:55). In most state lotteries, the participating individual buys a ticket ($1 to $5) in a weekly drawing, choosing six numbers. If those six numbers are chosen in the random selection, the individual wins. The attraction to participation is the possibility of winning a large amount of money (usually over $1 million) for a small investment. Over 100,000 retail establishments act as state-lottery ticket agents—newsstands, supermarkets, gasoline stations, restaurants, hotels, and so on—thus integrating lotteries into the neighborhood, where they become "part of the ordinary life" (*ibid.*:62–63). State lotteries are permitted for the purpose of raising revenues. In 1988 over $17 billion was wagered in state lotteries (*Business Week*, 1989:114).

Legal *casinos* operate in Nevada and Atlantic City, New Jersey. Casinos offer such gambling activities as poker, blackjack, craps, roulette, and slot machines. These games can be divided into "games of pure chance" and "games of mixed chance and skill" (Abt *et al.*, 1985:69–71). In games of pure chance—such as roulette, craps, and slot machines—the player cannot win over the long term,

The "wheel of fortune" (roulette wheel) in a legal gambling casino.

but can slow the rate of loss by choosing those bets that produce the smallest advantage to the casino. In games of mixed chance and skill (there are no games of "pure skill" in casinos)—such as blackjack and poker—both luck and talent are important factors in determining whether one wins or loses. Blackjack (a card game whose object is to accumulate cards with a total face count closer to 21 than those of the dealer) provides an example. Chance is a factor in blackjack because the succession of cards dealt is irregular, following no consistent pattern. However, skill also can play a role. Some blackjack players have developed the talent of "counting," a skill enabling the player to memorize each card previously dealt. The player thus acquires knowledge of what remains in the deck, can gamble accordingly, and subsequently show a profit. Some counters have been so successful that they have been barred from casinos (Sasuly, 1982:241–242).

Casinos provide the arena for the greatest number of wagers. They are privately owned and, therefore, generate revenues for the state in the form of taxes. Although most people gamble via lotteries for the dream of striking it rich with only a minimum investment, individuals also frequent casinos, where they have some control over the outcome. As one frequent casino gambler stated (cited in Rosecrance, 1988:82):

> I know exactly what to expect when I go into the clubs. The games never change, the place is so predictable. I decide when to play and how much to put down. Nobody forces me into anything. I can quit any time I want, just cash in my chips and take off. At the clubs I'm in charge. I call the shots.

Finally, *pari-mutuel betting* is a form of legal betting on races where the winners divide the total amount bet—after deducting management expenses—in proportion to the sum each winner wagered individually. Pari-mutuel betting includes horse racing, greyhound racing, and *jai alai*. Horse racing, the most popular of the three, provides betting on thoroughbred, standardbred, and quarterhorse racing. Such betting occurs at the race track itself or at offtrack locations (such as a casino or a betting shop) (Sasuly, 1982:243–244). Some argue that considerable knowledge is required to bet successfully on the horses because it is essential to "know" the horses, jockeys, trainers, and so on. Greyhound racing consists of greyhound dogs chasing a mechanical rabbit around a track and individuals—as with horse racing—betting on which dog will win (first), place (second), and show (third). *Jai alai* fields teams of athletes who employ a curved basket-like bat to play a ball off the floor and walls of a three-sided court. *Jai alai* bettors attempt to choose the top three teams (Abt *et al.*, 1985:83–100).

One major purpose of pari-mutuel betting is, as with lotteries and casinos, to generate state revenues. Pari-mutuel betting generated legal revenues of more than $17 billion in 1988 (*Business Week*, 1989:114).

6.2 ———— DRUG USE/ABUSE

Psychoactive drugs are capable of altering and impacting mental processes and states. There are numerous psychoactive drugs—alcohol, tobacco (nicotine), amphetamines, tranquilizers, marijuana, cocaine, heroin. Space does not permit a discussion of each. Accordingly, we limit our examination to:

1. a historical sketch of why the production, distribution, and use of marijuana, cocaine, and heroin have been criminalized

2. the extent, use, and nature of the foregoing three illegal drugs today

3. the addiction-crime connection

4. the decriminalization and legalization movement

History, Extent, and Nature of Drug Use/Abuse

Throughout much of the 1800s, U.S. residents purchased opiates (opium, morphine, and heroin) over the counters of pharmacies, groceries, and general stores, and obtained them from physicians for tranquilization and the relief of pain. In fact, opiates "were as freely accessible as aspirin is today" (Breacher, 1972:3–20).

In 1875, however, the city of San Francisco enacted an ordinance outlawing opium "dens" (smoking houses). Prior to that time Chinese laborers, working for low wages building U.S. railroads, were "free" to smoke opium as they pleased and their dens were not outlawed. With the onset of the 1875–1880 depression, Chinese laborers became an obstacle to white workers' economic survival. As a result, whites organized against the opium-smoking Chinese.

Consequently, the San Francisco ordinance—and several other antiopium laws enacted in other cities—legally repressed the Chinese, thus serving the interests of the white working class (Helmer, 1975:32). Eventually (in 1909) Congress enacted the Opium Exclusion Act, thereby prohibiting importation of opium and/or its derivatives, except for medical purposes.

Similarly, in the early 1900s cocaine was widely used in the U.S. (it was a major ingredient of Coca-Cola). Yet racist beliefs that African Americans were especially prone to cocaine use—causing them to be particularly violent, criminal, and dangerous—grew widespread at the turn of the century (*ibid.*:47). As David Musto (1973:7) argues, however:

> Evidence does not suggest that cocaine caused a crime wave but rather that anticipation of black rebellion inspired white alarm. Anecdotes often told of superhuman strength, cunning, and efficiency resulting from cocaine. One of the most terrifying beliefs about cocaine was that it actually improved pistol marksmanship. Another myth, that cocaine made blacks almost unaffected by mere .32 caliber bullets, is said to have caused southern police departments to switch to .38 caliber revolvers. These fantasies characterized white fear, not the reality of cocaine's effects, and gave one more reason for the repression of blacks.

In addition to white fear, this association of African Americans with cocaine use and the Chinese with opium use tended to mystify the actual drug users during the early 1900s. Most persons addicted to opiates and cocaine were not African Americans and Chinese—but white, middle-aged, middle-class women. Moreover, their addiction largely resulted from "medical problems" rather than, as today, from a search for euphoria and excitement; furthermore, it was as frequent in rural areas as in urban areas (Goode, 1984:218).

Eventually, because of such racist fears, the Harrison Narcotics Act of 1914 was enacted. This Act taxed those who produced, imported, dispensed, and sold opium and cocaine (and their derivatives, such as heroin), and required these individuals to register with the Treasury Department. The Act was aimed primarily at regulating and controlling the traffic in narcotics. However, a series of Supreme Court decisions between 1919 and 1922 also made it illegal for physicians to prescribe narcotics to patients. Thus, it was the combination of these events and the Act itself that, as Oakley Ray (1983:36) points out, took

> the first step toward making it impossible for addicts to obtain their drugs legally. The result was the development of an illicit drug trade that charged users up to 50 times more than the legal retail drug price.

And as Erich Goode (1984:221) adds, following passage of the Harrison Act and the Supreme Court decisions, the United States

> witnessed the dramatic emergence of a criminal class of addicts—a *criminal class that had not existed previously*. The link between addiction and

crime—the view that the addict was by definition a criminal—was forged. The law itself created a new class of criminals.

Not only was a criminal class of opiate and cocaine users created by the Harrison Act and the Supreme Court decisions (this new class was composed primarily of lower- and working-class individuals; middle-class women turned to legal drugs, such as tranquilizers [Goode, 1984:221]), but those who inhaled marijuana also became victims of the law. Although marijuana was smoked for years by U.S. citizens and was not considered a social problem, all of a sudden in the 1930s it began to receive considerable attention. As with the Chinese during the 1875–1880 depression, Mexicans during the Depression of the 1930s were seen as a threat to white survival because they worked for lower pay. As a result, whites began to link marijuana use with the "degenerate and violent Mexican," and called for legal intervention. Politicians, police, and prosecutors likewise "protested constantly to the federal government about the Mexicans' use of the weed" (Musto, 1973:220). Thus, by the summer of 1936 it became obvious that the only way to appease whites in the Southwest was to enact some type of federal legislation (*ibid.*:225). The result was the 1937 Marijuana Tax Act, which regulated importation and use of marijuana and, as its own product, created a criminal class of marijuana users (Helmer, 1975:79). The possession of marijuana became a criminal act in exactly the same way as possession of opiates and cocaine did—not because of a thorough examination of the effects of marijuana on human behavior, but because of racist attitudes toward minorities thought to be its typical users (Goode, 1981:231).

By 1951, not only was an illegal drug market and a drug-using/abusing subculture firmly established in the U.S., but Congress was well on its way to repressing that subculture. In that year it enacted the Boggs Amendment to the Harrison Act, which introduced a law-and-order-stance on illegal drug use (including marijuana) by instituting minimum mandatory sentences and prohibiting suspended sentences and probation for second offenses (Ray, 1983:38). In addition, numerous laws enacted since then have continued to increase existing controls over the production, distribution, possession, and sale of what had been judged to be illegal drugs. Thus, behavior previously considered legitimate and legal was subsequently outlawed, the end result being the creation of a new class of criminals.

Eventually, the Comprehensive Drug Abuse, Prevention, and Control Act of 1970 repealed, replaced, and/or updated all pre-existing laws dealing with "dangerous drugs." This law placed all drugs controlled by the Act under federal jurisdiction (by the Justice Department rather than the Treasury Department), regardless of involvement in interstate commerce. The law did not, however, "eliminate state regulations; it just makes clear that federal enforcement and prosecution is possible in any illegal activity involving the controlled drugs" (*ibid.*:40). In addition, the law determined once and for all which drugs in circulation were to be considered dangerous, as well as who would make up the criminal class of drug users. As Graham (1975:107–122) argues in his analysis

TABLE 6-2 Estimated Percentages of High School Seniors Who Reported Ever Having Used Drugs, 1980–1987

	1980	1981	1982	1983	1984	1985	1986	1987
Cocaine	15.7	16.5	16.0	16.2	16.1	17.3	16.9	15.2
Heroin	1.1	1.1	1.2	1.2	1.3	1.2	1.1	1.2
Marijuana and hashish	60.3	59.5	58.7	57.0	54.9	54.2	50.9	50.2
Hallucinogens[1]	15.6	15.3	14.3	13.6	12.3	12.1	11.9	10.6
Sedatives[2]	14.9	16.0	15.2	14.4	13.3	11.8	10.4	8.7
Stimulants[2,3]	[4]	[4]	27.9	26.9	27.9	26.2	23.4	21.6
Tranquilizers[2]	15.2	14.7	14.0	13.3	12.4	11.9	10.9	10.9

[1] Figures adjusted for underreporting of PCP.
[2] Only nonmedical use is reported here.
[3] Figures adjusted for the inappropriate reporting of nonprescription stimulants.
[4] Data are not available for these years.
Note: Sample size ranged from 15,200 to 17,700.

Source: General Accounting Office, 1988, p. 5.

of the events leading to passage of the Act, its original intent was to control the distribution and use of *all* dangerous drugs. Nevertheless, after considerable lobbying by the pharmaceutical industry, the Act concentrated exclusively on drugs imported and/or produced easily by individuals (such as marijuana and heroin). Dangerous drugs produced by pharmaceutical manufacturers (such as amphetamines and tranquilizers like Valium and Librium) were not controlled, even though considerable congressional testimony indicated their use to be more widespread, incapacitating, dangerous, and socially disrupting than narcotic use.

In the 1980s, the U.S. witnessed new efforts by the federal government to control illegal drugs. Congress enacted the Comprehensive Crime Control Act of 1984 and the Anti-Drug Abuse Act of 1986. Each law strengthened existing drug statutes. The 1986 Act, in particular, increased the drug abuse control budget—from $1.2 billion in 1981 to $4 billion in 1987 (General Accounting Office, 1988:1)—and set forth once again that drugs like marijuana, heroin, and cocaine are the most dangerous, and those who use them the "real" drug abusers.

These laws, however, have had little success in deterring drug use/abuse. Nearly 40 percent of the population over 12 years of age admit using an illegal drug at least once in their lifetime (*ibid.*:5). Cocaine, heroin, and marijuana are the most widely used illegal drugs. For youth, Table 6-2 shows that cocaine and heroin use has remained relatively stable, yet for marijuana it indicates a downward trend in the 1980s. According to studies done by the National Institute on Drug Abuse (NIDA), this pattern—stable cocaine and heroin use and declining marijuana use—continued into the 1990s (Johnson, O'Malley, and Bachman, 1992).

Nevertheless, these NIDA data, which are based on self-report questionnaires administered in households and senior high school classrooms across the U.S., suffer similar methodological defects as "self-report studies" discussed in Chapter 2. In particular, the validity of the *responses* may be uncertain and, more importantly, the *respondents* themselves may not have been drawn from a representative sample of the population. Indeed, Elliott Currie (1993:25–35) recently pointed out that such NIDA studies are based on biased samples; namely, that part of the population where serious drug use is *least* likely to be found. He presents evidence that the homeless and those living in transient hotels and shelters have some of the highest rates of drug abuse, yet they are systematically missed in the above studies. For example, one study of runaway and homeless teenagers interviewed in eight states reported cocaine use five times higher than the NIDA senior high school respondents. Currie (*ibid.*: 30, 33) concludes that while:

> there is credible evidence that rising health consciousness and growing awareness of the adverse effects of drug abuse have altered the drug habits of the more secure strata of American society, no such evidence exists for the bottom quarter of the population. . . . The American drug problem continues to tower above those of the rest of the industrialized world, and it does so despite a truly extraordinary experiment in punitive control. We have unleashed the criminal justice system against drug users and dealers with unprecedented ferocity, but drugs continue to destroy lives and shatter communities to a degree unmatched outside the Third World.

Let us examine each of the three most widely used illegal drugs.

Cocaine—"the luxurious drug of the middle-class"—is the second-most-widely used illegal drug in the U.S., and is extracted from the leaves of the Latin American coca plant. It is a stimulant that produces a euphoric reaction. Most users snort cocaine, which consists of drawing the cocaine powder high into the nasal passages. This allows for rapid absorption into the bloodstream and subsequently the brain, leaving the user with a powerful, but brief, high.

Many people ingest "traditional" cocaine, but more and more people in the 1980s and into the 1990s, especially teenagers, turned to "crack." This type of cocaine is very potent and became widely available in 1985 and 1986. Crack is cocaine hydrochloride powder transformed into a base state for smoking. The powder is mixed with baking soda or ammonia and water, dried, broken into small "rocks," and then packaged for sale (General Accounting Office, 1988:8).

Extended use of cocaine is dangerous. Approximately 1.4 grams of cocaine is lethal in a 150-pound person; heavy cocaine users exhibit irritability, suspicion, paranoia, nervousness, unrelieved fatigue, lapses of attention, inability to concentrate, and hallucinations (Ray, 1983:301). Cocaine also increases the "heart rate and blood flow while simultaneously constricting blood vessels, thus increasing the risk of blood vessel damage and stroke" (Currie, 1993:334).

Heroin is produced from opium. For maximum effect it is usually "mainlined"—injected directly into the vein. It is a narcotic that, like cocaine, produces a euphoric reaction. Heroin is highly addictive; it quickly creates a craving for the drug, which can eventually lead to physical dependence. The drug has been found to suppress both respiratory and cardiovascular activity, and high levels of heroin ingestion can produce coma, shock, respiratory arrest, and even death

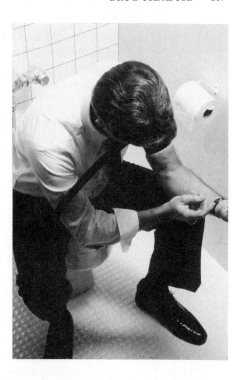

A narcotics user "shoots up."

(Inciardi, 1986:52). However, although the drug itself produces "little direct or permanent physiological damage," the dangers of heroin are chiefly related to amounts ingested and to users' disregard for standard practices of good health (for example, poor eating habits and lack of personal hygiene) (*ibid.*:64–65). Historically, heroin-related deaths almost doubled between 1983 and 1986 (General Accounting Office, 1988:11). Not surprisingly, both hepatitis and AIDS (acquired immunodeficiency syndrome) are associated with the sharing of needles by addicts. As Inciardi (1986:65) reports with regard to AIDS:

> Since this invariably fatal disease was first described in June 1981, intravenous drug users have emerged as its second highest "at-risk" category. In late 1985, they represented some 17% of the 11,919 known cases. In New York City, heroin users accounted for some 33% of the reported AIDS victims.

Finally, *marijuana*—the most widely used illegal drug in the U.S.—is derived from the dried leaves and flowering tops of the *cannabis sativa* plant. The dried parts are crushed and rolled into joints or packed in pipes for smoking. Marijuana does not appear to be addictive, nor are there tolerance or withdrawal symptoms associated with the drug. Moreover, the lethal dose is not known and no human fatalities have been linked to marijuana (Breacher, 1972:395; Goode, 1984:99–108). Of course, this does not mean that adverse effects are not linked to smoking marijuana. Although the drug is not yet fully understood, research indicates that marijuana (1) can injure mucosal tissue, (2) may be more carcinogenic than tobacco, and (3) hinders attention, long-term memory, and psychomotor skills associated with such activities as driving an automobile (Murray, 1986:23–55).

The Addiction-Crime Connection

An important question addressed by criminologists is whether addiction to drugs, such as heroin, leads to crime. Because of the illegal status of, and substantial demand for, addicting drugs, their cost is extreme. Accordingly, this can "push" individuals toward crime in order to support their habit. Nevertheless, most criminologists argue that this does not mean drug addiction *causes* crime among relatively law-abiding people or that most heroin addicts, for example, engage in crime only after becoming addicted. On the contrary, most men and women who eventually become heroin addicts commit crime "proportionally in excess of their numbers in the population before becoming involved with narcotics" (Goode, 1981:256). Indeed, study after study shows that drug use and crime begin "more or less *independently* without one clearly causing the other" (Currie, 1993:170). Nevertheless, arrest rates and self-report studies also show that higher crime rates occur when narcotic users become addicted and that substantially lower crime rates occur prior to addiction, or after addiction has ceased (Currie, 1993:164–190; Collins *et al.*, 1985; Gropper, 1985; Ball *et al.*, 1981; McGlothlin *et al.*, 1978). Moreover, an important study by James Inciardi (1986:122–132) compared narcotic users (primarily heroin) with non-narcotic users (alcohol, sedatives, marijuana, and/or cocaine) for frequency, diversity, and severity of crime committed in Miami between 1978 and 1981. His findings show that the narcotic users "committed more crimes, engaged in a greater diversity of offenses, and significantly larger proportions committed the more serious crimes of robbery and burglary" (*ibid.*:129). The overall conclusion, then, of the addiction-crime connection suggests that drugs do not cause criminality. As Currie (1993:179) states, "both crime and drug abuse tend to be spawned by the same set of unfavorable social circumstances, and they interact with one another in much more complex ways than the simple addiction-leads-to-crime view proposes." What the evidence does suggest, then, is that *addiction to narcotics like heroin clearly escalates criminal involvement.* It is not addiction *per se*, however, but addiction to a highly expensive and illegal commodity that escalates criminal involvement.

Decriminalization/Legalization

The preceding study by Inciardi (1986) also found that most narcotic users are never arrested. The 573 narcotic addicts committed a total of 215,105 offenses, yet only 609 (0.3 percent) offenses resulted in an arrest—one arrest for every 353 crimes committed. Inciardi (*ibid.*:131) concluded:

Drug-related crime is out of control, with law enforcement and the administration of justice incapable of managing it. Since less than 1% of the crimes committed result in arrest, it would appear that the efficient control of drug-related crime is well beyond the scope of contemporary policing.

Others, as well, argue that the criminal justice system has dismally failed in its effort to control illegal drug use. Not only have increased law-and-order policies gone bankrupt—leaving no measurable impact on the drug problem—but according to an American Bar Association report, such policies have "instead distorted and overwhelmed the criminal justice system, crowding dockets and jails, and deluding law enforcement and judicial efforts to deal with the major criminal cases" (cited in Gravley, 1988:3).

Because of the inability of the state to deal adequately with the growing drug abuse problem, many argue that the only alternative is *decriminalization*—the minimization, or actual removal of, criminal prohibitions for illegal drugs while still *regulating* their use. For instance, Edwin Schur (1979:460) has argued:

> One might believe, for example, that "drug addiction is immoral" or at least highly undesirable and, nonetheless, also conclude that on balance and in actual operation restrictive narcotics laws make a bad situation worse rather than better. If the basic concern is to develop policies that work to minimize the overall social harm associated with a given problem, then using the criminal law merely to express moral disapproval when the actual result of such use will be an exacerbation of the disapproved conditions readily becomes counterproductive.

Decriminalization of marijuana actually has already occurred. Back in 1973, Oregon began to treat marijuana possession of less than one ounce as a misdemeanor, with only a small monetary fine as a sanction. By 1984, 10 other states followed Oregon's lead, decriminalizing the possession of small quantities of marijuana (Goode, 1984:viii). In 1986 the Oregon Marijuana Initiative successfully placed a proposition on the state ballot that would have legalized the home growing of marijuana. Although defeated, the proposition received 27 percent of the vote (Gravley, 1988:10). Finally, throughout the country marijuana arrests have been dropping consistently since the mid-1970s. This fact led Goode (1984:257) to argue that

> for all practical purposes, the possession of marijuana has become decriminalized in the United States. Since present trends are moving in the direction of de facto legal acceptance of marijuana possession, it will not make a great deal of difference whether this attitude is officially recognized or not. Consequently, the debate over decriminalization is swiftly becoming obsolete.

In the late 1980s several conservatives joined forces with libertarians and called for *legalization* of all drugs and complete removal of all criminal sanctions for drug use, without subsequent regulation. Libertarians assert that the U.S. should abandon its attempt to "run other people's lives," stop imposing its beliefs on others, and realize that "there is all the difference in the world between deciding that you don't want to do something and trying to force other people to live your way" (Sowell, 1988:19). In other words, libertarians argue that people should be able to ingest whatever they choose as long as they do not violate the rights of others.

Conservatives, such as William F. Buckley and Milton Friedman, argue that prohibitive drug laws are really no match for the laws of supply and demand (Gravley, 1988:3). Not only does there continue to be a large demand for illegal drugs in the U.S. (over one-third of citizens have tried illegal drugs, 6.8 million use cocaine, and 25 million use marijuana, at least once a month [*ibid.*:3]), but because of the demand, many people become suppliers. This supply operation is so widespread and extensive—contributing substantially to the profits of criminal syndicates—that it is impossible to stop (see Chapter 8.2). Legalization is therefore the only answer for these conservatives.

Others also have argued for the legalization of drugs, especially heroin. Jeffrey Reiman (1984:27–30), for example, cites the fact that heroin is a relatively safe drug, especially when compared with such *legal drugs* as tobacco (nicotine) and alcohol. As Reiman (*ibid.*:27) states:

> There is no evidence conclusively establishing a link between heroin and disease or tissue degeneration such as that which has been established for tobacco and alcohol. On the basis of the scientific evidence available, there is every reason to suspect that we do our bodies more damage, more *irreversible* damage, by smoking cigarettes and drinking liquor.

Indeed, each year tobacco and alcohol, both of which are addicting, are responsible for 300,000 and 100,000 deaths, respectively. The use of all illegal drugs combined—cocaine, heroin, marijuana, LSD, and so on—accounted for only 3,403 deaths in 1987 (Ehrenreich, 1988:20). As Ehrenreich (*ibid.*) states:

> That's 3,403 deaths too many, but it's less than one percent of the death toll from the perfectly legal, socially respectable drugs that Americans—including drug warriors—indulge in every day.

In addition, Reiman (1984:29–30) argues that the illegal status of heroin creates additional harms to society. For example, because suppliers take serious risks, they charge outrageously high prices for addictive drugs. Because addicts need the drug to avoid withdrawal pains, they pay the high prices. What this creates is not merely users of heroin, but many users who deal in drugs as well in order to obtain the required money to satisfy their habit. Addicts, therefore, constantly look for new people to "turn on," which simply increases the market of heroin addicts.

Finally, Barbara Ehrenreich (1988:21) argues that drug prohibition has become even more dangerous than drug abuse, causing approximately 7,000 deaths each year—through drug-related crime, AIDS, and poisoned drugs—and an $80 billion-a-year economic loss to society. Without some type of legalization, Ehrenreich argues, we will continue to "feed our legal addictions" while maintaining a large subculture of addicts "who steal for heroin or kill for crack" (*ibid.*).

6.3   ABORTION, PROSTITUTION, AND PORNOGRAPHY

The question of whether abortion, prostitution, and pornography are victimless crimes has been debated for years, and the debate continues today. We analyze certain of the current issues and arguments for each of these "crimes."

Abortion

The 1973 Supreme Court decision in the case of *Roe v. Wade* established that women have the constitutional right to choose an abortion to end a pregnancy. In this decision the Court established that state laws restricting abortion "only as a *life-saving* procedure on behalf of the mother, without regard to pregnancy stage and without recognition of the other interests involved," are unconstitutional (Goldstein, 1988:347). The Court went on to argue that in the first trimester of pregnancy women have the right to choose abortion without interference from the state. During the second trimester the state cannot prohibit abortion, but may regulate abortion procedures in order to ensure the health of the mother. Finally, in the third trimester, abortion can be performed only to preserve the life or health of the mother (*ibid.*).

The public seems to support the Supreme Court's ruling. Approximately 84 percent of the public believe that "abortion should be legal either altogether or under certain circumstances" (Andersen, 1993:197). However, although the vast majority of the populace support a woman's right to decide on abortion, a slight majority also feel that abortion—even during the first three months of pregnancy—is murder. What this means, as Andersen (1988:203–204) points out, is "that although many people believe that abortion is morally wrong, they are in favor of leaving the choice to the individual concerned." Other evidence on the public's view of abortion includes the following (*ibid.*:204):

▲— Eighty percent support abortion in cases where the mother's health is seriously endangered.

▲— Eighty-three percent support abortion where pregnancy results from rape.

▲— Eighty-three percent support abortion where there is a serious chance of birth defect.

▲— Fifty-three percent support abortion where the woman is from a low-income family and cannot support any more children.

▲— Forty-eight percent support abortion when the woman is not married and does not want to marry the birth father.

A demonstration to maintain the legal right to abortion.

▲— Forty-seven percent support abortion when the woman is married but does not want any more children.

▲— Forty-one percent support abortion for any reason.

In addition, young and unmarried women—especially those in the age group 15–24—are more likely than other women to have an abortion (*Statistical Abstract of the United States,* 1992:74). Approximately 60 percent of all women undergoing abortions each year since 1973 have been between the ages of 15 and 24. Moreover, since 1980 slightly more than 50 percent of all abortions were performed at nine or fewer weeks of gestation, and 90 percent at 12 weeks or earlier (*ibid.*). It appears that for large numbers of young women abortion has been legitimized in U.S. society.

Nevertheless, abortion rights have gradually eroded since *Roe v. Wade.* The 1976 Hyde Amendment—upheld by the Supreme Court in 1980—eliminates federal Medicaid funds for abortion except in cases of rape and incestuous assault. Insurance coverage of abortion has been eliminated for members of the Peace

Corps, Defense Department, and residents of public hospitals and prisons (Herman, 1984:i). In 1985 all federal funding was cut to international family planning organizations that either counseled or offered abortion and, as discussed in Chapter 5, the premises of abortion providers have been the object of increasing harassment, violence, bombings, and arson (Glen, 1986:51–52).

Moreover, at least 24 states require that young women obtain the consent of one or two parents to proceed with an abortion (Clarke *et al.*, 1993). As Margaret Andersen (1992:195–196) points out, this is especially troubling once we consider the research on teenage sexuality, contraception, and parental relationships:

> Procrastination is the teenager's most frequent reason for delay in initiating contraceptive use; the second most frequent reason is fear that parents will find out. One-third of all teenagers delay going to a clinic because they fear their parents will find out. Regulations that limit the options available to young girls (or anyone else) seem unlikely, then, to solve the problems associated with teenage pregnancy.

In Chapter 4 we addressed the issue of child abuse. Here we add the unfortunate given that parental consent legislation actually may lead to physical abuse, and even death, of children. Indeed, parental notification of pregnancy "often precipitates a family crisis, characterized by severe parental anger and rejection of the minor" and, therefore, "it is reasonable to believe that some minors justifiably fear that they would be treated violently by one or both parents if they had to disclose their pregnancy to their parents" (Clarke *et al.*, 1993:83). Consequently, to avoid parents "finding out," young women in parental consent states may be compelled to seek imprudent measures to maintain the confidentiality of their pregnancy. The case of Becky Bell of Indiana is illustrative. Indiana requires girls under 18 to obtain the consent of one parent before they can have an abortion. However, not surprisingly, Becky Bell could not bring herself to tell either parent that she was pregnant. Consequently, "she died, the victim of an illegal abortion, an abortion doctors believe she may have given herself" (Halpern, 1990:43). The desire to maintain secrecy has been one of the leading reasons for illegal abortion deaths since the *Roe v. Wade* decision in 1973 (Clarke *et al.*, 1993:83).

It has been estimated that prior to legalization of abortion there were as many as 1–2 million illegal abortions each year in the U.S. (Tietze, 1981:21). In the year of the *Roe v. Wade* decision, there were 745,000 legal abortions; by 1988 the total had risen significantly to 1.575 million. However, from 1980 to 1983 the number of legal abortions remained quite stable (*Statistical Abstract of the United States*, 1992:74). Thus, legal or illegal, abortion seems to be a significant and popular means of fertility control in the United States.

In addition to abortion as a means of fertility control, evidence indicates that decriminalization of abortion has actually reduced infant and maternal mortality during pregnancy and childbirth. First, availability of safe and reliable abortions is considered the single most important factor in the decline in infant mortality. As Currie and Skolnick (1984:350) state:

> The growth in legal abortions reduced infant death among whites by about 1.6 per every 1,000 live births between 1964 and 1977, and by 2.5 per 1,000 for nonwhites, with the most rapid reductions coming in the 1970s, after the changes in the abortion laws.

Second, decriminalization of abortion has reduced deaths related to abortion, "cutting them by two-thirds between 1972 and 1975 alone" (*ibid.*:349–350). Third, maternal death from childbirth has decreased drastically, primarily due to better prenatal care, more publicly funded family planning services, and increased availability of abortion. Whereas at the end of World War II more than 200 women per 100,000 died during childbirth, the figure is now fewer than 10 per 100,000 births (*ibid.*:349). Finally, consider that 30 percent of all pregnancies are terminated by abortion (Henshaw, 1987:5) which, when undergone early in pregnancy, is considerably safer than childbirth. As LeBolt *et al.* (1982:188–191) reported in *The Journal of the American Medical Association*, since the *Roe v. Wade* decision, deaths due to legal abortions have fallen sharply, with only an accompanying gradual decline in childbearing deaths. Moreover, the number of legal abortions performed has increased continuously, while the number of live births has remained quite stable. The end result, according to these authors, is that women are about 10 times more likely to die from childbirth than from legal abortion. When compared with abortions performed at nine or fewer weeks of gestation—when, as we have seen, more than 50 percent of all abortions are performed—the risk of death from childbearing is more than 20 times higher than from abortion. Cates *et al.* (1982:196) agree with these conclusions: "Abortion through the fifteenth week of pregnancy is at least tenfold safer than childbearing. 'Natural pregnancy' is not safer for the woman than induced abortion."

Abortion did not become an issue in the U.S. until the late 1800s. Between 1800 and 1820 there were no laws related to abortion, and women commonly used either midwives or relatively safe "home remedies" to induce abortion. Women were not considered pregnant until "quickening" occurred—the point at which the fetus could be felt moving—and throughout the entire pregnancy the fetus was not considered a live human being. The first laws on abortion were enacted in the 1820s, but concentrated on outlawing certain unsafe methods of inducing abortion rather than abortion itself (Mohr, 1978:3–46). As more and more women began practicing abortion and

> as the practice changed from being invisible to being visible, from being quantitatively insignificant to being a systematic practice that terminated a substantial number of pregnancies after 1840, and from being almost entirely a recourse of the desperate and the socially marginal to being a commonly employed procedure among the middle and upper classes of

American society, state legislators decided to reassess their policies toward the practice (*ibid.*:117–118).

This policy reassessment was largely in response to agitation by male physicians, who fought strongly for antiabortion laws upon several grounds. First, they criticized midwives as incompetent to perform such medical procedures. During this period of time there existed a "popular health movement" whose backbone consisted of women healers who instructed audiences around the country in anatomy and personal hygiene—emphasizing preventive care that included such practices as frequent bathing, wearing loose-fitting clothing, and eating whole-grain cereals (Ehrenreich and English, 1973:25). These women were quite knowledgeable about abortion and birth processes, presiding over what was then a successful female-centered activity (Dye, 1980:98–99). However, male physicians, obtaining economic support from the newly created Rockefeller and Carnegie Foundations, attacked the popular health movement and midwives as incompetent "quacks." Their economic support effectively created medical schools that were closed to midwives. Thus, by the 1860s the white, male, upper-middle class physicians were regarded as *the* medical profession (*ibid.*:100; Ehrenreich and English, 1973:30–33).

Second, the statistics on falling birthrates and rising abortion rates in the U.S. communicated to these physicians that women who utilized abortion must be engaging in sexual intercourse without intending to procreate—simply having sex "for its own sake." And in 19th-century Victorian U.S. society—which defined women's place as in the home to nurture and care for children and husband and to engage in sexual intercourse only to have children—this was deemed threatening (Petchesky, 1985:78–84). As Mohr (1978:169) argues:

> To many doctors the chief purpose of women was to produce children; anything that interfered with that purpose, or allowed women to "indulge" themselves in less important activities, threatened marriage, the family, and the future of society itself.

Thus, sexual conservatism motivated male physicians to demand antiabortion laws. They argued vociferously against "respectable" women engaging in sex or controlling their sexuality. These physicians attacked abortion among upper-middle class "native" women while simultaneously supporting eugenic arguments to limit propagation of "lower-class," "unfit," immigrant women (*ibid.*:168). As Petchesky (1985:79) writes:

> Just as the Yankee woman was duty-bound to "propagate the race" and "defend the home," the immigrant, poor, or black woman, regarded as a carrier of disease and a breeder of "bad stock," was admonished to avoid reproducing.

Consequently, the male physicians' response to abortion was shaped further by class and racial biases. If respectable women engaged in abortion, physicians argued, they would find themselves outbred by unfit members of society—the poor, foreign born, racial minorities. Abortion was, in effect, seen as contributing to "race suicide" (Petchesky, 1985:82; Mohr, 1978:167).

For these reasons, then, male physicians strenuously lobbied state legislatures. From 1860 on, state after state enacted laws making abortion a crime for both the physician (or whoever performed the abortion) and the woman (Mohr, 1978:171–200). These laws remained in force until the 1960s.

Both Linda Gordon (1981) and Rosalind Petchesky (1985) have written about the changing conception of abortion in the 1960s and why abortion was eventually decriminalized in 1973. Gordon (1981:84–85) argues that the drive for legal abortion in the late 1960s and early 1970s was a response to three factors that developed during the period 1920–1960. First, there was an increase in teenage sexual activity without an accompanying increase in contraceptive use. Thus, "it was not technology that increased sexual activity but the behavior that increased the demand" for contraception and abortion (*ibid.*:84). Second, during this time there was a substantial increase in female-headed households as well as in families dependent on two incomes. Without adequate childcare facilities, this economic reality made it increasingly impossible for mothers to remain at home caring for an unplanned baby and led to an increased demand for abortion. Finally, Gordon argues that the lack of safe and effective contraception helped create the movement for legal abortion.

Petchesky (1985:101–132) adds to Gordon's explanation, arguing that in the late 1960s and early 1970s certain social conditions merged with a growing feminist movement. This merger created the foundation necessary for the development of legal abortion. Social conditions during the 1960s and the 1970s were such that women in the United States witnessed dramatic changes in their lives, including:

1. later marriage and childbearing among younger women
2. increasing levels of college attendance among women
3. rising labor-force participation by women
4. rising divorce rates and increased numbers of female-headed households
5. women's continued primary responsibility for children
6. continued lack of government-funded social services, such as child care
7. women's need to avoid unwanted pregnancy for health reasons, to control their sexuality, and for overall social self-actualization (*ibid.*:103–104)

According to Petchesky, these social conditions in the United States led to falling birthrates and to "a greater need for safe, reliable methods of fertility control among diverse groups of women" (*ibid.*:104).

The preceding social conditions helped spawn a number of movements calling for legalization of abortion. One such movement was the emerging second wave of the feminist movement in the 1960s, which championed the ideas of "abortion on demand" and "a woman's right to control over her body."

Feminists demanded the unconditional right to abortion. They vehemently opposed simply *reforming* the law through legalization of, for instance, "therapeutic abortions" or abortions only when a woman's health was in danger. Such reforms, feminists argued, would not give reproductive control to women. On the contrary, it simply would transfer control from the police to those who determined whether such medical conditions exist—namely, the male-dominated medical profession. Feminists argued further that this type of reform "implicitly suggested that women were incompetent to act as moral agents on their own behalf" (*ibid.*:126). Repeal, however, would abolish all restrictions that might be discriminatory and would not hinder a woman from obtaining an abortion. Repeal would give women the control, capacity, and right to make reproductive decisions, rather than allowing male physicians to control women's reproductive responsibility and, therefore, to act as the sole "moral gatekeepers" of society. Consequently, from 1968 to 1973 feminists directly pressured the medical profession, politicians, and the consciousness of society at large to repeal existing abortion laws. This feminist activism, Petchesky concludes, was critical in the establishment of legal abortion in the U.S. It was, in essence, the coming together of the social conditions just discussed and, in particular, the feminist movement generated by those conditions that, Petchesky and Gordon argue, laid the groundwork for the *Roe v. Wade* decision in 1973.

Notwithstanding, feminists are not completely satisfied with the *Roe v. Wade* decision; many believe it does not go far enough. For most feminists, the state must provide uniform, funded, and high-quality abortion services to all women—thus making abortion a "public responsibility" (*ibid.*:384). Moreover, most feminists agree that legal abortion is both minimal and indispensable for women because, although it does not create total reproductive freedom for women, it does help minimize certain negative aspects of their responsibility for pregnancy and, although it does not empower women or liberate their sexuality, it does allow women "the space to move from one point in [their] life to the next" (*ibid.*:385).

Prostitution

In the United States, as in most Western societies, there is a hierarchical system of sexual value. In other words, some forms of sexuality are defined as "normal" and "natural"; others are deemed "deviant." Marital, reproductive heterosexuals are alone at the top of the sexual hierarchy, followed closely by unmarried heterosexuals. Further down are those who prefer solitary sexuality, lesbians and gay males, prostitutes, transvestites, and sadomasochists (Rubin, 1984:279). Heterosexuals are rewarded with certified mental health, respectability, legality, social and physical mobility, institutional support, and material benefits. Those below heterosexuals in the hierarchy are often presumed to be mentally ill, disreputable, and criminal; their social and physical mobility is restricted; they have no institutional support; and they face economic sanctions (*ibid.*). In other words, U.S. culture emphasizes that "there is one best way to do it, and that everyone should do it that way" (*ibid.*:283).

The charmed circle:
good, normal, natural,
blessed sexuality

Heterosexual
Married
Monogamous
Procreative
Noncommercial
In pairs
In a relationship
Same generation
In private
No pornography
Bodies only
Vanilla

The outer limits:
bad, abnormal,
unnatural,
damned sexuality

Homosexual
Unmarried
Promiscuous
Nonprocreative
Commercial
Alone or in groups
Casual
Cross-generational
In public
Pornography
With manufactured objects
Sadomasochistic

FIGURE   The Sex Hierarchy
6-1   *Source: Rubin, 1984, p. 281.*

Figure 6-1 depicts the sexual hierarchy in the United States. In the final two sections we examine two types of sexuality that are part of the "outer limits" in the figure, prostitution (for money) and pornography.

Most people commonly think of prostitution simply as accepting payment for sexual services. However, this definition is so broad that some monogamous relationships (such as marriage) could be defined as prostitution. Indeed, some define *all* marriages as a form of prostitution. As one radical feminist states: "We have long held that all women sell themselves: that the only available role of a woman—wife, secretary, girlfriend—all demand the selling of herself to one or more men" (cited in Jaggar, 1983:264). We agree that *some* women (and men) may marry for money and that *some* spouses may sexually service their husband/wife in order to receive some type of remuneration. However, we focus our definition of *prostitution* on the consensual grant of *illegal* and *nonmonogamous* sexual services to clients for payment. Although both males and females may become prostitutes, most sociological research has concentrated on female prostitution. Following a brief discussion of male prostitution, the remainder of this section addresses female prostitution.

In terms of numbers, males are clearly the more involved gender in prostitution. This is true for several reasons. First, the transaction in female prostitution entails one female providing sexual services to a number of "johns," or male clients. Second, female prostitutes often work for, and support, a male (namely, a pimp). And third, male prostitutes are probably "as numerous as female prostitutes" (Allen, 1980:399). Consequently, males are the most common actors in prostitution.

According to David Luckenbill (1986:285–286) there exist several types of male prostitutes. First, male prostitutes can be categorized in terms of "sex identification" (whether the prostitute is a heterosexual or homosexual "hustler"), "sex role" (whether or not the prostitute adopts a masculine or feminine role during the transaction), and "sexual services" (the type of service(s) provided— fellatio, sadomasochism, and so on). In addition, Luckenbill (*ibid.*:285) identifies three major "modes of operation"—street hustler, bar hustler, and escort service:

> The street hustler stands around particular avenues, parks, bus stations, or bookstore entrances, attracts a customer from the passers-by, quickly arranges a sexual sale with him, and then moves to a private setting, to perform a brief sexual exchange. The bar hustler frequents particular gay bars or discos, attracts a customer from the patrons, socializes with him for a time, arranges a sale, and moves to a private place for sex. The escort operates through an escort or modeling agency; a customer contacts the agency and requests a "date," the agency operator and customer agree on the terms of the date, and the escort takes the job, contacting the customer at his residence and engaging in sex and other agreed upon activities, such as having dinner.

In the mid-1980s, street hustlers earned approximately $10–25 per "trick," bar hustlers from $50–70, and escorts between $90–140. Accordingly, escort male prostitutes are more likely to attract the higher-paying customers. Because they solicit and operate in a private setting, they are also more likely to minimize risks of operation—such as arrest (*ibid.*:286; see also Allen, 1980:404–407).

A recent study of male prostitution in London expands on Luckenbill's conclusions. Donald J. West and Buz de Villiers (1993) interviewed 50 "street hustlers" and 25 "bar hustlers," and reported in their book *Male Prostitution* that most of these teenage boys describe themselves as gay or bisexual. The vast majority initially resorted to prostitution when they were "either very short or, more often, desperately short of money, sometimes to the extent of having no access otherwise to food or shelter" (*ibid.*:161). Prostitution transactions most commonly emerged in their later teens, when youths are expected to begin providing for themselves. For many, lack of family support and education, as well as limited employment options, made prostitution a deceptively easy option, especially for those describing themselves as gay or bisexual. As West and de Villiers (*ibid.*:78) conclude, street and bar hustling is not the result of sexual abuse as a young child (as some have suggested), but rather develops from an "urgent need of money as their prime motive for entry into prostitution."

Female prostitution, throughout the 1800s, was condemned in the U.S., but was not classified as a criminal offense. In the early 1800s, community gangs engaged in the infamous "whorehouse riots," demolishing houses of female prostitution and battling female prostitutes in the streets. These riots did not end female prostitution but helped segregate it within the "red-light districts" of the growing urban slums (Rosen, 1982:4–5). As a result, in the 1860s and 1870s a reform movement emerged that concentrated on regulation of female prostitution. These "regulationists" argued for medical control, maintaining that such control would contribute to overall public health. During this period men were thought to possess an excessive sexual "drive"; women were considered to be asexual. Regulated female prostitution would therefore serve as an "outlet" for those men who could not control their alleged special "drive." Regulation involving both police and medical supervision was seen by its supporters as being in the best interests of both society and the prostitutes. Compulsory medical examinations for female prostitutes rather than the complete suppression of prostitution itself was viewed by regulationists as the answer to prostitution (Messerschmidt, 1987:244).

However, not everyone agreed with the regulationists. Women involved in the late 19th- and early 20th-century feminist movement opposed regulation. Feminists argued that regulation forced female prostitutes into vaginal examinations and licensing, thus providing men with the freedom to engage in sex with female prostitutes without acquiring venereal disease. They further showed that by not inspecting the men, regulation failed to regulate those men who were carriers of venereal disease—therefore not really protecting anyone. According to feminists, then, regulation actually served the interests of the men (customers) rather than the women (prostitutes) (*ibid.*). In the end, the movement *against* regulation in the United States proved so strong and successful that only one city (St. Louis) ever tried it, and the experiment there lasted for only four years (*ibid.*:245).

In spite of the "regulation" victory, feminists united with the conservative social purity movement of the time (a movement to reform sexual mores) to press for the actual *abolition* of female prostitution itself. This motley group consolidated into an abolitionist movement that embraced a program of social purity measures. Feminists argued that the alleged male "excessive drive" had to be eliminated. The abolition of female prostitution would contribute to this end by forcing men to control their "drive" and thereby raising men to the level of purity of women (*ibid.*:246–247).

Subsequently, in the early 1900s state legislatures began enacting laws aimed at closing down red-light districts. Iowa enacted the first law in 1909—the Red-Light Abatement Act—making it illegal to maintain a building for "immoral purposes." By 1917 31 states had enacted similar laws (Rosen, 1982:28–29). However, these laws failed to reduce female prostitution. On the contrary, because female prostitutes could not find "respectable work," new forms of prostitution emerged. As Rosen (*ibid.*:32) reports:

> Since brothels and parlor houses could no longer advertise their wares, rooming houses, flats, hotels, and massage parlors became the predominant sites for prostitution. To avoid detection, madams and prostitutes who had once catered to a wealthy clientele began to rely on the "call girl" system of prostitution, in which customers call to see a particular prostitute. In this way, connections could be made secretly without danger of police harassment. . . . For the majority of poor women, however, the closing of the houses meant increased streetwalking, which was immediately noticed in most American cities. Without recognized districts or brothels, prostitutes could no longer receive customers in the semiprotected environment of the brothel or district. Instead, they had to search for business in public places—hotels, restaurants, cabarets, or on the street.

This search for customers in public places made female prostitutes vulnerable to violent clients and police harassment. Consequently, control of female prostitution began to change hands. Because of the new conditions resulting from the abolitionist movement, female prostitutes turned to male pimps to help them ward off dangers, provide legal assistance, and offer some additional support. Eventually, the overall female prostitute/male "john" transaction became dominated by individual pimp entrepreneurs or male-dominated criminal syndicates (*ibid.*:33). Today, female prostitutes continue to search for customers in such public places as streets, bars, and hotels, and they work in a variety of private settings, such as massage parlors or brothels.

Women who work the streets often participate in prostitution subcultures, where they work together and rely on each other for safety and support. Within the subcultures they are emotionally and financially interdependent (Rosenblum, 1975:180). Moreover, many women who work the streets "laugh at the notion of having a pimp and say they only use men to give them back-up protection" (Andersen, 1988:258). However, Miller (1986:35–43) reports, in her in-depth examination of street women in Milwaukee, that most female prostitution is conducted in the context of "deviant street networks," or groups of individuals mobilized to carry out a variety of illegal behaviors, such as prostitution, larceny, check and credit-card fraud, auto theft, drug traffic, burglary, and robbery. Thus, although the women in Miller's study were involved in prostitution, there was also some diversity in their "hustling" activity.

Miller (*ibid.*:36) also reports that men clearly dominate the deviant street networks in Milwaukee. Commonly referred to as pimps, these men (while engaging in some property crime themselves) live off the earnings of the female prostitute and act as her agent and/or companion. The pimp usually controls two to three women, who are referred to on the streets as "wives-in-law" (*ibid.* :37–38). In return for their earnings, the pimp may provide companionship, someone to live and be with. One female prostitute defined her relationship with her pimp as "just knowing that you have somebody there all the time, not just for protection, just someone you can go to" (James 1982:304).

The pimp is not the only type of deviant street network "manager." Another type, referred to as the "man," works together with a single female prostitute, rather than two or three women. The "man," usually a husband or lover, not only shares the proceeds but is always close by, protecting his "woman" and supervising on-the-spot transactions (Cohen, 1980:56). As Cohen (*ibid.*) points out, the difference between the *pimp* and the *man* is that the prostitute works *for* a pimp but *with* a man.

The relationship between a female prostitute and pimp or man is not always conflict-free, and can result in *forced* prostitution. That is, if the female prostitute attempts to depart the relationship, she may find that her pimp or man becomes violent and brutal. Thus, many prostitutes are physically victimized by their "partner" (Barry, 1979:79).

Female prostitutes also work in settings other than "the streets." Two common private settings for female prostitution are massage parlors and brothels. The massage parlor prostitute usually, but not always, works for a male parlor manager who hires the masseuses, collects the clients' fees, keeps the books, and pays the masseuses. However, some massage parlors form "sisterhoods" to operate the parlor, sharing management duties and supporting one another. Most massage parlors in the U.S. are, of course, fronts for prostitution, in which the prostitute provides a massage and a variety of sexual services as well (Simon and Witte, 1982:244–246). The madam of a brothel operates somewhat like the massage parlor manager by hiring, firing, keeping records, and paying salaries. A typical brothel employs from two to four female prostitutes. But the brothel differs from the massage parlor in one important respect—it does not provide a legitimate service (such as a massage) and does not, therefore, have a legitimate front (*ibid.*:246).

Finally, some female prostitutes work for the manager of a bar or hotel, who pays the women a 40 to 50 percent commission. Prostitutes working in bars may also be part- or full-time barmaids, waitresses, or strippers (*ibid.*:246); the "high class" female prostitutes working in hotels are known as "call girls." Not all call girls work in hotels, however; some simply work solo out of their home or apartment.

It is estimated that streetwalkers comprise approximately 20 percent of all female prostitutes, call girls 15 percent, and that 65 percent work in an establishment of some type—25 percent in massage parlors, 15 percent in brothels, 15 percent in bars, and 10 percent in hotels (*ibid.*:253). Women who turn to prostitution tend to do better financially than they would working at a "straight" job. The yearly income ranged in the early 1980s from a low of $7,000 for some massage parlor prostitutes to $45,000 for call girls (*ibid.*:249).

As discussed earlier, in the late 1800s and early 1900s feminists organized to abolish female prostitution. Feminists today, however, are divided on the issue. Radical feminists, on the one hand, seem to maintain that the female prostitute is clearly the victim of prostitution, being exploited and treated simply as a sexual object by the pimp and customer alike. Kathleen Barry (1979:220), a radical feminist, goes so far as to refer to female prostitution as *female sexual slavery:*

> Because it is invisible to social perception and because of the clandestine nature of its practices, it is presently impossible to statistically measure the incidence of female sexual slavery. But considering the arrested sexual development that is understood to be normal in the male population and considering the numbers of men who are pimps, procurers, members of syndicate and freelance slavery gangs, operators of brothels and massage parlors, connected with sexual exploitation entertainment, pornography purveyors, wife beaters, child molesters, incest perpetrators, johns (tricks) and rapists, one cannot help but be momentarily stunned by the enormous male population participating in female sexual slavery. The huge number of men engaged in these practices should be cause for a declaration of a national and international emergency, a crisis in sexual violence. But what should be cause for alarm is instead accepted as normal social intercourse.

Thus, feminists argue that feminists should find a way for female prostitutes to *escape* their *plight* (Cole, 1987:35).

Many female prostitutes have publicly disagreed with this assessment of their situation. Margo St. James (1987:86), founder of Call Off Your Old Tired Ethics (COYOTE)—a female prostitute union that provides such legal services as bail and counseling for arrestees, as well as childcare services for prostitutes—says that the radical feminist view of the female prostitute as "victim" and "sexual slave" is patronizing and condescending. St. James (*ibid.*:82) argues that in

> private the whore has power. She is in charge, setting the terms for the sexual exchange and the financial exchange. In public, of course, she has absolutely no rights—no civil rights, no human rights. Prostitution laws are how women are controlled in this society.

Moreover, regarding their relationship with pimps and their man, three female prostitutes state that radical feminists (Scott, Miller, and Hotchkiss, 1987:205):

> use the pimp issue and the abuse issue as a way out, always pointing to him and pointing to the way we have to work as being very corrupt, when in fact these laws were the result of prostitutes being ostracized by society in general and specifically feminists.

Another female prostitute states (cited in Bell, 1987:119):

> I'm not condoning the men who do work several women, who are brutal—of course I'm not condoning that—but I would like to suggest to you that as adult women we have the right to choose a good man, a bad man. I don't want the culture telling me what man I can live with. I don't like knowing that the police can come and take my man away at any moment. I could go home now and find him gone. The inferiority with which we are regarded is directed as well at the clients and the pimps.

Finally, female prostitutes argue that a democratic morality should be used to judge all sexual acts. Female prostitutes do not see themselves as sexual objects, but rather as engaging in a specific type of sexuality that is stigmatized in this society. As Scott, Miller, and Hotchkiss (1987:208) put it:

> And we think the real thing is what works for the individual, and let's allow that individual to have that choice of what is the real thing for them. We don't want anyone telling us what kind of sex we can have, whether it's for money or not. And we certainly wouldn't tell anybody else what kind of sex they could have. We wouldn't go into a meeting of lesbians and say, "Well, we don't think that this kind of sex is right." Or we wouldn't go into a meeting at church and say, "Well, this kind of sex, if you're married and madly in love is not all right."

Increasingly, other feminists are supporting many of these views held by female prostitutes. While opposing gender inequality and, therefore, the male-dominated nature of the female prostitution "business" (just as they oppose gender inequality in other areas of society), these feminists do not argue for the dissolution of commercial sex because it does not benefit the women involved. Rather, they emphasize the need for society to provide all women with equal opportunities to enter any type of employment *if they wish* (Jaggar, 1983:180–181). Moreover, rather than viewing female prostitution as degrading and the prostitute as a passive victim, more and more feminists regard female prostitution as a legitimate form of sexuality. Accordingly, they argue that feminists must work to empower women within the sex industry itself. As Varda Burstyn (1985:169) argues: "Sex-workers themselves have to be protected and integrated into the women's movement and their needs and rights defended."

Pornography

Another sexually related topic under debate is pornography. Criminologist Ernest van den Haag (1969) wrote an essay in which he attempted to answer the question: "Is pornography a cause of crime?" Not only did van den Haag answer in the affirmative—arguing that pornography "can contribute to the formation of dispositions" or pornography can "precipitate the action, once the disposition has been formed for whatever reasons"—but he also maintained that it was important to censor pornography (*ibid.*:841). As van den Haag (*ibid.*:845) suggested:

Criminologists continue to debate whether "pornography" should be criminalized.

If we indulge pornography, and do not allow censorship to restrict it, our society at best will become ever more coarse, brutal, anxious, indifferent, de-individualized, hedonistic; at worst its ethos will disintegrate altogether.

One year later, the 1970 Commission on Obscenity and Pornography disagreed with van den Haag's position, concluding in its report that it had "found no evidence that exposure to explicit sexual materials plays a significant role in the causation of delinquent or criminal behavior among youth or adults" (Commission, 1970:27). In addition, the Commission (*ibid.*:25) pointed out that explicit sexual imagery may in fact increase "the frequency and variety of coital performance . . . and conversation about sexual matters." The Commission concluded that censorship was unwarranted.

In the 1980s pornography once again became an issue of governmental concern. The Attorney General's Commission on Pornography, headed by Edwin Meese, was formed in 1985 and released its report in July 1986. The Commission membership clearly reflected the Attorney General's political agenda. The panel was chaired by Henry Hudson, an antivice prosecutor from Arlington, Virginia, who was commended by President Reagan for "closing down every adult bookstore in his district" (Vance, 1986:76). Moreover, prior to being selected, seven of the 11 panel members had each indicated publicly their opposition to pornography and the importance of controlling it (*ibid.*).

The Meese Commission identified four types of sexual imagery: (1) sexually violent material; (2) nonviolent material depicting degradation, subordination, and humiliation; (3) nonviolent and nondegrading material; and (4) nudity. Not surprisingly, the Commission concluded that all sexual imagery is in some way harmful, but that the first two types are the most dangerous. Sexually violent material—defined as "actual or simulated violence presented in sexually explicit fashion with a predominant focus on the sexually explicit violence" (Meese Commission, 1986:323)—includes material depicting sadomasochistic themes, rape, and sexually motivated murder. After analyzing experimental laboratory research, the Meese Commission (*ibid.*:324) concluded that there is "a causal relationship between exposure to material of this type and aggressive behavior toward women." Regarding nonviolent material depicting degradation, subordination, and humiliation, the Meese Commission (*ibid.*:331) includes sexual imagery depicting women as (1) "existing solely for the sexual satisfaction of others," (2) "in decidedly subordinate roles in their sexual relations with others," or (3) "engaged in sexual practices that would to most people be considered humiliating." The Meese Commission (*ibid.*:332) concluded that experimental laboratory research indicates that substantial exposure to material of this type is

> likely to increase the extent to which those exposed will view rape or other forms of sexual violence as less serious than they otherwise would have, will view the victims of rape and other forms of sexual violence as significantly more responsible, and will view the offenders as significantly less responsible.

Thus, according to the Meese Commission, pornography causes males to be violent toward females.

Evidence for the alleged harmful effects of pornography was gathered primarily from the experimental laboratory research of two psychologists, Neil Malamuth and Edward Donnerstein. Although the Meese Commission accepted the findings of these researchers, it completely ignored the criticisms of this type of research made by other social scientists, as well as the psychologists' own admonition that care must be exercised in interpreting their findings. Caution, the psychologists argued, must be exercised because the duration of the effects of exposure to pornography in the laboratory (for instance, the attitudinal changes could disappear immediately upon leaving the lab) is unknown, and although pornography may reinforce and strengthen already existing beliefs and values, there is no evidence it causes predispositions toward violence (Donnerstein and Linz, 1986:56–59). Moreover, there are other problems associated with this research. For instance, what people *tell* researchers they believe, and what people *think* they will do, might differ from what they *actually* do. In other words, we cannot generalize from controlled laboratory situations to situations outside the laboratory: if people do one thing in the lab, this does not necessarily mean they will do it outside the lab. In contrast to the Meese Commission, Thelma McCormack (1985:192), in an exhaustive review of research on pornography, found "no systematic evidence to link either directly or indirectly the use of pornography with rape." And finally, in a more recent examination of research on "pornography" and violence against women, Michael Kimmel (1993:8) concludes:

> In aggregate studies and in the laboratories, researchers have not been able to isolate pornography as the cause of violence against women. The pervasiveness of rape and violence, even in the absence of a single causal mechanism, means that we have a larger and more diffuse constellation of masculine attitudes to confront.

In addition to its remarkable acceptance of the experimental laboratory research without probing its weaknesses, the Meese Commission was also criticized for its simplistic definitions. For example, the Commission included sado-masochistic (S/M) material as "violent pornography," yet it (Vance, 1986:81):

> called no witnesses to discuss the nature of S/M, either professional experts or typical participants. They ignored a small but increasing body of literature that documents important features of S/M sexual behavior, namely consent and safety. Typically, the conventions we use to decipher ordinary images are suspended when it comes to S/M images. When we see war movies, for example, we do not leave the theatre believing that the carnage we saw was real or that the performers were injured making the films. But the commissioners assumed that images of domination and submission were both real and coerced.

Moreover, it is circular reasoning to define "humiliating sexual practices" as those "that would to most people be considered humiliating." It also implicitly assumes that there is somewhat of a consensus about the nature of humiliating sexual practices. Yet, no evidence suggests such a consensus exists. In fact, the evidence suggests that one person's humiliating sexual practice is another person's sexuality. Nevertheless, the Meese Commission concluded that pornography is harmful and that it should be controlled through the vigorous enforcement of obscenity laws.

The U.S. Supreme Court has consistently ruled that pornography is not protected by the First Amendment of the Constitution, which prohibits any law from impending freedom of speech and press. In 1957 the Court ruled in *Roth v. United States* that if "the dominant theme" of any sexual imagery appeals to the "prurient interests" of the average person in a community, such material is deemed obscene (*Roth v. U.S.*, 354 U.S. 476 [1957]). Obviously, this decision has its problems. For example, it can be difficult to determine a dominant theme. Can we agree on the nature of "prurient interests"? What is the "average person"? Recognizing these problems, the Supreme Court attempted to be more precise in *Miller v. California* (1973). According to *Miller*, material is obscene if

1. the average person, applying contemporary community standards, would find that the work, taken as a whole, appeals to prurient interests

2. the work depicts or describes, in a patently offensive way, sexual conduct

3. the work, taken as a whole, lacks serious literary, artistic, political, or scientific value (*Miller v. California*, 413 U.S. 15 [1973])

Radical feminists, however, oppose pornography for other reasons than an alleged harm against the community. Radical feminists understand patriarchy (male control of the labor power and sexuality of women) as the central and causative system of inequality in U.S. society (see also Chapter 15.3). From this position they argue that "the organized expropriation of the sexuality of some for the use of others defines the sex, woman" (MacKinnon, 1982:516). For some radical feminists, heterosexual sexual relations "are characterized by an ideology of sexual objectification (men as subjects/masters; women as objects/slaves) that supports male sexual violence against women" (Ferguson, 1984:108). Consequently, the dominant philosophy for some radical feminists becomes: "Pornography is the theory, rape is the practice" (Morgan, 1980:134). Pornography is "central to the institutionalization of male dominance," some radical feminists argue, and maintains gender inequality by legitimating violence against, and objectifying and dehumanizing, women (MacKinnon, 1984:321–329). Some radical feminists also argue that pornography:

1. subordinates women through sex, harming women openly, publicly, and with social legitimacy

2. commodifies and objectifies women as possessions, to be controlled by men and used by men as men please

3. promotes violence toward women as pleasing, pleasurable, and enjoyable by *both* men and women

As such, radical feminists assert that pornography institutionalizes the second-class citizenship of *all* women, hampers the sexual equality of women, and helps maintain male control in all spheres of society—employment, education, politics, media, courts, and in the home (see the various articles in Lederer, 1980). As Zillah Eisenstein (1988:170–171) states:

> When pornography is defined as a problem of sex discrimination, one which denies women equality, it becomes clear that radical feminists' motive for eliminating pornography is not to protect women but to empower them.

In their efforts to ban pornography, radical feminists have united with various conservative groups. For these conservatives, the only "natural" form of sex is heterosexual monogamy. On this view, pornography is simply propaganda for nonprocreational sex. Thus, both radical feminists and conservatives "seek to exorcise pornography as if it were the devil incarnate" (Burstyn, 1984:32).

In 1983, Catharine McKinnon and Andrea Dworkin attempted to outlaw pornography—and thereby move beyond obscenity laws—by declaring, in the now-famous "Minneapolis Ordinance," that pornography is a form of sex discrimination and a violation of women's rights. The ordinance was enacted by the Minneapolis city council, but vetoed by the Mayor. A similar law was enacted in Indianapolis, but subsequently declared unconstitutional by a federal judge. The Minneapolis Ordinance defines pornography as "the sexually explicit subordination of women, graphically depicted, whether in pictures or in words," that includes one or more of nine categories of sexual imagery. The ordinance, if enacted, permitted individual women to initiate a civil lawsuit against pornographers who cause harm by trafficking in pornography, coercing people into pornographic performances, forcing pornography on a person, and assaulting or physically attacking someone due to pornography.

MacKinnon offered the case of Linda Marchiano ("Linda Lovelace" in the movie *Deep Throat*) as an example of the type of pornography covered by the law. If the law were implemented, that movie would be actionable on two counts: coercion into pornographic performance (because Marchiano alleges she was coerced into making the movie) and trafficking in pornography (because the movie allegedly presents women as sexual objects). As MacKinnon (cited in Duggan *et al.*, 1985:138) states, the film:

> subordinates women by using women . . . sexually, specifically as eager servicing receptacles for male genitalia and ejaculate. The majority of the film represents "Linda Lovelace" in, minimally, postures of sexual submission and/or servility.

MacKinnon (1984:335–340) argues further that the Minneapolis Ordinance does not abridge the freedom of speech of pornographers, but promotes the freedom of speech of women. In a gender-unequal society, MacKinnon states, the speech of the powerful (men) becomes dominant and, therefore, pornography (as "male speech") "invents women because it has the power to make its vision into reality, which then passes, objectively, for truth" (*ibid.*:337). Consequently, for MacKinnon (*ibid.*:340), a law like the Minneapolis Ordinance provides women a means with which to obtain access to speech (*ibid.*:340).

Feminists differ in their views on pornography and about the appropriate strategy to deal with it. Some socialist feminists, for example, hold a contrasting view of sexuality from the view held by radical feminists. Sexuality for such feminists is seen as "repressive," in the sense that the sexual desires and pleasures of people in this society are hindered because of the stigmatization of sexual minorities (the "outer limits" discussed earlier). What this repression does is keep the "majority 'pure' and under control" (Ferguson, 1984:109). Accordingly some socialist feminists (*ibid.*) assert that:

▲— feminists should repudiate any theoretical analyses, legal restrictions, or moral judgments that stigmatize sexual minorities and thus restrict the freedom of all

▲— feminists should reclaim control over female sexuality by demanding the right to practice whatever provides pleasure and satisfaction

▲— the ideal sexual relationship is between full consenting, equal partners who negotiate to maximize one another's sexual pleasure and satisfaction by any means they choose

Recognizing that pornography is embedded in a gender inegalitarian society, these socialist feminists nevertheless assert that we can likewise uncover progressive forces in pornography. Zillah Eisenstein (1988:163) argues that in pornography:

> females are displayed as subjugated, objectified women. Pornography's scope, however, is broader than this; it includes fantasy and rebellion as well. Multiple meanings coexist within pornography, and they crisscross the realms of real and ideal.

Duggan *et al.* (1985:145) likewise argue that pornography serves a number of social functions that benefit women, such as ridiculing conventional sexual mores and advocating sexual adventure, sex outside marriage, sex for no reason other than pleasure, casual sex, anonymous sex, group sex, voyeuristic sex, illegal sex, and public sex. Finally, Paula Webster (1981:50) points out that pornography contains important messages for women because "it does not tie women's sexuality to reproduction or to the domesticated couple or exclusively to men."

Some socialist feminists see the radical feminist attack on pornography as simply a means of attacking a sexual minority—namely, S/M. For example, the Minneapolis Ordinance defines S/M sexuality as subordination of women when the law includes such sexual acts as women "tied up" or "presented in postures of sexual submission." Although condemning S/M per se, radical feminists simultaneously argue for a "politically correct" sexuality—namely, "fully consenting, equal partners who are emotionally involved and do not participate in polarized roles" (Ferguson, 1984:108). As Gayle Rubin (1984:301) states, what antipornography feminists are doing is simply replacing "married, procreative heterosexuality at the top of the value hierarchy" with their own type of sexuality but simultaneously attacking heterosexuality as being oppressive to women. Duggan *et al.* (1985:138–139) explain, using the example of *Deep Throat*, how this is accomplished:

> The notion that the female character is "used" by men suggests that it is improbable that a woman would engage in fellatio of her own accord. *Deep Throat* does draw on several sexist conventions common in advertising and the entire visual culture—the woman as object of the male gaze, and the assumption of heterosexuality, for example. But it is hardly an unending paean to male dominance, since the movie contains many contrary themes. In it, the main female character is shown both actively seeking her own pleasure and as trying to please men; a secondary female character is shown as actually directing encounters with multiple male partners. . . . At its heart, this analysis implies that heterosexual sex itself is sexist; that women do not engage in it of their own volition; and that behavior pleasurable to men is repugnant to women.

These same authors argue that the Ordinance never explicitly defines what is meant by "the sexually explicit subordination of women." This deficit exemplifies a reality touched on earlier: one person's subordination can easily be another person's sexuality. As Duggan *et al.* (*ibid.*:140) go on to point out:

> To some, *any* graphic sexual act violates women's dignity and therefore subordinates them. To others, consensual heterosexual lovemaking within the boundaries of procreation and marriage is acceptable, but heterosexual acts that do not have reproduction as their aim lower women's status and hence subordinate them. Still others accept a wide range of nonprocreative, perhaps even nonmarital, heterosexuality but draw the line at lesbian sex, which they view as degrading.

Duggan *et al.* (*ibid.*:144–146) argue that people should oppose this type of legislation because sexual imagery does not cause more harm to women than do other aspects of a sexist culture and, pornography, even in a sexist society, does serve some positive functions for women. However, these authors (*ibid.*:146–151) go beyond this argument, correctly reasoning that passage of such laws would impede, rather than enhance, feminist goals—that is, such laws would (1) do nothing to improve the material conditions of women's lives, (2) divert attention from support for other laws that would enhance women's condition (such as the Equal Rights Amendment and comparable worth legislation), and (3) force pornography underground (rather than eliminate it), worsening the working conditions in the available sex industry.

REVIEW

This chapter examined five types of public-order "crimes"—gambling, drug use/abuse, abortion, prostitution, and pornography. There is considerable debate as to whether these behaviors should be criminalized by the state. Nevertheless, it is clear that the state selectively enforces public-order laws.

Gambling

1. There are two major types of gambling: illegal and commercial.

2. Some argue that all gambling is "immoral" and should be criminalized; others argue that gambling is "moral" and should be made available to all who wish to gamble. Still others point out that the state defines certain forms of gambling as "immoral" and other types as "moral"—thereby selectively enforcing morality to its own benefit.

3. The three major types of commercial gambling are state lotteries, casinos, and pari-mutuel betting.

Drug Use/Abuse

1. The criminal law itself contributes to the creation of an illegal drug market and subculture.

2. The most widely used illegal drugs are cocaine, heroin, and marijuana, whose dangers are attributed primarily to their illegal status.

3. Drugs do not cause crime, yet addiction to narcotics such as heroin clearly escalates criminal involvement.

4. Some argue that drug-related crime is so out of control, and the distribution of illegal drugs sufficiently unstoppable, that the only answer is to decriminalize, or even legalize, the drugs that are presently illegal.

Abortion, Prostitution, and Pornography

1. In *Roe v. Wade* (1973), the Supreme Court established that women have a constitutional right to abortion.

2. The public overwhelmingly supports the *Roe v. Wade* decision.

3. The history of abortion in the United States shows that it first became illegal after 1860 because of pressure from the male-dominated medical profession.

4. Certain social conditions in the 1960s and 1970s, as well as the second wave of the feminist movement, led to the decriminalization of abortion in 1973.

5. Prostitution and pornography are within the "outer limits" of the sexual hierarchy.

6. Both males and females are involved in prostitution, men more frequently than women.

7. The major types of male prostitution are street hustler, bar hustler, and escort service.

8. The abolitionist movement of the early 1900s led to the control of prostitution by pimps and male-dominated criminal syndicates.

9. Contemporary female prostitutes search for customers in such public and private settings as the streets, bars, hotels, massage parlors, and brothels.

10. Radical feminists, other feminists, and prostitutes debate whether prostitution is a "victimless" crime.

11. In 1970 the Commission on Obscenity and Pornography concluded that pornography was harmless; in 1986 the Attorney General's Commission on Pornography argued the opposite.

12. Researchers have argued several shortcomings in the latter Commission's methodology for reaching conclusions.

QUESTIONS FOR CLASS DISCUSSION

1. Discuss whether the terms "victimless" or "complaintless" crimes adequately describe the nature of public-order "crimes."

2. We identified certain means by which the state selectively enforces morality. Can you identify any others? What impact does such selective enforcement have on the notion of public-order "crimes"?

3. Should heroin, cocaine, and marijuana be decriminalized, legalized, or more seriously controlled?

4. Should prostitution be legalized in all states?

5. Does "pornography" oppress women?

RECOMMENDED READINGS

Abt, Vicki, James F. Smith, and Eugene Martin Christiansen (1985). *The Business of Risk: Commercial Gambling in Mainstream America.* Lawrence, KS: University of Kansas Press. A summary and discussion of commercial gambling in the United States.

Barry, Kathleen (1979). *Female Sexual Slavery.* Englewood Cliffs, NJ: Prentice-Hall. A good example of the radical feminist position on pornography.

Bell, Laurie (ed) (1987). *Good Girls/Bad Girls: Feminists and Sex Trade Workers Face to Face.* Seattle: The Seal Press. This book provides an interesting dialogue between a variety of feminists and women who work in the commercial sex industry.

Burstyn, Varda (ed) (1985). *Women Against Censorship.* Toronto: Douglas and McIntyre. This collection contains scholarly pieces by feminists on pornography and anti-censorship strategies for dealing with pornography.

Currie, Elliott (1993). *Reckoning: Drugs, the Cities, and the American Future.* New York: Hill and Wang. The most in-depth examination of drug use/abuse and what to do about it in the United States.

Lederer, Laura (ed) (1980). *Take Back the Night: Women on Pornography.* New York: William Morrow. A collection of writings on pornography; written primarily from a radical feminist perspective.

Miller, Eleanor (1986). *Street Woman.* Philadelphia: Temple University Press. This book contributes to our understanding of the role of prostitution in "deviant street networks."

Petchesky, Rosalind (1984). *Abortion and Women's Choice: The State, Sexuality, and Reproductive Freedom.* Boston: Northeastern University Press. An in-depth discussion of the history and nature of abortion in the United States.

Schur, Edwin and Hugo Adam Bedau (1974). *Victimless Crimes: Two Sides of a Controversy.* Englewood Cliffs, NJ: Prentice-Hall. An early classic debate on the controversial issues surrounding the notion of "victimless" crimes.

West, Donald J. and Buz de Villiers (1993). *Male Prostitution.* New York: The Haworth Press. The best study of male prostitution available.

CHAPTER 7

WHITE-COLLAR CRIME

7.1 Occupational Crime
Occupational Theft
Collective Embezzlement
Occupational Fraud

7.2 Corporate Crime
Corporate Violence
Corporate Theft
Transnational Corporate Crime

7.3 Criminal Corporations
From Legitimate to Criminal Corporation
Long-Firm Fraud
Laundries and Conduits

Preview

Chapter 7 introduces:

☞ what sociologists mean by white-collar crime.
☞ the different types of white-collar crime.
☞ the nature, extent, and costs of white-collar crime.
☞ how white-collar crimes differ from the crimes already examined.

Key Terms

collective embezzlement	insider trading
corporate crime	occupational crime
corporate theft	occupational fraud
corporate violence	occupational theft
criminal corporations	physician fraud
deceptive advertising	price-fixing
embezzlement	transnational corporate crime
employee theft	white-collar crime
financial fraud	

W*hen we think of crime, our thoughts usually focus on the types of crimes already discussed in this book—interpersonal crimes of violence and property and public-order offenses. This is natural because official agencies of social control (police and courts) concentrate on these behaviors (thus attracting media attention) and because these crimes are the most frequently studied by sociologists and criminologists.*

However, although the crimes discussed in Chapters 4 and 5 generate considerable fear and suffering in society—and thus it is critical to understand why they occur and how they can be controlled—the white-collar crimes discussed in this chapter are clearly more harmful not only to U.S. society but also to other societies.

Sutherland (see also Chapter 12.4) was the first sociologist in the United States to conceptualize the problem of white-collar crime. Given the contemptuous attitude toward the law and business ethics displayed by the "robber barons" (such as Daniel Drew and John D. Rockefeller) in the late 1800s and the widespread and publicized fraud of the 1920s and 1930s, Sutherland focused his classic study on "crime committed by a person of respectability and high social status in the course of his occupation" (Sutherland, 1949:2). Demonstrating that white-collar crime was widespread and endemic to U.S. business, Sutherland's findings forced him to concentrate almost exclusively on one type of white-collar crime—corporate crime. However, after Sutherland, sociologists and criminologists expanded the definition of white-collar crime to include not only corporate crimes, but also occupational crimes and criminal corporations.

Occupational crimes *are committed by individuals in the course of their occupations for direct personal gain. These crimes are usually, but not always, committed against an employer. Embezzlement is an example of an occupational crime.*

Corporate crimes *differ from occupational crimes in that they are not committed for direct personal gain—although certain individuals may benefit indirectly from the act. Rather, these crimes primarily benefit the corporation. We define corporate crimes as illegal and/or socially injurious acts of intent or indifference that occur for the purpose of furthering corporate goals, and that physically and/or economically abuse individuals in the United States and/or abroad. Collusion of top executives of utility corporations to fix prices is an example of corporate crime.*

Criminal corporations *constitute the third type of white-collar crime. Corporate crimes occur within legitimate corporate operations, but criminal acts also arise from criminal corporations—corporations deliberately set up, managed, or taken over for the exclusive purpose of conducting criminal activity (Box, 1983:22). A company set up to obtain goods on credit with the deliberate intent of never paying for them is an example of a criminal corporation.*

It is important to note that these three types of white-collar crime are both similar and different from the crimes already discussed in Chapter 4 and 5. Like other crimes, white-collar crimes involve theft and violence. That is, commission of white-collar crimes results in loss of property and/or physical injury and death. But white-collar crimes are different from other crimes in three important ways. First, white-collar crimes entail far more victimization—in terms of economic loss and lives injured and lost—than do the crimes discussed earlier. Second, white-collar crimes occur in the course of doing business, or working for a business; interpersonal violence and property and public-order offenses do not. Third, victimization resulting from white-collar crimes is less apparent— although once again, far more severe—than the one-on-one type of victimization result- ing from, for example, interpersonal crimes of violence. Indeed, most of us who suffer the pains of white-collar crimes—corporate crimes in particular—are unaware of our own victimization.

7.1 ———— Occupational Crime

Occupational crime occurs in the workplace and is motivated by direct personal gain: primarily occupational theft and fraud. *Occupational theft* stems from an abuse of trust between the employee and employer. We examine two types of occupational theft: employee theft and embezzlement. Both types affect consum- ers by increasing the cost of commodities; they also affect some businesses negatively. *Occupational fraud* is a deliberate workplace deception practiced for the purpose of obtaining personal financial gain. This type of fraud is ubiquitous; we explore the major aspects of occupational fraud through examples from the fields of medicine and securities.

Occupational Theft

In preindustrialized societies—such as feudal England in the 17th century— people had common rights to such necessities as the gathering of wood, the killing of game, and the grazing of animals. But with the transition from feudalism to capitalism, these "rights" were translated into "property." As Jason Ditton (1977:41) states: The "annexation of common rights . . . naturally culminated in the simultaneous creation of 'property,' and the propertied classes, and the ultimate criminalization of customary practices." As land previously open to everyone's use became the private property of a few, wood gathering became wood theft, game rights became poaching, and grazing rights became trespassing (*ibid.*:44). In addition, this privatization, as Ditton (*ibid.*:43) explains

> released into urban life a working population not only used to receiving part of their "wages" in kind . . . but also one still stinging from the effects of the abrupt and cruel negation of those practices in the countryside. As one might expect, and empirical evidence supports this, a major source of irritation to factory owners who took on such "idle" rural laborers was their penchant for making off with parts of the workplace or the fruits of their labor there, in addition to their wages.

Indeed, the preindustrial cultural tradition of common rights was carried over into industrialized society. Workers expected "wages-in-kind"—extras to supplement their actual earnings. In 18th-century England, for instance, workers in manufacturing industries "constantly borrowed, bartered, and sold small quantities of materials among themselves," a good portion of which was stolen from the workplace (Henry, 1987:142). As Stuart Henry (*ibid.*:142) argues:

> Criminalization of the consumption of a part of one's daily labor was redefined in conjunction with capitalist development of the factory to become employee theft and embezzlement; the trading of embezzled goods came to constitute a hidden economy.

In other words, accompanying the rise of capitalism was the emergence of two major forms of occupational theft: employee theft and embezzlement. We consider each form and its relation to the trade in stolen goods discussed in Chapter 5.1.

Employee theft—stealing merchandise and job-related items from one's workplace—is one of the most pervasive and costly crimes in the United States. Self-report studies suggest that between 75 and 92 percent of employees *admit* to some sort of theft from the workplace (Henry, 1981:12). One study found that only 25 percent of employees are honest at all times in the workplace (Comer, 1985:5).

The cost of employee theft is enormous. Most employees steal minor items; yet when these items are multiplied for many workers, the cost becomes substantial. "Inventory shrinkage" (loss from employee theft, shoplifting, poor paperwork, and vendor theft) adds approximately 15 percent to the price of all retail goods. Most of this loss is attributable to employee theft. According to Lloyd W. Klemke (1992:10), 40 percent to 50 percent of inventory shrinkage is attributable to employee theft, 31 percent to shoplifting, and 15 percent to 30 percent due to accounting errors. Overall, researchers estimate that employee theft costs $100–200 billion annually and that one-third of all small businesses fail due to expenses stemming from employee theft (Conway and Cox, 1987:8–9).

It is convenient to assume that employee theft is primarily a problem of lower-level employees. This is not the case. A 1974 investigation of employee crime attributed 62 percent of losses to thefts by company supervisors (Jaspan, 1974:v). Comer (1985:5) reports that "the most dangerous" thefts "are those which occur at higher management levels." In 1987, Baker and Westin (1987:10) found that petty employee theft (loss of small amounts of office supplies, tools, and so on) tends to be committed by all employees; however, at least 38 percent of management or senior staff are the principal source of major employee theft (loss of thousands of dollars in raw materials and components, supplies, tools, products, and so on).

Two classic studies by Ditton (1977a) and Mars (1983) enhance our understanding of the relationship between occupation and employee theft. Ditton considers employee theft a form of what he calls "part-time crime." However, part-time crime is not simply a matter of time commitment inasmuch as a part-time criminal may well

> spend more hours and minutes breaking the law than somebody involved full-time in crime. The crucial distinction is that whereas the full-time

criminal's legitimate occupation is perceived by him [or her] to be merely nominal, the part-time criminal sees his [or her] illegitimate activities in the same way, as nominal (*ibid.*:91).

In other words, part-time criminals may spend more hours planning and executing their crime than full-time criminals, but this activity is *perceived* by them as inconsequential to their full-time legitimate activity at work.

In a participant observation study of bread salesmen at Wellbread Bakery, Ditton (*ibid.*:92–113) found that part-time employee theft entailed three activities: fiddling, stealing, and dealing. "Fiddling" is the practice by salesmen (those who sell and deliver bakery goods) of overcharging customers by either increasing the price or reducing the number of items for the standard price. Ditton found that fiddling was tolerated—even overtly recommended—by management because the loser is the customer rather than the company. "Stealing" is theft from the company itself. Although production workers have "pilfering rights" to a daily loaf of bread, salesmen are excluded from this dubious privilege. As Ditton (*ibid.*:101) explains:

> It is assumed that production staff have no outlet other than domestic consumption of pilfered loaves, and that this empirical feature of the practice will de facto limit the amount of bread that they will take. Salesmen, on the other hand, are assumed to have guaranteed occupational access to facilities (a round of customers) which would encourage them systematically to escalate their thefts beyond tolerable levels. Thus, for salesmen at Wellbread's, we may define a successful steal as the removal of some sort of asset skillfully, unobserved, and without permission. Salesmen steal both convertible consumer goods for resale to their customers, and nonconvertible assets, such as plastic bags and clipboards, which, as tools of the trade, make occupational life easier.

"Dealing"—the third employee theft activity identified by Ditton—is the clandestine unofficial "distribution of other people's goods to the mutual interest and profit of those covertly involved" (*ibid.*:106). Dealing involves the collusion of salesmen and other employee staff in arranging a profit-making venture. For example, the bread dispatcher may provide extra trays of bread to a salesman without "booking it." Subsequent to the sale of the extra trays, both the salesman and the dispatcher share the profits (*ibid.*:107–113). Dealing involves the amateur trade (or fencing) in stolen goods from the workplace.

Ditton's book relates how crime can provide an outlet for creativity in monotonous and alienated work environments, as well as challenge the "official" view of crime as being predominantly a lower-class, nonoccupational phenomenon.

Mars' most important contribution distinguishes among types of employee theft and links these to types of jobs. Mars divides workers into four different types (hawks, donkeys, wolves, and vultures) distinguished by such elements as the amount of job autonomy, extent of isolation from others, and the degree of control over one's labor power. Mars (*ibid.*:26–28) also examined the amount of collectiveness in the workplace, which varies according to how a workplace prioritizes the interests of the group over the individual and is distinguished by such elements as the frequency with which people interact with others, whether contacts occur within a mutually interconnecting network, and the scope of group social life outside the workplace.

"Hawks" are professionals, executives, and small business persons who maintain individuality, autonomy, and control over their labor power, but have infrequent contact with others. Therefore, it is much easier for hawks to "bend the rules" to their personal advantage. Work-related expenses provide an example. A journalist, for instance, may claim first-class travel but actually go second class, or falsify costs of entertainment and meals as business expenses. More extremely, one journalist said: "It's not uncommon for you to say you're dashing . . . somewhere for a story. You look up fares plus a few beers for fictitious informants and a taxi or two and bang it in for expenses" (cited in Mars, 1983:47).

"Donkeys" have little autonomy, are not isolated from others, and have no control over their labor power. Moreover, donkeys do not work within a group setting with frequent interaction. Supermarket cashiers and workers "on long and noisy mass-production belts" are examples of donkeys. Because of the structured nature of these jobs, employee theft is more restricted than it is for hawks. Supermarket cashiers, for instance, are limited to undercharging—or not charging at all—friends and family who frequent the store where they work, or simply "taking from the till." As one cashier expressed to Mars (*ibid.*:66): A theft may occur "when your mother or friend comes in. Then they get away with a load of stuff and you put hardly anything through the till."

"Wolves" are similar to donkeys in the sense of having little autonomy and lacking control over their labor power; but they are different in that their jobs require a group of workers. For both hawks and donkeys, control over theft belongs to the individual. For wolves, however, theft is under group control. Airport baggage handlers and longshoremen are examples of wolves. If dockworkers, for example, want to steal cargo, to do so they need the support of the group. This is so both because they work as a group and because they must divide their labor so that some workers steal cargo while others distract supervisors. As Mars (*ibid.*:103) explains:

> Theoretically, all these men can pilfer cargo. Yet supervision of unloading by the ships' officers at one end and the shed superintendent at the other greatly reduces *individual* opportunities. Those with *access* therefore need the *support* of those who do not have access, to distract the attention of the supervisors, to provide cover, to "clear" documents and to enable the swift removal and distribution of goods once they have been pilfered.

Finally, "vultures" have considerable individual autonomy, yet that autonomy operates within a loosely structured work group setting. Waiters, truck drivers, and hotel workers are examples of vultures. Such occupations enjoy a degree of independence yet rely on support from coworkers. For example, Mars (*ibid.*:112) found a coordinated group of truck drivers who arranged the "private delivery" of stolen company goods on company time.

Overall, Mars' work identifies how type of occupation and workplace setting help determine type of occupational theft. Indeed, his classification of hawks, donkeys, wolves, and vultures involves a combination of employee theft and embezzlement.

As with conventional property theft, much of employee theft involves trade in stolen goods. Friends, relatives, and workmates form "trading networks" in which goods are stolen and subsequently sold (Henry, 1978:17–41). For example, the cashier "donkey" referred to earlier may, once store detectives are out of view, signal (*ibid.*:18)

> a friend who is buying various goods. The cashier rings up some of the items, but lets the rest through. The extra goods obtained in this way may be shared out later between the cashier and her friend, or they may be passed on to a friend's friend for sale in a local office or factory.

Thus, the overall amateur trade in stolen goods involves a variety of theft-related techniques—from conventional property theft discussed in Chapter 5.1, to the stealing and dealing of stolen goods among "ordinary people in honest jobs" (*ibid.*:20). Indeed, sometimes these techniques overlap. Henry (*ibid.*:26–27) describes a plumber who contracts out his labor to a variety of industrial firms. Coming into contact with a large number of people, he can "fence" or "deal" stolen goods provided him by a shoplifter friend. Consequently, type of job not only determines the nature of employee theft—as Mars points out—but also creates opportunities for dealing stolen goods. The amateur trade in stolen goods—whether the stolen goods originate from conventional property theft or employee theft—creates a hidden economy governed primarily by social relationships rather than economic gain (Henry and Mars, 1978:245–251). This hidden economy was discussed more thoroughly in Chapter 3.1.

Embezzlement, similarly to employee theft, also involves a violation of employer/employee trust. However, embezzlement differs from employee theft in that it involves taking money—rather than merchandise and job-related items—for one's personal use. The supermarket cashier "donkey," for example, has the opportunity to steal both merchandise (employee theft) and money (embezzlement).

Embezzlement ranges from simply "taking from the till" to "manipulating the books," but people in certain occupations can embezzle more than those in others. Individuals who occupy top business or bank positions—such as loan officers, accountants, computer operators, and vice-presidents—have a much greater opportunity for embezzling large sums of money than do cashiers, bank tellers, sales clerks, or other lower-level employees. Consequently, individuals in the position to embezzle, and who actually do embezzle large sums of money, frequently are viewed by employers as some of the most important people in the company.

It is extremely difficult to determine exactly how much money is lost to embezzlement each year. Because businesses do not, for obvious reasons, want the crime aired publicly, embezzlement is severely underreported. Nevertheless, *The Wall Street Journal* estimates that losses from bank embezzlements alone total more than $1 billion a year (McCoy, 1987:23). Bank failures are one result. In a study by the House Government Operations Committee, embezzlement was found to be one of the major reasons underlying three-fifths of the 75 bank failures between 1980 and 1983 (Green and Berry, 1985:274). In 1986, according to *Business Week*, there were 144 bank failures caused by embezzlement (De-George, 1987:49). Yet we must remember that not only businesses are victims of embezzlement. Banks and other businesses simply pass along their losses to us—consumers—in the form of higher fees and service charges.

An example of embezzlement entailing "taking from the till" is a department store cashier who stole "one nickel, dime or quarter from every roll of change she made over a period of 20 years; she was able to purchase a home with the money she stole" (Conklin, 1977:6). However, most embezzlements of this type are not as lucrative. In 1987, for example, 21 former employees of 15 south Florida banks and savings and loan associations were indicted on charges of embezzling $1.2 million. The individuals charged included a vice-president and a comptroller, but most were tellers charged with embezzling—"from the till"—only a few thousand dollars each (*The New York Times*, 1987:39).

A recent case of embezzlement involving "manipulation of the books" is that of a Mitsubishi Bank of California executive who embezzled almost $45 million from 1980 to 1984 by creating more than 135 fictitious loans and misappropriating substantial sums of money from two corporate accounts. The embezzled money was used to pay gambling debts and to purchase stock (Stevenson, 1987:D1, D4).

Much embezzlement results from the use of computers: the technology makes it easier to manipulate books because it is so difficult to detect and trace. Moreover, only about 15 percent of computer embezzlements are ever reported. Thus, like other embezzlements, we must rely on estimates to determine the magnitude of this crime. According to one estimate, the average computer crime nets approximately $400,000, and from $100 to $300 million in computer theft occurs each year (Coleman, 1989:83). Nearly one-half the businesses surveyed in 1984 by the American Bar Association reported being victimized by computer crime, and employees account for 70 percent to 90 percent of all cases of computer crime (Green and Berry, 1985:272; Albanese and Pursley, 1993:42).

Examples of computer embezzlement are wide-ranging. A bank teller at New York's Union Dime Savings Bank embezzled approximately $1.4 million over three years by manipulating accounts and putting inaccurate information into the computer (Parker, 1976:192–203). In 1987 a branch manager at Family Bank of Ogden, Utah, provided money for a gambler by engaging in computer embezzlement; the manager used the bank's computers to set up phony accounts through which he channeled $4 million to the gambler. According to McCoy (1987:23), the scheme was only uncovered because the bank's president, unable to find a magazine to carry with him into the restroom, picked up a sheaf of computer records instead and discovered that a usually dormant account held some $800,000.

Collective Embezzlement

The above discussion identified embezzlement as a crime committed by employees *against* the company. However, a new type of embezzlement emerged from the savings and loan scandal, what Kitty Calavita and Henry Pontell (1990:321) have termed "collective embezzlement." This type of embezzlement entails "the siphoning off of funds from a savings and loan institution for personal gain, at the expense of the institution itself *and with the implicit or explicit sanction of its management*" (*ibid.*:321). In other words, like traditional embezzlement, collective embezzlement is a crime against the company. Yet collective embezzlement differs from traditional embezzlement in that it is endorsed, approved, and accomplished by management itself. It is, in short, "crime *by* the corporation *against* the corporation" (*ibid.*:322).

The savings and loan scandal is the most expensive white-collar crime in U.S. history and will most likely cost the U.S. government between $300 and $500 billion over the next decade (Waldman, 1990: 4). Ultimately, however, U.S. taxpayers are the victims of this crime because the money embezzled did not belong to the embezzlers. As Michael Waldman (*ibid.*:3) points out, "it was *ours*, because we, as taxpayers, insured the deposits in their banks. The result is an unprecedented government bailout, with an estimated cost of up to $15,000 per taxpayer."

In 1980, Congress increased the amount for which the Federal Savings and Loan Insurance Corporation (FSLIC) would insure S&L accounts from a maximum of $40,000 to $100,000 per deposit. Additionally, Congress phased out controls on interest rates. Subsequently, S&Ls raised their interest rates, thus attracting wealthy depositors who did not face any risk of loss; should an S&L fail, the U.S. government (and therefore taxpayers) would reimburse depositors up to $100,000 per deposit. Combined with the Reagan Administration's deregulation policies of "getting government off our backs," the conditions were ripe for this new form of occupational crime.

According to U.S. government reports, crime or misconduct played a crucial role in 70 percent to 80 percent of the S&Ls bailed out and two prominent examples of collective embezzlement are "buying sprees" and "straw borrower loans" (Calavita and Pontell, 1990: 315, 322–23).

An example of a buying spree is the case of Erwin "Erv" Hansen, president of Centennial Savings and Loan in northern California. According to Stephen Pizzo, Mary Fricker, and Paul Muolo (1989: 36–37), Hansen embezzled S&L funds to purchase such things as antique furniture ($130,000), a penthouse in San Francisco ($773,487), a Mercedes limousine ($77,000), five cars for his family ($90,000), and a $137,000 Rolls-Royce for himself. In 1983, Hansen threw a Christmas party for his friends, described by Pizzo *et al.* (*ibid.*: 25–26) as:

> the most lavish Christmas party anyone could recall. "Elegant Renaissance Faire" was the theme. Couples gasped as jesters proclaimed their entry into the hall, now transformed into an Elizabethan forest of 300 living trees sparkling with 75,000 tiny white lights. Candlelight shimmered through piped-in fog that simulated the moors and woods of Nottingham. Oriental rugs covered the floor.
>
> Once seated among the trees, the 500 guests were entertained by a hundred roving Robin Hoods, fiddlers, jugglers, jesters, and pantomimes. Waiters and waitresses, one for every two guests, wore Elizabethan costumes—swagger-plumed hats, ruffled laced bodices, yards of velvet. They rolled the ten-course, three-hour meal into the hall on flaming carts, meats cracking on open spits, each course heralded by twelve trumpeters.
>
> Men and women visiting the rest room were attended by shoeshine boys for the men and maids-in-waiting with an array of makeup and perfumes for the women. Dancing continued until three o'clock in the morning, and to this day many say it was the most romantic evening of their lives.

Because of the outright looting (collective embezzlement), Centennial eventually became insolvent, costing the FSLIC an estimated $160 million (Calavita and Pontell, 1990: 322).

In the case of straw borrower loans, the owner/officer of an S&L will extend a loan to a "straw borrower" (someone indirectly connected to the S&L) who receives a kickback for obtaining the loan and then returns the remaining money to the lender. One such owner/officer, Don Dixon (owner of all the stock of Vernon S&L in Texas), put together "an intricate network of at least 30 subsidiary companies for the express purpose of making illegal loans to himself," and overall, the Vernon collective embezzlement cost taxpayers approximately $1.3 billion (*ibid.*:323).

Occupational Fraud

In Chapter 5.2 we discussed different types of fraud committed against the government and through the use of checks and credit cards. We now discuss two types of occupational fraud—physician fraud and insider trading—committed for direct personal gain in the course of one's occupation.

According to a past president of the Federation of State Medical Boards, at least one of every 20 physicians is a severe disciplinary problem and one of nine is repeatedly guilty of practices unworthy of the profession (Jesilow, Pontell, and Geis, 1985:154). Most physicians are honest; some, however, defraud through unnecessary prescription of pharmaceutical drugs, unnecessary surgical procedures, and overtreatment of Medicare and Medicaid patients. We examine each in turn.

Approximately 25 percent of all antibiotic prescriptions in U.S. hospitals are prescribed unnecessarily, resulting in about 10,000 potentially fatal reactions (Coleman, 1989:113). Moreover, because many physicians own pharmacies and/or stock in drug repackaging firms, some engage in selling the products they prescribe. Coleman (*ibid.*:114) describes how some physicians buy drugs from manufacturers and then put on their own labels. The "owner-physicians" of these drug repackaging firms then exploitatively prescribe their own drugs at substantially inflated prices. Coleman (*ibid.*:114) further points out: "Not surprisingly, there is evidence that physicians who make a financial profit from the products they prescribe are likely to prescribe them more often."

In addition to fraudulent prescription of pharmaceuticals, some physicians perform unnecessary surgeries. Unnecessary surgeries cost the people of the United States approximately $4 billion annually, and it is estimated that 10 percent of all surgeries performed in the United States are unnecessary (Jesilow, Pontell, and Geis, 1993:19). Moreover, estimated deaths each year from unnecessary surgeries range from 12,000 to 16,000 (Reiman, 1984:61).

A prime example of fraudulent surgery is coronary bypass surgery. A recent study, reported in *The New York Times*, concluded that a substantial number of patients who receive the operation do not actually need it. According to the findings, approximately 25,000 of the 170,000 bypass operations each year do not improve a patient's chances of survival over the next six years. The study concluded that "at the end of six years, 92 percent of those who had surgery and 90 percent of those treated only with medications were still alive" (Brody, 1983:A28). This represents what some regard as a substantial growth in the incidence of unnecessary surgeries. As Cooke and Dworkin (1981:42) express it: "The 1970s and the 1980s will be remembered as the decades when the medical profession trained so many surgeons that they ran out of patients who needed surgery and began to do it on those who didn't."

The preceding view is supported by Scully's (1980a, 1980b) important study of surgical residents. She found that a prerequisite of successful surgical residency "was the ability to find patients and persuade them that surgery was in their best interest" (*ibid.*:90). Performing unnecessary hysterectomies was one of the most common forms of surgical residency abuse—for example, a hysterectomy to remove small, benign uterine fibroids that often disappear without surgery or remain intact without symptomology. Scully asked surgical residents how they would treat a nine- to ten-week asymptomatic uterine fibroid. The following is a representative answer (cited in *ibid.*:90–93):

> I don't think it would be right to say you have a horrible disease or you have cancer or anything like that, so I have to do this surgery. I would explain to her that she has fibroids that are nine- to ten-week size, that she isn't going to have a family any more, she doesn't want a family any more, that these fibroids may sometime in the future grow bigger, may get symptoms, may cause her trouble, she may need surgery at some point in time, and if she would like to have surgery done now, it can be

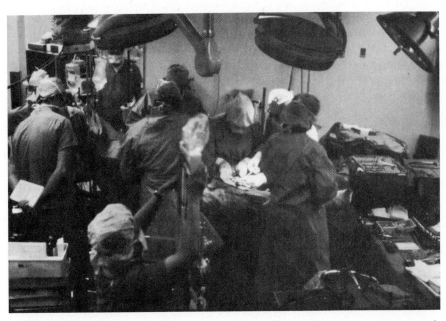

Surrounded by nurses and assistants, a surgeon performs a hysterectomy. Many such operations are not medically necessary.

easy surgery, vaginally. As a consequence she won't have any more children, but she won't have any fibroids and she won't have any potential for disease.

Moreover, studies indicate a relationship between hysterectomy surgery, physician fraud, and racist sterilization. Contemporary findings show that the hysterectomy rate among never-married black women is three to four times higher than the rate for never-married white women, and that the South has the highest hysterectomy rate in the country (Andersen, 1988:206–207). Clinical reports further suggest that although physicians often recommend this surgery to their patients, they also provide them with incorrect information about the overall effects of the surgery. This physician fraud seems to occur more often with minority and poor clients, resulting in the following statistics (*ibid.*:191, 206):

▲— Approximately 43 percent of women living in East Harlem have had either a tubal ligation or a hysterectomy.

▲— Approximately 50 percent of welfare mothers have been sterilized, representing one-third more sterilizations than for other women.

▲— Among women of childbearing years, 36 percent of black women, 24 percent of Native American women, and 21 percent of white women have been sterilized.

Comparative studies demonstrate that the number of practicing surgeons is related to the amount of surgery performed. For example, there are twice as many surgeons in the United States per 100,000 population as there are in England and Wales. Not surprisingly, there are also twice as many operations performed per person in the United States as there are in England and Wales. But this does not ensure that U.S. residents are healthier; mortality rates in England are equal to or lower than those in the United States for all ages (Coleman, 1989:113).

Finally, physician fraud also occurs in Medicaid (for the poor) and Medicare (for the elderly) programs, costing an estimated $61 billion a year (Jesilow, Pontell, and Geis, 1993:12). When physicians know that medical costs will be paid for the poor and elderly, "there is a great deal to be gained by doing as much work as possible, needed or not, and doing it at a minimum cost" (Jesilow *et al.*, 1985:159). As a result, some doctors operate "Medicaid mills"—clinics that use assembly-line, move-them-through procedures—and also frequently falsify claims. For example, a physician in Washington state recently obtained tens of thousands of dollars from the Medicaid system by "treating" approximately 50 to 60 patients every day (Coleman, 1989:117).

A shocking example of Medicaid fraud is the case of a California ophthalmologist found guilty of performing unnecessary cataract surgery on the poor to obtain Medicaid fees. For the affluent the surgery was performed skillfully and successfully; for the poor it was performed in "slipshod fashion." For example, in one case the physician totally blinded a 57-year-old woman when he performed unnecessary surgery on her *one* sighted eye (Jesilow, Pontell, and Geis, 1993:19–20). Moreover, approximately 50 percent of the $3 billion annual Medicare costs for cataract surgery pays for fraudulent practices (Spolar, 1985:11–12). Paul Jesilow, Henry Pontell, and Gilbert Geis (1993) recently investigated Medicaid fraud. In their book *Prescription for Profit*, they draw on case file material from California and New York (the two states with the largest number of violators), finding four primary categories of crimes committed by physicians caught violating Medicaid programs (*ibid.*:105):

> (1) billing schemes, which include billing for services not rendered, charging for nonexistent office visits, or receiving or giving kickbacks; (2) poor quality of care, which includes unnecessary tests, treatments, and surgeries as well as inadequate record keeping; (3) illegal distribution of controlled substances, which include drug prescriptions and sales; and (4) sex with patients whereby physicians under the guise of "therapy" received payments for sexual liaisons with their patients.

Psychiatrists constitute a disproportionate share (in relation to other medical specialists) of Medicare and Medicaid fraud. Examples of physician fraud by psychiatrists include charging patients for individual therapy when patients are actually involved in group therapy, charging a fee for "treatment" that is in reality sexual relations between psychiatrist and "patient," and charging for therapy that simply constitutes the prescription of pharmaceutical drugs (Geis *et al.*, 1988:25–27; Geis *et al.*, 1984; Jesilow *et al.*, 1993:133).

A second type of occupational fraud is insider trading, a form of securities fraud. *Insider trading* occurs when one uses "inside information" (information unavailable to the public) to gain a personal advantage over others in the buying and selling of stock. Individuals obtain such inside information because of their occupational position. For example, if one company plans to take over another, a large number of people are usually involved in the decision making (lawyers, corporate executives, and others). All these people know that if the takeover occurs, the value of each company's stock will change. Thus, prior to takeover, some of these people may take advantage of their "inside information," using it to buy and/or sell stock prior to public disclosure. This is illegal.

One of the earliest insider trading cases involved the Texas Gulf Sulfur Company. In 1963 large deposits of copper and zinc were discovered by company engineers. Employees with access to this information (prior to public disclosure) abused that privilege to profit personally by buying considerable amounts of the company's stock. The employees were convicted of insider trading, the court concluding that all potential investors should have equal access to this type of information, and that company employees—"insiders"—should not have an advantage over the public at large (Bequai, 1975:26).

In the 1980s several other insider trading cases came to public attention, including the following (Green and Berry, 1985:273; *The New York Times,* 1987a:D2; Sterngold, 1987:D1, D4):

▲— Paul Thayer, official of LTV Corporation and former deputy secretary of defense, admitted committing insider trading in 1985.

▲— Thomas Reed, former Reagan national security aide, used inside information to convert a $3,000 stock option into a $427,000 gain in two days.

▲— Dennis Levine, managing director of Drexel Burnham Lambert (an investment banking firm), and Ivan Boesky, Wall Street's most successful arbitrageur—two of the major actors in an informal 1986 network— exchanged information on mergers, takeovers, and corporate restructurings in order to execute trades prior to public disclosure. It is alleged that Boesky profited more than $50 million and Levine almost $13 million from this insider trading network.

▲— Part of the Levine/Boesky network was Martin A. Siegel, who sold takeover information to Boesky from August 1982 until February 1986.

▲— In 1987 it was uncovered that Timothy Tabor (ex-vice-president of Kidder, Peabody), Richard Wigton (Kidder vice-president), and Robert M. Freeman (head of arbitrage at Goldman, Sachs and Co.), were also involved in the network, exchanging takeover information that allegedly earned its participants millions of dollars.

Overall, it is estimated that about one-half the stock market reaction to forthcoming takeovers occurs prior to announcement date and, therefore, insider trading continues to be a frequent crime (Green and Berry, 1985:273; *The Wall Street Journal,* 1993; *The New York Times,* 1993).

7.2 ———— CORPORATE CRIME

We define corporate crime as (1) illegal and/or socially injurious acts of intent or indifference (2) that occur for the purpose of furthering the goals of a corporation and (3) that physically and/or economically abuse individuals in the U.S. and/or abroad. Thus, corporate crime includes not only illegal acts but also socially injurious acts that lie outside the jurisdiction of criminal or regulatory law. Moreover, corporate crime includes harmful acts that result from indifference to the consequences of certain actions as well as from the deliberate intent to harm. By including "indifference," we follow Box (1983:21) who explains that if

> a person intends doing *someone* harm, it cannot be assumed that s/he displays a disdain towards humanity, although it is clearly directed towards the particular intended victim. However, if indifference characterizes the attitude a person has toward the consequences of his/her action, then s/he is indifferent as to who suffers—it could literally be anybody—and this does display disdain for humanity in general. In this sense, the intent to harm someone may be less immoral (or at least no more immoral) than to be indifferent as to whom is harmed.

Finally, our definition notes that corporations perpetrate violence and theft on members of U.S. society, and sometimes on other societies as well. Corporate crime victimizes large numbers of people throughout the world, and it is considerably more harmful and dangerous than the crimes we have already discussed in this and other chapters.

We are not alone in our concern about corporate crime. U.S. residents—according to opinion polls and studies—seem to believe that corporate crime is widespread and not something to be taken lightly (Cullen *et al.*, 1987:43). The most comprehensive study to date on corporate crime, by Marshall Clinard and Peter Yeager (1980), substantiates these concerns. Clinard and Yeager analyzed federal, administrative, civil, and criminal actions either initiated or completed by 25 federal agencies against the 447 largest publicly owned manufacturing corporations in the U.S. In addition, these sociologists conducted a smaller study of the 105 largest wholesale, retail, and service corporations, for a total of 552 corporations studied (*ibid.*:110). Clinard and Yeager limited their investigations to *actions initiated* against corporations for violations (roughly equivalent to arrests or prosecutions) and *actions completed* (equivalent to convictions). Although they uncovered only "the tip of the iceberg of total violations" (*ibid.*:111), nevertheless, Clinard and Yeager found considerable corporate crime. Sixty percent of the corporations had at least one action initiated against them, 42 percent of the corporations were multiple offenders, and the most frequent violators averaged 23.5 violations per corporation (*ibid.*:116). In short, corporate crime is, indeed, widespread.

We turn now to certain specific types of corporate crime.

Corporate Violence

In this section we examine corporate violence against workers, consumers, and the general public. We begin with workers.

Every year approximately 6,000 U.S. workers are killed in job-related accidents, as many as 100,000 die from exposure to dangerous substances, at least 10 million suffer injuries while on the job (3 million of which are severe), and 390,000 contract new cases of job-related diseases (Cullen *et al.*, 1987:67).

Some criminologists argue that workers are injured and die on the job not because of their own carelessness (although this does occur) but, rather, because of the conditions under which workers must labor, such as production quotas (Reiman, 1984:56). The organization of the workplace, then, primarily determines possible worker negligence and carelessness. In addition, Schraeger and Short (1978:413) reported in the late 1970s that approximately 30 percent of all industrial accidents were the result of safety violations and another 20 percent were caused by unsafe, yet legal, working conditions. More recently, Messerschmidt (1986:100) reviewed studies on corporate violence against workers and found that between 35 and 57 percent of job-related accidents occurred because of safety violations. However, all the preceding figures are based primarily on company reports. Because a company's insurance rating and costs are related to the frequency of injuries, illnesses, and deaths in the workplace, corporations have an incentive to hide accidents. Indeed, studies show that many do (*ibid.*:101; Berman, 1978:108). Consequently, the preceding figures most likely understate the seriousness of corporate violence. Even so, the figures clearly indicate that corporate violence in the workplace exceeds the amount of interpersonal violence in U.S. society. We pointed out in Chapter 4 that we are actually safer in the street than indoors; the evidence presented here suggests that we are safer almost anywhere than the workplace.

An example of corporate violence caused by the intentional violation of safety standards is the case of Film Recovery Systems, Inc. (Frank, 1985; see also Frank and Lynch, 1992). Workers at the Film Recovery plant who worked around cyanide—poisonous if swallowed, inhaled, or absorbed through the skin—were not protected with adequate equipment (gloves, boots, aprons, and so on) and effective ventilation. In fact, the plant air was thick with an odorous "yellow haze" of cyanide fumes (*ibid.*:22). On February 10, 1985, Stephen Golab, a worker at the plant, collapsed on the plant floor and died. During the autopsy of Golab, when the

> medical examiner made the first incision, a strong almond-like smell came out of the body, indicating cyanide poisoning. Subsequent blood tests revealed that Golab had a blood cyanide level of 3.45 micrograms per milliliter, a lethal dose (*ibid.*).

Three executives of Film Recovery were eventually convicted of murder and 14 counts of reckless conduct (*ibid.*:23). As Frank (*ibid.*:24) points out, the judge in the case

> found that the three convicted defendants were "totally knowledgeable" of the hazards of cyanide. Judge Banks reiterated the evidence substantiating his findings that each of the three executives knew the dangers of

cyanide and understood that their failure to provide proper protective equipment created a strong probability of death or great bodily harm.

The conviction of the Film Recovery executives, the first of its kind in this country, touched off a number of prosecutions of corporate officials throughout the country. In 1986 executives of Peabody Southwest, Inc. and Sabine Consolidated, Inc. were charged with negligent homicide because three workers were buried alive in two separate construction-trench cave-ins (Cullen *et al.*, 1987:314). In 1984 the president of Maggio Drilling, Inc. was charged with involuntary felony-manslaughter because of alleged unsafe working conditions resulting in the death of a worker who suffocated while digging an elevator shaft (*ibid.*). Finally, in 1985 three executives of Jackson Enterprises were charged with involuntary manslaughter because of alleged unsafe working conditions causing an employee to die from carbon monoxide poisoning (*ibid.*).

Despite such prosecutions, corporations continue to expose workers to dangers, such as the "silent killers." Workers are sometimes victims of corporate violence simply because they hold a job with a company that does not adequately protect them from such dangerous substances as chemical compounds, asbestos fibers, and cotton dust. Asbestos, for example, was a suspected "silent killer" as early as 1918 when a number of life-insurance companies disallowed policies to asbestos workers because of their high death rate (Epstein, 1978:83). In the 1950s a connection between asbestos and lung cancer was found by British epidemiologist Richard Doll (*ibid.*:84). The asbestos industry funded 11 studies in an attempt to rebut this link; however, 52 independent studies found asbestos to pose a major threat to human health (Coleman, 1989:35). More recently, the National Institute for Occupational Safety and Health (NIOSH) (Cullen *et al.*, 1987:69) reports that 10 to 18 percent of the 12 million U.S. citizens exposed to asbestos will die from the lung disease *asbestosis*, 11 percent of workers exposed to asbestos will most likely develop cancerous tumors, and approximately 6,000 asbestos-related lung cancers will occur every year. As sociologist James Coleman (*ibid.*:35) states: "Such evidence suggests that the asbestos industry knowingly perpetrated a massive fraud on its workers and the public."

Since at least the 1960s medical studies have shown that *byssinosis* (or brown-lung disease) is a severe health problem for textile workers; yet the textile industry remains insensitive to its effect on worker health (some 85,000 textile workers suffer impaired breathing due to acute byssinosis) (Mokhiber, 1988:4). By the late 1980s textile workers continued to offer detailed testimony on the extreme levels of cotton dust that fills the mills (Guarasci, 1987).

As noted earlier in this chapter, women of color and poor women have been especially victimized by physician fraud, high percentages having been forced to undergo sterilization. Similarly, in business today many working-class women, to survive economically, are forced into sterilization. Unlike men—who seldom are forced to make this choice—women are often required to surrender their right to produce children in order to work (Messerschmidt, 1986:103). For instance, five women who worked for American Cyanamid Corporation were forced to undergo sterilization or lose their jobs (*ibid.*:103). Rather than making the workplace safe, the company simply excluded the women. Moreover, American Cyanamid is not unique. In the 1980s

> a number of corporations such as General Motors, B. F. Goodrich, St. Joe's Minerals, Allied Chemical, and Olin, had policies that banned women, but not men, from certain jobs unless they could prove they were sterile (*ibid.*:103).

Men also have been forced into sterilization because of the working conditions they endure. For example, in 1961, when Dow Chemical marketed DBCP (a soil fumigant), research at that time indicated that the pesticide was a sterility hazard. However, Dow failed to inform workers of this danger and, as a result, in 1977 many workers (approximately 3,000) who worked with DBCP became sterile in plants from California to Arkansas to Alabama (Castleman, 1979:590). Mokhiber (1988:140) reports that DBCP workers

> stood upon platforms over 1,000-gallon containers known as batch tanks so that they could monitor the mixing of DBCP with diluting chemicals. To the side of the tanks, other workers would measure the finished DBCP product as it poured into cans for sale. There was no ventilation system to disperse the fumes from the chemicals.

Eventually the three largest chemical companies stopped producing DBCP, but a smaller company, Amvac, saw this as a profitable opportunity (Seager, 1993:73–74). As their annual report for 1977 stated (*ibid.*:74), because of the extensive

> publicity and notoriety surrounding DBCP, it was [our] opinion that a vacuum existed in the marketplace that we could temporarily occupy. . . . [We] further believed that with the addition of DBCP, sales might be sufficient to reach a profitable level.

As consumers, we also are subject to victimization from corporate violence. The case of the Dalkon Shield, an IUD, is a telling example. The Dalkon Shield was manufactured, promoted, and marketed in the face of company files containing several hundred negative reports from physicians and others about its safety. Although these reports represented firm evidence linking the Dalkon Shield with 75 cases of uterine perforation, ectopic pregnancies, and at least 17 deaths, they were never made public (Braithwaite, 1984:258). Approximately 2.86 million Shields were distributed in the United States, and the vast majority of women who used this IUD developed the dangerous infection known as pelvic inflammatory disease (Mintz, 1985:20).

Myriad products—from hazardous toys to dangerous automobiles—have been found harmful to consumers (Simon and Eitzen, 1986:97–114). A horrific example of corporate violence against youthful consumers is the drug thalidomide that was marketed as a safe treatment for "morning sickness" during the early stages of pregnancy. Approximately 8,000 pregnant women who took the prescription drug gave birth to terribly deformed babies. The corporation that patented and distributed the drug deliberately falsified test data and concealed the facts about the drug's serious side effects (Box, 1983:24). Two victims of this case of corporate violence are described below (Jackall, 1980:357; Mokhiber, 1988:408).

> *Terry* was born without arms or legs, had a protruding eye that had to be surgically removed, and at the age of sixteen was only two feet tall.

> *Alex* was born with a deformed and shortened arm; one hand did not have a thumb but the other hand had an extra finger. His palate had a hole in it; his face was paralyzed on one side; he had only one ear, and it was terribly deformed; his brain was damaged, and he was deaf and mute.

Production of an unsafe automobile, the Ford Pinto, is a notorious illustration of corporate violence against consumers. As Simon and Eitzen (1986:4) point out:

> Ford knew that this car had a defective gasoline tank that would ignite even in low-speed rear-end collisions, yet the company continued its sales. Ironically and tragically Ford continued to sell this defective and dangerous car even though the problem could have been solved for a cost of $11 per vehicle.

It is reported that as many as 900 burn deaths occurred as a result of the exploding Pinto (Dowie, 1977:20).

In the early 1970s the Firestone 500 steel-belted radial tire was produced and sold, and throughout that decade the company continued to receive evidence of its danger to motorists. The tire was plagued with sudden blowouts and the separation of its tread from the steel-belted inner layer. Although the tire had been linked to thousands of automobile accidents and at least 41 deaths, Firestone responded with a "concerted campaign to keep the truth from the public" (Coleman, 1989:42).

Another example of the occasional dangers of automobile transportation concerns recently released documents revealing that, prior to production, internal General Motors' records repeatedly warned company executives that the rear-wheel brakes of its 1980 X-cars had a tendency to lock prematurely, causing the cars to spin out of control. As Hills (1987:7) points out, despite

> more than 1,700 complaints, and at least 71 known injuries and 15 deaths, GM . . . bitterly fought the government's attempt to force a recall to repair, without any charge to the owners, of over one million 1980 X-cars.

Finally, a recent example of corporate violence against consumers is the C.R. Bard Company of Murray Hill, New Jersey, which *deliberately* sold faulty surgical devices to consumers and used unsuspecting heart patients as "guinea pigs" to test new products not approved by the Food and Drug Administration.

Business as usual: Corporate violence routinely invades the home.

The devices injured dozens of patients and killed at least one (*Portland Press Herald*, 1993).

We turn now to a discussion of violence against the general public, not only specific consumers. Corporate pollution provides an easy first illustration of this type of corporate crime. The case of Love Canal is no doubt the most familiar. From the late 1930s until 1953, Hooker Chemical Company dumped hundreds of tons of toxic waste into the abandoned Love Canal, near Niagara Falls, New York (Tallmer, 1987:113). In 1953, Hooker sold the dump site to the local school board, which in turn sold it to a private developer. The canal was filled in, and eventually houses were built on top of the chemical dump. Some 20 years later, "as leaching wastes began to be linked to miscarriages, birth defects, and other ailments, more than 200 families fled their homes" (*ibid.*:113).

U.S. corporations produce 88 billion pounds of toxic waste each year, and the Environmental Protection Agency (EPA) estimates that 90 percent of it is disposed of improperly (Coleman, 1989:36). Thus, Love Canal is not unique. In Times Beach, Missouri, the EPA found dioxin levels 100 times those considered safe, forcing the federal government to purchase the entire town and move the people out (*ibid.*:39).

Probably the worst hazardous waste condition in the United States—more serious than Love Canal and Times Beach—is, as Russell (1988) reported, the chemical contamination of a small Arkansas community, Jacksonville, referred to by local residents as "Dioxinville." Approximately 20 chemicals have been found in Jacksonville's air, 12 of which were also found in the Love Canal area. But the major problem in Jacksonville is *dioxin,* one of the most lethal substances ever produced. Dioxin has been found to cause cancer and fetus-malforming effects in animals at concentrations as low as 10 to 100 parts per trillion; the EPA considers dioxin dangerous to humans when it measures one part per billion. As Russell (*ibid.*:9) points out, just "one part per million is therefore 1,000 times more toxic. In Jacksonville, dioxin was measured . . . at concentrations as high as 111 parts per million," or 111,000 times as toxic as the EPA danger level.

Jacksonville is contaminated with at least 30,000 barrels containing dioxin waste. From 1946–1957, Reasor-Hill Chemical Corporation buried drums of chemical waste in an open field near its plant in Jacksonville. In 1961 the plant was acquired by the Hercules Chemical Corporation, which continued to bury drums of chemical waste and began discharging processed wastewater—from production of chlordane and Agent Orange™—into a nearby creek. By 1979 it became publicly known that the plant and surrounding area were contaminated with dioxin. Today, dangerous levels of dioxin (higher than one part per billion) have been found in soil samples (taken from residents' yards), as well as in the air, the city sewer system and lagoons, the sediments of the nearby floodplain, and in fish and wood ducks (*ibid.*).

This disaster could have been avoided. Dow Chemical Company knew as far back as 1965 about the dangers of dioxin. As Green and Berry (1985:263) report:

> One memorandum from Dow's toxicology director warned then (1965) that the chemical could be "exceptionally toxic"; the company's medical director said that dioxin-related "fatalities have been reported in the literature." Dow's response was to discuss these problems with its competitors at a March meeting, but *not* to inform the government or public because the situation might "explode" and spur more federal regulation of the chemical industry.

Dow's cover-up helped make the violence at Love Canal, Times Beach, and Jacksonville inevitable. Yet the story of hazardous waste does not end here. More and more often we find our drinking water contaminated by hazardous toxic waste sites. Little wonder that one of every five public water systems is contaminated to some extent, mainly because of toxic chemicals seeping from waste dumps (Shavelson, 1988). Consider the following examples (*ibid.*:71–77; Asinoff, 1985):

▲— In certain parts of Tucson, Arizona, the water is contaminated with trichloroethylene.

▲— In Suffolk County, New York, pesticides found in the water have been linked to nerve damage.

▲__ In Picher, Oklahoma, the water is poisoned with cadmium and lead.

▲__ In Toone, Tennessee, the drinking water in one community was found to contain waste chemicals—such as carbon tetrachloride—known to cause cancer and kidney and liver disease in animals.

▲__ In Woburn, Massachusetts, a cluster of child leukemia deaths has been tied to chemical contamination of drinking water.

▲__ In Middlesboro, Kentucky, headaches, nausea, rashes, and miscarriages are thought to be linked to contaminated drinking water.

▲__ In Lathrop, California, dangerous pesticides have poisoned the drinking water.

Contaminated drinking water is only a tip of the corporate violence iceberg. As Jodi Seager (1993:72) notes:

> American chemical companies admitted that they annually leak or vent 196 "extremely hazardous" compounds into the air. The U.S. Environmental Protection Agency (EPA) cautiously estimates that as few as 15 to 45 of the hundreds of released air toxins directly cause up to 1,700 cases of cancer each year. American industry alone generates annually 280 million tons of lethal garbage and 10.3 billion pounds of toxic chemicals that are spewed each year into the air, discharged into public waters, and flushed into the sewers—enough to fill 8,000 Love Canals.

Corporate Theft

Corporate theft is similar to other forms of theft—in the sense that property is taken from people—yet it is significantly different, primarily because it does not entail a face-to-face confrontation and it is not easily apparent that a crime has been committed. Three of the most costly and prevalent forms of corporate theft are deceptive advertising, financial fraud, and price-fixing. We look briefly at each.

According to the Federal Trade Commission Act, *deceptive advertising* occurs when advertisements are "misleading in a material respect" (Coleman, 1989:16). This means that advertising can in fact be false, as long as it is not deceptive. In other words, it is illegal for advertising to be both false and deceptive, or just simply deceptive. When Jello™ claims that "Every kid in America loves Jello brand gelatin," they are clearly making a false statement. However, "exaggerated claims" (hype) such as this have been interpreted by the courts as not deceptive because it is believed that no reasonable person would take the statement seriously (*ibid.*). Nevertheless, many corporations have simultaneously lied and deceived for decades. For example, Anacin™ was found to be the subject of deceptive advertising in that its manufacturer claimed that Anacin (Simon and Eitzen, 1986:88):

▲— relieved nervousness, tension, stress, fatigue, and depression

▲— was stronger than aspirin

▲— brought relief within 22 seconds

▲— was highly recommended over aspirin by physicians

▲— was more effective for relieving pain than any other analgesic available without prescription

Moreover, corporations have also violated the law by engaging in deception without outright lying. For example, the bottom of a bowl of Campbell's "chunky style" soup used in a TV commercial was lined with marbles, creating the illusion that the soup was much thicker and chunkier than it actually was (Coleman 1989:16).

Corporate executives can engage in a form of fraud that serves the interests of the corporation, *financial fraud*. Such was the case with the Equity Funding Corporation of American (EFCA). Beginning operations in 1960, by the mid- to late-1960s EFCA was seen as a "success story"—its stock had risen from $6 per share in 1964 to $80 per share in 1969. In 1973, however, the "success" was found to have been the result of fraud: the corporation sold 64,000 fraudulent policies, falsified its assets and earnings in annual reports, sold counterfeit bonds, and forged death certificates (Dirks and Gross, 1974; Blundell, 1976).

A more recent example of corporate financial fraud is the case of the invest-ment firm E. F. Hutton and Company. Hutton officials pleaded guilty in 1985 to defrauding some 400 banks by writing checks in excess of amounts it had on deposit. Hutton officials then moved funds—to cover these amounts—from one bank to another, thereby avoiding overdrafts. In effect, what Hutton officials did was simply provide the company with interest-free loans (Nash, 1985:5; Claybrook, 1986:35). As Cullen *et al.* (1987:56) point out: the entire "operation involved nearly $10 billion; on some days the company enjoyed $250 million in illegal 'loans.' "

In 1988, E. F. Hutton pleaded guilty to two felony counts of laundering hundreds of thousands of dollars for criminal syndicate figures and business people seeking to evade payment of taxes. According to *The Washington Post*, investigators found that "customers would bring suitcases full of cash to Hutton brokers," who would then transfer the money to secret overseas bank accounts (Kurtz, 1988:A3).

Both financial institutions and criminal syndicates profit from money laun-dering. It is against the law not to report cash transactions in excess of $10,000. Financial institutions evade this required federal disclosure by fraudulently con-verting large amounts of cash (sometimes provided by criminal syndicates) into bonds worth $9,999 or less, or they secretly launder it in foreign bank accounts. Financial institutions are attracted to obtaining money from criminal syndicates because large sums of money can be used for future investments and/or interest-earning loans. Criminal syndicates benefit from money laundering because, in essence, this process changes "dirty" money into "clean" money. We more thoroughly analyze the relationship among financial institutions, criminal syndicates, and money laundering in Chapter 8.

Price-fixing, costing consumers between $30 and $200 billion every year, is probably the most expensive form of corporate theft (Green and Berry, 1985a:705). The basic purpose of antitrust laws is to impede corporations from colluding to fix prices (price-fixing) by ensuring that competition keeps prices as low as possible. Profits above those that would be produced in a competitive industry are illegal (Messerschmidt, 1986:108). However, the value of illegal profits is astounding (as the preceding figures demonstrate). Probably the most famous price-fixing incident is the case of Heavy Electrical Equipment, in which 29 corporations—such as General Electric and Westinghouse—conspired to fix prices, primarily on government contracts (Pearce, 1976:78; Green *et al.*, 1972:155). The illegal costs paid by purchasers of the electrical equipment in this case alone totaled $1.75 billion per year for seven years (Hills, 1971:162). Some recent examples of price-fixing, and the extraordinary financial burden this crime places on consumers today, are listed by Cullen *et al.*, (1987:60):

▲ $35 million in overcharges in the Seattle-Tacoma area because of collusion among bread companies.

▲ Losses of as much as $9 million in a three-year period when Arkansas dairy companies set prices on milk sold to public schools and other state institutions.

▲ Millions lost from a plot to rig prices of plumbing fixtures.

▲ A cost of $51 for 100 tetracycline tablets, which dropped to $5 after exposure of a price-fixing conspiracy.

▲ Savings to consumers of over $225 million after a price-fixing case was launched against a blue-jeans manufacturer.

▲ A massive bid-rigging scheme by highway and paving contractors that resulted in millions of dollars in overcharges and in fines of $50 million, 400 convictions, and 141 prison sentences.

The following dialogue illustrates what appears to be solicitation of a price-fixing arrangement. The taped conversation occurred on February 1, 1982, and is between Howard Putnam, president of Braniff Airlines, and Robert Crandall, then president of American Airlines (Green and Berry, 1985:260):

PUTNAM: Do you have a suggestion for me?
CRANDALL: Yes, I have a suggestion for you. Raise your goddamn fares 20 percent. I'll raise mine the next morning.
PUTNAM: Robert, we . . .
CRANDALL: You'll make more money and I will, too.
PUTNAM: We can't talk about pricing.
CRANDALL: Oh, bullshit, Howard. We can talk about any goddamn thing we want to talk about.

Transnational Corporate Crime

Transnationals—large corporations that maintain business operations in more than one country—are clearly the worst corporate offenders. The Clinard and Yeager (1980:119) study discussed earlier found that small corporations (annual sales of $300–499 million) accounted for only 10 percent of violations, medium-sized corporations (annual sales of $500–999 million) for 20 percent, but large corporations (annual sales of $1 billion or more) for almost 75 percent of all violations. Moreover, large corporations accounted for 72.1 percent of the serious and 62.8 percent of the moderately serious violations (*ibid.*:119).

Of the 15 largest corporations in the world in 1978 (the time of Clinard and Yeager's study), three were car manufacturers, eight were oil companies, and one was a chemical producer (Box, 1983:76). The largest corporations, then, are the worst offenders in view of Clinard and Yeager's (*ibid.*:119) finding that "the oil, pharmaceutical, and motor vehicle industries" are the "most likely to violate the law."

Large corporations invest heavily outside the United States. As Michalowski and Kramer (1987:35) reported:

> Three-fourths of all U.S. companies with sales over 100 million dollars had manufacturing facilities in other countries by 1975. By 1977 developing nations had surpassed developed ones in dollar value as locations for manufacturing by U.S. industries. Reimportation of overseas assembly by U.S. companies increased five-fold between 1969 and 1983, and in the textiles and electronics industries more than half of all current sales by U.S. corporations are now assembled abroad.

This transnational nature of U.S. corporations has resulted in considerable Third World corporate crime, ranging from bribery to export of hazardous products to dangerous working conditions. Goff and Reasons (1986:210) provide salient examples of transnational corporate bribery that occurred in the 1970s:

▲__ Ashland Oil admitted paying more than $300,000 to foreign officials, including $150,000 to President Albert Bernard Bongo of Gabon to retain mineral and refining rights.

▲__ Burroughs Corporation admitted that $1.5 million of corporate funds may have been used for improper payments to foreign officials.

▲__ Exxon Corporation admitted paying $740,000 to government officials and others in three countries, and that its Italian subsidiary made $27 million in secret but legal contributions to seven Italian political parties.

▲__ Gulf Oil Corporation admitted paying $4 million to South Korea's ruling political party, and giving $460,000 to Bolivian officials—including a $110,000 helicopter to late President René Barrientos—for oil rights.

▲__ Lockheed Aircraft admitted giving $202 million in commissions, payoffs, and bribes to foreign agents and government officials in the Netherlands,

Italy, Japan, Turkey, and other countries, and that $22 million of this sum went for outright bribes.

▲— McDonnell Douglas admitted paying $2.5 million in commissions and consultant fees between 1970 and 1975 to foreign government officials.

▲— Merck and Company admitted giving $3 million, largely in "commission-type payments," to employees of 36 foreign governments between 1968 and 1975.

▲— Northrop admitted (in part) SEC charges that it paid $30 million in commissions and bribes to government officials and agents in the Netherlands, Iran, France, West Germany, Saudi Arabia, Brazil, Malaysia, and Taiwan.

▲— G. D. Searle admitted paying $1.3 million to foreign government employees from 1973 to 1975 to "obtain sales of products or services."

▲— United Brands admitted paying a $1.25 million bribe to Honduran officials for reduction of the banana export tax. It also admitted paying $750,000 to European officials (investigators say the payment was made to head off proposed Italian restrictions on banana imports).

This enormous volume of bribery in the mid-1970s led in 1977 to enactment of the Foreign Corrupt Practices Act, which attempts to prevent such conduct. Yet transnational bribery continues. For example, in 1984 the Justice Department investigated the Bechtel Group for bid rigging and for illegal payments to a South Korean utility company that was awarding contracts for nuclear plant construction, and in the 1990s the media continued to report violations of the Foreign Corrupt Practices Act (Green and Berry, 1985:266; *The Wall Street Journal*, 1993a, 1992a, 1992b).

Bribery is clearly profitable for transnationals and the political elites in Third World countries, yet it perpetrates serious harm on a good portion of the rest of the people in these countries. Braithwaite (1979:126) convincingly argues that transnational bribery is one of the most destructive and injurious crimes today because of its unequal and antidemocratic consequences:

> When a government official in a Third World country recommends (under the influence of a bribe) that his country purchase the more expensive but less adequate of two types of aircraft, then the extra millions of dollars will be found from the taxes sweated out of the country's impoverished citizens. For a mass consumer product, the million dollar bribe to the civil servant will be passed on in higher prices to the consuming public. While it is conceivable that bribes can be used to secure the sale of a better and cheaper product, the more general effect is to shift the balance of business away from the most efficient producer and in favour of the most corrupt producer. The whole purpose of business-government bribes is, after all, the inegalitarian purpose of enticing governments to act against the public interest and in the interest of the transnational.

Transnational corporations are also involved in "dumping" on other countries certain hazardous products banned or not approved for sale in the United States (Messerschmidt, 1986:112). U.S.-based transnationals frequently sell to other nations defective medical devices, lethal drugs, known carcinogens, toxic pesticides, contaminated foods, and other products ruled unfit for use and/or consumption in the U.S. (Dowie, 1987:47). For example, the contraceptive Depo-Provera—banned in the United States because of its severe side effects—was dumped in 70 foreign countries, especially in the Third World (*ibid.*:51–52).

A. H. Robins dumped approximately 1.71 million Dalkon Shields in 40 foreign countries (Mintz, 1985:21), and the Agency for International Development purchased approximately 700,000 Dalkon Shields for distribution in the Third World (Mintz, 1986:2). These Shields were sold by Robins to the Agency for International Development at a 48-percent discount and were packaged *unsterilized* (Braithwaite, 1984:258). They were then distributed by AID to a variety of countries in Africa, Asia, the Middle East, the Caribbean, and Central and South America, where medical techniques are underdeveloped and consumer protection laws are practically nonexistent. Obviously, tens of thousands of women worldwide have been victimized by this corporate crime (Messerschmidt, 1986:113).

Corporations also dump chemicals, such as pesticides, on foreign markets. Taking just one example, DDT—a pesticide banned in the United States—in the mid-1980s was being sold particularly in Central and South America, only to return home on such imported food as bananas and coffee (Asinoff, 1985:3). According to Russell Mokhiber (1988:185):

> U.S. chemical companies ship overseas at least 150 million pounds a year of pesticides that are totally prohibited, severely restricted, or never registered for use in this country. While data on the effects of this practice are incomplete, evidence indicates a problem of major proportions. The World Health Organization estimated in 1973 that 250,000 pesticide poisonings, 6,700 of which are fatal, occur each year in the Third World. The Oxford Committee on Famine Relief estimated in 1982 that the toll had risen to 375,000 poisonings with a resulting 10,000 deaths each year.

Transnationals have also—in addition to bribery, corruption, and dumping—relocated dangerous working conditions to other countries. Transnationals search for areas of the world where pollution controls and worker safety regulations are minimal or nonexistent. As Barry Castleman (1979:570) points out: "runaway hazardous shops" are leaving the United States for those areas of the world where illegal actions in home countries are permissible. For example, in 1972, Amatex (a Millford Square, Pennsylvania, asbestos yarn mill) moved its entire factory to Aqua Prieta, Mexico, because Mexico has no laws protecting workers who work around asbestos (*ibid.*:576). The following account is what one observer found in the Aqua Prieta plant five years after the Millford Square plant was shut down (cited in *ibid.*:576):

Asbestos waste clings to the fence that encloses the brick plant and is strewn across the dirt road behind the plant where children walk to school. Inside, machinery that weaves yarn into industrial fabric is caked with asbestos waste and the floor covered with debris. Workers in part of the factory do not wear respirators that could reduce their exposure to asbestos dust.

Other examples abound (Mattelart, 1983:102; Michalowski and Kramer, 1987:36; Asinoff, 1985:3):

▲— The only U.S. producer of arsenic, Arasco, moved to Mexico and Peru when the Occupational Health and Safety Administration (OSHA) proposed to lower the workplace limit for airborne arsenic exposure from 500 to 4 micrograms per cubic meter of air.

▲— After the soil fumigant DBCP was banned in the U.S. because it causes sterility in male workers, the production of this pesticide was moved to Mexico. Subsequent investigations report cases of sterility among Mexican workers.

▲— Raybestos-Manhattan acquired 47 percent of the stock in a Venezuelan asbestos plant for the purpose of taking advantage of Venezuelan law that allows higher levels of airborne asbestos fibers than are allowed in the United States.

▲— In India, workers at an asbestos-cement plant designed by the Manville Corporation were exposed daily to hazardous asbestos material and protected by only rudimentary safeguards. Outside the factory, children played in discarded piles of asbestos.

▲— In Indonesia, at a Union Carbide battery plant outside Jakarta, health and safety provisions were reported as so poor that at one point more than one-half of the work force of 750 were diagnosed as having kidney diseases linked to mercury exposure.

Clearly, several U.S.-based transnational corporations are causing substantial harm to large numbers of people throughout the world. Recognition of this harm, in particular by the developing nations, led the United Nations (U.N.) to adopt worldwide business standards for transnational corporations (Michalowski and Kramer, 1987:41–45). The U.N. is in the process of implementing a set of rules that attempt to govern the international behavior of large corporations. In fact, a Draft Code of Conduct on Transnational Corporations has been produced that "constitutes a set of international norms for the conduct of transnational business—a new set of political definitions concerning the behavior of transnational corporations" (*ibid.*:44). Although the Code has not yet been adopted formally by the U.N. General Assembly, the major areas and topics covered by the code include the following (*ibid.*:44):

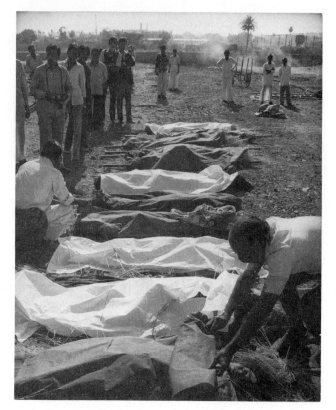

Mass murder, corporate style: On December 3, 1984, toxic gas leaked from a Union Carbide insecticide plant in Bhopal, India, killing more than 3,500 Indians and injuring 200,000 others.

A. General and Political

1. Respect for national sovereignty and observance of domestic laws, regulations, and administrative practices.
2. Adherence to economic goals and development, objectives, policies, and priorities.
3. Adherence to sociocultural objectives and values.
4. Respect for human rights and fundamental freedom.
5. Noninterference in internal political affairs.
6. Noninterference in intergovernmental relations.
7. Abstention from corrupt practices.

B. Economic, Financial, and Social

1. Ownership and control.
2. Balance of payments and financing.
3. Transfer pricing.
4. Taxation.
5. Competition and restrictive business practices.
6. Transfer of technology.
7. Consumer protection.
8. Environmental protection.

This code of conduct is clearly an important first step in the control of transnational corporate crime.

7.3   CRIMINAL CORPORATIONS

Earlier we defined criminal corporations as those deliberately set up, managed, or taken over for the exclusive purpose of conducting criminal activity. Although this type of white-collar crime is the least investigated by sociologists, certain important studies have been conducted. We consider three specific studies by Block and Bernard (1988), Levi (1981), and Kwitny (1987).

From Legitimate to Criminal Corporation

Block and Bernard's (1988) study of crime in the waste-oil industry provides a splendid example of a corporation that was for years legitimate, yet in the late 1970s turned criminal. In a detailed case study, Block and Bernard (*ibid.*:114–120) provide the following information.

Russell Mahler legally owned and operated four waste-oil refineries for 30 years, eventually producing as much as 6 percent of U.S. output of re-refined lubricants. However, in the latter part of the 1970s, the re-refining of waste oil for reuse as lubricants became uneconomical. In fact, the economic situation was so severe that the entire waste-oil industry was threatened with bankruptcy. At the same time, the legal disposal of toxic wastes became very expensive because Congress enacted the Resource Conservation and Recovery Act. This Act sets minimum standards and regulations for disposing of hazardous waste, thus increasing its price. The combined effect of these economic and legal circumstances created (*ibid.*:120)

> economic pressure to dispose of toxic wastes by cheap but illegal means. Waste oil dealers already had facilities for the storage and disposal of waste products and could illegally sell a mixture of toxic waste as fuel with minimal chances of being caught. Thus, a new illegal means for making money was presented to waste oil dealers at the same time that their traditional, legal means for making money suddenly disappeared.

Indeed, Mahler's business changed from a legitimate waste-oil dealership to one that "cocktailed" toxic waste with waste oils, either selling the resulting mixture as fuel oil or illegally dumping it in different parts of the Northeast (*ibid.*:116–117).

Long-Firm Fraud

Levi's (1981) study of what he calls "long-firm fraud" is important because it increases our understanding of criminal corporations. Levi identifies long-firm fraud as occurring when a corporation obtains goods from suppliers for the purpose of reselling these goods at a profit—with, however, the deliberate intention of never paying for the goods.

Levi found two major types of long-firm fraud: "preplanned" and "slippery-slope." Preplanned long-firm frauds define corporations deliberately set up to defraud suppliers. Slippery-slope long-firm frauds define established legitimate corporations turned into—for a variety of reasons—criminal corporations that defraud their suppliers.

The would-be long-firm fraudster, whether preplanned or slippery-slope, has two main concerns: obtaining goods on credit and disposing of such goods before creditors demand the return of their money or goods. Satisfying these concerns is much easier for the slippery-slope fraudster, inasmuch as an established legitimate corporation already has access to goods on credit and to trade outlets for their resale. For the preplanned long-firm fraud this is not the case, inasmuch as the corporation begins anew, and must therefore provide references (usually accomplished by furnishing suppliers with the names of nonexistent firms that appear to trade with the criminal corporation). In other words, the corporation involved in preplanned long-firm fraud creates its own credit references, obtains the goods, resells them quickly, and disappears with the profits. Levi also found that for many such corporations to get started, they must establish contacts with a number of "organizers," such as " 'bent' bank managers," "shady businessmen," and "big-time criminals." Once the required capital is obtained, individuals can set up their own corporation or simply, as Levi (*ibid.*:8) points out

> purchase an existing perfectly respectable firm or limited company, pref-
> erably on credit terms, and then, usually without informing suppliers of
> the change in ownership, obtain extensive credit on the basis of the
> former owner's reputation before finally absconding with the proceeds.

Laundries and Conduits

Kwitny's (1987) investigation of the Australian Nugan Hand Bank illustrates a criminal corporation as well. The Nugan Hand Bank was founded in Sydney in 1973 by Frank Nugan, a 30-year-old heir to an Australian fruit-processing fortune, and by Michael Hand, a 31-year-old former Green Beret and CIA operative from the Bronx. As Kwitny (1987:43) points out, the "Nugan Hand Bank never did any banking." From the very beginning, Nugan Hand obtained its "seed capital" from the "high fees charged for performing illegal services and from the fraudulent procurement and subsequent misappropriation of investments from the public" (*ibid.*:94). It was, in short, "a giant theft machine," laundering billions of dollars around the world, helping finance the heroin trade (the bank even had a branch in Chiang Mai, Thailand, the center of opium trade in the famous Golden Triangle), engaging in tax fraud, as well as in the theft of at least $50 million from investors (*ibid.*:76 and passim).

Most striking is Kwitny's detailed evidence of the bank's role as a conduit for U.S. intelligence. Indeed, a number of individuals working for the bank came from Washington: its president was retired U.S. Admiral Earl F. Yates; its legal counsel was former CIA director William Colby; a consultant for the bank was former deputy director of the CIA, Walter McDonald; an ex-advisor to Henry Kissinger and Zbigniew Brzezinski—Guy Pauker—was an advisor to the bank. Finally, a "commodities trader" on the staff—Andrew Lowe—was, according to Kwitny, one of Australia's biggest heroin importers.

In January of 1980, Frank Nugan, a rifle in his hands, was found dead in his 1977 Mercedes. Nugan's briefcase was in the car, and contained a list of prominent political, sports, business, and entertainment personalities. Next to each such name was a handwritten dollar amount, mostly five- and six-figure sums. Also found, on Nugan's lap, was a Bible (he was a staunch fundamentalist), with a piece of paper (interleaved at page 252) that bore the names of Robert Wilson (the ranking Republican on the House Armed Services Committee) and ex-CIA director William Colby. Finally, in Nugan's back pocket was Colby's business card, noting Colby's scheduled visits to Australia, Hong Kong, and Singapore (*ibid.*:19–22).

Following the death of Frank Nugan (officially listed as suicide) and the disappearance of Michael Hand four months later, investigations of the bank by the Australian Government have confirmed most of Kwitny's conclusions. We have more to say (Chapters 8 and 9) about Nugan Hand—especially its connections to the intelligence community, criminal syndicates, and the "Contra-gate" scandal in this country.

REVIEW

This chapter examined different types of white-collar crime—occupational crime, corporate crime, and criminal corporations. These crimes are similar to crimes previously discussed because they also entail theft and violence. However, they differ from other crimes because (1) they cause far greater victimization, (2) they occur in the course of doing business or working for a business, and (3) their type of victimization is less apparent. Certain of the more important points of this chapter are outlined as follows.

Occupational Crime

1. There are two major types of occupational crime: theft and fraud. Occupational theft includes employee theft and embezzlement, which differ in what is stolen—merchandise and job-related items or money, respectively.

2. Employee theft and embezzlement—two of the most costly crimes in the United States—occur in different ways depending upon the type of job and range from simply stealing merchandise to "taking from the till" and "manipulating the books" to collective embezzlement.

3. Two types of occupational fraud are physician fraud and insider trading. The former occurs through prescription of pharmaceutical drugs, surgical procedures, and treating Medicare and Medicaid patients. Insider trading results when "insiders" gain special advantage in the buying and selling of stock.

Corporate Crime

1. Corporate violence causes considerable worker illness, injury, and death; corporations perpetrate violence on consumers and the general public.

2. Three of the most costly and prevalent forms of corporate theft are deceptive advertising, financial fraud, and price-fixing.

3. Transnational corporations are the worst corporate offenders.

Criminal Corporations

1. Some corporations are deliberately set up, managed, or taken over for the explicit purpose of engaging in criminal activity.

2. Examples of criminal corporations discussed include the waste-oil industry, long-firm fraud, and the Nugan Hand Bank.

QUESTIONS FOR CLASS DISCUSSION

1. Why is it valuable to study white-collar crime?

2. How do various types of work help determine specific types of occupational theft? How does the thesis advanced by Ditton and Mars relate to your own job? Your parents' jobs?

3. Describe how corporate violence and theft differ from the types of violence and theft discussed in Chapters 4 and 5.

4. Discuss the differences and similarities between criminal corporations and the other types of white-collar crime examined in this chapter.

5. Are there other forms of white-collar crime not covered in this chapter? Would these forms fit one of the three types identified here?

RECOMMENDED READINGS

Braithwaite, John (1984). *Corporate Crime in the Pharmaceutical Industry*. Boston: Routledge & Kegan Paul. An analysis of corporate crime in one of the top industries in the world.

Clinard, Marshall and Peter Yeager (1980). *Corporate Crime*. New York: Free Press. The best study of corporate crime since Sutherland's famous work of the 1940s.

Ditton, Jason (1977). *Part-Time Crime.* New York: Macmillan. An entertaining and highly informative book about employee theft.

Frank, Nancy K. and Michael J. Lynch (1992). *Corporate Crime, Corporate Violence.* Albany, NY: Harrow and Heston. An excellent theoretical examination of corporate violence against workers, consumers, the community, and the environment.

Jesilow, Paul, Henry N. Pontell, and Gilbert Geis (1993). *Prescription for Profit: How Doctors Defraud Medicaid.* Berkeley: University of California Press. Provides an insightful examination of physician fraud.

Levi, Michael (1981). *The Phantom Capitalists.* London: Heineman. An examination of an ignored area of white-collar crime—criminal corporations.

Mars, Gerald (1983). *Cheats at Work.* Boston: Unwin. Discusses the relation between the type of job and the type of occupational theft.

Schlegel, Kip and David Weisburd (eds.) (1992). *White-Collar Crime Reconsidered.* Boston: Northeastern University Press. A collection of essays of recent research and theory on white-collar crime.

Simon, David and D. Stanley Eitzen (1991). *Elite Deviance.* Boston: Allyn and Bacon. The most thorough discussion of corporate and political crime yet published.

Sutherland, Edwin (1983). *White-Collar Crime: The Uncut Version.* New Haven: Yale University Press. The classic, first study of white-collar crime by one of the most famous criminologists of all time.

CHAPTER 8

SYNDICATED CRIME

8.1 A History of Syndicated Crime
"Mafia" in Sicily
Syndicated Crime in the United States, 1800–1930
A National Crime Syndicate?

8.2 Syndicated Crime Today
Patron-Client Relationships
Crime Networks

8.3 Principal Forms of Syndicated Crime
Syndicates and Illegal Goods and Services
Syndicates and Legitimate Businesses
Syndicates and the State

Preview

Chapter 8 introduces:

☞ the history of syndicated crime in the United States.
☞ the structure and extent of syndicated crime in the United States today.
☞ the principal forms of syndicated crime and their social costs.

Key Terms

bookmaking
crime networks
criminal syndicate
labor racketeering
loan sharking

mafia
money laundering
numbers
patron-client relationships

T*he core of* **syndicated** *crime (commonly referred to as "organized crime") is, primarily, the provision of illegal goods and services in a society that displays a continued and considerable demand for such goods and services. Syndicated crime has developed a structure that makes it possible to provide such goods and services on a regular basis. This structure can best be understood as a variety of* **syndicates**—*associations of people such as businesspeople, police, politicians, and criminals—formed to conduct specific illegal enterprises for the purpose of making a profit. These enterprises include illegal gambling, illegal drug distribution, loan sharking, illegal disposal of hazardous waste, as well as such other illegal activities as money laundering, labor racketeering, and prostitution. However, the specific structure of a syndicate depends on its specific illegal activity (Albini, 1971:47). Thus, although criminal syndicates are highly organized, a syndicate engaged in the distribution of illegal drugs, for example, is structured differently than one engaged in illegal gambling.*

In this chapter we examine three major aspects of syndicated crime: its history, its structure, and the principal activities engaged in by criminal syndicates today. We begin with a history of syndicated crime.

8.1 _____ A HISTORY OF SYNDICATED CRIME

When we commonly think of "organized crime" (what we call syndicated crime), usually the first term that comes to mind is "the Mafia." However, we rarely ask ourselves where this term originated or whether it is appropriate to use such a term to describe syndicated crime in the United States. In this section we attempt to answer these two questions.

"Mafia" in Sicily

The word "Mafia" is not found in Italian or Sicilian writings until the 19th century, and even then it designated a *method* rather than an *organization* (Albini, 1971:83–152). To understand this method, we must look at Sicily during the 1800s. During feudalism in the 19th century (1812–1833), Sicilian peasantry lived on land controlled by absentee landlords. The centralized Italian State attempted to curb the power of feudal landlords and emancipate its peasantry from traditional feudal obligations (Blok, 1974:10). Not surprisingly, the landlords did not cooperate with the centralized power in Italy, and sought to maintain control over both the feudal estates and the peasantry. To accomplish this the landlords worked with a group of ambitious middle-class persons—the *gabelloti*—who paid the "absentee feudal owners a lump-sum rent for the whole estate," and then "sublet it at a profit to the peasantry" (Hobsbawn, 1959:38). The *gabelloti* ensured continued payment to the landlords while providing protection over the estates. In this way they served as mediators between the landlords and the peasantry. Moreover, because of their geographic location *vis-à-vis* the peasantry and landlords, the remoteness of a centralized power (in Italy), and the rural character of feudal Sicily, the *gabelloti* were the only authoritative "organ" for local law and order. In short, they controlled and monopolized the links among peasant, landlord, and a remote centralized government. As Eric Hobsbawn (*ibid.*:35) points out in his important work *Primitive Rebels*, the *gabelloti*

> provided a parallel machine of law and organized power; indeed, so far as the citizen in the areas under its influence was concerned, the only effective law and power. In a society such as Sicily, in which the official government could not or would not exercise effective sway, the appearance of such a system was as inevitable as the appearance of gang-rule, or its alternative, private posses and vigilantes in certain parts of *laissez-faire* America.

The *gabelloti* in Sicily then played an important role as organ of social control—in the absence of official bodies—and in fact enjoyed a high degree of social acceptance within Sicilian communities. Consequently, a *method* of patronage developed whereby the *gabelloti* held sufficient power to maintain law and order and to control feudal estates, whereas the peasantry (in return) offered services and loyalty to the *gabelloti*. As Albini (1971:133) explains, a *gabelloti*

> entrenched himself in a patronage system which continues today. As a client to his landowner in return for certain favors he promised continued suppression of the peasant. As a patron to the peasant he promised work and the continuation of contracts.

It was this method of patronage that came to be identified as "Mafia," and the role of the *gabelloti* as "mafioso." Because it represents a system of patron-client relationships, mafia is a method, not an organization (*ibid.*:135, 140). As Dwight Smith (1976:82–83) notes:

> Events in Sicily that we have subsequently called Mafia were essentially localized patron-client relationships . . . to which the word "Mafia" was generally applied. It existed in the absence of a strong governmental presence. The mafioso person served to mediate, in a heavily stratified economy, between absent landlords and landless peasants; inevitably, men of a mafioso character obtained influence that extended also into political affairs. The system was dependent upon patronage and upon the ability of a "man of respect" to utilize violence when necessary, to maintain his authority as middleman.

Other research supports this conclusion (see, for example, Blok, 1974; Hess, 1973).

Syndicated Crime in the United States, 1800–1930

Thus, Mafia evolved from certain political, economic, and social conditions. Not being an organization per se, it was not "imported" to the U.S. Yet, this does not mean that syndicated crime was not an important phenomenon in the

U.S. during the 1800s and early 1900s. In fact, crime was clearly organized in the various vice districts of the growing urban centers. As Samuel Walker (1980:107) argues: "There was a large demand for liquor (regardless of the day or hour), gambling, and prostitution. To meet this demand vice districts flourished in every major city." Syndicates providing these illegal goods and services blossomed everywhere. They were well organized and run primarily by Irish, Jewish, and Italian working-class entrepreneurs.

Policy gambling provides an example. Policy gambling is based on the illegal drawing of numbers—usually around 12—upon which players place bets, hoping that from one to four numbers of their choosing will be among the 12 drawn. This form of illegal gambling was a well-organized part of criminal syndicates early in U.S. history. For instance, at about the time of the Civil War, a number of politicians, gamblers, and businesspeople in New York City accumulated $1 million to organize policy shops in that city (Haller, 1976:105). Moreover, by 1900 other large cities (like Chicago) had policy writers in a sizable number of stores, saloons, and barbershops; policy writers collected bets and delivered the money twice daily to a headquarters where the winning numbers were then "drawn" by means of a wheel (*ibid.*). During this time, criminal syndicates made substantial profits from policy gambling, and "the policy runners or writers operating on commission, could be assured of a steady income" (*ibid.*:105).

Similarly, the cocaine trade was organized and coordinated by a variety of criminal syndicates. As a trade it was decentralized into importers, wholesalers, and retailers "who formed, re-formed, split, and came together again as opportunity arose and when they were able" (Block, 1979:94). Criminal careers in the cocaine trade were not structured in one centralized and particular organization, but rather in an increasing network of small but efficient criminal syndicates. Some of these syndicate members had interests in other drug-related illegal syndicates as well as in other types of syndicates, such as gambling. Finally, the cocaine trade was not structured along ethnic lines; Block (*ibid.*) found substantial evidence of interethnic cooperation among cocaine importers, wholesalers, and retailers.

The vice districts, and subsequently syndicated crime, flourished because corruption pervaded city government and everyone involved benefited: citizens had their liquor, gambling, sex, and drugs; ethnic groups had a means of social mobility; police and city officials benefited through financial gain (Walker, 1980:107). Thus, from the Civil War onward (perhaps even earlier), provision of illegal goods and services was *syndicated*, having well-established political and police connections. In fact, as time went on, the boundary between politician and syndicated criminal became more and more obscure as "ward bosses were in a good position to engage in racketeering and racketeers and their nominees could move into political positions" (McIntosh, 1973:56). As Haller (1976:106) has shown concerning gambling during this period:

> It was not simply that gambling syndicates influenced political organizations, but that gambling syndicates sometimes were the local political organizations. Local bookmakers or policy writers served as precinct

One of the largest distilleries ever found in the United States during Prohibition.

captains, while the leaders of syndicates became ward leaders and often won election as alderman or state representatives. By the early twentieth century it would not be possible to understand the structure of local politics without a knowledge of the structure of gambling syndicates.

In short: "The operations of the early criminal syndicates were carefully coordinated with, and often even controlled by, local machine politicians and police" (Nelli, 1987:16–17).

Enactment of the Volstead Act in 1919 made it illegal to produce, distribute, and sell alcoholic beverages. With law enforcement effectively neutralized, and the demand for alcohol continuing unabated, Prohibition (1920–1933) provided the context for the rapid development of a new illegal enterprise: importing, manufacturing, bottling, wholesaling, distributing, and retailing illegal alcoholic beverages. Initially, bootlegging was chaotic and uncoordinated. By the middle of the 1920s, however, syndicates grew in strength and increasingly coordinated the bootlegging activities. In fact, bootlegging, like the cocaine trade, became regional, national, and international.

To supply the large urban markets, bootlegging syndicates required improved coordination and organization. For example, Max Hassel—an owner of breweries in Reading, Pennsylvania, and Camden and Atlantic City, New Jersey—provided beer throughout the Delaware Valley and Philadelphia (Haller,

1976:115). Similarly, in a single four-month period in 1926 and 1927, "Boo Boo" Max Hoff's bootlegging syndicate produced and diverted 350,000 gallons of pure alcohol throughout the Northeast and Midwest (*ibid.*). The Mill Creek Distillery, established in Cuba in 1929, further illustrates the national and international ties of bootlegging syndicates (*ibid.*:116):

> Investors in the distillery included Leon Gleckman, perhaps the leading bootlegger in Minneapolis; representatives of Ansonia Copper and Iron Works of Cincinnati, a manufacturer of stills and other apparatus for making alcohol; G. L. Bevan of Montreal, through whom there were ties with major Canadian distilleries that exported for the American market; Charles Haim of New York, who may also have been a partner in "Boo Boo" Hoff's enterprises in Philadelphia. Mill Creek manufactured both Scotch and rye whiskey. To transport the liquor into the United States, Mill Creek owned or chartered ships to take the liquor off ports such as New Orleans, from which contact boats carried the liquor to shore. Mill Creek also exported liquor directly to ports such as New York in cartons labeled ink or canned fruit. And Mill Creek sold liquor to George Gough of Belize, British Honduras. . . . Thus, the investments in Mill Creek were part of a complex set of relationships that linked New Orleans, Minneapolis, and New York bootleggers with Canadian and West Indian smugglers.

During Prohibition (1920–1933), criminal syndicates grew into larger organizations involving more participants than any other criminal grouping. They also developed a much more complex division of labor. As depicted by Mary McIntosh (1973:42), criminal syndicates developed:

> the form that any organization theorist would suggest was most appropriate to their kind of business; that is, to coordinate and control one or a series of complex but routinized and continuous activities.

This does not mean that criminal syndicates became highly centralized into one organization, under the direction of an alleged Italian Mafia. All evidence indicates the contrary. In fact, data on individuals considered the leading syndicate criminals during Prohibition indicate that they included a variety of ethnic groups—from Jews and Italians to the Irish and Polish (Haller, 1976:109; Block, 1983:129–160; Nelli, 1987:19).

Some criminologists argue, however, that toward the end of Prohibition syndicated crime became extremely centralized and controlled chiefly by Italians. According to this view, a national crime syndicate controlled by a small group of Italians was the "final product of a series of 'ganglord wars' in which an alliance of Italians and Sicilians first conquered other groups and then fought each other" (Cressey, 1969:9). It is to the validity of this argument that we now turn.

A National Crime Syndicate?

Donald Cressey (1969) argues in his well-known book *Theft of the Nation* that a nationwide, centralized control of illegal goods and services came into existence in 1931. As a result of the so-called "Castellammarese War":

> In 1931 leaders of Sicilian-Italian organized crime units across the United States rationally decided to form monopolistic corporations, and to link these corporations together in a monopolistic cartel (*ibid.*:35).

Basing his account "principally on the memoirs of one soldier, Joseph Valachi," Cressey (*ibid.*:37–45) presents the following argument. In 1929, Giuseppe Masseria controlled Sicilian-Italian syndicated crime in New York City. A group called the "Castellammarese" (named after a specific geographical area in Sicily) rebelled against this control, Salvatore Maranzano becoming the leader of the rebels. Throughout 1929 and 1930 a series of feuds and assassinations occurred between the two groups, Masseria declaring war against the Castellammarese on November 5, 1930. Within five months Masseria's "soldiers" realized they were outnumbered, and some of his "key men"—including Charles "Lucky" Luciano—secretly surrendered to Maranzano. To demonstrate their new loyalty, these men successfully arranged to have Masseria executed in April 1931.

According to Cressey, Maranzano immediately appointed himself the "Boss of Bosses" ("Godfather") and "established the notion that there would be bosses beneath him, each with an underboss and a *'caporegima,'* or 'lieutenant,' who, in turn, would have 'soldiers' working for him" (*ibid.*:42). Luciano was allegedly rewarded with a position as a boss, Vito Genovese becoming Luciano's underboss. However, within five months, so the argument goes, Luciano and Genovese grew disenchanted with Maranzano's demands for unquestionable allegiance, eventually aligning themselves with "four Jews"—Louis Buchalter, Meyer Lansky, Benjamin "Bugsy" Siegel, and Jake Shapiro—as well as Al Capone from Chicago. On September 11, 1931, Maranzano was assassinated, this day becoming the so-called "Mafia Purge Day" because, as Cressey (*ibid.*:44) argues:

> On that day and two days immediately following, some forty Italian-Sicilian gang leaders across the country lost their lives in battle. Most, if not all, of those killed on the infamous day occupied positions we would now characterize as "boss," "underboss," or "lieutenant." Perhaps it is for that reason that the "purge day" terminology emerged.

Luciano then substituted the "Boss of Bosses" position with the *"consigliere of six,"* which consisted of the six most influential syndicated criminals in the U.S. Thus, what had previously been, according to Cressey, a local alliance of gangsters in the major U.S. cities became, in 1931, a nationally organized network under the control of an exclusive Italian "board of directors."

In 1951 this conspiracy theory was officially recognized by the U.S. government when it was crystallized in the infamous Kefauver Committee (1951) report, which examined the possibility of a national crime syndicate in the U.S.

Even though *all* the syndicated criminals testifying before the committee denied membership in, or knowledge of, a "Mafia" (Albanese, 1985:31), the Committee (1951:150) concluded that there "is a nationwide crime syndicate known as the Mafia, whose tentacles are found in many large cities"; it centralizes and controls syndicated crime in the United States, and its leadership is found in "a group rather than in a single individual."

In 1963, Joseph Valachi testified before the Senate Subcommittee on Investigations, and outlined the "Mafia Purge Day" story (related earlier) to the Committee. In addition, Valachi gave his view of the structure of syndicated crime at that time, arguing that it was centrally controlled by an Italian organization, "Cosa Nostra" (U.S. Senate, 1963: *passim*).

Cressey (1969:x–xi) echoed Valachi, arguing that "the Mafia" was superseded by "Cosa Nostra" (our thing), and structured as follows:

1. A nationwide alliance of at least 24 tightly knit "families" of criminals exists in the United States. (Because the "families" are fictive, in the sense that members are not all related, references to them are within quotation marks.)

2. Members of these "families" are all Italians and Sicilians, or of Italian and Sicilian descent; those on the Eastern Seaboard, especially, call the entire system "Cosa Nostra." Each participant thinks of himself as a "member" of a specific "family" and of Cosa Nostra (or some equivalent term).

3. The "families" are linked to each other, and to non-Cosa Nostra syndicates, by understandings, agreements, and "treaties," and by mutual deference to a "Commission" made up of the leaders of the most powerful "families."

4. The "boss" of each "family" directs the activities, especially the illegal activities, of the members of his "family."

Most recently, the President's Commission on Organized Crime (1986:35–58), although recognizing the existence of a wide variety of criminal syndicates, simply echoed Cressey—and thereby Valachi—by arguing (without evidence to support it) that an alleged "Cosa Nostra" is the largest and most influential criminal group in the United States.

However, several criminologists question these conclusions. Alan Block (1983), for instance, criticizes Cressey for relying on the testimony of *one* gangster, Valachi. Also, he has reinvestigated the so-called "Mafia Purge Day" story. Block therefore went beyond simply questioning the competence of Cressey's source, investigating whether the event actually took place. Block surveyed newspapers in eight cities—New York, Los Angeles, Philadelphia, Detroit, New Orleans, Boston, Buffalo, and Newark—for any stories (two weeks before and two weeks after Maranzano's death) of gangland murders "remotely connected" to the Maranzano assassination. Block (*ibid.*:6) found various accounts of the Maranzano murder but could find only three murders of "gangsters" that might have been connected to the Maranzano killing. Thus, Block concluded that the killing of three gangsters did not constitute a purge, and he is perplexed as to the origin of Cressey's figure of 40. Additionally, in newspaper stories reporting the killing of Maranzano, it was disclosed that Maranzano was killed for simply *informing* on fellow gangsters for illegally importing aliens, not to rid the "Boss of Bosses" of power (*ibid.*:7–8). Similarly, research by Nelli (1981:179–218) uncovered no evidence to support the "Mafia Purge Day" thesis.

Beyond questioning evidence on the so-called "Mafia Purge Day," Block also analyzed syndicated crime in New York City between 1930 and 1950. These two decades are critical because this is the period between the alleged purge of the "Mafia" and the rise of the so-called "Cosa Nostra" (1930s) on the one hand and, on the other hand, the Kefauver Committee's endorsement of the centralization thesis (1950). What did Block find?

First, although clear that some criminal syndicates became increasingly centralized and hierarchically controlled between 1930 and 1950, Block found *no* evidence indicating the emergence of a national crime syndicate in the sense of "Cosa Nostra." Instead, two types of criminal syndicates operating in New York City during this time period were uncovered, *enterprise* and *power* syndicates (*ibid.*:13). Enterprise syndicates are groups of people organized into illegal enterprises; power syndicates are "loosely structured, extraordinarily flexible associations centered around violence and deeply involved in the production and distribution of informal power" (*ibid.*:13). Enterprise syndicates organize the production and distribution of illegal goods and services, such as narcotics and gambling. These syndicates tend to be large, with a complex division of labor, a centralization of authority, and a hierarchy of command. In contrast, power syndicates have no clear division of labor, for their specific purpose is to maintain power over others through extortion—obtaining control through the use or threat of violence. Block (*ibid.*:129–199) demonstrates that certain of the more energetic power syndicates—controlled by such people as Charles "Lucky" Luciano, Arthur "Dutch Schultz" Flegenheimer, and Louis "Lepke" Buchalter—attempted to exploit enterprise syndicates for extortionary purposes. However, rather than resulting in a centralized "Cosa Nostra," this move by the power syndicates was *disruptive*, creating the conditions for the gangsters' eventual downfall. The case of "Lucky" Luciano is illustrative.

Prior to 1933 in New York City, prostitution was well organized and centralized in enterprise syndicates. There were approximately six "bookers" (individuals who organized the prostitution business and "booked" prostitutes into brothels) who had numerous brothels—and the madams and prostitutes who staffed them—under their control. Luciano's power syndicate "conspired to carry this centralization to an extreme," attempting to control the entire operations of "bonding" (providing bail for arrestees) and "booking."

A prostitute made approximately $85 for a week's labor. However, a prostitute had to pay $10 each week to a bonder, who would then guarantee bail if she were arrested. In 1933, Luciano forced the bonders out of business, and his organization took control. The elimination of the bonders led to centralization and control of the bookers. As Block (*ibid.*:144) points out, Luciano's power syndicate used extortion, such as terrorizing

> booker Dave Miller with threats of murder unless he paid $10,000. . . . Pete Harris was similarly threatened and told he must pay $250 a week to "a 'mob' being formed to 'protect' the bookers." Harris settled his problem by paying $100 a week to stay in business. The other major bookers including Weiner, Charlie Spinach, and Montana were also "taken over." . . . By the end of 1933 . . . the bonders had been totally replaced and the bookers were now employees of the Luciano syndicate.

Once in control, however, Luciano's power syndicate became rapacious. For instance, with regard to posting bond the syndicate decided to put up only one-half of the bond, the other one-half coming from the particular madam affected. When the defendant (prostitute) appeared at trial—and the bond money was returned—the syndicate kept the entire amount, returning nothing to the madam. This "exploitation of madams was one of the key disruptive issues under the new syndicate" (*ibid.*:147). As time passed, madams were less and less likely to cooperate (bookers joined them) and attempted to conceal brothels from the syndicate. This rebellion by madams and bookers was so strong that by 1935 Luciano reportedly wanted out of the prostitution business because the profit was not worth the trouble. Indeed, Luciano's power base was reduced considerably, and in February 1936 he was prosecuted successfully by Thomas Dewey for compulsory prostitution. Luciano received a sentence of 30 to 50 years (*ibid.*:68–69). As Block (*ibid.*:147–148) concludes, the Luciano power syndicate

> took a fairly centralized operation, the booking system, and subjected it to intense pressures which threatened to disrupt the entire trade. It turned on the key personnel in the trade with the exception of the prostitute herself who was already cruelly exploited, and initiated various methods of financially squeezing both bookers and madams who resorted to cheating and ultimately to testifying against their bosses. . . . It was clearly an effort at extreme centralization that attacked what was already a stable system of organized prostitution. . . . As neither the price structure nor the volume of trade changed under the Luciano syndicate, profits for the entrepreneurs of violence could only come from the pockets of the formerly independent syndicate leaders and madams. Indeed, one might want to argue that without substantial changes in the economics of organized prostitution, it had about all the centralization it could take by 1933.

Syndicated prostitution continued, "but never under the centralized direction of a power syndicate" (*ibid.*:148). Overall, Block found no evidence of the emergence of a national crime syndicate in New York between 1930 and 1950.

Frank Pearce's (1976:124–131) important examination of the legendary Al Capone provides yet another example of historical inaccuracy. Although clear that Capone was a central figure in such illegal activities as bootlegging and labor racketeering, there is no evidence that he became a "boss" in an alleged national crime syndicate in the early 1930s. In fact, Pearce shows that syndicated crime's involvement in corruption and, therefore, its close relationship with the police and politicians, undermined "legitimate" business endeavors at the time. It was this phenomenon that actually led to Capone's downfall. As Pearce (*ibid.*:128–129) writes:

> Many businessmen had begun to feel that City Hall could no longer be relied upon to provide the "rational legal" form of administration that they required to run their businesses. Chicago's judges were corrupt, her administration was inefficient, civic contracts were awarded to the highest briber; the infrastructure was starting to break down. The true magnitude of the city's crisis became clear in 1930 when it was found to be $300 million in debt.

In addition to a corrupt and bankrupt state, businesspeople were also concerned about Prohibition, and supported its repeal. Legal alcohol, they argued, would relieve social tensions, lessen class hatred, and provide tax revenues for the state. Thus, businesspeople appealed to the federal government to intervene in Chicago, and in 1929 federal proceedings began against Capone for tax evasion (Eliot Ness and his Justice Department Raiders soon destroyed his breweries). Three years later—in 1932—Capone was sentenced to 10 years in Alcatraz; in 1933, Prohibition was repealed.

As with New York then, Pearce found no evidence of leading syndicate criminals in Chicago becoming involved in a national crime syndicate. Moreover, with the downfall of Capone—as with Luciano—criminal syndicates were not even bruised, continuing to operate such activities as extortion, loan sharking, gambling, drugs, and labor racketeering.

Given that it is highly unlikely a national crime syndicate emerged between 1930 and 1950, most criminologists also argue that it is doubtful such a syndicate emerged after 1950. Numerous scholars—such as William Moore (1974), Joseph Albini (1971), and Daniel Bell (1964)—found no evidence of a national crime syndicate in the 1950s, arguing that the Kefauver Committee's "Mafia" conclusion was based simply on assumptions and conjecture, not empirical evidence. Moreover, from Kefauver to the present, no reliable evidence indicates the existence of a national crime syndicate. For such to exist, one criminal syndicate would have to retain monopoly control of all syndicated criminal activity—from illegal gambling to the illegal drug trade, from labor racketeering to the illegal disposal of hazardous wastes. While there is evidence of some large-scale syndicates—some of which are dominated by Italians and call themselves "Mafia" (there are also syndicates other than Italians that use this designation, such as the "Black Mafia" and "Mexican Mafia")—no such monopoly exists (Block, 1991:11–14). As Jay Albanese (1985:64) concludes after an exhaustive review of research on syndicated crime: "It is difficult to understand, therefore, the continuing belief in a nationwide criminal conspiracy when no one has been able to produce reliable evidence of it."

8.2 _____ SYNDICATED CRIME TODAY

The endless contemporary demand for illegal goods and services in the U.S. creates perfect conditions for criminal syndicates to flourish and prosper. These syndicates are not controlled by an Italian-dominated national crime syndicate. Rather, they are diverse and autonomous. For example, the President's Commission on Organized Crime (1986:75–128) found the following racial and ethnic membership in syndicated crime: Chinese, blacks, Mexicans, Italians, Vietnamese, Japanese, Cubans, Colombians, Irish, Russians, Canadians, and a variety of others. Thus, there is no specific ethnic stereotype synonymous with syndicated crime (Nelli, 1987:27). Two excellent sociological studies—by Joseph Albini (1971) and William Chambliss (1988)—help us further understand the structure of syndicated crime in the United States today. We briefly summarize their conclusions.

Patron-Client Relationships

Albini (1971:263–304) argues that syndicated crime in the U.S. is characterized by patron-client relationships. Syndicated criminals differ in the kinds of relationships they establish among themselves, between themselves, and with those who protect them. For Albini, no rigid formal structure is prevalent; syndicated criminals simply make use of whatever resources or persons are necessary to accomplish their goals. Moreover, every criminal syndicate has several powerful individuals who serve as "patrons" to the criminal clientele; patrons wield force and deliver favors. Yet, as Albini (*ibid.*:265) further argues:

> A powerful syndicate leader in the west at a particular time may be influential in his area because he has excellent protection in his city and because he provides funds for a multitude of new criminal enterprises, giving other syndicated criminals continued sources of revenue. Yet he may have no power whatsoever over other syndicated criminals in other parts of the country.

In addition, powerful syndicate figures may serve as "clients" to others more powerful, especially those with legal power to offer protection in return for payoffs. In other words, the "entire system involves various levels of patron-client relationships" that are constantly permeated with conflict, cooperation, and accommodation (*ibid.*). Syndicated crime therefore is never formally or rigidly bureaucratized; rather, it maintains numerous and complex criminal and noncriminal patron-client relationships. As Albini (*ibid.*:300) concludes, syndicated criminal enterprises

> are generated at all levels of patron-client relationships and they are primarily held together by the fact that each participant is basically motivated by his own self-interest. Power within the system depends upon the individual's rise in the number of significant patron-client relationships he is able to establish.

Albini's perspective on the structure of syndicated crime is supported by other research that employs a variety of methodologies, such as participant observation, interviews with informants, and analysis of the government's syndicated crime files (Bynum, 1987:7).

Crime Networks

In his book *On the Take*, Chambliss (1988) extends Albini's thesis a little further. He documents how businesspeople, politicians, and members of the criminal justice system are involved in "the subterranean, often invisible" industry built upon, for example, illegal gambling, drugs, loan sharking, business fraud, and prostitution (*ibid.*:2). As shown in Figure 8-1 Chambliss studied syndicated crime in Seattle, finding that the vice district was prospering and controlled *not* by "Cosa Nostra," but by

> a loose affiliation of businessmen, politicians, union leaders, and law-enforcement officials who cooperate to coordinate the production and distribution of illegal goods and services, for which there is a substantial demand (*ibid.*:151).

Thus, financiers (who finance the operations) and middle-level organizers (who supervise the racketeers) unite in a loosely structured "crime network" for the purpose of financial gain. Rather than the existence of a highly centralized "Cosa Nostra," Chambliss' research indicates that criminal syndicates are organized by those who primarily benefit from the criminal activities—those "legitimate" members of society who hold business, political, and criminal justice positions.

The importance of both Albini's and Chambliss' research, then, is that it shows that the overall structure of syndicated crime has changed little since the 1800s. Syndicated crime is not centrally organized in a national crime syndicate, and "upright" businesspeople and public officials continue to play a regular and significant role in the organization and perpetuation of criminal syndicates. We turn now to the principal forms of syndicated crime today.

8.3 ———— PRINCIPAL FORMS OF SYNDICATED CRIME

There are various estimates of the annual gross income of syndicated crime. For example, the President's Commission on Organized Crime (1986:423) calculated annual gross income at approximately $66 billion. This figure means that syndicated crime is one of the major U.S. industries, having approximately the same income as all U.S. metal producers (such as iron, steel, aluminum) as well as the textile and apparel industries, and a larger income than the paper and rubber and tire industries (*ibid.*). The Commission's estimate, however, is based only on syndicated crime's *illegal* activities. When *legal* activities are included, the gross annual income of this U.S. "industry" increases considerably. James Cook (1980:60), using a variety of sources on legitimate and illegitimate enterprises,

Financiers

Jewelers   Attorneys
Realtors   Businessmen
Contractors   Industrialists

Bankers

Organizers

Businessmen	**Politicians**	**Law-Enforcement Officers**
Restaurant owners	City councilmen	Chief of police
Cardroom owners	Mayors	Assistant chief of police
Pinball-machine license	Governors	Sheriff
holders	State legislators	Undersheriff
Bingo parlor owners	Board of supervisors members	County prosecutor
Cabaret and hotel owners	Licensing bureau chief	Assistant prosecutor
Club owners		Patrol division commanders
Receivers of stolen property		Vice-squad commanders
Pawnshop owners		Narcotics officers
		Patrolmen
		Police lieutenants, captains, and sergeants

Racketeers

Gamblers	Pimps	Prostitutes	Drug distributors	Usurers	Bookmakers

FIGURE 8-1 Seattle's Crime Network

Source: Chambliss, 1988, p. 74.

estimated the annual gross income of syndicated crime to be as high as $150 billion. Although Cook's estimate was based on 1979 figures, if syndicated crime's revenues have grown at the rate of inflation, it grossed as much as $226 billion in 1986 (President's Commission on Organized Crime, 1986:419).

We consider next the principal forms of syndicated crime that generate this enormous income. Specifically, we examine:

1. Four types of illegal sale and distribution of goods and services—illegal gambling, illegal drugs, loan sharking, and illegal hazardous waste disposal.

2. Syndicated crime's involvement in legitimate business through direct investment, racketeering, and money laundering.

3. Syndicated crime's involvement with the state, such as corruption and performing political favors.

Syndicates and Illegal Goods and Services

The first type of illegal sale and distribution of goods and services is *gambling*. Since the 1800s illegal gambling has been an important source of income for many criminal syndicates. In the 1940s and early 1950s, criminal syndicates found that substantial profits could be made in the Las Vegas *legal* gambling business as well. As Humbert Nelli (1987:23) reports, many syndicate leaders

> quickly recognized the opportunities in Las Vegas and invested (either openly or through fronts) in the casino-hotels that sprang up during the 1950s. In the process they turned Las Vegas into the most lucrative gambling spa in the world.

We have more to say about Las Vegas later when we discuss syndicated crime's involvement in corruption.

It is estimated that the income generated by syndicated crime through illegal gambling is somewhere between $29–$33 billion each year in the United States (President's Commission on Organized Crime, 1986:447; *Business Week*, 1989:114). There are two major types of illegal gambling: "numbers" and "bookmaking." Numbers is a form of lottery in which the customer (bettor) places a bet by choosing three numbers between 000 and 999. The customer usually bets from $1 to $10, receiving from a "numbers runner" a receipt with the chosen number and the amount of the bet written on it. The runner, who has several copies of the receipt, passes one to the "pickup," who then carries it to the "bank" or to the accounting room of the numbers operation. The customer, if a winner (that is, if she or he predicted correctly the three numbers in their chosen order), is paid a fixed multiple (such as 500 to 1) of the amount bet. A common procedure for determining the winning number is the "Brooklyn" method, which is based on the last three digits of the total amount of money a particular racetrack handles on a specific day. Another method calculates the three-digit number from the winning dollar amounts paid on a $2 wager on the first, fifth, and seventh races at a particular racetrack (Reuter, 1983:45–54). Approximately $5.5 billion was wagered on the numbers in 1988 (*Business Week*, 1989:114).

The structure of a numbers syndicate is not especially complex. At the bottom, of course, are the customers who make wagers with either "mobile runners" (those who travel over a territory to accept bets) or "stationary runners" (those who accept bets at their place of business—such as a bar, newsstand, or small business). Runners are usually paid a commission of 25 percent of their receipts (because they have the highest risk of apprehension) and also receive tips of, on the average, 10 percent of the winning payoffs. The pickup operates as an area manager, tabulates daily collections, maintains records of runners, and makes payoffs from the bank. The pickups receive between 5 and 10 percent of total receipts. Finally, the pickup transfers the day's receipts to the bank, which is the main organizer and manager of the numbers game. The banker usually employs a staff to audit the games and arranges payoffs to the police, bailbondsmen, and lawyers. For a game that pays 500 to 1, bankers earn a profit of approximately 14.5 percent (Simon and Witte, 1982:212–214).

Bookmaking, the second major type of illegal gambling, is the organized illegal betting on horse racing and sporting events. The major source of syndicated crime's bookmaking income is the latter category—primarily football (college and professional), basketball (college and professional), and baseball (professional only). Reuter (1983:17) provides an example of how sports betting works:

> Most sports bets are on the outcome of a single game. For basketball or football, one team is usually given a handicap of a certain number of points, called the "spread." Assume the Los Angeles Rams are handicapped by 8 points in their game against the Chicago Bears. This means that the person who wishes to bet on the Rams wins his bet only if the Rams win by more than 8 points. If the Bears win or lose by less than 8 points, bets on the Bears are paid. If the Rams win by exactly 8 points, all bets are returned to the bettors; to avoid this return, the spread is frequently a half-point value, such as 7 1/2.

Approximately $26.8 billion was wagered on sports and horse bookmaking in 1988 (*Business Week*, 1989:114).

The four major players in a bookmaking syndicate are the customer (bettor), runner, clerk, and bookmaker ("bookie"). The runner transfers money from the customers to the bookmaker; the clerk transcribes and records transactions. The bookie is the controlling figure, "setting the terms of the bets and the limits on the size of bets. He also provides capital to cover expenses and losses" (Reuter, 1983:20). Furthermore, the bookie may have others working in the syndicate in addition to a clerk and several runners. For instance, some bookies have what is referred to as a "tabber" who keeps "tabs" on the bets and changes the spreads when necessary (Simon and Witte, 1982:216). For both numbers and bookmaking, the best available evidence indicates that these illegal gambling syndicates operate autonomously, and are not centrally controlled under the exclusive direction of one organization (Reuter and Rubinstein, 1978:63–74; Reuter, 1983:14–84).

A second type of illegal sale and distribution of goods and services is the *illegal drug* business (primarily heroin, cocaine, and marijuana), which reaps tremendous profits for syndicated crime. Take heroin, for example. It has been estimated that for approximately four hours each day, 365 days a year, $400 worth of heroin is sold every minute on 115th Street in New York City—resulting in a financial exchange amounting to $24,000 an hour, $96,000 a day, and $672,000 a week (Timmer, 1982:386). According to Block and Chambliss (1981:33), annual gross sales of heroin alone exceed $30 billion.

Overall, the illegal drug industry operates like importing, wholesaling, and retailing businesses. It is organized and coordinated by a variety of criminal syndicates—not one exclusive criminal elite. As a former police commissioner of New York City stated (cited in Block and Chambliss, 1981:57):

The illegal drug industry today can more accurately be compared structurally to the garment industry. Many sources of raw materials exist. Many organizations, large and small, buy and process the raw materials, import the product into this country, where it is sold to and processed and distributed at retail by a host of outlets, some large and small, chain and owner-operated. . . . Organization in the drug business is largely spontaneous, with anybody free to enter it at any level if he has the money, the supplier and the ability to escape arrest or robbery.

Simon and Witte (1982:128–134) have examined the structure of the heroin, cocaine, and marijuana distribution systems. Heroin seems to be the most organized of the three, with a few criminal syndicates sharing in monopolizing *importation* of heroin into the U.S. For instance, Moore (1977:100) estimated there were approximately 25 importers supplying New York City. Simon and Witte found the heroin industry inside the U.S. comprised a variety of small syndicates, thus creating a long vertical distributional structure. As they point out, small syndicates ("distribution units," they call them) serve somewhere between 5 and 20 customers, and enjoy certain advantages over large monopolies because (*ibid.*:130)

they require just a small number of transactions, they discourage information leaks, they facilitate supervision and discipline of customers, and they allow for quick and efficient adjustments in behavior. Furthermore, these distributional units will be well isolated from one another so that each dealer can limit information on his activities to just a few trusted customers, both for his own protection and to exploit some of his monopoly advantages.

Even though these distribution units are small, they nevertheless maintain different levels between production and sales, each level relatively insulated from other levels. At the top (as stated earlier) are the heroin *importers,* who coordinate large shipments of heroin into the U.S. Importers have high operating costs because success is somewhat based on employing skilled smugglers. Importers almost never see or touch the actual heroin; they simply coordinate the shipment of uncut and undiluted heroin to a criminal syndicate in the U.S., which then distributes it to a variety of *wholesalers.* The wholesalers dilute the purity of the heroin—usually with quinine, mannite, and/or lactose—thereby doubling the volume and weight of the heroin mixture. Eventually the heroin is reduced in purity to approximately 25 percent, and then divided into "street-ounce" sizes (a little less than one full ounce). These packages are then sold to a variety of what may be called "street syndicates," who also dilute the purity, reducing it to approximately 10–15 percent heroin, selling "half-ounces" or "bundles" to users.

Mieczkowski's (1986) work on heroin street sales indicates there are three major players in street syndicates, all of whom are not heroin users: runners, guns, and crew bosses. "Runners" are given allocations of heroin from the crew

Billy, Marie, and their 6-month-old daughter survive on drug dealing. Billy—a "runner"—is notified of incoming drug shipments through a beeper.

boss to sell on the street at a variety of locations. Runners maintain a specific "selling position" on the sidewalk or in an alley, and sell their heroin to customers (*ibid.*:651). "Guns" are armed members of the syndicate who station themselves close to the sales areas to provide security for runners. As Mieczkowski (*ibid.*:652) states: "Guns observe and monitor the street transactions. Should anything go awry, guns are expected to intervene." The "crew boss" manages the street syndicate, distributes the heroin to runners, and collects funds obtained by runners. Crew bosses either go "into the field" to collect the money or runners report to crew bosses at specific locations. The average "wage" of a runner is approximately $800 per week (if the runner works a five-day week); crew bosses average almost $1,500 per week. The crew bosses in Mieczkowski's study were approximately 18 to 19 years of age, the runners were several years younger. It is also the job of crew bosses to obtain quantities of heroin on a regular basis. This requires coming into contact with wholesalers, who either require payment for the heroin "up front" or after the street sales are completed.

Overall, Simon and Witte's and Mieczkowski's research is important because it reveals that the overall structure of the heroin distribution system is based on patron-client relationships. The runner requires the patronage of a crew

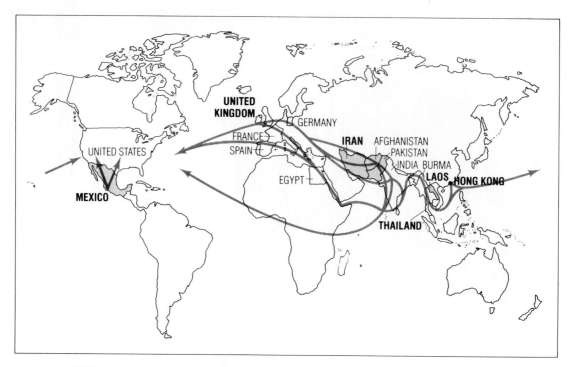

FIGURE   **Major Heroin Smuggling Routes into the United States**
8-2   *Source: General Accounting Office, 1988, p. 10.*

boss and the crew boss the patronage of a supplier (*ibid.*:661); in turn, the supplier (or wholesaler) requires the patronage of an importer.

According to Simon and Witte (1982:158, 171–174), cocaine and marijuana distribution systems in the U.S. are very similar to the heroin system in that they maintain a long vertical distribution system with well-insulated syndicates, each servicing a small number of customers—or clients—below them. For cocaine, each participant dilutes the drug, thereby increasing its volume and price. By the time the mixture reaches the street, it is rarely over 5–10 percent pure. Marijuana is seldom diluted, but is repackaged into smaller parcels as it passes from one level to the next.

The vast majority of heroin, cocaine, and marijuana sold in the U.S. comes from foreign countries. Figures 8-2, 8-3, and 8-4 illustrate smuggling routes from the major drug-producing countries of the world. The figures show that the major heroin producers are the countries of the "Golden Crescent" area of Southwest Asia (Afghanistan, Iran, and Pakistan), Mexico, and the "Golden Triangle" area of Southeast Asia (Laos, Burma, and Thailand). The major cocaine producers are Bolivia, Colombia, and Peru, and of marijuana, Colombia and Mexico.

Syndicates in these (and in other) countries work with a variety of syndicates in the U.S. to organize importation of the specific drug into this country. For

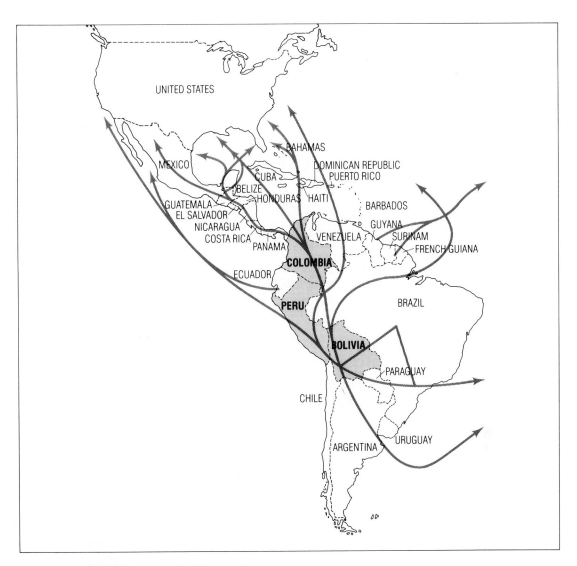

FIGURE
8-3

Major Cocaine Smuggling Routes into the United States

Source: General Accounting Office, 1988, p. 14.

example, in the late 1980s it was reported in *The New York Times* and in other media sources that a major Colombian syndicate—commonly referred to as the "Medellin Cartel"—supplies approximately 75 percent of the cocaine used in the U.S. It is alleged that this Colombian cocaine usually passes through Panama on its way to the U.S. In fact, according to a U.S. Justice Department indictment of General Manuel Noriega—former ruler of Panama—Noriega allegedly worked closely with this Colombian syndicate, providing it with secure airstrips,

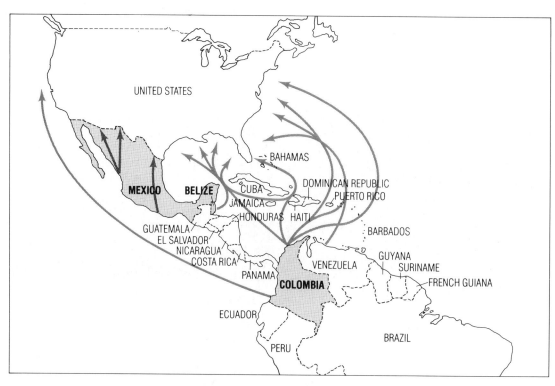

FIGURE   Major Marijuana Smuggling Routes into the United States
8-4   *Source: General Accounting Office, 1988, p. 16.*

allowing syndicate fugitives to remain in Panama if they were sought by law-enforcement officials in other countries, and transforming certain Panamanian banks into "money laundering centers" for the syndicate (Shenon, 1988:A5).

Loan sharking is a third type of illegal sale and distribution of goods and services. For many individuals and small businesses in urgent need of money, legitimate sources of obtaining that money—such as relatives and banks—are not possible. Consequently, in times of financial crisis many such people must turn to loan sharks, who loan money at extremely high interest rates and who require rapid repayment of all loans. Larger loans seem to have lower interest rates than smaller ones. For instance, Reuter (1983:96–97) reports that a $1,000 loan usually requires repayment in 12 weekly sums of $100, or 20 percent interest per week; however, the interest rate for a $20,000 loan may be as low as 1 percent per week. Large borrowers are usually small businesses, speculators or promoters, and gamblers (Simon and Witte, 1982:229).

Most loan sharks also require some type of collateral—such as the ownership documents to the borrower's automobile—which lessens the need for engaging in violence to obtain repayment (Reuter, 1983:98–99). Loan sharks usually attempt to avoid violence, inasmuch as violence is likely to attract an official response. A more common strategy for a loan sharking criminal syndicate is

The disposal of hazardous waste in an illegal manner has become big business in the United States.

loaning money to a legitimate business with the understanding that if repayment is not forthcoming, the syndicate simply takes over the business (Kwitny, 1979:*passim*).

Loan sharking may be directed by syndicates involved in a variety of criminal activities. Or it may simply involve individuals with large quantities of cash—from either legitimate or illegitimate ventures—available for use in further money-making endeavors, such as creating their own loan sharking syndicate. For the latter type, loan sharking becomes a means of "moonlighting," whereby they employ a variety of individuals in their syndicate: attorneys, accountants, enforcers, runners (who contact borrowers), law-enforcement officials, and so forth. For example, Simon and Witte (1982:230–231) report that one loan shark in New York City employed 19 runners (all held legitimate full-time jobs as well) and five bookkeepers (each kept records on three or four runners).

Finally, *illegal disposal of hazardous waste* is well organized in the U.S. (Block and Scarpitti, 1985). It is estimated that 150 million metric tons of toxics are generated each year (10 billion pounds in New Jersey alone) and that the number of toxic waste dump sites is approximately 120,000 (Scarpitti and Block, 1987:117). Neutralizing toxic chemicals and burying toxic wastes in sealed eco-logically safe sites is remarkably expensive. In 1976 Congress enacted the Re-source Conservation and Recovery Act, which sets standards and regulations for the control of hazardous wastes. One result of this Act has been a drastic increase in the price of waste disposal (Block and Bernard, 1988:118). Thus, businesses that produce such waste may turn to criminal syndicates organized to dispose of it illegally and, therefore, at a more reasonable (namely, less expensive) cost. Indeed, immediately following the new disposal guidelines, "midnight dumpers" opened for business, and "charged under-market prices because they simply dumped the toxic wastes anywhere and everywhere" (*ibid.*:118). Illegal disposal of hazardous wastes becomes a means of minimizing costs for a business while earning huge profits for criminal syndicates. As Scarpitti and Block (*ibid.*:121–122) point out:

> From New York to New Mexico, from New Jersey to Florida, a pattern of waste racketeering may be observed. In fact, a recent survey by the U.S. Senate Permanent Subcommittee on Investigations (1984) revealed that about one-third of the states, including the largest and most industrialized, appear to be experiencing the problem.

Criminal syndicates dump hazardous wastes into landfills, sewers, rivers, farms, and elsewhere, and may either contract out their labor to a legitimate business or the syndicate itself may own a legitimate waste disposal company (*ibid.*:120). Either way, syndicates effectively conceal their illegal activity.

Syndicates and Legitimate Businesses

In addition to illegal sale and distribution of goods and services, criminal syndicates work with legitimate businesses. There are three major means by which syndicated crime effects this involvement: direct investment, money laundering, and racketeering.

Criminal syndicates often reinvest their profits from the illegal sale and distribution of goods and services in legitimate enterprises. The President's Commission on Organized Crime (1986:424) reported syndicate investments in (1) construction; (2) waste removal; (3) garments; (4) food processing, distribution, and retailing; (5) legal gambling; (6) hotels; (7) bars; (8) liquor retailing and wholesaling; (9) entertainment; (10) business and personal services; (11) motor vehicle sales and repair; (12) real estate; (13) banking; and (14) various other wholesale and retail businesses. The advantages of investing in legitimate businesses include less risk than expanding an illegal operation, opportunities for concealing illegal activities (as we have seen concerning illegal disposal of hazardous wastes), and avenues for paying income taxes.

In addition to investing in legitimate businesses, legitimate businesspeople sometimes become involved in working relationships with syndicate-owned businesses. The case of Frank Perdue demonstrates one way this relationship can develop (Rowan, 1986:37–38). Perdue, owner of a large chicken processing plant, was approached by representatives of a syndicate-owned business—Dial Poultry Company—who wanted to buy his product. At first he refused to sell to Dial because it was owned and controlled by a criminal syndicate. However, eventually Perdue realized that—because Dial served a substantial number of retail butchers—if he became involved, he could gain a competitive advantage in the legal chicken market. This he did, engaging in a close business relationship with Dial. So close did this relationship become that when workers at one of his plants attempted to organize a union, Perdue asked the owners of Dial to help quell the labor unrest!

Much of what is earned by criminal syndicates from the illegal sale and distribution of goods and services is in *cash*, and usually in small bills. Before this "dirty" money (illegally earned) can be spent or invested in legitimate businesses, it must be turned into "clean" money. Criminal syndicates accomplish this by engaging in *money laundering*. This is the process "by which one conceals the existence, illegal source, or illegal application of income, and then disguises that income to make it appear legitimate" (President's Commission on Organized Crime, 1984:7). Money laundering ranges from the small individual drug dealer who wishes to exchange smaller-denomination bills for larger ones, to the large criminal syndicate that obtains enormous sums of money from numerous illegal activities.

Under the Bank Secrecy Act, financial institutions must report all currency transactions of $10,000 or more. When a financial institution fails to do this, it is engaging in money laundering. Syndicated crime's involvement in the illegal flow of drugs provides an excellent example of how money laundering occurs, benefiting both financial institutions and criminal syndicates. Although examples of money laundering are legion, we summarize only one case reported in the President's Commission on Organized Crime (*ibid.*:31–42) and one case reported more recently.

The case referred to as "The Pizza Connection" resulted in the indictment of 38 people in April 1984 for heroin trafficking and money laundering. These individuals were accused of using U.S. pizza parlors to distribute heroin smuggled from Southeast Asia's Golden Triangle. Couriers deposited tens of millions of dollars in cash at banks in New York City. The New York banks then transferred the funds to a variety of banks in other countries, such as Switzerland. From these foreign banks the money was channeled to various narcotic sources to pay for conversion of opium to heroin, to finance additional "drug" laboratories, and to support and profit the overall network of heroin trafficking. By transferring the funds around the world, the process of money laundering is considerably more difficult to detect.

One of the couriers, Franco Delle Torre, deposited almost $5 million (in $5, $10, $20 bills)—over a six-week period—in an account at the brokerage firm Merrill Lynch Pierce Fenner and Smith. The deposits apparently were so important to the brokerage firm that Merrill Lynch's

> security employees determined that Delle Torre's funds could not be afforded proper security, and arrangements were made to escort the money from Delle Torre's hotel directly to Bankers Trust, where Merrill Lynch maintained accounts (*ibid.*:33).

Eventually, however, Merrill Lynch closed the account, and Delle Torre simply moved his laundering operation to the Manhattan offices of the brokerage firm E. F. Hutton and Company. For six months in 1982, Delle Torre made 18 different cash deposits totaling $13.5 million in a Hutton account. Security personnel at Hutton similarly provided Delle Torre protection from his hotel room to the depository institution. As noted in Chapter 7.2, in 1988 E. F. Hutton pleaded guilty to this money laundering scheme.

The "Pizza Connection" case reveals not only the close relationship between syndicated crime and legitimate businesses but also the *international* nature and context of this relationship. Approximately $5–15 billion of the $50–75 billion in illegal drug money generated in the United States each year quite likely moves into international financial channels. As the President's Commission on Organized Crime (*ibid.*:13) found:

▲— More than two-thirds of the $5–15 billion is moved on behalf of foreign traffickers bringing drugs to the United States, as well as on behalf of Colombians and Mexicans involved in distributing cocaine and heroin in the United States. The remainder comes from funds earned by U.S. drug dealers and distributors.

▲— About one-third of the illegal drug money moves overseas in the form of currency, and much of the remainder is wired abroad after being deposited in the U.S. banking system.

▲— More than two-thirds of the $5–15 billion probably passes through Colombia, or the offshore banking centers of the Caribbean Basin, mainly Panama, the Bahamas, and the Cayman Islands.

The case of the Bank of Credit and Commerce International (BCCI) illustrates further the international networking of drugs and money laundering. According to *The New York Times*, BCCI was the seventh-largest privately held financial institution in the world, operating 400 branches in 73 countries. In October 1988 some 85 people in seven U.S. cities, as well as the bank itself, were indicted for money laundering. The bank allegedly laundered $14 million in narcotic funds, mostly serving Colombia criminal syndicates involved in the cocaine trade. The money laundering scheme involved shifting money around the world in order to make it difficult to trace (Schmalz, 1988:A56). Once the money was deposited, BCCI wired it to a variety of foreign banks in France, Britain, Luxembourg, Uruguay, Panama, and the Bahamas, placing the money in certificates of deposit (CDs). The CDs were used as a basis for setting up phoney loans to syndicated crime figures for slightly smaller amounts than the CDs. According to *Time* magazine, BCCI then "collected the CDs as 'payment' for the loans, pocketing the difference in the face amounts as a commission" (Castro, 1988:66). In this way syndicate crime obtained "clean" money and BCCI made a substantial cost-free profit.

In the early 1990s, it was revealed that BCCI had a clandestine division in the bank known as the "black network" (Beaty and Gwyne, 1991). This network functioned as a global intelligence and enforcement squad for the bank, while simultaneously operating a lucrative illegal arms trade and drug transport business. The network attracted deposits from drug syndicates, tax evaders, corrupt government officials, and frequently worked with governmental intelligence agencies, including the CIA. For example, BCCI kept secret CIA accounts so that the CIA could finance covert aid to the U.S.-backed *Contras* in Nicaragua and the Mujahedin rebels in Afghanistan. In turn, the CIA acquiesced to BCCI's involvement in the heroin trade in Pakistan and the cocaine trade in Central America (*ibid*. See Chapter 9).

In addition to direct investment and money laundering, criminal syndicates are also involved with legitimate businesses through *labor racketeering*, "the infiltration, domination, and use of a union for personal benefit by illegal, violent, and fraudulent means" (President's Commission on Organized Crime, 1986a:9). As we have learned, labor racketeering is not new, having been a major activity of syndicated crime in the 1920s. Moreover, in the 1950s the Kefauver Committee, investigating "Improper Activities in Labor-Management Activities," documented systematic racketeering in the bakers, butchers, carpenters, distillery workers, hotel and restaurant employees, operating engineers, teamsters, and textile workers unions (Moore, 1974:68–79).

Labor racketeering continues to be a major activity of syndicated crime today. Traditional forms of racketeering that continue to proliferate include (1) entering into "sweetheart contracts" with employers, (2) looting workers' benefit funds, and (3) extorting "strike insurance" payments from businesses. In addition to these traditional forms of racketeering, criminal syndicates wield "union power to facilitate marketplace corruption and to give businesses an advantage in the marketplace" (President's Commission on Organized Crime, 1986a:10). We briefly summarize the Commission's evidence on each racketeering form (*ibid.*:12–23).

A "sweetheart contract" results from a criminal syndicate's extensive infiltration of a union, ensuring it the opportunity to control the union and consequently to collude with management, permitting employers to violate collective bargaining provisions. In return for payoffs to syndicate figures who negotiate such contracts, the employers have, for example, the privilege of using nonunion labor, a guarantee that workers will not be organized by specifically unwelcome unions, and the right to select union representatives with whom to negotiate. These sweetheart contracts seem to be flourishing in such industries as construction, trucking, and garments (*ibid.*:18).

Concerning workers' benefit funds (which cover pension, health, and welfare benefits for retired, disabled, and needy workers), infiltration of unions by criminal syndicates has resulted in the systematic looting of these funds to provide syndicate figures and their friends with such perks as "no show" jobs, homes, automobiles, travel expenses, stocks and bonds, and capital for legitimate investment. The International Brotherhood of Teamsters (IBT)—which has a long history of benefit-fund abuse—provides a shocking example (*ibid.*:99–166). In the early 1960s, Jimmy Hoffa (then president of the Teamsters Union) shared pension-fund kickbacks with Allen Dorfman, a former asset manager and service provider to the Teamsters Central States Pension Fund. Hoffa was convicted of jury tampering in 1964. Prior to beginning his prison sentence, according to the President's Commission on Organized Crime (*ibid.*:99) Hoffa:

> convened a meeting of the Fund trustees to state, unequivocally, that Allen Dorfman was his spokesman while he, Hoffa, served time in jail. Hoffa and Dorfman were the moving forces behind the Central States Pension Fund's entry into speculative real-estate loans in Las Vegas, an action that eventually robbed the Teamsters of millions of pension fund dollars and resulted in the government's decision to place the Fund in receivership.

Other presidents of the Union—such as Roy Williams and Jackie Presser—in association with criminal syndicates, have similarly looted the Teamsters pension fund. For example, Jackie Presser placed his uncle, Allen Friedman, on the Union payroll at a $1,000 weekly salary, even though Friedman did not work for the union. In addition, Presser arranged to pay a syndicate-controlled firm—Hoover-Gorin and Associates—$1.3 million per year and a $350,000 yearly retainer to do advertising and public relations work that seems never to have been performed (*ibid.*:107–108). Even before assuming the Teamsters' presidency, "Jackie Presser had compiled an extensive record" of syndicate crime associations, benefiting "from their support in his elevation to the IBT Presidency in 1983" (*ibid.*:90).

Criminal syndicates may also extort "strike insurance" from employers in return for the promise to keep the business "running as usual" (namely, free from labor strife). In other words, the employer pays a criminal syndicate a fee to keep labor peace. For example, it was recently uncovered that syndicate figures "created and owned a series of labor-leasing companies throughout the country" (*ibid.*:110–111). These companies provided workers and labor peace to the corporations that hired them. Criminal syndicates received contractual payments and the corporations minimized their labor costs. If a corporation did not voluntarily hire one of these syndicate companies, corrupt union officials created labor disputes to suggest the need for labor peace and, therefore, syndicated crime's leased labor.

As a union member one has the right to nominate candidates, vote in elections and on different referenda, attend membership meetings, participate in deliberations, and meet and assemble freely with other union members. Notwithstanding, the President's Commission on Organized Crime (*ibid.*: 114) found that syndicate-influenced unions, such as the Teamsters

> rely on fear and violence to deny these rights to members. The violence takes many forms, literally ranging from verbal harassment to murder, to quell all forms of dissent, criticism, and opposition. Violence need not be an everyday occurrence. Occasional "examples" are often sufficient to

persuade members that any opposition may create a substantial risk of injury or death.

When criminal syndicates control a union, they also have the power to participate in market corruption schemes. The construction industry of New York City provides a prime example of how this type of corruption occurs (*ibid.*:21):

> New York construction businesses cooperating with organized crime have formed a cartel, and the union is the enforcing agent. General contractors are told what suppliers to use and who the subcontractors will be. If a contractor does not comply, either he will never get the job (having been purposely underbid by the cooperating companies) or he will get the job but never be able to complete it. Construction contractors have told Commission representatives that they simply cannot go into the New York market because they are underbid or cannot get work done when they get a bid.

> Between 1981 and 1985 several criminal syndicates imposed a 2-percent "tax" on New York City contractors who poured concrete for structures exceeding $2 million. These criminal syndicates in fact operated a cartel that not only rigged bids for supplying the concrete but also decided in advance which company would offer the winning bid; other "participating" companies were forced to place extremely high bids. The 2-percent tax alone produced $3.5 million in profits on 72 construction jobs. These criminal syndicates made over $71 million from 10 big construction jobs, including the luxurious apartment building in Manhattan known as Trump Plaza (Rowan, 1986:28).

Syndicates and the State

Finally, criminal syndicates are involved with the state in two essential ways: providing political favors for the state and colluding with state officials (such as the police and politicians). We consider each of these.

The use of syndicate figures to perform political favors for the state goes back to the time of "Lucky" Luciano. As David Simon (1981:360) points out, this began

> during World War II when the underworld figures in control of the New York docks were contracted by navy intelligence officials in order to ensure that German submarines or foreign agents did not infiltrate the area. It was thought that the waterfront pimps and prostitutes could act as a sort of counterintelligence corps. The man whose aid was sought for this purpose was Lucky Luciano, and he was reportedly quite successful in preventing sabotage or any other outbreaks of trouble on the New York docks during the war. In 1954, Luciano was granted parole and exiled for life in exchange for the aid he provided during the war.

Other historical examples abound (Pearce, 1976:148–152; Church Committee, 1975:40–41; McCoy, 1972:263; Hinckle and Turner, 1981:34–38):

▲— In France, in 1950, the CIA recruited syndicate figures to create a "criminal terror squad" to force recalcitrant Marseilles dockers to load ships with arms for use in Vietnam. For their assistance to the state, these syndicate figures were "allowed" to continue refining heroin in Marseilles and then export it to the United States.

▲— In the 1960s the CIA recruited anti-Castro, right-wing, syndicate figures to assassinate Fidel Castro. Such notables as John Roselli, Sam Giancana, and Santo Trafficante, Jr., as well as Rafael "Chi Chi" Quintero, Felix Rodriguez, Frank Sturgis, and E. Howard Hunt were all involved in the assassination plans.

▲— In the middle to late 1960s syndicate figures worked together with the CIA to develop the Golden Triangle area as a major source for growing opium. In return for fighting the Pathet Lao opposition forces, the Meo tribespeople of the area were compensated by the CIA's own airline—Air America—which helped to transport the opium to heroin laboratories, and ultimately into the arms of GIs in Vietnam and users in the United States.

The overall viability and profitability of criminal syndicates have been based historically on a symbiotic relationship between syndicate figures and state officials. Earlier in the chapter we discussed this close relationship during the 1800s and early 1900s. Since then this relationship has continued, as a variety of governmental commissions and academic researchers have uncovered widespread corruption between state officials and criminal syndicates. For example, in 1931 the National Commission on Law Observance and Enforcement found that "nearly all of the large cities suffer from an alliance between politicians and criminals" (cited in Chambliss and Seidman, 1982:278). John Gardiner's (1970) study of Reading, Pennsylvania, found that for decades criminal syndicates in that city systematically worked closely with mayors, city council members, police officers and chiefs, and judges. After an investigation of police corruption in New York City, the Knapp Commission (1972:22) concluded:

> We found corruption to be widespread. . . . In the five plainclothes divisions where our investigation was concentrated we found a strikingly standardized pattern of corruption. Plainclothesmen, participating in what is known in police parlance as a "pad," collected regular bi-weekly or monthly payments amounting to as much as $3,500 from each of the gambling establishments in the area under their jurisdiction, and divided the take in equal shares. The monthly share per man . . . ranged from $300 and $400 in midtown Manhattan to $1,500 in Harlem. When supervisors were involved they received a share and a half. . . . Evidence before us led us to the conclusion that the same pattern existed in the remaining divisions we did not investigate. . . . Corruption in narcotics

enforcement lacked the organization of the gambling pads, but individual payments . . . were commonly received and could be staggering in amount. . . . Corrupt officers customarily collected scores in substantial amounts from narcotic violators. . . . They ranged from minor shakedowns to payments of many thousands of dollars, the largest narcotics payoff uncovered in our investigations having been $80,000. . . . The size of this score was by no means unique.

Chambliss' (1988) study of Seattle demonstrated that syndicated crime in that city flourished with the support and cooperation of a number of state officials. And as Block and Chambliss (1981:112) show, the frequency of major scandals linking criminal syndicates with leading political and legal figures suggests that Seattle is not alone:

> Detroit; Chicago; Denver; Reading, Pennsylvania; Columbus and Cleveland, Ohio; Miami; New York; Boston; and a hoard of other cities have been scandalized and cleansed innumerable times. Yet organized crime persists and thrives.

Moreover, a cursory scan of leading newspapers continues to provide evidence of state officials involved with criminal syndicates. For instance, from the late 1980s to the early 1990s (*The New York Times*, 1993a; *Chicago Tribune*, 1993; *The New York Times*, 1988a:A31; *The New York Times*, 1988b:B5; *The Wall Street Journal*, 1987:10):

▲__ A Baltimore police officer was found to be working for a heroin syndicate, selling heroin over one of the department's emergency communications telephone lines.

▲__ A New York City policewoman was found to be a participant in a heroin syndicate that had sales of up to $2 million a month.

▲__ A Chicago county judge pleaded guilty to fixing cases, receiving a "salary" of $1,000 per month from a syndicate for three years.

▲__ A New York City police detective pleaded guilty to selling secret police information about syndicated crime to a variety of syndicate members, including John Gotti.

▲__ Two Chicago police officers served as "middlemen" for two large drug dealing criminal syndicates.

This intimate and symbiotic relationship goes beyond the local level, reaching governors, senators, and possibly even the White House. Some examples include (Chambliss and Seidman, 1982:278; Alexander, 1985:90):

▲__ Former Governor of Maryland, Marvin Mandel, was found guilty of fraud and racketeering.

▲__ Criminal syndicate money flowed "copiously" into the campaigns of Hugh J. Addonizio, formerly a member of Congress from New Jersey and Mayor of Newark, who was later convicted for receiving kickbacks extorted from city businesses.

▲— In 1982, Allen Dorfman and Roy Williams (then IBT president) were convicted for attempting to bribe Howard Cannon, then Democratic Senator from Nevada.

Moreover, regarding the White House, some researchers argue that since at least the 1940s, former President Richard Nixon socialized, and been involved in business endeavors with, a number of syndicate members (Block *et al.*, 1972:12). As Chambliss (1988:157–158) points out:

> Nixon had long-standing and very close ties to a number of people whose business profits derived at least in part from illegal businesses. Regardless of how heavily involved in crime enterprises these associates and partners of Nixon were, it is tempting to speculate that they were involved enough in such places as Dade County, Florida; the Bahamas; Costa Rica; and Las Vegas, and in such enterprises as drug trafficking, stock frauds, bank swindles, and gambling casinos to have the wherewithal to run illegal businesses profitably.

Chambliss (*ibid.*:158–164) goes on to argue that when Nixon came to power in 1968 he undertook a campaign against certain criminal syndicates—namely, those allied with the Democratic Party, particularly Meyer Lansky's syndicate. Lansky, who contributed to the campaigns of such Democrats as Lyndon Johnson, Hubert Humphrey, John Connolly, Richard Daley, and Edmund Brown, was suddenly indicted by "Republican-controlled grand juries" in Las Vegas for tax evasion and in Florida for perjury. These important areas of syndicate activity then shifted to the control of such Nixon associates and friends as Howard Hughes and Bebe Rebozo. In addition, Teamster officials, Chambliss argues, shifted their support to Republicans. In return, Nixon granted Jimmy Hoffa executive clemency in 1971, which eventually led to Hoffa's release from prison. Moreover: "Several years later it was reported that Nixon could get $1 million from the Teamsters. He told John Dean that this fund could be used for hush money" to silence the Watergate burglars (*ibid.*:164).

Block and Chambliss (1981:34–38) discuss further "the final attack on Lansky." According to these authors, pressure was applied on Turkey by the Nixon White House to decrease its production of opium, and the Bureau of Dangerous Drugs was encouraged to reduce heroin traffic from Latin America and France—routes largely controlled by Meyer Lansky. Pressure was not, however, applied to the Golden Triangle to stop growing opium and to cease transforming it into heroin for shipment to the United States. In fact, argue Block and Chambliss, although the amount of heroin coming to the U.S. from Turkey declined almost 50 percent from 1968 to 1972, the amount coming from Southeast Asia increased 20–30 percent. This pressure to reduce the flow of heroin from Turkey and France—and "open it up" from the Golden Triangle—was in direct conflict with Meyer Lansky's interests. As Block and Chambliss (*ibid.*:36) state: "It is no wonder, then, that Meyer Lansky gave more than $250,000 in campaign contributions for Hubert Humphrey's presidential campaign in 1968 in an attempt to stop Nixon." Humphrey, of course, lost the election. Narcotics Bureau arrests and seizures of heroin coming from Europe increased, so that by 1972, 2,700 pounds of heroin had been seized, "almost 15 times as much heroin as had been seized only four years before" (*ibid.*). Eventually the Golden Triangle area came under the control of Santo Trafficante, Jr., a Lansky rival. Trafficante, as noted earlier, had worked with the CIA in a plot to assassinate Castro, and therefore had already established ties to the Nixon White House. In Southeast Asia, Trafficante worked with the *Chiu Chow* syndicate, whose leader managed the Laotian Pepsi-Cola Company. The president of Pepsi-Cola in the United States "has been one of Richard Nixon's longest and most important friends and financial supporters" (*ibid.*:35). By 1972 (*ibid.*:36–37):

> The Nixon administration had seriously disrupted the established monopoly. Furthermore, the emerging control over the Southeast Asian supply was becoming firmly established. At this point, the Attorney General and the President proposed yet another reorganization of the narcotics enforcement process. The reorganization culminated in the formation of the Drug Enforcement Administration. The seizure of heroin immediately plummeted to 900 pounds in 1973, and in 1974 it fell to less than 600 pounds. Dr. John Ingersoll resigned his post as head of the bureau and accused the Nixon administration of interfering with the agency.

Whether we agree or disagree with the Block and Chambliss argument, there is no doubt that they have put together an interesting thesis.

Nixon, however, is not the only president implicated by researchers and journalists as a "friend" of shady individuals and dealing. Former President Ronald Reagan has had certain associations with people reportedly connected to syndicated crime. First, a number of his original cabinet members were allegedly associated with syndicated crime. For instance, according to Holly Sklar and Robert Lawrence (1981:1), former Reagan National Security Advisor Richard V. Allen

> consulted or had business dealings with convicted resource swindler John L. King; Howard Cerny, an attorney for stock swindler Robert Vesco; and acted as a go-between with the State Department and the CIA for an Azorean separatist group with alleged organized crime connections.

Moreover, according to these same authors (*ibid.*), six FBI informants made independent allegations concerning Raymond Donovan's (ex-Secretary of Labor under Reagan) ties to criminal syndicates, which an FBI investigation neither refuted nor substantiated.

Second, Reagan has had an intimate relationship with Walter Annenberg, son of Moses Annenberg, the previously powerful and economically successful publisher of the Nationwide News Service that, in the 1920s, catered to bookies (Haller, 1976:122–123). In 1939, Moses and Walter were indicted for federal tax evasion and for selling pornography illegally through the mail. Moses eventually agreed to divest control of the "news" wire, settle his tax liabilities by paying $8 million, and go to prison for three years (*ibid.*:123; Block *et al.*, 1972:13). Moses' son, Walter, became publisher of the *Philadelphia Inquirer*, *Seventeen*, and *TV Guide*, and was appointed Ambassador to Britain by Richard Nixon (Block *et al.*, 1972:13). Moreover, former President Reagan spends almost every January 1st at Walter Annenberg's Palm Springs estate to celebrate the New Year (Scott, 1988:2).

Finally, Reagan's close associate and friend, as well as past chair of both the Republican National Committee and the 1984 Reagan-Bush re-election committee—former Senator Paul Laxalt of Nevada—allegedly has had certain close associations with syndicate figures. As Robert Friedman (1984:32–39) reported in 1984, Morris "Moe" Dalitz (named by the Kefauver Committee as being involved in syndicate activities), Al Sachs (alleged to be involved in illegal casino profiteering operations), and Rudy Kolod (convicted in an extortion-murder plot), all contributed generously to Laxalt's campaigns for governor and senator. When governor, Laxalt allegedly helped Howard Hughes—whose corporation collaborated with criminal syndicates in several casino and resort speculations in Las Vegas and the Caribbean (Simon and Eitzen, 1986:65)— "become the largest landowner and casino operator in Clark County, Nevada" and "Governor Laxalt's Gaming Control Board waived investigations of Hughes' finances required by the state gaming and control board" (Friedman, 1984:36). Finally, Laxalt allegedly lobbied on behalf of Jimmy Hoffa—at Allen Dorfman's urging—asking Nixon to pardon him (*ibid.*:38). As discussed earlier, Hoffa and Dorfman shared Teamster pension fund kickbacks, and as the President's Commission on Organized Crime (1986b:90) points out, Hoffa was "indisputably" a direct instrument of syndicated crime, the first Teamsters "leader over whom organized crime had a 'powerful hold.'" Laxalt also was

> instrumental in winning Teamsters President Jackie Presser's backing for Ronald Reagan's 1980 presidential campaign, and he helped arrange for Presser to join Reagan's transition team as a 'senior economic advisor' " (Friedman, 1984:38).

REVIEW

This chapter provided an understanding of the nature, extent, types, and costs of syndicated crime in the U.S. The first section outlined a brief history of syndicated crime. The second section discussed the structure of syndicated crime in the United States today. The third described in greater depth the structure of various syndicates, examining this structure in light of the principal activities of syndicated crime. Some of the more important points of this chapter follow.

A History of Syndicated Crime

1. The term "Mafia" originally described a method rather than an organization.

2. Syndicated crime can best be conceptualized as a variety of criminal syndicates, or associations of people (from all walks of life), formed to conduct specific illegal enterprises.

3. Early in U.S. history criminal syndicates were local in scope, primarily involved in such illegal enterprises as gambling and prostitution, and worked in a symbiotic relationship with state officials.

4. The passage of the Volstead Act in 1919 provided the context for the rapid development, increased size, and more complex division of labor of criminal syndicates.

5. It is quite unlikely that a national crime syndicate has ever existed in the United States.

Syndicated Crime Today

1. The work of sociologists—such as Joseph Albini and William Chambliss—reveals that criminal syndicates flourish and prosper today, and that businesspeople and state officials continue to play a regular and significant role in them.

2. Albini argues that syndicated crime in the U.S. is characterized today by "patron-client" relationships while Chambliss documents how numerous businesspeople, politicians, and members of the criminal justice system are involved in crime networks.

Principal Forms of Syndicated Crime

1. Syndicated crime is one of the major "industries" in the United States, at least in terms of gross annual income.

2. There are two major types of illegal gambling: "numbers" and "bookmaking."

3. The illegal drug industry (heroin, cocaine, and marijuana) operates like importing, wholesaling, and retailing businesses.

4. Loan sharking is usually directed by small, locally organized syndicates.

5. Criminal syndicates have moved into the substantial control of waste disposal in at least one-third of the states.

6. Criminal syndicates directly invest some of their profits in legitimate businesses.

7. Criminal syndicates are also extensively involved in labor racketeering and money laundering.

8. Criminal syndicates provide political favors for the state and continue to maintain a symbiotic relationship with state officials.

QUESTIONS FOR CLASS DISCUSSION

1. How did the term "Mafia" originate? Is it applicable today?
2. Summarize Cressey's argument concerning the national crime syndicate, and then outline the major criticisms of his position. Explain which position you support and why.
3. We presented evidence on the structure of syndicated crime in the United States today. Why do you think such a structure exists?
4. In the media, locate examples of syndicated crime, and then compare these to our analysis here. How are they similar? Different?

RECOMMENDED READINGS

Albini, Joseph (1971). *The American Mafia: Genesis of a Legend.* New York: Appleton-Century-Crofts. This book contains a discussion of the history of the term "Mafia," as well as the patron-client structure of syndicated crime.

Block, Alan (1983). *East Side-West Side: Organizing Crime in New York, 1930–1950.* New Brunswick, NJ: The definitive research on syndicated crime in New York City during a neglected, but highly important, period in the history of syndicated crime.

Block, Alan (ed) (1991). *The Business of Crime.* Boulder: Westview Press. Provides an array of government documents on the role criminal syndicates have played in the U.S. economy.

Block, Alan and Frank Scarpitti (1985). *Poisoning for Profit: The Mafia and Toxic Waste in America.* New York: William Morrow. An examination of syndicated crime's involvement in a new area, hazardous waste disposal.

Bynum, Timothy S. (ed) (1987). *Organized Crime in America: Concepts and Controversies.* New York: William Tree Press. An edited volume containing a variety of articles on different controversial syndicated crime topics.

Chambliss, William J. (1988). *On the Take: From Petty Crooks to Presidents* (second edition). Bloomington, IN: Indiana University Press. A study of the structure of syndicated crime in Seattle, Washington.

Cressey, Donald (1969). *Theft of the Nation.* New York: Harper and Row. The classic, although problematic, analysis of the rise and alleged continuance of a national crime syndicate.

Pearce, Frank (1976). *Crimes of the Powerful.* London: Pluto Press. This book contains a chapter on the history of syndicated crime in the United States.

Reuter, Peter (1983). *Disorganized Crime.* Cambridge, MA: MIT Press. This book has a very thorough discussion of the illegal gambling and loan sharking businesses.

CHAPTER 9

POLITICAL CRIME

9.1 Political Crimes Against the State
Violent Political Crimes Against the State
Nonviolent Political Crimes Against the State

9.2 Domestic Political Crimes by the State
State Corruption
State Political Repression

9.3 International Political Crimes by the State
International Crimes by the CIA
The Iran-*Contra* Scandal

Preview

Chapter 9 introduces:

☞ what sociologists mean by "political crime."
☞ the extent, nature, and costs of political crime.
☞ the various types of political crime, including crimes against the state and crimes by the state.

Key Terms

civil disobedience
corrupt campaign practices
election fraud
international law

political bribery
political crime
political kickbacks

Criminologists rarely recognize the category "political crime." When they do, however, they usually conceptualize political crime as crime committed against the state. The work of well-known criminologist Austin Turk is a good example of this view. In his book **Political Criminality: The Defiance and Defense of Authority**, Turk (1982:34) argues that the concept of political crime should be reserved only for subordinate groups who challenge state authorities through dissent and violence. In his words:

> Direct challenges to authority will at some point—depending upon the seriousness of the challenge as perceived and interpreted by the authorities—become intolerable enough to them to be either openly or "operationally" defined as *political crimes* (*ibid.*).

Turk explicitly concentrates his definition on crimes committed **against** the state, arguing that crimes committed **by** the state—and the instigators and perpetrators of such crimes—should not be identified as a category of political crime. For Turk (*ibid.:35*):

> No matter how heinous such acts may be, calling them political crimes confuses political criminality with *political policing* or with *conventional politics*, and therefore obscures the structured relationship between authorities and subjects [emphasis added].

There are two difficulties with Turk's conceptualization. First, by labeling crimes by the state and its authorities simply as "political policing," Turk assumes that the state reacts only **after** subordinate groups have engaged in some challenging, illegal political behavior. However, as we show in this chapter, the state, and its representatives, oftentimes **initiate** illegal attacks upon legally functioning—albeit politically challenging—subordinate groups. Second, although crimes by the state and its officials may indeed be "conventional politics"—which becomes especially apparent once we discuss the frequency of the state's illegalities—Turk's failure to label this "politics" as harmful and/or illegal serves to obscure the real nature of such actions. As we assert in the following argument the state's "conventional politics" not infrequently results in violations of domestic and international law. In short, we agree with Clinard and Quinney (1973:158) when they claim: "It need not be paradoxical that those who make and enforce the law are lawbreakers."

Accordingly, our definition of political crime is threefold, entailing not only crimes against the state (violations of law for the purpose of modifying or changing social conditions) but also crimes by the state, both domestic (violations of law and unethical acts by state officials and agencies whose victimization occurs inside the U.S.) and international (violations of domestic and international law by state officials and agencies whose victimization occurs outside the U.S.).

9.1 _____ POLITICAL CRIMES AGAINST THE STATE

Political crimes against the state are carried out for the purpose of changing or modifying existing social conditions. When individuals and/or groups believe a particular social condition (or overall social structure) is problematic in some important way, they may attempt to modify the social order, or alter it entirely, by means that violate criminal law. Political crimes against the state differ from other crimes discussed in this book in that they are not engaged in for personal gain. Rather, they are committed in behalf of a specific group (class, race, gender, political party, for example). Moreover, political crimes against the state are usually intentionally overt and public, rather than covert and secret.

Political crimes against the state, then, involve intentional violations of criminal law for political purposes, as well as various acts criminalized by the state for the purpose of curbing political dissent. Political crimes against the state may also be violent or nonviolent in nature. We consider first some examples of violent political crimes against the state.

Violent Political Crimes Against the State

Social groups have turned to violence in a bid to modify or change the social order throughout U.S. history (Graham and Gurr, 1969; Skolnick, 1969; Hofstadter and Wallace, 1970; Rubenstein, 1970). In fact, the U.S. was born of politically violent crimes against the British government. For example, by encouraging, and then engaging in, the Revolutionary War (1775–1783), colonists violated the British law of treason, which made it illegal to levy war against the King (Maier, 1972:19).

Native Americans in the U.S. have likewise resorted to violence to oppose state policies and to change social conditions. Although the examples are legion, consider briefly the case involving the Lakota Sioux and General George Armstrong Custer. In 1868 the U.S. government signed the Fort Laramie Treaty with the Lakota, guaranteeing the Lakota tribal sovereignty and assuring them perpetual control over

> unceded Indian territory from which whites are excluded, stretching from the Missouri River west to the Powder River hunting grounds into the Wyoming Big Horn Mountains and from the Canadian border South into Nebraska (Garitty, 1980:262).

However, the treaty was repeatedly broken by the U.S. government. In 1874 Custer trespassed onto Lakota land to confirm the existence of gold in the Black Hills of South Dakota. Gold was indeed found, and Custer's cavalry allowed thousands of "gold-hungry miners" to scrape the Black Hills clean (Johansen and Maestas, 1979:125). As a result, in 1876 the Lakota, Cheyenne, and Arapaho assembled at Little Big Horn in Montana. This gathering has been reported to be "the largest gathering of native peoples ever to have taken place in the hemisphere" (Garitty, 1980:263). Led by Gall, Two Moons, Dull Knife, and Crazy Horse, the Native Americans responded to the trespassers by killing Custer and 204 of his men because they had "violated the sanctity of the Black Hills" (Johansen and Maestas, 1979:29). This did not stop the U.S. government from violating the treaty; they continued to do so until 1889, when the Great Sioux Nation, in violation of the treaty, was reduced to five small reservations in western South Dakota (Ortiz, 1977:92). Overall, between 1776 and 1871

Violations of treaty rights by the U.S. government led to the battle of the Little Big Horn in 1876.

the U.S. government ratified 371 treaties with native Indian nations (Weyler, 1982:65). Figure 9-1 traces the results of U.S. government violations of those treaties. The Lakota example is important not only for indicating the use of violence to change social conditions and to oppose state policy, but also for understanding that groups often resort to violence *in response* to state violence and/or criminality.

The struggle for Native American control of their land, culture, and treaty rights continues today, and has, throughout the years, led to such actions as occupations (for example, Alcatraz Island in 1969 and the Bureau of Indian Affairs offices at Wounded Knee, South Dakota, in 1972) and firefights with the Federal Bureau of Investigation (FBI) (such as Pine Ridge, South Dakota, in 1975, which we discuss later in this chapter) (Messerschmidt, 1986:*passim*; Churchill and Vander Wall, 1988:*passim*).

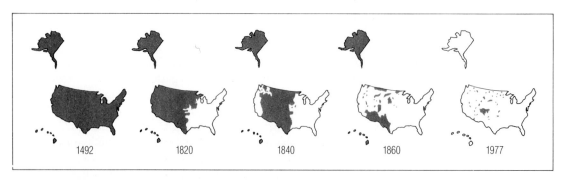

1492   1820   1840   1860   1977

FIGURE   **American Indian Land within the United States**
9-1   *Source: Weyler, 1982, p. 65.*

Similarly, farmers in the U.S. have engaged in violence to change existing conditions. Prior to 1800, farmers were involved in numerous rebellions, the Shays' Rebellion being one of the most famous. In the late 1700s many farmers experienced severe social and economic problems, forcing many to borrow money at extremely high interest rates to survive. Moreover, in order to meet their growing debts "they mortgaged their future crops and went still deeper into debt" (Parenti, 1983:63). And, as Parenti (*ibid.*:64) points out:

> Among the people there grew the feeling that the revolution against the English crown had been fought for naught. Angry armed crowds in several states began blocking foreclosures and forcibly freeing debtors from jail. They gathered at county towns to prevent courts from sentencing honest men to jail for being unable to pay mountainous debts and ruinous taxes. Disorders of a violent but organized kind occurred in a number of states. In the winter of 1787, debtor farmers in western Massachusetts led by Daniel Shays took up arms. But their rebellion was forcibly put down by the state militia after skirmishes that left eleven men dead and scores wounded.

Farmers recently have been involved in several violent acts to oppose state policy. For example, in the late 1970s the state of Minnesota built an electric transmission system that centered on an 800,000-volt powerline extending from the Canadian border to the southernmost part of Minnesota. The farmers who lived adjacent to the line immediately began to complain of such health problems as nose bleeds, fatigue, headaches, irritability, skin rashes, and high blood pressure when the line was operating. The Minnesota farmers also reported a sharp increase in aborted calves, general infertility among livestock, and a decrease in milk production when the line was operating. Grazing livestock consistently kept their distance when the line was transmitting; other farmers along the line route reported television interference, shriveled crops, ungerminated seeds, and unripened corn. Thereafter, the farmers resorted to violent acts to take down the line. Because the state would not respond to their verbal demands, many Minnesota farmers developed sabotage squads (referred to as "bolt weevils" and "wire worms") that toppled the poles that supported the powerline, shot out the power generators along the powerline route with rifles, and disabled the powerline through other means (Casper and Wellstone, 1981:180–188).

Workers also have historically engaged in violence to change certain working conditions. The extraordinarily unsafe, lengthy, and alienating working conditions in the 1800s and early 1900s led many workers to turn to labor violence in order to make their grievances effective. A good example was the 1886 struggle for the eight-hour day that resulted in substantial violence between striking workers and the police. In May of that year a major rally was held at Haymarket Square in Chicago; when the last speaker had finished, a bomb exploded among the police, killing one and wounding many others. The police responded by firing into the crowd. The labor movement in the late 1800s and early 1900s—

for the eight-hour day and other job demands—resulted in many long and bloody battles (Brecher, 1980:36–47; Lens, 1973:55–65).

Women also have engaged in violence at times in an attempt to change social conditions. For example, during the U.S. suffrage movement (to give women the right to vote) a number of feminist marches turned to mob violence between the demonstrators and outside agitators (O'Neil, 1969: 76–81). However, the suffrage movement in the U.S. was clearly not as militant as it was in England. The British suffragettes (the Women's Social and Political Union) engaged in a specific strategy of violence—such as breaking windows, arson, and vandalism—to achieve political ends; their motto was "Deeds not Words" (Heidensohn, 1985:23–24). Recently, certain feminist groups in the U.S. have engaged in such violent acts as setting afire, or bombing, shops selling pornographic materials. For example, in 1980 in Seattle, women's antipornography groups stink-bombed several pornography bookstores and, in that same year in New York City, "three porn movie houses were firebombed" (Morgan, 1980:138).

Other examples of violent political crimes against the state abound. For instance, many of the African-American urban rebellions in the 1960s and 1970s were motivated by political concerns for civil rights. During the same period, groups such as the Weather Underground—an organization that broke off in 1969 from the Students for a Democratic Society—turned to violence as a means for political change. The Underground announced the following in 1969 (cited in Evans, 1983:255):

> Kids know that the lines are drawn; revolution is touching all of our lives. Tens of thousands have learned that protest and marches don't do it. Revolutionary violence is the only way.

Finally, in 1986, six members of the United Freedom Front were convicted of violent, politically motivated crimes. According to *The New York Times*, the six were found guilty of bombing (unoccupied) military centers and corporate buildings that were either defense contractors or companies doing business in South Africa (Buder, 1986:B3).

Nonviolent Political Crimes Against the State

Most political crime against the state is not violent. Individuals and groups in the U.S. historically have engaged in such actions as civil disobedience and demonstrations of a nonviolent nature, but which sometimes result in criminalization by the state. Consider a few examples.

The efforts of Martin Luther King, Jr., and the civil rights movement of the early 1960s to end racial segregation in the U.S. were based on an explicitly nonviolent strategy. Dr. King's major weapon was *civil disobedience*, or refusing to obey certain laws because they are considered unjust. In his famous "Letter from Birmingham Jail," King puts forth his arguments for such actions (cited in Washington, 1986:293–294):

> There are two types of laws: there are *just* and there are *unjust* laws. I would agree with St. Augustine that "An unjust law is no law at all." Now what is the difference between the two? How does one determine when a law is just or unjust? . . . Any law that uplifts human personality is just. Any law that degrades human personality is unjust. All segregation statutes are unjust because segregation distorts the soul and damages the personality. It gives the segregator a false sense of superiority, and the segregated a false sense of inferiority. . . . So segregation is not only politically, economically, and sociologically unsound, but it is morally wrong and sinful. . . . So I can urge men to disobey segregation ordinances because they are morally wrong. . . . I hope you can see the distinction I am trying to point out. In no sense do I advocate evading or defying the law as the rabid segregationist would do. This would lead to anarchy. One who breaks an unjust law must do it *openly*, *lovingly*, and with a willingness to accept the penalty. I submit that an individual who breaks a law that conscience tells him is unjust, and willingly accepts the penalty by staying in jail to arouse the conscience of the community over its injustice, is in reality expressing the very highest respect for law.

Individuals can also engage in civil disobedience, not for the purpose of changing the law being broken but, rather, to protest—and hopefully put a stop to—particular state policies. For example, in 1976 members of the Clamshell Alliance engaged in civil disobedience by organizing a "sit-in" at the construction site of the Seabrook, New Hampshire, nuclear power plant. On May 1 of that year, 1,414 people occupied the construction site (for the purpose of halting construction of the plant) and were arrested for trespassing, more than half refusing bond and spending about two weeks in National Guard armories. The resulting publicity inspired other groups around the country, and a massive antinuclear movement eventually emerged (Dwyer, 1983:153–154).

Another example of this type of civil disobedience involved student and community demonstrators at the University of Massachusetts in the fall of 1986. The demonstrators—who included former President Carter's daughter, Amy, and ex-"yippie" leader Abbie Hoffman—engaged in a sit-in at a campus building used to recruit agents for the Central Intelligence Agency (CIA). Carter, Hoffman, and others, arrested for trespassing and disorderly conduct, were tried in April 1987. Although the demonstrators admitted at trial that they had trespassed on university property, they were nevertheless allowed by the judge to assert the criminal defense of necessity and won acquittal. This affirmative defense can be used to prove that a defendant's "illegal" acts were justified—in this case to stop a more dangerous crime: the recruiting of CIA agents who would, according to the demonstrators, most likely engage in significantly more heinous and illegal activities. After presenting the testimony of various experts on CIA criminality around the globe, the jury acquitted the demonstrators (Tushnet, 1988:2).

Individuals and groups may also engage in nonviolent protests and demonstrations against state policies that are not specifically directed at violating any law. Yet, because the state regards such behavior as threatening, it enforces certain laws chosen for the purpose of curbing the dissent. For example, the trial of the Chicago Eight—which grew out of nonviolent demonstrations against the Vietnam War conducted at the 1968 Democratic convention—resulted in the demonstrators being charged with "conspiracy." The state does not have to prove that an activity was actually planned, only that the conspirators communicated in some way (Clinard and Quinney, 1973:156). All Chicago Eight defendants were acquitted of conspiracy but received numerous contempt citations because of their behavior during the course of the trial. As Clinard and Quinney (*ibid.*:156) note:

> Whether or not the defendants are convicted, the conspiracy law is an effective form of political harassment whereby those who threaten the system can be detained for long periods of time at great personal expense.

9.2 ———— DOMESTIC POLITICAL CRIMES BY THE STATE

Domestic political crimes by the state are violations of law and unethical conduct by state officials or agencies whose victimization occurs within the boundaries of the U.S. We discuss two types: state corruption and political repression. *State corruption* is illegal or unethical use of state authority for personal or political gain (Benson, 1978:xiii); *political repression* is illegal or unethical conduct by state officials or agencies for purposes of repressing domestic political dissent.

State Corruption

State corruption exists at city, state, and national levels, and consists of a wide range of state-directed activities—such as purchasing goods and services, use of public funds and property, tax assessment and collection, regulation of commercial activity, zoning and land use, law enforcement, and so on (Simon and Eitzen, 1986:170–177). We focus on four types of state corruption: political bribery, political kickbacks, election fraud, and corrupt campaign practices.

Political bribery is the acceptance of money or property by state officials in return for favors (*ibid.*:169). Politicians, for example, have myriad opportunities for involvement in bribery, accepting money for such services as introducing special forms of legislation, voting a specific way on already introduced legislation, and voting in favor of a government contract. Probably the best-known recent case of bribery of politicians is the ABSCAM case. This FBI "sting" operation, which took place in the early 1980s, resulted in the conviction of seven members of Congress for accepting bribes from undercover FBI agents posing as Arab sheiks. The "sheiks" met the members of Congress in hotel rooms, offering them substantial amounts of money or stock for favorable legislation on business ventures. Only one of the eight politicians present refused the bribe (*ibid.*:176–177).

State officials, other than politicians, are also in a position to accept bribes. The police, for example, have a long history of involvement in corruption. From at least the 1890s, a legion of investigative committees has consistently unearthed substantial and wide-ranging forms of police bribery (Coleman, 1989:95–96). In the 1980s bribery in law enforcement once again came to national attention. In 1988, for example, seven Boston police detectives were convicted on 57 counts of bribery totaling $18,000 over an eight-year period (*Boston Herald*, 1988:26). Moreover, according to *The New York Times*, over 100 law-enforcement drug-related bribery cases come before state and federal courts each year (Shenon, 1988a:A12). The cases range from rural police in Georgia to the FBI (*ibid.*):

▲— In several rural Georgia areas certain sheriffs accepted bribes of $50,000 each to allow drug smugglers to land planes on stretches of abandoned highway.

▲— A member of the Justice Department's Organized Crime Strike Force provided drug dealers with the identities of government informants for $210,000.

▲— An FBI agent accumulated over $850,000 in money, real estate, and other property for not only allowing drug dealers to sell cocaine, but selling it himself.

▲— A customs agent was paid $50,000 for each marijuana-packed automobile he allowed to cross from Mexico into the United States without inspection.

Judges and lawyers have similarly been found to be involved in bribery. An investigation of the Circuit Court of Cook County, Illinois, for example, revealed that judges were found to provide specific dispositions or consideration to a case in exchange for money or other things of value and "lawyers would pay off judges for permission to 'hustle' clients in large volume criminal courtrooms" (Valukas and Raphaelson, 1988:4). In one particular court (*ibid.*:4):

> a corrupt chief judge assigned other judges to the "big rooms" (courts where driving under the influence cases were heard) based on their willingness to accommodate the corrupt defense lawyers who practiced there. These defense lawyers were called "miracle workers" because they never lost a case. These same lawyers got their results by paying judges, often through middlemen, for favorable disposition of their clients' drunk driving cases. Often the arresting police officer was also paid to testify in a way that created a reasonable doubt. The weakened evidence gave the corrupt judge "something to hang his hat on" in finding the defendant not guilty.

State officials may also participate in *political kickbacks* (namely, receive payment for help in obtaining a government contract). A good example of this type of corruption involves ex-Vice President Spiro Agnew, who began receiving kickbacks from contractors, architects, and engineers when he was Baltimore County Executive in 1962. The kickbacks continued when he became governor of Maryland, and "as late as 1971, when Agnew was vice president, he received a payment in the basement of the White House" (Simon and Eitzen, 1986:171).

More recently, it was uncovered in New York that various contracts for public services were "given out not to the low bidder but to the company that best lines the pockets of those making the contracting decision" (Weld, 1988:ii).

Many politicians have also been involved in *election fraud*—such as illegal voting, false registration, stuffing ballot boxes, and the like—which had its beginning in the heyday of political machines in the late 1800s (*ibid.*:187). Some more contemporary examples include the following (*ibid.*:187–188; Douglas, 1977a:115):

▲— Harry Truman likely would not have been elected senator from Missouri if he had not received 50,000 fraudulent votes provided by "The Pendergast Machine" in Kansas City.

▲— John Kennedy was assured victory in 1960 when Chicago Mayor Richard Daly and his machine stuffed ballot boxes with Kennedy votes.

▲— Lyndon Johnson won his 1948 Senate race in Texas by 202 fraudulently obtained votes.

▲— Approximately $5,000 was allegedly used to purchase black votes for Jimmy Carter in the 1976 California primary.

Finally, *corrupt campaign practices* appear relatively widespread in the U.S. For example, politicians tend to be extremely loyal to those who contribute to their campaign. In 1981, Senator Robert Dole, chair of the Senate Finance Committee, would not support tax loopholes for 333 Chicago commodity traders. Yet when these same traders contributed over $70,000 to Dole's 1984 campaign, he reversed himself and won the traders their loophole (Judis, 1988:7). Moreover, all congressional members who received $30,000 or more in campaign contributions from the dairy industry lobby voted for dairy subsidies, and 97 percent of those members receiving $20,000–$30,000 supported the bill (*ibid.*).

Campaign contributions are also made to presidential candidates, ultimately for the purpose of influencing state policy. For example, the milk producers contributed over $300,000 to Nixon's re-election campaign, later determined to be tied directly to a promise—eventually carried out—to increase the price support for dairy products (Coleman, 1989:52–53). In addition to the foregoing, in June 1972 a group of ex-CIA Bay of Pigs operatives was caught breaking into the Democratic party's national headquarters in the Watergate building in Washington, D.C. Subsequent investigations revealed that the burglary was only part of an extensive campaign of political corruption "involving political espionage, electoral sabotage, wiretapping, theft of private records, and illegal use of campaign funds—planned and directed by members of Nixon's campaign staff and White House staff" (Parenti, 1983:173). In August 1974, in order to avoid an impeachment trial, Nixon resigned from office and eventually was pardoned of all crimes associated with Watergate by then-President Gerald Ford.

Corrupt campaign practices may also have been part of the 1980 Reagan-Bush campaign for the presidency. On November 4, 1979, the U.S. embassy in Tehran was taken over by pro-Khomeini forces. Sixty-six U.S. citizens were held captive until, mysteriously, January 20, 1981. Only two hours after President Reagan's inauguration on that day—the 444th day of captivity—the hostages were released. Why were the hostages released at that particular time? Abbie Hoffman and Jonathan Silvers (1988) think they know why. Fearing in the final weeks of the 1980 presidential campaign that President Carter would come up with an "October Surprise"—somehow bring home the hostages, thus almost guaranteeing his re-election—the Reagan-Bush campaign, Hoffman and Silvers argue, quite possibly managed to stop such an event from occurring. What follows is a summary of Hoffman and Silvers' argument.

In May 1984 the House Subcommittee on Human Resources, investigating "Unauthorized Transfers of Nonpublic Information during the 1980 Presidential Election," concluded in its report that what began as a simple inquiry into the alleged theft of Carter's debate briefing book unearthed an immense quantity of unethical—if not illegal—behavior by the Reagan-Bush campaign. For example, the subcommittee found that by October 1980, senior Reagan advisors had *informants* at the CIA, the Defense Intelligence Agency, the National Security Council, the White House Situation Room, and at military bases around the country for purposes of reporting any aircraft movements related to the hostages in any way. In short, by "the fall of 1980, the Carter White House was riddled with moles, spies and informers" for the Reagan-Bush campaign (*ibid.*:151).

In addition to monitoring the possibility of a Carter "October Surprise," Reagan-Bush campaign officials may also have attempted to deal directly with the Iranians themselves. Basing their argument on *anecdotal evidence*, Hoffman and Silvers contend that in September 1980 Richard Allen (who would become Reagan's first National Security Advisor), Robert McFarlane (then a consultant on Iran for the Senate Armed Services Committee), and campaign advisor Laurence Silberman met a representative of the Iranian government at the L'Enfant Plaza Hotel in Washington, D.C. According to Hoffman and Silvers, Allen and Silberman admit that this meeting did take place, yet contend that they specifically *rejected* an offer by the Iranian that Iran could obtain release of the hostages to the Reagan-Bush campaign prior to the election. In any event, it seems neither Silberman nor Allen reported the meeting to the Carter White House. Moreover, others, according to Hoffman and Silvers, disagree with these Reagan-Bush officials, arguing that a deal was indeed made with Iran. For example, Bassar Abu Sharif, Yasir Arafat's chief spokesperson, is on record saying that "Reagan people" contacted him during the first (1980) campaign, requesting "the PLO to use its influence to delay the release of the American hostages from the embassy in Tehran until after the election" (cited in *ibid.*:152). Further, Barbara

Honegger, a former policy analyst in the Reagan White House, has stated that Allen "cut a deal" with the Iranians on the hostages in Iran prior to the election. And former President of Iran, Abolhassan Bani-Sadr (exiled in France), states that those at the Washington meeting "agreed in principle that the hostages would be liberated after the election, and that, if elected, Reagan would provide significantly more arms than Carter was offering" (cited in *ibid.*:153). In other words, prior even to taking office, Reagan-Bush campaign officials may have attempted to guarantee victory by "cutting a deal" with Iran. In exchange for keeping the hostages until Inauguration Day, Hoffman and Silvers argue, Reagan-Bush officials pledged that Iran would receive U.S. military arms and supplies. Others support Hoffman and Silvers' argument (Honegger, 1989; Sick, 1991). In particular, Gary Sick (1991) adds that William Casey, Reagan's campaign manager, met with Iranian arms dealer Cyrus Hashemi in Madrid and Paris on July 26 and 27, 1980, to hammer out the deal.

The "October Surprise" argument is not without substance. The hostages were released on Inauguration Day, and that same year, on July 24, Israel contracted with Iran to sell them more than $100 million worth of U.S. arms (Marshall *et al.*, 1987:172). As noted in the last section of this chapter, McFarlane, Casey, and Israel played important roles in the initial phases of the arms-for-hostages deal that eventually erupted as the Iran-*Contra* scandal.

Nevertheless, the above allegations prompted investigations by both the U.S. Senate and House. Neither inquiry found credible evidence of a secret deal. In fact, according to Lee H. Hamilton (1993:17), chair of the House October Surprise Task Force:

> there was virtually no credible evidence to support the accusations. Specifically, we found little or no credible evidence of communications between the 1980 Reagan campaign and the Government of Iran and no credible evidence that the campaign tried to delay the hostages' release.

Yet Sick (1993:17) responded to the House report by arguing that William Casey's activities were not adequately substantiated. For example, Sick (*ibid.*:17) claims that "the report says Mr. Casey could not have attended a Madrid meeting the weekend of July 26–27 because he was at the Bohemian Grove outside San Francisco. Yet the committee's own evidence places him at the Grove the following weekend, from Aug. 1 to Aug. 3." Casey's passport mysteriously vanished—therefore not available to the Task Force—and crucial pages were missing from his loose-leaf calendar. Thus, Sick (*ibid.*:17) concludes that questions remain, and he hopes "the task force will open its files to outside independent investigators to the maximum extent permissible by law."

State Political Repression

Federal agencies such as the FBI and the CIA have been involved in numerous illegal activities, many of which relate to political repression. For instance, although legally the CIA has no domestic security and law-enforcement functions, it has (1) opened and photographed the mail of over 1 million private citizens for 20 years, (2) broken into homes and offices, stealing documents and installing illegal surveillance devices, and (3) equipped, trained, and supported local police forces (Parenti, 1983:170–171). Similarly, since its inception in 1938, the FBI has been involved in a variety of illegal activities related to the repression of political dissent.

Historically, one of the first responsibilities of the FBI was to investigate "subversion," which was entirely unrelated to the enforcement of federal criminal laws (Church Committee, 1976:30). In 1938, for instance, the FBI *illegally* investigated subversion in (1) the maritime, steel, coal, clothing, garment, fur, automobile, and newspaper industries, (2) educational institutions, (3) organized labor, (4) youth groups, (5) black groups, (6) government affairs, and (7) the military (*ibid.*:32). Explicit illegality included wiretapping, bugging, mail-openings, and breaking and entering. Through such illegal behavior the FBI gathered information on "radical" individuals and groups, and forwarded it directly to the White House (*ibid.*:36–38).

The major thrust of the FBI since at least 1941, however, has been its counterintelligence program, more commonly known as COINTELPRO. Although the FBI's counterintelligence function is restricted by law to "hostile foreign governments, foreign organizations, and individuals connected to them" (Churchill and Vander Wall, 1988:37), the FBI clearly went beyond that mandate to include not only intelligence gathering but also strategies and tactics for the purpose of disrupting and "neutralizing" organizations that, the FBI felt, were threatening to the social order. As William C. Sullivan, former head of the FBI Counterintelligence Division, stated in the mid-1970s (cited in Church Committee, 1976:66): "We were engaged in COINTELPRO tactics, to divide, conquer, weaken, in diverse ways, an organization. We were engaged in that when I entered the Bureau in 1941."

Between 1940 and the early 1960s, COINTELPRO activities were primarily directed at the U.S. Communist Party and the Socialist Workers Party (*ibid.*:67). In the 1960s and early 1970s the FBI investigated new groups, implementing some 2,370 separate COINTELPRO actions (Kunstler, 1978:721). Some of the groups embraced by COINTELPRO activities were the Puerto Rican independence movement, the civil rights movement, Students for a Democratic Society, and the Black Liberation movement. Because of space limitation, it is impossible to discuss the effects of COINTELPRO on each of these movements. Therefore, we focus on one particular case, the FBI's campaign against Martin Luther King, Jr.

In 1962 the FBI claimed that Dr. King and the civil rights movement had been duped by the communists. This claim was eventually proved false (Garrow, 1981:59–60). Nevertheless, in December 1963—four months after the famous civil rights march on Washington and King's "I Have a Dream" speech—a nine-hour meeting was convened at FBI headquarters to discuss various "avenues of approach aimed at neutralizing King as an effective Negro leader" (Church

Committee, 1976:220). Agents throughout the country were instructed to continue gathering information on King's personal life "in order that we may consider using this information at an opportune time in a counterintelligence move to discredit him" (*ibid.*). According to David Garrow (1981:115), the FBI went through the Southern Christian Leadership Conference's (SCLC) trash in hope of finding incriminating evidence against that organization and King. The FBI investigated Dr. King's bank and charge accounts, instituted electronic surveillance of King's apartment and his office, attempted to win cooperation with the Bureau from certain SCLC employees, sent threatening forged letters in King's name to SCLC contributors, and attempted to intensify the well-known mutual dislike between King and NAACP head Roy Wilkins. However, the Bureau was unable to produce any incriminating evidence against the SCLC or King himself.

Undaunted, on January 5, 1964, FBI agents planted a microphone in King's bedroom at the Willard Hotel in Washington, D.C. Over the next two years the FBI installed at least 14 additional bugs in King's hotel rooms across the country, sometimes accompanied by physical and photographic surveillance (Church Committee, 1976:220). Alleging that the resulting tapes revealed "meetings" with prostitutes, the FBI then fabricated an anonymous letter to King, enclosing a copy of one of the tapes, and sent them to King on the eve of his receiving the Nobel Peace Prize (*ibid.*:220–221). The letter, in part, reads as follows (cited in Garrow, 1981:125–126):

> King,
> In view of your low grade . . . I will not dignify your name with either a Mr. or a Reverend or a Dr. . . . No person can overcome facts, not even a fraud like yourself . . . I repeat—no person can successfully argue against facts. You are finished . . .
> King, there is only one thing left for you to do. . . . You are done. There is but one way out for you. You better take it before your filthy, abnormal fraudulent self is bared to the nation.

When this effort by the Bureau failed to force King to commit suicide—as he himself allegedly interpreted the purpose of the message (Church Committee, 1976:221)—the FBI "leaked" the tapes and photographs to a number of leading newspapers in the United States (Wise, 1976:303–306; Bray, 1980:109–111).

Unhindered by the FBI's virulent attacks and efforts to halt his political movement, King traveled to Sweden to receive the Nobel Peace Prize. During his stay in Europe, and upon his return to the U.S., the Bureau continued its activities (Church Committee, 1976:221–222). The "neutralization" program actually continued until King's death. As late as March 1968, FBI agents were instructed to neutralize King because he might, according to the Bureau, become a "messiah" who could "unify and electrify the militant black nationalist movement" (*ibid.*:223). Moreover, as Churchill and Vander Wall (1988:57) point out:

Dr. Martin Luther King
Jr. receives the Nobel
Peace Prize.

Given the nature of the Bureau's campaign to neutralize King, there remain serious questions—unresolved by subsequent congressional investigations—as to the FBI's role in King's assassination in Memphis on March 31, 1968.

Indeed, the FBI had long ago (1964) determined that New York attorney Samuel R. Pierce (an extreme conservative) should be King's successor; he would be, according to one FBI document, the " 'right kind' of leader" (cited in *ibid.*:395).

Most methods employed by the FBI under COINTELPRO were, according to the Church Committee investigating FBI illegalities (Church Committee, 1976:137), "secret programs . . . which used unlawful or improper acts" to carry out desired goals. Beyond falsification of information and documents and illegal surveillance, the FBI conducted hundreds of illegal burglaries against "threatening" individuals and organizations, stealing private files and documents (*ibid.*). Moreover, through COINTELPRO the FBI conducted disinformation campaigns, used "agent provocateurs" to disrupt political (primarily leftist) organizations, and was implicated in the assassination of such dissident political group leaders as Fred Hampton of the Black Panther Party (Churchill and Vander Wall, 1988:64–77).

Although COINTELPRO was allegedly abolished in 1971, FBI illegalities continued. The case of Leonard Peltier is extraordinary in this regard. Leonard Peltier is, and was in the 1970s, a member of the American Indian Movement (AIM), a national movement of Native Americans striving to restore their traditional culture and reclaim the rights guaranteed them by treaties entered into over a period of 100 years. In 1975, Peltier was living at the Pine Ridge Indian Reservation in South Dakota (along with approximately 30 other AIM members and supporters) when, on the morning of June 26, two armed FBI agents entered the reservation allegedly in search of a young Native American accused of stealing a pair of cowboy boots. A firefight occurred between members of AIM and the FBI. Shortly thereafter, both agents and an AIM member were dead. There was never an investigation of the killing of the AIM member, yet four Native Americans were charged with the murder of the two agents. Only one, Leonard Peltier, was convicted. The charges against one of the original defendants were dropped allegedly due to a lack of evidence; the other two were brought to trial in Cedar Rapids, Iowa, in the summer of 1976. Both were eventually acquitted amidst controversy concerning FBI misconduct in the prosecution of their case (Messerschmidt, 1986:38–41).

Prior to the Cedar Rapids trial, Peltier sought political asylum in Canada, where he was apprehended by the Royal Canadian Mounted Police at the request of the FBI. He petitioned the Canadian government to grant him status as a political refugee, contending that it would be impossible for him to receive a fair trial in the U.S. because of his political beliefs and activities. The FBI's response to Peltier's petition was to provide the Canadian authorities with two fabricated "eyewitness" affidavits signed by a Lakota woman, Myrtle Poor Bear. It was later revealed at Peltier's trial, but out of the presence of the jury, that Myrtle Poor Bear never knew Leonard Peltier, had never seen him before, was more than 50 miles away from the crime scene on the day of the firefight, and was most likely coerced by FBI agents to sign the affidavits (*ibid.*:78–87). The Canadian government honored the U.S. extradition request.

Unhappy with the acquittal in Cedar Rapids, and thus the "performance" of the federal judge in that case, the federal government obtained a change of venue to Fargo, North Dakota. Here the FBI found the judge they wanted. Virtually the entire defense, which had justified an acquittal in Cedar Rapids, was ruled inadmissible by the judge in Fargo. But more importantly, according to a detailed examination of the trial record (*ibid.*:37–128), the prosecution enjoyed free rein to manipulate highly inconsistent and contradictory circumstantial evidence, and the entire trial was ˙saturated with the suppression of evidence, the coercion of testimony and, quite possibly, judicial impropriety. It was under these circumstances that Leonard Peltier was convicted and sentenced to serve two consecutive life terms for the murder of two FBI agents.

Peltier appealed the conviction to the Eighth U.S. Circuit Court of Appeals in St. Louis. Although noting, for example, that the Myrtle Poor Bear affair was "disturbing," the court upheld his conviction. Several more appeals were heard, each fruitless. In the final appeal to the Eighth Circuit, the judges stated the following in their decision (cited in Churchill and Vander Wall, 1988:326):

J. Edgar Hoover FBI Building—FBI headquarters.

"We recognize that there is evidence in this record of improper conduct on the part of some FBI agents, but we are reluctant to impute even further improprieties to them." As Churchill and Vander Wall (*ibid.*) respond:

> Thus, it was deemed more appropriate that Leonard Peltier remain locked away in a maximum security cell rather than expose the FBI to further scrutiny concerning the way in which it had obtained its conviction, even *after* a clear pattern of Bureau misconduct had been demonstrated.

Because of the foregoing, many people worldwide believe that Peltier's arrest, prosecution, and continued confinement are the result of his political activities as a leader of AIM. Although Peltier remains behind bars: (1) he was selected to receive the International Human Rights Prize by the Human Rights Commission of Spain, (2) over 50 members of Congress have twice signed "Friend of the Court" briefs supporting Peltier's right to a new trial, (3) over 50 members of the Canadian Parliament signed a petition asking the U.S. government to order a new trial (six of the Canadian endorsers held cabinet posts at the time of Peltier's extradition), (4) human rights organizations, such as Amnesty International, have supported Peltier's request for a retrial and have recommended that an independent Commission of Inquiry be established to look into the case, and (5) over 14 million people worldwide have signed petitions demanding a new trial for Peltier.

The FBI seems to have abandoned the viciousness of the COINTELPRO era in the 1980s, but is still involved in intelligence gathering and overall monitoring of (primarily) leftist organizations in the U.S. The Committee in Solidarity with the People of El Salvador (CISPES) is a case in point.

Through the Freedom of Information Act, the Center for Constitutional Rights in New York obtained FBI files on CISPES, documenting political intelligence gathering and political harassment of individuals and groups associated with CISPES and working to change U.S. foreign policy in Central America. The files also reveal that 52 of the 59 FBI field offices were involved in the massive investigation. Initially the FBI attempted to substantiate that CISPES was an agent of a foreign government and, therefore, in violation of the Foreign Agents Registration Act. When this failed, the FBI—with approval from then-Attorney General William French Smith—mounted a new investigation on the premise that CISPES was probably a "terrorist" organization. The FBI, however, never found any evidence to support this thesis either. In fact, field reports came into FBI headquarters indicating that those involved in CISPES and related organizations were "legitimate" and "respectable" people involved in such activities as demonstrations, lobbying, protests, rallies, newsletters, and occasionally conducting nonviolent civil disobedience—all protected by the First Amendment.

The FBI, however, did not stop there, but went on to develop two rationales that allowed the investigation to continue. Ann Buitrago (1988:3) summarizes the rationales:

> The "Covert Programs" Rationale: To explain away its negative results, the FBI reasoned that all the peaceful legal activities on which CISPES' broad support was based merely represented an *overt* program designed to cover a sinister *covert* program of which most CISPES members were unaware.
>
> The "Front Groups" Rationale: The old concept of "front groups" was dredged up to enable the investigation to expand beyond CISPES chapters and affiliates to any of the hundreds of organizations whose work brought them in touch with CISPES or its members. The usefulness to the FBI of the notion of "front groups" was that even though a given group was clearly not involved in terrorism but only in public education and/or protest, it could continue to be investigated because it might be a CISPES "front."

These rationales had the effect of driving the investigation further and deeper. Under the guise of looking for "fronts" and "covert terrorists," the FBI employed the following techniques to investigate CISPES (*ibid.*:7–8):

1. FBI informers infiltrated organizations and were sent to meetings and demonstrations.

2. Record checks were made of FBI files, other police records, school records, phone books, and student-faculty directories.

3. Frequent physical surveillance of people, residences, meeting places, offices, and demonstrations took place, often accompanied by photographic surveillance.

4. CISPES-related literature was collected and reviewed.

5. Radio programs were monitored.

6. License plate numbers of vehicles at or near demonstrations, public events, and conferences were traced and the names of owners were investigated.

7. FBI interviews were attempted of CISPES leaders, members, former members, and members of other groups "knowledgeable" of CISPES.

In addition, the FBI worked closely with several right-wing groups, helping to develop further the privatization of intelligence gathering. For instance, right-wing groups—such as the Young Americans for Freedom (YAF) and CARP (followers of Sun Yung Moon)—would routinely gather "intelligence" and pass it on to the FBI. In one case a YAF document on the CISPES National Convention was sent to FBI headquarters, where it was disseminated to 32 field offices (Center for Constitutional Rights, 1988:3).

Ironically, the only "covert program" uncovered during this operation was conducted by right-wing groups and the FBI. In fact, the FBI's "terrorist" investigation was viewed by those investigating the case as simply a cover for conducting domestic security programs aimed at disrupting organizations critical of U.S. foreign policy. According to Buitrago (1988:4–5), hostility toward CISPES "pours out of these documents." For example (*ibid.*), the field office at:

> Dallas wrote frequently about the need to devise investigative activity "*against* this organization"; New Orleans fired off a tirade against CISPES and individuals who "display contempt against the U.S. government," calling for them to be deported or denied reentry if they ever left the country.

At least one FBI agent refused to go along with this investigation. In January 1988, Jack Ryan, an FBI agent for 22 years, was fired because he refused to investigate peace groups opposed to U.S. policy in Central America. As Ryan stated (cited in Hopkins, 1988:14): "Investigating this as domestic terrorism or domestic violence is absurd. . . . What our Government's doing is wrong in Central America. I don't want to be a part of it." Ryan was fired just 10 months before his retirement.

9.3   INTERNATIONAL POLITICAL CRIMES BY THE STATE

In 1947, President Harry Truman signed into law the National Security Act, providing not only for the Central Intelligence Agency (CIA) but the National

Security Council (NSC) as well. The primary responsibility of the CIA, according to this Act, is to gather foreign intelligence and transmit it directly to the White House; the NSC was set up ostensibly as a civilian advisory group to the President on domestic, foreign, and military policies related to national security. However, both the CIA and the NSC have used their respective powers to go beyond their legislative mandates, engaging in a variety of covert operations almost from their inception. These covert operations have, at times, violated U.S. laws—such as the Neutrality Act, which makes it a crime to prepare a means for, or to furnish weapons for, military expeditions against any foreign country with which the U.S. is at peace (Tushnet, 1988:3). In addition, both the CIA and the NSC have, at times, violated international law. International law embodies "various treaties, agreements, customary law principles, and general legal principles that serve to judge the actions and behavior of various nation-states that have agreed to them" (Frappier, 1984:3). The United Nations Charter, which most nations signed after World War II, is an essential part of international law. In particular, Article 2(4) of the U.N. Charter—which states that no country has the right to intervene in the internal affairs of another country—has been violated continually by the CIA, and most recently by the NSC.

In this final section we present examples of violations of both domestic and international law by the CIA. Following this we turn to CIA and NSC violations of domestic and international laws during the Iran-*Contra* affair. Both cases represent *international political crimes by the state* because, although they may violate both domestic and international law, the resulting victimization occurs outside of the United States.

International Crimes by the CIA

In 1953 the CIA engaged in its first extensive operation to overthrow a democratically elected foreign leader. This occurred in Iran, where the legitimately elected and reform-minded prime minister, Mohammed Mossadegh, was toppled by the CIA. Mossadegh nationalized several large foreign-owned oil companies, thus challenging U.S. interests in the region (Prados, 1986:92–98). Even though Mossadegh offered compensation, Secretary of State John Foster Dulles, and his brother Allen Welsh Dulles (then director of the CIA), supported President Eisenhower's decision to reinstate the Shah as head of Iran. Once in power, the Shah—Reza Pahlavi—was considerably more favorable to U.S. economic interests. For example, he allowed U.S. oil companies to take over almost 50 percent of Iran's oil production, and U.S. arms merchants (such as Richard Secord, who would emerge as a leading figure in the Iran-*Contra* scandal in the 1980s) negotiated over $18 billion in weapon sales over the next 20 years (Moyers, 1988:9).

In 1957 the CIA helped set up the Iranian secret police (SAVAK), which stalked Iranian dissidents and earned a worldwide reputation for extreme sadism and frequent use of torture. From its inception, SAVAK agents "received special training at the Marine base in Quantico, Virginia, and attended orientation programs at CIA headquarters in Langley, Virginia" (Chomsky and Herman, 1979:49). While the Shah was in power, close to 1,500 people were arrested *monthly*, and on only one day, June 5, 1963, SAVAK and the Shah's army allegedly killed as many as 6,000 citizens (Simon and Eitzen, 1986:158). As noted earlier, future Iran-*Contra* operative Richard Secord (working with Albert Hakim) was chief of the U.S. Air Force's Military Advisory Assistance Group in Iran in 1975, which represented U.S. defense contractors selling the technology of control to the Shah (Sheehan, 1988:212). Secord proved an excellent representative. In 1977 alone, Iran purchased $4.2 billion worth of arms, "making Iran the largest foreign buyer of U.S. arms"; for the entire decade, the Shah purchased more than $17 billion worth of military equipment (Marshall *et al.*, 1987:152).

In addition, political prisoners (arrested and incarcerated because they disagreed with government policy) numbered as high as 100,000 each year in Reza Pahlavi's Iran. Amnesty International, the human rights organization, reported 20 years after the coup (the Shah still in power) that Iran (cited in Chomsky and Herman, 1979:13):

> has the highest rate of death penalties in the world, no valid system of civilian courts and a history of torture which is beyond belief. No country in the world has a worse record in human rights than Iran.

The Iranian people, as we all know, rebelled against the Shah in 1979, shouting such slogans during demonstrations as "Death to the Shah" and "Death to the American Satan" (Moyers, 1988:9). Historically, the emergence of the Shah's outrageous repression, the subsequent rise of Khomeini, the hostage crisis, and the subsequent Iran-*Contra* scandal can all be seen as direct outcomes of the 1953 CIA policy in Iran (*ibid.*).

In 1954 the CIA turned its attention to Guatemala, overthrowing its president, Jacobo Arbenz, who received 65 percent of the vote in a democratic election (Herman, 1982:176). Not only did Arbenz maintain democratic institutions—such as allowing workers the right to unionize—he also launched a massive land reform program. Given that less than 3 percent of the landowners held more than 70 percent of the land when Arbenz was elected, he nationalized more than 1.5 million acres—including land owned by his own family—and turned it over to peasants (Moyers, 1988:9). A considerable portion of this land belonged to a U.S.-based corporation, United Fruit Company, which immediately worked with the Dulles brothers in Washington to remove Arbenz from office (*ibid.*:10). The CIA organized a contingent of "rebels," led by Castillo Armas, who crossed over the Honduras border on June 18, 1954. Although Arbenz' military attempted to hold off the rebels, it was unable to defend against CIA B-26 and P-47 air raids on Guatemala City (McClintock, 1985:28). Arbenz fled the country, and on July 8, 1954, was replaced by Armas, who immediately overturned the reformist policies of the Arbenz government, returning the land to United Fruit and other landowners. Virtually all beneficiaries of the agrarian reform movement under Arbenz were dispossessed, entire cooperatives dissolved, literacy programs suspended, teachers fired, and "subversive" books burned (*ibid.*:29). As Moyers (1988:10) points out, the CIA's "Operation Success" entailed even more:

> The CIA had called its covert action against Guatemala, "Operation Success." Military dictators ruled the country for the next 30 years. The United States provided them with weapons and trained their officers. . . . Peasants were slaughtered, political opponents were tortured, suspected insurgents shot, stabbed, burned alive or strangled. There were so many deaths at one point that coroners complained they couldn't keep up with the workload. "Operation Success."

Approximately five years after "Operation Success," the CIA began planning another covert action, this time in Cuba. As noted in Chapter 8, prior to 1959, syndicate figures—in particular, Santo Trafficante, Jr.—were heavily invested in narcotics trafficking, gambling, and prostitution in Cuba. Fulgencio Batista, then dictator of Cuba, profited substantially from these syndicate ventures (Kruger, 1980:141–142). On January 1, 1959, however, Fidel Castro's revolution forced Batista, and much of syndicated crime, out of Cuba. Immediately the CIA moved to overthrow the Castro government, recruiting right-wing anti-Castro Cubans who had fled the country to do the dirty work (Hinckle and Turner, 1981:59–60). Under the title "Operation 40," this group organized by the CIA carried out terrorist acts against Cuba and conspired to assassinate various leaders in the Cuban government. Part of the program involved hiring Robert Maheu—an associate of Howard Hughes and a private investigator who worked for the CIA—to recruit syndicate figures John Roselli, Sam Giancana, and Santo Trafficante, Jr., to orchestrate the assassination of Castro for $150,000 (Wyden, 1979:41–42). Also involved in "Operation 40" were people later identified with the Iran-*Contra* scandal, such as Rafael "Chi Chi" Quintero and Felix Rodriguez (both anti-Castro Cubans working for the CIA) (Marshall *et al.*, 1987:37–38). Thus, "Operation 40" consisted of a well-organized sabotage, invasion, and assassination force, later known as Brigade 2506, which was based and trained by the CIA in both the United States and Guatemala.

In mid-April 1961 a major invasion of the Bay of Pigs in Cuba took place, but was unsuccessful (Hinckle and Turner, 1981:80–81). At the last minute President John Kennedy—fearing the attack would be identified as a U.S. operation if air cover were provided to the anti-Castro Cubans—halted the air strike, leaving Brigade 2506 defenseless upon landing at the Bay of Pigs (Ranelegh, 1987:355–376). Nevertheless, the plan to assassinate Castro continued.

The assassination operation became known as JM/WAVE, was based in Miami, and consisted of some 300 agents and 4,000–6,000 Cuban exile operatives (Kruger, 1980:145–146). In addition to at least eight attempted assassinations of Castro, this CIA-directed unit was involved in *daily violations* of the law—from the National Security Act to the Neutrality Act—as well as statutes involving firearms possession and perjury (Prados, 1986:211). JM/WAVE involved terrorist attacks against Cuban infrastructure—such as railroads, oil and sugar refineries, and factories—as well as, for example, contaminating exported Cuban sugar with chemicals at San Juan, Puerto Rico, and at other ports, and sabotaging shipments of machinery and spare parts en route to Cuba (*ibid.*:212). Raids against Cuban targets continued until 1965 (*ibid.*:215–217).

When JM/WAVE was dismantled in 1965, the CIA left behind "a highly trained army of 6,000 fanatically anticommunist Cubans allied to organized crime," who eventually merged into terrorist organizations such as Alpha 66 and Omega 7 (Kruger, 1980:207). These organizations ultimately became known as the "Cuban Refugee Terrorist Network," involving overlapping memberships in the different groups. According to Edward Herman (1982:65–66) in his examination of terrorism, this network was responsible for a substantial number of terrorist acts in the Western Hemisphere. Trained by the CIA in the "arts of bomb construction, demolition, and efficient murder as part of the secret war against Cuba," the network was found to be responsible for 25–30 bombings in Dade County, Florida, in 1975 alone (*ibid.*). In addition, Herman (*ibid.*) argues that this network has assassinated diplomats in Lisbon, Mexico City, New York City, and Washington, D.C. Ironically, certain Bay of Pigs veterans in this network financed their underground terrorist operations through involvement in the illegal drug trade. Indeed, according to Kruger (1980:146), a primary reason JM/WAVE was closed down was "because one of its aircraft was caught smuggling narcotics into the United States." Criminologist Howard Abadinsky (1989:209) adds that certain of these anti-Castro Cubans "imported only enough cocaine to satisfy members of their own community, but by the mid-1960s, the market began to expand, and they began to import the substance in greater quantities." And, as Marshall, Scott, and Hunter (1987:134) contend:

> America's drug problem today is arguably, in large measure, an out-growth of the "secret war" against Fidel Castro begun under Presidents Eisenhower and Kennedy. . . . The connection isn't fanciful. Over the years, federal and local law enforcement officials have found CIA-trained Cuban exiles at the center of some of this nation's biggest drug rings. They had the clandestine skills, the Latin connections, the political protection and the requisite lack of scruples to become champion traffickers.

In 1965 many of those involved in the Miami JM/WAVE operation were transferred to Laos, where the CIA organized its secret Meo tribe army (Kruger, 1980:146). CIA offices were set up in Vientiane and Long Tieng, both cities becoming new centers of the heroin trade (*ibid.*). During this time, one of the most active heroin laboratories was in Vientiane and was under the direction of Huu Tim Heng, who also built a Pepsi-Cola bottling plant on the outskirts of the city (McCoy, 1972:186). This plant, however, never bottled a single Pepsi, but rather served as a front for the purchase of chemicals vital to the processing of heroin (*ibid.*:186–187). Moreover, one Vang Pao, head of the Meo secret army, was extensively involved in heroin production, operating a heroin plant at Long Tieng, in Laos (*ibid.*:248–249).

As noted in Chapter 8, the CIA used the Meo tribespeople to combat leftist Pathet Lao forces in Laos. The only air transport in the area was the CIA's Air America. These planes ensured an adequate food supply to the Meo tribespeople through regular rice drops, thus allowing the Meo to "devote all their energies to opium production (*ibid.*:283). The opium was purchased by Vang Pao's officers and flown to heroin plants in Long Tieng and Vientiane by Air America (*ibid.*). Ultimately, the heroin was distributed to GIs in Vietnam and users in the U.S. (*ibid.*:263). Indeed, syndicate figures invaded Southeast Asia, helping create the then-major producer and exporter of heroin around the world—the Golden Triangle (*ibid.*:210–217; Kruger, 1980: 147–149). (See Figure 9-2.) It is estimated that approximately 20 percent of U.S. troops were addicted to heroin during their tour of duty in Vietnam (Stanton, 1976:557). Moreover, as Bellis (1981:19) argues:

> Between 1965 and 1970 the estimated number of active heroin addicts in the United States grew from about 68,000 to some 500,000. Extremely high and rapidly spreading incidence and prevalence were taken as indicators of "epidemic" heroin abuse, which grew to peak rates in American cities between 1969 and 1972.

It has been alleged further by Sheehan (1988:18–24) that much of the money generated by this drug trade was laundered through the Nugan Hand Bank (discussed in Chapter 7.3). Nugan Hand operated a branch in Chiang Mai, Thailand (in the Golden Triangle), and several of the bank's officials—such as ex-CIA Director William Colby—worked for the U.S. government at one time.

In 1968, "Operation Phoenix" (in Vietnam) was orchestrated by William Colby, who at the time was working for the CIA (Branfman, 1978:112). Although "Phoenix" was originally formed to incarcerate and assassinate members of the Vietcong—the National Liberation Front—it engaged in the massive roundup, incarceration, murder, and torture of thousands of Vietnamese citizens. Colby, according to Branfman (*ibid.*:113), established "quotas for the number of Vietnamese to be 'neutralized' each month." In the end, over 40,000 enemy civilians were murdered in a three-year period, 1968–1971, and thousands more tortured (Chomsky and Herman, 1979:322–328).

By 1972 the CIA had moved its covert operations to Chile, for the purpose of overthrowing the democratically elected socialist, Salvadore Allende. In the late 1960s the CIA had worked closely with International Telephone and Telegraph (ITT)—because of ITT's heavy investments in Chile—to prevent Salvador Allende from being elected President; if elected, Allende had pledged to nationalize ITT. The CIA "spent some $13 million to block Allende's election, including $350,000 to bribe members of the Chilean Congress . . . to vote against Allende" (Simon and Eitzen, 1986:215). When this failed and Allende was elected in 1970, the CIA, working with the State Department, did all it could to destabilize the Chilean economy through such practices as reducing U.S. aid to Chile (while increasing aid to the Chilean military); eliminating loans from U.S. banks and

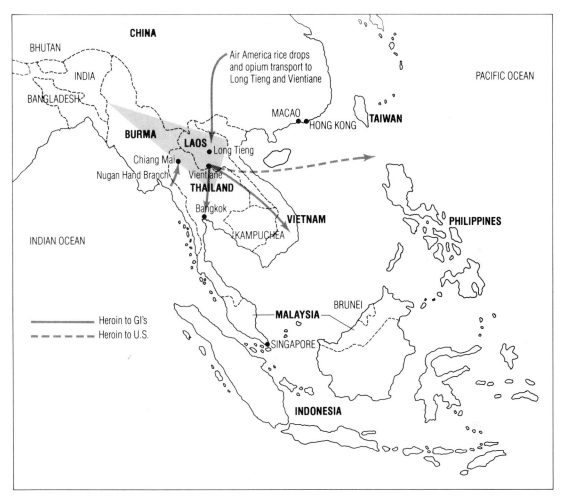

FIGURE   **CIA-Meo Tribe Rice-Heroin Connection in the Golden Triangle**

9-2   *Source: Adapted from McCoy, 1972, pp. 249–281.*

encouraging international financial institutions, such as the World Bank, to do the same; cutting supplies of and parts for U.S.-made machinery in Chile; and organizing a worldwide boycott of all Chilean products (Coleman, 1989:71). In addition to destabilizing its economy, the CIA worked with high officials in the Chilean military to overthrow Allende, which it did in 1973, resulting in the death of approximately 30,000 Chileans and President Allende himself (*ibid.*:71–72). A military dictatorship under the direction of Augusto Pinochet subsequently came to power. Immediately, the nationalization policies of Allende were overthrown, many democratic institutions were dismantled, and repression by the Pinochet regime grew rampant. Between 1973 and 1976, for example, over 100,000 people were detained for political reasons in Chile—over 20,000 of them eventually killed during incarceration, and an even larger number tortured (Herman, 1982:115). According to Amnesty International's *Report on Torture, 1975–1976* in Chile under Pinochet (cited in *ibid.*:113):

> The most common forms of physical torture have been prolonged beating (with truncheons, fists or bags of moist material), electricity to all parts of the body, and burning with cigarettes or acid. Such physical tortures have been accompanied by the deprivation of food, drink and sleep. More primitive and brutal methods have continued to be used. On 19 December, one prisoner was found dead, his testicles burned off. He had also been subjected to intensive beating and electricity. One day later another prisoner who died from torture had the marks of severe burns on the genital organs.

During Pinochet's active and brutal repression of dissent in Chile, Congress approved George Bush, in 1976, to head the CIA (Maas, 1986:8–9). Under Bush's control, the agency continued its involvement in shady, covert operations, a few of which are listed below (Corn, 1988:157–160):

▲— The CIA secretly provided weapons and money to "our side of the Angolan war," much of the money never reaching the rebels but, rather, pocketed by President Mobutu Sese Seko of Zaire.

▲— The CIA secretly worked to destabilize the "democratic-socialist" Jamaican government of Michael Manly, spending an estimated $10 million trying to overthrow the prime minister.

▲— Bush allegedly met, and kept on the CIA payroll, General Manuel Noriega of Panama, even though the U.S. possessed evidence linking Noriega to drug dealing and other criminal activities.

Perhaps most disturbing of all is the CIA's possible connection to "Operation Condor" while Bush was at its helm. In 1976, six Latin American states—Argentina, Bolivia, Brazil, Chile, Paraguay, and Uruguay—"entered into a system for the joint monitoring and assassinating of dissident refugees in member countries" (Herman, 1982:69). The program was sponsored and organized by Pinochet's secret police, DINA, which provided the initial funding and centralized coordination for the operation. Herman (*ibid.*:70) illustrates how Condor initially worked in Uruguay and Argentina:

> Under Operation Condor, political refugees who leave Uruguay and go to Argentina will be identified and kept under surveillance by Argentinian "security" forces, who will inform Uruguayan "security" forces of the presence of these individuals. If the Uruguayan security forces wish to murder these refugees in order to preserve western values, Argentine forces will cooperate. They will keep the Uruguayans informed of the whereabouts of the refugees; they will allow them to enter and freely move around in Argentina and to take the refugees into custody, torture

and murder them; and the Argentinians will then claim no knowledge of these events.

Hundreds of Latin Americans were abducted and subsequently murdered under Operation Condor (*ibid.*).

This network of murderers eventually extended its operations outside the borders of Latin American nations. Indeed, the murders of Orlando Letelier (former Chilean Ambassador to the U.S. under Allende) and Ronnie Moffit, in Washington, D.C., were likely part of this expanding operation. On September 21, 1976, a devastating bomb exploded under the automobile of Letelier, killing both Letelier and Moffit, who was a fellow at the Institute for Policy Studies where Letelier worked. According to John Dinges and Saul Landau (1980:239) in their book, *Assassination on Embassy Row*, under George Bush the CIA helped halt such Condor operations in other countries (for example, Portugal and France) by informing intelligence liaisons in these countries of Condor's movements. However, the CIA did nothing to stop the Letelier-Moffit murders, even though it quite possibly knew ahead of time that Condor terrorists were in the country (*ibid.*:382–384). Moreover, Dinges and Landau (*ibid.*:386) argue that there exists some evidence indicating possible CIA complicity in the assassinations. First, the authors maintain that although the CIA eventually obtained evidence indicating this was most likely a Condor operation organized by DINA, instead of providing that information to the press, the CIA leaked stories to a variety of leading newspapers and magazines stating that the CIA had concluded that DINA had nothing to do with the assassinations. Second, the authors argue there is evidence that alleges the CIA withheld, destroyed, and concealed key evidentiary documents indicating possible CIA sabotage of an FBI investigation of the assassination (*ibid.*:387). Third, the CIA allegedly leaked documents primarily to right-wing columnists, who in turn attempted to discredit Letelier by portraying him as a Cuban agent and, therefore, a KGB spy (*ibid.*:388). All this should not be surprising, inasmuch as the CIA had trained many members of Condor (for example, during the Bay of Pigs fiasco) and had brought to power its sponsor, the Pinochet regime itself. Indeed, two and one-half years later, the head of Chile's secret police and two of its officials were indicted for the murder of Letelier (Corn, 1988:163).

Finally, the CIA's newest "secret" war also is possibly financed through the heroin trade. In the 1970s most of the heroin in the U.S., as pointed out, came from the Golden Triangle geographical region. At that time, Afghanistan and northwestern Pakistan were virtually untapped opium areas, and heroin use was practically unknown in these countries (Lamour and Lamberti, 1974:177; Lifschultz, 1988:492). However, CIA support for Afghan rebels involved the Golden Crescent region (see Figure 9-3), which has now become one of the major heroin-producing areas of the world. The CIA arms pipeline from Karachi in the south through Pakistan to the Afghan mujahedeen in the north, according to *The Nation*, is "also one of the principal routes for the transport of heroin to Karachi for shipment to Europe and the United States" (Lifschultz, 1988:495).

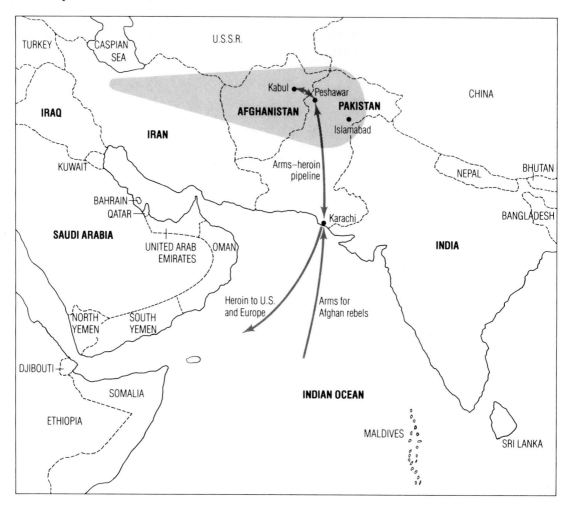

FIGURE   **Probable CIA-Supported Arms-Heroin Pipeline in the Golden Crescent**

9-3   *Source: Adapted from Lifschultz, 1988, pp. 495–496; Sciolino, 1988, p. 110; Bellis, 1981, p. 86.*

Moreover, *The New York Times* reported that a great deal of the poppy crop grows in areas controlled by Afghan rebels or in areas where they have influence (Sciolino, 1988:10). As Bellis (1981:86) reported in the early 1980s:

> Not surprisingly, the unleashing of this opium flow from Afghanistan coincided perfectly with the arrival of the CIA on the Afghan-Pakistan border—to support and arm the tribes who were both producing opium and fighting the Russian invaders.

Indeed, according to a recent General Accounting Office (1988:13) status report on drug abuse and drug trade, in the first six months of 1986, of the heroin in the U.S., 19 percent came from the Golden Triangle and 40 percent from the Golden Crescent. In other words, as the CIA moved its operations from Southeast Asia to Southwest Asia, so, it seems, has the heroin trade.

The Iran-*Contra* Scandal

We turn now to the Iran-*Contra* scandal to exemplify international political crime by the state. Because this is such a recent event—and thus sociologists and criminologists have not had sufficient time to research it thoroughly—we rely on a variety of research efforts, journalistic accounts, and legal briefs to piece together the unfolding evidence. With this in mind, we analyze one of the most absurd political crimes in the history of the United States.

In February 1979 the U.S. State Department, under President Jimmy Carter, recalled more than half its officials from Nicaragua and suspended all new economic and military aid to that country. In July of that year a revolution occurred in Nicaragua, whereby the dictator Anastasio Somoza was ousted and the Sandinista National Liberation Front (FSLN) assumed power (Black, 1981).

In early March 1981, President Ronald Reagan, according to *The Washington Post*, authorized covert CIA activities against Nicaragua (Oberdorfer and Tyler, 1983:A10). CIA Director William Casey then met with Argentina junta members, who subsequently supplied approximately 100 military officials to train the first Nicaraguan opposition forces—approximately 500 strong—in urban terrorist tactics and guerrilla war (Marshall *et al.*, 1987:10–11). The CIA worked with the Argentinians and other governments in Central America to build a paramilitary force against Nicaragua (Oberdorfer and Tyler, 1983:A10; Emerson, 1988:121). That same year (1981), Reagan authorized $19.95 million for this paramilitary force, which at the time was composed primarily of the ex-National Guard and other loyalists of Somoza (*ibid.*). Eventually, this creation of the White House and the CIA became the Nicaraguan Democratic Front (FDN), or the first of several *contra* groups.

Toward the end of 1981, debate in Congress and throughout the country led to widespread criticism, and increasing scrutiny, of White House intentions in Central America, especially in Nicaragua. By December 21, 1982, Congress was so skeptical that it enacted the first Boland Amendment to the Defense Appropriations Act, terminating the use of any public money for the purpose of toppling or destabilizing the Nicaraguan government (Scheffer, 1987:714). Nevertheless, it seems the Reagan Administration chose to ignore the Boland Amendment by *secretly* seeking new ways to train and arm the *contras*.

One such way was "Operation Elephant Herd" (Emerson, 1988:133–134), wherein the CIA clandestinely obtained, on September 22, 1983, $12 million worth of military equipment (for deployment against Nicaragua) from the U.S. military. At least 40 attacks employing Elephant Herd equipment against Nicaraguan targets occurred in 1984, the most well known occurring on March 7 and consisting of speedboats armed with Bushmaster 25-millimeter cannon-guns firing on and destroying numerous oil facilities and storage tanks at various Nicaraguan ports. Moreover, during this time the CIA also engaged in the mining of Nicaraguan harbors, resulting in the following (Gutman, 1988:198–199):

> Two small fishing boats at the Caribbean port of El Bluff were the first to detonate the mines and sank on February 25. . . . A Dutch dredger was seriously damaged at Corinto on the Pacific coast on March 1, a week later a Panamanian freighter detonated a mine. On March 20, a Soviet oil tanker reported damage at Puerto Sandino on the Pacific coast.

In addition, the CIA prepared and distributed to the *contras* an "assassination manual" in direct variance with Executive Order 12333 signed by President Reagan in 1981, which specifically prohibited political assassinations, directly or indirectly, by intelligence agencies or entities of the U.S. government. The manual instructed the *contras* in the "selective use of violence" to "neutralize carefully selected and planned targets such as court judges, police, and state security officials" and to "kidnap all officials or agents of the Sandinista government." Moreover, the manual stated that "if possible, professional criminals will be hired to carry out selective 'jobs' " (cited in Woodward, 1988:388–389).

In June 1986 the World Court (the United Nations International Court of Justice) ruled that these actions by the U.S. government violated international law. U.S. aid to the *contras*, its support of attacks on Nicaraguan oil installations and ports, and the mining of Nicaragua's harbors constituted, according to the Court, "force against another state." By organizing and supporting the *contras*, the United States had violated Nicaraguan sovereignty, amounting "to an intervention of one state in the internal affairs of another." Finally, the World Court ordered the United States "to cease and to refrain" from violating international law, and held further that the United States was obligated to pay reparations to Nicaragua. The United States continues to ignore the rulings (Pfost, 1987:75).

Largely because of the foregoing crimes, in August 1984 Congress enacted a stronger Boland Amendment, which prohibited any administrative agency or entity involved in "intelligence activities" from "supporting, directly or indirectly, military or paramilitary operations in Nicaragua by any Nation, group, organization or individual" (cited in Scheffer, 1987:714). Congress also halted all military aid to the *contras* (Gutman, 1988:18).

The *contras*, however, were not without funds. In fact, considerable anecdotal evidence suggests that the *contras* were involved from the beginning in the illegal drug trade to support their cause (Marshall *et al.*, 1987:134–139). In April 1988, for example, Senator John Kerry's Senate Subcommittee on Terrorism, Narcotics and International Operations began exploring *contra* drug ties throughout the 1980s. One year later, the subcommittee—in its report *Drugs, Law Enforcement and Foreign Policy*—concluded the following (U.S. Senate, 1989:36):

> It is clear that individuals who provided support for the *contras* were involved in drug trafficking, the supply network of the *contras* was used

by drug trafficking organizations, and elements of the *contras* themselves knowingly received financial and material assistance from drug traffickers.

It has also been alleged that the "Medellin Cartel" (discussed in Chapter 8.3) contributed at least $10 million to the *contra* cause between 1982 and 1985 (Cockburn, 1987:154). The money was allegedly laundered primarily in Panamanian banks, and then distributed to the *contras* by Ramon Milian-Rodriguez, according to his testimony before Senator Kerry's subcommittee (*ibid.*). Milian-Rodriguez was invited to President Reagan's 1981 inauguration. Between August 1982 and May 1983 (according to detailed records found in his briefcase upon arrest by U.S. authorities), Milian-Rodriguez flew from Miami to Panama 47 times, transporting a total of $151 million most likely obtained from Colombian cocaine sales and bound for Panamanian banks under the control of Panamanian dictator General Manuel Noriega (*ibid.*; Eddy, Sabogal, and Walden, 1988:340). Thus, it is unlikely that the *contras* were "hurting" financially.

Nevertheless, according to *The Washington Post*, Oliver North (NSC liaison to the CIA), who claimed that the Boland Amendments did not apply to the NSC, proposed to Robert McFarlane (national security advisor) in early 1984 (he subsequently accepted) that they build a private funding and supply network for the *contras* (Ignatius, 1986:D1). The project initially entailed North "crisscrossing the globe" in 1984 and 1985, obtaining funds from private individuals in the U.S. and wealthy right-wing leaders in other countries (Marshall *et al.*, 1987:12). For example, the Saudi royal family reportedly gave at least $32 million to the *contras;* the Sultan of Brunei reportedly deposited $10 million in a Swiss bank account controlled by North; both Israel and South Korea gave "generously to the *contras*" in terms of finances and arms; with the help of the World Anti-Communist League (WACL)—an organization with a strong right-wing and Nazi component (Anderson and Anderson, 1986)—and its leader, John Singlaub, Taiwan contributed at least $2 million to North's Swiss bank account (Marshall *et al.*, 1987:13–14; Sheehan, 1988:113). North also solicited funds from wealthy people in the U.S., such as Joseph Coors and Ellen Garwood, the latter contributing over $2,500,000 in 1986 for the purchase of weapons and ammunition (Moyers, 1988:22).

In the spring of 1984 a number of U.S. citizens were taken hostage in Lebanon, CIA Beirut station chief William Buckley receiving the most publicity (Sheehan, 1988:177). Inasmuch as Buckley was kidnapped by members of the pro-Khomeini Lebanese faction of the Hizbollah, the U.S. State Department imposed heavy restrictions on the export of aircraft, aircraft spare parts, and other military goods and technology to Iran (*ibid.*:177). Accordingly, the combination of U.S. hostages in Lebanon and Iran's need for U.S. arms and spare parts (the Shah had relied extensively on U.S. military hardware) created an alternative method with which to attract finances and arms for the *contras*.

Michael Ledeen, an NSC "consultant" with extremely close ties to Israel, suggested exploring an opening to Iran by way of Israel (Marshall *et al.*, 1987:174–182). Subsequently—three weeks after the hijacking of a TWA jet bound for

Beirut on June 14, 1985—David Kimche, director-general of the Israeli Foreign Ministry, was in Washington arguing that U.S. hostages could be released only via generous shipments of weapons to Iran. In August 1985, McFarlane told Kimche the U.S. would support an Israeli shipment of arms to Iran and would replenish Israel for what was shipped. Ledeen was charged with handling arrangements to receive the hostages (*ibid.*).

Two arms shipments—coordinated with Iranian "moderates" by Manucher Ghorbanifar (formerly SAVAK commander and Iranian arms dealer)—were delivered to Iran on August 19 and September 14, the Reverend Benjamin Weir released from captivity on the latter date. Another shipment of arms was to follow in November, but this delivery ran into logistical problems when (to avoid public exposure) the arms were sent from Israel to Portugal for transfer to Iran. Portugal denied air clearance because the delivery was contrary to stated U.S. policy. Thus, because no arms were received, no hostages were released (Sheehan, 1988:180–181).

Frustrated, on November 18, 1985, North asked Richard Secord (who had organized the secret war in Laos and coordinated the sale of U.S. arms to the Shah of Iran) to take over management of the arms shipments to Iran. North also arranged for transfer of $1 million from a well-known Israeli arms dealer to a Swiss bank account controlled by Secord and Albert Hakim (a business partner of Secord who, earlier in his career, sold surveillance equipment to the Shah for use by his secret police, SAVAK) (*ibid.*:181). Approximately $150,000 of this money was used to purchase arms for Iran; the remaining $850,000 went to the *contras*, and to Secord and Hakim in the form of profit (*ibid.*:183).

On December 11, 1985, McFarlane resigned his office and John Poindexter was appointed new national security advisor (Marshall *et al.*, 1987:182). Subsequently, Poindexter, CIA Director William Casey, North, Secord, and Hakim worked closely with Israel in shipping arms to Iran with the hope of obtaining the hostages' release and simultaneously generating sufficient profits to help support the *contras* in Nicaragua. In early 1986, Poindexter and North arranged for Secord and Hakim—posing as agents of the U.S. government—to receive funds in payment for weapons to be shipped to Iran, to transmit those funds to the CIA, and then to transport replacement weapons from the U.S. to Israel. This arrangement permitted Secord and Hakim expanded control over the proceeds from the sale of arms in order to divert substantial amounts of money not only to the *contras*, but to their own pockets as well.

An example of the foregoing arrangement occurred in January 1986 (Sheehan, 1988:186–188). North and Secord decided to transfer arms (TOW missiles) from a domestic storage facility to Kelly Air Force Base in Texas. Secord would travel to Texas, accept the missiles, and arrange their transportation via Southern Air Transport (a CIA-owned airline) to Israel; from Israel the missiles would go to Iran. Manucher Ghorbanifar agreed to purchase the missiles for $10,500 each. Initially, Iran bought $10 million worth, or approximately 1,000 missiles, the money being deposited in a Swiss bank account. Secord and Hakim, however, paid the U.S. government only $3,469 per missile, less than half the regular price. This amounted to approximately $3.7 million. The profit generated by *underpaying* the U.S. government and *overcharging* the Iranians ($6.3 million) went to the *contras* (in the form of weapons and supplies) and to Secord and Hakim (in the form of personal enrichment). Indeed, both Hakim and Secord explained during the Iran-*Contra* hearings that making money was one of their major reasons for engaging in the covert operation (cited in Moyers, 1988:23, 25):

MR. HAKIM: Not only was I presented with an opportunity to help my country, the United States, and my native land, Iran, but at the same time I had the opportunity to profit financially.

GENERAL SECORD: We were in business to make a living, Senator. We had to make—we had to make a living. I didn't see anything wrong with it at the time; it was a commercial enterprise.

Throughout the remainder of 1986, Secord, North, and Hakim arranged additional shipments and diversions of funds to the *contras*. As a result, on July 26, 1986, Reverend Lawrence Jenco and on November 2, 1986, David Jacobsen were released by their Lebanese captors. On the following day the entire arms network was exposed by the Lebanese magazine, *Al-Shiraa* (Sheehan, 1988:192).

The supply operation in Central America was managed by Robert Owen, North's "man in the field," who worked to coordinate contacts with the *contras* and the private aid network. The arms were apparently shipped to the Ilopango and Aguacate military bases in El Salvador and Honduras, respectively, as well as to a large ranch in Costa Rica (Sheehan, 1988:*passim*). Rafael "Chi Chi" Quintero ran the Aguacate base and Felix Rodriguez the Ilopango base (Calonius, 1987:27; Cockburn, 1987:154). From these drop-off points, pilots and "kickers" (cargo handlers) made air drops to *contras* both inside and outside Nicaragua (Calonius, 1987:27). From April to October 1986, for example, at least 25 arms drops were made inside Nicaragua (*ibid.*:28).

On October 5, 1986, two pilots and a kicker (Eugene Hasenfus, a veteran of Secord's covert air supply operation in Laos [Marshall *et al.*, 1987:28]) were shot down while flying over Nicaragua. Only Hasenfus survived (Calonius, 1987:28). The flight originated from Ilopango base (managed by Felix Rodriguez). According to *The Washington Post*, Rodriguez allegedly carried out the program under the direction of Donald Gregg, George Bush's national security advisor (Hoffman, 1986:A20). Indeed, immediately after the downing of the aircraft it is alleged further that Rodriguez telephoned Gregg's Washington, D.C., office (on both October 5 and 6) to inform him of what was at that time a missing plane (Cockburn, 1987:224). Moreover, Rodriguez personally met with Bush on a number of occasions. One such meeting, held on January 24, 1985, was described by *The Washington Post* (Hoffman, 1986:A1) as follows:

It was a typical meeting of the type Vice President Bush often holds in private: a small group, involving participants with firsthand knowledge of intelligence and global trouble spots. Bush, the former director of

Central Intelligence, often asks for "raw" intelligence material on a subject, the kind of information he could get from Felix Rodriguez.

The meeting was held January 24, 1985, in Bush's office. It included his national security affairs advisor, Donald P. Gregg. Also attending were Lt. Col. Oliver North of the National Security Council and Rodriguez.

The Hasenfus plane may also have been involved in several drug runs (Marshall *et al.*, 1987:138). Anecdotal evidence suggests that many supply planes utilized a drug trafficking connection on return flights to the United States (*ibid.*:136–139; Sheehan, 1988:107–108; Cockburn, 1987:172–173). Moreover, anti-Castro Cuban veterans of the 2506 Brigade—who participated in the 1961 Bay of Pigs invasion—may also have been involved in the drug trade, operating from the ranch in Costa Rica (Marshall *et al.*, 1987:136–139; Sheehan, 1988:101). In addition, the Subcommittee on Terrorism, Narcotics and International Operations found that the *contra*-drug links included (U.S. Senate, 1989:36):

▲— Involvement in narcotics trafficking by individuals associated with the *contra* movement.

▲— Participation of narcotics traffickers in *contra* supply operations through business relationships with *contra* organizations.

▲— Provision of assistance to the *contras* by narcotics traffickers—including cash, weapons, planes, pilots, air-supply services, and other materials—on a voluntary basis.

▲— Payments by the U.S. State Department to drug traffickers of funds authorized by Congress for humanitarian assistance to the *contras*, in some cases after traffickers had been indicted by federal law-enforcement agencies on drug charges and in others while traffickers were under active investigation by these same agencies.

Regarding payments to traffickers, the State Department actually selected four companies owned and operated by narcotics traffickers to supply humanitarian assistance to the *contras* (*ibid.*:43):

▲— SETCO Air: established by Honduran drug trafficker Ramon Matta Ballesteros.

▲— DIACSA: Miami-based air transport company operated as the headquarters of a drug trafficking enterprise for convicted drug traffickers Floyd Carlton and Alfredo Caballero.

▲— Frigorificos de Puntaremas: owned and operated by Cuban-American drug traffickers.

▲— Vortex: air service and supply company partly owned by admitted drug trafficker Michael Palmer.

Each company was under contract to the State Department in spite of the fact that federal law-enforcement agencies knew the individuals controlling the companies were involved in the narcotics trade (*ibid.*:43). A portion of the profits realized from the overall drug smuggling operation into the U.S. and elsewhere was used to purchase additional weapons for the *contras* (*ibid.*; Moyers, 1988:88). Indeed, in its conclusion, the subcommittee (*ibid.*:136) argued: "The U.S. government failed to address the drug problem because to do so might have interfered with the war in Nicaragua."

In other words, just as with the heroin secret war connections in the Golden Triangle and possibly the Golden Crescent areas, it seems that the CIA and the NSC were quite possibly involved in a *cocaine-contra* connection in Central America. We do know that cocaine became "the most serious problem drug of the 1980s"; the number of U.S. citizens over the age of 12 who were current cocaine users between 1982 and 1985 increased 38 percent. Moreover, the use of "crack," a highly potent and addictive form of cocaine, became widely practiced in 1985 and 1986 (General Accounting Office, 1988:7–8). Interestingly, it was exactly during the height of the alleged *contra* arms-for-drugs trade in Central America that cocaine use peaked in the United States—and most of the cocaine coming into the U.S. during this period came from Colombia (see Figures 9-4 and 9-5).

Most distressing of all, of course, is the fact that while profits were secured in a variety of ways (such as illegally selling arms and drugs), many people were killed and lives destroyed in the process. On the one hand, the eight-year Iran-Iraq war—in which Iran made use of the weapons it received from the U.S.—resulted in the deaths of millions of Iraq's soldiers and citizens. On the other hand, in Nicaragua the *contras* conducted a campaign of terror. Certain organizations—from Witness for Peace (a religious-based group that maintains a permanent presence along the Nicaraguan border to monitor *contra*-Nicaragua activity) to America's Watch and Amnesty International (two human rights organizations)—have documented atrocities committed by the *contras* against Nicaraguan civilians. Moreover, although we are told by the mass media that the *contras* were "freedom fighters" and the "moral equivalents of our founding fathers," Noam Chomsky (1985:12) has shown that the foreign press—primarily in Canada and Western Europe—had a different view. From reading such press we learn of

> "the *contras'* litany of destruction": the destruction of health and community centers, cooperatives, kindergartens and schools. . . . And we can learn of a 14-year-old girl who was gang raped and then decapitated, her head placed on a stake at the entrance to her village as a warning to government supporters; of nurses who were raped, then murdered; a man killed by hanging after his eyes were gouged out and his fingernails pulled out; a man who was stabbed to death after having been beaten, his eyes gouged out and a cross carved in his back after he fled from a hospital attacked by the *contras;* another tortured then skinned; another cut to pieces with bayonets by *contras* who then beheaded his 11-month-old baby before his wife's eyes.

Former Assistant Attorney General of the State of New York Reed Brody (1985) headed a fact-finding mission to Nicaragua in 1984 and 1985, which

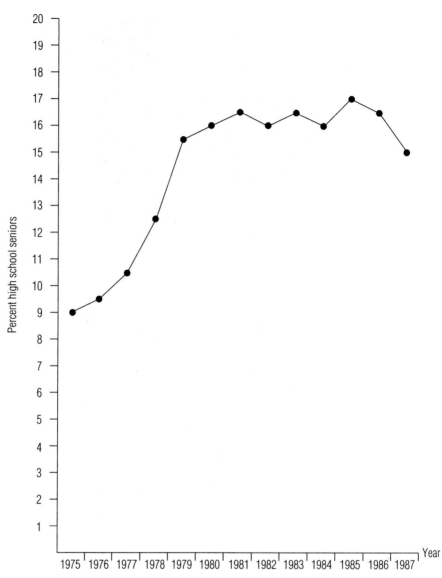

**FIGURE
9-4**   **Trends in Lifetime Cocaine Use Among High School Seniors, 1975–1987**

Source: General Accounting Office, 1988, p. 5; National Institute on Drug Abuse, 1987, p. 47.

obtained testimony from victims and eyewitnesses of *contra* attacks against civilians. His report corroborates and confirms Chomsky's analysis of foreign press reports. Brody (*ibid.*:21–22) found that *contra* activity often included:

▲— attacks on purely civilian targets that resulted in the killing of unarmed men, women, children, and elderly

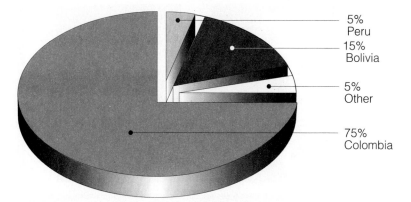

5%
Peru

15%
Bolivia

5%
Other

75%
Colombia

FIGURE   **Probable Sources of Cocaine Available in the United States, 1985–1986**
9-5   "Other" countries include Argentina, Brazil, and Ecuador.
Source: General Accounting Office, 1988, p. 9.

▲— premeditated acts of brutality including rape, beatings, mutilation, and torture

▲— individual and mass kidnapping of civilians . . . for the purpose of forced recruitment into the *contra* forces and for the creation of a hostage-refugee population in Honduras

▲— assaults on such economic and social targets as farms, cooperatives, food storage facilities, and health centers, including a particular effort to disrupt the coffee harvests through attacks on coffee cooperatives and on vehicles carrying volunteer coffee harvesters

▲— intimidation of civilians who participated or cooperated in government or community programs such as distribution of subsidized food products, rural cooperatives, education, and local self-defense militias

▲— kidnapping, intimidation, and even murder of religious leaders who supported the government, including priests and clergy-trained lay pastors

Thus, although the Iran-*Contra* affair was a covert operation hidden from the people of the United States, it was clearly not secret to its victims.

The diversionary plan was revealed on November 25, 1986, by Attorney General Edwin Meese. In time, Oliver North was fired and John Poindexter resigned. On March 11, 1988, Robert McFarlane pleaded guilty to four misdemeanor counts of withholding information from Congress about the Administration's *contra* supply efforts (but was eventually pardoned by former President George Bush) and agreed to serve as a prosecution witness in the criminal investigation of the Iran-*Contra* affair (Shenon, 1988b:A1). On March 16 of that same year Poindexter, North, Secord, and Hakim were indicted, jointly accused of conspiracy to defraud the United States, of stealing government property, and of wire fraud (Shenon, 1988c:A1). These co-conspirators engaged in the

The "Gang of Four": clockwise from top left, John Poindexter, Richard Secord, Albert Hakim, and Oliver North.

foregoing crimes, according to the indictment, because they "deceitfully and without legal authorization" organized a program to support the *contras* despite congressional ban on such aid, as set forth in the Boland Amendments (*ibid.*:D27). The prosecution elected to try each co-conspirator separately. Albert Hakim eventually pleaded guilty to a misdemeanor and John Poindexter was convicted on five counts of lying to Congress and obstructing congressional investigations. After conspiracy and fraud charges were dismissed, North was eventually convicted of only three charges: aiding and abetting the obstruction of Congress, destroying documents, and accepting an illegal gratuity, and Richard Secord pleaded guilty to one felony count of making false statements to Congress. Secord was sentenced to two years probation, and both Poindexter's and North's convictions were overturned on appeal because their testimony to the Iran-*Contra* Congressional Committee was allegedly unfairly used against them at their trials.

However, we believe the Iran-*Contra* scandal involved numerous other violations of domestic and international law not covered by either the indictment or North's and Secord's trials. Domestically (in addition to the Boland Amendments), through the sale of arms to Iran the co-conspirators likely violated the Arms Export Control Act, which prohibits the export of arms to states supporting terrorism (Scheffer, 1987:699). Indeed, Secretary of State George Shultz stated on January 23, 1984, "that Iran is a country which has repeatedly provided support for acts of international terrorism" (cited in *ibid.*:699–700). Moreover, with regard to military assistance to the *contras*, the co-conspirators likely violated the U.S. Neutrality Act, which (as explained earlier) prohibits any U.S. citizen, whether in public office or not (including the President), from supporting (initiating, organizing, and/or funding) hostile expeditions against other nations with which the U.S. is at peace (Pfost, 1987:76–77). Internationally, the U.N. Charter was also likely violated. In 1965 the U.N. adopted its "Declaration of the Inadmissibility of Intervention in the Domestic Affairs of States and the Protection of Their Independence and Sovereignty." The declaration prohibits (*ibid.*:71) in part:

▲— any State from intervening, directly or indirectly, for any reason whatsoever, in the internal or external affairs of any other State

▲— the use of economic, political, or any other type of measure to coerce another State in order to obtain from it the subordination of the exercise of its sovereign rights or to secure from it advantages of any kind

▲— efforts to organize, assist, foment, finance, incite, or tolerate subversive, terrorist, or armed activities directed toward the violent overthrow of the regime of another State

REVIEW

This chapter examined the nature, extent, types, and costs of political crime in the U.S. in terms of: (1) political crimes against the state (violations of the law for the purpose of modifying or changing social conditions), (2) domestic political crimes by the state (violations of the law by state officials and/or agencies whose victimization occurs *inside* the U.S.), and (3) international political crimes by the state (violations of domestic and international law by state officials and/or agencies whose victimization occurs *outside* the U.S.).

Political Crimes Against the State

1. Political crimes against the state involve intentional violations of criminal law for political purposes, as well as various acts criminalized by the state for the purpose of curbing political dissent.

2. Political crimes against the state may be violent or nonviolent.

3. From the Revolutionary War onward, various groups in the U.S. have used violence in an attempt to modify or change the social order.

4. Historically, various groups in the U.S. also have been engaged in such nonviolent actions as civil disobedience and demonstrations, involvement which sometimes results in their criminalization.

Domestic Political Crimes by the State

1. Domestic political crimes by the state are violations of law by state officials and/or agencies whose victimization occurs inside the boundaries of the U.S.

2. Two major types of domestic political crimes by the state are corruption (political bribery, political kickbacks, election fraud, and corrupt campaign practices) and political repression (illegal repression of dissent).

International Political Crimes by the State

1. International political crimes by the state are violations of domestic and international law by state officials and/or agencies whose victimization occurs outside the boundaries of the U.S.

2. Historically, both the CIA and the NSC have been involved in international political crimes—from illegally intervening in the affairs of other nations, to sabotage, to assassinations.

QUESTIONS FOR CLASS DISCUSSION

1. Should the concept of political crime encompass crimes *against* the state and crimes *by* the state? Why?

2. Explain the difference between violent and nonviolent political crimes against the state. Discuss why you believe the state may want to criminalize each crime.

3. Choose two examples from each category of political crime by the state (domestic and international) and explain why you think they occur in U.S. society.

RECOMMENDED READINGS

Cavender, Gray, Nancy C. Jurik, and Albert K. Cohen (1993). "The Baffling Case of the Smoking Gun: The Social Ecology of Political Accounts in the Iran-Contra Affair." *Social Problems* 40(2):152–166. An important study of "information management" by the media of the Iran-*Contra* scandal.

Chomsky, Noam (1988). *The Culture of Terrorism*. Boston: South End Press.

This book outlines some of the social and political forces behind international political crimes by the state.

Churchill, Ward and Jim Vander Wall (1988). *Agents of Repression.* Boston: South End Press. A documentation of the FBI's vendetta against political dissent in the United States.

Dinges, John and Saul Landau (1980). *Assassination on Embassy Row.* New York: Pantheon Books. An examination of the assassination of Orlando Letelier and Ronnie Moffit.

Frappier, John (1984). "Above the Law: Violations of International Law by the U.S. Government from Truman to Reagan." *Crime and Social Justice* 21–22:1–36. An article on the violations of international law by the U.S. state since World War II, with a focus on the 1980s.

Herman, Edward (1982). *The Real Terror Network.* Boston: South End Press. A discussion of U.S. intervention in the affairs of other nations and the effects of these violations of international law upon citizens of these countries.

Kwitny, Jonathan (1987). *The Crimes of Patriots: A True Tale of Dope, Dirty Money and the CIA.* New York: Norton. A very readable investigation of the Nugan Hand Bank, and its relation to money laundering and crimes by the CIA.

Marshall, Johnathan, Peter Dale Scott, and Jane Hunter (1987). *The Iran-Contra Connection: Secret Teams and Covert Operations in the Reagan Era.* Boston: South End Press. The most detailed discussion of the Iran-*Contra* scandal, placing it in the context of a long tradition of U.S. covert activities.

Messerschmidt, James (1986). *The Trial of Leonard Peltier.* Boston: South End Press. An in-depth examination of the trial of AIM activist Leonard Peltier.

Tunnell, Kenneth D. (ed) (1993). *Political Crime in Contemporary America.* New York: Garland. A collection of essays discussing a variety of political crimes in the United States as well as important theoretical issues about political crime.

Turk, Austin (1982). *Political Criminality: The Defiance and Defense of Authority.* Beverly Hills, CA: Sage. A significant contribution to the literature on political crime (limited solely to political crimes against the state).

PART THREE

CRIMINOLOGICAL THEORY

CHAPTER 10

THE ORIGINS OF CRIMINOLOGICAL THEORY

Preview

Chapter 10 introduces

☞ the origins of modern criminological theory.
☞ the key writings of the early criminologists.

Key Terms

born criminality

classical criminology

dangerous classes

Enlightenment

moral statistics

neoclassical criminology

penal strategies

positivist criminology

scientism

social mechanics

utilitarianism

T*he ideas and concepts of the first criminologists originated in response to a variety of social conditions. These conditions included the legal and penal practices of the era, and the concerns of government and influential sections of European society regarding the perceived dangers posed by the "dangerous classes."*

We do not assess directly the merits of these writings here. Worthwhile though such assessments undoubtedly would be, our chief focus is on the background and social context of the era in which modern criminology began.

10.1 ———— THE ENLIGHTENMENT AND CLASSICAL CRIMINOLOGY

The origins of modern criminological theory can be traced to the writings of Enlightenment philosophers, especially in France, during the second half of the 18th century. To understand why these writings arose when they did we begin with the notorious case of Jean Calas, a prosperous French cloth merchant who was wrongly convicted and then executed in 1762 for the murder of his son. The sentence of execution required that Calas

> in a chemise, with head and feet bare, will be taken in a cart, from the palace prison to the Cathedral. There, kneeling in front of the main door, holding in his hands a torch of yellow wax weighing two pounds, he must make the *amende honorable*, asking pardon of God, of the King, and of justice. Then the executioner should take him in the cart to the Place Saint Georges, where upon a scaffold his arms, legs, thighs, and loins will be broken and crushed. Finally, the prisoner should be placed upon a wheel, with his face turned to the sky, alive and in pain, and

repent for his said crimes and misdeeds, all the while imploring God for his life, thereby to serve as an example and to instil terror in the wicked. (quoted in Beirne, 1993:11–12).

The Enlightenment theorists opposed Calas' execution and all other punishments like it. Their opposition had two sources. First, they objected to the form of the punishment because it was cruel and inhumane. Second, they disagreed with prevailing views of the relation between crime and punishment. At this time, in much of Europe, the definition of crime was the Word of God revealed in the dogma of Roman Catholicism. Serious crimes were often seen to result from a pact made by individual sinners with supernatural forces such as the devil, demons, and evil spirits. Catholic doctrine held that the role of lawful authorities was to eradicate the devil from the body of the condemned so that others would not be infected with their sins. The application of physical pain took a great variety of forms and was widely used both as a method of punishment and also as a form of inquisition to establish an accused's innocence or guilt. An example of this process is given by Michael Kunze (1987) in his book *Highroad to the Stake.* Kunze (1987:260) describes the barbarous forms of inquisition used to extract confessions of witchcraft from members of a peasant family in 17th-century Germany. Kunze reports that only after her hands had been bound behind her back, fastened to a rope that ran over a pulley connected to the ceiling, and she left dangling upside down in midair, did Agnes Pappenheimer (a girl of 10) confess that she and her mother were both witches.

Throughout Europe those accused of crimes were overwhelmingly poor and enjoyed little or no protection from legal systems consciously and unashamedly designed to serve monarch, government, church, and men of property. In England, for example, even as late as 1820 there were as many as 200 capital offenses, the great majority for crimes against property (Hay, 1975:18). During these judicial dark ages, the precise punishments for many crimes were not even contained in the legal codes. The enormous discretionary powers of judges were exercised arbitrarily and were quite often open to bribery and corruption. Moreover, even animals were occasionally subjected to these judicial irrationalities. Indeed, there is much evidence that until about 1800 in Europe and colonial America pigs, horses, and a variety of other species were formally prosecuted in criminal courts for crimes and, if convicted, were executed with the full majesty of the law. One such example is the public execution in 1386 of an infanticidal sow in the French city of Falaise. Having been duly tried in a court of law, presided over by a judge with counsel attending, the sow was dressed in human clothes, mutilated in the head and hind legs, and executed in the public square by an official hangman on whom had been bestowed a pair of new gloves befitting the solemnity of the occasion (Beirne, 1994).

The Enlightenment's reforming spirit emerged in France in the middle of the 18th century and grew into a widespread philosophical and humanist movement. The movement professed that reason and experience, rather than faith and superstition, must replace the excesses and corruption of feudal societies. Its demands were championed by the related logic of two new doctrines—

A saint exorcising a demon.

the doctrine of the social contract and the doctrine of free will. The Enlighten-ment's chief theorists included Voltaire, Montesquieu, Helvétius, Rousseau, and Diderot in France; Kant in Germany; and Ferguson, Adam Smith, and Hume in Scotland.

The doctrine of the social contract was an attempt to avoid Thomas Hobbes'

(1588–1679) belief that society was based on the nasty and brutish fact of *bellum omnium contra omnes* (the war of all against all)—all citizens pursuing their own narrow self-interests. How then could government be justified? What was the role of law in such a society? The Enlightenment philosophers responded to such questions by asserting that society was held together by a contract between citizens and property owners. The fulfillment of this contract, their argument continued, required establishment of governmental authority. Only with such a contract could society exist. Citizens must surrender some measure of their individuality so that the government can enact and enforce laws in the interests of the common good; the government, in return, must agree to protect the common good but not to invade the natural, inviolable liberties and rights of individual citizens. Henceforth, the lives of the citizenry were to be regulated and protected not by theology but by "the rule of law."

The doctrine of free will held that all men (women were generally not included at this time) rationally and freely chose to engage in the social contract. This *utilitarian* view further asserted that those who challenged the social contract, those who decided to break its rules, and those who pursued harmful pleasures and wickedness were liable to be punished for their misdeeds.

Criminologists at this time also began to protest the specific barbarities and inequities characteristic of feudal systems of justice, like the continued use of capital punishment. This classical criminology was part of the broad Enlightenment movement. We now examine the writings of the two most influential classical theorists, Cesare Bonesana Beccaria (1738–1794) and Jeremy Bentham (1748–1832).

Beccaria: *Of Crimes and Punishments* (1764)

At first glance it could not have been suspected that Cesare Beccaria's *Of Crimes and Punishments* (1764) would become so influential. Little of Beccaria's book was original, and its proposals for reform borrowed heavily from the existing humanist and rationalist texts of Enlightenment philosophers. Even the idea for his book was suggested to Beccaria by his friend Pietro Verri. Beccaria knew very little about criminal law and punishment when he began to write *Of Crimes and Punishments,* and his ideas were developed only after long discussions and much prodding by Pietro and Pietro's brother, Alessandro. The finished product consisted less of reasoned arguments for reform than of a controversial program of reform. Because of Beccaria's singular and continuing importance in the history of criminology, we quote major points from *Of Crimes and Punishments* at length.

Excerpts from Beccaria's *Of Crimes and Punishments*

2. The Origin of Punishments, and the Right to Punish
    No man ever freely sacrificed a portion of his personal liberty merely in behalf of the common good. That chimera exists only in romances.

Cesare Beccaria (1738–1794).

If it were possible, every one of us would prefer that the compacts binding others did not bind us; every man tends to make himself the center of his whole world. . . .

Laws are the conditions under which independent and isolated men united to form a society. Weary of living in a continual state of war, and of enjoying a liberty rendered useless by the uncertainty of preserving it, they sacrificed a part so that they might enjoy the rest of it in peace and safety. The sum of all these portions of liberty sacrificed by each for his own good constitutes the sovereignty of a nation, and their legitimate depositary and administrator is the sovereign. But merely to have established this deposit was not enough; it had to be defended against private usurpations by individuals each of whom always tries not only to withdraw his own share but also to usurp for himself that of others. Some tangible motives had to be introduced, therefore, to prevent the despotic spirit, which is in every man, from plunging the laws of society into its original chaos. These tangible motives are the punishments established against the infractors of the laws. . . .

It was, thus, necessity that forced men to give up part of their personal liberty, and it is certain . . . that each is willing to place in the public fund only the least possible portion, no more than suffices to induce others to defend it. The aggregate of these least possible portions constitutes the right to punish; all that exceeds this is abuse and not justice. . . . (pp. 11–13)

6. Imprisonment

An error no less common than it is contrary to the purpose of association—which is assurance of personal security—is that of allowing a magistrate charged with administering the laws to be free to imprison a citizen at his own pleasure, to deprive an enemy of liberty on frivolous pretexts, and to leave a friend unpunished notwithstanding the clearest evidences of his guilt. Detention in prison is a punishment which, unlike every other, must of necessity precede conviction for crime, but this distinctive character does not remove the other which is essential—namely, that only the law determines the cases in which a man is to suffer punishment. It pertains to the law, therefore, to indicate what evidences of crime justify detention of the accused, his subjection to investigation and punishment. . . . (p. 19)

12. Torture

A cruelty consecrated by the practice of most nations is torture of the accused during his trial. . . .

No man can be called *guilty* before a judge has sentenced him, nor can society deprive him of protection before it has been decided that he has in fact violated the conditions under which such protection was accorded him. . . . (p. 30)

16. The Death Penalty

It is not the intensity of punishment that has the greatest effect on the human spirit, but its duration, for our sensibility is more easily and more permanently affected by slight but repeated impressions than by a powerful but momentary action. . . .

The death penalty becomes for the majority a spectacle and for some others an object of compassion mixed with disdain; these two sentiments rather than the salutary fear which the laws pretend to inspire occupy the spirits of the spectators. But in moderate and prolonged punishments the dominant sentiment is the latter, because it is the only one. The limit which the legislator ought to fix on the rigor of punishments would seem to be determined by the sentiment of compassion itself, when it begins to prevail over every other in the hearts of those who are the witnesses of punishment, inflicted for their sake rather than for the criminal's. . . . (pp. 46–47)

19. Promptness

The more promptly and the more closely punishment follows upon the commission of a crime, the more just and useful will it be. . . . (p. 55)

20. The Certainty of Punishment

One of the greatest curbs on crimes is not the cruelty of punishments, but their infallibility, and consequently, the vigilance of magistrates, and that severity of an inexorable judge which, to be a useful virtue, must be accompanied by a mild legislation. The certainty of punishment, even if it be moderate, will always make a stronger impression than the fear of another which is more terrible but combined with the hope of impunity. (p. 58)

23. Proportion Between Crimes and Punishments

It is to the common interest not only that crimes not be committed, but also that they be less frequent in proportion to the harm they cause society. Therefore, the obstacles that deter men from committing crimes should be stronger in proportion as they are contrary to the public good, and as the inducements to commit them are stronger. There must, therefore, be a proper proportion between crimes and punishments. . . . (p. 62)

24. The Measure of Crimes

[T]he true measure of crimes is . . . the *harm done to society*. . . . (p. 64)

41. How to Prevent Crimes

It is better to prevent crimes than to punish them. This is the ultimate end of every good legislation, which, to use the general terms for assessing the good and evils of life, is the art of leading men to the greatest possible happiness or to the least possible unhappiness. . . .

Do you want to prevent crimes? See to it that the laws are clear and simple and that the entire force of a nation is united in their defense, and that no part of it is employed to destroy them. See to it that the laws favor not so much classes of men as men themselves. See to it that men fear the laws and fear nothing else. For fear of the laws is salutary, but fatal and fertile for crimes is one man's fear of another. . . .

Do you want to prevent crimes? See to it that enlightenment accompanies liberty. . . . (pp. 93–95)

We must stress, contrary to traditional wisdom, that the image of crime and punishment in Beccaria's book is not one based exclusively on free will (Beirne, 1993:12–64). Borrowing liberally from the emerging determinism of the Glaswegian philosopher Francis Hutcheson, Beccaria believed—as did many others of his era—that human action was based on both free will *and* determinism. Indeed, attached to his humanism was Beccaria's attempt to apply to the study of crime and punishment some of the deterministic principles found in natural science, mathematics, probability theory, and the early forms of psychology. This project Beccaria termed the "science of man."

In Beccaria's recommendations are the seeds of policies present in criminal justice systems around the world today, including the U.S. His book was the first widely read text that urges the machinery of criminal justice be answerable to rules of due process; that sentencing policies reflect the harm inflicted on society by a given crime (essentially, that punishment "fit" the crime); and that punishment be prompt, certain, and contain a measure of deterrence. His major recommendations can be summarized as follows:

▲— The right of governments to punish offenders derives from a contractual obligation among its citizens not to pursue their self-interest at the expense of others.

▲— Punishment must be constituted by uniform and enlightened legislation.

▲— Imprisonment must replace torture and capital punishment as the standard form of punishment.

▲— Punishment must fit the crime. It must be prompt and certain, and its duration must reflect only the gravity of the offense and the social harm it caused.

Upon publication, *Of Crimes and Punishments* had a great impact on much of Europe and colonial America. As Henry Paolucci records: "[A]lmost at once, as if an exposed nerve had been touched, all Europe was stirred to excitement" (1963:x). Part of Beccaria's fame doubtless derived from the fact that in 1766 his book was condemned for its extreme rationalism and placed on the *Index Prohibitorum* (the Papal Index of forbidden books) by the Catholic Church. Beccaria's influence was most visible in the new classical legal codes of Austria, Denmark, France, Poland, Prussia, Russia, and Sweden. In the fledgling United States of America, the Constitution embraced Beccarian principles, as did the Bill of Rights. Beccaria's ideas were widely quoted by Thomas Jefferson, John Adams, and others (Jones, 1986:43–46). Upon reading *Of Crimes and Punishments*, English reformer Jeremy Bentham was driven to declare: "Oh! my master, first evangelist of Reason . . . you who have made so many useful excursions into the path of utility, what is there left to do?—Never to turn aside from that path" (cited in Paolucci, 1963:x–xi).

However, that Beccaria had not left all reformist stones unturned was soon evident in Bentham's original contributions to classicism. Before considering whether Beccaria's ideas were as enlightened as they are generally made out to be, we turn our attention to the other pillar of classical criminology, Jeremy Bentham, and to his writings on punishment and prisons.

Bentham: Punishment and the Panopticon

Jeremy Bentham (1748–1832) was a gifted and passionate young man who graduated from Oxford University at the age of 12 and who later became a law student in London. Bentham never practiced law, but instead became the prolific author of numerous texts on moral philosophy, usury, punishment, jurisprudence, prison reform, and the police. A keen critic of the English constitution, and even more so of the U.S. Constitution, he traveled extensively throughout Europe and corresponded frequently with many leading intellectuals and political figures of his day.

Although much in his writings was original, Bentham owed intellectual debts to Beccaria, inevitably, and also to Scottish philosopher David Hume (1711–1776). Bentham was inspired by Beccaria to campaign for a rational, humane, and codified system of law. However, whereas Beccaria had simply compiled a list of humane reforms to the barbaric practices of criminal justice, Bentham intended to place them on a solid philosophical foundation. While a law student, Bentham first read Hume's moral philosophy, and was greatly impressed by it. Hume argued that the basic quality of moral action was its tendency to produce happiness—but that, as freewilled and social beings, members of a society derive pleasure from the happiness of others. Consequently, individual members of society should pursue not only their own pleasure but that of others. He argued that the happiness, pleasures, and security of individuals—of whom a society is composed—are the sole ends that laws should protect and promote. This utilitarian principle—the greatest happiness to the greatest number—became the cornerstone of Bentham's writings. Dissatisfied with existing legal and moral philosophy, Bentham engaged in the lifelong project of making his law solve all social and political problems. We turn now to his campaign to reform punishment and prisons.

Punishment

In the theory of punishment outlined in his book *An Introduction to the Principles of Morals and Legislation,* Bentham (1780:152–203) assumed that potential criminals consciously *calculate* the profits and losses that arise from committing a crime. Similarly, he suggested, lawmakers should calculate the measures required to prevent and punish crimes. Bentham argued that in promoting the law of utility, legislators should prevent mischiefs such as crimes by means of various sanctions, including that necessary evil, punishment. Crimes, Bentham argued, could be prevented either through positive sanctions (rewards) or negative sanctions (punishment).

Notwithstanding, Bentham urged that punishment should not be inflicted at all in certain circumstances (1780:170–178):

▲— where it is *groundless*—where, on balance, the act itself is not really mischievous

▲— where it is *inefficacious*—where it cannot act so as to prevent the mischief

▲— where it is *unprofitable*, or too *expensive*—where the cost of the punishment outweighs the cost of the harm it seeks to prevent

▲— where it is *needless*—where the mischief may be prevented, or cease of itself, without punishment

Bentham argued that when punishment is worthwhile, legislators should follow four rules of utility in calculating the proportion (balance) between crime and punishment. First, the ultimate goal is the prevention of all crime. To achieve this goal the pleasure derived from any crime should always be just outweighed by the pain inflicted by the punishment for its commission. Second, a person about to commit a crime should be persuaded by the very threat of punishment either not to commit that crime at all or to commit a lesser offense.

Third, a person who has actually decided to commit a crime should be persuaded by the threat of punishment to do no more mischief than is necessary. In no case should punishment for a crime be more than necessary to prevent its occurrence. Fourth, legislators should try to prevent crime as cheaply as possible.

The Panopticon

In criminology, Bentham is most famous for the invention of his macabre Inspection-House, otherwise known as the Panopticon (Greek, meaning "all seeing"). In the preface to *Panopticon*, Bentham (1787, I:i–vii) wrote that the principles of his Panopticon represented an unequalled power of mind over mind. The Panopticon was explicitly created to be an engine of power that would discipline all of society.

The objectives of the Panopticon were to punish the incorrigible, guard the insane, reform the vicious, confine suspects, employ the idle, maintain the helpless, cure the sick, and offer training in any branch of industry and education. The scope of the Panopticon therefore embraced not only prisons but also workhouses for the poor, factories, madhouses, hospitals, and schools. Bentham believed that the ingenious architectural principles of the Panopticon would enable morals to be reformed and

> health preserved; industry invigorated; instruction diffused; public burdens lightened; Economy seated as it were upon a rock; the Gordian knot of the Poor-Laws not cut but untied—all by a simple idea in Architecture! (1787, I:i).

And, of course, crime would be eliminated!

We should remember that until the late 18th century, prisons were crudely designed and not intended for prolonged incarceration. Their uses were limited to holding-institutions for torture before trial, for debtors, for confinement prior to execution, and (especially in England and France) for the period between conviction and transportation to a penal colony. Bentham argued that the prison must be transformed from its position as one among many marginal and temporary institutions within the system of criminal justice to its permanent center. His plan for a penitentiary Panopticon began with a three-storied circular or polygonal building (Bentham, 1787, III:5–33). The circumference of the building contained the prisoners' cells, which were divided from one another by partitions in the form of radii issuing from the circumference toward the center. The prisoners were thus isolated from one another. At the center of the building was a three-storied central tower, the Inspectors' Lodge for the prison guards. Because the windows of the tower were draped with blinds, the prisoners were unable to see the inspectors in the tower. The prisoners were therefore to be seen without seeing, subject to "uninterrupted exposure to invisible inspection" (*ibid.*:3,88). Moreover, Bentham planned for the Panopticon to be built at a strategic location in a metropolitan area—in this way a visible reminder to free citizens of the foolishness of their wrongdoing.

These architectural principles Bentham supplemented with a strict regimen of visits by prisoners to the prison chapel for moral and religious instruction. Every minute of the prisoners' day was subject to discipline, order, and isolation in order to encourage inward self-reflection and moral reformation of character. Bentham's detailed plans for prisoners' lives within the Panopticon included rules for a crushing uniformity in the segregation of inmates by sex and class; in diet, clothing, and bedding; in the ventilation, shading, cooling, and airing of cells; in the health, cleanliness, and exercise of prisoners; in the precise distribution of time; and in forms of punishment. The governor was charged with ensuring that all prisoners were taught some marketable skill; the profits from what they produced, through a system of contract labor, were to contribute to the financial management of the prison. Additionally, Bentham offered suggestions for the conduct of prisoners' lives after prison: their continued release was made conditional on "acceptance by a bondsman" (payment of bail) and successful fulfillment, for a specified term, of apprenticeship in a worthy trade or occupation.

At first Bentham's innovative plans for the Panopticon were well received; they were debated in Parliament and, in 1794, several sites in England were purchased for the construction of his penitentiary houses. However, no Benthamite Panopticon was ever completed in England partly because, according to some (Phillipson, 1923:129–130), King George III opposed it and Parliament deemed it too expensive. Moreover, no pure Benthamite Panopticon was built in continental Europe—despite a frenzied program of prison construction between 1780 and 1840—and the two Panopticons undertaken in the United States (one in Pennsylvania, the other in Illinois) were eventually abandoned as impractical.

Bentham's writings on crime and criminal justice were ignored and forgotten in the 50 years after his death. However, Bentham's lasting influence lay less in actual implementation of architectural plans than in widespread acceptance of principles of punishment and prison. Indeed, it has been recorded that "[t]he work of Jeremy Bentham exerts an influence upon our time perhaps more diversified than that of any other modern philosopher" (Lafleur, 1973:vii).

Toward the Disciplinary Society

Significant questions remain about the nature of the reforms initiated by classical writers such as Beccaria and Bentham. How progressive was classical criminology? Whose interests did its ideas serve? Why did the proposals of Beccaria and Bentham gain widespread acceptance, rather than those of other now-forgotten writers?

Most accounts of the origins of modern criminology begin, as here, with the writings of Beccaria and Bentham. Clearly it was their classical ideas about penal reform that gained official attention, their ideas that were implemented in practice. But ideas about penal reform are rarely implemented simply because they are believed somehow to be better than those of their competitors; they are implemented also because they tend to serve certain interests and to achieve certain aims. Doubtless the self-declared humanism of the classical writers commanded a measure of respect among most, if not all, sections of European society and the United States. Their demand that capital punishment and judicial torture be abolished, for example, was a progressive feature that had few opponents.

However, we must recognize that both Beccaria and Bentham championed ideas that were conservative *even in the context of their own times.* Their proposals were narrow ones, consciously chosen from within the broad range of rational, humanist, and materialist ideas that comprised the Enlightenment. As Philip Jenkins (1984:117) writes: "Beccaria's book . . . was handling debates which had led others to much more dangerous conclusions." Chief among such conclusions was the view of established figures—such as Montesquieu, Rousseau, and Hume—that legislation reflected not the will of a whole nation but the narrow interests of owners of property, land, and industry. In this view crime itself was to a certain extent seen as a result of social inequality. If crime somehow was caused by social inequality, then it was but a short step to such radical ideas as English anarchist William Godwin's (1756–1836) *Political Justice* and the eccentric Marquis de Sade's (1740–1814) *Juliette.* Godwin, for example, wrote that crime consisted of "offences which the wealthier part of the community have no desire to commit" (quoted in Jenkins, [*ibid.*:123]). Both Godwin and de Sade urged that because most crime resulted from inequalities of property and wealth, communism, rather than imprisonment, was its proper cure. Among men of wealth and property such a recommendation was not fit for serious discussion.

Neither Beccaria nor Bentham intended to introduce penal reforms that would threaten the inequality of property. Beccaria's *Of Crimes and Punishments* was a plea for the supremacy of law rather than of religion and superstition. Implemented throughout Europe, his proposals were legal and administrative solutions to the problem of crime. But, as noted in his *Panopticon,* Bentham planned to extend Beccaria's proposals far beyond the confines of the criminal justice system. The Panopticon was devised as an engine of regulation whose machinery was to be used to discipline the lives of those who deviate from any aspect of established order. The ultimate aim of classical criminology, therefore, was not that punishment should be less but that it should be better and more efficient.

10.2 ———— THE EMERGENCE OF POSITIVIST CRIMINOLOGY

The second great theoretical movement in modern criminology was *positivist criminology.* The term "positivism" refers to a method of analysis based on the collection of observable scientific facts. Its aim is to uncover, to explain, and to predict the ways in which observable facts occur in uniform patterns. Positivist analysis can thus be applied to such things as the movement of stars through the heavens, the fertility of rabbits, and, indeed, to the entire subject matter of natural sciences such as physics, chemistry, and biology. Many scholars believe that positivist analysis can also be used to study people. Thus, the term "positivist

TABLE 10-1   **Classical and Positivist Criminology—A Comparison**

CLASSICAL CRIMINOLOGY	POSITIVIST CRIMINOLOGY
1. The focus of criminological study should be the act of crime.	1. The focus of criminological study should be the criminal.
2. Human action is based on free will, the "motivation" for which can be determined by psychological factors.	2. Human action is largely deterministic.
3. Crime is an action voluntarily engaged in by free-willed individuals; their motivation can be determined by psychological factors.	3. Crime is an action into which individuals are propelled by social, economic, and "mental" forces largely outside their control.
4. The punishment should fit the crime.	4. The punishment should fit the criminal.

criminology" is used generally to refer to the search for uniformities in the area of crime and criminal justice. Table 10-1 provides a convenient comparison between the major principles of classical criminology and positivist criminology.

Positivist criminology emerged in the writings and observations of various European authors in the second quarter of the 19th century. It is difficult to identify the precise moment when positivist criminology was created. Undoubtedly one of its forerunners was phrenology. The primary champions of phrenology were the Germans Franz Joseph Gall (1758–1828) and his pupil John Gaspar Spurzheim (1776–1832). This movement focused on the psychiatric concern with relationships among the organic structure of the brain, illness, and social behavior. But the phrenologists never regarded crime or criminals as the focus of their studies.

We can say confidently that as a self-conscious effort to apply positivist principles to the study of crime, positivist criminology began with the ideas of French and Belgian statisticians in the 1820s. These ideas were a response to a perceived crisis in classical criminology, and it is to certain of the dimensions of this crisis that we now turn.

The Crisis of Classicism: The Dangerous Classes

The emergence of positivist criminology in early 19th-century France was an important response to changes in the system of criminal justice that occurred, rapidly in some respects and gradually in others, between the middle of the 18th and the beginning of the 19th centuries.

As noted, on one side of this transformation were the barbaric practices of feudal society, especially of the French *ancien régime*. At the center of the new system was a network of institutions of confinement ushered in by classical writers such as Beccaria and Bentham. These institutions had been created to control and to oversee the entire population. They were intended to operate on their inmates with the same monotonous precision as schools, barracks, and monasteries. Their expanding inventory included hospitals, workhouses, asylums, reformatories, houses of correction, and prisons. Their official aim was moral reformation through the deprivation of liberty. Their "delinquent" and "pathological" inmates included syphilitics, alcoholics, idiots and eccentrics, vagabonds, immigrants, prostitutes, and petty and professional criminals. Inaugurated in 1810, the French prison system was based on a complex classification of inmates, and included military prisons, debtors' prisons, agricultural colonies, transportation, and the galleys. These components operated in concert with a new criminal code, a professional police force (*gendarmerie*), a system of passport and identity cards, and an extensive network of paid informers and spies (Foucault, 1979:280; Stead, 1983:47–48).

Positivist criminology itself emerged from the convergence of two areas of government activity in France. From the criminal justice system, criminology acquired a secure position of status, a measure of financial support, and considerable interest among the citizenry in its pronouncements about the social distribution and causes of crime. From the statistical movement, criminology acquired its intellectual orientation and recognition by the scientific community of its methods of analysis (Beirne, 1993:71–75).

During the Restoration (1814–1830), the separate activities of the criminal justice system and the statistical movement joined in a common concern: the failure of the new institutions of confinement (such as prisons) to regulate the conduct of the *dangerous classes*. The "dangerous classes" was a derogatory term applied by law-abiding citizens to describe—with a mixture of fear and disgust—those members of the working classes, the unemployed, and the unemployable who seemed to pose a threat to law and order. Criminals, especially thieves, formed a large part of the dangerous classes. That the expanding network of prisons had significantly failed to control the criminal activities of the dangerous classes was apparent in at least three ways (Beirne, 1987:1144–1148).

First, such failure was implicit in the continued and growing presence in urban areas of large numbers of poor, unemployed, and working-class thieves whose desperate conditions were immortalized in such works as Victor Hugo's *Les Misérables* and Charles Dickens' *Oliver Twist*. In Paris, for example, despite a doubling of its population between 1800 and 1850, the city remained structurally intact. It is not difficult to imagine how quickly this population explosion manifested itself in the incidence of infant mortality and related social problems of accommodation, food supplies, unemployment, public order, and crime. It has been estimated that in 1800 the only source of income for 30,000 Parisians was robbery; Balzac's *Code des gens honnêtes* recorded that 20 years later there were 20,000 professional criminals and as many as 120,000 "rogues" in Paris (Frégier, 1840; Chevalier, 1973:448).

Second, the continued presence of the dangerous classes led to widespread fear of criminality among the law-abiding citizenry. Reports of crime were widely circulated by newspapers and government inquiries—and eagerly devoured by their audiences. During certain winters of cold and destitution, the fear of crime turned to panic and terror. This widespread fear of crime was heightened by working-class insurrections and, as Tombs (1980:214) has suggested, it quickly became an unquestioned tenet of middle-class thought that crime and revolution were symptoms of the same disease.

Third, after 1815 increases in the official crime rate lent support to fearful public opinion. For example, a sudden increase was recorded in felony offenses, primarily in theft and disturbances of public order (Wright, 1983:48–50; Duesterberg, 1979:29–31). Between 1813 and 1820, the number of convictions in the criminal tribunals nearly doubled. Even more telling was the fact that many members of the dangerous classes were continually shuttled back and forth between incarceration and free society. This process was apparent in rising rates of recidivism, which implied that prisons were failing in their duty to reform the moral character of their inmates. "In 1820 it was already understood," writes Foucault (1980:40), "that the prisons, far from transforming criminals into citizens, serve only to manufacture new criminals and drive existing criminals ever deeper into criminality."

Failure of the new system of prisons to regulate the conduct of the dangerous classes stimulated considerable statistical research into their lives. The vital statistics of their lives, both inside and outside prison, were scrutinized by government investigators and independent researchers from the public health movement. For inquiries into prison conditions, one question was paramount: "Should (or could) the prisoners be returned to society and, if so, how?" (Petit, 1984:137). However, it was soon apparent that this question could not be answered with information derived solely from prison conditions. Inquiry broadened, therefore, to consider the larger population that passed through successive layers of the criminal justice system. In 1825 the French government commissioned the first national statistical tables on crime, the annual *Compte général* (General Account). This account was first published in 1827, immediately after a winter in which crime and death rates increased equally and during which public fear and terror were the major themes of police reports and newspaper articles throughout Paris (Chevalier, 1973:3). The *Compte* included information on the annual number of known and prosecuted crimes against persons and property, whether the accused (if prosecuted) were acquitted or convicted, as well as the punishments awarded. It also recorded the time of year when the offenses were committed and the age, sex, occupation, and educational status of both accused and convicted.

The French government reasoned that the hard facts in the *Compte's* tables could be used to understand the causes of crime and to apply appropriate corrective measures. These hopes were echoed by a loosely knit, somewhat amateurish group of social statisticians who were busy collecting data on such items as births, marriages, and deaths. One member of this group was the young Belgian astronomer Adolphe Quetelet (1796–1874).

Quetelet's criminology was one result among many of the failure of the new penal institutions. It is with Quetelet's writings on crime that we begin our journey into the development of positivism in criminological theory.

The Social Mechanics of Crime: Quetelet

Quetelet not only founded positivist criminology but also pioneered thinking in the fields of astronomy, meteorology, statistics, and sociology. Interestingly,

Quetelet contributed, indirectly, to inventing the new word "sociology": so embarrassed was prickly philosopher Auguste Comte with Quetelet's ("a mere statistician") use of his term "social physics" that, in 1828, Comte coined the term *sociology*.

Quetelet's criminology reflected two parallel areas of government activity: the failure to regulate the conduct of the dangerous classes and the new statistical movement and its concern with empirical social research. His genius in criminology lay in the fact that he integrated advances in statistical technique with widespread concern about the dangerous classes.

Quetelet was a brilliant student of astronomy and mathematics at the University of Ghent in Belgium. In 1823, during a visit to Paris, he learned of the potential for applying algebra, geometry, and the principles of astronomy to the understanding of social conditions. On his return to Belgium from Paris, Quetelet engaged in various projects, including a study of Belgian birth and mortality tables as the basis for constructing insurance rates. Soon thereafter he submitted plans for a national census and the collection of crime statistics in Belgium. In these early works, Quetelet attempted to show that the same law-like regularity existing in the heavens and the world of nature also existed in society. "In following attentively the regular march of nature in the development of plants and animals," Quetelet reasons, "we are compelled to believe . . . that the influence of laws should be extended to the human species" (1826:495).

The basis of Quetelet's efforts to understand crime lay in his search for law-like regularities in society. At first he sought these regularities in relatively simple data that were subject to predictable variation and which could be observed directly, such as mortality rates, the heights of 100,000 French soldiers, and the chest measurements of Scottish soldiers. From these observations, Quetelet calculated the averages (of height and the like) of his subjects. These averages he thought to be more accurate the greater the number of observations. In combination, the averages produced the image of a fictitious, statistically derived creature—the "average man."

> If the *average* man were ascertained for one nation, he would present the type of that nation. If he could be ascertained according to the mass of men, he would present the type of the human species altogether (Quetelet, 1831:3).

Soon thereafter, Quetelet (1831) turned his attention to crime and crime rates, publishing the findings in the short book *Research on the Propensity for Crime at Different Ages*. Herein he suggested it is reasonable to suppose that the volume of crime would vary from one year to another because individuals were so fickle in character. This would seem especially true of unpremeditated crimes such as murders committed during a quarrel. Careful to point out that social mechanics could never pretend to discover laws verifiable for all individuals, Quetelet argued that—when observed on a great scale through the prism of such statistical records as the *Compte*—the phenomena of crime obeyed the same law-like regularities as did physical phenomena.

Quetelet's analysis of the data in the *Compte* revealed considerable sophistication for his era; he realized that any scientific analysis of crime must assume "*a relationship pretty nearly invariable between offenses known and judged and the unknown sum total of offenses committed*" (1831:17). The size of this relationship, Quetelet suggested, would depend on the seriousness of offenses and on the actions of the criminal justice system in prosecuting offenders. Moreover, he indicated that if the causes influencing this relationship remained the same, their representation in official statistics would remain constant as well.

Quetelet's findings on the social distribution of crime were threefold: the constancy of crime rates over time, criminal propensities and causes of crime, and statistics and biology. We examine each in turn.

The Constancy of Crime Rates

Quetelet inferred from the astonishing regularity in French crime rates between 1826 and 1829 that the ratio of unknown crimes to recorded crimes was in practice constant (see Table 10-2). In addition to the constancy in the annual number of accused (tried) and convicted and in the ratios of accused to convicted, of accused to inhabitants, and of crimes against persons to crimes against property, Quetelet noted regularities in the number of accused who failed to appear in the courts, in the number of convictions in different types of courts, and in the number of convicts sentenced to death, imprisonment, or forced labor. Even the different methods of murder he reported to be constant from one year to another:

> [O]ne passes from one year to the other with the sad perspective of seeing the same crimes reproduced in the same order and bringing with them the same penalties in the same proportions. Sad condition of the human species! The share of prisons, chains, and the scaffold appears fixed with as much probability as the revenues of the state. We are able to enumerate in advance how many individuals will stain their hands with the blood of their fellow creatures, how many will be forgers, how many

TABLE 10-2   The Constancy of Crime, 1826–1829

YEAR ACCUSED	ACCUSED (TRIED)	ACCUSED OF CRIMES AGAINST		DISPOSITION	
		PERSONS	PROPERTY	GUILTY	% GUILTY
1826	6,988	1,907	5,081	4,348	62
1827	6,929	1,911	5,018	4,236	61
1828	7,396	1,844	5,552	4,551	61
1829	7,373	1,791	5,582	4,475	61
Totals	28,686	7,453	21,233	17,610	61

Source: Quetelet (1831, p. 20), amended.

poisoners, pretty nearly as one can enumerate in advance the births and deaths which must take place (Quetelet, 1831:69).

Criminal Propensities and the Causes of Crime

Quetelet inferred from the apparent constancy of crime rates recorded in the *Compte* that, even if individuals have free will, criminal behavior obeys scientific laws of the same sort as those that govern the motion of inanimate objects like stars. The disproportionate presence of certain categories in the *Compte* between 1826 and 1829 also indicated to Quetelet that young males, the poor, and those without employment or in lowly occupations had a greater propensity (or probability) than did others to commit crimes and to be convicted of them. These data led him to cast doubt on several standard accounts of the causes of crime. Quetelet noted that neither the presence of poverty nor the absence of formal education warranted the great causal importance commonly claimed for them: some of the poorest areas in France, and some of the areas with the lowest literacy rates, had among the lowest crime rates. For Quetelet, a more important factor than absolute poverty was the unequal distribution of wealth. Where great riches are amassed by a few, when an economy suddenly fluctuates, and when many individuals pass rapidly from well-being to misery:

> [T]hese are the rough alternations from one state to another that give birth to crime, especially if those who suffer from them are surrounded by subjects of temptation and find themselves irritated by the continual view of luxury and of an inequality of fortune which disheartens them (Quetelet, 1831:38).

Moreover, he continued, it was not education as such that altered the propensity to crime, but the type of education and the presence or absence of moral instruction (*ibid.*:37).

Quetelet found the two factors most strongly tied to criminal propensities to be age and sex. He noted, first, that the propensity for crime was strongest between the ages of 21 and 25. Quetelet observed a cyclical pattern in age-specific crime rates between infancy and old age. Physical immaturity permits only crimes whose victims offer little resistance, like indecent assault and rape. Middle age is associated with crimes involving greater planning, such as thefts on the public highways, murder by poisoning, and acts of rebellion. Finally, their powers somewhat enfeebled, elderly criminals commit crimes such as forgery and child molestation.

Second, in relation to sex, Quetelet noted that for those accused of property crimes the female/male ratio was 26:100, but that for crimes against persons it was 16:100. Quetelet explained this difference by arguing that crime requires the bringing together of motive, opportunity, and the ability to act. Women have lower propensities to crime in general, but higher rates of infanticide, because, he believed, they are motivated more by feelings of shame and modesty than are men. Moreover, according to Quetelet, women have fewer opportunities to commit crime because they lead more retiring lives and are less often influenced by alcohol. Women, he continued, are also physically weaker than men and, therefore, commit murder less often. To Quetelet's explanation should be added that women's lack of visibility in the *Compte* reflected the lenient judicial attitude toward women throughout the 19th century: women were more often successfully able to plead mitigating circumstances and were rarely sentenced to death. However, such "leniency" is itself an issue that requires explanation. In some cases leniency resulted from "chivalry"; however, it must be stressed that women who could not prove obedience to the standards of traditional womanhood (namely, marriage and economic dependency) tended to be treated quite repressively by the courts (Perrot, 1975).

Quetelet reasoned that the many causes of crime could be divided into three types: (a) accidental causes such as wars, famines, and natural disasters; (b) variable causes such as free will and personality that can oscillate between greater or smaller limits; and (c) constant causes such as age, gender, occupation, and religion. Moreover, because he saw crime as a constant and inevitable feature of social organization, Quetelet further claimed that society itself caused crime (Quetelet, 1842:6,108):

> Every social state presupposes, then, a certain number and a certain order of crimes, these being merely the necessary consequences of its organization. . . . *Society prepares crime, and the guilty are only the instruments by which it is executed.*

Quetelet's placement of criminal behavior in a formal structure of causality was a remarkable advance over the unsystematic speculations of his contemporaries. His intuition that society somehow caused crime marked a profound theoretical departure from the crude realism of public opinion and classical criminology, flying in the face of the theory that criminals freely chose to engage in wickedness. Yet because Quetelet's concept of social organization was based on the idea that society was only the sum of its individual components, his view of how propensities were translated into criminal activities remained conventional. This tendency in Quetelet's criminology was expressed in his linking of statistics and biology.

Statistics and Biology

In the early 1840s, especially after he became better acquainted with statistical advances in astronomy and mathematics, Quetelet insisted on the need to present not only the mean of a scale of given characteristics but also the upper and lower limits between which individuals oscillated. Minor or "natural" deviation around the mean Quetelet defined as deviation that should attract no unusual attention; extraordinary variation (such as, the height of giants and dwarfs) he saw as "preternatural . . . monstrous" (1842:x). In addition, Quetelet asserted that variation around the mean occurred not randomly but in a determined order that approximated the principle of normal distribution. This principle (also called Gaussian distribution) is an idealized mathematical concept describing the distribution of a variable with an infinite number of cases. It is symmetrical and unbounded at either end, and the mean, mode, and median are identical and divide the distribution into two equal parts. The distribution was first used in 1733 by Abraham de Moivre to describe probabilities in games of chance, and was first applied to social data by Quetelet (Muellet *et al.*, 1970:168).

Quetelet's application of the principle of normal distribution to crime altered the social thrust of his criminology and led directly to his rigid distinction between the statistical mean and "unusual" deviation. Unusual deviation now implied abnormality. Although Quetelet inferred from the normal distribution that "every man . . . has a certain propensity to break the laws" (1848:94), at the same time he believed that the criminal propensities of the "average man" were rarely, if ever, translated into criminal actions. Accordingly, the characters of individuals with propensities at the mean Quetelet described as law-abiding, medically and psychologically healthy, and morally temperate. The virtues of the average law-abiding citizen he contrasted with the criminality of vagabonds, vagrants, "primitives," "gypsies," "inferior classes," certain races with "inferior moral stock," and persons of low moral character. Eventually, Quetelet believed that unhealthy morality was manifest in biological defects and that those with such defects had high criminal propensities. Crime, he concluded, was "a pestilential germ . . . contagious . . . [sometimes] hereditary" (Quetelet, 1848:214–215).

We note that Quetelet could not identify the precise point at which variations from the law-abiding citizenry were transformed into the alien world of incorrigible criminality. In large measure the impetus to make this distinction derived from public hysteria generated by increasing rates of recidivism, annually confirmed throughout the 19th century by the *Compte*. Irrespective of what such official crime statistics actually measured, and why, the publicized increases in recorded rates of recidivism led to widespread belief in the existence of born criminals, habitually committed to a way of life dependent on the proceeds of crime.

10.3 ——— CRIMINAL ANTHROPOLOGY: LOMBROSO'S "BORN CRIMINAL"

It was into this ripening climate that the notion of the "born criminal" was first introduced, in 1876, by Italian army physician Cesare Lombroso (1835–1909) in his book *Criminal Man*. Between 1852 and 1856, Lombroso had been a medical student at universities in Pavia, Padua, and Vienna. During this time, after studying anatomy and pathology, he became concerned about Italy's high incidence of such diseases as cretinism and pellagra. When he began to research delinquents in the 1860s, Lombroso was convinced that only a scientific criminology (anthropometry) could avoid the superstitious belief in free will of classical criminology.

Cesare   Lombroso
(1836–1909).

The major sources of the claims in *Criminal Man* derived from a diverse positivist landscape that included the new prominence of the scientific method in social investigations, the claim by statisticians that science was objective and therefore factual and free of values, and the evolutionism of Charles Darwin's *Origin of Species*. To these positivist influences must be added Lombroso's lifelong hatred of "idealism"—namely, any view that explains human behavior by reference to spiritual or nonmaterial factors. Finally, mention should be made of the heated debates in Italy on the "Southern Question": Why was southern Italy so economically and culturally stagnant? One answer to this question was advanced by the Italian Communist Party, which asserted that the real problem was not the backwardness of the South but the racist myths circulated about the peasantry by the press and by conservative politicians to the effect that "the Southerners are inferior beings . . . lazy, incapable, criminal and barbaric" (Gramsci, 1926:444). This myth was shared by prominent members of the Italian Socialist Party, the worst tendencies of which were also espoused by Lombroso. According to Lombroso's own account of his intellectual development, he gradually began to realize that the only scientific criminology was one based on an analysis of the individual criminal. This he realized after a series of revelations, one of which came during his *postmortem* examination of the convicted thief Vilella:

> On [Vilella's] death one cold grey November morning, I was deputed to make the *postmortem*, and on laying open the skull I found on the occipital part, exactly on the spot where a spine is found in the normal skull, a distinct depression which I named *median occipital fossa*, because of its situation precisely in the middle of the occiput as in inferior animals, especially rodents. . . .
>
> This was not merely an idea by a revelation. At the sight of that skull, I seemed to see all of a sudden, lighted up as a vast plain under a flaming sky, the problem of the nature of the criminal—an atavistic being who reproduces in his person the ferocious instincts of primitive humanity and the inferior animals. Thus were explained anatomically the enormous jaws, high cheek-bones, prominent superciliary arches, solitary lines in the palms, extreme size of the orbits, handle-shaped or sessile ears found in criminals, savages, and apes, insensibility to pain, extremely acute sight, tattooing, excessive idleness, love of orgies, and the irresistible craving for evil for its own sake, the desire not only to extinguish life in the victim, but to mutilate the corpse, tear its flesh, and drink its blood (Lombroso, 1911:xxiv–xxv).

The arguments of *Criminal Man* stemmed from the "scientific" data largely outlined in its first two chapters. The first chapter reported on Lombroso's autopsies performed on 66 male delinquents in Italian anatomical museums. He examined several aspects of the cephalic indices of these corpses in great detail: their capacity, facial angle, occipital depression, brain, and extent of microcephaly. Lombroso found that these delinquents presented a significant number of deviations similar to those of insane persons examined in his clinic, to "blacks" in the U.S., to the Mongolian races, and above all, to prehistoric man. In the second chapter Lombroso engaged in an anthropometric analysis of the physiognomy of 832 living Italian delinquents. This second group of delinquents included both males and females selected from among the "most notorious and depraved" Italian criminals. Of this group, 390 of its members were compared with 868 Italian soldiers and 90 "lunatics." From these data Lombroso (1876) concluded that

> many of the characteristics found in savages, and among the coloured races, are also to be found in habitual delinquents. They have in common, for example, thinning hair, lack of strength and weight, low cranial capacity, receding foreheads, highly developed frontal sinuses . . . darker skin, thicker, curly hair, large or handle-shaped ears, a great analogy between the two sexes . . . indolence . . . facile superstition . . . and finally the relative concept of the divinity and morals.

For some criminologists Lombroso's discoveries established his new school as an academic science and him as its founder. With the publication of its own journal and key supporting texts by Ferri (1884) and Garofalo (1885), the *scuola positiva* formed an identifiable program. Although challenged by classical lawyers and by some socialists (such as Loria), Lombrosianism dominated public discussion of crime in Italy. Its reputation quickly extended beyond Italy to Germany, Russia, and France. Lombrosian findings were tested in France in the late 1880s and early 1890s, and favorably received by several converts (Duesterberg, 1979:319–321).

The Offensive Against Lombrosianism

But enthusiasm for Lombroso's concept of the "born criminal" was not universal. Criticisms of the concept were led by French sociologist Gabriel Tarde (1843–1904) and by a diverse coalition of lawyers and anthropologists including Topinard, Manouvrier, and Lacassagne; criticisms were also made by criminologists in the United States such as Frances Kellor, although somewhat later than those in Europe (see Chapter 11.1).

The offensive against Lombrosianism climaxed in 1889 at the Second Congress of Criminal Anthropology held in Paris. There, one of Lombroso's supporters, Garofalo, proposed that a commission of seven anthropologists—including representatives from both the classical and the new schools of criminology—engage in comparative family case studies of 100 born criminals, 100 persons with criminal tendencies, and 100 honest persons. Lombroso defiantly agreed to retract his notion of born criminality if the physical, mental, and psychological characteristics of the first group proved identical with either of the others. Although this proposal was accepted, it was not carried out; apparently it was impossible to distinguish among the three groups with sufficient accuracy.

Tarde's Criticisms of the "Born Criminal"

Three influential criticisms of the "born criminal" were put forward by the French judge and criminologist Gabriel Tarde. First, he argued that there was no agreement about the characteristics of born criminals. In their anatomy, physiology, and pathology, born criminals represented a mass of contradictory evidence. For example, one of Lombroso's disciples, Marro, had compared 456 "malefactors" with 1,765 "honest" persons, and reported that criminals' cranial capacity, stature, and weight were sometimes greater than average and sometimes less (Tarde, 1890:220). Again, anthropologist Topinard reported that pictures of criminals collected by Lombroso reminded him of photos of his own friends (*ibid.*)!

Second, Tarde showed that one of the born criminal's key attributes—moral atavism (embracing lunacy, degeneracy, and epilepsy)—was absent in many cases. He noted that the Italian provinces registering the highest rates of bodily illnesses and deformities typical of degeneracy were in fact the most moral provinces—in northern Italy. Moreover, in the provinces with the highest crime rates—in southern Italy—the inhabitants tended to exhibit excellent health. "Does this mean," Tarde humorously asked, "that degeneracy constitutes the best condition for the increase of morality?" (*ibid.*:237).

Third, Tarde attempted to shift the empirical terrain from one field to another. He suggested, for example, that variations in crime rates in different areas of France were caused not by different concentrations of born or habitual criminals, but by local variations in the incidence of such factors as poverty and alcoholism (Tarde, 1886:155–156). Another example of this tactic was Tarde's attempt to reinterpret the finding that born criminals often indulged in the practice of tattooing. He (Tarde, 1890:66) explained this practice as

> traditional among certain barbarous tribes coming into contact with our civilized people, sailors or soldiers, [and] . . . communicated as a fashion to the latter, and then to the prisoners, as a result of the habitual isolation and the long periods of idleness favorable to its propagation. . . . [T]hus prisons sometimes become, they are almost bound to, true studies of tattooing.

However, Tarde's criticisms offered no alternative explanation of habitual criminality. Indeed, Tarde believed that individual criminals were sometimes abnormal, inferior, and degenerate beings. Tarde's contributions were his empirical criticisms suggesting that not all criminals were born to their misdeeds. His efforts led not to the complete defeat of Lombrosianism in France, but to a serious decline in its intellectual influence.

In turn, the attempt to rescue the causal purity of the notion of the born criminal increasingly led Lombroso to a thoroughly eclectic notion of causality in which an infinite number of factors could predispose someone to criminality. Indeed, in one of his last major statements, Lombroso said that "[e]very crime has its origin in a multiplicity of causes, often intertwined and confused, each of which we must . . . investigate singly" (1902:1). These expanded causes included such factors as climate, temperature, age, poverty, occupation, race, and gender.

Lombroso also retreated from his claim that all criminals were atavistic beings. A new classificatory system recognized a variety of criminal types: the born, the epileptic, the criminaloid, the occasional, the passionate, and the female. About the latter, for example, Lombroso began with the idea that although female criminality increases with the advance of civilization and education, most women are not criminal (Lombroso and Ferrero, 1893:1–102). This is so because women are both (a) physically more "conservative," brought about by "the immobility of the ovule compared with the zoosperm" (*ibid.*:109) and, therefore, physically less ferocious than men; and (b) socially more "withdrawn," because they bear the larger share of child rearing and thus necessarily lead a more sedentary life. The physical characteristics of female criminals, such as prostitutes, tend to resemble those of male criminals. Extending this paternalistic logic, Lombroso argued that because most female criminals have their crimes suggested to them by men (e.g., by a lover or a husband), the best deterrent to female criminality lies in an appeal to women's natural vanity—such as cutting off their hair.

10.4 _____ **HEREDITY VS. ENVIRONMENT: GORING'S *THE ENGLISH CONVICT* (1913)**

Lombrosianism exercised little influence in England, but it was there that the most widely regarded refutation of it occurred: Charles Goring's (1913) *The English Convict: A Statistical Study.* In the history of criminology few books have commanded such high esteem. Upon publication it immediately entrenched itself as a methodological classic. Among many prison officials, statisticians, and criminologists, its 528 pages and 286 methodological tables were accepted as a staunch, positivist bulwark against the theoretical superstitions of Lombrosianism. The eminent statistician Karl Pearson, for example, suggested that "it is not too much to say that in the early chapters of Goring's work he clears out of the way forever the tangled and exuberant growths of the Lombrosian School" (1919:xviii).

The English Convict combined the focal concerns of three hitherto more or less separate areas of activity. To begin with, it continued the English tradition of prison research pursued by medical doctors such as J. Bruce Thomson, David Nicolson, and John Baker. This tradition involved the empirical calculation of "criminal propensities," often couched in the language and rhetoric of psychiatry: What mental and psychological factors distinguished prisoners from the law-abiding citizenry? Second, mention must be made of the British statistical movement. From the 1830s onward, the primary mission of many statisticians had been the quantification of social facts in order to address a wide range of such controversial issues as public health, child labor, factory conditions, education, and crime. Goring's contribution to these two traditions was the application of innovative statistical techniques to the study of criminals. Third, Goring's work was strongly influenced by the tradition that began with Charles Darwin's *Origin of Species* and that, in the 1890s, culminated in the findings of evolutionary and mathematical zoologists, including those of Francis Galton and W. F. R. Weldon. Galton's (1889) work on ancestral resemblance in sweet peas, for example, had shown that peas of a certain type, weight, and genetic structure tended to pass on their specific characteristics to their progeny. Weldon (1894–1895) found in his research on shrimps and crabs that creatures with deviant organs, such as long carapaces, tended to die early. From such findings was derived the belief that the content of social activity was itself inherited through genes and that those with deviant genes would be unable to adapt adequately to social life.

Eugenics

Straddling these three traditions was the desire of the professional middle class to stem the political and economic decline of the British Empire through rejuvenation of the physical stock and moral character of the British people. One platform in this social and political agenda was *eugenics* (Greek: good genes). It was hoped that eugenist principles could be applied to a broad spectrum of social undesirables, including the physically unfit, alcoholics, the very poor, the morally and mentally depraved, and habitual criminals.

The basic assumption of the eugenists was that distribution of social, moral, and intellectual qualities could be discerned in humans with the same procedures used to identify distribution of physical qualities in the world of nature. Galton pioneered the view that in any nation the natural human talents that comprise "civic worth" were distributed according to certain statistical laws. The distribution of worth was further assumed to be spread throughout society and its presence or absence manifest in such indicators as wealth and pathologies, respectively. In *Hereditary Genius*, Galton (1869) argued—with retrospective confirmation sought from his cousin's *Origin of Species*—that it was almost exclusively the "naturally" worthy who achieved social prominence, and this despite whatever obstacles they might encounter; conversely, the naturally "worthless" never succeeded in rising above their lowly positions, and this despite all government or private supports.

Eugenist proposals were of two sorts. Positive eugenics suggested that the middle and upper classes should be provided with incentives to intermarry and produce offspring, on the grounds that ordinarily only in these strata were intelligent and hard-working citizens found. Negative eugenics demanded that social undesirables (such as habitual criminals) should be isolated, sterilized, or occasionally castrated, because their useless offspring were a drain on national resources.

Testing Lombrosianism

These diverse traditions merged in Goring's *The English Convict*. In 1903, Charles Goring, a junior medical officer in the English prison service, was made coordinator of a government-sponsored project, begun in 1901, to test the factual reality of the concept of born criminals. Goring himself outlined certain problems with Lombroso's criminology: (a) that it was unscientific, (b) that Lombroso had never studied criminals using a proper statistical analysis of a large series of carefully collected data, and (c) that Lombroso had failed properly to compare the characteristics of criminals with those of noncriminals. Goring also believed that Lombroso had wrongly assumed that some people were naturally criminal and some actions inherently criminal. Both assumptions confused statistically unusual (i.e., rare) qualities with abnormal ones. Goring thus objected to "the unfortunate tendency to theorize as to the existence of abnormal types of human beings" (Goring, 1913:23–24). Such important questions could be solved only by careful statistical analysis.

Goring's testing of Lombrosianism involved three phases: (1) a statistical analysis to determine the presence of 37 Lombrosian characteristics in the criminal population, a group represented by 2,348 male convicts; (2) a comparison of the findings in the first phase with the characteristics of the "noncriminal public," represented by control groups including a company of soldiers, English and Scottish undergraduate students, and the staff and inmates of two separate hospitals; and (3) an analysis of the general physique of criminals. Goring found no significant differences between the average physical characteristics of criminals and those of his control groups. Indeed, he joked that from knowing only a student's cephalic measurements, a better judgment could be made as to whether the student was studying at an English or a Scottish university than a prediction as to whether the student would become a university professor or a convicted felon (*ibid.*:145)! Goring (*ibid.*:173) concluded that in

> the present investigation we have exhaustively compared . . . criminals as a class, with the law-abiding public. . . . *[N]o evidence has emerged confirming the existence of a physical criminal type, such as Lombroso and his disciples have described—our inevitable conclusion must be that there is no such thing as a physical criminal type.*

However, Goring did report that most criminals were physically inferior (in height and weight) to the general population. He reasoned that such differences could be explained perhaps by the process of "selection"; for example, those with inferior physiques were less likely to avoid arrest, given that the police were appointed only from among those with superior physiques. However, Goring (1913:200) further suggested that

> this physical inferiority, although originating in and fostered by selection, may tend with time to become an inbred characteristic of the criminal classes, just as, with the passage of generations, the upper classes of the noncriminal community have become differentiated in physique from those lower on the social scale.

Toward Mental Deficiency

The notion of an "inbred characteristic" was pivotal to Goring's work. With it, Goring ended his testing of Lombrosianism and began to insert his findings about "born criminality" into the arguments of the British eugenics movement.

In so doing, Goring discussed the social distribution of mental qualities, including temperament, intelligence, and mental capacity. In relation to the estimated 0.45 percent mental defectives in the general population, he asserted that 10–20 percent of the criminal population displayed some degree of mental defect and that many types of criminals displayed a decline in general intelligence quite similar to their increasing physical defectiveness. Goring linked these findings to the distribution of socioeconomic indicators of worth. "In every class and occupation of life, it is the feeble-minded, and the inferior forms of physique—the less mentally and physically able persons—which tend to be selected for a criminal career" (Goring, 1913:261). Goring concluded it likely that, if reducible to one condition, mental defectiveness would be the common antecedent of such other pathologies as alcoholism, epilepsy, insanity, and sexual promiscuity.

We must note that for most European criminologists, a definite line of demarcation had been drawn between biological and sociological causes of crime. Although most eugenists dismissed altogether the relevance of sociological factors, Goring nevertheless engaged in an analysis of the relative importance of several "adverse environmental conditions"—including employment, education, family life, and social class, of mental defectiveness and of heredity—upon the recidivism of convicts and the types of their crimes. In this second line of analysis Goring assumed that sociological factors, on the one hand, and mental capacities and heredity on the other, were independent of each other. For Goring it followed that to measure the effect of one factor, the effect of others must be controlled or eliminated. Goring therefore assumed, as did Weldon and other biologists, that maladaptive, deviant, or defective qualities of individuals in a given species were not influenced by social environment. "Our interim conclusion," he argued (*ibid.*:288)

> is that, relative to its origin in the constitution of the malefactor, and especially in his mentally defective constitution, crime in this country is only to a trifling extent (if to any) the product of social inequality, of adverse environment, or of other manifestations of what may be comprehensively termed the "force of circumstances."

Goring also noted that as many as 68 percent of the male offspring of criminals themselves became criminal. Was this the result of genetic inheritance of criminal propensities or of the influence of one's family? Controlling for the influence of family contagion—by eliminating it from his calculations—Goring found the intensity of the inherited factor in criminality to be extremely significant and the intensity of family contagion to be almost negligible. "Criminality," Goring (*ibid.*:368) concluded, is inherited

> at much the same rate as are other pathological conditions in man. . . . [T]he influence of inheritance, and of mental defectiveness [are] by far the most significant factors we have been able to discover in the aetiology of crime.

Finally, Goring offered some familiar eugenist proposals for the crusade against crime: appropriate education to modify criminal tendencies, segregation and supervision of the unfit to modify the opportunities for crime, regulation of the reproduction of constitutional qualities (feeblemindedness, inebriety, epilepsy, deficient social instinct, and others), and examination of convicts' lives outside prison (*ibid.*:273).

We conclude that *The English Convict* failed to refute Lombroso's concept of the born criminal. Indeed, Lombroso's concept of born criminality still had fervent followers in the U.S. even in the 1930s (see Chapter 12.1). Goring's dubious achievement simply replaced Lombroso's atavistic criminal with one born with inferior weight, stature, and mental capacity. Goring's ultimate contribution actually paralleled that of Lombroso—criminals had psychiatric defects that were reproduced through hereditarian mechanisms.

10.5 _____ NEOCLASSICAL CRIMINOLOGY

Thus far we have described the origins of the two most influential forms of modern criminology, classicism and positivism. These two versions of criminology competed strongly for legislative and popular attention throughout Europe and North America. Yet in combination they produced unworkable dilemmas for the machinery of criminal justice.

Penal Dilemmas

Classical and positivist criminology harbored fundamental differences of perspective on four key points (see Table 10-1). Especially after the rise of Lombrosianism in the mid-1870s, the classicists and the positivists engaged in heated, bitter, and prolonged dispute. The outcome of this dispute—the precise contours of which varied from one country to another—had telling practical significance for bases of criminal responsibility, objectives of punishment, and preferred styles of punishment. In short, the intractable differences between classical and positivist criminologies, far from being confined to an academic arena, caused practical penal dilemmas whose resolution entailed a series of compromises agreed upon by the major institutions of criminal justice.

The serious implications of the conflict between the classicists and the positivists was best understood by French magistrate and criminologist Gabriel Tarde. In his book _Penal Philosophy_, Tarde (1890:Chs. 1–2) took issue with the sterile debate between the classicists and the positivists over the respective merits of free will and determinism. Neither doctrine, he argued, was justified either theoretically or practically. The doctrine of free will held that the individual, uninfluenced by any external factors, chose to do one thing rather than another with complete freedom and foresight. This was clearly absurd, Tarde indicated, given the obvious truth of the positivist insight that crime varied according to such factors as gender, age, and socioeconomic position. The doctrine of determinism had arisen, Tarde continued, largely as a reaction to the exaggerated free-willed individualism of the classicists. Determinism viewed the individual as a machine incapable of free choice. But Tarde replied that quite apart from such factors as gender, age, and socioeconomic position, individuals were authentic beings who somehow were the "authors" of their actions. Tarde therefore concluded that neither doctrine was adequate as a basis for a coherent system of penal responsibility.

Tarde attacked certain effects classicism had on the style of criminal justice. First, he denied that free will as such should be the basis of criminal responsibility. Individuals should be held _accountable_ for their actions whether or not they exercise free will. Every individual, Tarde asserted, has unique psychological, social, and familial characteristics. Therefore, the basis of criminal liability, and the relation between liability and punishment, should be a combination of the social harm caused by accountable offenders and the offenders' unique personal

characteristics. Second, Tarde objected to many classical legal reforms as impractical. If individuals had unique characteristics, they should not be subjected to
uniformity of treatment by the criminal justice system. Legal distinctions should
be made, for example, between men and women, children and adults, violent
offenders and property offenders, first-time offenders and habitual criminals,
and the sane and the insane.

Tarde also attacked the positivists, chiefly because their determinism greatly
contributed to the ineffectiveness of the criminal justice system. If the positivists'
concept of the criminal was accepted as the basis of criminal law, Tarde believed,
only two unacceptable strategies would be available for dealing with criminals:
either complete forgiveness of a crime or extermination of the criminal. Clearly,
if the actions of criminals were "caused" by factors outside their control, rehabilitation was not a practical possibility—certainly not in the case of "born criminals." The influence of determinism was found in the increasing laxity shown
criminals by prosecutors, judges, and juries. Such laxity was apparent in the
judicial tendency to reduce criminal charges from felonies to misdemeanors
which, Tarde (1886a:63–71) argued, artificially reduced the crime rate and, in
its turn, caused more than a threefold increase in the number of misdemeanors.

The key dilemma facing judges, legislators, and the criminal justice system,
then, was this: How can justice be administered on a coherent and systematic
basis? How can the partial truths of classicism and positivism be recognized
without accepting the most dangerous implications of their respective extremes?

Neoclassical Compromises

The typical response of the criminal justice system to these two critical questions
has been doctrinal and procedural compromise. The compromise—devised
roughly between 1880 and 1920, and led by Tarde and his pupil Raymond
Saleilles (1898)—is known as *neoclassicism*. In effect, neoclassicism has become
the basis of criminal responsibility and punishment in most Western countries.

The exact terms of the neoclassical compromise between classicism and
positivism varied from one country to another (Garland, 1985: Ch.3), but shared
six general features (Beirne, 1993:170–174):

1. The concept of *character* replaced the extremes of free will and
   determinism as the source of criminality. An offender's character was
   open to analysis by experts from the fields of law, medicine, psychiatry,
   probation, criminology, and social work. Because the links between
   character and crime could be influenced by an infinite variety of factors,
   crime therefore should be understood through multicausal (multifactorial)
   analysis.

2. There should be an *equivalence* between the seriousness of crime and the
   degree of punishment pronounced. Punishment should be exemplary but
   not vengeful.

3. *Imprisonment* must be the normal method of punishment, and a variety of penitentiary systems should be employed. The criminally insane and the recidivists should be segregated from other prisoners. There should be increased use of visitation and probation.

4. The treatment of the criminal character should not be uniform but *individualized*. Specific treatment, both in prison and during post-release programs, should be administered to offenders according to the nature and the degree of an individual's incorrigibility of character.

5. Every punishment should include a measure of *deterrence* for future miscreants. Deterrence is unworkable only for the insane.

6. The *death penalty* should be abolished for nearly all crimes.

10.6 ———— ASSESSMENT: CLASSICISM AND POSITIVISM TODAY

Classicism and positivism were the two great systems of early criminological theory. Each was based on a fundamentally different view of human action (free will, or "free" will determined by psychology v. determinism). Each identified a different object of analysis for criminology (crime v. the criminal). Each provided a different focus on punishment: one demanded punishment fit the social harm caused by crime (classical criminology), the other demanded punishment fit the criminal (positivist criminology).

As the remaining chapters of Part Three argue, the intellectual history of modern criminology is largely one of positivism's triumph over classicism. So thoroughgoing has been this triumph that even neoclassical criminology—which emerged as a compromise solution to the extremes of both classicism and positivism—has developed in positivist terms. With few exceptions (see Chapters 13.3, 14.3), the several variants of positivism have dominated the thinking of most criminologists regarding crime and crime policies. Most criminological theory is modeled on the positivist methods of the natural sciences. Thus, criminal behavior tends to be viewed rather like the behavior of billiard balls (they move, predictably, according to certain laws of motion): the subject of criminology—the criminal—behaves according to certain sociological, historical, psychological, or economic laws. The vast majority of crime policies, likewise, are based on the assumption that given changes in the sociological, historical, psychological, and economic causes that propel an individual into crime, individuals can be redirected toward lawful behavior. The appeal of positivism in criminology is overwhelming. Moreover, disregarding such anti-intellectual claims as "individuals commit crimes *only* because they enjoy doing so, and because of no other reason," it is impossible to deny positivism's enormous explanatory powers.

But there have been mounting signs, in the last decade or so, that the fortresses of criminological positivism are not impregnable. Put simply, if positivist criminology has accurately identified the causes of crime, why do state anticrime policies repeatedly fail? Reflecting the pessimism that seems the obvious answer to this question—they fail because we have failed to grasp the true causes of crime—criminologist James Q. Wilson (1985:51) has gone so far as to suggest we should perhaps abandon altogether the search for the causes of crime. As policymakers, he reasons, all that criminologists can do today is devise anticrime policies that assume potential criminals are rational actors who weigh the costs and benefits of engaging in crime. Wilson therefore asks us to return to the rational calculus of classical criminology. Let us devise policies that deter free-willed actors from committing crimes. In arguing for a return to the principles of classicism on the practical grounds of policy making, Wilson writes that

> [t]he criminologist assumes, probably rightly, that the causes of crime are determined by attitudes that in turn are socially derived, if not determined; the policy analyst is led to assume that the criminal acts *as if* crime were the product of a free choice among competing opportunities and constraints. The radical individualism of Bentham and Beccaria may be scientifically questionable but prudentially necessary.

Wilson's plea for prudent use of the classical criminology of Bentham and Beccaria returns us to the beginning of this chapter. Although no modern criminological research adopts the pure model of free-willed classicism, many studies have recently appeared that focus on the deterrent effect of punishment. Although we cannot explore the complicated issues associated with deterrence in this book, we note the significant influence of classical deterrence in current research on topics as diverse as the killing of police officers (Bailey and Peterson, 1987), drinking and driving (Ross, 1982), and gun ownership (Green, 1987). We conclude by noting further that not one of the studies found sufficient evidence to support the view that specific legislation deters criminal behavior.

REVIEW

This chapter introduced the earliest theories of modern criminology, each of which has had a great impact on the subsequent development of criminological theory. Each theory defines certain of the ways in which criminologists understand crime today.

Classical Criminology

1. Classicism was the first form of modern criminology. It began as part of the Enlightenment's opposition to barbarism and arbitrariness in the criminal justice system.

2. The first text of classical criminology, Beccaria's *Of Crimes and Punishments* (1764), was extremely influential on penal practice and quite conservative in its basic intentions.

3. The principles of utilitarianism were developed by Bentham. His views on punishment and imprisonment were widely accepted in theory if not always in practice. Bentham is best remembered for his "model" prison, the Panopticon.

The Emergence of Positivist Criminology

1. Positivist criminology began in France in the 1820s as a response to a "breakdown" in the classical system of penality, chiefly evident in the failure of the new systems of incarceration to regulate the conduct of the "dangerous classes."

2. The most influential form of early positivism was Quetelet's social mechanics of crime, which derived from the convergence of the concerns of criminal justice, astronomy, and statistics.

3. Quetelet's criminology employed natural science methods to identify the constancy of crime rates, criminal propensities, and the causes of crime.

4. Although his criminology was in some respects far in advance of his time, Quetelet ultimately believed that crime had biological causes.

Criminal Anthropology: Lombroso's "Born Criminal"

1. In 1876, Lombroso popularized the concept of the born criminal in his book *Criminal Man*. This biological concept radically opposed the free-willed individual of classicism.

2. Lombroso believed that born criminals have atavistic features that distinguish them from the law-abiding citizenry.

3. The crusade against Lombrosianism was led by Tarde, whose critical endeavors in the 1880s and 1890s caused a decline in the influence of Lombrosianism throughout much of Europe.

Heredity vs. Environment: Goring's *The English Convict* (1913)

1. Goring's *The English Convict* (1913) is often viewed as the definitive refutation of Lombrosianism. The book was Goring's attempt to disentangle the respective influences of heredity and social environment on the activities of criminals.

2. The major traditions that influenced Goring's work were English prison research, the statistical movement, and the eugenics movement. These influences were crystallized in Goring's analysis of his data on English convicts at the Biometric Laboratory in London.

3. Goring's analysis of the physical features of English convicts, and his comparisons between them and control samples of nonconvict populations, led him to reject decisively Lombroso's concept of born criminality.

4. Through assumptions derived from eugenics, Goring also found that English criminals engaged in crime because of alleged mental deficiencies

rather than for sociological reasons. This was, of course, quite compatible with Lombrosianism.

Neoclassical Criminology

1. By the 1890s it was clear that a serious dilemma faced the machinery of criminal justice. Conflict between the classical and the positivist schools created a dangerous vacuum in penal policies.

2. The neoclassical school of criminology attempted to fill this vacuum with a coherent system of criminal responsibility based on accountability, individualization of punishment, and treatment programs.

3. Neoclassical criminology was led by Tarde and Saleilles. Although the exact terms of the compromise between classicism and positivism varied from one country to another, today its general outlines remain the dominant features of most Western systems of criminal justice.

QUESTIONS FOR CLASS DISCUSSION

Refer again to the grisly execution of Jean Calas in France in 1762, recounted at the beginning of this chapter. Less than a century later in the 1830s, a very different penal style is visible in rules for the House of Young Prisoners in Paris, among which are the following (cited in Foucault, 1979:6–7):

Art[icle] 17. The prisoners' day will begin at six in the morning in winter and at five in summer. They will work for nine hours a day throughout the year. Two hours a day will be devoted to instruction. Work and the day will end at nine o'clock in winter and at eight in summer.

Art. 18. Rising. At the first drum-roll, the prisoners must rise and dress in silence, as the supervisor opens the cell doors. At the second drum-roll, they must be dressed and make their beds. At the third, they must line up and proceed to the chapel for morning prayer. There is a five-minute interval between each drum-roll.

Art. 19. The prayers are conducted by the chaplain and followed by a moral or religious reading. This exercise must not last more than half an hour.

Art. 20. Work. At a quarter to six in the summer, a quarter to seven in winter, the prisoners go down to the courtyard where they must wash their hands and faces, and receive their first ration of bread. Immediately afterwards, they form into work-teams and go off to work, which must begin at six in summer and seven in winter.

Art. 21. Meal. At ten o'clock the prisoners leave their work and go to the refectory; they wash their hands in their courtyards and assemble in divisions. After the dinner, there is recreation until twenty minutes to eleven.

Art. 22. School. At twenty minutes to eleven, at the drum-roll, the prisoners form into ranks, and proceed in divisions to the school. The class lasts two hours and consists alternately of reading, writing, drawing and arithmetic.

Art. 23. At twenty minutes to one, the prisoners leave the school, in divisions, and return to their courtyards for recreation. At five minutes to one, at the drum-roll, they form into work-teams. . . .

Art. 28. At half-past seven in summer, half-past eight in winter, the prisoners must be back in their cells after the washing of hands and the inspection of clothes in the courtyard; at the first drum-roll, they must undress, and at the second get into bed. The cell doors are closed and the supervisors go the rounds in the corridors, to ensure order and silence.

1. Describe the major differences between the two styles of punishment characterized respectively by the execution of Calas (in 1762) and by the rules for the House of Young Prisoners in Paris (*circa* 1837).

2. This transformation of penal styles largely reflects changing theories on the causes of crime. Describe the broad transformation in such theories between the Enlightenment and Goring's *The English Convict* (1913).

3. Is one penal style more "humane" than the other?

4. What do these different penal styles imply about the possibility of the treatment and correction of criminals?

RECOMMENDED READINGS

Beirne, Piers (1993). *Inventing Criminology.* Albany, NY: SUNY Press. A history of concept formation in criminology from 1764 to 1914. Questions the very existence of classical criminology.

Garland, David (1985). *Punishment and Welfare: A History of Penal Strategies.* Aldershot: Gower. Although a difficult book for undergraduate students, its analysis of British criminology between 1870 and 1914 is the finest of its kind.

Hart, H. L. A. (1982). *Essays on Bentham: Jurisprudence and Political Theory.* New York: Oxford University Press. An overview of Bentham's theory of law and political obligation.

Jenkins, Philip (1984). "Varieties of Enlightenment Criminology." *British Journal of Criminology,* 24(2):112–130. Discusses the respective criminologies of Beccaria, anarchist William Godwin, and the Marquis de Sade. Jenkins argues that criminological theories are successful not because they are necessarily "correct" but because they have political influence unavailable to their competitors.

Klein, Dorie (1973). "The Etiology of Female Crime: A Review of the Literature." *Issues in Criminology*, 8(2):3–30. Criticizes the concept of female criminality typically held by criminologists from Lombroso onward.

Nye, Robert A. (1984). *Crime, Madness, and Politics in Modern France*. Princeton: Princeton University Press. The first four chapters dissect the development of positivism in France; the links among criminal law, medicine, and concepts of justice; and the 19th-century debate on whether criminality is a product of heredity or social environment.

CHAPTER 11

THE EMERGENCE OF SOCIOLOGICAL CRIMINOLOGY

11.1   Toward a Social Psychology of Crime: Gabriel Tarde
Criticisms of Social Mechanics
Imitation and Crime
Collective Behavior and Crime
Assessment

11.2   Toward a Sociology of Law and Crime: Émile Durkheim
Law and Social Solidarity
The Nature of Crime
Anomie, Egoism, and Crime
The Evolution of Punishment
Assessment

11.3   Classical Marxism: Marx and Engels on State, Law, and Crime
Key Concepts of Marxism
State and Law
Crime and Capitalism
Criminalization as a Violation of Rights
Crime and Demoralization
Crime and Primitive Rebellion
Crime and Communism
Assessment

Preview

Chapter 11 introduces:

☞ the major strands in the emergence of sociological criminology:
social psychology, sociology, and classical Marxism.

☞ the criminological theories of Gabriel Tarde, Émile Durkheim, Karl Marx, and Friedrich Engels.

Key Terms

anomie	mode of production
communism	repressive and restitutive law
ideology	social classes
imitation	social solidarity

11.1 ——— TOWARD A SOCIAL PSYCHOLOGY OF CRIME: GABRIEL TARDE

In Chapter 10 we learned that French criminologist Gabriel Tarde believed, like public opinion, that rising rates of recidivism were one of the most serious aspects of criminality. However, unlike public opinion, Tarde thought these rates could not be explained by the habitual criminality of Lombroso's born criminals (see Chapter 10.3). Attempting to devise a social theory of crime that would explain more about the incidence and causes of criminality than did born criminals, Tarde began by criticizing the leading alternative to Lombrosianism—Quetelet's "social mechanics."

Gabriel Tarde (1843–1904).

Criticisms of Social Mechanics

Tarde regarded Quetelet's uncritical worship of the scientific method as a great barrier to the proper analysis of crime. First, he suggested it was simplistic to believe that a multitude of free wills culminated in a constant and predictable crime rate. A better explanation of statistical constancy, Tarde (1890a:299) claimed, was that people regularly imitated each other's behavior. Second, new data in the government's *Compte général* convinced Tarde that crime rates actually were not constant. Like other European nations after the 1840s, France experienced a significant increase in recorded crime—the number of crimes trebled and the number of misdemeanors doubled. Finally, Tarde suggested that Quetelet's theories on the causes of crime also were wrong. Because there were always numerous counterexamples to established "causes" of crime (including poverty, lack of education, and so on), Tarde insisted that Quetelet had not produced a plausible explanation either of rising crime rates or, indeed, of crime itself.

Toward this end, Tarde's starting point was the concept of "imitation."

Imitation and Crime

Tarde reasoned that crime—like all other social phenomena—was influenced by the processes of *imitation*. "Imitation" is a mental process Tarde defined as "the powerful, generally unconscious, always partly mysterious, action by means of which we account for all the phenomena of society" (Tarde, 1890a:322). Imitation applies to the different psychological states and beliefs of individuals. It is a process in which individuals behave as if they were in a trance, as in sleep-walking.

According to Tarde, the process of imitation always operates in a social context. Socially and historically it is present in urbanism and in the growth of cities, in national institutions, and even in international warfare. It cuts across all social, racial, and religious boundaries. It infiltrates all aspects of social life, from art to architecture and from music to militarism. It produces both good and evil. It encourages crime.

Tarde (1890:331–338) argued that crime originates in the "higher ranks" and descends to the "lowest ranks." The masses are typically tied through imitative bondage to the ideas and fancies of their social superiors. Drunkenness, smoking, moral offenses, political assassination, arson, and even vagabondage are, according to Tarde, crimes that originated with the feudal nobility and were transmitted, through imitation, to the masses. Criminal propensities therefore typically travel downward and outward—from the powerful to the powerless, from urban centers to rural areas.

Why, then, despite a common exposure to the same set of imitative processes, do some people commit crimes and others do not? Tarde asserted that individuals are not born into criminality but socialized into it: "Perhaps one is born vicious, but it is quite certain that one *becomes* a criminal" (Tarde, 1890a:256). Thus some people are born with psychological qualities that predispose them to crime.

Those born with vicious dispositions, for example, are more likely to become violent than those born with passive natures. To the presence of predisposing qualities, Tarde adds the necessary component of "a special kind of fever" (*ibid.*:261). This fever he variously described as a fermentation, an agitation, and a disturbance.

Despite his preference for an individualistic or psychological theory of crime, Tarde consistently identified two sociological factors that in practice had causal status in his criminology. First—and far more so than any of his contemporaries—Tarde isolated urbanism as the greatest arena for spread of crime through imitation. He showed that cities have the highest rate of homicide motivated by greed; it is there where murderer and victim are likely to be utter strangers, and where recidivism is most pronounced. Urban life encourages the greatest decadence in customs: the formation of political sects, increasing rates of assassination, murder and suicide, crimes against children and crimes by children, rape, and vandalism. It is in urban life that the psychological states associated with criminal intent are most evident.

For Tarde a second cause of crime is the violence fostered by mass collective behavior. Such violence exemplifies the processes of imitation and is closely tied to the impersonal social relations of modern urban life.

Collective Behavior and Crime

Tarde's analysis of collective behavior reveals a frantic dislike of any body of people larger than a small and orderly gathering. For example, he suggested that (Tarde, 1892:358):

> The crowd, even among the most civilized populations, is always a savage or a faun, still worse, an impulsive and maniacal beast, a plaything of its instincts and unconscious habits, occasionally an animal of a lower order.

On another occasion (Tarde, 1890a:323):

> A *mob* is a strange phenomenon. It is a gathering of heterogeneous elements, unknown to one another; but as soon as a spark of passion, having flashed out from one of these elements, electrifies this confused mass, there takes place a sort of sudden organization, a spontaneous generation. This incoherence becomes cohesion, this noise becomes a voice, and these thousands of men crowded together soon form but a single animal, a wild beast without a name, which marches to its goal with irresistible finality.

Tarde often used such concepts as somnambulism (sleepwalking), paroxysm (a fit), and mental contagion (imitation) to explain the abnormality and the dangerousness of crowds in late 19th-century France. In his writings on collective behavior Tarde tended to equate mob violence with organized activities of the French working class (such as strikes). "The conduct of a crowd," Tarde

(1892:372–373) declared, "largely depends on the social origin of its members, on their profession, class or caste." Moreover, "Urban crowds are those whose contagion achieves the highest degree of speed and intensity . . . their members . . . drawn from those detached from family and tradition" (*ibid.*:373). Appalled by events such as a strike by mill workers in his native region of Périgord, by anarchist uprisings in 1871 (the "Paris Commune"), and by a wave of bombings, Tarde (1893) asserted that the emotional turbulence of crowd behavior was perfectly expressed in the deluded actions of striking workers, rioters, and revolutionary political movements. Such actions Tarde characterized as proletarian, anarchic, irrational, and feminine.

Certain prejudices Tarde shared with sociologist Émile Durkheim. Before considering Durkheim's analysis of crime, we briefly assess Tarde's contribution to the development of criminology.

Assessment

Tarde's criminology was an intriguing attempt to place both the sociological and the psychological dimensions of life into a unitary perspective. In his own era, Tarde's perspective was of enormous influence. More so than any other perspective at the end of the 19th century, Tarde's social psychology of crime was responsible for forging a compromise between the extremes of classical and positivist schools of criminology. His theories on the causes of crime anticipated and influenced later developments in criminology (see Clark, 1969:47; Lukes, 1973:303). Tarde's concept of imitation, and his theories about urban life and crowd behavior, for example, explicitly influenced certain of the most important theoretical developments in criminology in the U.S.—among them the Chicago school of criminology (see Chapter 12.2), Merton's theory of anomie (see Chapter 12.3), Sutherland's theory of differential association (see Chapter 12.4), and subcultural perspectives on delinquency (see Chapter 13).

11.2 ———— TOWARD A SOCIOLOGY OF LAW AND CRIME: ÉMILE DURKHEIM

Émile Durkheim (1858–1917) was one of the founders of sociological criminology, and his analyses of crime and punishment exert a powerful influence in the world of criminology today. Durkheim's writings were a successful attempt to integrate a theory of crime with a theory of law.

Durkheim was born in Lorraine, France. Discarding the Jewish orthodoxy of his family, he enrolled at the École Normale Supérieure in Paris. Later, Durkheim was appointed professor of social science and sociology at Bordeaux University and, eventually, at the Sorbonne in Paris. He was a prodigious scholar whose innovative concepts and arguments spanned a great diversity of topics. The breadth of Durkheim's interests is best seen in the titles of his major books: *The Division of Labor in Society* (1893), *The Rules of Sociological Method* (1894),

Émile Durkheim (1858–1917).

Suicide (1897), *Professional Ethics and Civil Morals* (1900), and *The Elementary Forms of Religious Life* (1912).

Durkheim's writings on law and crime probably have had more intellectual influence on the development of criminology in the United States than any other body of thought. In much of his sociology Durkheim tried to answer the difficult questions about how order and stability could be restored to France as it made the disruptive transition from a preindustrial social structure to modern and more complex forms of social organization in the 19th century: What are the preconditions of an ordered, stable, and moral society? What conditions produce social disorder? A logical consequence of Durkheim's search for the sources of social order was a concern with situations in which order and stability seemed to be lacking and which were manifest in such "pathologies" as crime and deviance.

Before outlining Durkheim's writings on law and crime, we emphasize a theme that spanned his entire work—a sociological method. For Durkheim, societies can be analyzed properly only through the scientific method of positivism. Like Quetelet's social mechanics (see Chapter 10.2), Durkheim's positivism involved a search for law-like regularities in social behavior in the same way that natural scientists seek to generalize about animal behavior and about the motion of inanimate objects. Unlike Tarde, Durkheim insisted that, sociologically, generalizations about social behavior can be made independently of individual variations in free will, psychological state, and motivation. Indeed, much of Durkheim's (1894:50–84) book *The Rules of Sociological Method* is a polemical attack on the view that individuals and their beliefs and values are at the center of social life.

Durkheim's positivist method stemmed from his insistence that "[t]he first and most basic rule is *to consider social facts as things" (ibid.*:60). Durkheim's chief intention here was to distinguish sociology from such other sciences as biology, politics, and psychology by making the "social fact" its object of study. But for Durkheim social facts are not to be confused with the psychic phenomena that exist only in individual consciousness; in reality, although we are often victims of the illusion that we act with free will, our actions are usually imposed on us externally. Durkheim (*ibid.*:52) defined social facts as "manners of acting, thinking and feeling external to the individual, which are invested with a coercive power by virtue of which they exercise control over him." Social facts are thus obligatory and coercive. They have this character not because they are practiced by many people but because they are practiced collectively. "Social phenomena," Durkheim (*ibid.*:70) wrote, should thus "be considered in themselves, detached from the conscious beings who form their own mental representations of them."

For Durkheim, in other words, social phenomena (such as law and crime) have an objective existence of their own and exist quite independently of the individuals who experience them. This is a crucial insight, as we shall learn.

Law and Social Solidarity

Durkheim analyzed law in many of his writings, but his most extended treatment occurs in *The Division of Labor* (1893). Here Durkheim tried to find the sources of social order ("social solidarity") in modern industrial societies and to determine the changes they undergo during evolution from lower to higher stages of civilization.

Durkheim's starting point was that social development lies along a continuum, with primitive societies of "mechanical solidarity" at one end and modern societies of "organic solidarity" at the other. *Mechanical solidarity* is typical of simple societies with only a limited role specialization or division of labor. Members of such societies are quite similar to each other in their ways of acting, thinking, and feeling. They live within a shared consensus of beliefs and values— the "collective conscience"—in which collective life dominates and replaces individualism. During the course of social evolution, as roles within the division of labor became more specialized, social solidarity is transformed from a mechanical to an organic basis. *Organic solidarity* is thus typical of societies with an advanced division of labor and whose members have diffuse ways of acting, thinking, and feeling—in which individualism dominates and replaces collective life. The cohesion of such societies derives from complex patterns of interdependence among the members based on the morals of different occupational categories and also on increasing respect for individual differences.

In his search for the sources of social order, Durkheim realized that social solidarity, which is abstract and internal to consciousness, does not lend itself to exact observation or precise measurement. Thus, to classify and compare the different forms of social solidarity he believed it necessary to use another, more visible aspect of social life that varies directly with solidarity. Durkheim (1893:24) argued that "[t]o arrive at this classification, as well as this comparison, we must therefore substitute for this internal datum, which escapes us, an external one which symbolizes it, and then study the former through the latter." That visible symbol, he asserted, is law. Durkheim (*ibid.*:25) continued:

> Social life, wherever it becomes lasting, inevitably tends to assume a definite form and become organized. Law is nothing more than this organization in its most stable and precise form. Life in general within a society cannot enlarge in scope without legal activity simultaneously increasing in proportion. Thus we may be sure to find reflected in the law all the essential varieties of social solidarity.

Durkheim never explicitly defined the essential qualities of law. But he implied that it differs from other forms of social regulation (including custom, ritual, ceremony, and professional obligation) because it alone exercises an organized pressure on individuals to conform to its commands. This pressure appears in the form of *sanctions*. To classify the different types of law, which themselves correspond to the different types of social solidarity, Durkheim reasoned that one must only classify different types of sanctions. Two forms of legal sanction correspond to the two forms of social solidarity: repressive sanctions and restitutive sanctions, which Durkheim termed respectively "repressive law" and "restitutive law."

Durkheim held that *repressive law* is chiefly associated with societies of mechanical solidarity. It is religious in origin, and largely identical with penal and criminal law. The violation of repressive law ushers in the use of repressive sanctions. These sanctions consist in inflicting suffering or loss on individuals for having offended the strong sentiments of the collective conscience. Because repressive sanctions tend to be enforced by the whole of society, no special or organized institution (lawyers, courts, police, and so forth) is needed to enforce them. Durkheim provided numerous examples to show that the vast majority of the commands of ancient legal systems—such as the last four books of the Pentateuch (*Exodus, Leviticus, Numbers,* and *Deuteronomy*), the laws of Manou, the Ten Commandments, and the Twelve Tables of ancient Rome—are solely directed to sentiments offended by crimes.

During the evolution from mechanical to organic solidarity, Durkheim argued, the volume of penal law in legal systems declines relative to other forms of law. He noted that certain crimes, such as those offending sexual and traditional sentiments, have almost disappeared (*ibid.*:109–110). With the evolutionary decline of collective sentiments and the growth of individualism, repressive law is gradually ousted by *restitutive law*. This law consists not in the infliction of pain but in "*restoring the previous state of affairs*, reestablishing relationships . . . disturbed from their normal form" (*ibid.*:29). Restitutive law, growing continually in volume and intensity, results not from breaches of the collective conscience but from conflicts among different occupational groups (for example, guilds, unions, and professional associations) in the division of labor. Its violation involves enforcement of the *status quo ante* (previously existing state of affairs). Moreover, in contrast to repressive law, restitutive law is specialized through its two basic forms (Durkheim, 1893:154–171). *Positive law* reflects the cooperation required in a complex division of labor, and includes contract, administrative, domestic, and commercial legislation. *Negative law* involves the rules between persons and objects that enjoin others not to interfere in certain proprietary rights of the owner, and includes property and tort legislation.

The Nature of Crime

Durkheim's analysis of relationships between law and sanctions was a critical tool for understanding social solidarity. In pursuing the latter goal he was led to analyze the nature of crime. As a sociologist, Durkheim rejected definitions of crime based on legalistic criteria. Such criteria—as well as crime based on criteria such as evil, social harm, violations of justice, and so forth—he regarded as inadequate for the scientific purposes of sociological investigation.

What, then, is crime? To begin, no action is intrinsically or universally criminal. For Durkheim, the common denominator of all crimes is that they are "acts repressed by prescribed punishments" (1893:31). This is what distinguishes a crime from a minor offense such as a tort or a breach of etiquette. In societies of mechanical solidarity an act is defined as criminal because of the universal social reaction that condemns it. As Durkheim (1893:39–40) argued in *The Division of Labor:*

> An act is criminal when it offends the strong, well-defined states of the collective consciousness. . . . [W]e should not say that an act offends the common consciousness because it is criminal, but that it is criminal because it offends that consciousness.

From this it seemed to follow that to investigate the nature of crime one must examine the nature of punishment.

What functions, then, does punishment serve? Central to Durkheim's criminology is his linking of crime and punishment. Thus: "If our definition of crime is exact it must account for all the characteristics of . . . punishment" (*ibid.*:44). Durkheim (*ibid.*:52) defined punishment as "a reaction of passionate feeling, graduated in intensity, which society exerts through the mediation of an organized body over those of its members who have violated certain rules of conduct."

Durkheim rejected popular beliefs that the function of punishment is simply revenge, deterrence, or the reformation of the character of criminals. The true function of punishment is to maintain and strengthen social solidarity. Each time a crime is committed, the subsequent condemnation of it by penal law reaffirms the values of the collective conscience or the shared consensus of a community's beliefs and values. In this way "honest people" are convinced of the moral righteousness of their conformity to law and of the "inferiority" of criminals. With great insight, Durkheim (1893:63) therefore concluded that "punishment is above all intended to have its effect upon honest people."

Durkheim made three specific claims about the nature of crime: (a) crime is normal, (b) crime is inevitable, and (c) crime is useful.

Crime Is Normal   Durkheim caused considerable outrage by claiming that crime is a normal phenomenon, as normal as birth and marriage. Durkheim's (1894:85–107) discussion of this seemingly unusual claim is found in the third chapter ("Rules for the Distinction of the Normal from the Pathological") of his book *The Rules of Sociological Method* in which he tried to restructure "the fundamental facts of criminology." Durkheim's starting point—like the starting point of his sociology in general—was his concept of the "social fact" (Durkheim, 1894:97):

> *A social fact is normal for a given social type, viewed at a given phase of its development, when it occurs in the average society of that species, considered at the corresponding phase of its evolution.*" (emphasis in original)

In other words, in a given social context and against the background of a given level of social development, the very generality of social facts indicates that they must be normal phenomena. At any given moment society has a "normal" or statistically average volume of births, for example, or of marriages and deaths. For Durkheim, it is only statistical deviations from such averages that are abnormal. Because crime is a social fact, Durkheim complained that criminologists err in seeing it only as a pathological or morbid phenomenon. Generally, crime should not be viewed as deviance or as sickness—what is abnormal to the biologist or to the pathologist is not necessarily so to the sociologist.

For Durkheim, then, crime as such is rarely abnormal. Crime occurs in all societies, is closely tied to the facts of collective life, and its volume tends to increase as societies evolve from lower to higher phases. However, Durkheim was careful to add that although crime is a normal social fact, in a given context its rate might be abnormal.

Crime Is Inevitable   To begin with, Durkheim admitted that his idea about the normality of crime surprised and upset him. Eventually, he reasoned that no society can ever be entirely rid of crime. To illustrate this point, Durkheim (1894:100) asked that we imagine a community of saints in a perfect and exemplary monastery:

> [I]n it crime as such will be unknown, but faults that appear venial to the ordinary person will arouse the same scandal as does normal crime in ordinary consciences.

Moreover, universal and absolute conformity to rules is impossible because each member of society faces variation in "the immediate physical environment . . . hereditary antecedents . . . [and] social influences" (*ibid.*:100). Crime is therefore inevitable. Even if all the actions regarded as criminal at one moment suddenly disappeared, new forms of crime would at once be invented. For example, if increasing public sentiment against a particular sort of crime (for example, theft) declines, public reaction to and condemnation of lesser actions of the same sort (such as mere misappropriation) intensify accordingly. "Nothing is good indefinitely and without limits" (*ibid.*:101).

Crime Is Useful   Durkheim first claimed that crime is normal and inevitable in *The Division of Labor*. But in *The Rules* he took the argument a stage further (1894:98) in suggesting that

> to classify crime among the phenomena of normal sociology is not merely to declare that it is an inevitable though regrettable phenomenon arising from the incorrigible weakness of man; it is to assert that it is a factor in public health, an integrative element in any healthy society.

In addition, then, to claiming that crime is normal and inevitable, Durkheim argued that crime is useful to society. This is so, he reasoned, because crime is indispensable to the normal evolution of law and morality. Indeed, if crime is not a sickness then punishment cannot be its remedy. The nature of crime and punishment must therefore lie somewhere else than in the area of wrongdoing and its correction. If there were no crimes—if there was no deviation from social norms—Durkheim reasoned, this could only happen if the collective conscience had reached an intensity, an authoritarianism, unparalleled in history. In other words, a society with "no crime" must be an extremely repressive one.

For Durkheim, crime is useful because often it is a symptom of individual originality and a preparation for changes in law and morality. Durkheim cited the fate of Socrates as an example of crime's utility. Socrates (470–399 B.C.), perhaps the most original of all Greek philosophers, committed the "crime" of independent thought. Having been charged with not believing in the official gods of the Athenian state and with corrupting the minds of the young, Socrates committed suicide by drinking hemlock. Durkheim (*ibid.*:102) suggested that "Socrates' crime served to prepare the way for a new morality and a new faith— one the Athenians . . . needed [inasmuch as] the traditions by which they had hitherto lived no longer corresponded to the conditions of their existence." Today's criminal may be tomorrow's philosopher!

Anomie, Egoism, and Crime

Durkheim applied his sociological insights to the analysis of two specific forms of deviance—suicide and homicide. First, he tried to show that suicide—usually regarded as the supreme act of individual deviance—has profoundly sociological rather than psychological or biological causes. Indeed, Durkheim (1897:299) claimed that variations in suicide rates can *only* be explained sociologically. His general concern was to show that the suicide rate of any society depended on the type and extent of social organization and integration. In any society each social group (*ibid.*:299–300) really has a collective inclination for the act, quite its own, and the source of all individual inclination, rather than their result. It is made up of the currents of egoism, altruism or anomy running through the society under consideration. . . . These tendencies of the whole social body, by affecting individuals, cause them to commit suicide.

Durkheim's explanation of varying suicide rates is structured around four distinct (although in practice often overlapping) types of suicide:

▲__ *Egoistic suicide (ibid.*:152–216) results from a weakening of the bonds between an individual and society. It is a special type of suicide caused by excessive individualism. Its incidence recedes only with the sort of increase in collective sentiments produced by wars and political crises. Social groups prone to egoistic suicide include Protestants (whose religious beliefs foster individualism), the unmarried, the childless, and the widowed.

▲__ *Altruistic suicide (ibid.*:217–240) results when individuals have insufficient inner strength to resist the demands of a social group into which they are overly integrated. Durkheim's examples of altruistic suicide include Hindu widows, who place themselves next to their husbands on their funeral pyre, and slaves, who are expected to die with their masters.

▲__ *Anomic suicide (ibid.*:241–276) results from a sudden crisis in economic or familial life. Thus, in situations such as sudden impoverishment or unexpected riches, or immediately after family members are divorced, there is an abrupt change in expectations that causes massive personal or social upheaval. In the aftermath of these situations, those who cannot adjust to their suddenly altered position become more suicide-prone (and see Chapter 12.3).

▲__ *Individualized suicide (ibid.*:277–294) presents certain individualized characteristics, either in mental state or in the way it is achieved. Durkheim's predisposing mental states include melancholy, passion, and irritation. But he insisted that, in their turn, these might also have social causes.

Second, Durkheim (1900) analyzed the offense of homicide, wherein he suggested that civilized peoples always consider three broad moral attitudes as duties—respect for life, property, and the honor of others. In primitive societies homicide is the most serious breach of moral duty because it is viewed as an offense against the whole of society—an offense against what is sacred. Offenses against individual property or individual honor are considered far less serious than offenses against the social order as a whole—and sometimes they are not considered offenses at all. In ancient Greece, Rome, and Judea, for example, victims of crimes other than homicide had to pursue their own redress, and could allow the guilty party to pay a sum of money as a form of satisfaction. Durkheim suggested that during social evolution, and especially with the onset of Christianity, something of a reversal occurs in the hierarchical order of these duties. With the growth of modern societies, collective sentiments generally are reduced in intensity, the sentiments centering on the individual achieving prominence. Homicide therefore remains the supremely forbidden act because it violates the individual. Given that homicide is so abhorred, Durkheim (1900:112–115) claimed that homicide rates tend to decline relative to the advance of civilization. At the same time, rates of other offenses against the individual, whether against person or property, tend to increase.

Durkheim was confident that homicide rates decreased with modernization because of the growth of individualism (namely, the great respect afforded the person by public opinion). But Durkheim (1900:114) knew that this explanation was too general:

> The decline in the rate of homicide at the present day has not come about because respect for the human person acts as a brake on the motives for murder or on the stimulants to murder, but because these motives and these stimulants grow fewer in number and have less intensity (*ibid.*:117).

How then does one explain cases in which the general rule about declining homicide rates does not apply? To explain counterexamples, Durkheim introduced statistical evidence showing how other variables influence homicide rates. In any given society these other variables include rural/urban differences, wars, religious membership, political crises, and state power. For example, Durkheim (1900:118–119) argued that Catholic countries (such as Italy, Spain, and Hungary) tend to have higher homicide rates than Protestant countries because the latters' religious beliefs are more individualistic and, therefore, promote greater respect for the sanctity of individual life.

The Evolution of Punishment

In his important essay "Two Laws of Penal Evolution," Durkheim (1901) offered a sophisticated theory of the history of punishment, returning him squarely to his earlier concern with law and crime in *The Division of Labor*. This final theory on the sources of punishment, and of changes in its justifications and forms, was a marked improvement on earlier analyses (Hunt, 1978:79–85). Indeed, in his entire criminology it was only here that Durkheim considered that *political* factors sometimes influence the way in which certain behavior is defined as criminal.

In the essay, Durkheim modified his earlier argument to suggest that forms of punishment have varied historically in two ways, quantitatively and qualitatively. Each form is governed by a separate law, and Durkheim (1901:102) formulated the first as follows:

> **Law 1:** *The intensity of punishment is greater the more closely societies approximate to a less developed type—and the more the central power assumes an absolute character.*

Durkheim's first law contains two propositions. The first concerns the concept of "development": societies are more or less advanced according to their level of social complexity, or the intensity of their division of labor. Here Durkheim repeats his argument that less developed societies are dominated by repressive laws and barbaric forms of punishment, especially capital punishment. In such societies punishment is severe because most crimes are seen as religious violations that threaten the collective conscience. The second proposition concerns absolutist forms of political power: the exercise of governmental power without checks and balances. This authoritarian form of power (hypercentralization) exists in different types of society, early and modern, but occurs only when it is seen as a *right*. "Such was the state of the criminal law until the middle of the eighteenth century. There then occurred, throughout Europe, the protest to which Beccaria gave his name" (Durkheim, 1901:113).

Durkheim's first law proceeds to argue that with social development the severity of punishment generally declines. This occurs not because authorities become more lenient but because there is a change in the type of crime. In less developed societies crime is seen as a threat to collective life and, therefore, punishment is severe; in more developed societies crime is seen as a threat to individuals only, and punishment is correspondingly less. However, by identifying the importance of the relationship between state power and punishment, Durkheim can now explain certain factual counterexamples to his earlier analysis. For example, he claims, interestingly, that in societies dominated by political absolutism, crimes retain a primarily sacrilegious character (*ibid.*:120–129). In other words, for Durkheim, authoritarian societies act punitively and repressively not because they are not socially developed but because their organs of political power regard crime religiously—as an attack on the social order as a whole.

Durkheim's second law refers to qualitative changes in punishment (*ibid.*:114):

> **Law 2:** *Deprivations of liberty, and of liberty alone, varying in time according to the seriousness of the crime, tend to become more and more the normal means of social control.*

Durkheim illustrated the workings of the second law with several examples taken from ancient Greece and modern France. He established that the death penalty had disappeared completely from some legal codes and that "virtually the whole field of punishment is now found to consist in the suppression of liberty for limited periods of time or for life" (*ibid.*:116). Durkheim explained this change by arguing that there is no need for incarceration in less developed societies. There a crime affects the entire community and, because responsibility for it is communal, all members of the community ensure that the offender does not escape before trial. However, with the disintegration of ancient societies—after which crime became more of an offense against an individual rather than society as a whole—some method of pretrial detention was needed to ensure that offenders were held accountable.

Thus, Durkheim advanced the brilliant argument that the prison emerged from changing *forms* of crime. However, Durkheim realized this explanation was incomplete. "To explain an institution, it is not enough to establish that when it appeared it served some useful end; for just because it was desirable it does not follow that it was possible" (Durkheim, 1901:117). So, Durkheim proceeded to explain the growth of the prison in terms of his first law concerning the less repressive nature of punishment. Prisons arose because of the transformation in criminal responsibility from a collective to an individual basis. Some of the first prisons were "hole[s], in the form of a pit where the condemned wallow in refuse and vermin" (*ibid.*:119). But prisons gradually became milder in nature, reflecting the general decline in the severity of punishment. Imprisonment—responding to the changed basis of criminal responsibility—became milder and the typical form of punishment in developed societies for the reasons that punishment as a whole became less severe and that a vacuum had been left by the abolition of severe forms of punishment.

Durkheim (*ibid.*:120) therefore concluded that "[t]he qualitative changes in punishment are in part dependent on the simultaneous quantitative changes it undergoes." His two laws of penal evolution thus turn out to be interdependent. The same circumstances that bring about changes in the bases of criminal responsibility in early societies also create the apparent need for widespread use of imprisonment in modern societies!

Assessment

Quite aside from the power and scope of its analysis of crime, Durkheim's criminology has exerted tremendous influence on the subsequent development of sociological criminology. This influence has been most obvious in the writings of the Chicago school of criminology (see Chapter 12.2), Merton's theory of anomie and social structure (see Chapter 12.3) and Hirschi's theory of control and crime (see Chapter 14.1). Moreover, contemporary criminologists continue to draw on Durkheim's insights.

Durkheim's continuing influence derives from two crucial features of his criminology. First, more than anyone before him, Durkheim identified the sociological links among crime, law, punishment, and social organization. He showed that in any given society the amount and the types of crime directly relate to the basic ways in which that society is organized. Societies, Durkheim insisted, should be understood historically. Second, Durkheim suggested that crime must be explained sociologically rather than in terms of an individual's psychological state or biological nature. Sociologically, crime is a normal and inevitable feature of social organization. Its functions lie not only in the area of sanctions but also in the creation and enforcement of solidarity.

Criticisms of Durkheim's criminology tend to focus on two questions. First: Did Durkheim correctly describe the historical transformation in styles of punishment? Second: How did Durkheim's own personal and political agenda influence the propositions set forth in his various theories?

The first question has been debated largely in terms of whether or not the facts of the evolution of punishment fit Durkheim's theory of crime. For example, in a well-known study that examined legal evolution in 51 societies, Schwartz and Miller (1964; see also Garland, 1983:38–40) concluded that simple societies generally are not characterized by the predominance of penal sanctions but, contrary to Durkheim's claim about the evolution of punishment, by restitutive law. Despite such difficulties in using empirical evidence to test Durkheim's theory, it is reasonable to conclude, as do Vold and Bernard (1986:155; and see Foucault, 1977:3–69), that:

> Durkheim may have derived his idea [of the evolution of punishment] from the fact that punishments in European societies were becoming much less severe at the time, due to the reforms introduced by Beccaria and other classical theorists. But the extremely harsh punishments that had been imposed prior to those reforms were not associated with simple, undeveloped societies, but rather with absolute monarchies.

Additionally, Durkheim is frequently criticized for the many biases that allegedly entered his sociological method in general and his criminology in particular. Durkheim has thus been scolded because his preoccupation with the sources of social order apparently led him to neglect the sources and expressions of social conflict. For example, Hunt (1978:91) has complained that Durkheim's general orientation "is marked by a number of important absences or gaps," such as the relationships between law on the one hand, and power, domination, and the state on the other. Such criticism appears somewhat misplaced, however; it seems inappropriate to condemn an author whose interests or emphases merely happen to be different from one's own (Garland, 1983:37–41).

Nonetheless, it is indeed true that Durkheim's criminology is based on certain assumptions: for example, that law tends to stem from and reflect widely held social values, that crime is a breach of shared social values, and that it is not necessary to examine the political factors that influence the definition of certain actions as criminal. Exposure of such assumptions was to some degree an important theme in the views held by Marx and Engels. To their writings we now turn.

11.3 ——— CLASSICAL MARXISM: MARX AND ENGELS ON STATE, LAW, AND CRIME

An introduction to the emergence of sociological criminology would be seriously incomplete without an analysis of the perspectives of the authors of classical Marxism, Karl Marx (1818–1883) and his colleague and friend Friedrich Engels (1820–1895). Before outlining the various claims Marx and Engels made concerning the nature of crime, we consider briefly certain key concepts of their writings.

Karl Marx (1818–1883).

Key Concepts of Marxism

Marxism is a social and political movement in which theory plays a uniquely central role: its theory is the mind of Marxist analysis, and the working class is its heart. Marxism is thus intended as a practical guide to political action. In what follows the term "Marxian" refers to the writings of Marx and Engels themselves and the term "Marxist" to the general body of theory that has developed from Marxian writings.

The development of Marxian theory can be traced to Marx and Engels' initial acceptance, subsequent rejection, and ultimate transcendence of early 19th-century German idealist philosophy. In his very first writings in the 1840s, Marx strongly opposed the idea that history and social change reflect such *idealist* factors as God, the intellect, reason, the spirit, and the progress of civilization. Against idealist concepts of human history, Marx gradually developed a *materialist* concept of historical change. His materialism combined the ideas of English political economists (such as Malthus, Ricardo, Bentham, and Say) and French socialists (including Saint Simon, Lassalle, and Fourier), forging them into a new theory termed "historical materialism." Today, this theory is known as "Marxism."

Marxism is based on the concept that although human beings make their own history, they do not do so entirely as they choose. "The history of all hitherto existing society," Marx and Engels (1848:108) declared in a famous passage from their *Communist Manifesto*, "is the history of class struggles." Class struggles, therefore, are the chief source of historical development. During such struggles social classes actively create and recreate the conditions of their existence. At the same time, the very existence of social classes means that members of a society cannot live exactly as they would choose. Social classes, therefore, also constrain social relationships. Class position is an important determinant of such basic life events as social mobility, consciousness, level and types of education and income, leisure patterns, and (as we see later) the likelihood of incarceration.

What, then, did Marx and Engels understand by the term "social classes"? To grasp this term properly we begin with their concept of *mode of production*, which is carefully analyzed by Marx (1868) in his lengthy book *Capital*. Analytically, the concept of mode of production entails two major elements: the *means of production* and the *social relations of production*.

The element "means of production" refers to specific types of technology, capital, labor, tools, machinery and equipment, monetary system, and land. In combination, these items are the necessary raw materials for producing commodities. And all these materials, combined in different ways, are required to produce commodities as different as bicycles and criminology textbooks. They are subject to almost infinite variety. Commodities such as reading materials, for example, can be produced on stone tablets, papyrus, parchment, biodegradable paper, and computer floppy disks. In addition, commodities can be produced, exchanged, and sold on a small or a large scale and by capital-intensive or labor-intensive means.

The element "social relations of production" refers to the many ways in which members of a society relate both to the possession (legal or otherwise) of the means of production and also to the distribution of the commodities that result from the process of production. For example, the productive process can occur in the institutional context of private or communal relationships; it can occur at home, in fields, or in factories; its participants can be slaves, free laborers, white-collar workers, bankers, landed gentry, industrialists, and state bureaucrats. The productive process can act more or less discriminately along lines of gender. It can be unaffected by or be dominated by political authority or government.

The means of production and the social relations of production, in combination, comprise a *mode of production*. Marx and Engels identified several distinct modes of production in their theory of history—primitive communal, slave, feudal, Asiatic, capitalist, socialist, and communist. Engels usually, but Marx almost never, saw such modes of production as definite stages through which all societies evolved. In other words, several modes of production can exist within one society. For example, until at least the Civil War in the 1860s, slave, feudal, and capitalist modes of production all coexisted in the United States. Again, during the 1920s, feudal, capitalist, and socialist modes of production all coexisted in the Soviet Union. However, in any given society, one mode of production tends to dominate and lend its character to other aspects of social relationships (Marx, 1857–1858:106–107).

Any given society, depending on its dominant mode of production, has typical social classes. Under capitalism, Marx's primary focus, typical classes include the *lumpenproletariat* (the perennially unemployed, those "unfit" for work), the working class (skilled and unskilled workers), the middle class, and the capitalist class (those who own *capital*: industrialists, financiers, commercial speculators, and landlords). In capitalist societies the basic class struggle is between the capitalist class (bourgeoisie) and the working class (proletariat). The economic site of this particular struggle is the productive process; it occurs over the distribution of the fruits of this process. The capitalist class, on the one hand, strives to maximize profit from the unpaid labor of the working class. Its income lies in rent, interest, and industrial profit. The working class, on the other hand, strives to maximize wages. It attempts to do so by reducing the length of the working day, by compelling employers to pay higher wages, and by wresting from the capitalist class such concessions as health insurance, work-safety regulations, and job security. The goals of the capitalist class and the working class are thus mutually exclusive. Typically, the one maximizes its return from the productive process at the expense of the other.

For Marx and Engels, then, social classes are determined chiefly by their economic position within a given mode of production. The relationships among different classes are rarely fixed: they can be extremely fluid, varying according to changes in the political and economic power of one side or another. However, in Marxian analysis the basic source of conflict in capitalist societies is between those who own the means of production and those who have no source of income other than their labor. This exploitive situation is inherently unstable and, Marx and Engels asserted, tends to lead in the direction of socialism. Under socialism the means of production are socialized, and class struggles begin to evaporate.

We note here the great importance of political power to the maintenance, development, or rupture of a mode of production and the class relationships associated with it. Maintenance of class relationships ultimately depends on coercion. Sometimes this coercion is quite naked; usually it is a subtler process. The relationship between economic position and political power—and, indeed, between economic position and many other aspects of social life—Marx often depicted in terms of the metaphorical "base and superstructure." In a famous passage from the preface to his *Contribution to the Critique of Political Economy*, Marx (1859:503–504) described the relationship between economy and politics in the following terms:

> In the social production of their life, men enter into definite relations that are indispensable and independent of their will, relations of production which correspond to a definite stage of development of their material productive forces. The sum total of these relations of production constitutes the economic structure of society, the real foundation, on which rises a legal and political superstructure and to which correspond definite forms of social consciousness. The mode of production of material life conditions the social, political and intellectual life process in general. It

is not the consciousness of men that determines their being, but, on the contrary, their social being that determines their consciousness.

The mode of production thus conditions the life process in general; the mode of production conditions the processes of life by a mechanism Marx and Engels term "ideology." *Ideology* has several meanings in their writings. First, it refers to any set of structured beliefs, values, and ideas. Examples include bourgeois ideology, proletarian ideology, and legal ideology (see Marx and Engels, 1845; Marx, 1868,I:35–83). Bourgeois ideology, for example, refers to beliefs and values typically held by bourgeois (capitalist) classes, such as thriftiness and respect for private property. In capitalist society, the ideas of the capitalist class tend to be the ruling ideas.

Second, ideology was sometimes used to describe a set of mistaken or false beliefs. "Ideology is a process," wrote Engels, "accomplished by the so-called thinker consciously, it is true, but with a false consciousness" (1893:496). Marx often attacked religious beliefs ("the opium of the masses"), not only because he believed they alienated people from each other but also because religious beliefs wrongly assumed the existence of God. In the same context, Marx sometimes contrasted ideology with science: ideology is false belief; science is correct belief.

Finally, and most difficult, the term "ideology" refers to a set of beliefs that both reflect social reality and simultaneously distort it. To help understand this dual process think of a straight stick standing upright in a pool of water. In this situation the image conveys the appearance that the stick is bent. Thus, the image is both a reflection of physical matter (governed by the laws of optics) and a distortion of it (the stick is not actually bent). This final meaning of ideology, then, refers to a process whereby beliefs, deriving from real social relationships, hide or mask the precise nature of such relationships. Certain ideas, such as those associated with justice, fulfill the ideological function of masking from exploited classes the nature of their oppression and its precise source.

This final meaning of ideology was especially important for Marx and Engels' analysis of state and law. In their analysis, a key role in the dominance of bourgeois ideology—hence, in the maintenance of capitalist modes of production—is played by the institutions and doctrines of state and law.

State and Law

By "state," Marx and Engels refer broadly to all central and local organs of political authority and ideological processes that underpin their legitimacy. Marx, for example, refers to "centralized State power, with its ubiquitous organs of standing army, police, bureaucracy, clergy and judicature" (1871:217). Generally, Marx and Engels view the state both as a product of society at a certain level of development and as an institution that seemingly stands above society. However, this apparent ability to stand above society, and represent itself as neutral and independent of class struggles, is in fact an ideological distortion inasmuch as the state, and its various components, actually are manipulated by the dominant class.

The state thus has a *class* character, and Marx and Engels frequently refer to the "class character of the state." In capitalist societies the state is typically a weapon or instrument manipulated by the capitalist classes, though Marx realizes that state activities are not always so straightforward. For example, in one analysis of French politics of the late 1840s and early 1850s, Marx (1852) describes a situation in which the dominant economic class is unable to manipulate the state in its own interests; for a brief period of time the French state represented not the interests of the capitalist class (or even of the working class) but the interests of the millions of smallholding peasants (Marx, 1852:478). In this scenario the state is a prize actively pursued by contestants in the class struggle.

Law is a crucial component of the state apparatus. In class societies law is endowed by Marx and Engels with a number of distinct functions (Cain and Hunt, 1979:144–152). First, law tends, as we have seen, to reflect and promote the interest of the dominant class in private property. It does so by promoting and protecting *all* private property, thereby obscuring the fact that the vast majority of property is owned by only a tiny fraction of the population. Law fulfills this function through constitutions, statutory and case law, and by enforcing compliance with its commandments—supported by agencies of the criminal justice system. Second, law operates as a central mechanism of bourgeois ideology. Through such notions as "justice" and "fair play," law promulgates the idea that it is independent of economic and political interests, and that it can mediate conflicts in the interests of the whole society. But in class societies law cannot do this: to apply law fairly and equally in a society of inequality is merely to perpetuate inequality (Marx, 1843). Legal doctrines such as "the rule of law" and "equality before the law" are thus no more than fictions designed to lull the populace into believing that law truly does stand above society as an impartial arbiter. As Engels (1886:371) put it:

> But once the state has become an independent power *vis-à-vis* society, it produces forthwith a further ideology. It is indeed among professional politicians, theorists of public law and jurists of private law that the connection with economic facts gets lost for fair. Since in each particular case the economic facts must assume the form of juristic motives in order to receive legal sanction; and since, in so doing, consideration of course has to be given to the whole legal system already in operation, the juristic form is, in consequence, made everything and the economic content nothing.

Finally, law acts as an apparatus of repression; it does so when the struggle between classes becomes particularly acute. Typically, this function is activated when the legal system represses the working class and its organized political movements. Marx's (1868) *Capital*, for example, documented how the legal system is manipulated so as to repress working-class political movements—

such as Chartism[1]—or to avoid reforms in working conditions enacted by the Factory Acts.[2]

Against this background we consider Marxian writings on crime.

Crime and Capitalism

Marx and Engels' treatment of crime differed greatly from the approach to crime found in the writings of the Enlightenment and in the literature of classical criminology. Where social contract theory had argued that law is based on a covenant between government and citizens, Marx and Engels suggested that law has an ideological basis. Against the Enlightenment belief in the free-will basis of crime, Marx and Engels opposed the social and determined character of crime. Moreover, in the context of an article attacking capital punishment and praising Quetelet's social mechanics of crime, Marx (1853) argued that both the volume and the types of crime in modern society were produced by the fundamental conditions of *bourgeois* society.

Marx and Engels' sociological analysis of the links between crime and capitalism contained three separate dimensions: criminalization as a violation of natural or human rights, crime and demoralization, and crime and primitive rebellion. Each dimension is quite suggestive, especially so given the widespread acceptance of individualistic explanations of criminality by their contemporaries.

Criminalization as a Violation of Rights

In certain of Marx's writings the process of criminalization was described somewhat moralistically as a violation by the state of some natural or inalienable human rights. Thus, in commenting on a decrease in the official crime rate in Britain between 1855 and 1858, Marx (1859a) complained:

> This apparent decrease of crime, however, since 1854, is to be exclusively attributed to some technical changes in British jurisdiction; to the

---

[1]Chartism (1838–1848), led by several members of Parliament and the London Working Men's Association, began as a movement whose charter demanded various electoral reforms, including universal suffrage (for men!). The Chartist movement quickly grew into a mass rebellion against British capitalism, its demands expanding to the legal recognition of unions and popular control in the workplace and over education. Some of its leaders were eventually transported to British penal colonies.

[2]The Factory Acts (1802–1891) were a series of laws enacted to improve working conditions in factories and mines in Britain. Hailed as model legislation, the Factory Acts were intended to be enforced by a quasi-independent state body, the Factory Inspectorate. However, the Inspectorate was rarely staffed by committed inspectors and enjoyed neither proper funding nor a judiciary sympathetic to its charge of prosecuting "white-collar criminals." The Acts, therefore, were largely symbolic, and helped pave the way to the present situation in which white-collar offenses (for instance, violations of ethical business practices and work-safety regulations) tend to be "accepted as customary, are only rarely subjected to criminal prosecution and, indeed, are often not regarded as really constituting crimes at all" (Carson, 1979:38).

Juvenile Offenders' Act . . . and to the Criminal Justice Act of 1855, which authorizes the Police Magistrates to pass sentences for short periods, with the consent of the prisoners. Violations of the law are generally the offspring of economical agencies beyond the control of the legislator . . . [but] it depends to some degree on official society to stamp certain violations of its rules as crimes or as transgressions only. This difference of nomenclature, so far from being indifferent, decides on the fate of thousands of men, and the moral tone of society.

In one of his very first articles—written when a radical journalist in Prussia— Marx (1842:131) attacked censorship laws because they violated real freedom of expression. By "real" freedom Marx meant not only freedom to do certain things but also freedom not to be exploited by others. In another article— which led him eventually to study economic relationships—Marx (1842a; and see Linebaugh, 1976) discussed a Prussian law on the theft of wood enacted by the Rhineland Assembly. Despite a serious shortage of firewood and a depression in the local wine industry, this draconian law made it a criminal offense for anyone to collect and pilfer fallen wood in private forests. Marx attacked this law as blatantly undermining what had been a customary *right* of the Rhenish peasantry since the 16th century.

Crime and Demoralization

We note a second, perhaps more important, way in which Marxian writings argued that criminalization is a violation of rights. Many of Marx and Engels' writings analyzed the capitalist mode of production, and it is difficult not to believe they thought capitalist production unjust (Young, 1978). Thus, Marx wrote in the *New York Daily Tribune*, commenting on the lot of the Irish peasantry: "There must be something rotten in the core of a social system that increases its wealth without diminishing its misery, and increases in crimes even more rapidly than in numbers" (1859a). For Marx, the social system associated with capitalist production was unjust partly because it permits others (namely, capitalists) to profit from the labor of workers.

It is a simple matter of historical record that from the birth of industrialization to the time when Engels (1845) wrote *Condition of the Working Class in England*, British capitalism spawned the most gruesome living and working conditions for the mass of the population. Sometimes these conditions led to competition among members of the working class, and hence to crime (Engels, 1843:442). In Marxian analysis these conditions led, straightforwardly, to massive demoralization. This psychological condition, in its turn, led either to crime or to rebellion.

The linking of crime and demoralization is a vivid and recurring theme in many of Marx and Engels' more polemical passages. Thus, Engels (1845:411– 412) wrote that the working class is:

Friedrich Engels (1820–1895).

cast out and ignored by the class in power, morally as well as physically and mentally. The only provision made for them is the law, which fastens upon them when they become obnoxious to the bourgeoisie. Like the dullest of brutes, they are treated to but one form of education, the whip, in the shape of force, not convincing but intimidating. There is, therefore, no cause for surprise if the workers, treated as brutes, actually become such. . . .

In another passage Engels (1845:421–422) blamed the appalling conditions at home and at work for the criminality of the working class in Manchester. These conditions produced demoralization that, in turn, fostered widespread "[d]runkenness, sexual irregularities, brutality, and disregard for the rights of property" (Engels, 1845:421). According to Engels (*ibid.*:423), the bourgeoisie had left the working class only the pleasures of alcoholic and sexual excesses

> while imposing upon it a multitude of labors and hardships, and the consequence is that the working-men, in order to get something from life, concentrate their whole energy upon these two enjoyments, carry them to excess, surrender to them in the most unbridled manner.

Elsewhere, Engels (1845:412) suggested a different form that demoralization might take:

> True, there are, within the working class, numbers too moral to steal even when reduced to the utmost extremity, and these starve or commit

suicide . . . [actually] numbers of the poor kill themselves to avoid the misery from which they see no other means of escape.

Crime and Primitive Rebellion

One alternative to demoralization was rebellion. In *Capital*, Marx (1868) documented the rebellion of the British working class against the harsh emergence of industrial capitalism. As a class, British workers first manifested opposition to the bourgeoisie when they resisted the introduction of machinery or, in the case of the Luddites, either smashed it or even attempted to assassinate manufacturers (Engels, 1845:508). "Theft," said Engels (1845:502–503), "was the most primitive form of protest."

Although Marx and Engels identified certain working-class crime as rebellion—a crude and unconscious form of political protest—they did not, perhaps surprisingly, look on such activity with much favor. Doubtless they shared with their contemporaries a puritan assessment of the activities of the dangerous class (see Chapter 10.2)—crime offended Victorian morality. In addition, Marx and Engels condemned such forms of rebellion as having no value for working-class revolutionary consciousness. Thus, Engels lamented that working-class crime is "the earliest, crudest, and least fruitful form of this rebellion" (1845:502). Elsewhere, Marx and Engels (1848) analyzed class allies upon which the working class could realistically seek to depend for growth of its revolutionary movement. Within that context, they (*ibid.*:118) complained:

> The "dangerous class," the social scum, that passively rotting mass thrown off by the lowest layers of the old society, may, here and there, be swept into the movement by a proletarian revolution; its conditions of life, however, prepare it far more for the part of a bribed tool of reactionary intrigue.

Crime and Communism

How did Marx and Engels foresee the nature of crime in the future communist society? To begin with, throughout their writings was scattered a rudimentary image of life in the future communist society. This new, emancipated life would above all be determined by a revolution in the relationship between labor and the freedom of leisure. However, Marx and Engels rarely described the characteristics of the future communist society, largely because they refused to identify utopian blueprints for an unknown future. The model for what they believed might be possible under communism was the 1871 Paris Commune. The Commune was established during an armed working-class insurrection in Paris between March 18 and May 28, 1871. During the insurrection—mounted against widespread political oppression of the French working-class movement—the workers created a revolutionary government, a "dictatorship of the proletariat," that disarmed the police and instituted broad social reforms. Marx commented (1871:229) about these reforms:

> Wonderful, indeed, was the change the Commune had wrought in Paris! . . . No longer was Paris the rendezvous of British landlords, Irish absentees, American ex-slaveholders and shoddy men [and] Russian ex-serfowners. . . . No more corpses at the morgue, no nocturnal burglaries, scarcely any robberies; in fact, for the first time since the days of February 1848, the streets of Paris were safe, and that without police of any kind.

In Marxian writings the longest description of the nature of crime in communist society is given by Engels (1845:248–249), and is worth quoting at some length:

> Present-day society, which breeds hostility between the individual man and everyone else, thus produces a social war of all against all which inevitably in individual cases, notably among uneducated people, assumes a brutal, barbarously violent form—that of crime. In order to protect itself against crime, against direct acts of violence, society requires an extensive, complicated system of administrative and judicial bodies which requires an immense labor force. In communist society this would likewise be vastly simplified, and precisely because . . . the administrative body in this society would have to manage not merely individual aspects of social life, but the whole of social life, in all its various activities, in all its aspects. We eliminate the contradiction between the individual man and all others, we counterpose social peace to social war, we put the axe to the *root* of crime—and thereby render the greatest, by far the greatest, part of the present activity of the administrative and judicial bodies superfluous. . . . Advancing civilization moderates violent outbreaks of passion even in our present-day society, which is on a war footing; how much more will this be the case in communist, peaceful society! Crimes against property cease of their own accord where everyone receives what he needs to satisfy his natural and spiritual urges, where social gradations and distinctions cease to exist. Justice concerned with criminal cases ceases of itself, that dealing with civil cases, which are almost all rooted in property relations or at least in such relations as arise from the situation of social war, likewise disappears; conflicts can then be only rare exceptions, whereas they are now the natural result of general hostility, and will be easily settled by arbitrators. The activities of the administrative bodies at present have likewise their source in the continual social war— the police and the entire administration do nothing else but see to it that the war remains concealed and indirect and does not erupt into open violence, into crimes . . . [I]t is vastly more easy to administer a communist society rather than a competitive one.

Assessment

Marx and Engels' writings are an important part of the development of sociological criminology. Their writings, like Durkheim's, have endured among criminologists because they offer a radical approach to crime in capitalist societies. Crime, in their view, is not caused by moral or biological defects in individuals but by fundamental defects in a society's social organization.

Marx and Engels saw crime, as Durkheim did, as an inevitable feature of existing social organization. However, unlike Durkheim, they believed that crime is inevitable because it is an expression of basic social and class inequalities. Working-class crime, especially, results from demoralization, and occasionally turns to primitive rebellion. The extent of crime and its forms, they suggest, should be understood in the context of the specific class relationships, state, and law associated with a given mode of production. Yet Marx and Engels did not explain crime simply by reference to economic factors, as many commentators wrongly claim. As noted, they clearly understood that crime involves a political process whereby the state criminalizes certain conduct, and in so doing often reflects the interests not of society as a whole but of certain groups within it. Crime, Marx and Engels sometimes suggested, was a form of rebellion against this process. This realization, however poorly articulated by Marx and Engels, was taken up by criminologists in the 1970s and 1980s (see Chapters 14.4, 15.2, 15.3).

It is significant that Marx and Engels never seriously addressed certain basic questions about the nature of crime. Why, for example, are some actions defined as criminal but others are not? Because they gave no consideration to this definitional question, Marx and Engels tended to accept, as did most of their Victorian contemporaries, that crime indeed represents a violation of moral or good conduct. In arguing, therefore, that the *lumpenproletariat* and the unskilled working class—those groups who allegedly contribute least to society because they are neither involved in the productive process nor politically organized—engage in the great bulk of this conduct, they generally ignored the different types of crime committed by different classes. Finally, the writings of Marx and Engels contain no analysis of the links between crime and other forms of social inequality (see Chapter 3).

REVIEW

This chapter outlined the early forms of sociological criminology, which derived many theories and concepts from problems identified in the basic social organization of societies. This linking of crime and social organization was, and is, the key feature of sociological criminology. The ideas analyzed in this chapter indelibly imprinted the subsequent development of criminological theory in the United States and elsewhere.

Toward a Social Psychology of Crime: Gabriel Tarde

1. Tarde developed a theory about the causes of crime that attempted to combine individualistic and sociological concepts. Tarde was the leading critic of such biological theories of crime as Lombrosianism.

2. Tarde's social psychology opposed both the Lombrosian concept of *born criminality* and Quetelet's concept of the regularity of crime. Tarde applied the concept of *imitation* to crime, thereby suggesting that, in addition to the importance of sociological factors, individual mental states also contributed to the growth of crime.

3. Influenced by the growth of socialist and anarchist insurrections in France, Tarde pinpointed the imitative behavior of crowds and mobs as one of the leading causes of violence in modern urban societies.

Toward a Sociology of Law and Crime: Émile Durkheim

1. French sociologist Émile Durkheim was one of the founders of sociological criminology, and his writings represented an extremely successful attempt to integrate a theory of crime with a theory of law. His analysis of crime and punishment exerts great influence on modern criminology.

2. Durkheim's sociological method was based on the idea that societies can be fully understood only by the scientific method of positivism. Like Quetelet's social mechanics, Durkheim's criminology attempted to find regularities in criminal behavior.

3. Durkheim's criminology began with the belief that types of law and types of social solidarity were intimately connected. Mechanical solidarity is associated with repressive law; organic solidarity is associated with restitutive law. During the evolution from mechanical to organic solidarity, the volume of repressive law declines relative to other forms of law. This is another way of restating the broad transformation in penal strategies that accompanied the Enlightenment and classical criminology (see Chapter 10.1).

4. Durkheim argued that the function of punishment is to maintain and strengthen social solidarity rather than to repress crime. Crime is a normal, inevitable, and useful form of social activity. Detailed analyses of crime in Durkheim's works concentrate on suicide and homicide. Both these crimes testify to the sociological causes of crime, and especially to the effects of anomie and egoism on them.

5. Durkheim argued that forms of punishment have varied in history according to two laws. Quantitatively, punishment has tended to be repressive the less developed the society and the more absolute the power of the central authority. Qualitatively, the more developed the society the more imprisonment tends to become its dominant form of social control.

Classical Marxism: Marx and Engels on State, Law, and Crime

1. Marx and Engels founded the international communist movement. Their writings on state, law, and crime were set in the context of their sociological analysis of modern capitalist societies.

2. The key concepts of Marx and Engels' sociology are social classes, mode of production, means of production, social relations of production, and ideology. It is the articulation of these concepts that defines the movement of social relationships in history (although their primary concern was with capitalist societies).

3. Marx and Engels generally insisted that the institutions of state and law, and the doctrines that emerge from them, serve the interests of the dominant economic class. The state arises from class struggles, and gives the false appearance of independence from social classes. Law is endowed with several functions: it defends and enforces existing property relationships, and in class societies does so in the context of unequal ownership of property; it acts as an ideological mechanism, promoting respect for private property; and in moments of acute class struggle, it acts as a mechanism of repression.

4. Marx and Engels offered a view of crime and capitalism that differed greatly from the social contract and free-will theorists of the Enlightenment. They defined crime in three ways: as a violation by the state of natural or human rights, as a form of demoralization resulting from the gruesome conditions of industrial capitalism, and as a form of primitive rebellion.

5. Marx and Engels tentatively believed that with the abolition of private property and, accordingly, with the disappearance of the class character of the state, crimes would almost disappear under communism.

6. Marx and Engels provided no well-formed theory of crime. However, Marxian writings contain several comments and observations relevant to a radical approach to crime (and see Chapter 15.2).

QUESTIONS FOR CLASS DISCUSSION

1. Is crime normal?
2. Is crime inevitable?
3. Can you describe the social organization of a future society in which crime has disappeared entirely?

RECOMMENDED READINGS

Greenberg, David (1993) (ed). *Crime and Capitalism: Readings in Marxist Criminology*. Palo Alto, CA: Mayfield, Greenberg's (pp. 1–35) introduction to this edited collection sets the concept of crime in the context of Marx and Engels' broader concerns with the analysis of social formations and class struggles.

Hunt, Alan (1978). *The Sociological Movement in Law*. London: Macmillan. Pp. 60–92 contain a critical appraisal of Durkheim's sociology of law and crime.

Hunt, Alan and Maureen Cain (1979). *Marx and Engels on Law*. London: Academic Press. Pp. 145–152 contain the editors' introduction to important reprinted passages (pp. 153–201) of Marx and Engels' views on state, law, crime, and punishment.

Lukes, Steven (1973). *Émile Durkheim: His Life and Work*. London: Penguin. The standard intellectual biography of Durkheim.

CHAPTER 12

THE EMERGENCE OF CRIMINOLOGY IN THE UNITED STATES

12.1 The Early History of Criminology in the U.S., 1895–1915

12.2 Crime and Social Ecology
    Introduction to the Chicago School of Criminology
    Shaw and McKay's *Juvenile Delinquency and Urban Areas*
    (1942)
    Assessment: The Poverty of Empiricism

12.3 Social Structure, Anomie, and Deviance
    Merton's Typology of Modes of Individual Adaptation
    Assessment

12.4 The Contributions of Edwin Sutherland
    Differential Association
    Differential Social (Dis)Organization
    The Professional Thief (1937)
    White Collar Crime (1949)
    Assessment

Preview

Chapter 12 introduces:

    ☞ certain key themes and prejudices of the diverse analyses of crime
       that prospered in the U.S. before 1915.
    ☞ the social factors that contributed to the emergence of
       criminology in the U.S.

☞ the innovative methods and concepts of the Chicago school of social ecology, culminating in the findings of Shaw and McKay's (1942) important work *Juvenile Delinquency and Urban Areas.*

☞ Merton's theory of "anomie," which offers a sociological explanation for the high rates of deviance and crime in the U.S.

☞ the contributions of Edwin Sutherland—in particular his theories of differential association and differential social organization, and his books *The Professional Thief* (1937) and *White Collar Crime* (1949).

Key Terms

anomie

Chicago school of criminology

differential association

social disorganization

social ecology

white-collar crime

C*hapters 10 and 11 introduced the most influential theories of crime fashionable in much of Europe at the dawn of the 20th century. These theories are important partly because they acted as stepping-stones in the historical development of modern criminology. Additionally, they continue to exert a powerful influence on the ways in which we understand crime today.*

*Moreover, this **historical** introduction to criminological theory should provide a valuable lesson in intellectual humility: the sobering realization that our understanding of crime has not advanced much beyond that of theories put forward over 100 years ago. Yet this dubious progress is not peculiar to the discipline of criminology. Taken as a whole, the social sciences have been notoriously unsuccessful in putting forward **any** confirmed generalization on social behavior (MacIntyre, 1981:84–102)! Criminology's "failure," then, is shared with other social sciences.*

We begin Chapter 12 with certain of the diverse explanations of crime favored before 1915, just prior to the growth and professionalization of criminology in the United States.

12.1 _____ THE EARLY HISTORY OF CRIMINOLOGY IN THE U.S., 1895–1915

Prior to the emergence of the Chicago school of sociology in the decade after 1915, the study of crime had few institutional facilities with which to develop a systematic intellectual content. It is therefore very hard to isolate a precise event, a particular book, or an exact period of time to which we can confidently trace the first appearance of a criminology indigenous to the United States.

However, following the end of the Civil War in 1865, there appeared a multitude of published opinions concerning crime. These were voiced in amateurish ways by persons with vested interests in crime and criminality: prison reformers, medical doctors, psychiatrists, journalists, politicians, social reformers, philanthropists, and moral crusaders. Some treatises—such as those associated with proposals by the Pennsylvania Quakers for the "humanitarian" reform of prisons and punishment—were enlightened for their era (Walker, 1980:11–34; Dumm, 1987:65–86). Yet we do not suggest that Quaker proposals were enlightened in an absolute sense, only that they were enlightened when compared with alternative proposals of the same era. Indeed, it is highly debatable whether the humanitarian basis of the modern penitentiary marks a real advance over preclassical forms of punishment (see Chapter 10.1; Foucault, 1979; Rothman, 1971:54–108).

The ideological leanings of these early works have been usefully charted by Boostrom (1974). Behind these works, he suggests, lay four basic beliefs that paved the way for the development of a criminology whose focus would become the "correction of criminals" (*ibid.*:2–3):

1. ... [T]he idea that crime is an alien phenomenon in American society. Crime was claimed to be a phenomenon principally associated with alien, non-WASP groups. Crime was also seen as associated with the growth of urban-industrial centers stimulated by technological progress.

2. ... [T]he effort of correctional reformers to dissociate their ideas and panaceas from those of radical groups such as socialists.

3. ... [T]he effort to differentiate progressive correctional reform ideas from the perspective of Social Darwinism. Correctional reformers lobbied for creative government intervention (the positive state) to solve social problems while conservative Social Darwinists argued for the limitation of government to reactive police powers.

4. ... [T]he establishment of the idea that the solution of the crime problem in modern society would require social support for special "scientific" expertise and intervention.

The all-too-generous biases of these early works did not meet the concerted intellectual focus characteristic of an autonomous academic discipline. Intellectually, the vast majority of writings on crime in the U.S., up to and including the turn of the 20th century, took the nature of crime and criminality entirely for granted. Crime was pathological activity unquestioningly committed by criminals. Sociological questions about the nature and possible normality of crime were neither raised nor, it seems, even recognized as part of serious inquiry. Moreover, the understanding of crime, and especially of its causes, tended to be combined with the explanatory framework of whatever concepts seemed appropriate to the problems at hand. And these concepts tended to be borrowed piecemeal from those of European phrenology, medicine, and psychiatry. Biological concepts were especially in fashion; and Darwinism, degeneracy, imbecility, moral insanity and, especially, Lombrosianism, all exerted powerful influences on the public mind (Fink, 1938; Rafter, 1992). Indeed, long after its apparent discredit in Europe, Lombrosianism retained a powerful hold on the U.S. public's imagination (see Chapter 15.1).

The piecemeal, or multifactorial, thrust of much criminology of this era is exemplified by the work of Chicago sociologist Frances Kellor. Although Kellor's studies were unusual in that they addressed female criminality, her perspective conventionally combined Lombrosianism, psychology, and environmental sociology in the search for a scientific criminal sociology. In the 1890s, for example, Kellor visited female penitentiaries and workhouses to assess how well Lombroso's concept of born criminality applied to women. Aided by a mobile laboratory, Kellor (1899) compared 21 physical and psychological characteristics of 61 female criminals with 55 students. Regarding physical differences, although she largely disagreed with the assertions of the learned Italian doctor, Kellor concluded that female inmates were differentiated among themselves: "immoral women," such as prostitutes, were found "mentally and physically . . . more defective than the criminal" (*ibid.*:543). At the same time, Kellor stressed the importance of sociological factors in understanding female criminality, including age, marital status, nationality, religion, occupation, and class origin. For Kellor, these social and economic factors were almost always more critical than biological forces. For example, she found prostitution largely caused not by some innate female depravity but by limited economic circumstances. Kellor's multifactorialism led her to the tentative conclusion that some women are criminal because of natural immorality, others because of domestic infelicity, and still others because of poor education; female recidivists tended to have "degenerate habits which enthrall them" (*ibid.*:678–679). Kellor also believed, as Estelle Freedman stresses, that "[u]nder a similar [moral] standard and given equal opportunities . . . members of both sexes would commit the same crimes" (1981:115).

We stress that, in an important respect, all early authors of treatises on crime shared a common interest: their paternalistic concern with the correction and reformation of "criminals." Despite their paternalistic thrust, it was, nevertheless, reformist motives that eventually induced commentators on crime to become part of a wider and more recognized movement for the development of social science and, especially, sociology.

The intellectual and institutional rise of sociology was fostered by three major factors (Hinkle and Hinkle, 1954; Oberschall, 1972; and Schwendinger and Schwendinger, 1974):

1. The Progressive Era (1890–1910)—a combination of secular and Christian (especially Protestant) reform movements inspired by the professional middle classes (lawyers, doctors, teachers and so on) and designed to improve the lot of the poor in the wake of the problems associated with the ill effects of industrialization and urbanization.

2. The rapid expansion of the university system in the U.S. and, at the same time, the institutionalization of the social sciences at elite universities (Columbia, Johns Hopkins, Yale, Harvard, Chicago) between the mid-1870s and 1915. The first course in sociology probably was offered in 1876 by Sumner; the first book on sociology was Lester Ward's (1883) *Dynamic Sociology*. The first book on criminology to use sociology specifically as one of its multifactorial perspectives probably was Kellor's (1901) *Experimental Sociology*.

3. The state's recognition, between 1865 and 1905, of new academic associations for the professional security and advancement of the social science community, including the American Social Science Association, the American Economic Association, the American Historical Association, the American Sociological Society.

Criminology itself emerged from the Progressive Era's general concern with the alleviation of social problems.[1] Institutionally, its position in universities across the U.S. derived from its inclusion within the movement for the expansion of sociology, and its voice was actively promoted by such professional associations as the National Prison Association and the National Conference of Charities and Corrections (later, of Social Work). This voice was enhanced in 1909, at a conference in Chicago, with the founding of the American Institute of Criminal Law and Criminology and the *Journal of Criminal Law and Criminology*. Between 1895 (the publication of Max Nordau's *Degeneration*) and 1915 (the publication of John Gillin's *Social Pathology*), the vague subject matter of criminology was transformed by a deluge of empirical studies addressing the criminality of immigrants, of the dangerous classes, and of "negroes." Intellectually, these studies involved a selective reliance on sociological perspectives that excluded everything in the realm of theoretical speculation. This was not the time, or so it must have seemed, to speculate on grandiose sociological questions (What is society? How is social order possible? Is crime "normal"?), whether they were asked by criminologists in the United States, such as Cooley, or in Europe, such as Durkheim.[2] Instead, there was a new emphasis on such empirical social categories as poverty, alcoholism, and family upbringing (Rafter, 1988), each seen as a potential factor in criminality in a continually expanding but, in principle, endless

---

[1] The pre-1915 history of U.S. criminology is relatively uncharted territory. Guillot (1943) summarizes many of the links in the chain of factors held to induce crime between 1860 and 1885. Boostrom (1974) provides the best overall view of the relation between the eclectic concepts used to understand crime before 1900 and the emergence of a self-proclaimed scientific criminology. Gibbons (1979:18–37) relies largely on secondary sources, but provides solid commentary on the early contributions of Parmalee, Gillin, Parsons, and Sutherland.

[2] In 1909, The American Institute of Criminal Law and Criminology resolved that important treatises on criminology in foreign languages should be made readily accessible to scholars in the U.S. (essentially, translated into English). The several translated books that resulted from this resolution (namely, by Tarde, Lombroso, Saleilles, Gross) were all leaders, in one way or another, of the neoclassical compromise between free will and determinism (see Chapter 10.5).

Ellis Island official questioning an Italian immigrant.

chain of causality. Typically, the various links in the causal chain were tied to the criminality of social, economic, political, and religious "outsiders": immigrants, persons of color, heretics, lunatics and imbeciles, the undeserving poor, the feebleminded, the naturally unfit, and others.

Pronouncements of criminologists on the causes of crime, titillated by the mass media for popular consumption, were naturally assured a large public audience. The focus on the individual as the appropriate object of study and the reformation of the criminal character through individualization of punishment as its legitimate goal assured criminologists considerable financial support by both state and private agencies. The appearance, about the end of the First World War, of several texts (such as Parmalee's [1918] *Criminology*) that urged the use of scientific principles as its basic method gained a measure of support for criminology from the academic and scientific communities.

As a part of the movement for social reform, and as a fledgling member of the academic community, criminology was now charted on a respectable course. We consider, now, the development of the Chicago school of social ecology, the first U.S. "school" of criminology.

12.2 _____ CRIME AND SOCIAL ECOLOGY

By the term *social ecology* (or *human ecology*), we refer to a type of research that examines (1) different geographical *areas* of cities, communities, and neighborhoods and (2) the area concentrations, regularities, and patterns of social life in such fields as work/leisure, health/sickness, and conformity/deviance. In this section we outline the ecological approach to crime practiced by the Chicago school of criminology between the mid-1920s and early 1940s.

Introduction to the Chicago School of Criminology

In Chapter 11 we identified two explanatory frameworks instrumental in the development of sociological criminology. First, a sociopsychological explanation focused on the individual and, specifically, on the ways in which society cultivates the latent tendencies of those psychologically predisposed to crime (see Chapter 11.1). Second, a sociological explanation focused on the patterned and regular ways in which social structures themselves exert pressures on groups toward crime (see Chapter 11.2). The investigations of the Chicago school of criminology included both explanatory frameworks, sociopsychological and sociological, often combining them in the same piece of research. Broadly, the Chicago school's work in the field of crime investigated: (1) the life histories of juvenile delinquents, interpreted both through personal accounts of their delinquent acts and with the aid of sociopsychological and, occasionally, clinical techniques, and (2) the geographical and social distribution of delinquents and delinquency rates. Many members of the Chicago school came from a common background that can be summarized as rural or small town, midwestern, Christian in upbringing, and reform-oriented or even liberal in its political views; their investigations therefore led directly, and were expected to lead, to policies for social reform.

The Chicago school of criminology was part of the post-Progressive Era social science movement, many aspects of which evolved at the University of Chicago. Between 1915 and the early 1940s, sociological research in the United States was dominated by various academic disciplines at the University of Chicago, especially those of political science and sociology. This domination resulted from several factors, chief among them the nature of the city of Chicago itself. By the 1920s and 1930s, in little more than a century, Chicago had changed completely beyond recognition. From a small town of little more than two square miles and 200 inhabitants, Chicago expanded to become the second-largest industrial metropolis in the U.S., with a corporate area of 211 square miles and a population of over 3.3 million, extending some 25 miles along Lake Michigan and from eight to 10 miles inland. During this expansion, tremendous changes occurred in the social composition of many neighborhoods in the city. These changes were especially visible in neighborhoods in and adjacent to the central business district and in areas of rapid industrial growth. "About the only thing that could be thought beautiful about . . . Chicago," a Chicago sociologist pointedly commented, "was fresh and lively Lake Michigan" (Faris, 1967:21). To journalists, social reformers, and sociologists, the ever-changing and fascinating patterns of daily life in Chicago were a barometer of the human condition itself. German sociologist Max Weber, visiting the city in 1904, is reported to have "found it incredible and compared it to a man whose skin had been peeled off and whose intestines were seen at work" (Bulmer, 1984:xvi).

In the intellectually stimulating atmosphere of Chicago, a considerable number of creative scholars combined their talents and applied their energies to a sociological analysis of the harsh consequences of "urbanism," and especially to those problems generated by living in the inner city. Prominent among them were such famous names as W. I. Thomas, Ernest Burgess, Robert Park, and George Herbert Mead. Affiliated with the department of sociology—as graduate students, teachers, and quasi-independent researchers under the leadership of Park and Burgess—were such criminologists as William Healy, Frederick Thrasher, Paul Cressey, John Landesco, Clifford Shaw, and Henry McKay (Bennett, 1981:104–210).

The Chicago school brought to its research on urbanism innovative, vigorous and eclectic methods of analysis. In the history of empirical research, these methods fell, chronologically, midway between (although curiously unrelated to) investigations that relied on large social surveys and those that employed scientific measurement techniques. Members of the Chicago school used a dazzling array of methodological techniques in their research. Their *quantitative* methods included somewhat unsystematic but nevertheless advanced statistical analyses that were quite sophisticated for the time. Their *qualitative* techniques included the use of life-history documents, case studies, investigative journalism, media materials, in-depth interviews, and participant observation. Above all, Chicago sociologists believed in following Park's recommendation to get their feet wet with *real* research (Bulmer, 1984:108), taking great pride in conducting research in "the open," or in "the field" (on the streets, in opium dens, in brothels, in parks, wherever), rather than in laboratories, faculty offices, or libraries.

In effect, the Chicago school firmly believed that the new methodological techniques of fieldwork would provide the basis for a factual, theory-free analysis of society. In this they agreed with French moral statisticians, such as Quetelet, that "facts speak for themselves" quite independently of theoretical interpretation (see Chapter 10.2). However, the Chicago school's "facts" did not speak for themselves. Behind their facts lay the guiding hand of an important theoretical assumption: that the social ecology of urbanism could proceed within the same framework as the ecological study of plant and animal life. This assumption was present, sometimes beneath the surface and sometimes quite overtly, in numerous writings of the Chicago school—from the early research of Park (1915) and Burgess (1925) on urban spatial analysis to Shaw and McKay's (1942) famous

Juvenile Delinquency and Urban Areas. The assumption was used to help describe how industrial and commercial expansion invades and disturbs the "metabolism" of "natural areas" (local communities) in the city. The guiding ecological assumption of the Chicago school has been described effectively by Vold and Bernard (1986:160–161):

> The term *ecology*, as it is used today, is often linked to the idea of protecting the natural environment. In its original meaning, however, it is a branch of biology in which plants and animals are studied in their relationships to each other and to their natural habitat. Plant life and animal life are seen as an intricately complicated whole, a web of life in which each part depends on almost every other part for some aspect of its existence. Organisms in their natural habitat exist in an ongoing balance of nature, a dynamic equilibrium in which each individual must struggle to survive. Ecologists study this web of interrelationships and interdependencies in an attempt to discover the forces that define the activities of each part.
>
> Human communities, particularly those organized around a free-market economy and a laissez-faire government, could be seen to resemble this biotic state in nature. Each individual struggles for his or her survival in an interrelated, mutually dependent community. The Darwinian law of survival of the fittest applies here as well.

After World War I (1914–1918), Chicago sociologists turned their ecological attentions to a variety of social problems. Exacerbated by the severe hardships of the Great Depression, Prohibition, and by the well-publicized rise of gangland warfare and union racketeering, crime itself came to be seen as a major social problem in Chicago. Crime, therefore, was one of the chief topics studied by members of the Chicago school. One of the most famous of the early studies— W. I. Thomas and Florian Znaniecki's (1918–1920) *The Polish Peasant in Europe and America*—used personal documents and life histories to examine the difficulties which immigrants faced in adjusting to life in America. Another study— W. I. Thomas' (1923) *The Unadjusted Girl*—collected information from 3,000 interviews to establish that all social behavior, including that of female delinquency, apparently derived from one or all of four motives or "wishes": the wish for new experience, for security, for response, and for recognition. As such, implied Thomas, delinquency and lawful activity were merely "functional alternatives" directed to the satisfaction of the same goals. *The Unadjusted Girl* marked a rare concern among criminologists with the "criminality" of young females. However, feminists find scant value in Thomas' book; the analysis is thoroughly sexist (females are entirely incidental to Thomas' concern with the four "wishes" [and see Schwendinger and Schwendinger, 1971:786–790]). Thrasher's (1927) *The Gang* strongly implied that, although there are many gang types, *delinquent* gang activity represented a normal part of the process of adjustment between adolescence and adulthood. Delinquency, Thrasher found, was the best method of adjustment available to adolescents in deprived inner-city areas.

Clifford Shaw contributed two directions of research to the Chicago school before completing his famous *Juvenile Delinquency and Urban Areas* with Henry McKay in 1942. In one direction, heralded in his book *Delinquency Areas*, Shaw (*et al.*, 1929) argued that the physical destruction and social deterioration of inner-city areas led to the disintegration of the community and, ultimately, to the loss of community ability to police itself. Social disorganization, in other words, caused increases in juvenile delinquency. In a second direction, Shaw demonstrated how seemingly important it was for a researcher, when attempting to explain juvenile delinquency, to listen to delinquents' own definitions of their activities. Why did juveniles, according to *their* own explanations (rather than those of such other interested parties as teachers and police officers), engage in delinquency? Indeed, to answer this question Shaw collected more than 200 life histories of juvenile delinquents. In 1930, Shaw published *The Jack-Roller*, a widely read account of "a delinquent boy's own story." This was followed by (Shaw, 1931) *The Natural History of a Delinquent Career*, a book that contradicted public condemnation of a convicted rapist and armed robber depicted by the press and by popular indignation as a brute and a beast. Instead, insisted Shaw, this felon should be understood in terms of the values transmitted to him by numerous juvenile institutions and by his economically insecure and disorganized community in Chicago. Finally, we note *Brothers in Crime* (Shaw, McKay, and McDonald, 1938), an in-depth study of the social backgrounds, criminal careers, and personality characteristics of the five Martin brothers, children of foreign-born immigrants. This book represented a sympathetic and appreciative view of five "criminal careers" determined by the cultural conflict into which immigrant families were thrust by poverty, by lack of education, and by the aggravating effects of such control agencies as juvenile institutions.

This sort of criminology seemed, and actually was, very different from much that preceded it. Aside from their innovative methods of study, members of the Chicago school did not assume that those who committed crimes were malicious miscreants. On the contrary, in the works referenced thus far, it was generally concluded that delinquents were normal juveniles in abnormal environments. In reaching this broad conclusion, we believe the Chicago school made considerable progress over the opinionated explanations of their predecessors.

We turn now to what was, in some respects, the greatest achievement of the Chicago school's contribution to criminology—Shaw and McKay's (1942) book *Juvenile Delinquency and Urban Areas*.

Shaw and McKay's *Juvenile Delinquency and Urban Areas* (1942)

Clifford Shaw and Henry McKay conducted the research for *Juvenile Delinquency and Urban Areas* while they were affiliated with the department of sociology at Chicago's Institute for Juvenile Research. *Juvenile Delinquency and Urban Areas* applied to the city of Chicago the detailed statistical analyses pioneered a century earlier by French moral statisticians (see Chapter 10.2); it is arguably the most famous book ever published on the relationship between crime and urbanization.

Its sophisticated statistical analyses attempted to sort out the tangled links among the dynamics of urban growth, community problems, and rates of juvenile delinquency. Among the crucial questions about juvenile delinquency that Shaw and McKay sought to explore were:

1. Do juvenile delinquency rates and adult crime rates vary together in different types of cities?

2. Do rates of juvenile delinquency correlate with the rates of juvenile recidivism?

3. Do juvenile delinquency rates vary with the economic, social, and cultural characteristics of local communities?

4. Do juvenile delinquency rates vary with patterns of immigration?

5. How do economic and social conditions influence the development of juvenile delinquency as a cultural tradition in certain neighborhoods?

6. How can juvenile delinquency be prevented and treated?

Shaw and McKay approached these questions in four stages. First, they identified various physical and social demographic changes in Chicago neighborhoods. On the one hand, the physical changes comprised such factors as growth of the central business district and invasion of traditional local communities in the course of industrial and commercial expansion. With this expansion, Chicago landlords typically failed to repair rented dwellings in surrounding areas because of expectations that rising property prices—caused by the increased demand of industry and commerce for scarce land—would eventually yield fat profits. As a result, the interstitial areas (the "zone of transition") surrounding the central business district and industrial developments of Chicago were subject to increasing physical deterioration. This deterioration, Shaw and McKay perceived, was manifest in the number of substandard and dangerous buildings that survived in the zone of transition.

On the other hand, the changes in Chicago's social composition derived largely from the fact that from the 1880s to the 1930s the population in Chicago's zone of transition was in relative decline while the population in its expanding suburbs was increasing. Employing census data, Shaw and McKay (*ibid.*:32–42) found that a disproportionate number of those in professional and clerical occupations resided in the affluent suburbs, far from the central business district and industrial development. Correspondingly, a disproportionate number of industrial workers and the poor were concentrated in areas of physical deterioration. These deteriorated areas also contained the greatest number of families on welfare (*ibid.*:32).

In combination, the physical and social changes in Chicago spawned a far-reaching geographic segregation of the population. Shaw and McKay discovered further that patterns of immigration were part of a related process of economic and occupational segregation. The native white population not only enjoyed the highest economic status but tended to live in comfortable suburban houses;

the residents of deteriorated zones of transition tended to have the lowest economic status. This latter group included: (a) white European immigrants (especially from Czechoslovakia, Germany, Greece, Italy, Ireland, Poland, and Russia) and (b) African Americans, many of whom were "internal immigrants" who had migrated to Chicago from rural areas. Each immigrant group tended to be concentrated in a particular section of Chicago, although African American families were more dispersed throughout the deteriorated neighborhoods than were European immigrants. Upon arrival in the "New World," each impoverished immigrant group tended to be pushed into the areas of lowest economic status. Eventually, however, most groups (but not African Americans, Latinos, and Native Americans) worked their way to the suburbs, their places in the deteriorated neighborhoods simply filled by subsequent arrivals. To paraphrase the jargon of social ecology: as industry and commerce extend their habitat, the metabolism of existing natural areas is dominated or destroyed; surviving areas, in succession, are organically reconstituted as part of another natural area. As Shaw and McKay (*ibid.*:42) inferred about this complicated process:

> In the process of city growth, areas within Chicago have been differentiated in such a way that they can be distinguished by their physical or economic characteristics or, at any given moment, by the composition of their population.

Moreover, they suggested (*ibid.*):

> Associated with these differences and with the more subtle variations in the attitudes and values which accompany them are found marked variations in child behavior. These are reflected in differential rates of delinquents. . . .

Second, Shaw and McKay focused on the distribution of delinquency in Chicago. The juveniles in their data were of three types:

1. alleged male juvenile delinquents (namely, those under 17) brought before the Juvenile Court of Cook County

2. juveniles actually committed to correctional institutions

3. all boys dealt with by the juvenile police probation officers, with or without court appearances

Although the objection (of which Shaw and McKay were aware) could be made that these three types represented only a sample of those apprehended, rather than of all juvenile delinquents, this sample was larger than any other study to date. Moreover, their data were compiled from different periods of time: (a) 9,860 alleged Chicago juvenile delinquents for the period 1934–1940, (b) 8,411 for 1927–1933, (c) 8,141 for 1917–1923, and (d) 8,056 for 1900–1906. Their use of time-series data, Shaw and McKay reasoned, permitted comparisons of delinquency rates not only in the same area for different periods, but also in areas some of which had undergone great sociodemographic changes and some of which had remained relatively stable.

Their findings, displayed with spectacular diagrams and shaded maps, were most revealing. Employing a series of spot maps that located the homes of all the delinquent boys reported in their data, Shaw and McKay showed that certain areas of Chicago had large concentrations of juvenile delinquents, whereas in other areas the delinquents were greatly dispersed (see the spot map in Figure 12-1). The areas of heaviest concentration were generally those near the central business district or those within or near areas zoned for industry and commerce.

Shaw and McKay divided the map of Chicago into 140 units, each approximately one square mile in size. They then computed delinquency rates for each unit (a delinquency rate was the number of delinquent boys in any given unit expressed as a percentage of the total of boys in that unit). Significantly, the units with the highest delinquency rates were found to be those near the central business district and those adjacent to areas zoned for industry or commerce (see the rate map in Figure 12-2).

Shaw and McKay further demonstrated that delinquency rates throughout Chicago varied in a strikingly uniform pattern (see the zone maps in Figure 12-3): the center of the city had the highest delinquency rates and the units at the extreme periphery the lowest; in between, with few exceptions, the rates regularly decreased the farther away from the center. This finding—that delinquency rates actually declined as one moved from the center to the periphery of the delinquency zones in Chicago—is analyzed in greater detail later in this section. For now, we quote Snodgrass' (1976:12) perceptive comment on the relationship between this empirical finding and Shaw's upbringing in rural Indiana:

> The fact that delinquency rates "thinned" as one traveled the gradient toward rural Illinois was not empirical alone; it had a solid basis in Shaw's personal history and ideology. The gradient implied that the farther away one went, the fewer pathologies one found. Back home in Indiana one did not find delinquency, but wild-oats and corn-bred mischievousness. . . .

Third, Shaw and McKay presented data showing that juvenile delinquency was not at all an isolated social problem. Analyses revealed that, area by area, juvenile delinquency rates were strongly correlated with such other community problems in Chicago as high rates of school truancy (*ibid.*:90), young adult offenders (*ibid.*:93–99), infant mortality (*ibid.*:99–101), tuberculosis (*ibid.*:101–104), and mental disorders (*ibid.*:104–106). In other words, Shaw and McKay found that areas in Chicago with certain social problems also tended to have higher rates of juvenile delinquency. Moreover, these same areas had the highest juvenile recidivism rates and relatively more delinquents who were later arrested as adults (*ibid.*:138–139).

Shaw and McKay were careful to point out that their correlational analyses should not be confused with causal analysis. For them, the high correlation between delinquency rates and certain sociodemographic characteristics of Chicago neighborhoods did not mean that these characteristics *cause* delinquency.

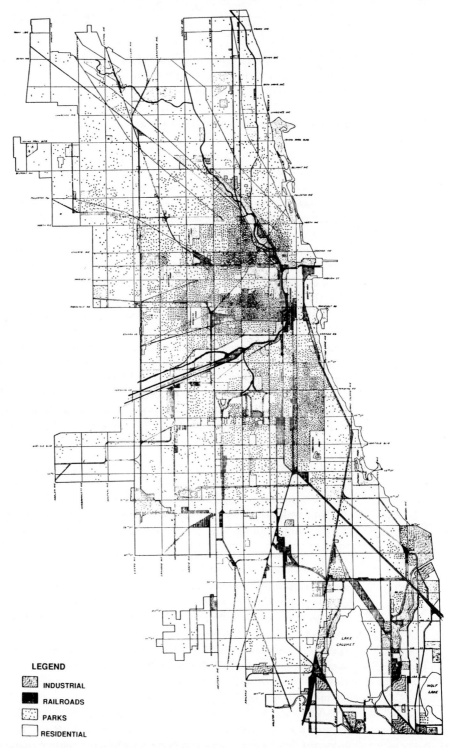

FIGURE
12-1

Places of Residence of 8,411 Male Juvenile Delinquents, Chicago, 1927–1933

Source: Illinois Institute for Juvenile Research, Department of Sociology, in Clifford R. Shaw and Henry D. McKay, 1942, 1969, p. 51.

LEGEND

INDUSTRIAL

RAILROADS

PARKS

RESIDENTIAL

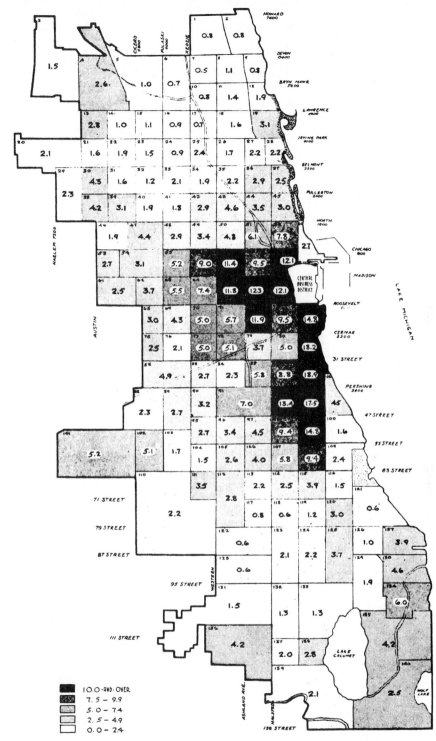

FIGURE
12-2

Delinquency Rates of 8,411 Male Juveniles, Chicago, 1927–1933

Source: Illinois Institute for Juvenile Research, Department of Sociology, in Clifford R. Shaw and Henry D. McKay, 1942, 1969, p. 54. Prepared with the assistance of the Works Administration.

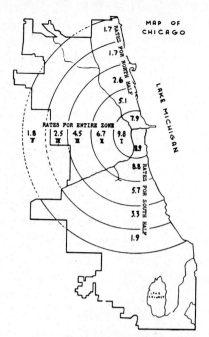

Zone rates of male juvenile delinquents, 1927–33 series

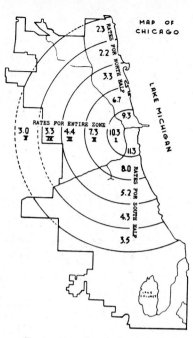

Zone rates of male juvenile delinquents, 1917–23 series

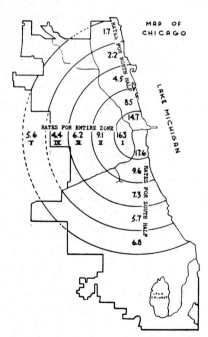

Zone rates of male juvenile delinquents, 1900–1906 series

FIGURE   Male Juvenile Delinquency Rates, Chicago, 1900–1933

12-3   *Source: Adapted from Clifford R. Shaw and Henry D. McKay, 1942, 1969, p. 69.*

For example, Shaw and McKay recognized that although the proportion of the foreign-born and the African American population was higher in areas with high delinquency rates, this statistical finding did not mean that the delinquency rates of these populations were higher *because* they were foreign-born or African American. They were higher, in part, because the high turnover of immigrant populations caused a withdrawal of residents' identification with their community and, correspondingly, a lack of pride in their neighborhood. Curiously, areas with high delinquency rates continued to have high rates irrespective of which groups inhabited them. Thus, between 1884 and 1930, eight inner-city Chicago areas underwent no changes in delinquency rates relative to other areas, despite the fact that the dominant population in these areas changed from Germans, Irish, English/Scots, and Scandinavians, to Italians, Poles, and Slavs (*ibid.*:156–157). This stability in delinquency rates, in the face of changing ethnic compositions, supported "emphatically the conclusion that the delinquency-producing factors are inherent in the community" (*ibid.*:315). The delinquency rates for these groups were high, Shaw and McKay (*ibid.*:164) somewhat vaguely continued, "because of other aspects of the total situation in which they live." The explanation of delinquency, Shaw and McKay (*ibid.*:14) promisingly insisted, must be

> in the first place, in the field of the more subtle human relationships and social values which comprise the social world of the child in the family and community. These more distinctively human situations, which seem to be directly related to delinquent conduct, are, in turn, products of larger economic and social processes characterizing the history and growth of the city and of the local communities which comprise it.

In the fourth and final stage of analysis, Shaw and McKay (*ibid.*:170–189; 315–357) attempted to extend the importance of the relationship between "social values" and "larger economic and social processes" to their explanation of the causes of juvenile delinquency. In areas with low delinquency rates (essentially, generally middle-class areas and those with high economic status), on the one hand, Shaw and McKay suggested there was general consensus on conventional values and attitudes toward such things as the welfare of children, the desirability of education, constructive leisure-time activities, and conformity to law. In such middle-class areas, moreover, respect for social values was expressed and cultivated by a variety of voluntary social control organizations such as parent-teacher associations, women's clubs, service clubs, churches, and neighborhood centers. Children who lived in such an environment tended to be insulated from direct contact with deviant forms of adult behavior and, in general, were "exposed to and participate[d] in a significant way in one mode of life only" (*ibid.*:171). In areas with high delinquency rates (generally, working-class areas and those with low economic status), on the other hand, Shaw and McKay suggested there was wide diversity in norms and standards of behavior. This diversity resulted from the different cultural beliefs and practices of migrant groups and unassimilated immigrant groups, and also from the moral values of predatory youth gangs and organized crime. In these areas, Shaw and McKay (*ibid.*:171–172) summarized:

> Moral values range from those that are strictly conventional to those in direct opposition to conventionality as symbolized by the family, the church, and other institutions common to our general society. The deviant values are symbolized by groups and institutions ranging from adult criminal gangs engaged in theft and the marketing of stolen goods . . . to quasi-legitimate businesses and the rackets through which partial or complete control of legitimate business is sometimes exercised. . . . Thus, within the same community theft may be defined as right and proper in some groups and as immoral, improper, and undesirable in others. In some groups wealth and prestige are secured through acts of skill and courage in the delinquent or criminal world, while in neighboring groups any attempt to achieve distinction in this manner would result in extreme disapprobation. Two conflicting systems of economic activity here present roughly equivalent opportunities for employment and for promotion. Evidence of success in the criminal world is indicated by the presence of adult criminals whose clothes and automobiles indicate unmistakably that they have prospered in their chosen fields. The values missed and the greater risks incurred are not so clearly apparent to the young.

For Shaw and McKay, in other words, areas with high delinquency rates were those whose children were exposed to (1) conflicting sets of moral values, (2) adult role models whose material success derived from participation in criminal activities, and (3) a social tradition of delinquency that was a hallmark of the life of the local community. Boys constantly surrounded by this social milieu were thus routinely exposed to delinquent life-styles.

However, the mere existence of criminal organizations did not explain why some boys were tempted to join and others were not. "Under what conditions is the conventional community capable of maintaining its integrity and exercising such control over the lives of its members as to check the development of the competing system?" (*ibid.*:317). To put Shaw and McKay's question another way: What causes juvenile delinquency?

In their conclusion Shaw and McKay attempted to answer this question—a question that, as we learn in the following section, dominated much thinking about juvenile delinquency for the next two decades. Shaw and McKay once again emphasized that the major difference between Chicago areas with high and low rates of officially recorded delinquency was that the former tended to be more impoverished and the latter more affluent.[3] Despite this difference, boys in all areas of Chicago—both rich and poor—were "exposed [in school

---

[3] Their studies (*ibid.*:193–312) also analyzed similar data for the metropolitan areas of Philadelphia, greater Boston, Cincinnati, greater Cleveland, and Richmond (Virginia), some of which included data on delinquent girls. In each case Shaw and McKay documented a delinquency distribution that paralleled their findings in Chicago.

and elsewhere] to the luxury values and success patterns of our culture" (*ibid.*:319). However, success by legitimate means was difficult to achieve for boys in low-income areas inasmuch as they usually lacked the opportunities and skills required to be successful. Boys from low-income families thus calculated, quite rationally, that the best means for achieving success lay in acts of delinquency and crime. Juvenile delinquency is therefore *rational* activity, and delinquent boys are by no means necessarily disorganized, maladjusted, or antisocial. As Shaw and McKay (*ibid.*:319) explained:

> In the low-income areas, where there is the greatest deprivation and frustration, where, in the history of the city, immigrant and migrant groups have brought together the widest variety of divergent cultural traditions and institutions, and where there exists the greatest disparity between the social values to which the people aspire and the availability of facilities for acquiring these values in conventional ways, the development of crime as an organized way of life is most marked. Crime, in this situation, may be regarded as one of the means employed by people to acquire, or to attempt to acquire, the economic and social values generally idealized in our culture, which persons in other circumstances acquire by conventional means.

Assessment: The Poverty of Empiricism

Shaw and McKay's findings in their famous study have had enormous influence on criminology, as has the methodological legacy of the Chicago school in general. "It would be difficult to overestimate the significance of the delinquency studies carried on by Clifford Shaw and Henry McKay," assesses Gibbons (1979:40), because "[t]he results of their inquiries provided much of the intellectual capital on which criminologists have continued to draw, even to the present time." Indeed, ecological analysis shows every sign of increasing its influence during the 1990s.

Doubtless a tribute to their signal importance, the method and findings of *Juvenile Delinquency and Urban Areas* have been reinterpreted endlessly by successive generations of criminologists. Criticisms of this research can be divided roughly into two sorts, empirical and theoretical. Consider three empirical criticisms.

First, consider the relationship between the source of Shaw and McKay's data and their finding that rates of juvenile delinquency tend to be highest in the low-income and working-class neighborhoods of cities. These data on the distribution of delinquency rates came from records of such official agencies as juvenile courts and juvenile probation officers. Although Shaw and McKay (*ibid.*:44) realized that many juveniles commit serious offenses that go undetected or for which they are not apprehended, they failed to acknowledge that crime rates are not pre-given, objective facts. Crime rates are always *socially constructed* (see Chapter 2). Delinquency rates, for example, reflect not only the illegalities of juveniles but also the reporting activity of the public and the decision to accept an act as an offense by a law enforcement officer. One reason why delinquency is so often found concentrated in working-class areas is that working-class adolescents are more likely than others to have their offenses reported to the police and, if reported, more likely to be arrested, to enter the criminal justice system, and to leave it as officially defined delinquents.

Moreover, recent self-report studies and victimization surveys show that although lower-class neighborhoods contain a disproportionate amount of violent crime, delinquency as a whole is not concentrated among working-class adolescents. Status offenses and property crimes, in particular, are far more evenly distributed throughout the class structure than Shaw and McKay imagined.

Second, consider that Shaw and McKay's data on delinquency distribution derived from the *residences* of juveniles who entered the criminal justice system. Subsequent research on urban social spaces, beginning with Newman's (1973) *Defensible Space*, has demonstrated the critical importance of the locations where crimes are committed (crime sites) rather than the residences of those who commit them—a fact of obvious importance in the case of white-collar, organized, and political crimes (see Chapters 7–9). Investigation of the geography of crime sites has uncovered the importance of the following problems, here summarized by Vold and Bernard (1986:178):

> the distance between the crime site and the offender's residence; the relationship between specific offenses and various characteristics of the crime site, such as land-use policy, climate and seasonality, population density, city size, and so on; the reasons offenders select certain crime sites; and the way these sites can be designed so as to prevent the occurrence of crime.

Third, consider Shaw and McKay's claim that delinquency rates remained stable despite great changes in the social composition of Chicago neighborhoods. If we ignore such factors as class bias in the construction of delinquency rates, it is possible that this claim was true for the specific period investigated (namely, 1906–1940). However, even if true for this period, there is no good reason to suppose, as Shaw and McKay did, that delinquency rates will be stable in other places and times (Lander, 1954). Indeed, it is likely that delinquency rates after 1945 in Chicago itself did not conform to the pattern predicted for them by Shaw and McKay (Bursik, 1984). Ultimately, we cannot be sure of the exact meaning of any claim about the stability of socially constructed crime rates. Does such a claim mean that the rate of actual illegalities remained stable? Does it mean, instead, that the actions of law enforcement officers remained constant? In posing these questions we are forced to raise anew a central question of the discussion in Chapter 2: What, precisely, do crime rates measure?

Theoretical criticisms of *Juvenile Delinquency and Urban Areas* tends to object that its findings are empiricist. Such criticisms do not imply, or do not imply only, that its findings are empirically wrong (which, as we have seen, they sometimes are), but that Shaw and McKay mistakenly believed the findings were strictly factual (essentially, that they existed independently of theoretical assumptions). However, in two respects Shaw and McKay's findings about delinquency were deeply structured by theoretical assumptions that lurked below the surface of their argument.

Recall that social ecologists tend to see urban development as a process in which areas of industrial and commercial expansion interfere with the metabolism of adjacent areas. Certain natural areas of transition—undergoing invasion, dominance, and succession—have high delinquency rates. As *Juvenile Delinquency and Urban Areas* attempted to show, this interference was manifest in the growth of juvenile delinquency and in other indices of social disorganization in inner-city neighborhoods. However, Shaw and McKay also believed that, like the processes of change in plants and animal life, the surrounding areas eventually would return to a harmonious state of equilibrium through the mechanisms of natural selection and symbiosis. When, and if, immigrants acquired the skills required for survival in a hostile environment, it was hypothesized that they would move up the social ladder and then move out to the suburbs. However, this often did not happen in Chicago, Shaw and McKay reasoned, because the inner-city areas lacked sufficient community controls to restore their natural state. The sources of disorganization thus lay with the residents rather than with the profit-seeking decisions of industrialists.

However, quite aside from the difficulties of applying concepts about change in plant life to processes of change in social life, the concept "social disorganization" remains unclear. It belies an important theoretical assumption. As Taylor, Walton, and Young (1973:124) have objected:

> When the biological analogy in ecology is translated into social terms, we are presented with a view of "organization," the overall society . . . and with a picture of social disorganization within certain residual or transitional areas—disorganization which is defined by reference to the organization that characterizes the dominant society.

Although Shaw and McKay were quite aware of the great diversity of life-styles in Chicago, they nevertheless tended to start with an image of conventional life-styles and then describe those that deviated from convention as disorganized and, occasionally, as socially pathological (and see Kobrin, 1951). Sociologically, however, societies and communities can never be disorganized as such. Disorganization is a label that is *always* conceived of, explicitly or implicitly, in relation to some theoretically conceived yardstick of organization. Sometimes this conception is quite explicit (such as when someone says that unregulated industrial expansion is immoral *because it destroys the communality of residential neighborhoods* or that, compared with the orderly life-styles of the residents of Chicago's fashionable Gold Coast, life in the slums is disorganized). Sometimes, as in Shaw and McKay's analysis of delinquency and deviance in Chicago slum neighborhoods, the concept of social organization is implicit only. Shaw and McKay implicitly assumed, *and wrongly so*, that the life-styles and values of those in natural areas of transition were disorganized. Like their eclectic predecessors before 1915, whose common focus was the study of social problems, Shaw and McKay ultimately assumed that juvenile delinquency was necessarily disorganized or deviant activity.

Moreover, the objection can rightly be made that in *Juvenile Delinquency and Urban Areas* the causal chain leading to delinquency suffers from theoretical confusion. Shaw and McKay made no attempt to follow through on the implications of their original insight—that industrial expansion, neighborhood destruction in zones of transition, and juvenile delinquency might be parts of the same causative process. In other words, although they correctly identified the socially harmful effects of unregulated industrial and commercial expansion on community life, they instead chose to argue that these effects were generated by a breakdown in the values of the affected communities. For Shaw and McKay it was not dilapidated housing, overcrowding, poor hygiene, and inadequate leisure facilities (all effects of unregulated urban growth) that caused delinquency. Delinquency was caused by a breakdown in the values of the delinquents, in those of their families, and in those of their communities as a whole. Their analysis failed to view delinquency and capital movements as anything other than aspects of a temporary, coincidental process. Thus Snodgrass (1976:11) rightly complained:

> A number of observations could have been made about this "process" (even the term "transitional" implied that it was a process that took place without conflict). The most obvious was the "discrepancy" in the distribution of land, property, power, wealth, health and longevity between the residents of the high delinquency area and the business elites of the commercial center. The fact that life resources were held by one class, the fact that landowners allowed their property to deteriorate, the fact that capitalist enterprises and other vaunted institutions invaded and destroyed communities, that this "process" was carried out "legitimately" and without concern for human dislocation and welfare, and that the residents were politically impotent and resourceless (and could offer no resistance) are all points unmentioned and apparently unnoticed.

Finally, we note that Shaw and McKay concluded their analysis with a discussion of the implications of their findings for the prevention and treatment of delinquency. Their proposal to form an *area project* led directly to creation of the legendary community-based Area Project that began in South Chicago (Schlossman and Sedlak, 1983). Disregarding the popular theory that delinquency typically results from individuals of wayward or deprived moral character, Shaw and McKay (*ibid.*:322–326) recommended that the Project be "initiated and carried on by the concerted efforts of citizens and local residents interested in improvement of the community life in all its aspects" (*ibid.*:322). Because Shaw and McKay pinpointed the immediate causes of delinquency as cultural variation and conflict in the realm of values, so too their recommendations were intended to encourage certain values (self-reliance, self-respect, status, and so forth) that, for them, were lacking in low-income and in high-delinquency areas.

However, the harsh reality of Chicago quickly marred this romantic vision. About its predictable lack of success in combatting crime, Snodgrass has written that "the CAP was cosmetic rather than surgical; the approach was almost trivial in the face of the realities of Chicago politics and economics" (1976:16).

In the next section we outline a theory of crime and deviance that in certain ways appears as a marked advance on the school of social ecology, Merton's (1938) theory of social structure and anomie. Merton emphasized, or so it seemed, what Chicago criminologists generally had ignored—a *theoretical* explanation that linked deviance and crime to the class structure.

12.3 ———— SOCIAL STRUCTURE, ANOMIE, AND DEVIANCE

It is difficult to exaggerate the importance of Robert Merton's (1938) short article "Social Structure and Anomie," in which he strongly opposed biological and individualistic explanations of deviance and crime. Merton focused, rather, on the *rates* of such conduct. In developing this focus, Merton relied on Durkheim's concept of anomie (see Chapter 11.2) to explain how and why "some social structures exert a definite pressure upon certain persons in the society to engage in nonconforming rather than conforming conduct" (*ibid.*:255). But whereas Durkheim had stressed that anomic states arise from unregulated human desires, Merton pinpointed the importance of the relationship between means and goals.

Merton's central hypothesis was that, sociologically, deviant behavior is a symptom of a specific sort of *social disorganization*: a lack of fit between culturally prescribed aspirations and socially structured avenues for achieving them. Although his essay could in principle be applied to several different societies, it is clear that Merton chiefly had in mind the United States and, especially, the goals enshrined in the so-called "American Dream."

Merton's argument begins with two important elements of social and cultural structures. The first element is the culturally defined *goals* held out as legitimate objectives for all members of a society. These goals are "the things worth striving for." The second element is the regulations, controls, and procedures for moving toward goals, which are termed *institutionalized means* or norms. A well-regulated, or stable, society has a balanced equilibrium between means and goals. In a stable society, both means and goals are accepted by everyone and are available to all. Social integration effectively occurs when individuals are socialized into accepting that they will be rewarded for the occasional sacrifice of conforming to institutionalized means and when they actually compete for rewards through legitimate means. Malintegrated, or unstable, societies stress the goals without stressing the means, or vice versa. In some societies institutionalized means are not integrated with important social values. In some societies, such as the U.S., provisions for making the means of achieving the goals available to all are insufficient. Certain means, such as vivisection or medical experimentation, although perhaps technically more efficient in achieving goals, are sometimes unacceptable. Yet people often turn to technically more efficient means if other institutionalized means are unavailable. The more widespread the practice of using noninstitutionalized means, the more a society destabilizes or, put another way, the more widespread becomes anomie.

Competitive sports illustrate the processes that lead to anomie. If success in sports is construed as "winning the game at all costs," rather than winning by the rules, the use of illegitimate but technically more efficient means is more attractive to participants. As Merton (*ibid.*:259) put it:

> The star of the opposing football team is surreptitiously slugged; the wrestler incapacitates his opponent through ingenious but illicit techniques; university alumni covertly subsidize "students" whose talents are confined to the athletic field. The emphasis on the goal has so attenuated the satisfactions deriving from sheer participation in the competitive activity that only a successful outcome provides gratification. Through the same process, tension generated by the desire to win in a poker game is relieved by successfully dealing one's self four aces or, when the cult of success has truly flowered, by sagaciously shuffling the cards in a game of solitaire.

Moreover, Merton suggested that if "concern shifts exclusively to the outcome of competition, then those who perennially suffer defeat may, understandably enough, work for a change in the rules of the game" (*ibid.*:257). Merton believed that the United States is a society in which great emphasis is placed upon certain success-goals without a corresponding emphasis upon institutionalized means.

This *lack of fit* occurs in three ways. First, as in competitive sports, means are often elevated to ends (for example, money is commonly viewed as an end in itself rather than as a means to achieve a goal). Moreover, its acquisition is a goal that can never be met. All income brackets constantly want more money and when they get more of it, they want still more. In other words, the goals of the American Dream are beyond nearly everyone's reach. Second, the lot of the multitudes who never achieve success-goals is made doubly worse because they not only fail to succeed but tend to endure penalties for such "failure." Through the socializing agencies of family, school, and peer groups we are bombarded constantly with such slogans as "There is no such word as 'fail,'" "Never be a quitter," and "You can make it if you try." Coupled with this pressure to maintain lofty goals, there are very real penalties paid by those who draw in or reduce their ambitions. The cultural manifesto, Merton argued, is clear: Never quit, never stop trying, never lower your horizons.

The third description of the *lack of fit* between means and goals in the United States Merton never fully articulates, although at several points it reaches the surface of his argument. Merton hints that because of a maldistribution of power (*ibid.*:263) certain segments of the population—such as individuals in the lower social strata—are continually denied access to legitimate, institutionalized means. Despite such slogans as "Anyone can be president" or "Work hard and

TABLE
12-1

A Typology of Modes of Individual Adaptation

MODES OF ADAPTATION	CULTURE GOALS[1]	INSTITUTIONALIZED MEANS[1]
I Conformity	+	+
II Innovation	+	−
III Ritualism	−	+
IV Retreatism	−	−
V Rebellion	±	±

[1] + signifies acceptance, − signifies rejection, ± signifies rejection of prevailing values and substitution of new values.

Source: Merton, Robert (1938, p. 263).

you are rewarded with monetary success," these goals are almost impossible to achieve for those at the bottom or at the margins of society. Tragically, failure tends to be defined as a consequence not of social inequality but of individual ineptitude or lack of ambition.

Merton's scenario of the American Dream contemplates a society egalitarian in its ideology but unequal in terms of availability of the means of achieving success-goals. U.S. society, therefore, is imperfect and badly integrated; its social and cultural structures inevitably produce strain and tension.

Merton's Typology of Modes of Individual Adaptation

What are the consequences of this strain on the individual? Merton identified five different responses to the strains and tensions of social life in the U.S. (see Table 12-1): conformity, innovation, ritualism, retreatism, and rebellion.[4] We stress that Merton did not conceive of these responses as psychological conditions, but as structural responses to the strain of anomie. The ways in which individuals respond to anomie in part vary, in Merton's formulation, according to their position in the class structure.

I Conformity   This is the most common practice. Although Merton did not explain why the majority of the members of society typically conform, he suggests that "were this not so, the stability and continuity of the society could not be maintained" (*ibid.*:264). However, Merton was concerned chiefly with the four deviant adaptations to the tensions generated by the gap between means and ends.

II Innovation   The *combination* of cultural emphasis on success-goals and rigidity of the U.S. class structure, Merton insisted, produces an innovative

---

[4] Merton never clarified whether "conformity" was a *response* to strain and tension or an *avoidance* of such problems. Whichever the case, Merton ignored the important problem of whether individuals engage in conformist conduct because they have chosen freely to do so or, on the contrary, because they have been manipulated into doing so by such socializing agencies as family, school, peer, group, media, and so forth.

deviant adaptation. This is the most common deviant response, and the most important for criminology. Innovation is deviant behavior that uses illegitimate means to achieve socially acceptable goals. Many crimes against property (such as burglaries, robberies, and larcenies) are clear examples of innovative acts. Because innovative responses are distributed throughout the U.S. class structure there is, Merton suggests, no simple correlation between crime and poverty (*ibid.*:269–271). The pressures to succeed operate at *all* points in the class structure; innovative deviance occurs throughout the social structure—from robber barons and white-collar criminals to common criminals in the lower social strata. However, Merton continued, innovative deviance in the U.S. is concentrated largely in the skilled and unskilled working class. It is there, more than at any other class location, that the gap between goals (which *all* are urged to achieve) and means is most acute.

In his theory of innovative deviance, Merton assumed that innovators are persons who have been improperly socialized. Had they been properly socialized, had they properly internalized the need to follow institutionalized norms, their behavior, of course, would by definition be conformist. An alternative for those who have fully internalized the institutionalized values, but who still crave the impossible-to-achieve aspirations of the American Dream, is a dogged involvement with institutionalized norms at the expense of success-goals. This alternative Merton terms "ritualism."

III Ritualism   Merton defined ritualism as "the abandoning or scaling down of the lofty cultural goals of great pecuniary success and rapid social mobility to the point where one's aspirations can be satisfied" (*ibid.*:273–274). It is the response of conformist bureaucrats who "take no chances." Ritualism is expressed in such clichés as "I'm not sticking *my* neck out" and "Aim low and you'll never be disappointed." Ritualism is practiced most often by members of the lower middle class, where "parents typically exert continuous pressure upon children to abide by the moral mandates of society, and where the social climb upwards is less likely to meet with success than among the upper middle class" (*ibid.*:275).

IV Retreatism   This is an adaptation (or maladaptation) that relinquishes culturally prescribed goals and does not conform to institutionalized means. It is an escape mechanism that often arises when, after having internalized the importance of following legitimate means toward acceptable goals, an individual suffers repeated failure in goal achievement *and* is unable to resort to proscribed means. Retreatists constitute the "true aliens": they are "*in* the society but not *of* it" (*ibid.*:277). They include psychotics, autistics, pariahs, outcasts, vagrants, vagabonds, tramps, chronic drunkards, and drug addicts. The retreatist adaptation, Merton insists, is by and large a private and isolated response rather than a public one.

V Rebellion   This involves alienation from legitimate means and values. In contrast to retreatism, rebellion is a collective activity. For a rebellious disposition to be transformed into organized political action, legitimate means and values must be viewed as arbitrary or mythical, loyalty to them must be withdrawn, and an allegiance must be developed to new groups possessed of a new myth. The new myth has two functions. First, it must identify the source of large-scale frustration in society itself rather than in the individual. Second, it must be directed to the founding of a society with closer links among merit, effort, and reward (*ibid.*:279–281). The precise mix of these criteria, Merton could have added, is subject to almost infinite variety, and includes anarchists, communists, and the Ku Klux Klan.

Assessment

Merton's analysis of the pressures and strains in the U.S., and of the way in which they lead to different deviant responses, including crime, was a brilliant polemic against those who believe that the causes of crime are found in such individualistic factors as defective personality or malformed biology. It was, moreover, a thoroughgoing indictment of the rampant social inequality endemic to U.S. society. Merton's argument about strain and anomie remains one of the most powerful sociological explanations of deviance and crime; it is perhaps the single most cited journal article in modern sociology (Clinard, 1964:10). As we learn in the remainder of this chapter, Merton's analysis has substantially influenced theories of delinquent subcultures.

However, several criticisms must be made of Merton's analysis of the relations among social structure, anomie, and deviance. First, crucial parts of his argument hinge on unstated and unproven assumptions. For example, it is questionable whether acceptance of middle-class norms and values in U.S. society is as widespread as Merton depicts. Accepted by whom? For what reason? Are middle-class norms and values in Manhattan the same as those in rural Wisconsin? Again, Merton's argument that deviance is a *response* to structural strain assumes that no forms of deviant activity have authenticity in their own right. Some deviant activities are engaged in for no apparent reason other than the fact that they are enjoyable.

Second, although Merton's analysis focuses on the psychic effects of strain on individuals at different points in the class structure, there is no indication of the structural causes of strain themselves. We should not, of course, criticize Merton for not outlining something he never intended to examine—but this remains an important omission in his theory of social structure and anomie. It is especially important if we are concerned with issues of social policy and crime. If crime is caused by tensions and strain generated by a society that, for most people, routinely fails to deliver the promises of the American Dream, then how can crime be reduced? Should structural strain be seen as the starting point of a chain of causation that ends in crime and deviance? What are the causes of strain? Can nonconformist conduct be reduced by psychiatric counseling or prescription pills?

Third, recall that Merton's analysis was directed explicitly to success-oriented societies like the U.S. In such societies, the structural strain that produces nonconformist responses, and that culminates in anomie, derives from the gap between availability of means and ideology of equal opportunity. Strain is most intense for those with the least opportunity to partake in the promises of the American Dream (namely, lower-class individuals). Merton therefore suggests that nonconformist conduct (essentially, crime and deviance) is concentrated in the lower class. But this conclusion is at best tentative and, at worst, false. It is true that crimes of lower-class individuals are far more likely to be detected by the police and to lead to arrest (see Chapter 3.1). Yet only in this limited sense is the (property) crime rate of the lower class greater than that of other classes. This does not mean, however, that the actual volume of crime committed by the lower class is greater than that of other classes. Indeed, if the strains of life really operate as suggested, then Merton is left with the problem of explaining why it is that most members of society engage in law-abiding activities far more than in deviance. To a certain extent this very issue was the focus of the criminology of Merton's contemporary, Edwin Sutherland; we consider now his contributions to U.S. criminology.

12.4 ———— THE CONTRIBUTIONS OF EDWIN SUTHERLAND

No introduction to modern criminology is complete without recognizing the enduring contributions made by sociologist Edwin Sutherland (1883–1950). Sutherland was raised in Nebraska and Kansas; his mother was active in Christian service and his father was a Baptist minister and historian (Geis and Goff, 1983:xxi–xxiii). By his own account, Sutherland (1942:13–14) began an academic career with primary training in political economy and political science and a major interest in the study of labor problems. In 1906, Sutherland took a course in criminology at the University of Chicago, where the basic textbook was Henderson's (1893) *Dependent, Neglected and Delinquent Classes.* As a sociologist at the University of Illinois, he taught courses in criminology between 1913 and 1921. Thoroughly dissatisfied with existing textbooks, Sutherland began serious work in criminology in 1921 by drafting an overview of the state of the field. This overview resulted in the first reasonably systematic textbook in U.S. criminology, Sutherland's (1924) cautious yet progressive *Criminology.* In this book Sutherland claimed that the criminologist should not assume the correctness of such popular and legal categories as "crime," "criminality," and "crime rates" (1924:11–30). Instead, he argued, sociology should provide the primary perspective of criminology, and its focus should be both law and crime.

Sutherland's sociological interest in such questions as "What is crime?" and "What is the relationship between crime and law?" was apparent throughout the main body of his work from the mid-1920s to the late 1940s. No one criminologist contributed more to the theoretical development of criminology in the U.S. than Edwin Sutherland did during these two decades. In what follows we divide his sociological criminology into four areas: differential association, differential social organization, his book *The Professional Thief,* and white-collar crime.

Differential Association

In the early editions of his book *Criminology,* Sutherland clearly believed, as did the majority of his contemporaries, that the causes of crime were in principle infinite. However, by the mid-1930s his belief in multicausality had weakened as further study convinced him to integrate existing findings about the causes of crime into a general theory of crime. In this regard Sutherland was greatly influenced by the pessimistic although, he largely agreed (Schuessler, 1973:230), correct findings of a widely read report released by the Rockefeller-funded Bureau of Social Hygiene in New York City. The report's most damning accusation (Michael and Adler, 1933) was that criminology in the U.S. was entirely lacking in scientific generalizations about the causes of crime. What Sutherland termed the *theory* (or "principle") of *differential association* resulted from his ambitious search for a general theory of the causes of crime. As he later reflected:

> It was my conception that a general theory should take account of all the factual information regarding crime causation. It does this either by organizing the multiple factors in relation to each other or by abstracting from them certain common elements. It does not, or should not, neglect or eliminate any factors that are included in the multiple factor theory (Sutherland, 1942:18).

The specific content of Sutherland's theory of differential association derived from Tarde's theory of imitation (see Chapter 11.1), from the Chicago school's concept of social disorganization, and from George Herbert Mead and W. I. Thomas' sociopsychological emphasis on the importance of meanings in social interaction. Although we do not address social psychology as such, it is worth quoting Vold and Bernard's (1986) summary of the elements in Mead's theory that influenced Sutherland's theory of differential association:

> In Mead's theory a cognitive factor—"meanings"—determines behavior. Concrete experiences in the person's life, such as social or economic position, unemployment, racial discrimination, peer pressures, physical abuse, or a learning disability, can mean very different things to different people. Mead regarded meaning as the central factor in the explanation of behavior and assessed the influence of psychological or social conditions in terms of the meaning those conditions have for the individual (*ibid.*:211).

Sutherland's theory of differential association was first explicitly stated in 1939 and, after modification, appeared in its final version in 1947. In its last formulation, Sutherland meant the theory to explain both the *process* by which a given person learns to engage in crime and also the *content* of what is learned.

The theory of differential association can be summarized as follows (Sutherland, 1947:6–8). First, criminal behavior is learned, like all other behavior, within intimate personal groups in an interactive process of communication. This means that criminality is not inherited biologically. Second, the learning of criminal behavior includes instruction in the techniques of crime and the motivational values favorable to committing it. These values are learned from definitions of the legal codes as favorable or unfavorable. The principle of differential association asserts that a person becomes criminal when definitions favorable to violation of law exceed definitions unfavorable to violation, and when contacts with criminal patterns outweigh contacts with anticriminal patterns. Exposure to such definitions and contacts varies in frequency, duration, priority, and intensity. Finally, writes Sutherland (*ibid.*:8):

> While criminal behavior is an expression of general needs and values, it is not explained by those general needs and values, since noncriminal behavior is an expression of the same needs and values. Thieves generally steal in order to secure money, but likewise honest laborers work in order to secure money. The attempts by many scholars to explain criminal behavior by general drives and values, such as the happiness principle, striving for social status, the money motive, or frustration, have been and must continue to be futile since they explain lawful behavior as completely as they explain criminal behavior.

Sutherland's theory has appealed greatly to sociologists because its basic argument seems to offer a precise sociological explanation of why some people engage in crime and others do not. It allows no space, for example, for the idea that criminals are persons with abnormal biological constitutions or psychiatric tendencies. Persons who engage in crime do so because they have associated, *socially* and *culturally*, more (in frequency, duration, priority, and intensity) with pro-criminal patterns than with anticriminal patterns. In this framework crime is a deviant action that is learned by normal persons who have been influenced by a specific cultural process.

Sutherland's theory of differential association has been, and continues to be, one of the most fertile causal accounts of crime. As recently as 1984, Chambliss described it as "the most influential of all sociological perspectives on criminal behavior" (quoted in Gaylord and Galliher, 1988:1; and see Matsueda, 1988). One of differential association's great strengths is that it is a general theory that seeks to account for both criminal and noncriminal behavior. And, as discussed in some depth in Chapter 13, Sutherland's theory has encouraged analysis of both forms of behavior. Analysis of criminal behavior is found especially in theories about the causal relationships between crime and subcultural ideas and values (see Chapter 13); theories of noncriminal behavior, specifically addressing the question "Why do so many people not commit crimes?" have focused on the behavioral processes of control and learning (see Chapters 14.1, 14.2).

The theory of differential association has gained tremendous respect. It has also generated substantial controversy. Sutherland's collaborator, Donald

Cressey, has argued persuasively that some of this controversy is quite unwarranted (Sutherland and Cressey, 1970:78–87). For instance (*ibid.*:78–79), certain critics (such as Vold, 1958:194; DeFleur and Quinney, 1966) mistakenly suggested that the theory of differential association fails to realize that not all persons who associate with criminals actually become criminals themselves. Indeed, a careful reading of "Proposition #6" in Sutherland's theory argues that it is not mere association with criminals and criminal patterns that causes crime. In fact, Sutherland fully realized that associating with criminals was not a sufficient condition for engaging in crime. Persons commit crime, Sutherland stressed, "because of an excess of definitions favorable to violation of law over definitions unfavorable to violation of law" (1947:6–7).

Some critics have suggested that Sutherland's theory does not apply at all to various sorts of crime, especially those involving no social milieu of procriminal associations (including heroin addiction contracted in a hospital [Lindesmith, 1947]). Gaylord and Galliher report that at one point Sutherland himself did not feel that "his theory could account for 'adventitious' crimes, criminal acts that were accidental, casual, or trivial in nature" (1988:151). But, they perceptively counter:

> It is unclear what these adjectives mean when applied to crimes. Is one to believe that Sutherland thought that they were accidental in the sense that they did not have causes? Or that they were engaged in by nonprofessional criminals? Or by persons lacking a criminal identity? (*ibid.*).

However, behind the repeated misreadings of its basic terms lie three serious problems with the explanatory adequacy of differential association theory. First, the terms of the theory are so deliberately abstract that testing of them has proven extremely difficult. How, for example, can we actually measure an "excess" of definitions favorable to violation of law over definitions unfavorable to violation of law? What, precisely, are "associations" with "criminal patterns"? Should such associations include the influence of deep-rooted, socially harmful tendencies like racism and sexism—some of which have even been expressed in law and espoused by government officials and law enforcement officers? Questions such as these clearly reveal that the terms of Sutherland's theory are insufficiently precise.

Second, the actual causal chain in Sutherland's theory arguably rests on a tautology. Logically, if we assume that human beings are not automata, then to say that crime is engaged in by persons who are motivated to engage in it or who learn to engage in it is not to say very much at all.

Third, the premises of Sutherland's theory are highly controversial. The image of the social actor postulated by Sutherland is that of an empty vessel with no history, no beliefs, no preferences, and no capacity for choice. Into this vessel Sutherland sought to pour "pro-" and "anti-" criminal tendencies. If (for some unstated reason) there is an excess of pro-criminal tendencies poured into this human vessel, then, the theory of differential association suggests, the vessel engages in crime. Because of this rigid determinism the theory does not, indeed cannot, address the problem of *why* certain persons associate more with pro-criminal patterns than with anticriminal patterns. Yet this problem must certainly be incorporated into any theory that seeks to generalize about the causes of crime.

In two respects, at least, Sutherland was aware that his theory of differential association was seriously incomplete. He knew that individuals differed in their *responses* to pro-criminal patterns and that, therefore, elements of social psychology relating to differences in personality traits must be included in a revised version of the theory (Sutherland, 1942:25–29; Sutherland and Cressey, 1949:83–87). He also knew that it was one thing to explain why a particular individual engages in crime but quite another to explain why some social groups have higher or lower crime rates than others. Toward the end of his career, Sutherland gave some indications of the direction in which he would have addressed this latter difficulty concerning his theory of differential association. These are found in his concept of "differential social organization" (or "differential group organization"). Because criminologists (including Cressey in Sutherland and Cressey, 1949:87–91) are tempted to read more coherence into this concept than Sutherland himself could give it, we proceed with considerable caution.

Differential Social (Dis)Organization

Although his theory of differential association seemed to apply to the criminal behavior of individuals, Sutherland was also concerned with the question of why crime tended to be concentrated among certain groups in society. In his recollection of the development of the theory of differential association, Sutherland referred to the importance of three questions:

> One of these questions was, Negroes [*sic*], young-adult males, and city dwellers all have relatively high crime rates: What do these three groups have in common that places them in this position? Another question was, Even if feebleminded persons have a high crime rate, why do they commit crimes? It is not feeblemindedness as such, for some feebleminded persons do not commit crimes. Later I raised another question which became even more important in my search for generalizations. Crime rates have a high correlation with poverty if considered by areas of a city but a low correlation if considered chronologically in relation to the business cycle; this obviously means that poverty as such is not an important cause of crime. How are the varying associations between crime and poverty explained? (1942:15)

Sutherland (1947:8–9, 69–80) began to examine these sociological questions, albeit tentatively, in the context of his last statement of differential association. Although almost wholly unintegrated, Sutherland argued that because of the industrial revolution social organization in the U.S. had moved from a simple to a more complex and differentiated type. At the same time there had been a relaxation in the uniformity of social control. Traditional social controls, such as those uniformly exercised within the family and local community and by religion, were increasingly challenged by the rise of economic and political individualism, by increased social mobility, and by material acquisitiveness. In the U.S. this process of social disorganization or, more accurately, reorganization (*ibid.*:75), had been exacerbated by successive waves of immigration, and had resulted in culture conflict between different communities. Crime was one expression of this conflict. Crime rates would be higher in communities where traditional social controls were lacking and that contained some social groups organized for criminal behavior. Crime was also, therefore, an expression of such differential social organization.

Through these incoherent remarks Sutherland was trying to convey the idea that differential social organization explains the *origin* of crime and differential association its *transmission* from one person to another. A final twist appeared in Sutherland's (1949) last major book, *White Collar Crime*, in which he attempted, briefly and tantalizingly, to integrate his incoherent combination of differential association and differential social (dis)organization with Merton's concept of anomie:

> Differential association is a hypothetical explanation of crime from the point of view of the process by which a person is initiated into crime. Social disorganization is a hypothetical explanation of crime from the point of view of the society. These two hypotheses are consistent with each other and one is the counterpart of the other. Both apply to ordinary crime as well as to white-collar crime.
>
> Social disorganization may be either of two types: anomie, or the lack of standards which direct the behavior of members of a society in general or in specific areas of behavior; or the organization within a society of groups which are in conflict with reference to specified practices. Briefly stated, social disorganization may appear in the form of lack of standards or conflict of standards (*ibid.*:255).

The Professional Thief (1937)

Sutherland's interest in the varying associations between crime and economic position led him to explore the crimes of those whose social position had little to do with poverty. This interest was expressed in his research on professional thieves and on white-collar crime.

Sutherland's book *The Professional Thief* was based on the recollections of Broadway Jones, alias "Chic Conwell," a professional thief, ex-drug addict, and ex-con from Philadelphia (or perhaps Boston) who had worked for 20 years as a pimp, pickpocket, shoplifter, and confidence man. Although most of the book was actually written by Conwell, Sutherland edited it for publication and wrote two interpretive chapters. Conwell's recollections provide a fascinating glimpse into the underworld of professional thieves, and include details of criminal *argot* (slang), the roles of members in the *mob* (criminal group), rackets, the *fix* (techniques of avoiding conviction and/or doing time in prison), and thieves' images of the police, the law, and society at large. According to Conwell, the work habits of professional thieves are very similar to the practices of those engaged in lawful business activities (Sutherland, 1937:140):

> Professional stealing as a business is much like any other business. The conversation among thieves in a police station, prison, or hangout is concerned principally with their business, and it is no different in that respect from the conversation of monument salesmen in their meetings. Business possibilities, conditions, and returns are the foremost subjects of conversation, and just as the salesman learns of fertile territory, new methods, new laws which affect the business, so does the thief.
>
> It involves as much hard work as any other business. There is little thrill about it. . . . It is no more thrilling than the work of the factory slave.

According to Sutherland's analysis of Conwell's depiction of the professional thief, the profession of theft has five basic features: technical skill, status, consensus, differential association, and organization (*ibid.*:197–228).

1. *Technical Skill*   Like bricklayers, lawyers, and physicians, professional thieves have a stock of abilities and skills. Wits, *front*, speaking ability, manual dexterity, and specialization are all needed to plan and execute crimes, to dispose of stolen goods, and to fix those cases in which arrests occur.

2. *Status*   Like other professionals, the professional thief occupies a certain status based on such factors as ability, knowledge, dress, manners, wealth, and power. Professional thieves therefore often show contempt toward amateur, small-time, and "snatch-and-grab" thieves.

3. *Consensus*   Professional thieves usually share similar values that aid them in their criminal careers. Their reactions to certain events tend to be similar, including such things as prospective victims and *squealing* on other thieves. "These reactions are like the 'clinical intuitions,'" Sutherland (*ibid.*:202) diagnosed, "which different physicians form of a patient or different lawyers form of a juryman on quick inspection."

4. *Differential Association*   For reasons of security and safety, professional thieves often maintain a barrier between themselves and all others. They tend to associate chiefly with members of their own professional group. The group defines its own members because only professional thieves are received into it.[5]

5. *Organization*   Because technical skills, status, consensus, and differential association form a core of knowledge informally shared by thieves in a

---

[5] This was the first time that the term "differential association" was employed by Sutherland, and its use here is much narrower than in its later usage. See further Snodgrass (1973:4–5).

network of cooperation, professional theft is organized crime (essentially, crime that is organized).

Sutherland's *The Professional Thief* is a classic in the history of criminology for two critical reasons. First, it provides an image of crime that is a decided alternative to the stereotypical picture of disreputable activities engaged in by poorer members of the working class. Indeed, Sutherland's portrayal of crime in this book points to the considerable skills and abilities needed to be a professional thief and to the code of ethics extant among professional thieves. This is a far cry from the popular image of criminals as mentally defective personalities or as biologically deformed individuals. In addition, it shows that the world of professional thievery is a fairly exclusive club, one to which all the learning principles of differential association fully apply.

Second, the analysis in *The Professional Thief* carries through to its logical conclusion the Chicago school's theory that criminologists should investigate criminality "in the flesh" and "on the street" rather than in the comfort of their armchairs. As Snodgrass writes: "*The Professional Thief* . . . is [still] the most authoritative statement on the subject of stealing as an occupation, and it is one of the few studies which has relied on the collaborative contribution of the criminal himself" (1973:1; and see Jackson, 1964; King and Chambliss, 1984; Taylor, 1984).

White Collar Crime (1949)

We have seen how Sutherland (1945) argued, in his article "Is 'White Collar Crime' Crime?" that socially injurious acts (such as white-collar offenses) should be part of the proper subject matter of criminology regardless of how such acts are defined in legal terms (see Chapter 1.2). In this section we outline the findings of Sutherland's (1949) courageous book *White Collar Crime*. This book amplified certain of his concerns in *The Professional Thief* and extended the scope of differential association theory to "white-collar crime," a term that Sutherland coined and introduced into the English language. It was Sutherland's last major venture in criminology, and it was to be his most important contribution.

Sutherland had become distressed, at least since the mid-1930s, that criminology had devoted nearly all its energies to analyzing the crimes of the poor (Geis and Goff, 1983). In the opening sentence of *White Collar Crime*, he dryly remarks that "criminal statistics show unequivocally that crime, as popularly understood and officially measured, has a high incidence in the lower socioeconomic class and a low incidence in the upper socioeconomic class" (Sutherland, 1949:3). Sutherland complained that official statistics of crime, most case studies, and Shaw and McKay-inspired analyses based thereon gave a distorted picture of the social distribution of criminality. These statistics and studies wrongly implied, for example, that poverty was the chief cause of crime. Yet Sutherland felt sure, from his preliminary studies of embezzlers and of the diverse crimes committed by large U.S. corporations, that criminality was far from being the preserve of the poor. Just as much as the poor, if not more so, it was the rich who committed crimes. In this attempt to reverse the familiar object of U.S. criminology—away from the crimes of the poor and toward those of the rich— lay the heart of Sutherland's revelations in *White Collar Crime.*

Sutherland defined white-collar crime as "a crime committed by a person of respectability and high social status in the course of his occupation" (1949:7). His studies of white-collar crime have two main thrusts, neither of which had been explored adequately before his description of them. The first is an estimate of the extent of white-collar crime, the second a theoretical explanation of the causes of white-collar crime.

Sutherland introduced *White Collar Crime* by asserting: "The thesis of this book, positively stated, is that persons of the upper socioeconomic class engage in much criminal behavior" (1949:7). His exposé of white-collar crime included a battery of staggering statistics provided by U.S. government agencies. For example, according to the U.S. Comptroller of the Currency, 75 percent of all banks examined had violated banking laws. According to the Federal Trade Commission, commercial bribery was a prevalent and common practice of many industries. "The financial cost of white-collar crime," Sutherland estimated from the sparse data available prior to his study, "is probably several times as great as the financial cost of all the crimes which are customarily regarded as the 'crime problem' " (*ibid.*:9). However, the great bulk of Sutherland's data in *White Collar Crime* consisted of his own findings collected during two decades. These data concerned decisions of federal, state, and municipal courts and administrative commissions involving the 70 largest manufacturing, mining, and mercantile corporations in the U.S. Among the worst corporate offenders were such giants as American Sugar Refining; American Tobacco; Armour; DuPont; Ford; General Electric; General Motors; Gimbel; A&P; International Harvester; Loew's; Montgomery Ward; National Steel; Procter & Gamble; Sears, Roebuck; U.S. Steel; Warner Bros.; Westinghouse Electric; and Woolworth. Sutherland reported in painstaking detail that in the preceding 20 years:

> each of the 70 large corporations has 1 or more decisions against it, with a maximum of 50. The total number of decisions is 980, and the average per corporation is 14.0. Sixty corporations have decisions against them for restraint of trade, 53 for infringement, 44 for unfair labor practices, 43 for miscellaneous offenses, 28 for misrepresentation in advertising, and 26 for rebates (*ibid.*:15).

Of the 70 largest industrial and commercial U.S. corporations, 97.1 percent were recidivists in that they had two or more decisions against them. In addition, Sutherland revealed that the Federal Trade Commission, by order of Congress, reported that during the 1914–1918 and 1939–1945 world wars many corporations had violated wartime regulations (*ibid.*:174–191). These violations included price regulation abuse, overcharging and fraudulent profiteering in war-related materials, tax evasion, restraint of trade, illegal maintenance of competitive positions, violations of embargoes and neutrality, and even treason (for example, illegally revealing classified information to the enemy). As Sutherland concluded:

> The large corporations in time of war, when Western civilization was endangered, did not sacrifice their own interests and participate wholeheartedly in a national policy, but instead they attempted to use this emergency as an opportunity for extraordinary enrichment of themselves at the expense of others (*ibid.*:191).

With these data Sutherland demonstrated that in order to maximize their profits, U.S. corporations routinely committed crimes against consumers, competitors, stockholders and other investors, inventors, employees, and the state itself. Corporations tended to commit more crimes the greater their age, the larger their size, and the more their economic position was monopolistic, antiunion, and dependent on advertising (*ibid.*:258–263).

Sutherland complained vigorously that the criminal behavior of the lower socioeconomic class differs from the criminal behavior of white-collar and corporate offenders chiefly in the respective ways that society deals with them. The former are typically processed by the criminal justice system, the latter by quasi-judicial review boards and administrative agencies. The typical outcome for the former is prison, but for the latter a warning, an order to desist, or a fine (and see Chapter 7). Indeed, these very different outcomes tend to hide the criminal nature of white-collar crime from the public, from the press, and from criminologists themselves.

We note also that in his explanation of white-collar crime, Sutherland preferred to ignore almost entirely both the economic form that this crime typically took and also the ways in which economic cycles (such as the 1930s Great Depression) stimulated economic and other abuses by the powerful. Sutherland attempted to explain the causes of white-collar crime in terms of his earlier general theory of crime. "The significant thing about white-collar crime," he emphasized, "is that it is not associated with poverty or with social and personal pathologies which accompany poverty" (1949:7). Because he had shown how very often white-collar crimes occur, he therefore believed that a general theory linking crime, poverty, and the latter's related pathologies to be entirely invalid. The only factors common to the crimes of the rich and the poor, he theorized, were differential social organization and differential association (*ibid.*:255–257, 240–255). Differential social organization fosters white-collar crime because it underpins the anomic ideology that free enterprise should not be regulated by government. Because of this ideology, neither the U.S. government nor the community is well organized to counter white-collar and corporate crime. Differential association fosters the transmission of white-collar crime because profit-seeking corporations rapidly mimic the techniques of their successful competitors and because specific techniques of violating the law are passed from one executive to another. These techniques are themselves part of a widespread corporate ideology favorable to violation of law, an ideology exemplified by such maxims as "We are not in business for our health" and "Business is business."

Sutherland's classic text has had a strange history in the subsequent development of criminology in the U.S. It was "the publishing highlight of the 1940s in criminology" (Geis and Goff, 1983:xxviii), was very favorably reviewed on publication—even though neither his publisher nor his university would permit publication of the actual names of convicted corporations—and then subjected to sympathetic empirical criticisms. The latter included studies of violations in the meat-packing industry (Hartung, 1950) and in black markets during rationing in World War II (Clinard, 1952).

Following this initial outburst of enthusiasm, however, criminologists returned to their traditional neglect of crimes of the powerful in the U.S. Only in the 1970s did criminologists "rediscover" the analysis of white-collar crime (see Chapter 7), and only with the publication of Clinard and Yeager's (1980) *Corporate Crime* has a thorough examination of corporate illegalities been returned to the criminological agenda. Only recently has Sutherland's *White Collar Crime* received the recognition it so thoroughly deserves. On the dust jacket of the uncensored version of *White Collar Crime* (not published until 1983!), Sutherland's classic text is described by Ralph Nader as a "remarkable and courageous work of criminological scholarship" and by Donald Cressey as "the most significant book ever published in American criminology." We agree.

Assessment

Sutherland may be genuinely regarded as a pioneer who contributed immeasurably to the development of criminology, for two major reasons. First, his questioning of the basic subject matter of criminology—and its extension to social harms not always perceived, defined, or processed as crimes—was a valuable insight inadequately appreciated by many criminologists even today. Second, his search for a general theory of crime, however difficult to achieve, was one of the first attempts by a criminologist to make *explicit* the ever-present role of sociological theory in all studies of crime. These two contributions guided Sutherland's search for the factual revelations in his books *The Professional Thief* and *White Collar Crime*, both milestones in criminology. As we shall learn, Sutherland's theoretical focus on the origin (differential social organization) and on the transmission (differential association) of criminal values was soon to influence new lines of inquiry in criminology, including analysis of delinquent subcultures (see Chapter 13) and of the processes of control (see Chapter 14.1) and learning (Chapter 14.2).

REVIEW

This chapter outlined the early forms of criminological theory in the U.S. The institutional position of criminology in the U.S. was dramatically transformed during the Progressive Era (*circa* 1890–1910). Before the Progressive Era, criminology was conducted in an unorganized and amateurish way; afterward, it found a secure and well-founded base in the universities. U.S. criminology rapidly gained global dominance, although its domination of criminological theory has created some hardship for the development of comparative criminology (see Chapter 16). U.S. dominance is so great that perhaps three-quarters of all professional criminologists now live and work in the United States.

The Early History of Criminology in the United States, 1895–1915

1. Intellectually, the vast majority of pre-1900 writings on crime took the nature of *crime* and *criminality* entirely for granted.

2. In addition to native concern with the crimes of immigrants, blacks, and other outsiders, early writings on crime borrowed piecemeal from European concepts of crime, especially those connected with biology.

3. Criminology emerged generally from the Progressive Era's (1890–1910) social reformism. It depended specifically on the support of the social science movement, the rise of various professional associations, and mass media stimulation of public interest in its pronouncements on the causes of crime. Gradually, criminology admitted the relevance of social factors to its investigations.

Crime and Social Ecology

1. Initially, sociological criminology in the U.S. was almost exclusively identified with the perspective of social ecology developed by the Chicago school from 1920 onward. Chicago was an important site of the progressive movement, and the city naturally lent itself to the study of social problems, including crime.

2. The Chicago school adopted and spread several innovative research techniques, including both quantitative and qualitative methods. The latter involved life-history documents, case studies, investigative journalism, media materials, in-depth interviews, and participant observation. These methods, it was believed, would produce objective, value-free knowledge.

3. The crowning achievement of the Chicago school was Shaw and McKay's (1942) *Juvenile Delinquency and Urban Areas*. This study concluded that many social problems, including juvenile delinquency, were concentrated in zones of transition populated by white lower-class immigrants and by blacks. This concentration was correlated with such other factors as rates of adult crime, school truancy, disease, and mental disorders, and it remained highly stable despite resident turnover in the zones of transition. Certain of these problems, it was felt, could be alleviated by a change in the local community's values.

4. The Chicago school has been extremely influential in the development of sociological criminology. Nevertheless, it has been criticized for its factual errors and its empiricist theory.

Social Structure, Anomie, and Deviance

1. This section examined Merton's (1938) influential article "Social Structure and Anomie." Merton's analysis of deviance and crime drew on the work of Durkheim and the Chicago school.

2. Merton argued that certain societies, like the U.S., are unstable because they fail to provide adequate means for achieving socially approved goals.

3. Failure to achieve socially approved goals leads to various structural responses: conformity, innovation, ritualism, retreatism, and rebellion.

4. Because it is based on various unproven assumptions, the validity of Merton's analysis of deviance is somewhat suspect.

The Contributions of Edwin Sutherland

1. Edwin Sutherland wrote one of the earliest textbooks on criminology. Justifiably called the "Dean of American criminology," Sutherland attempted to combine an explicit sociological theory of crime with detailed empirical analyses. Significantly, he attempted to extend the proper subject matter of criminology beyond state-defined categories of social injury.

2. Sutherland's general theory of differential association attempted to explain both conformity and deviation. It held that a person engages in crime because of an excess of definitions favorable to violation of law over definitions unfavorable to violation of law. Crime is thus learned behavior. By merging social disorganization theory with differential association theory, Sutherland attempted, largely unsuccessfully, to explain the origins of crime and its cultural transmission.

3. In *The Professional Thief* (1937) and *White Collar Crime* (1949), Sutherland pioneered analyses of certain crimes not often considered crimes either by the public or by criminologists, and often not processed as crimes by the criminal justice system. The former examined the crimes and cultural world of professional thieves; the latter examined the occupational crimes routinely committed by white-collar executives in large corporations. In both books, Sutherland explained the transmission and persistence of these crimes with the theory of differential association.

4. Sutherland's theories of the causes of crime have proven very difficult to test, largely because their content is imprecise and their scope is so general. Yet they remain the starting point for much analysis of crime today (see Chapter 14.1, 14.2).

QUESTIONS FOR CLASS DISCUSSION

1. In the late 1920s, lawyer Jerome Michael and philosopher Mortimer Adler were commissioned by Columbia University Law School and by the Bureau of Social Hygiene in New York City to write a report on the desirability of establishing an institute of criminology in the United States. In the course of their lengthy final report, Michael and Adler scrutinized the scientific status of existing criminology, and concluded that "the work of criminologists has not resulted in scientific knowledge of the phenomena of crime" (1933:54). Do you agree with this statement?

2. Was Shaw and McKay's (1942) *Juvenile Delinquency and Urban Areas* scientific? How does a scientific explanation of crime differ from other types of explanation, such as a religious one? Are sociological and scientific explanations of the same sort? Can we understand the causes of social behavior (for example, crime) in the same way that natural scientists, such as biologists and physicists, understand the behavior of animals and inanimate objects?

3. When Shaw and McKay pinpointed the links between juvenile delinquency and the social organization of Chicago neighborhoods, were these links causative or correlational?

4. Does Merton's typology of deviance actually explain variations in crime rates?

5. Discuss the following (Sutherland, 1947:7–8):

    The attempts by many scholars to explain criminal behavior by general drives and values, such as the happiness principle, striving for social status, the money motive, or frustration, have been and continue to be futile since they explain lawful behavior as completely as they explain criminal behavior. They are similar to respiration, which is necessary for any behavior but which does not differentiate criminal from noncriminal behavior.

6. Is white-collar crime real crime?

RECOMMENDED READINGS

Bennett, James (1981). *Oral History and Delinquency: The Rhetoric of Criminology.* Chicago: University of Chicago Press. Pp. 104–210 give an account of the oral life histories method practiced by Chicago criminologists.

Bulmer, Martin (1984). *The Chicago School of Sociology: Institutionalization, Diversity, and the Rise of Sociological Research.* Chicago: University of Chicago Press.

This authoritative history of the Chicago school outlines its methodological contributions to the rise of empirical social research.

Gaylord, Mark S. and John F. Galliher (1988). *The Criminology of Edwin Sutherland.* New Brunswick, NJ: Rutgers University Press. A detailed history of Sutherland's theory of differential association.

Geis, Gil and Colin Goff (1986). "Edwin H. Sutherland's White-Collar Crime in America: An Essay in Historical Criminology." *Criminal Justice History: An International Annual,* 7:1–31. Recreates the development of Sutherland's concept of white-collar crime and of the publishing fiasco surrounding *White Collar Crime.*

Laub, John H. (1983). *Criminology in the Making: An Oral History.* Boston: Northeastern University Press. A unique series of interviews probing the emotions, ideas, attitudes, and feelings of selected U.S. criminologists.

Taylor, Ian, Paul Walton, and Jock Young (1973). *The New Criminology.* London: Routledge & Kegan Paul. Contains some trenchant criticisms of Mertonian anomie theory (pp. 91–110) and the social ecology of Shaw and McKay (pp. 110–114).

CHAPTER 13

DELINQUENT SUBCULTURES AND SUBCULTURES OF DELINQUENCY

13.1 Delinquent Subcultures
Cohen's *Delinquent Boys* (1955)
Delinquency, Lower-Class Culture, and Opportunity
Assessment

13.2 Matza's *Delinquency and Drift* (1964)
The Positive Delinquent
The Subculture of Delinquency
Delinquency and Drift
Assessment

13.3 Control Theory
Containment
Control
Assessment

Preview

Chapter 13 introduces:

☞ the ways in which—beginning in the mid-1950s—criminologists have attempted to explain the origins, beliefs, and activities of male, lower-class, delinquent subcultures.
☞ explanations of violent delinquent subcultures.
☞ the anti-positivist theory of David Matza, which argues that delinquents are not nearly so committed to their activities as subcultural theorists have supposed.
☞ control theory as an explanation of delinquency.

Key Terms

containment	reaction formation
control	status frustration
drift	subculture
middle-class measuring rod	techniques of neutralization

13.1 ——— DELINQUENT SUBCULTURES

Chapter 12 examined Merton's (1938) theory of anomie and Sutherland's (1947) theory of differential association. Following the 1939–1945 war hiatus, these two theories exercised enormous influence over criminology. During the 1950s many criminologists examined the subcultural settings in which deviant values coexist with dominant social values. These subcultural theorists took their theoretical perspectives directly from the earlier writings of Merton and Sutherland. The central question of the subcultural theorists repeated Durkheim's question: Given the widespread persistence of deviance, what functions do deviant values serve for those who subscribe to them? This section outlines the key answers given to this question.

As research on delinquent subcultures developed during the 1950s, it gradually recognized the importance of a variable seldom referred to and never properly examined by the Chicago school—the influence of social class. We begin our outline of subcultural theory with Albert Cohen's (1955) book *Delinquent Boys*.

Cohen's *Delinquent Boys* (1955)

Albert Cohen's *Delinquent Boys* was based on the premise that juvenile delinquency is "a major practicable problem of every sizeable American community" (1955:19). All attempts to control the growth of juvenile delinquency had failed largely, Cohen argued, because not one of the three leading theories of delinquency had accurately identified its causes. Cohen (*ibid.*: 32–33) stressed that the Chicago school had overemphasized the social disorganization of the zones of transition (and see Kobrin, 1951; and Chapter 12.2) and that these areas were not nearly so lacking in community spirit as researchers such as Shaw and McKay had imagined. Moreover, Cohen was critical of Mertonian anomie theory (see Chapter 12.3 and Cohen, 1965) because it had failed to come to grips with the content of juvenile gangs. Cohen further believed that Merton had ignored the fact that delinquent gangs do not simply use deviant means to achieve culturally approved goals. Far from it, he insisted, delinquent gangs often seem to engage in violence simply for "the hell of it" (*ibid.*:35–36). And Sutherland's theory of differential association, too, failed to explain why some juveniles join gangs and others do not (see Chapter 12.4). Moreover, Cohen felt that Sutherland had taken for granted the *existence* of juvenile gangs: Where do they come from? What are their origins? Why do delinquent gangs exist in some social settings but not in others?

About Sutherland, with whom he had done graduate study at Indiana, Cohen (quoted in Laub, 1983:189) recorded his feeling that the theory of differential association

> has to do with how people come to acquire the delinquent or criminal culture through a process of association. But, I asked, Where does it come from? How do you explain the existence of the culture? . . . But [Sutherland] didn't think that was much of a question. Somewhere he said, actually he wrote it too, that the southern practice of dropping the r's is explained by the southern practice of dropping the r's—that's all you have to know—which incidentally is wrong. It sounds on the face of it that it might say something but the point is, some speech practices become extinct, others spread and you get novelties linguistically. Some catch on, others don't. So it really wasn't a very good answer.

For Cohen, then, existing theories in criminology did not explain much about delinquent behavior. No theory had seriously examined the values and beliefs of juvenile gang members and the nature of their activities. Very little indeed was known about the causes of juvenile delinquency. Why do some juveniles, and not others, join delinquent gangs? Why do gangs do what they do? Why do gangs persist in urban neighborhoods?

Cohen's *Delinquent Boys* tried to answer such questions by beginning with the idea that the world of juvenile delinquents is enveloped in a *subculture*. Although the term "subculture" had been in use among anthropologists at least since the 1870s, it was Cohen who first applied it to the study of delinquency (Wolfgang and Ferracuti, 1967:95–99). Culture, for Cohen, refers to the knowledge, beliefs, values, codes, tastes, and prejudices that persist in the social relations people regularly have in their interactions with each other. A subculture, then, refers to a set of beliefs (and so forth) that differs in some way from the main or dominant culture. Taking part in delinquent acts is a major aspect of delinquent subcultures. As Cohen himself defined it (*ibid.*:13), a delinquent subculture is

> a way of life that has somehow become traditional among certain groups in American society. These groups are the boys' gangs that flourish most conspicuously in the "delinquency neighborhoods" of our larger American cities.

According to Cohen, the subculture of delinquent boys has six major characteristics in the United States (*ibid.*:24–48):

1. Its activities are (a) *nonutilitarian:* gang members steal, for example, not only because they necessarily want or have a use for something, but

sometimes simply for the hell of it; (b) *malicious:* delinquents take delight in others' discomfort, in terrorizing "good" children, and in flouting teachers and their rules (such as, defecating on a teacher's desk); and (c) *negativistic:* delinquent conduct is right by the standards of the subculture precisely because it is wrong by conventional standards.

2. *Versatility:* gang members rarely specialize in types of delinquent acts, as do adult criminals and solitary delinquents.

3. *Short-run hedonism:* gang members have little interest in long-run goals, a fact that reflects their lower-class origins. Typically, they "hang around," "chew the fat," and "wait for something to turn up."

4. *Group autonomy:* gang members are intensely loyal to their own gang, very hostile to others, and resist even the efforts of their families to control them.

5. *Working-class membership:* although cautious about relying on official crime statistics, Cohen nevertheless agrees that juvenile delinquency— especially the juvenile subculture—is overwhelmingly concentrated in the working class.

6. *Male:* although Cohen recognizes the existence of female gangs, and of solitary delinquency engaged in by females, he agrees with official statistics showing that delinquent subcultures are masculine dominated (and see Chapter 3.2).

Cohen reasoned that a good theory of delinquent subcultures must explain the existence of these six subcultural characteristics. But it must also explain *why* subcultures typically flourish *where* they do in the class structure.

Cohen argued that subcultures exist because they provide a solution to certain problems of adjustment shared by a group of individuals. Why, then, is the delinquent subculture mostly found in working-class environments? In his explanation, Cohen begins with the position of the family unit in the local community. He notes that, although the boundaries between working-class and middle-class families are sometimes indistinct, nevertheless, child-rearing practices do vary between different classes. Crucially, all children are not equally well prepared to satisfy the standards by which U.S. society evaluates their passage to adulthood. Working-class parents, for example, place less emphasis than do middle-class parents on development of analytical skills, education, self-denying discipline, and long-term planning for adult status and career; they place more emphasis on physical prowess in groups and learning through "having fun." However, because *all* children are evaluated by middle-class standards, some children are doomed to be seen as failures in *middle-class terms.*

The prevailing middle-class standards (the *middle-class measuring rod*) by which all children are evaluated, especially in schools, include: ambition; individual responsibility; outstanding achievement, especially academic or athletic; industry and thrift; foresight; manners, courtesy, and personality; control of physical aggression; constructive leisure; and respect for property (*ibid.*:88–91).

Because middle-class children tend to acquire these skills from their parents and peers far more than do working-class children, most adolescent failures are drawn from the working class. Above all it is in the school—that supremely middle-class institution—that working-class boys fail. Failure in school often results in *status frustration*, which causes feelings of "guilt, self-recrimination, anxiety, and self-hatred" (*ibid.*:126). Because the working-class boy finds himself at the bottom of the status hierarchy, according to Cohen, he is now in the market for a solution (*ibid.*:119).

According to Cohen it is within the working-class delinquent subculture that the otherwise-unadjusted working-class boy successfully finds a solution to his lack of status in middle-class life. The delinquent subculture, therefore, operates as an "adjustment mechanism" for many working-class adolescents. Adjustment occurs through a process of *reaction formation*, in which the academic success typically denied working-class boys is contemptuously redefined as the "bookish knowledge" of "sissies"; whereas "street knowledge," which is learned from friends in the delinquent gang, is regarded as superior to other forms of knowledge. In general, as previously outlined, the virtues of the working-class gang include the practices regarded by the middle class as vices: nonutilitarian, malicious, and negativistic activities. The gang confers high status on those of its members who practice these activities, a much-needed status for working-class adolescents that is typically denied them when they participate in an alien middle-class world.

Finally, Cohen addressed two further problems about delinquency, which were almost completely ignored in his era, and largely so in ours: female delinquency (*ibid.*:137–147) and middle-class delinquency (*ibid.*:157–169).

Regarding female delinquency, Cohen suggested that because females are not socialized into being successful in the male-dominated realms of society, young females do not have the adjustment problems characteristic of male, working-class "failures." Although young females can eventually find additional satisfaction in a career, successful relationships with the opposite sex are the primary means by which they derive status. Their activities focus, therefore, on popularity with boys, dating, beautification, charm, clothes, and dancing. Although involvement in a delinquent subculture can increase the masculine status of a boy, it can only do harm to the feminine status of a girl. Cohen concludes that for a boy the delinquent response, " 'wrong' though it may be and 'disreputable,' is well within the range of responses that do not threaten his identification of himself as a male" (*ibid.*:140).

Regarding middle-class delinquency, Cohen rightly points out that its very existence must embarrass those who argue that a poor or working-class background is the chief cause of delinquency *in general*. He therefore speculates that this embarrassment may stem from inadequate concepts of social class (namely because lower-class and middle-class families may in fact be *culturally* closer to each other than is usually admitted, boys from both groups might be responding to the same cultural tensions). Another possibility, according to Cohen—which ties in well with other aspects of his theory—is that middle-class delinquent

"Bloods" gang member: Criminologists have traditionally ignored female delinquency.

subcultures respond to the same tensions of gender identification as do their working-class counterparts. As Cohen (*ibid.*:164) now argues, in sociopsychological terms:

> Because of the structure of the modern family and the nature of our occupational system, children of both sexes tend to form early feminine identifications. The boy, however, unlike the girl, comes later under strong social pressure to establish his masculinity, his *difference from*

female figures. Because his mother is the object of the feminine identification which he feels is the threat to his status as a male, he tends to react negativistically to those conduct norms which have been associated with mother and therefore have acquired feminine significance. Since mother has been the principal agent of indoctrination of "good," respectable behavior, "goodness" comes to symbolize femininity, and engaging in "bad" behavior acquires the function of denying his femininity and therefore asserting his masculinity. This is the motivation to juvenile delinquency.

Consequently, Cohen reasons that males from middle-class homes may join delinquent gangs as well.

It is appropriate now to mention an obvious difficulty with Cohen's analysis. We noted that Cohen's explanation of the sources of delinquent subcultures was inspired largely by Mertonian anomie theory. Indeed, much of the importance of Cohen's work lies in the original way in which it extended to delinquent boys an explanation of Merton's category of the rebellious deviant. At root, however, both Merton and Cohen shared the view that deviance (Merton) and delinquency (Cohen) arise as a *reaction* of the lower classes to their failure in middle-class terms. In this view, working-class activities, such as boys' delinquency, are wholly parasitic on middle-class practices. Indeed, what this view of delinquency ignored was precisely what the Chicago school of ecology had emphasized (at least in principle)—the importance of granting authenticity to the values of the deviants themselves. In other words, do working-class delinquents themselves regard their activities as a response to "failure"?

Cohen failed to provide empirical evidence that working-class delinquents accept middle-class success goals. In what sense, we are compelled to ask, does the subculture of working-class juvenile delinquency actually reject middle-class values? This question was soon addressed by other subcultural theorists; to their answers we now turn.

Delinquency, Lower-Class Culture, and Opportunity

Cohen's *Delinquent Boys* rapidly stimulated numerous responses from criminologists and a wealth of new research into the diverse origins, functions, and forms of delinquent subcultures. There follows an outline of the most influential arguments of this research.

The first major criticism of Cohen's findings was developed by Walter Miller (1958) in his article "Lower Class Culture as a Generating Milieu of Gang Delinquency." The bulk of Miller's data came from reports of daily contact with ghetto youth in a large eastern city during a three-year, service-research project into the control of juvenile delinquency. The subjects of the study were both black and white, male and female, and in early, middle, and late adolescence.

Miller suggested that adolescent members of delinquent gangs, and of other forms of "street corner society," are not psychopaths, nor are they physically or mentally defective. Far from it. Gang members are often drawn, Miller observed, from the most "able" sections of the community. Why, then, do they commit crimes? Reasoned Miller:

> The most general answer is that the commission of crimes . . . is motivated primarily by the attempt to achieve ends, states, or conditions which are valued, and to avoid those that are disvalued within their most meaningful cultural milieu (*ibid*.:346).

For achieving these ends, gang members tend to choose the most accessible means available to them. Miller argued that the lower-class way of life has a set of ends, or focal concerns, that include trouble, toughness, smartness, excitement, fate, and autonomy. These focal concerns, he stressed, differ greatly from those of the middle classes. For example, whereas the middle class might value achievement in high school examinations, the lower class values the smartness embodied in the capacity to outfox, outwit, or con others. The distinctive focal concerns of the lower class derive from aspects of its structural position in U.S. society. According to Miller, 40–60 percent of the U.S. is influenced directly by lower-class culture, and of this, 15 percent comprise the "hard-core lower class group" (*ibid*.:334, n.3). Above all, this latter group is characterized by its distinctive family unit—the female-headed household (see Chapter 3.2). The female-headed household is one that "lacks" a permanent male parent or that has no male parent involved in child care and family support.

According to Miller, the major factor that pushes lower-class boys into joining delinquent gangs is the widespread presence of female-headed households in their cultural milieu. Why is this so? Miller depicts the lower-class boy as the victim of a female web of neglect. Because he is surrounded by females, the lower-class boy suffers from acute identity crises, especially those crises associated with problems of gender-role identification (see Chapter 3.2). Miller argues that the female-headed household does not provide "a range of essential functions—psychological, educational, and others" (*ibid*.:342) for the lower-class boy. These functions, Miller concludes, are typically provided by the most accessible means available: the corner group and the gang. The focal concerns of the gang parallel those (smartness, and others) of lower-class life in general. But the gang also embraces two further concerns that in combination explain their territoriality and their positive values: (1) belonging, or adherence to the rules of the gang; and (2) status, (derived from smartness, and others) *as it is defined within the cultural framework of lower-class society.*

Miller therefore reasoned that the delinquent gang functions to resolve crucial problems generated by the cultural, and especially the family, milieu of lower-class boys. But for Miller, unlike Cohen, the gang resolves these problems in its own cultural framework rather than in reaction to the cultural standards of the middle class. We note, however, that there is no evidence that boys in single-parent (female- or male-headed) households, for example, are more likely to be deprived emotionally or psychologically than boys in two-parent households (see Chapter 3.4; and Currie, 1985:182–221). Despite the antifeminist leanings of his argument, Miller casts serious doubt on the validity of Cohen's theory in one important respect. Recall that Cohen assumed that lower-class boys *react* to failure in middle-class worlds (such as school) and, *as a result*, seek status in the more familiar setting of the delinquent subculture. What Miller questions, quite correctly, is Cohen's assumption that the lower-class boy has no authentic values that identify gangs as good things to belong to simply *because they are good things to which to belong.*

Miller was part of a group of delinquency theorists (the Chicago school, Merton, and Cohen) who took the style and direction of delinquent subcultures, or gangs, very much for granted.

However, this great simplification was uncovered by Richard Cloward and Lloyd Ohlin (1960) in their book *Delinquency and Opportunity.* To explain why some juveniles violate conventional norms does not explain variations in the particular form of their deviant actions (such as theft, violence, drug use/abuse, and so forth). Why, for example, do some gangs allegedly focus on violence, some on theft, and still others on drug use/abuse? Following Merton's theory of anomie, Cloward and Ohlin asserted that delinquent subcultures arise because of a gap between the aspirations of lower-class youth and the possibility of their achieving those aspirations through legitimate means. However, the effects of the gap between aspirations and frustrated achievement vary from one individual to another. The direction of variation depends on two basic *types* of legitimate aspiration—aspirations for higher status (achieved by membership in the middle class) and for greater economic success (*ibid.*:90–94). Table 13-1 outlines Cloward and Ohlin's four major categories of male lower-class youth.

According to Cloward and Ohlin, both Type I and Type II boys aspire to middle-class status. However, Type II boys regard a change in their reference groups as more important than greater economic success. Cloward and Ohlin agree with Cohen that when faced with frustrated opportunities for upward social mobility, boys of these two types are the ones most likely to react against middle-class values. This is so because these boys are the ones who most want to be accepted by the middle class. Type III boys, who want more economic success (namely money) but who are neither interested in middle-class values or in becoming middle class, seek higher status in their own cultural milieu. They want " 'big cars,' 'flashy clothes,' and 'swell dames' " (*ibid.*:96). It is this

TABLE 13-1   Cloward and Ohlin's Classification of Lower-Class Youth

CATEGORIES OF LOWER-CLASS YOUTH	ORIENTATION OF LOWER-CLASS YOUTH	
	TOWARD MEMBERSHIP IN MIDDLE CLASS	TOWARD IMPROVEMENT IN ECONOMIC POSITION
Type I	+	+
Type II	+	−
Type III	−	+
Type IV	−	−

Source: Cloward and Ohlin (1960, p. 95).

group that comprises the majority of delinquents. Type IV boys are street-corner boys who are not interested in social mobility in any sphere. These boys drop out, in other words, without dropping into anything else. Although they are sometimes criticized for lack of ambition, these boys rarely get into trouble with the law.

Cloward and Ohlin's astute analysis of delinquent subcultures clearly avoided an error made by Cohen. It did not assume, as Cohen's had, that the cause of most juvenile delinquency is the failure of lower-class youth to succeed in middle-class institutions such as schools. Even though they may fail, and even though they may be alienated from the school, lower-class delinquents do not become delinquent solely because of failure in school. The causative factors in delinquency are likely to be more complicated than the process suggested by Cohen. As Cloward and Ohlin indicated (*ibid.*:97):

> Type III youth are alienated from the school because of a conflict regarding *appropriate* success-goals; this conflict simply reinforces their own definitions of criteria of success [i.e., making money versus making it into the middle class]. If these youngsters subsequently become delinquent, it is chiefly because they anticipate that legitimate channels to the goals they seek will be limited or closed.

Finally, Cloward and Ohlin argue that the illegitimate means of achieving success are not evenly distributed within working-class communities. They identify three sorts of delinquent subculture participated in by Type III boys: (1) the *criminal subculture*, (2) the *conflict subculture*, and (3) the *retreatist subculture*.

The Criminal Subculture   The legitimate aspirations of delinquency-prone boys are satisfied illegitimately in neighborhoods where a criminal subculture already exists. A criminal subculture has its own success models, learning techniques, and gradations of status (mainly by age). Its leading members are also part of the conventional culture of the community, thus lending the subculture a measure of stability and legitimacy. Its focus is the rational, albeit illegal, provision of opportunities for income through activities such as theft. In areas where no established criminal subculture is available, the typical avenue for potential delinquents is membership in either a conflict or a retreatist subculture (*ibid.*:161–171).

The Conflict Subculture   The environs of the conflict subculture typically are poor, disorganized, transient, and unstable. The activities of the conflict subculture make it extremely visible to the media and to the public. These activities focus on interpersonal violence, gang warfare, and the physical destruction of property (*ibid.*:171–178).

The Retreatist Subculture   The retreatist subculture is the last avenue for boys who experience failure in both legitimate activities and also in the illegalities of the criminal and conflict subcultures. The focus of the retreatist subculture is the retreat into persistent drug use/abuse. Of course, not all lower-class youth who experience status and economic deprivation engage in drug use/abuse. But those who choose to use and abuse drugs persistently are those who either (a) experience the double failure just described or (b) cannot revise their aspirations downward yet continue to experience the strain of frustrated opportunities (*ibid.*:178–186).

The apparent implications of certain of the findings of Cloward and Ohlin's study were actively pursued as policy by the Federal Government. As Vold and Bernard (1986:201) describe:

> After Robert Kennedy, who was then attorney general of the United States, read Cloward and Ohlin's book, he asked Lloyd Ohlin to help develop a new federal policy on juvenile delinquency. The result was the passage of the Juvenile Delinquency Prevention and Control Act of 1961, which was based on a comprehensive action program developed by Cloward and Ohlin in connection with their book. The program included improving education, creating work opportunities, organizing lower-class communities, and providing services to individuals, gangs, and families. The program was later expanded to include all lower-class people and became the basis of Lyndon Johnson's War on Poverty.

Billions of dollars were spent on the War on Poverty and other social welfare programs, but it was eventually abandoned by President Nixon on the grounds that it showed no clear results. In fact, the reasons why the program was abandoned are many and complex, including conservative objections that government should not be in the business of eliminating social inequalities. It must be considered seriously whether the subcultural theorists, because they had failed to identify the causes of juvenile delinquency, therefore misunderstood the set of policies that should be implemented to contain it.

Assessment

As noted, theories of delinquent subcultures largely developed in the 1950s as an attempt to answer various questions ignored in the research of the Chicago school. Yet, like their predecessors in the Chicago school, the subcultural theorists have continued either to ignore the delinquency of young females or typically to view it in masculine terms (see Chapters 15.3, 3.2; and Klein, 1980; Campbell, 1984). Additionally, they have ignored the delinquency of middle-class youth (see Chapter 3.4 and Vaz, 1967).

How much of an advance was the new subcultural criminology of the 1950s over the earlier tradition of the Chicago school? As David Matza (1964:63) reported, the sociologists of delinquent subcultures provided two fundamental insights about the nature of delinquency. First, they showed that delinquency typically is not a solitary enterprise but a group activity. Second, they showed that delinquent activities, rather than being engaged in by biologically or psychologically deformed individuals, typically develop in the sociological context of particular territorial locales. Often they develop in neighborhoods with cultural traditions associated with established gangs. In his history of criminological theory in the U.S., Don Gibbons reflects widespread sentiment over Cohen's description of gang behavior when he writes, for example:

> The cornerstone of his argument remains unchallenged: that serious, repetitive, organized, subcultural delinquency is a working-class phenomenon in the United States, qualitatively different from peer behavior in other strata or in most other cultures (1979:101).

Although we do not fully agree with Gibbons' assessment, we do agree that the criminology of the subcultural theorists was a real advance over earlier work in at least two respects. First, the subcultural theorists explicitly raised what the Chicago school left dormant: the relation between lower-class opportunities and the social and economic inequality of the U.S. class structure. Moreover, the subcultural theorists implicitly condemned the economic inequalities, the blocked opportunities, and the strains that result from class structure. The problem remains, however, as to whether they were correct in concluding that benevolent social programs could contain the juvenile delinquency that resulted from these economic conditions. Second, in some cases subcultural theory displayed considerable sensitivity to issues not previously raised. It recognized, for example, that juvenile delinquency took a number of forms and was engaged in for a variety of reasons.

However, in assessing the merits of subcultural theory, we also note that its findings provoked widespread criticism. Certain early critics, in particular Kitsuse and Dietrick (1959), argue that Cohen, for example, overemphasizes the extent to which the delinquency of lower-class boys is a *reaction* to failing in middle-class terms. Perhaps most working-class boys simply do not care about middle-class values. Do working-class boys have no authentic cultural traditions of their own? Others object that the activities of delinquent gangs are utilitarian rather than nonutilitarian (for example, Bordua, 1961) and far more diverse in character than thought to be (Short, 1962). Still others object that not enough emphasis has been placed on the deviant psychological characteristics of juvenile gang leaders. For example, Lewis Yablonsky (1962) charges (without evidence) that gang leaders are typically sociopaths.

Clarence Schrag (1962) argues that the theory of differential opportunity is too general in the face of real world complexities. Schrag (*ibid.*:169) objects that Cloward and Ohlin's theory fails to explain why, even in Type II and Type III communities, a substantial number of working-class boys do not join delinquent gangs. Why do some working-class boys join gangs, but others do not? Schrag also points out that, especially in neighborhoods with high delinquency rates, delinquent gangs are far more diverse, more fluid, and less organized than Cloward and Ohlin maintain. Thus, Schrag (*ibid.*:173) emphasizes:

> Many gangs do not exhibit the degree of cultural integration suggested by the theory. They often adopt distinctive titles, special items of

apparel, and other symbols of identity long before they have a stabilized membership or any high degree of organizational autonomy. Fluid membership, spatial mobility, and considerable versatility with respect to objectives and internal organization are characteristic of many of our delinquent gangs.

David Matza and Gresham Sykes (1961) disagree with the subcultural theorists' portrayal of middle-class values as being centered on the Protestant ethic of hard work and abstemiousness. There is, they argue, a wide range of respectable subterranean values that both the middle class and the working class have in common, including the search for kicks and the identification of masculinity with toughness. In other words, Matza and Sykes question whether the activities of delinquent gangs really are deviant if those same activities find cultural support within the middle class.

13.2 ——— MATZA'S *DELINQUENCY AND DRIFT* (1964)

In what at the time seemed to some criminologists a complete annihilation of subcultural explanations of delinquency, David Matza eloquently charged that subcultural theory has failed altogether to understand the causes of juvenile delinquency. In his book *Delinquency and Drift*, Matza (1964:1–32) forcefully attacks the core assumptions of the lengthy positivist tradition that stretches from Quetelet's social mechanics (see Chapter 10.2) to the ideas of the subcultural theorists. At the same time, in this book, as well as in his *Becoming Deviant* (Matza, 1969) and in his writings with Gresham Sykes (Sykes and Matza, 1957; Matza and Sykes, 1961), Matza offers an alternative theory of delinquency.

The key concepts in Matza's theory of delinquency are (1) the *positive delinquent*; (2) *the subculture of delinquency* (subterranean convergence, the situation of apprehension, and the situation of company); and (3) *delinquency and drift* (neutralization, will, and preparation and desperation).

The Positive Delinquent

According to Matza, positivist criminology makes three explicit assumptions about crime and criminality. Each assumption, he argues, is wrong. Matza points out that positivist criminology assumes the proper focus of criminological study should be the criminal rather than the criminal law. This assumption has involved a search for all sorts of motivational and socioeconomic causes of crime. However, the assumption ignores that crime is, above all, not only an action but also an *infraction* (namely, law breaking). In neglecting to study the legal and other institutions that define certain actions as infractions (in essence, crime and deviance), positivist criminology has "for close to a century display[ed] little concern for the essence of crime—infraction" (*ibid.*:5).

Moreover, positivist criminology has been unduly preoccupied with copying the methods of the natural sciences (*ibid.*:8–11). Rejecting the free-will philoso-phies of classical criminology (see Chapter 10.1), the positivists have assumed, as a matter of faith, that all human action is determined by scientific law and that, therefore, humans are largely incapable of choice between different paths of action. "The positive delinquent does not exercise choice," Matza writes (*ibid.*:11), "his action is constrained [and he] must behave in a delinquent manner because of the determinants that have shaped him." Matza admits that this approach of hard determinism, found especially in biological theories of crime, has given way in recent times to soft determinism. This modified analysis of delinquent subcultures endows individuals with the capacity to exercise choice but, Matza continues, advocates of soft determinism still basically believe that criminality is *caused.* This more subtle form of determinism is at the heart of linking crime with poverty, differential association, and the values of delin-quent subcultures.

Further, argues Matza (*ibid.*:11–12), positivist criminology assumes that criminals are fundamentally different from the law-abiding citizenry. With the exception of 18th-century classical criminology, this assumption has been a central feature of all previous criminology. From this assumption it follows that criminals are thus constrained by a set of circumstances that simply do not apply to the law-abiding. However, Matza objects (*ibid.*:12):

> A reliance on differentiation, whether constitutional, personal, or sociocultural, as the key explanation of delinquency has pushed the stan-dard-bearers of diverse theories to posit what have almost always turned out to be empirically undemonstrable differences.

Matza concludes that this doomed attempt to distinguish between the crimi-nal and the law-abiding has resulted in, or perhaps paralleled, several other errors by the positivists. Because subcultural theorists assume that the values of delinquents differ from those of nondelinquents, for example, insufficient atten-tion has therefore been paid either to the values of society at large or to smaller units within it, such as the family (*ibid.*:19–20). To study crime, Matza implies, we must look far beyond the immediate social environment where infraction is detected. Moreover, positivist criminology accounts for too much delinquency. It has been an "embarrassment of riches" that predicts far more delinquency than actually occurs. If delinquents really were as different from the law-abiding and as committed to the values of their subculture as the positivists assume (*ibid.*:22)

> involvement in delinquency would be more permanent and less transient, more pervasive and less intermittent than is apparently the case. Theories of delinquency yield an embarrassment of riches which seemingly go unmatched in the real world. This accounting for too much delinquency may be taken as an observable consequence of the distorted picture of the delinquent that has developed within positive criminology.

Matza's criticisms of the positivists' skeletal assumptions are extraordinarily revealing. Matza's book *Delinquency and Drift*, however, did much more than simply criticize the explanations of subcultural theorists; as with several other texts in the emerging societal reaction and labeling perspectives (see Chapter 14.3), it also put forward an alternative image of delinquency.

The Subculture of Delinquency

The basis of Matza's alternative theory of delinquency is that *there is a subculture of delinquency but that it is not a delinquent subculture*. Matza begins by saying that subcultural theorists are wrong to see the relationship between the values of a subculture of delinquency and mainstream culture as one of opposition. Things are not so neat and tidy. By and large the vast majority of delinquents are children; it would therefore be surprising indeed if the subculture of delinquency were made up of children strongly opposed to the values of conventional mainstream culture. Matza believes, in other words, that juvenile delinquents typically are not very different from other juveniles, and their values are likely to be quite similar to nondelinquent youths.

These similarities between the conventional culture and the subculture of delinquency Matza terms "subterranean convergence." In many of their basic ideas the subculture of delinquency and the conventional culture converge: in cowboy masculinity, in the search for kicks and for excitement, in the Bohemian celebration of the primitive, and in the persistence of territorial sentiments in certain localities of large cities.

Matza suggests that the subculture of delinquency is of two minds regarding delinquency: one allows and encourages its members to behave illegally and to gain prestige from doing so; the other reveals that it remains basically committed to the important values of conventional culture. Both frames of mind must be examined if the subculture of delinquency is to be understood accurately. Moreover, Matza continues, conventional culture is often not quite as conventional as it is made out to be. Conventional culture is complex and many-sided. Its features consist not only of ascetic puritanism, middle-class morality, the boy-scout oath, and the like—but also of hedonism, frivolity, and excitement (*ibid.*:36–37).

Matza suggests that the way to understand the *two-mindedness* of the subculture of delinquency is to assess the posture of delinquents in a variety of circumstances (*ibid.*:40–59), especially in what he terms "the situation of apprehension" and "the situation of company." By the *situation of apprehension* Matza refers to the problem created if the subculture of delinquency and the conventional culture hold oppositional values: radical defenses of their activities will be offered by delinquents when arrested by the police or when brought before a juvenile court. If the members of a subculture of delinquency are committed to their delinquent activities and values, they will feel almost no shame or guilt upon detection by authority. Yet juveniles commonly express feelings of genuine contrition on apprehension. Such feelings cannot simply be dismissed as a manipulative tactic designed to appease authority. The contrition of juveniles, Matza concludes, "cannot be ignored if we are to avoid the gross stereotype of the delinquent as a hardened gangster in miniature" (*ibid.*:41). With the exception of a few bizarre oddities—regarded by ordinary delinquents as crazy—delinquents rarely desire either to attack the values of conventional culture or to defend those of the subculture of delinquency. Moreover, if delinquents are so different from nondelinquents, as subcultural theorists insist, why do the vast majority of them desist from delinquency at the end of their adolescence?

By *the situation of company* Matza refers to the understanding of delinquents when in the company of their peers. Matza suggests that the values of the subculture of delinquency are far more fluid and less clear than usually thought. He argues that these values are not, as such, learned formally by novice delinquents because there is no written or formal code of delinquent values to be learned. Actually, many things are not discussed openly, and must be inferred (often wrongly!) by novices from the hints and the cues of their friends. During entry into the subculture of delinquency, boys—there are very few females in Matza's *Delinquency and Drift*—suffer *status anxiety* about their masculinity. How can they learn the values of the subculture of delinquency without revealing that they are not yet the fully committed delinquents they believe all the other boys are? Matza suggests that they do this by cautiously sounding out other boys about masculinity and appropriate delinquent acts. Serious discussion of delinquency is almost always impossible for delinquents because of the anxiety it would produce about their own masculinity. Thus: "Do I really like you? Yea, come here and suck and I'll show you how much I like you." Or: "Do I think that stealing a car is a good thing? Man you a fag or something? Ain't you one of the boys?" Whatever the motive, Matza concludes, "The function of such remarks is to mislead the delinquent into believing that his subculture is committed to delinquency" (*ibid.*:54).

However, Matza is keenly aware that this comedy of errors cannot continue indefinitely. Most boys eventually discover, often from one close friend in whose company their anxieties can be relaxed, that almost no one is actually committed to the subculture of delinquency. They discover, in other words, that all along they were wrong to believe that delinquents are committed to their misdeeds. The importance of this eye-opening information is reinforced as juveniles become adults (as boys become "real men"). Achievement of real masculinity is marked by such new signs of status as jobs, wives, children, and mortgages. Acquisition of these "obvious" signs of masculinity allows the ex-delinquent to reject the values and activities of the subculture as "kids' stuff." Dwindling remnants of the old gang mix with the company of younger cohorts. But the great majority of members of the subculture of delinquency do not become adult criminals.

Delinquency and Drift

Recall that, against the determinism of the positivist tradition, Matza is eager to assert the presence of a certain degree of choice and free will in human action. This assertion he lodges in the concept of *drift*. Matza suggests that the delinquent is committed neither to the subculture of delinquency nor to the conventional culture. Instead, the delinquent chooses, more or less consciously, to drift between the one and the other, often many times in the course of a single day.

> Drift stands midway between freedom and control. Its basis is an area of the social structure in which control has been loosened [and where it is] coupled with the abortiveness of adolescent endeavor to organize an autonomous subculture. . . . The delinquent *transiently* exists in a limbo between convention and crime, responding in turn to the demands of each, flirting now with one, now with the other, but postponing commitment, evading decision. Thus, he drifts between criminal and conventional action (*ibid.*:28).

Matza's theory of delinquency and drift has three components: neutralization, will, and preparation and desperation.

Neutralization is the process by which potential delinquents are freed from conventional social and moral controls, and because of which they are then able to engage in delinquency (*ibid.*:60–62, 69–100; Sykes and Matza, 1957). Gresham Sykes and David Matza (1957) have argued that most juvenile delinquents are not nearly as committed to delinquent values and activities as subcultural theorists have supposed. Indeed, precisely because they are not really opposed to mainstream values, juveniles often display feelings of shame and guilt when their delinquency is detected and exposed. To shield them from such feelings, experienced delinquents teach novice delinquents a variety of techniques to rationalize and justify their behavior (for example, "I didn't mean it," "I didn't really hurt anybody," "They had it coming to them," "Everybody's picking on me," "I didn't do it for myself"). These techniques operate to deflect or to neutralize the disapproval of such authority figures as judges, juvenile police officers, and probation workers. According to Sykes and Matza there are five basic techniques of neutralization (*ibid.*:667–670):

1. Denial of Responsibility

> Insofar as the delinquent can define himself as lacking responsibility for his deviant actions, the disapproval of self or others is sharply reduced in effectiveness as a restraining influence. . . . It may also be asserted that delinquent acts are due to forces outside of the individual and beyond his control such as unloving parents, bad companions, or a slum neighborhood.

2. Denial of Injury

> The delinquent frequently, and in a hazy fashion, feels that his behavior does not really cause any great harm despite the fact that it runs counter to the law.

3. Denial of Victim

Even if the delinquent accepts the responsibility for his deviant actions and is willing to admit that his deviant actions involve an injury or hurt, the moral indignation of self and others may be neutralized by an insistence that the injury is not wrong in light of the circumstances. The injury, it may be claimed, is not really an injury; rather, it is a form of rightful retaliation or punishment.

4. Condemnation of Condemners

The delinquent shifts the focus of attention from his own deviant acts to the motives and behavior of those who disapprove of his violations. . . . [B]y attacking others, the wrongfulness of his own behavior is more easily repressed or lost to view.

5. Appeal to Higher Loyalties

Internal and external social controls may be neutralized by sacrificing the demands of the larger society for the demands of the small social groups to which the delinquent belongs such as the sibling pair, the gang, or the friendship clique. . . . The conflict between the claims of friendship and the claims of law, or a similar dilemma, has of course long been recognized. . . . If the juvenile delinquent frequently resolves his dilemma by insisting that he must "always help a buddy" or "never squeal on a friend," even when it throws him into serious difficulties with the dominant social order, his choice remains familiar to the supposedly law-abiding.

Techniques of neutralization, then, generally reduce the effectiveness of social and moral controls. They allow juveniles to engage in delinquency despite the disapproval of authority figures or of their conforming peers. At the same time, Sykes and Matza (*ibid.*:669) are careful to note that such techniques are not powerful enough to shield all delinquents from feelings of shame and guilt. Moreover, some delinquents are so isolated from the conforming world of the dominant culture that neutralization techniques are not even useful.

Matza argues that neutralization of the values of conventional culture is insufficient to ensure that a juvenile will actually drift into delinquency. For a delinquent act to occur, the juvenile must *will* it ("the impetus for the commission of a crime in classical criminology"—*ibid.*:182). Two factors that activate the will are *preparation* and *desperation* (*ibid.*:181–191). Preparation provides the will to repeat old infractions of law; desperation provides the will to commit new ones.

By *preparation* Matza refers to the behavioral and attitudinal skills a juvenile must have prior to committing a crime. To commit a robbery, for example, a youth must have a certain rudimentary level of strength, dexterity, speed, agility, and cunning in order to be successful. Also, a youth must not be apprehensive or "chicken" when about to violate the law; or, in the language of classical criminology, he must not be deterred by the threat of the imposition of law. Youths must believe that the police are relatively incompetent and that they are only relatively potent. In their preparation for delinquency, youths also learn that, even if their delinquency is detected, incarceration is unlikely.

By *desperation* Matza refers to what he suspects to be the primary motive in the will to delinquency: that youngsters feel they have no control over their lives. For youngsters with anxieties about their masculinity and membership in their peer group, a mood of fatalism and desperation is the natural consequence of experiencing lack of control. To assert control a boy cannot just do anything ("Shit, man, anybody can do that."). He must master his fate. He must make something happen. Often the subculture of delinquency stresses the importance of delinquency as a means of making things happen; sometimes it stresses the time-honored method of exploiting and conquering females. However, Matza concludes, the will to crime may be "discouraged, deterred, or diverted by countless contingencies" (*ibid.*:191).

Assessment

While Matza's work has inspired few full-length studies, a notable exception is Jack Katz's (1988) phenomenological *The Seductions of Crime*. Katz believes that, from the point of view of criminals, little can be understood about why they commit crime by positivist explanations that focus on "background" correlations like socioeconomic factors or whether they were dropped on their heads when they were babies. As Katz writes, "The statistical and correlational findings of positivist criminology provide the following irritations to inquiry: (1) whatever the validity of the hereditary, psychological, and social-ecological conditions of crime, many of those in the supposedly causal categories do not commit the crime at issue, (2) many who do commit the crime do not fit the causal categories, and (3) and what is most provocative, many who do fit the background categories and later commit the predicted crime go for long stretches without committing the crimes to which theory directs them" (*ibid.*:3–4). Instead, Katz argues, we need to understand the "foreground" of experience, the thrill, the magic and emotions that "seduce" persons to commit crime. Katz extends his ethnographic method to such crimes as murder, robbery, and shoplifting.

To return to Matza, one means of evaluating *Delinquency and Drift* is as an attempt to restore to juveniles a degree of free will denied them by the determinism of the positivist tradition. In a sense, Matza's criminology marks a return to one of the basic principles of classical criminology—our 18th-century point of entry into criminological theory (see Chapter 10.1). In criticizing the unwarranted determinism of positivist criminology, Matza tries to force us, instead, to appreciate the way in which deviants themselves view their activities. If certain youths consciously *choose* to drift between convention and delinquency, clearly their accounts of why they drift become an essential part of explaining their actions. Deviants have voices that should be heard. And taken seriously!

Is Matza's reformulation successful, or does his reformulation merely shift the causes of delinquency from one positivist area to another—from status frustration to masculine anxiety, for example? This is an extremely difficult question that has no simple answer. Matza's basic thesis is that delinquents drift between conventional and delinquent activities. Although this thesis has been subjected to extensive empirical tests by criminologists, generally these tests have focused on the importance that Matza has attributed to techniques of neutralization. The tests have explored two main questions: Do techniques of neutralization come before delinquent acts? Where do delinquents stand relative to delinquent and conventional values? In both cases the evidence is frustratingly inconclusive.

Richard Ball's (1966) research has provided somewhat limited support for Matza's concept of techniques of neutralization. Ball found that for a variety of property and personal offenses, the use of excuses (or neutralizations) by juveniles tends to appeal more to delinquents than to nondelinquents. Additionally, Ball's findings supported Matza's view that most delinquents do not adhere to a set of norms different from those of conventional culture. Nonetheless, Ball concluded from his data that it was impossible to determine whether techniques of neutralization are used before, during, or after delinquent acts. Although Travis Hirschi (1969:208; and Chapter 14.1) has confirmed that delinquents use neutralization techniques to reduce the power of conventional morality, he also claims, as opposed to Matza, that this process occurs after the delinquent act. Similarly, John Hamlin (1988) has argued that techniques of neutralization are motives that neutralize guilt following a delinquent act.

In the face of this controversy, it seems reasonable to conclude that some delinquents use techniques of neutralization *before* and others *after* their behavior has been detected and defined as deviant. For example, many people who cheat on their income tax returns rationalize their behavior beforehand by claiming "Everyone else is cheating the IRS, and I'm stupid if I don't do it." Carl Klockars (1974:135–161) and Darrell Steffensmeier (1986:237–249) have shown, in their biographical studies of professional fences, that certain thieves can neutralize their past *and* their future illegalities—if they are involved in a continuing criminal career—by reasoning that "I'm not hurting anyone when I steal, because insurance will always pay the loss" (and see Chapter 5.1). Listen to Sam, Steffensmeier's (1986:241) fence:

> I don't feel I hurt any little people 'cause most of the stuff did come out of business places and big places, which were insurance write-offs and which they will many times mark it double what it was. In a roundabout way, yes, the individual is going to pay for it, like with the higher transport and that. I would not feel bad about this. It's the same as, say, chiseling on income tax. You cheat Uncle Sam, but that's not the same as cheating this here person.

However, such partial confirmations of Matza's thesis on the use of neutralization techniques have been challenged by Michael Hindelang (1970; 1974). In his earlier study, Hindelang (1970) obtained the confidential information of

346 boys from a middle-class section of Oakland, California. In this study Hindelang asked his subjects to record the number of times they had committed any of 26 offenses (including theft, drug use/abuse, fighting, sexual deviance, and truancy in the previous year). In addition, the youngsters were asked whether they strongly disapproved, disapproved, were indifferent to, approved, or strongly approved the act. If Matza was correct, and delinquents are not committed to their misdeeds, then delinquent approval of an act should be similar to approval expressed by nondelinquents. Hindelang found that 13 of 15 activities examined showed a significant association between delinquent involvement and approval of delinquent acts. These findings clearly contradict Matza's thesis that delinquents do not substantively differ from nondelinquents in commitment to conventional culture.

Recall Matza's point that if delinquents really were so influenced by their subculture, it would be extremely difficult to explain the fact that most members of the subculture eventually abandon their delinquency. In other words, how can we account for the maturational reform of juvenile delinquents? Why do most juvenile delinquents become conformist adults? A possible explanation of maturation was in fact precisely the one suggested by Matza himself: most delinquents are never seriously committed to their delinquency in the first place. As David Greenberg (1981) has argued about this difficulty of accounting for maturational reform, it is not at all clear why most subculture carriers so soon abandon activities so highly prized within the subculture. Why, then, do gang members eventually desist from delinquent activities? Greenberg is quick to point out that as valuable as Matza's insight is, it opens up other nagging questions:

> There are valuable insights in [Matza's] account, but unresolved questions as well. . . . Why does desistance from violen[t] offenses occur later and more slowly than [from] theft offenses? Why are some juveniles so much more extensively involved in delinquency than others? Matza's remarkable presentation of the subjective elements in delinquency must be supplemented by an analysis of the objective, structural elements in causation, if such questions are to be answered (Greenberg, *ibid.*:120).

For Greenberg, therefore, Matza has not adequately considered the relation between social class and socioeconomic status, on the one hand, and the distribution of values on the other. Are *working-class* youths, for example, more likely to engage in neutralization techniques than youths from other sections of society? If so, why? As Taylor, Walton, and Young have written: "Delinquency is in part the result of an external situation of inequality, poverty and powerlessness and can be seen as an attempt to assert control and thereby to reestablish some sense of self" (1973:182). Ironically, in the U.S. the analysis of the sort of structural elements to which Greenberg (see also Cernkovich, 1978) refers has been undertaken only by Matza's antagonists, the subcultural theorists (Cohen, Cloward and Ohlin, and Miller). Greenberg's desire to look for structural explanations of delinquency is explored in Chapter 3.4.

13.3 _____ CONTROL THEORY

The concept of "social control" was pioneered originally by French sociologist Gabriel Tarde (see Chapter 11.1). In the U.S. the concept was used first by sociologists (Ross, 1901; Park and Burgess, 1921; MacIver and Page, 1949) and social psychologists (Mead, 1925; Cooley, 1930). In these early formulations, social control was understood in broad terms as all institutions and processes that guarantee social order. In some writings, such as those of MacIver—who looked for inspiration to German sociologist Max Weber—social control was depicted as a coercive device by which the will of the powerful was imposed on society. However, during the 1940s the concept of social control was given a much narrower reading. Two aspects of this narrower view were soon adopted as guiding themes in criminology. First, social control was stripped of its critical content and declared a functional necessity that contributed to the well-being of society. Without social control, functionalists claimed, anarchy and chaos would prevail in any society. Second, the concept was narrowed to include small groups (such as families, schools, and peers). The focus here was on the ways these groups socialized their members.

These narrower perspectives on social control are vividly present in certain of the criminological research to which we now turn. This research proceeds on the central assumption that crime is likely to occur when the social bonds between an individual and society are weakened or severed. In what follows we present the two best-known versions of control theory in criminology—Walter Reckless' (1961) *containment theory* and Travis Hirschi's (1969) *social control* (or *social bonding*) *theory*.

Containment

Walter Reckless (1940:58) suggested that variation in the respective crime rates of different social groups in the U.S. was caused by variations in the ability to *contain* norm-violating behavior in the face of social change and cultural conflict. This insight Reckless (1961:335–359) later developed as containment theory in his book *The Crime Problem*.

Reckless developed the theory of containment largely because of a major bias he detected in existing criminological theory. To Reckless' dismay, the vast majority of theories placed too much emphasis on the process of social disorganization in causing crime. To correct for this, Reckless argued that crime generally is prevented, or contained, as a result of two key processes: one occurs at the level of social organization, the other at the level of individual personality.

In attempting to correct what he saw as a misplaced bias toward factors of social organization at the expense of personality factors, Reckless relied on several new empirical studies of delinquency. According to these studies (e.g., Redl and Wineman, 1951:74–140; Reiss, 1951; Nye, 1958), delinquents often come from broken homes and have not been properly socialized or controlled by their families, peer groups, schools, and adult friends. These studies also found that recidivists have weak egos, weak personal controls, and poor self-concepts, whereas "good boys" (nondelinquents) tend to come from middle-class families or from families that are stable maritally, economically, and spatially. Moreover, good boys project a good self-concept, namely one that acts as an effective insulator against delinquency (Reckless, Dinitz, and Murray, 1956). The self-concept of good boys includes law-abiding and obedient self-evaluation together with positive responses to family life and parental (especially maternal) control (*ibid.*:922). Reckless suggests that a good self-concept represents

> a favorable internalization of presumably favorable life-experiences, including an acceptance or incorporation of the proper concern which significant others have had for the person. It acts selectively on experience and holds the line against adversities (pressures), the subculture of delinquency, wrong-doing, and crime (pull), as well as discontent and frustrations (pushes). The poor self-concept is a residue of less favorable growth, the acceptance of less concern or a different concern (value-wise) of significant others.

Reckless' theory of containment is a hierarchical structure focusing on individual ability to contain social and psychological conflict (1961:355–359). For Reckless, inner and outer containments occupy a position between the pressures and pulls of the social environment and the inner pushes of the individual personality (*ibid.*:355–356). At the top of the hierarchy is a layer of *social pressures* that bears down on the individual. These pressures include poverty, unemployment, economic insecurity, family conflict, minority group status, lack of opportunity, and class and social inequality. At the same level is a layer of *social pulls* that draws individuals away from their routines and accepted patterns of life. These pulls include influential deviants ("prestige individuals"), bad company, delinquent and criminal subcultures, and propaganda such as that purveyed by the mass media.

According to Reckless, immediately surrounding the individual is a barrier of *outer containment*. This barrier consists of effective family living and supportive groups, and includes such factors as morality, supervision, discipline, reasonable norms and expectations, and safety valves to release tensions. If this barrier is weak, the individual is quite susceptible to social pressures and pulls.

Inside the individual's consciousness is a barrier of *inner containment*. Deviance-prone individuals (essentially those with weak inner containment) are likely to possess some combination of bad self-control, weak ego, underdeveloped superego (conscience), poor self-concept, low frustration tolerance, no sense of responsibility, and inadequate goal-orientation. Inner containment is the last line of defense against internal and external pressures and pulls.

Finally, the bottom layer of the hierarchy consists of *psychological pushes*. These include varying degrees of hostility, aggressiveness, suggestibility, rebellion, guilt reactions, feelings of inadequacy and inferiority, sibling rivalry, and such organic difficulties as brain damage and epilepsy. According to Reckless (*ibid.*:356), certain of these psychological pushes are usually too strong for inner as well as outer containment.

Reckless' theory has been vulnerable to several objections. Some criminologists have rightly complained that important parts of his theory—such as a poor self-concept—are defined so vaguely that they are not testable (Schrag, 1971:82–89). What, precisely, is a poor self-concept? Is it, for example, the belief that one is no good? Or is it the belief that others believe that one is no good? How does one define bad company? How bad must company be for it to constitute bad company?

These difficulties notwithstanding, Reckless' containment theory fostered another, far more articulate theory of crime: Travis Hirschi's (1969) social control theory.

Control

Travis Hirschi's (1969) *Causes of Delinquency* is a prominent landmark in the developing literature on the sociology and social psychology of social control (for example, Reiss, 1951; Toby, 1957; Nye, 1958; Gold, 1963; Stinchcombe, 1964; Briar and Piliavin, 1965; Short and Strodtbeck, 1965). Hirschi thinks most sociological theories have failed to show that delinquency actually is caused by such factors as the strains of "[s]ex, race, social class, neighborhood, mother's employment, the broken home, size of family, and so forth . . . " (*ibid.*:65). Although these factors might be *correlated* with delinquency, Hirschi reasons, there is no evidence they actually *cause* it. In his theory of social control, Hirschi attempts to show that control theory, far more so than subcultural theories, explains the factors that lead to delinquency. Instead of looking for the causes of delinquency, he argues, it is much more fruitful to look for the causes of conformity. Instead of looking for some motivation to delinquency, delinquency turns out to be merely an absence of the causes of conformity.

Hirschi therefore starts with the seemingly biological proposition that most people have antisocial tendencies; however, these tendencies are actualized only if various sorts of social control are relaxed. Whether individuals are law-abiding or deviant depends on the extent of variance from the four factors that are critical in bonding them to society: (1) *attachment* to parents, school, and peers; (2) *commitment* to conventional lines of action; (3) *involvement* in conventional activities; and (4) *belief* in conventional values.

First, Hirschi theorizes, juveniles will be law-abiding if they have strong attachments to positive role models or significant others—their parents, school teachers, and law-abiding friends. Weak attachments to expectations of significant others can derive from such sources as lack of discipline on the part of parents and teachers, poor intellectual and social skills exhibited by the juvenile, disrespect for or indifference to expectations and opinions of significant others, and differential association with juvenile delinquents. Second, Hirschi maintains that for a system of social control to be effective, juveniles must fear punishment. He reasons that delinquents are likely to be juveniles who, during their difficult passage to adulthood, are less committed to completing their education or achieving a high-status career. Hirschi therefore disagrees with subcultural theories that identify frustrated aspirations as the main provocation for delinquency— although he fails to identify the factors that cause variance in juvenile attachment to conventional lines of action. Third, juvenile attachments and attitudinal commitments to positive role models and to conventional goals are likely to be reflected in the juvenile's daily involvement in conventional activities. The more juveniles are involved in such conventional activities as education and school-related activities, the more they are discouraged from engaging in delinquency, and vice versa. Fourth, Hirschi argues that belief in the goodness of certain values—such as respect for the law and for the police, and in the wrongness of such actions as juvenile delinquency—operates as a brake on delinquency. Finally, we note that Hirschi implies all four factors (attachment, commitment, involvement, and belief) are strongly interrelated:

> In general, the more closely a person is tied to conventional society in any of these ways, the more closely he is likely to be tied in the other ways. The person who is attached to conventional people is, for example, more likely to be involved in conventional activities and to accept conventional notions of desirable conduct (*ibid.*:27).

In *Causes of Delinquency*, Hirschi attempts to test his theory empirically. His test was based on a study of school records, police records, and questionnaire responses gathered from a large sample of juveniles (stratified by race, sex, school, and grade) in the San Francisco-Oakland area in the mid-1960s. Self-report items included many questions about juvenile attitudes toward family, school, and peers. Six items in the questionnaire were meant to serve as an index of delinquency. Three questions asked whether in the last year the juvenile had stolen anything worth less than $2, worth $2–$50, and worth over $50. Three questions asked if he or she had ever "taken a car for a ride without the owner's permission," "banged up something that did not belong to you on purpose," and (not counting fights with brothers and sisters) "beaten up on anyone or hurt anyone on purpose." (*ibid.*:54).

From these data Hirschi made a variety of generalizations about the links between social control and delinquency, each of which seemed remarkably at odds with previous theories. Consider a summary of the seven most important generalizations:

1. *Juveniles Engage Less in Delinquency the More They Are Attached to Their Families.* "The more strongly a youth is attached to his parents, the more strongly he is bound to their expectations, and therefore the more strongly he is bound to conformity with the legal norms of the larger system" (*ibid.*:94). Because the most important variable is the quality of family bonding, juveniles from broken homes are no more likely to be delinquent than juveniles from intact homes.

2. *Juveniles Engage Less in Delinquency the Better They Perform in School.* "The causal chain runs from academic incompetence to poor school performance to disliking of school to rejection of the school's authority to the commission of delinquent acts" (*ibid.*:132). Academic incompetence often is present with a general social disability that includes lack of skill in interpersonal relations.

3. *The Greater a Youth's Stake in Conformity, Then, Irrespective of the Delinquency of His or Her Peers, the Less Likely He or She Is to Be Delinquent.* Like many other investigators of lower-class, urban, male juvenile delinquency, Hirschi agrees that the relationship between personality characteristics and peer association patterns is a major theoretical problem. Do birds of a feather flock together? According to Hirschi, the evidence "strongly supports the view that the boy's stake in conformity affects his choice of friends rather than the other way around" (*ibid.*:159).

4. *Members of Delinquent Gangs Do Not Have Cohesive or Warm Associations with Fellow Gang Members.* According to Hirschi, the evidence for cohesiveness of delinquent gangs often is simply a romantic assertion on the part of the investigator. Moreover, the less cohesive a given gang, the more delinquent its activities are likely to be (*ibid.*:159–60).

5. *The Importance of Techniques of Neutralization in Delinquency Is Inconclusive.* Although 62 percent of the delinquents in Hirschi's data reported that "it is not all right to get around the law if you can get away with it" (*ibid.*:203), nevertheless, the likelihood of engaging in delinquency increases as concern for the morality of delinquent acts declines. This generalization implies that feelings of guilt decline—or the negation of shame increases—with the degree of involvement in delinquency. However, it is unclear whether this is due to the techniques of neutralization or to the finding that delinquents are likely to be those juveniles who lack close social bonds with their parents.

6. *There Is No Significant Causal Link Between Delinquency and Social Class.* Contrary to "strain" theories, Hirschi's empirical findings suggest that delinquency is distributed evenly throughout the class structure, even though racial minorities and the very poor are known to have higher arrest rates. Hirschi summarizes: "While the prisons bulge with the socioeconomic dregs of society, careful quantitative research shows again and again that the relation between socioeconomic status and the commission of delinquent acts is small, or nonexistent" (*ibid.*:66).

7. *In the U.S., No Section of Society Encourages Delinquency More Than Any Other.* Because delinquency is so evenly distributed throughout the class structure, there is no specifically lower-class subculture of delinquency. "The beliefs and values that feed delinquency are not peculiar to any social class or (nondelinquent) segment of the population" (*ibid.*:230; and see Chapter 3.1, 3.4).

Finally, we note that Hirschi (1983) has offered a partial reformulation of the theory of social control that extends the implications of his original theory and that focuses on child socialization rather than on adolescence. In this revised version Hirschi borrows from the Oregon Social Learning Center's treatment of families with problem children. He reports the Center's "commonsense" finding that "children must be *punished* for their misdeeds" (*ibid.*:53). Continuing forcefully to reject theories of crime that stress such factors as poverty, social class, and unemployment, Hirschi asserts that good child-rearing techniques and proper discipline are the chief ways to prevent or control juvenile delinquency. Good techniques include monitoring children, recognizing problems, and punishing misbehavior. Thus, inadequate child-rearing techniques and lax discipline are allegedly the chief factors in juvenile delinquency. These factors are especially present, Hirschi argues, among working mothers, in situations of child abuse (*ibid.*:58–65), among parents with criminal records, in large families, and in single-parent families. "The single parent (usually a woman) . . . is less able to devote time to monitoring and punishment, and is more likely to be involved in negative, abusive contacts with her children" (*ibid.*:62).

Hirschi proposes, somewhat vaguely, three policies directed to the control of problem children. First, child-rearing classes should be standard fare in high school so that future parents learn the rudiments of sound child-rearing techniques. Second, parents and teachers should combine their knowledge and their supervisory roles in order better to address child-rearing issues. Third, there must be appropriate governmental commitment to ensuring that families have incentives to raise law-abiding children. However, as Hirschi (*ibid.*:68) recognizes, these proposals are highly controversial. For instance, should the government penalize parents (and guardians) who do not employ sound child-rearing practices? If so, how severe a penalty is appropriate? Where should the dividing line be drawn between family privacy and governmental responsibility?

Assessment

Among many criminologists the control theory of crime continues to be extremely influential. In Hirschi's version, especially, it is a formalized theory whose several propositions easily lend themselves to empirical tests. It is a major source of current research and, until quite recently, has consistently received empirical support from researchers (Hindelang, 1973; Hepburn, 1977; Cernkovich, 1978:349–350; Krohn and Massey, 1980; Shoemaker, 1984:175–176; Van Voorhis, Cullen, Mathers, and Garner, 1988; Laub and Sampson, 1988). Moreover, it has influenced other researchers (such as Toby, 1983) to pinpoint the apparent importance of strict control—and the dire consequences of lax discipline—in institutions such as schools.

However, certain research has shown that some of Hirschi's key concepts should be refined. For example, Stephen Cernkovich and Peggy Giordano (1987:299–300) complain that Hirschi's concept of attachment is too vague. What exactly is attachment? How does one measure it? They suggest that to understand the subtle dynamics of family interaction, future researchers should (1) recognize the importance of different measures of attachment—including control and supervision, identity support (during adolescent crises), caring and trust, forms and degree of intimate communication, parental disapproval of peers, and conflict—and (2) explore the effects on delinquency of the variety of intact and broken family units—including both-parent, mother-only, father-only, father/stepmother, and mother/stepfather homes. Certain of these concerns have been addressed by Edward Wells and Joseph Rankin (1988). They argue that in the analysis of the control of delinquent behavior it is wrong to focus solely on indirect controls (or Hirschi's attachments). Wells and Rankin suggest that direct controls are also very important in controlling delinquency. Examples of direct controls include *normative regulation*, or how parents "lay down the law" about such things as who their children's friends can be and what they can wear; *monitoring*, or making sure that children follow parental rules; and *punishment*, or "picking up the rod" to sanction misbehavior and deviation (*ibid.*:268–270).

The relation between Hirschi's concepts of conformity, on the one hand, and his other key concepts (attachment, involvement, commitment, and belief), on the other, has also been strongly criticized. As discussed earlier, Hirschi asserted that juveniles are law-abiding or conforming if they have strong attachments to their positive role models. But, as Thomas Bernard (1987:416–418) has pointed out, Hirschi's statement confuses a definition of conformity with an explanation of conformity. As Bernard writes: "If conformity is *defined* as acts controlled by attachments, involvements, commitments, and beliefs, conformity cannot be *explained* by the same statement without simply restating the definition" (*ibid.*:417). In other words, Hirschi's reasoning appears to be circular. If we accept Bernard's criticism, it is not at all clear that the concepts of control theory explain anything at all.

Other criminologists have raised serious doubts about the validity of Hirschi's findings. In his longitudinal study of 2,213 boys between 1966 and 1968, Robert Agnew (1985) found that Hirschi's theory cannot explain serious forms of juvenile crime. In other words, even if control theory can explain minor crimes such as petty theft, it does not and cannot explain why some juveniles commit very violent offenses. Some other explanation is needed of these latter offenses. Moreover, Agnew also found that although at any given point in time delinquency may appear strongly correlated with Hirschi's control variables, in the long run, rather than delinquency being caused by weak social controls, delinquency itself can causally affect control! Agnew therefore concludes that "the explanatory power of Hirschi's social control theory has been exaggerated" (*ibid.*:58).

Criminologists have for several years engaged in a heated dispute over the causal relationships indicated by theorists of control. There are essentially two sides to this dispute, respectively championed by conservatives and liberals, and each side tends to characterize the claims of the other in somewhat crude terms. According to conservatives such as Hirschi and his followers, the allegedly high and rising U.S. crime rates have been caused by the lax discipline and the cultural permissiveness of 1960s liberalism. From this view, rising crime rates have been caused by the general permissiveness of liberal parents, the decline of religious values, the collapse of order in the nation's high schools, governments that have been too generous with the poor and with welfare recipients, and criminal justice systems that are too soft on criminals. In this conservative scenario the solution to the problem of crime lies in greater social control. Typical conservative policies for controlling crime include compulsory religious instruction from the elementary school upward, restoration of strict discipline (including corporal punishment) in the nation's high schools, reduction or elimination of government welfare programs in order to cultivate individual responsibility and to foster initiative among the "undeserving poor," and increased severity of penal sanctions (such as longer prison sentences and determinate sentencing).

On the other side of this dispute are the liberal critics of control theory (such as Currie, 1985). To the advocates of greater social control these critics reply that there is little or no evidence, either in the U.S. or abroad (and see Chapter 16.5), that strict discipline controls or deters delinquency. Moreover, strict discipline (including corporal punishment) may actually encourage delinquency, they continue, because its use teaches children that physical force is the appropriate way to solve interpersonal problems with others. It is no accident, the liberal argument concludes, that the U.S. has both the highest rate of violent crime and the highest rate of incarceration of all industrial nations. Punitive control and high rates of violent crime are both symptoms of the same problem: the U.S. is a thoroughly violent society even, ironically, in its response to violent crime. In the liberal scenario it is the thoroughgoing social, economic, and political inequality in the U.S. that is the chief cause of crime. To reduce crime its causes must be attacked by social policies that seek alternatives to imprisonment, that foster community spirit, that create employment for the poor, and that make adequate provision for the children of poorer families.

Although we do not explicitly assess the respective merits of the conservative and liberal viewpoints—admitting that the arguments supporting them are many and complex—we conclude this assessment of social control theory by noting one basic, perhaps fatal, criticism of the conservative viewpoint. Hirschi's theory of social control derives from an assumption about human nature that is probably undemonstrable and quite likely wrong: at the moment of birth, when society has not yet imprinted its values and its controls on our social characters, we are all aggressive and naturally violent animals. In this dark and pessimistic vision, as in the biblical theory of original sin, criminal behavior is something that parents, educators, and other agents of social control must work to avoid. But as Currie (1985:187) complains:

> Whatever one may think, on a purely philosophical level, about Hirschi's attitude toward human nature, it cannot tell us why some times, some places, and some groups are more criminal than others. In order to accomplish this, Hirschi must go on to blame a variety of changes in

contemporary values and attitudes for weakening parents' capacity to quash their children's unruly impulses.

Finally, recall in the beginning of this section we noted that the original concept of social control underwent considerable change when used by criminologists. In the hands of theorists of containment and control, such as Reckless and Hirschi, it has become almost exclusively identified with the links between crime and delinquency on the one hand and the processes of socialization in families and schools on the other. Dorothy Chunn and Shelley Gavigan (1988) have asserted that certain criminologists now claim social control itself is simply a means of repression, and that control theory is one aspect of that repression. This newer and skeptical view of social control (see Chapter 15.2) was partly precipitated by the rise of labeling and conflict theories, which we consider in the next chapter.

REVIEW

This chapter outlined subcultural perspectives on delinquency, dividing them into three sections. The first section described the key themes emerging in the sociology of delinquent subcultures during the 1950s, strongly influenced by earlier traditions of anomie and differential association. The second section examined the thesis of a specific subculture of violence. The third section presented David Matza's criticism of the positivist approach to juvenile delinquency. In his alternative formulation, Matza emphasized that juveniles consciously drift between the conventional culture and the subculture of delinquency.

Delinquent Subcultures

1. Beginning in the 1950s, Mertonian anomie theory led directly to further examination of the cultural settings that fostered juvenile delinquency.

2. Cohen's (1955) *Delinquent Boys* suggested that delinquent boys inhabit a subculture whose activities are nonutilitarian, malicious, and negativistic. Lower-class boys (rather than middle-class boys, or girls, in general) are doomed to fail in terms of middle-class standards, especially in school, and they react by participating in the creation of a delinquent subculture or by joining a bearer group of such a subculture. This reaction provides the status that the middle-class world denies them.

3. Cohen's findings were criticized by numerous scholars, including Miller (1958) and Cloward and Ohlin (1960). Miller suggested that Cohen had overemphasized the extent to which lower-class youth internalized middle-class values. Lower-class delinquent subcultures should therefore be understood in terms of the focal concerns of lower-class life, especially the female-headed household.

4. In *Delinquency and Opportunity*, Cloward and Ohlin responded that earlier theorists had simplified both the reasons why lower-class youth join

delinquent subcultures and the variety of such subcultures. Delinquents tend to be boys who desire greater economic success but who, not interested in becoming middle class, seek higher status in lower-class terms. Boys generally join a criminal subculture, if available; if not, they join a conflict subculture. Boys who fail in these subcultures, or for whom they are unavailable, tend to join the retreatist subculture.

Matza's *Delinquency and Drift* (1964)

1. Matza's (1964) *Delinquency and Drift* offered powerful criticisms of the lengthy positivist tradition stretching from Quetelet's social mechanics of crime to subcultural theories of delinquency discussed in this chapter. Matza argues that this tradition wrongly teaches that all activities of juveniles are determined by social and environmental forces over which they have absolutely no control. In a partial return to one of the principles of classical criminology, Matza claims that, in fact, juveniles rationally exercise choice over their activities, whether these are delinquent or conformist.

2. Matza stresses the existence of a subculture of delinquency that is not a delinquent subculture. Because most delinquents are children, it is not surprising that the values of the subculture of delinquency are not opposed to those of the conventional culture. For this reason most delinquents grow up to become conformist adults rather than adult criminals.

3. Delinquents drift in and out of delinquency and conventional behavior. They rationalize their delinquent activity by means of five main techniques of neutralization: denial of responsibility, denial of injury, denial of victim, condemnation of condemners, and appeal to higher loyalties. These techniques are supplemented by situations of preparation and desperation.

4. Matza has correctly identified serious problems in the positivist tradition. But there is little conclusive evidence that his image of a less constrained deviant is actually closer to social reality. Some critics have suggested that Matza has not paid sufficient attention to constraints of social class and racial inequality.

Control Theory

1. The two major forms of social control theory are containment theory and social control (or social bonding) theory. Control theory assumes that crime is likely to occur when the social bonds between an individual and society are weakened or severed.

2. Reckless' theory of containment is a hierarchical structure focusing on an individual's ability to contain social and psychological conflict. Inner and outer containments occupy a position between the pressures and pulls of the social environment, and the inner pushes of the individual

personality. Deviance-prone individuals tend to have weak inner and outer containments that result from some combination of factors such as bad self-control, weak ego, badly developed superego, and poor self-concept.

3. Containment theory has been criticized because several of its key concepts are either too vague or immune to empirical proof.

4. Hirschi's theory of control is based on the idea that rather than look for the causes of delinquency, it is better to look for the causes of conformity. Delinquency is an absence of the causes of conformity. Whether individuals are law-abiding or deviant depends on variation among four factors that bond them to society: (1) attachment to parents, school, and peers; (2) commitment to conventional lines of action; (3) involvement in conventional activities; and (4) belief.

5. Hirschi argues that good child-rearing techniques and proper discipline are the chief means of preventing and controlling delinquency.

6. Although it has been criticized, Hirschi's theory remains influential today. As with containment theory, its concepts are rather vague and difficult to test.

7. The policy implications of control theory are the subject of heated debate among criminologists. Conservatives argue that stern discipline and family values are the best means of delinquency prevention; liberals reply that such discipline has never been shown to deter crime. Liberals argue that to reduce crime its causes must be attacked by policies that seek alternatives to prison, foster community spirit, create employment for the poor, and adequately provide for children of poorer families.

QUESTIONS FOR CLASS DISCUSSION

1. To what extent does Albert Cohen's (1955) *Delinquent Boys* represent a rejection of the findings of Clifford Shaw and Henry McKay's (1942) *Juvenile Delinquency and Urban Areas*?

2. How do the respective explanations of the causes of juvenile delinquency advanced by Walter Miller (1958) and by Richard Cloward and Lloyd Ohlin (1960) represent an advance over Cohen's *Delinquent Boys*?

3. Discuss the following quotation from Kornhauser (1978:253):

> So abused have been the concepts of culture and subculture in explanation of delinquency that if these terms were struck from the lexicon of criminologists, the study of delinquency would benefit from their absence. It might then be possible more insistently to search for the roots of delinquency in social structure and situation.

4. Do delinquents *drift*?

5. Can the assumptions of David Matza's *Delinquency and Drift* accurately be described as a return to the assumptions of classical criminology?

RECOMMENDED READINGS

Kornhauser, Ruth Rosner (1978). *Social Sources of Delinquency*. Chicago: University of Chicago Press. Despite its tendency to read the recent history of delinquency theories through the partial lens of control theory (see Chapter 14.1), this surprisingly neglected book contains as provocative and informative criticisms of cultural-deviancy theory as can be found anywhere in current literature.

Matza, David (1964). *Delinquency and Drift*. New York: John Wiley. The authoritative theoretical critique of the field of juvenile delinquency in the U.S. See especially the devastating antipositivist comments on subcultural theories of delinquency (pp. 1–32).

———— (1969). *Becoming Deviant*. Englewood Cliffs, NJ: Prentice-Hall. This brilliant argument against the subcultural tradition never quite delivers the alternative theory of delinquency promised; moreover, the final third of the book suffers from Matza's weak attempt to analyze the relationships between the state (Hobbes' "Leviathan") and the meaning of deviancy in general. Although students often find this a most difficult book, we thoroughly recommend it.

CHAPTER 14

THEORETICAL DIVERSITY

14.1 Social Learning Theory
Differential Reinforcement
Assessment

14.2 The Labeling Perspective
The Social Meaning of Deviance
Societal Reaction
Primary and Secondary Deviance
Deviance Amplification
Stigma
Assessment

14.3 Conflict Theory
Crime and Criminalization
Criminal Law and Crime
The Carrier's Case
Assessment

14.4 Biocriminology and Crime
Genes and Crime
Studies of the XYY Chromosome
Studies of Twins
Studies of Adoptees
Biochemical Imbalances and Crime
Intelligence and Crime
Assessment

Preview

Chapter 14 introduces:

☞ the theoretical diversity in criminology that first appeared during the turbulent decade of the 1960s, and that continues today.

☞ four influential theories of crime: social learning theory, the labeling perspective, conflict theory, and biocriminology.

Key Terms

biochemical imbalances
criminalization
genes
IQ
labeling

primary deviance
secondary deviance
societal reaction
stigma

Chapter 14 examines four theories of crime that matured during the 1960s and 1970s. In combination, these theories represent the beginnings of the extraordinary theoretical diversity that now characterizes U.S. criminology. **Social learning theory** *developed, in part, from much of the existing criminological theory examined thus far. The* **labeling perspective** *and* **conflict theory** *have been influenced less by existing theories of crime than by various social and political movements that flourished in the 1960s.* **Biocriminology** *is an ancient theory that has recently had somewhat of a renaissance.*

14.1 ———— SOCIAL LEARNING THEORY

In Chapter 12.4 we examined Edwin Sutherland's theoretical focus on the origins and the transmission of delinquent values, and learned that he stimulated new lines of inquiry, one of which is social learning theory. With Sutherland's original insight in mind, subsequent empirical studies indeed seemed to confirm that the more serious a juvenile's delinquent involvement, the more likely he or she will be to have friends who are also delinquent (see, for example, Glueck and Glueck, 1950; Short, 1957, 1958; Glaser, 1956, 1960; Voss, 1964). This finding, however, does not explain *how* or *why* associational patterns influence delinquent involvement.

In arguing that Sutherland's theory of differential association and differential social organization cannot account for the process leading to individual criminality, Burgess and Akers (1966:130) recommended that criminologists try to utilize the genetic explanations of social behavior found in behavioral psychology. When such explanations are combined with structural explanations, such as subcultural and anomie theories, criminologists have termed them "social learning theory."

The basic premise of social learning theory is that social behavior is determined neither by inner personality drives nor by outer sociological and environmental factors. Rather, learning theorists believe that social behavior is a cognitive process in which personality and environment engage in a continuous process of reciprocal interaction. Modern learning theory was pioneered in laboratory settings, especially the operant conditioning theory of such behavioral scientists as B. F. Skinner (1953). Operant (or active) conditioning theory begins with the empirical fact that animal behavior is effected by its consequences, both negative and positive. Animals are easily trained to perform certain actions if they are rewarded for so doing. For example, dogs are usually trained to sit following the command "Sit!" if, after every time they sit, they receive positive reinforcement in the form of a bone or a friendly pat from their trainer. Desired behavior, in other words, is reinforced through a process of conditioned learning that emphasizes rewards or (for dogs who do not sit on command) punishments.

However, Bandura (1973) has shown that the process of social learning would be extremely tiring and hazardous if it depended solely on rewards and punishments. Although some behavior patterns actually are acquired through the process of rewarding and punishing direct experience, other behavior patterns are acquired by observing the behavior of significant others (family and peer group). As Bandura writes (*ibid.*:46):

> Of the numerous cues that influence how people will behave at any given moment, none is more ubiquitous or effective than the actions of others. People applaud when others clap, they exit from social functions when they see others leaving, they wear their hair like others, they dress alike, and on countless other occasions their behavior is prompted and channeled by the power of example. Modeling influences play an especially important role in the contagion of aggression. When behaving like others produces rewarding outcomes, modeling cues become powerful determinants of analogous behavior; conversely, when imitative actions are treated negatively but dissimilar behavior proves rewarding, models' responses prompt divergent performances in observers.

Differential Reinforcement

Several criminologists have indicated the importance of learning theory as an explanatory tool for understanding crime (e.g., Jeffery, 1965; DeFleur and Quinney, 1966; Burgess and Akers, 1966). In a direct application of Skinnerian theory, Clarence Ray Jeffery (1965) claimed that in any given social situation, whether an individual commits a crime depends largely on his or her past conditioning history, namely whether the individual has been reinforced (or rewarded) for crime. Jeffery's theory of *differential reinforcement* states:

A criminal act occurs in an environment in which in the past the actor has been reinforced for behaving in this manner, and the aversive consequences attached to the behavior have been of such a nature that they do not control or prevent the response (*ibid.*:295).

Crime is therefore a response to reinforcing stimuli. For example, the crime of robbery may produce either money or imprisonment (often both). If only money is produced, the behavior is likely to continue; if only imprisonment is produced, the aversive consequence is likely to deter the act. Thus, according to this explanation, crime depends chiefly on the process of differential reinforcement.

For Robert Burgess and Ronald Akers (1966), who attempted to reformulate Sutherland's theory of differential association, social behavior (including criminal behavior) responds chiefly to a complicated network of rewards and punishments. Any given behavior is likely to continue or to increase if it is followed more by rewards than by punishments; the same behavior is likely to decrease or to end if it is followed more by punishments than by rewards. Paraphrasing Burgess and Akers, criminal behavior is actually learned in seven stages (1966:146; and see Akers, 1973:46–47; and Akers, Krohn, Lanza-Kaduce, and Radosevich, 1979:637–639):

1. Criminal behavior is learned through direct conditioning or through imitation.

2. Criminal behavior is learned both in nonsocial reinforcing situations (for example, the physical effects of drug use) or nonsocial discriminative situations and through social interaction in which the behavior of others is either for or against criminal behavior.

3. The principal component of learning criminal behavior occurs in groups that comprise the individual's major source of reinforcements: peer friendship groups, the family, schools, and churches.

4. Learning criminal behavior—including specific techniques, attitudes, and avoidance procedures—depends on the effective and available reinforcers and the existing reinforcement contingencies.

5. The specific type and the frequency of learned behavior depends on the reinforcers that are effective and available, and on the norms by which these reinforcers are applied.

6. Criminal behavior is a function of norms that are discriminative for criminal behavior, the learning of which occurs when such behavior is more highly reinforced than is noncriminal behavior.

7. The strength of criminal behavior is a direct function of the amount, frequency, and probability of its reinforcement.

For Akers, all seven stages in this process must be examined. However, the central part of his theory lies in two factors concerning the learning of *acts and definitions:* (1) *differential reinforcement* and (2) *positive and negative definitions* (Akers, 1973:287–288). All social behavior is either strengthened by reward (positive reinforcement) and avoidance of punishment (negative reinforcement) or weakened by aversive stimuli (positive stimuli) and lack of reward (negative punishment). Whether a deviant act or a conforming act occurs depends on differential reinforcement (essentially past and present rewards or punishment both for the act and also for alternative acts.) However, in addition to learning an act, a person also learns if the act is defined as good or bad. The more a person defines an act as good, or as justifiable, the more likely he or she is to engage in it and the less likely he or she is to engage in alternatives. As Akers summarizes:

> A person participates in deviant activity then to the extent that it has been differentially reinforced over conforming behavior or defined as more desirable than conforming alternatives, or at least justified (*ibid.*:287–288).

As with Sutherland's theory of differential association, Akers' social learning theory clearly is intended as a *general* theory of crime. The broad scope of this theory is best seen in Akers' (1973) textbook *Deviant Behavior: A Social Learning Approach*. In this book Akers attempts to apply social learning theory to under-standing deviant behavior in general—"the principal forms of which . . . [include] drug use and addiction; homosexuality; prostitution; white-collar, professional, organized, and violent crimes; suicide; and mental illness" (*ibid.*:vii). In this book Akers applies the general principles of social learning theory to learning each form of deviance: (1) how a person first engages in the deviant act, (2) how that person progresses to more frequent engagement, (3) the substantive events that reinforce the act, and (4) the content of the definitions favorable to the act.

Consider two examples of Akers' application of learning theory: suicide and drug use. Suicide presents an interesting test case for a learning theory of deviance that relies on reinforcement as the major motivating element because, without exception, the act of taking one's own life cannot be reinforced for one's future behavior (One has none!). Moreover, on the whole, U.S. culture condemns suicide, which means that there exist very few definitions favorable to it. Nevertheless, Akers is confident the act of suicide is based on social learning, and offers a four-stage model as evidence (1973:245–252):

1. People learn that suicide appears to be a solution to personal problems. Everyone knows, or learns, that some people successfully eliminate their problems by hanging themselves, jumping off bridges, and by drug overdoses. A terminal illness, the loss of a loved one, financial ruin, and the existential *angst* are all situations in which suicide can be rationalized, justified, excused, or forgiven. These rationalizations are not defined as definitions favorable to the act of suicide, but often operate to neutralize unfavorable definitions.

2. People learn about specific techniques of suicide. We learn that a drug overdose (which sometimes can be interrupted after the drug is taken) is less likely to be successful than suicide by shooting. We also learn,

according to Akers, that certain techniques are considered more appropriate for one sex than another: the violence of shooting, for example, is a "masculine" technique, whereas a drug overdose is more "feminine."

3. People learn that the act of suicide receives considerable attention. Thus, some proportion of suicidal behavior is not actually intended to result in death but in attention from loved ones. Suicide resulting from previously learned nonfatal suicidal behavior is common. In some cases of suicide without prior attempts, the act of suicide derives from imitation—psychiatrists, therefore, have high rates of suicide compared with most other occupations.

4. Whether a person tries to commit suicide again depends in part on the reaction of others. Thus:

> They may increase their attention to him without necessarily solving the crises and thus reinforce further attempts, or they may reinforce his belief that there is no hope. In either case he is likely to attempt again, and one of these attempts may be fatal (*ibid.*:251).

Another well-known test of social learning theory was conducted by Akers *et al.* (1979) in a study of teenage deviance—drug (marijuana) and alcohol use/abuse. This study was based on a self-report questionnaire administered to 3,065 male and female teenagers attending grades 7 through 12 in seven communities in three midwestern states. It strongly confirmed social learning theory: the probability of abstinence from drug and alcohol use/abuse decreases and the frequency of use/abuse increases when individual teenagers (1) associate more with using/abusing rather than abstaining peers and adults, (2) are more rewarded than punished for use/abuse, and (3) are exposed more to favorable than to unfavorable definitions of use/abuse (*ibid.*:639). These three factors, they concluded, explained 55 percent of the differences between users/abusers of and abstainers from alcohol, and 68 percent of the differences between users/abusers of and abstainers from marijuana (*ibid.*:642).

Assessment

Apart from his sustained research and that of a small group of followers, Akers' social learning theory has not gained significant influence (Conger, 1978; Pfohl, 1985:272). The basic principles of social learning theory, and its explanation of why some persons commit criminal and deviant acts, has still not been widely or deeply tested. There are three major reasons for its somewhat quiet passage through the corridors of criminological research, two of which are external to the contents of social learning theory and one of which is internal.

Social learning theory arose when deterministic causation was unfashionable in criminology. We have seen already (Chapter 13.3), for example, the devastating challenge posed by David Matza's view that delinquency is not caused by deterministic forces but that juveniles episodically *drift* into (and out of) delinquency. This detachment from deterministic theories was reinforced, in turn, by the tremendous popularity of the labeling perspective, which seemed to imply that crime should not be understood as having causes at all. Moreover, it is probable that many criminologists shy away from social learning theory because of the ethical difficulties associated with its policy implications. If criminal tendencies, including violence, are chiefly *learned*, it seems to follow that they can just as easily be unlearned through behavior modification. Controversial examples of behavior modification treatment include drug-based therapy, ECT, chemotherapy, and confrontational juvenile correctional programs such as Visionquest. Although none of these strategies has proven very effective, all arouse widespread ethical controversy because they appear to foreshadow a return to the violent criminal justice system of the dark and distant past.

Finally, we note that social learning theory, as with Sutherland's theory of differential association, was devised by Akers as a *general* theory of crime. The attractiveness of social learning theory, like all general theories, derives from its simplicity. How nice and convenient it would be to discover that the cause of all crime lies in learned behaviors! However, even though in some abstract sense it may be correct to say that all behavior is learned, this does not tell us why certain (learned) behavior is criminal and other behavior is not. Crime involves considerably more than someone learning to engage in certain behavior. The behavior itself must also be defined as criminal, a process that is an integral part of explaining crime and that has little indeed to do with learning. This final point is emphasized by the labeling perspective, to which we now turn.

14.2 ———— THE LABELING PERSPECTIVE

During the decade of the 1960s, the legitimacy of political authority in the U.S. was challenged by many college students, liberal intellectuals, women's movements, and members of minority racial groups. Questions about U.S. foreign policy in Vietnam and elsewhere, about domestic civil rights, and about the stark social, economic, racial, and gender inequalities in the world's richest society quickly filtered through to sociological perspectives on crime and criminal justice. Certain radical intellectuals (such as Marcuse, 1964) argued that social inequality and injustice in the U.S. could be removed only by the powerless, deviant, outcast, criminal populations typically studied by criminologists. These populations, it was determined, had nothing to lose and everything to gain from a revolutionary overthrow of the existing social order. Reflecting this turbulent political climate, sociologists and criminologists opened a Pandora's box using a key provided by Robert S. Lynd's (1939) famous question: "Knowledge for what?" In such an inegalitarian society as the U.S., why is criminology typically concerned with crimes of the powerless rather than with crimes committed by the government, by white-collar executives, and by corporations? *Who* defines certain behavior as criminal? And *why?* In a society like the U.S.—where "the rich get richer and the poor get prison" (Reiman, 1979)—whose side are *we* (the "we" who study crime with detached objectivity) on?

The criminologists who first examined such politicized questions were mainly younger scholars attached to *the labeling perspective* (which we examine now) and *conflict theory* (which we examine next). By and large, as the labeling perspective developed, its neutral posture toward deviants was transformed into a celebration of deviant activity as evidence of the virtue of social diversity. Many deviant activities began to be seen in a different and more interesting light. The "opening up" and "demystifying" implied by the concept of deviance involves a very different relationship between the deviant and the student of deviant behavior. In coming out of their criminological closets, labeling theorists tended to see in alcoholism, criminality, and mental illness, for example, individuals who had been victimized by society and who were potential rebels against its values.

It is not easy to pin down the key concepts of the labeling perspective. Unlike many other approaches to crime, the labeling perspective does not come prepackaged with a set of instructions for assembly. There is even disagreement, for example, about the very term "the labeling perspective," which has also been described as "societal reaction," "sociology of deviance," "social interactionism," "the neo-Chicago school," and "the new deviancy theory." Our use of "the labeling perspective" is thus only a simple convenience for all these terms. The term "the labeling *perspective*," moreover, is preferable to "labeling theory" because, as most of its supporters and critics agree, there is no formalized *theory* of labeling.

Although the labeling perspective is a mixture of several intellectual traditions, we can isolate three key concepts held by a majority of those using this perspective: (1) the social meaning of deviance, (2) societal reaction, and (3) stigma.

The Social Meaning of Deviance

Following in the footsteps of the Chicago school of the 1920s and 1930s (see Chapter 12.2)—and drawing on the social psychology (phenomenology and symbolic interactionism) of George Herbert Mead, his student Herbert Blumer, and others—those researching deviance from the labeling perspective have united around the central importance of *meanings* in everyday life. Social reality itself is seen as an ongoing, fluid process that is constructed according to the outcome of the meaning that we attach to our interaction with others, on the one hand, and the meanings that they, on the other, attribute to us. Crime and deviance, then, are not pre-given, objective categories, but negotiable statuses. Thus, in interactionist or participant observation studies, the researcher participates in the social interaction of drug users/abusers, alcoholics, mental patients, and others in order to "appreciate" the meanings that those defined as deviant attribute to their own activities. As we saw in Chapter 13.2, this was partly the view of deviance advocated by Matza's work.

The emphasis on meanings takes a number of twists and turns in the labeling perspective. At one level, the labeling perspective is skeptical that our knowledge can ever be objective and value-free. Because social behavior means different things to different people, it follows that it is impossible to have the sort of complete knowledge about social interaction that, for example, a natural scientist may have about the movement of inanimate objects such as billiard balls. It is thus no accident that many of the studies in the labeling tradition have rejected the use of the scientific method. At another level (as we shall soon learn), it is clear that because meanings do not exist in a social vacuum, the meanings, perceptions, and opinions of certain individuals or groups are taken more seriously than those of others. Although reality is socially constructed, therefore, not all members of society have an equal voice in deciding precisely how it is constructed. Taking a sympathetic cue from the way in which society devalues deviants and outsiders, the labeling perspective typically sides with the underdog and the outcast.

A well-known and excellent example of the centrality of meaning in the labeling perspective is provided by Howard Becker's (1963) book *Outsiders.* Becker (*ibid.*:46–58) argues (relying somewhat on learning theory) that marijuana users must learn to experience the meanings and effects of using marijuana if they are to get high "properly":

1. *Learning the Technique*   Users must learn the proper technique for smoking marijuana. The technique is not the same as that for smoking tobacco, for example. "If nothing happens," Becker reports, "it is manifestly impossible for the user *to develop a conception* of the drug which can be used for pleasure, and use will therefore not continue" (*ibid.*:47) [emphasis added]. According to the 50 users interviewed in Becker's study: "Without such a conception marijuana use was considered meaningless and did not continue" (*ibid.*:48).

2. *Learning to Perceive the Effects*   Becker suggests that the actual smoking of marijuana with the proper technique is not enough to get high. Users must learn to perceive the effects of being high: "The new user may not get high and thus not form a conception of the drug as something which can be used for pleasure" (*ibid.*). Marijuana users *must perceive* hunger, laughter, tingling, and dizziness as important and valuable parts of the process of getting high. Becker reported that in each case where one of his subjects continued to use marijuana, "the user had acquired the necessary concepts with which to express to himself the fact that he was experiencing new sensations caused by the drug" (*ibid.*:51). Only by acquiring these concepts does marijuana use acquire meaning for the user as a pleasurable activity.

3. *Learning to Enjoy the Effects*   Like the taste of oysters, cigarettes, and dry martinis, there is nothing automatically pleasurable about marijuana-produced sensations. Only when the user learns to perceive marijuana use as enjoyable—which often involves redefining the meaning of some early

sensations of fear, or of sickness, for example—does marijuana become and remain an object that the user conceives as capable of producing pleasure.

Becker's research on marijuana use emphasizes that cognition is an important part of social interaction, that social reality is constructed by the meanings embedded in everyday life. Indeed, Becker goes so far as to claim that the subjective experience of drugs is structured much more by social meanings and perceptions than by biological and pharmacological factors! If a situation is perceived and defined as real, then it is real in its consequences. Moreover, as human and social beings, each of us differs in the meaning that we attach both to our own behavior and to that of others. At different times, and to different people, our behavior (such as wearing punk clothing) may be perceived as interesting, or exotic, or daring. At other times, the very same behavior may be seen as dangerous, abnormal, sick, delinquent, or criminal. The labeling perspective insists that such perceptions are the only real difference between behavior that is seen, respectively, as normal or as deviant.

Becker argues that it is a mistake to see deviance simply as the infraction of some agreed-upon rule. To look at deviance in this way is to ignore the fact that what counts as deviance is largely a function of the ability of groups with political power to impose their concept (or meaning) of right and wrong on the behavior of other groups. Because there is great diversity in the values of groups with political power there is, therefore, great cross-cultural and cross-temporal variety in what officially (let alone unofficially) counts as deviance (and see Chapter 16). Homosexuality, for example, is perceived as morally deviant in some cultures but in others it is tolerated and in still others (such as classical Greece and Rome) its practice is regarded as a positive virtue (Greenberg, 1988). In other words, suggests Becker, to understand deviance one must recognize that a given form of deviance is typically only *statistically* abnormal. As Becker argues:

> *Social groups create deviance by making the rules whose infraction constitutes deviance*, and by applying those rules to particular people and labeling them as outsiders. From this point of view, deviance is *not* a quality of the act the person commits, but rather a consequence of the application by others of rules and sanctions to an "offender." The deviant is one to whom that label has successfully been applied; deviant behavior is behavior that people so label (*ibid.*:9). [emphasis in original]

Societal Reaction

In arguing that "deviant behavior is behavior that people so label," Becker does not claim that such acts as homicide would not exist without the label that is often attached to them. That would be patently absurd. Rather, he is pointing to the important role of societal reaction in the designation of certain acts as deviant or criminal. For example, although the physical act of killing another human being can occur without societal reaction to it, whether a given killing is labeled as murder, manslaughter, accidental death, or justifiable homicide crucially depends on the meaning attributed to it by a social audience. From Becker's perspective, therefore, it follows that society itself "creates" deviance because it is society that defines it as such.

Half a century ago, Frank Tannenbaum (1938:17–18) pointed out how there is often a shift in society's reaction to delinquency and to delinquents, a process he described as the "dramatization of evil." Tannenbaum argued that the community's condemnation of *delinquent behavior* often becomes transformed into a view of the offender as a *delinquent person.* The evil that is seen in a delinquent act, in other words, is easily transferred from the act to the person engaging in it. Boys who vandalize school are seen as "bad boys." In attempting to understand the mechanisms of this transformation, Edwin Lemert has distinguished between primary and secondary deviance. To Lemert's distinction we now turn.

Primary and Secondary Deviance

In his books *Social Pathology* and *Human Deviance, Social Problems, and Social Control,* Lemert (1951:75–78; 1967:40–64) has used the sociopsychological concepts of *primary* and *secondary* deviation to understand the process of deviance. Lemert proposed this distinction in order to draw attention to the difference between what he terms on the one hand the "original" and on the other the "effective" causes of the deviant attributes and actions "associated with physical defects and incapacity, crime, prostitution, alcoholism, drug addiction, and mental disorders" (1967:40).

According to Lemert, primary deviance has original causes that are numerous in their possible sources. *Primary deviance* can be caused by a host of social, cultural, psychological, and physiological events (such as many of those referred to from Chapter 10 onward). Primary deviants do not undergo any change in their psychological makeup or in the way they act as members of society. *Secondary deviance* is caused by the way in which society reacts to some of those who engage in primary deviance. After they are apprehended, Lemert points out, primary deviants suffer a variety of consequences, many of which focus on the application to them of such deviant labels as sick, cripple, criminal, insane, and so on. Youth in trouble with the police, for example, often are labeled as bad or delinquent. Such labels can have important consequences—for friendship, for job opportunities, and for self-image. Sometimes the effect of deviant labels is so powerful—either through a self-fulfilling prophecy or through the negative consequences of stigma (which we examine soon)—that labeled individuals are forced to reorient their lives around the label. Secondary deviants accept their new identity as a "deviant," and act in accordance with the societal reaction to their primary deviance. Secondary deviance thus becomes a powerful tool for explaining recidivism.

Following Lemert and Becker, labeling theorists do not therefore study the causes of crime in the way they are approached by most theories examined thus far in this book. Indeed, labeling theorists generally tend to evade altogether questions of individual causation. When they deal with what to other criminologists looks suspiciously like causation, or when they are pushed to examine the implications of their research, it is clear that labeling theorists are concerned chiefly with the way *society itself causes deviance*. In other words, they are interested in how and why society labels certain behaviors deviant. Lemert, for example, has argued that whereas previous studies of deviance tended to rest heavily upon the idea that deviance leads to social control:

> I have come to believe that the reverse idea, i.e., social control leads to deviance, is equally tenable and the potentially richer premise for studying deviance in modern society (1967:v).

Lemert never suggested that societal reaction to primary deviance itself causes subsequent deviance, but he seems to have come very near to this position. However, the diverse ways in which society reacts to and actually creates deviance have been examined in various studies. Consider certain key findings of research on societal reaction.

According to the labeling perspective it is the *response* to certain behavior—rather than the behavior itself—that is the crucial element in the designation of deviance. Much of the time the process of deviance creation is a routine and humdrum affair that commands little comment by the media. This is especially so for most property crimes and many crimes against public order. The great bulk of offenders processed by the criminal justice system—those accused of public drunkenness, larceny-theft and fraud, driving under the influence, and disorderly conduct—receive almost no attention in the media (see Chapter 1.1).

Every so often, however, a society becomes engrossed in a process of public frenzy directed to certain forms of crime and deviance. Well-known examples of this intense process include the 16th- and 17th-century witch hunts in Europe and in colonial America, the moral crusade against prostitution between 1890 and 1920, the Nazi slaughter of Jews in the 1930s and 1940s, the McCarthyite search for communists in the 1950s, and the campaign against child abuse in the 1980s. Stanley Cohen's (1972) seminal book *Folk Devils and Moral Panics* has highlighted the fact that societies appear to be subject, every now and then, to outbreaks of moral panic. As Cohen (*ibid.*:9) explains:

> A condition, episode, person or group of persons emerges to become defined as a threat to societal values and interests; its nature is presented in a stylized and stereotypical fashion by the mass media; the moral barricades are manned by editors, bishops, politicians and other right-thinking people; socially accredited experts pronounce their diagnoses and solutions; ways of coping are evolved or (more often) resorted to; the condition then disappears, submerges, or deteriorates and becomes more visible.

Deviance Amplification

Cohen's research shows how the media, the police, and various moral entrepreneurs conspired to create a panic over the activities of two youth gangs (the

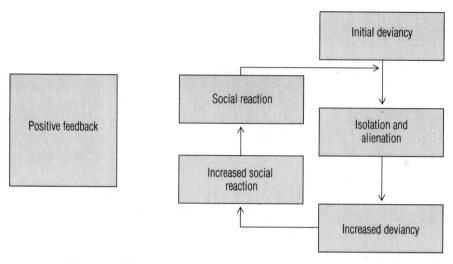

FIGURE   **The Amplification of Deviance**
14-1   Source: *Jock Young, 1971, p. 34.*

Mods and the Rockers) in southern England in the mid-1960s. Since the 1970s a similar, far more controversial panic has arisen over soccer hooliganism in Britain (Redhead, 1987). In each case the media and the agencies of social control acted in such a way as to fan out of all proportion what was originally a fairly small problem. This part of the process has been termed "deviance amplification" (Wilkins, 1964).

One well-known study that illustrates the major features of the process of deviance amplification has been conducted by British criminologist Jock Young (1971). The subjects of Young's participant observation study were marijuana users in the Notting Hill Gate area of London in the late 1960s. Young shows how the socially harmless activity of marijuana use was transformed into a social problem through the complicated web of interaction among the mass media, the public, the police, and the users themselves (see Figure 14-1).

Young describes how the mass media made marijuana use a social problem through sensationalistic and lurid accounts of the lives of marijuana users. The media's portrayal of marijuana users as sick, unwashed, promiscuous weirdos completely committed to drug use was a stereotype that inflamed popular indignation during 1967. As with Cohen's (1972) study of the Mods and Rockers discussed previously, Young shows how this media pressure led police to amplify the very problem they vigilantly sought to curb. Intensive police action (specifically arrest, with the view of segregating them from the "normal" community) against Notting Hill marijuana users led to an organized defensive posture in the drug-using community. Drug users united around a shared sense of injustice concerning harsh sentences and mass media stereotypes. Drug use became a symbol of defiance against an unjust and intolerant society. As Young (*ibid.*:46) writes:

As police concern with drug-taking increases, drug-taking becomes more and more a secret activity. Because of this, drug-taking in itself becomes of greater value to the group as a symbol of their difference, and of their defiance of perceived social injustices. . . .

Drug-taking and trafficking *thus move from being peripheral activities . . . to become a central activity of great symbolic importance. The stereotype begins to be realized, and fantasy is translated into reality.* [emphasis added]

In other words, police activity amplifies the new social problem of drug taking. But Young shows that this police-generated amplification does not stop here. As the drug takers are more and more driven underground, the profits from selling marijuana begin to rise steeply. Where formerly the sale of marijuana was a low-key and low-profit activity often conducted largely among friends, now the activity is taken over by "the criminal underworld" (*ibid.*:47). This organized underworld

becomes more interested in the drug market, overtures are made to importers; a few pushers come under pressure to buy from them and to sell a wider range of drugs, including heroin and methedrine. A drug pyramid . . . begins to emerge. Once again fantasy is translated into reality (*ibid.*).

The media uses the rising number of drug convictions to fan public indignation about marijuana use even further. Increased pressure is then put on the police to stamp out this new evil. Expanded police drug units ensure greater detection of marijuana users. Once again the number of drug convictions soars. The vicious cycle is firmly established.

Young's research demonstrates, then, that the police actually amplify the deviant activities they mean to control. Moreover, Gary Marx (1981) has shown there are three types of interdependence between rule enforcers (such as police, prosecutors, and judges) and deviants that involve the possibility of deviance amplification: (1) escalation, (2) nonenforcement, and (3) covert facilitation.

(1) The situation of escalation can arise from initial attempts at social control. Marx (*ibid.*:223) points out, for example, that "police involvement in family conflict, crowd, and automobile chase situations can contribute to violations where none was imminent, or it can increase the seriousness of these situations." The mere presence of police officers at the scene of a domestic disturbance, for instance, can easily escalate a potentially dangerous situation into an overtly violent one. High-speed police vehicle chases, which sometimes result in injuries or death, can lead to manslaughter charges where none would otherwise have existed. But escalation can also arise from post-apprehension efforts in the process of social control. A defendant's need to make bail can lead to illegal attempts to raise money. Innocent defendants (and others) who lie on the witness stand can be fined or jailed. Prisoners sometimes have their sentences extended for bad behavior in prison. Another source of post-apprehension escalation is the stigma that accompanies the label of "deviant" or "criminal."

(2) The situation of nonenforcement is less direct than escalation. According to Marx (*ibid.*:226–231), the nonenforcement of rules is difficult to identify because often it is hidden and illegal. Marx (*ibid.*:227) documents that police may adopt a policy of nonenforcement with respect to (a) informants who provide information about the law breaking of others and/or help to facilitate a controlled commission of a crime, (b) vice entrepreneurs who agree to keep their own illegal behavior within agreed-upon limits, (c) individuals who either directly regulate the behavior of others using resources police lack or means they are denied or who take actions desired by authorities but considered too politically risky for them to undertake.

(3) In a situation of covert facilitation, rule enforcers take an active role in encouraging others to break rules (Marx, 1981:231–233). Such facilitation takes several forms. In one the police go undercover to buy or sell illegal goods and services. For example, the police may pose as johns in order to arrest prostitutes or try to buy drugs in order to arrest drug dealers. Or the police may use a decoy, such as a female police officer in civilian clothes, in order to create a robbery and/or assault, or pose as the representatives of a foreign country in order to trap unwitting members of Congress taking a bribe to secure political influence in Washington. The situation of covert facilitation can even be used inside a police department to detect corrupt police officers. In New York City alone, recent examples of this tactic include (*ibid.*:232–233):

> planting "lost" wallets near randomly selected police officers to see if they would be turned in intact; offering bribes to arresting officers; putting through a contrived "open door" call to an apartment where marked money was prominently displayed to see if two officers under suspicion would steal it (they did); establishing phony gambling operations to see if police sought protection money; and having an undercover officer pose as a pusher to see if other undercover narcotics agents paid out the full amount of "buy" money they claimed.

Stigma

As noted, one of the insights of the labeling perspective is that whether or not individuals are regarded as deviant depends on societal reaction to their behavior. Moreover, partly because of this reaction to their behavior (primary deviance), some—although by no means all—deviants are pushed into further (or secondary) deviance. This redirection of behavior occurs in a variety of ways. We now consider why societal reaction to deviance often results in, and can actually stem from, the fact that those who deviate from the norm tend to be stigmatized.

Stigma is a term invented in ancient Greece. Goffman (1963:1) relates that, for the Greeks, stigma referred to

> bodily signs designed to expose something unusual and bad about the moral status of the signifier. The signs were cut or burnt into the body and advertised that the bearer was a slave, a criminal, or a traitor—a

blemished person, ritually polluted, to be avoided, especially in public places. Later, in Christian times, two layers of metaphor were added to the term: the first referred to bodily signs of holy grace that took the form of eruptive blossoms on the skin; the second, a medical allusion to this religious allusion, referred to bodily signs of physical disorder.

Stigma is therefore a sign of disgrace imposed on an individual. It is a way of spoiling a person's real identity, marking him or her as someone to be avoided. The process of stigma operates in numerous settings and can be applied as a label to numerous persons: in medicine to those with physical deformities (cripples, gimps, dwarfs, giants) or mental deviancy (weirdos, lunatics, crazies); in education to those who achieve low grades in school (retards, dumbos, failures) or, sometimes, those who achieve high grades (egg heads, nerds, brains); in religion to those who do not believe in the "one and true" God (witches, heretics, pagans); and in the criminal justice system to those convicted of crimes (ex-cons, recidivists, career criminals). In these examples stigma is a sign denoting someone who is disqualified, by varying degrees, from full social acceptance. It can affect self-esteem, self-concept, and future behavior. Returning to the central importance of meaning, we emphasize that stigma can vary in the meaning that it has both to the person stigmatized and to the social audience.

Stigma is not really an attribute but a point within a set of social relationships. Goffman provides the example of an individual who wants to join the military and, because he has a physical infirmity, hides his physical condition from the army recruiters. Later, "the same individual, embittered and trying to get out of the army, may succeed in gaining admission to the army hospital, where he would be discredited if discovered as not really having an acute sickness" (1963:3–4). We should add that had the individual remained in the military, fought in a war, and been wounded, his physical condition would doubtless have been the mark of a war hero. Moreover, the meaning of stigma also varies according to such factors as gender and social class. For example, the same behavior for which females with deviant sexual appetites receive condemnation (nymphos, loose women, sluts) is often for men a source of praise and esteem (stags, studs, lady killers).

What are the effects of stigma? Richard Schwartz and Jerome Skolnick (1964) have argued that the effectiveness of legal sanctions against stigmatized individuals often varies according to the social position of the defendant penalized. To demonstrate this they examined the effects of sanctions on unskilled workers charged with assault and on physicians accused of medical malpractice.

In the first study Schwartz and Skolnick concocted four employment folders, each containing one potential job applicant applying for an unskilled job in the Catskill resort area of New York State. One hundred sample firms were each sent one of the four employment folders (each employment folder was reviewed by 25 potential employers) in an attempt to determine what sorts of applicants were likely to receive offers of employment. The basic information available on the one candidate in each of the four employment folders indicated that the applicant was single, male, high-school trained, 32 years of age, of unspecified race, with some experience in unskilled work. However, each employment folder differed in one important respect: the applicant's record of criminal involvement: (1) The first folder indicated that the applicant had been tried and sentenced for assault. (2) The second folder indicated that the applicant had been tried for assault *but* acquitted. (3) The third folder indicated that the applicant had been tried for assault *and* acquitted—but contained a letter from the trial judge certifying the defendant's innocence under the constitutional presumption of innocence. (4) The fourth folder made no mention of any criminal involvement.

The employers' responses to these different employment folders were of two kinds: *positive* responses referred to employers who expressed a willingness to consider an applicant; *negative* responses referred to employers who refused to consider a candidate. The findings of this study were not surprising. Of the 25 employers shown the last folder, nine responded positively. But of the 25 employers shown the first folder, only one responded positively. As Schwartz and Skolnick lament: "This is a rather graphic indication of the effect which a criminal record may have on job opportunities" (*ibid.*:107). The results of the "acquittal" group of folders, the second and third employment folders, were less obvious. The second folder produced only three positive responses; when accompanied by a judge's letter (the third folder), this increased to six. This finding tends to show that, at least in the case of employment opportunities, prospects are reduced simply by an applicant having been tried in criminal court. "From a theoretical point of view, this result indicates that permanent lowering of status is not limited to those explicitly singled out by being convicted of a crime" (*ibid.*:108). Legal determination of innocence, in other words, is an effective barrier to job prospects!

In their second study Schwartz and Skolnick obtained the insurance records of, and then questioned, 58 of the 69 Connecticut physicians who were defendants in malpractice suits. The 58 physicians turned out to be comparable with physicians in Connecticut as a whole in terms of age and professional experience. The physicians ranged from the lowest professional stratum to chiefs of staff and services in Connecticut's most highly regarded hospitals. The subjects of the second Schwartz and Skolnick study differed from the first in several ways: type of offense, social position of the accused, social support available to the accused, and relationship of the accused to their employers. Of the 58 malpractice cases examined, physicians clearly won 38 (of which 19 were dropped by the plaintiff[s]); of the remaining 19 cases, 11 were settled out of court for small amounts, four for roughly the amounts claimed by the plaintiff(s), and four resulted in judgments for the plaintiff(s) in court.

Of considerable interest is the lack of negative effects from these malpractice suits on the physicians' practices. Of the 58 physicians, 52 reported no negative effects, and five of the remaining six reported their practice actually improved after the suit! Schwartz and Skolnick point out that these results can be explained by the protective environment surrounding medical work (*ibid.*:112). For example, physicians who reported improvements in their practices after a suit (such as an increase in fees) had been referred more patients by sympathetic fellow physicians. When local medical societies took any action, it was almost always to assist a physician in defense of the suit.

Schwartz and Skolnick's findings have been supported by a similar study in Holland. In this study, Wouter Buikhuisen and Fokke Dijksterhuis (1971) found that two groups of convicts (those convicted once for theft and those convicted for drunken driving) received significantly fewer positive responses than nonconvicts in their job applications to 75 large companies. Although both studies clearly imply that stigma differs in its effect on such factors as job opportunities, Schwartz and Skolnick's study points to the fact that the effects of stigma are in fact quite variable. They show that unskilled workers suffer much more from the stigma accompanying accusations of assault than do physicians from the effects of accusations of medical malpractice. The higher the social status, so their study implies, the easier it is to counteract the effects of labeling.

What are the different ways in which people respond to being stigmatized? How do stigmatized individuals—to pose Goffman's graphic question—"negotiate" their "spoiled identities" (1963:9; and see Garfinkel, 1956)? Research addressing these two questions is inconclusive. The response to stigmatization clearly varies according to certain factors, but their relative weights have not as yet been fully determined. One important factor seems to be the stage in a "deviant career" in which a negative label is applied. For example, some children may be told by their parents or by their teachers, "You are no damn good." If the children internalize such warnings they may, through self-fulfilling prophecy, actually become "no damn good" (Polk and Schafer, 1972). But this is far from being inevitable. The stigmatizing effect of the label attached to primary deviation is one of the most important factors in the occurrence of secondary deviation, and is often used to explain cases of recidivism. Consensus on this issue seems to hold that the earlier in a deviant career a label is applied, the less likely is secondary deviation to occur. Cameron (1964) found that first-time shoplifters, for example, tend not to engage in shoplifting again because of the effect of the label. But the effect of the label also depends on how sensitive the victim is to the meaning of the label—and this is obviously subject to wide variation. Some juvenile gang members, for example, may actually take pride in expulsion from school or in apprehension by the police.

Sometimes it is relatively easy for stigmatized individuals to hide or to "correct" their stigma. Nowadays, for example, persons with certain forms of deviant attributes, such as physical deformities or illiteracy, can seek surgical or educational remedies to reform or hide their apparent defects. However, as Goffman (1963:9) suggests, these strategies are not always completely successful:

> Where such repair is possible, what often results is not the acquisition of fully normal status, but a transformation of self from someone with a particular blemish into someone with a record of having corrected a particular blemish.

The effects of stigma also partly depend on the institutional context in which it is conferred. In his book *Asylums*, for example, Goffman (1961) reports that in "total institutions"—such as mental hospitals, where "a large number of

The preconceptions of stigma.

like-situated individuals, cut off from the wider society for an appreciable period of time, together lead an enclosed, formally administered round of life" (*ibid.*:xiii)—it is very difficult to shrug off the effects of stigma. Goffman reported that in the mental institution he studied for three years (St. Elizabeth's Hospital in Washington, D.C.), whenever patients exhibited "normal" behavior, the staff often interpreted that very normalcy as a sign that they were "abnormal"! According to recent research (for example, Link, Cullen, Frank, and Wozniak, 1987), former mental patients often encounter public preconceptions that they are dangerous—not on the basis of their behavior but because of the label attached to them.

Following the lead of Schwartz and Skolnick, it is reasonable to conclude that responses to stigmatization are strongly associated with social class and relative powerlessness. The exact nature of this association, however, is unclear. Allen Liska (1987:132–133; see also Jensen, 1972; Thornberry, 1973; Ageton and Elliott, 1974), for example, writes:

> Since blacks occupy a negative social status and are not well integrated into society, they are not very sensitive to official reactions of society. Labeling may have its maximum effect on people well integrated into society; hence, the effects of labeling should be maximal for first offenders, the middle-class, and whites and minimal for prior offenders, the lower class, and blacks (Liska, 1987:132–133).

However, although negative labeling arguably can be seen as affecting those with higher social status (namely, whites) more than those with lower social status (for example, African Americans), it is also true that the former have greater resources for counteracting stigma than do the latter. The question of whether certain social groups are better equipped to counteract the effects of labeling returns us to another question raised by Lemert's distinction between primary and secondary deviance: Is the person on whom the label "criminal" is conferred likely to be propelled into more crime or deterred from future criminal behavior? Once again the evidence is inconclusive. On the one hand, the labeling perspective as a whole implies that negative labels lead to further deviant activity. On the other hand, there is some evidence to suggest that labeling has very little effect on future behavior (such as Tittle, 1975; Rausch, 1983).

Assessment

The labeling perspective continues to be an important influence in criminology, primarily because it emphasizes the fact that terms like "deviance" and "crime" are applied selectively to social behavior. Moreover, the labeling perspective has uncovered the ironic ways in which the process of societal reaction can actually amplify the very problems it seeks to eliminate. Although this can occur in many ways, the two chief forms are the stimulation of moral panics and the effects of stigma. Social control, in other words, is often counterproductive.

There are two serious difficulties with the labeling perspective. One concerns a broad problem with the way in which social meanings tend to be theorized. The other concerns the general failure—or the unwillingness—of the labeling perspective to pursue to its logical conclusion its basic insight that deviance and crime are in the eye of the beholder.

As we have seen, the labeling perspective insists on the importance of the meaning of social interaction to all participants. On this view, social reality is a malleable process flowing from the subjective meanings attached by participants to their actions. In his research on marijuana use, for example, Becker showed that novice marijuana users get properly high only after they have learned from veteran users to understand what it means to get high. However, in most labeling studies there is a tendency to assume that meanings are generated quite apart from the influence of such other, potentially determining, factors as history and biology.

Consider again Becker's emphasis on the relevance of meanings in the process of becoming a marijuana user. Quite apart from the importance of Becker's own contribution to the labeling perspective, we return to his research because it seems to offer a powerful confirmation of the importance of meaning in social interaction: getting high has little to do with the pharmacological properties of drugs and much to do with learning the meaning of getting high. However, Geoffrey Pearson and John Twohig (1976) have questioned the virtual absence of pharmacological factors in Becker's ethnography of drug use/abuse. They advanced the interesting idea of asking drug users/abusers what they thought of Becker's account of how marijuana smoking is experienced from the inside. Do drug users/abusers see themselves in Becker's account of how they learn to get high?

> One man, an experienced drug user, summarized for us one of the key issues. Becker had suggested that novices need to learn to perceive the effects. What was his own experience? "Perceive the effects??? Wow! (prolonged laughter) The effects were just ... WHAAM!!! ... like a hammer at the back of the head. ... That guy Becker should change his dealer!" He had smoked for the first time with his brother and a group of friends. From what he said, he had smoked rather a lot of cannabis resin rolled into large tobacco "joints." He was "blocked," he said, for what seemed like a very long time and eventually fell asleep listening to music. His dramatically phrased experience that the pharmacological effects of cannabis pressed themselves upon him (without subcultural mediation) is representative of a large group of drug users who did not recognize themselves in Becker's phenomenology" (*ibid.*:122).

Pearson and Twohig turn the tables on Becker and suggest that the mistaken conclusions of his never-never land derive from three sources. First, Becker mistakenly assumed that sociological accounts of drug use/abuse are always superior to biological and pharmacological accounts. To assume this superiority from the beginning is nothing short of sociological imperialism. (Hence the ease with which the preceding interviewee could ridicule Becker's account of how drug users/abusers learn to perceive the effects of drugs.) Second, Becker's underemphasis on the toxicity of drugs is a phony radicalism in line with the left-liberal demand to legalize "soft" drugs. If drug highs are not pharmacologically but *socially* induced then, Becker implies, highs can be taught to be experienced in safe and more creative ways. Third, the thesis of "the social construction of even the most intimate aspects of personal experience reflects the fear ... that advanced industrial society overwhelms every nook and cranny of private life" (*ibid.*:125).

Another difficulty with the labeling perspective is that its adherents have never pursued its own ambitious agenda. If terms like "deviance" and "crime" are applied selectively to social behavior then, it would seem to follow, it is critical to examine the criteria of selection. This examination involves thoroughgoing political questions about the interests served by criminal law, questions which those working in the labeling perspective occasionally have raised but almost never addressed properly. As sociologist Alvin Gouldner complained (1970:107):

> Becker's school thus views the underdog as someone who is being mismanaged, not as someone who suffers and fights back. Here the deviant is sly but not defiant; he is tricky but not courageous; he sneers but does not accuse; he "makes out" without making a scene. Insofar as this school of theory has a critical edge to it, this is directed at the

caretaking institutions who do the mopping-up job, rather than at the master institutions that produce the deviant's suffering.

In his book *Controlology*, Jason Ditton (1979:1–37; and see Liazos, 1972) confirms our criticism that the labeling perspective has never pushed its own original insights to their logical conclusion. Ditton complains (*ibid.*:5):

> The total rejection of positivism by followers of the labeling perspective either had no effect at all on the institutionalized study of crime or, at best, the massive theoretical critique was distilled into an additional factor ("the reaction") to be henceforth co-opted in the unchanged rhetoric of mathematical calculation. . . . It has always been content instead to snipe at convention from the theoretical sidelines—happy to stand on the lunatic fringe and lob distracting stories of strippers, nudists, gays, teddy boys, nutters, dwarfs, and druggies at the central juggernaut of state-sponsored criminology.

In this assessment Ditton therefore bemoans the fact that the labeling perspective never became the labeling *theory*. If criminal behavior really is what agents of social control define it as, then, concludes Ditton, the term "contrology" better reflects what we should be studying rather than the term "criminology"!

14.3 ———— CONFLICT THEORY

In this section we examine conflict theory, a theory of crime that overlaps with the labeling perspective. Conflict theory derives from a broad theory encompassing the nature of power and authority in society as a whole. To understand what conflict theory says about crime, criminalization, and criminal law, we review certain general ideas that conflict theorists hold about the nature of social conflict.

Conflict theory usually is approached by thinking of it in relation to its polar opposite, consensus theory. The debate over consensus and conflict theories has a lengthy intellectual history. According to Bernard (1983:30–45), the debate can be traced to the ancient Greeks—specifically to the differing interpretations of politics found in Plato's *Republic* and Aristotle's *Politics*. In its modern form, the debate between conflict and consensus theorists pivots on three questions: How is social order possible? What is the nature of power? What is the nature of authority? The many answers given to these questions often hinge on the answers to certain other questions: What is human nature? What are the causes of social inequality? What is a "good" or a "just" society?

According to consensus theory, a democratic society is held together by its members' common acceptance of such basic values as virtue, honor, right, and wrong. These are the basic values on which most people agree most of the time. Because of this common agreement concerning the most important values, social order proceeds in a harmonious and predictable fashion. This means that social change occurs only very slowly, and in a nondisruptive, evolutionary fashion.

Conflicting ideas about what is a "good" and "just" society: Police carry an elderly woman from train tracks after she was arrested for "stopping passage of a train." She and 105 other antinuclear protesters stopped the so-called "White Train" for two and a half hours in Vancouver, Washington.

In such a situation power and authority tend to be invested in persons with intellectual or moral capabilities—persons knowledgeable about and attentive to the public good and the national interest. According to conflict theory, on the other hand, there is little agreement on basic values. Society is composed of many competing groups, each of which has different interests to promote. Conflict, rather than stability, is the paradoxical feature of social order, and social change occurs in disruptive, revolutionary ways. Power and authority tend to be self-perpetuating domains of life that reflect deep-seated patterns of social, economic, and political inequality. Law, in this conflict scenario, is merely a weapon the powerful use to enforce their private interests, often at the expense of the public interest.

The immediate background to the conflict criminologists' view of crime and law is provided by writings of sociologists and political scientists on the nature and sources of social inequality in modern societies. Ralf Dahrendorf (1959), for example, has argued that in modern industrialized societies, the source of most social conflict lies in competition among interest groups to influence political authority. Dahrendorf insists that in societies as diverse as the U.S., the former U.S.S.R., and Britain, it is governmental elites who are always the core of the ruling class. It is through the executive, legislative, and administrative branches of government that such other interest groups as managerial and capitalist elites must go in order to have their interests cloaked in the authority of law (*ibid.*:301–307). C. Wright Mills' (1956; see also Kolko, 1962; Domhoff, 1967) famous book *The Power Elite* applied the principles of conflict theory to the distribution of power in the U.S. According to Mills, the center of power in the U.S. is found at the intersecting point of three "power elites" (see Figure 14-2). These elites are composed of persons in command of the major organizations and hierarchies of society. Their members are the people whose positions in the corporate economy (the chief executives), the political system (the political directorate), and the military (the warlords) enable them to make decisions of major consequence for the whole society and, often, for the rest of the world as well. The few members of the elites possess most of what there is to possess—money, power, prestige, and the way of life to which these commodities lead. This way of life includes such features as common social and psychological interests, similar educational backgrounds at Ivy League schools, membership in the same gentlemen's clubs, and Protestant religious

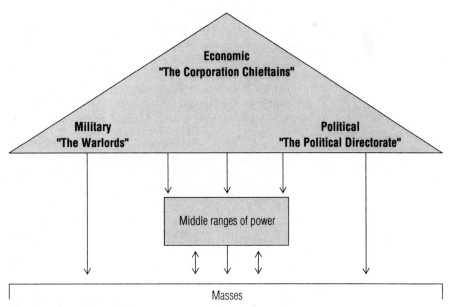

FIGURE   **C. Wright Mills' Power Elite**
14-2   *Source: David Lane,* Politics & Society in the USSR *(London: Martin Robertson, 1978), p. 195.*

affiliation. In the middle levels of power—below the three power elites yet separated from the mass of ordinary people—are advisers, consultants, and professional opinion makers. Their role is to influence the masses to accept the legitimacy of the very unequal distribution of power in the United States. The masses themselves, for Mills, are the more-or-less passive recipients of the commands and interests of the power elite.

Neither Dahrendorf nor Mills spelled out in any great detail the way in which the U.S. power structure influenced the field of crime, law, and penal policies. However, that task has been taken up by a number of conflict criminologists, whose respective contributions to conflict criminology we now outline.

Crime and Criminalization

The best introduction to conflict criminology is the pioneering work of Thorsten Sellin. We have already noted (Chapter 1.2) the importance of Sellin's (1938) concept of conduct norms to the continuing debate over the proper definition of crime. We now focus on another aspect of Sellin's argument in his book *Culture Conflict and Crime*: the role of *conflict* in understanding crime. This is generally recognized as the first argument that cultural conflict actually causes crime.

Sellin suggested that the advance of civilization (namely, of urbanization and industrialization) vastly increases the potential for social and cultural conflict. Instead of the well-knit social fabric of less technologically developed cultures, modern society contains many competing groups, poorly defined interpersonal relationships and, especially in cities, social anonymity. The rules (conduct norms) of such a society increasingly lack the sort of moral force possessed by the rules that grow out of deep-rooted, unified community sentiments. Sellin argues:

> To a large number of persons who live in such a culture, certain life situations are governed by such conflicting norms that no matter what the response of the person in such a situation will be, it will violate the norms of some social group concerned (*ibid.*:59–60).

For Sellin, crime was one of the many consequences of the conflicting conduct norms and social disorganization of modern society. Culture conflict exists when a person is caught between conflicting cultural rules. Two forms of cultural conflict, especially, tend to result in crime. *Primary culture conflict* arises when there is a clash between the norms of different cultures. This can occur when the law of one group is extended to cover the territory of another, or when members of one cultural group migrate to another (*ibid.*:63–67, 104). *Secondary culture conflict* arises from the process of differentiation and inequality in the parent culture (*ibid.*:105–107). Sellin cites as examples of secondary culture conflict the clash between law enforcement and the second generation of immigrant families over the rules governing views of gambling, prostitution, and liquor.

Whereas Sellin emphasized the importance of cultural conflict as a cause of crime, George Vold (1958:203–219; see further Vold and Bernard, 1986:270–277) has pointed to the role of what he terms "group conflict" and "political organization." Vold believes that in any society people in similar social situations group together to further their interests through collective action. Groups come into conflict with other groups when the goals of one can be achieved only at the expense of others. "The prohibitionist wishes to outlaw the manufacture and sale of alcoholic beverages; the distillers and brewers wish unrestricted opportunity to make and sell a product for which there is a genuine economic demand" (*ibid.*:208). In turn, distillers and brewers face competition over goals from other groups such as trade unionists (who want to raise wages and improve working conditions) and environmentalists (who do not want distillery chemicals to pollute the atmosphere, the soil, or the land). Environmentalists, in turn, face competition from groups who claim that economic progress should not be restricted by undue government interference. In a democratic society, Vold continues, each of the many interest groups attempts to secure its own interests by lobbying the legislature to enact laws in its favor. Groups that muster the greatest number of votes effectively enact new laws that enforce their interests and which, at the same time, curb the behavior and goals of competing groups. In other words, (*ibid.*:209):

> The whole political process of law making, law breaking, and law enforcement becomes a direct reflection of deep-seated and fundamental conflicts between interest groups and their more general struggles for the control of the police power of the state. Those who produce legislative majorities win control over the police power and dominate the policies that decide who is likely to be involved in violation of the law.

For Vold, therefore, crime is behavior committed by minority groups whose regular actions and goals have not been secured by legislative process. Juvenile delinquency, for example, is minority behavior unacceptable to the more powerful adult world. Those who reject the majority view tend to be criminalized. Because patterns of criminalization reflect the different degrees of political power wielded by different social groups, Vold argues that much crime should be understood as having a political nature. This is obviously the case for such crimes as result from political revolution and social protest movements. But it is also true for such other, less obvious cases, as the clash of interests between management and workers, and the struggle of racial minorities and women to secure their interests in racist and sexist societies. Vold concludes:

> There are many situations in which criminality is the normal, natural response of normal, natural human beings struggling in understandably normal and natural situations for the maintenance of the way of life to which they stand committed (*ibid.*:218).

Vold's focus on the role of power in the process of criminalization has been expanded by the influential contributions to conflict theory of Richard Quinney (1970; 1977; Quinney and Wildeman, 1977). In his book *The Social Reality of*

Crime, Quinney (1970:15–25) states the six propositions of his conflict theory of crime:

PROPOSITION 1 (definition of crime) Crime is a definition of human conduct created by authorized agents in a politically organized society.

PROPOSITION 2 (formulation of criminal definitions) Criminal definitions describe behaviors that conflict with the interests of the segments of society with the power to shape public policy.

PROPOSITION 3 (application of criminal definitions) Criminal definitions are applied by the segments of society with the power to shape the enforcement and administration of criminal law.

PROPOSITION 4 (development of behavior patterns in relation to criminal definitions) In segmentally organized society behavior patterns are structured in relation to criminal definitions, and within this context persons engage in actions with relative probabilities of being defined as criminal.

PROPOSITION 5 (construction of criminal conceptions) Conceptions of crime are constructed and diffused in the segments of society by various means of communication.

PROPOSITION 6 (the social reality of crime) The social reality of crime is constructed by the formulation and application of criminal definitions, the development of behavior patterns related to criminal definitions, and the construction of criminal conceptions.

Thus, according to Quinney, a theory of the social reality of crime must analyze both crime and criminal law. First, following the insights of the labeling perspective, Quinney claims that the defining quality of crime lies in the definition of crime rather than in criminal behavior as such. This definition is applied by legislators, police, prosecutors, and judges; it is always applied in the context of a society characterized by diversity, conflict, coercion, and change. Society is divided along political lines rather than being an entity based on consensus and stability. Persons become criminal when others define their behavior as criminal. The study of crime, in other words, has nothing to say about the biological or the psychological characteristics of those labeled as criminal.

Second, criminal definitions exist because the interests of some segments (or groups) of society are in conflict with the interests of others. Segments with greater power can have their definitions formulated in law and imposed on those with lesser power. According to Quinney, the greater the degree of social conflict, the more likely it is that the powerful will criminalize the behavior of powerless groups that conflict with their interests.

Third, the content of laws and their application tend to reflect the interests of the powerful because the powerful typically control or manipulate members of law enforcement and judicial machinery.

Fourth (following learning theory), Quinney claims that different societal groups typically learn to do different things. The less frequently people engage in law making and law enforcing, the more frequently their actions are defined

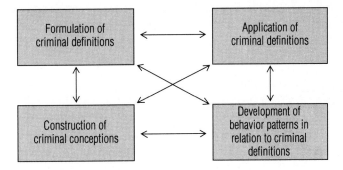

FIGURE 14-3   Model of the Social Reality of Crime

Source: Richard Quinney, 1970, p. 25.

as criminal. Moreover, increased experience with criminal definitions increases the likelihood of doing things that are subsequently defined as criminal.

Fifth, Quinney suggests that there is a variety of conceptions or opinions about what actions should be criminalized. However (echoing Karl Marx's credo that "the ideas of the ruling class are the ruling ideas"), Quinney points out that the opinions of the most powerful are in fact the most powerful opinions. Through the mass media the opinions of the powerful are communicated to others as the opinions that must be obeyed.

Finally, Quinney defines the social reality of crime as a composite of the definition in the first proposition and the four middle propositions (see Figure 14-3).

Quinney applies his theoretical perspective on the social reality of crime to a variety of situations: the religious and political foundations of criminal law; the behavior of judges, the judiciary, and the police; and such diverse conduct as defined by the laws of theft, antitrust laws, food and drug laws, sexual psychopath laws, and legislation protecting morality and public order.

Austin Turk has also made influential contributions to conflict theories of crime, especially in his book *Criminality and Legal Order.* Turk's theory is most insightful in attempting to show how the conflict theorists' picture of social order is useful to theorize the process of *criminalization.* Turk's (1969:32–34) complicated argument begins with the Dahrendorf-like assumption that the social order of modern societies is based on the relationships of conflict and domination between *authorities* and *subjects.* Authorities are those who make the most important legal decisions about the social order; subjects are those who have little or no influence on the process of decision making or on its substantive content. Slum dwellers, for example, have virtually no control over decisions affecting their life chances in such vital areas as tenancy and welfare.

Turk argues that conflicts between authorities and subjects occur over a wide range of social and cultural norms. Law is a crucial mechanism for resolving (essentially, emergency treatment but not a cure) many conflicts over what are acceptable values and behavior. Criminalization is the process by which authorities confer an illegal status on the behavior of subjects (resisters) that, for any number of reasons, they wish to prohibit. Authorities are either first-line (police) or higher-level enforcers (prosecutors, trial court judges, and appellate court judges). Against biological or psychological explanations of crime, Turk therefore stresses that

> criminality is not something which anyone *does* but rather something that *happens* in the course of interaction among various parties (including all kinds of norm markers, interpreters, enforcers, and violators) (*ibid.*:53).

Turk's theory of criminalization is designed to answer two questions (*ibid.*:64–75): Under what circumstances do subjects become criminals? When are subjects dealt with harshly?

Turk's answer to these questions has three parts. He argues, first, that the more significant a law is to authorities, the more likely it is that resisters will be criminalized. This scenario, of course, assumes that the various enforcers agree to waive their respective discretionary powers not to arrest, not to prosecute, and not to find mitigating circumstances. The more the two enforcer levels agree that violation of a law is offensive, the more likely police are to arrest, prosecutors are to prosecute, courts are to condemn, and judges are to punish and to punish severely. But what happens when different levels of the enforcement machinery hold different opinions about the offensive nature of a violation of law? Suppose that police and judges, for example, disagree about whether or not certain violations are worth enforcing. Or suppose the police feel that although certain behavior is morally reprehensible, there is little point to enforcement because the judges will not hand down harsh sentences to resisters. In such cases, Turk argues, offenders are unlikely to proceed beyond the arrest stage, where the police are more likely to deal with offenders illegally, informally, and with physical force. "Ultimately," he reasons, "it is the first-line enforcers, the police, who determine what proportion of an offensive population of norm resisters will actually be defined as criminals" (*ibid.*:67).

Second, Turk argues that the probability of criminalization varies according to the respective power of enforcers and resisters. Turk points out:

> Power differences between enforcers and norm resisters vary from relationships in which the enforcers are virtually all-powerful to cases where enforcers and resisters are about equal in resources, including effective organization, manpower, skills, funds, weaponry (*ibid.*:67).

One would expect perhaps that the relatively greater the power of enforcers the more likely they are to criminalize offensive behavior. Paradoxically, however, for Turk the probability of criminalization has a curvilinear relationship with power differences between enforcers and resisters. Turk suggests that the degree of criminalization of resisters depends largely on how threatened the enforcers feel by resisters. He argues that the greater the power of enforcers relative to resisters, the less likely is it that conflict results in criminalization; the closer their respective amounts of power, the more likely is it that the enforcers resort to criminalization. Thus:

Where the opposition is seen to be virtually powerless, normal legal procedures are likely to be unofficially abrogated in favor of summary and less costly procedures, so that official criminality rates may actually be lower than for somewhat more powerful resisters (*ibid.*:69).

Finally, Turk asserts that the probability of criminalization is influenced by what he terms "the realism of conflict moves" (*ibid.*:70–75). By this Turk means that criminalization of resisters' activities sometimes serves the interests *neither* of enforcers nor resisters. Because realism depends on knowledge of what it takes to be successful in a conflict, the act of criminalization is therefore often a sign of failure. It would not be particularly astute on the part of the police, for example, if arrests created martyrs that increased the size of the opposition. By the same token, from the point of view of resisters, arrests might be very useful! Again, criminalization is less likely to occur the more sophisticated the resisters. If resisters wish to decrease the probability of criminalization, they will not draw attention to their offensive behavior. For example, they will not allow enforcers to exploit public concerns about the danger that their activities represent.

Criminal Law and Crime

We have seen that criminalization is one of the key concepts of conflict theory, and that it describes a political process whereby certain behavior is designated as criminal. Crime is behavior that is criminalized through the application of criminal law. For conflict theory, then, we cannot understand crime without simultaneously understanding the role of criminal law in society (and see Chapter 1.3). We now examine certain ways in which conflict theorists have understood criminal law.

One of the best-known conflict accounts of criminal law is contained in William Chambliss and Robert Seidman's (1971) *Law, Order, and Power.* Although the book was intended as an analysis of the workings of law in general (both civil law and criminal law), we focus chiefly on its account of the workings of criminal law. Chambliss and Seidman's book contains a comprehensive application of conflict theory to (1) the creation of law, (2) the general principles of law, and (3) the implementation of law. The analysis of law is approached with the underlying assumption that "the central myth about the legal order in the United States is that normative structures of the written law represent the actual operation of the legal order" (*ibid.*:3). The law in the books, in other words, is not at all the same thing as the law in action. Chambliss and Seidman continue:

This myth of the operation of the law is given the lie daily. We all know today that blacks and the poor are not treated fairly or equitably by the police. We know that judges have discretion and in fact make policy (as the Supreme Court did in the school desegregation cases). We know that electoral laws have been loaded in the past in favor of the rich, and the average presidential candidate is not a poor man, that one-fifth of the senators of the United States are millionaires.

It is our contention that, far from being primarily a value-neutral framework within which conflict can be peacefully resolved, the power of the state is itself the principal prize in the perpetual conflict that is society. The legal order . . . is in fact a self-serving system to devise and maintain power and privilege.

As 19th-century philosopher Anatole France once remarked: "The majestic equality of the law allows both the rich and the poor to sleep under bridges if they so choose!" Chambliss and Seidman's detailed analysis of the relationships among conflict, power, and the purposes of law is extended to such institutions as legislatures, appellate courts, and the police. But perhaps the most telling sections of their analysis concern appellate courts.

Although many citizens see how easily the decisions of Congress can be swayed by lobbyists and special interest groups, most of us reject the idea that appellate courts are open to such persuasion. Yet Chambliss and Seidman suggest that the various inputs into the rule-making processes of the appellate courts are "necessarily biased in favor of ensuring that courts as institutions are more available to the wealthy than to the poor, and tend to produce solutions in the interests of the wealthy" (*ibid.*:113). These biases cluster around several variables, the two most important of which are (1) the selection of issues with which judges are confronted and (2) their personal characteristics and socialization (*ibid.*:89–112).

Because most appellate cases are initiated by individual litigants, it follows that the majority of such appeals are actually brought by those with sufficient funds to afford them. Thus, most appellate cases, such as in the area of trusts and corporate law, concern legal problems of the relatively wealthy. Conversely, legal problems of the poor rarely come to the attention of appellate courts. Nowhere is this bias reflected more than in the area of criminal law and police powers. The poor are arrested, interrogated, abused, and incarcerated more often than any other societal group (and see Chapter 3.1). But the problems the poor routinely encounter throughout the criminal justice system almost never reach appellate courts. Quite simply, argue Chambliss and Seidman (*ibid.*:91), the poor lack the funds to hire lawyers to initiate the necessary legal proceedings. Indeed, to protect themselves from such malpractice as the abuse of police powers, the poor must almost exclusively rely on the charitable endeavors of such groups as the American Civil Liberties Union.

Moreover, the highest state and federal appellate court judges typically come from exclusive and advantaged backgrounds. One study reports that 81 percent of U.S. Supreme Court justices had fathers who were proprietors, wealthy farmers, or professional men (*ibid.*:96, citing Schmidhauser, 1959). Most lawyers are trained by the case law method that, although imparting a questioning attitude to any given case, instills an acceptance of basic legal arrangements as they presently exist. This legal conservatism surfaces in those who become judges in the form of decisions that are closely tied to precedent. Successful judges are political animals who have assiduously learned not to rock the boats of the rich and influential.

Conflict criminologists have written extensively about how differential power and conflicts of interest are reflected in the content and operation of criminal law (for surveys see Galliher, 1980; Hagan, 1980). Their accounts of the links among power, conflict, and law span diverse historical periods and a variety of societies. An excellent example of such themes concerns a change in the law of theft (the *Carrier's Case* of 1473) in medieval England (Hall, 1969)—an instructive, if controversial, example of the crude power and conflict that lie behind the majesty of the law.

The Carrier's Case

The facts in Jerome Hall's (1969; and see Chambliss, 1964) account of the *Carrier's Case* of 1473 are as follows. A "carrier" (Old English term for courier or transporter) had been hired as a bailee to transport certain bales of cotton to the English port of Southampton. However, during the journey he took the bales to another place, broke them open, and took the contents. The bailee was apprehended, charged, and convicted of larceny by a majority of judges in the Court of Star Chamber.

This innocent-looking case marked an important innovation in the English law of larceny. Prior to the *Carrier's Case*, the element of trespass had to be demonstrated by the prosecution in order that a defendant be convicted of larceny. At that time legal opinion agreed that (1) trespass was an essential element of larceny, (2) a person having possession of property could not commit a trespass upon that property, and (3) a bailee has possession (Hall, 1969:34). The common law recognized no criminal liability in a person legally entitled to possession of an item who later converts it to his or her own use (the rationale being that owners should protect themselves by selecting a trustworthy carrier [*ibid.*:50]). These three precedents therefore created a serious problem: because the carrier had been legally consigned the bales, they were in his possession. There was then no legal precedent by which the carrier could be convicted of larceny! However, by clever intellectual juggling (known as a legal fiction) it was ruled that the mere opening of the bales ended the carrier's legal possession of them. In this way some of the most important English judges, who were hearing the case, ruled that the carrier was in fact guilty of larceny. The law of larceny was thus expanded to include this and similar factual situations.

The *Carrier's Case* is important not only because it shows how judges in fact make law, but because it also shows how extralegal factors influence judges when they make law.

Hall identifies various political and economic conditions that thrust themselves upon the court in the *Carrier's Case*. It is interesting to note that in the indictment against the carrier no specific mention was made of the contents of the opened bales. Hall produces evidence, however, to show that these contents were almost certainly either wool or cloth—no ordinary commodities during the 15th century. Indeed, wool and cloth were the products of the most important industry in England at that time, an industry encouraged by a king deeply committed to solidifying his rule at home by gaining the economic and political support of European merchants who traded in these commodities. According to Hall, King Edward IV (the reigning monarch of England) desperately needed to regulate and elevate the standards for security and honesty in the transportation of commodities bound for foreign markets. It is therefore quite likely that the king persuaded the court to expand the law of theft even though legal precedent did not permit it to do so.

Why did the judges do so? According to Hall, it was a matter of simple political expediency. During the 15th century the court of Star Chamber, like most other judicial bodies, was very subservient to the political will of the king. Thus, although at the time of the *Carrier's Case* judges wanted to assert their independence from the monarch (Edward IV), they were politically unable to do so. The result was a legal decision dictated by political interests.

The *Carrier's Case* illustrates the conflict theorists' claim that behind the majestic impartiality of the law often lies the power of an elite or a ruling class. When the situation requires, as in the *Carrier's Case*, and in numerous other cases from antiquity forward, the criminal law's thin veneer of neutrality is readily stripped away.

Assessment

Vold and Bernard (1986:290–294) summarized the three major ways in which, according to conflict theory, the differential enactment of criminal laws affects official crime rates. First, in a situation where different societal groups hold different values (such as on the desirability of heroin use), the most powerful groups succeed in having their values enacted through legislation and enforced on others. Second, even where agreement exists as to values, the content of the criminal law can affect crime rates if the law protects a certain distribution of valued property. In societies where property is distributed unequally, for example, the criminal law protects property of the "haves" from theft by the "have nots." Third, the criminal law may fail to protect the socially harmful actions of powerful groups (and see Chapter 7.2). As Vold and Bernard rightly remind us: "By any objective measure the socially harmful and victimizing behavior of more powerful people vastly exceeds [that] . . . of less powerful people" (*ibid.*:293).

Conflict explanations of crime, criminal law, and criminalization have been tested often and, to a certain extent, confirmed by criminologists. Confirmatory test cases include such diverse examples as laws concerning vagrancy (Chambliss, 1964), alcohol (Gusfield, 1963), drugs (Reasons, 1974; Galliher and Cross, 1983), prostitution (Roby, 1969), and bias in court decisions (Hagan, 1974; Chiricos and Waldo, 1975; Lizotte, 1978). In each case the ability of one segment of society to impose its moral view on another was a crucial element in the passage of a given law. We note also a study by David Jacobs and David Britt (1979) on police use of deadly force. This study addresses a crucial operational component of the criminal justice system: the relationship between inequality and officially sanctioned violent death. Jacobs and Britt attempted to test the proposition that violence, or the threat of violence, is the crucial element upholding the unequal relationships found in nearly all societies today. They point out:

> Because conflict theorists hold that the state's monopoly of violence is controlled by those who benefit from inequality, it follows that the control agents of the state should be more likely to use extreme force when economic inequality is most pronounced (*ibid.*:403).

Controlling for such confounding factors as the police being more likely to use violence in areas with high rates of violent crime, Jacobs and Britt concluded that states with the most unequal income distribution were the most likely to have the highest number of police-caused homicides. Moreover, a variation of this conflict hypothesis has been shown by Steven Messner (1980; Kennedy, Silverman, and Forde, 1991; and see Chapter 16.3) to apply in many societies around the world. According to Messner in a sample of 110 societies, high homicide rates were positively correlated with, and perhaps caused by, the social conflict that results from high levels of income inequality.

Conflict theory as such, at least in the ways in which it developed and as we have described it here, no longer really exists in criminology. Indeed, although the many conflict studies of law and crime in the 1960s and 1970s continue to exert great influence in criminology, scant new research was undertaken explicitly from this perspective during the 1980s. Of the theorists mentioned here, only Turk (1982) and Bernard (Vold and Bernard, 1986: 286–290) have continued to expand conflict theory.

The chief reason for the demise of conflict theory as it existed during the 1960s and 1970s is its reliance on so many vague and unproven general assumptions. It clearly requires a great leap of faith to assume, for example, either that law always arises from conflict or that crime always expresses conflict, or that the process of criminalization always serves the interests of the powerful. Most criminologists today realize that arguments based on such general assumptions are seriously open to doubt. Indeed, we note that conflict theory has rarely been precise in defining such crucial terms as "power" and "conflict." What, precisely, is "conflict"? Do all conflicts involve "power"?

The world of law and crime is often far more complicated than suggested by the *a priori* generalizations of conflict theory. Consider the problem posed by recent research on the relationship between judges' social backgrounds and sentencing policies, which reveals quite clearly that sometimes at least (When? Why?) there is no simple relationship between the two. In a study of superior court judges in Georgia, for example, Martha Myers (1988; see also Balbus, 1973) has shown that judicial background (in this case age, religion, years as prosecutor, and local background) has little *direct* bearing on sentencing outcomes: "Rather, its effect is subtle and indirect, discernible only after considering social background in conjunction with the offender's attributes and behaviors" (*ibid.*:668). Yet Myers discovered pronounced disparities in certain areas of sentencing. Thus, although blacks were generally more likely than whites to be incarcerated, judges who were ex-prosecutors were more likely to incarcerate white offenders. Again, violent offenders received relatively long prison sentences from nonlocal judges and lenient sentences from Baptist and fundamentalist judges.

Quite apart from whether the claims of conflict theory should be seen as confirmed, disconfirmed, or simply too abstract to be testable, its chief legacy is its introduction of a "political" dimension largely lacking in earlier criminology. To this we will return in Chapter 15.

14.4 _____ BIOCRIMINOLOGY AND CRIME

At least since the time of Greek antiquity it has been widely believed that physical appearance is a sign of moral character, personality, and temperament. According to criminologists Sheldon and Eleanor Glueck (1956:1), such beliefs are quite common in folklore, in philosophical speculation, and in literature. Familiar examples abound: Shakespeare's energetic shrew-tamer Petruchio, the jealousy and envy of the lean and hungry Cassius, the indolence and gluttony of the obese knight Sir John Falstaff, the villainies of the deformed King Richard III.

In recent years the supposed links between biology and crime have been theorized in a great variety of ways (Jeffery, 1979; Wilson and Herrnstein, 1985). In what follows we outline how criminologists have investigated the influence of genes, biochemical abnormalities, and intelligence.

Genes and Crime

The links between genes and crime have been investigated in several ways, including studies of the XYY chromosome, of twins, and of adoptees. Consider the evidence presented in each of these three areas.

Studies of the XYY Chromosome

Among adults in the U.S., males are five to 10 times more likely than females to be arrested for serious crimes recorded in the *Uniform Crime Reports*. Roughly the same gender disparity occurs in all societies with records of crime. Although this implies that gender is an important predictor of crime, we will see that it does not necessarily mean that the association between gender and crime has genetic causes.

Gender is determined by one of the 23 pairs of chromosomes possessed by each human being. In the gender-determining pair of chromosomes, genetically normal females have two X chromosomes (known as XX) and genetically normal males have one X and one Y chromosome (known as XY). Research on the claimed genetic causes of the association between gender and crime has tended to focus on such deviant chromosomal complements as the trichromosomal XXY (Klinefelter's) and XYY (supermale) syndromes. Only one in 3,000 males is XXY; only one in 1,000 males is XYY.

A possible link between XYY males and violent crime was widely circulated in a study of a Scottish special-security mental institution in 1965 (Jacobs, Brunton, and Melville). In this study Patricia Jacobs and her colleagues reported that eight (3.9 percent) of 203 "mentally subnormal male patients with dangerous, violent and criminal propensities" were XYYs, suggesting that XYYs were three and one-half times more likely to be violent criminals than the general population. The Scottish study has been followed by some 200 other studies of the XYY syndrome, which have more or less conclusively established that:

▲— XYY males are significantly more likely than XY males to be institutionalized in prisons and mental hospitals.

▲— XYY males are significantly taller than both the general population and their siblings and parents (see, for example, Nielsen, 1971; Owens, 1972).

▲— XYY males are moderately less intelligent than XY males based on their respective performances on a variety of intelligence tests.

However, what these pieces of evidence actually mean about the rate at which XYYs commit crimes is not very clear. Their higher rate of institutionalization does not necessarily mean that XYY males actually *commit* more crimes than XYs or that they are more likely than XYs to suffer mental illnesses. On the contrary, as some criminologists have argued, XYY males are more likely than other lawbreakers to be arrested, labeled, and stigmatized because of their unusual height and their occasional bizarre appearance (Taylor, Walton, and Young, 1973:45–46). Similarly, it is possible that the lower intelligence scores of XYY males reflect not a higher crime rate but a relative inability to avoid arrest and conviction.

Certain of these difficulties were addressed in the largest study of the XYY syndrome undertaken to date, that of Herman Witkin (Witkin *et al.*, 1976) and his colleagues in Denmark. The study attempted to determine whether (1) XYY males have higher crime rates than the general population, and (2) if so, whether there are intervening variables, such as aggressiveness and intelligence, that mediate the relationship between an extra Y chromosome and higher rates of antisocial behavior such as crime. The subjects of the study were 28,884 Danish males born in Copenhagen between 1944 and 1947. Data were gathered about educational levels, criminal records, and sex chromosomes of the tallest 4,139 males in the study. For this latter group it was determined that there were 12 XYYs (whose average height was less than indicated by previous studies) and 16 XXYs; the vast majority of the remainder was a control group of normal XYs. Significantly, 41.7 percent of the XYYs (five of 12 cases), 18.8 percent of the XXYs (three of 16 cases), and 9.3 percent of the XY control group had been convicted of one or more crimes (*ibid.*:174). The XYYs therefore did have higher conviction rates than the general population—although, once again, this does not mean they necessarily committed more crimes. Moreover, this finding must be understood in the context of three other findings:

▲— First, XYYs were no more likely than XYs to be convicted of crimes of violence. The elevated crime rate among XYYs was due solely to their higher rate of property offenses. Indeed, this finding has been partially confirmed by a subsequent study of nonalcoholic adoptees in Sweden (Bohman, Cloninger, Sigvardsson, and von Knorring, 1982:1240), wherein it was reported that hereditable criminality is characterized not by the commission of aggressive acts but by a small number of petty property offenses. In concert, these two findings tend to cast serious doubt on the earlier belief that XYYs are more violent than other sections of the population.

▲— Second, degrees of criminality related significantly to scores on intelligence tests for both XYYs and XYs. However, the XYYs scored appreciably lower than the XYs on intelligence tests. Although Witkin *et al.* do not argue that lack of intelligence causes crime, they do suggest that the XYY complement has broad adverse developmental consequences (*ibid.*:185). In other words, because XYYs seem to have lower-than-average intelligence, they may be less adept at avoiding arrest and imprisonment.

▲— Finally, several XYYs committed crimes in ways that made their detection and apprehension very likely. For example, one of the XYYs often burglarized homes while the owners were on the premises. Implicitly, such carelessness derives from the low intelligence scores of XYYs.

In sum, we stress two points. First, current studies of XYY males do not tell us that XYYs commit more violent crimes than males with other chromosomal complements—only that their crimes are more likely to be detected and more likely to result in their institutionalization. Second, the undoubted fact that males are universally more violent than females is not necessarily explained by chromosomal differences. As we argue in Chapter 15.2, the greater violence of men is most likely the result of social conditions associated with gender inequality—such as toleration and even encouragement of violence by young males.

Studies of Twins

Studies of twins are a potential source of excellent data about the relationship between biology and crime. Twins are either identical or fraternal. Identical twins (who are monozygotic [MZ]) are the result of one fertilized egg. Fraternal twins (who are dizygotic [DZ]) are the result of two fertilized eggs, and share the same genetic characteristics as do brothers and sisters. In principle, the study of twins should provide us with the controlled experimental conditions required to disentangle genetic and environmental influences on criminal behavior. Because the genetic structure of MZ twins is identical and that of DZ twins is dissimilar, if the rate of criminal concordance (association) among MZ twins is higher than that among DZ twins, the case for a genetic influence on crime would be strengthened.

One of the earliest studies of the respective rates of criminal concordance among MZ and DZ twins was conducted by German physician Johannes Lange (1929). Lange studied 30 pairs of Bavarian twins, of whom 13 were MZs and 17 DZs. He discovered that of the 13 MZ pairs, both twins had been convicted of a crime in 10 cases and one twin had been convicted in three cases; of the 17 DZ pairs, both twins had been convicted in two cases, and among the remainder only one twin had been convicted. In addition, Lange determined that DZ twins were not more likely to be convicted of a crime than the general population. From these data Lange concluded that "under our present social conditions heredity does play a role of paramount importance in the making of the criminal" (*ibid.*:173). At the same time, Lange warned that some environmental influence must have been at work in the three cases where only one MZ twin had been convicted.

Lange's findings were essentially confirmed by a succession of other twins studies, whose findings are summarized in Table 14-1 (and see Rowe and Osgood, 1984). The largest and best-designed study of twins undertaken has been conducted by Karl Christiansen (1977a) in Denmark, in which he addressed the criminal behavior of 3,586 unselected twin pairs born in eastern Denmark between 1881 and 1910. Of the 7,172 twins, 926 had been convicted of a crime, of delinquency, or of a minor offense. Christiansen found the concordance rate

TABLE 14-1   Summary of Twins-Criminality Studies[1]

	MONOZYGOTIC		DIZYGOTIC	
	NUMBER OF PAIRS	PAIRWISE CONCORDANCE PERCENT	NUMBER OF PAIRS	PAIRWISE CONCORDANCE PERCENT
Lange (1929	13	76.9	17	11.8
Legras (1932)	4	100.0	5	0.0
Rosanoff *et al.* (1941)				
Adult criminality	45	77.8	27	22.2
Juvenile delinquency	41	97.6	26	80.8
Stumpfl (1936)[2]	18	64.5	19	36.8
Kranz (1936)	32	65.6	43	53.5
Borgström (1939)	4	75.0	5	40.0
Yoshimasu (1962)[3]	28	60.6	18	11.1
Dalgaard and Kringlen (1976)[4]	31	25.8	54	14.9

[1]Tienari's results are not entered in this table because he has no group of dizygotic pairs.
[2]A monozygotic concordant pair is found in both Stumpfl's and Kranz's samples.
[3]The figures from Yoshimasu (1962) stem from two investigations in 1941 and 1947.
[4]Crime in the strict sense.

Source: Christiansen, 1977, p. 72.

for MZ males was 35 percent and for DZ males 13 percent; for MZ females it was 21 percent and for DZ females 8 percent (*ibid.*:97). Although these concordance rates were lower than reported in earlier studies, note that male and female MZs still have a concordance rate approximately three times higher than DZs. This finding suggests, in other words, that genetic factors play some part in predisposition to criminal behavior.

However, it is premature to conclude—as some criminologists recently have (see, for example Wilson and Herrnstein, 1985:90–95; Mednick, Gabrielli, and Hutchings, 1987:74)—that the link between genetics and crime has been firmly established by existing studies of twins. Because of several important methodological problems in twins studies (some of them noted by Christiansen [1977a] himself), such a conclusion is simply unwarranted. Among the most important methodological problems in twins studies are the following:

▲— Many studies were completed half a century ago, when the standards for distinguishing between identical and fraternal twins were not as rigorous as today. Although modern studies can exceed 95 percent accuracy in determining twinship (Wilson and Herrnstein, 1985:92), this was not so in the past.

▲— Several twins studies (in Table 14.1, Lange, 1931; Stumpfl, 1936; and Kranz, 1936) were conducted at a time when the Nazi movement put German researchers under great pressure not to report findings that disconfirmed the relationship between criminality and biology (and race, degeneracy, and the like). A similar problem perhaps also applies to the study by Yoshimasu (1962), who reported research conducted in Japan during the difficult years 1941 to 1947.

▲— Many studies differ considerably in their definition of "concordance."

▲— Twins studies have not consistently used the same indicator of crime; the variety of indicators includes self-report data, reports to the police, arrests, and convictions. Other twins studies refer not to crime but to aggression or even to delinquency. Moreover, the subjects of these indicators have variously included adults, children, males, and females, sometimes with no distinction by age or gender as to type and seriousness of offense.

The greatest weakness of twins studies lies in the ultimate theoretical inability to control for the impact of sociological influences on crime. To appreciate this weakness, assume for a moment that MZ twins actually have higher concordance rates for criminality than do DZ twins. Should this be explained by genetic factors? Not necessarily. It is entirely possible that MZ twins—who look more alike than do DZ twins, who often wear identical clothes, and whose identities are often confused by friends and teachers—engage in similar behavior (including criminal behavior) for sociological rather than biological reasons. If true, this sociological fact alone could explain the higher concordance rates for criminality of MZ twins. To compensate for this weakness, one would need to conduct a controlled experiment in which the MZ twins were raised in different social environments. Part of the conditions required for such an experiment have been met in studies of crimes committed by adoptees. To this we now turn.

Studies of Adoptees

Because, as we have seen, it is extremely difficult to control for environmental influences on the criminal behavior of twins, researchers have looked increasingly to the situation of adoptees. The critical question examined by studies of adoptees is whether the criminal behavior of adoptees resembles the behavior of their biological parents or that of their adoptive parents. The case for a genetic influence on crime would be strengthened if the criminal offspring of noncriminal adoptive parents were disproportionately the criminal offspring of criminal biological parents. This finding would be further strengthened if the criminal adoptive offspring knew nothing of the criminal records of their biological parents.

A number of suggestive studies have recently examined this question in the U.S. and in Sweden. For example, Raymond Crowe (1975) reported a disproportionate rate of antisocial personality types among 37 Iowan adoptees with criminal biological mothers. Remi Cadoret (1978) found that antisocial behavior in 246 Iowan adoptees was significantly related to such behavior in their biological parents. And a Swedish study reported a significant relationship between criminal biological parents and criminal adoptees, but only for property crimes (Bohman, Cloninger, Sigvardsson, and von Knorring, 1982).

The most comprehensive study of adoptees (largely males) was conducted by Sarnoff Mednick, William Gabrielli, and Barry Hutchings (1987) in Denmark, in which the researchers obtained information on 14,427 cases of nonfamilial adoption recorded at the Danish Ministry of Justice between 1924 and 1947. Their index of criminal involvement was based on court convictions for violations of the Danish Criminal Code for those aged 16 and over, and included data on date of conviction, specific law(s) violated, and penalty imposed. Similar information was obtained on criminal involvement of the adoptees' biological and adoptive parents. Two findings emerged from this study. The first concerns the respective probabilities of adoptee conviction if biological or adoptive parents had or had not been convicted. As seen in Table 14-2, if neither the biological nor the adoptive parents had been convicted, only 13.5 percent of their sons were convicted. If only the adoptive parents had been convicted, 14.7 percent of the adoptees were convicted. However, if only the biological parents had been convicted, then 20 percent of the adoptees were convicted. The highest rate of adoptee conviction (24.5 percent) occurred when both biological and adoptive parents had been convicted. These figures appear to suggest, according to Mednick *et al.* (*ibid.*:79), that some biological influence is transmitted from criminal biological parents that increases an adoptee's probability of being convicted.

The second finding of this Danish study concerns the relationship between

TABLE 14-2   **Cross-Fostering Analysis: Percentage of Adoptive Sons Convicted of Criminal Law Offenses[1]**

HAVE ADOPTIVE PARENTS BEEN CONVICTED?	HAVE BIOLOGICAL PARENTS BEEN CONVICTED?	
	YES	NO
Yes	24.5 (of 143)	14.7 (of 204)
No	20.0 (of 1,226)	13.5 (of 2,492)

[1]Numbers in parentheses represent the total number for each cell.

Source: Mednick, Gabrielli, and Hutchings, 1987, p. 79.

biological influence and degree of recidivism. No relationship was found between the number of adoptive parents' convictions and the number of adoptees' convictions. However, as seen in Figure 14-4, there is a strong positive correlation between the number of biological parents' convictions and the number of adoptees' convictions—but only for property offenses. In other words, the data suggest that biological factors influence not only whether an adoptee has a criminal involvement but also the nature of that involvement.

Interestingly, Mednick *et al.* (*ibid.*:85–86) also analyzed the relationship between adoptees with criminal involvement, on the one hand, and the respective socioeconomic statuses of their biological and adoptive parents, on the other. Here they found that when biological and adoptive parents both had a high socioeconomic status, adoptees had a very low rate of criminal involvement;

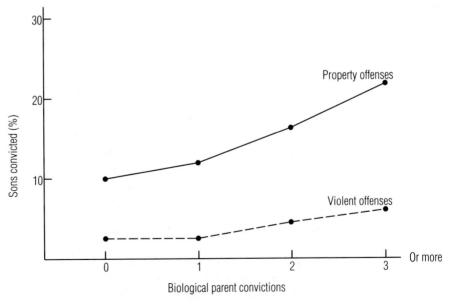

FIGURE 14-4   **Biological Parent Convictions and Adoptee Convictions**

Source: Mednick, Gabrielli, and Hutchings, 1987, p. 81.

when biological and adoptive parents both had a low socioeconomic status, adoptees had a very high rate of criminal involvement.

These data in the Danish study suggest, overall, that if there is a biological influence on criminal involvement, its importance is significantly modified by environmental factors such as socioeconomic status. We are, once again, left in a state of limbo. If the influence of biological factors on crime can be modified by social environment, what precisely do we mean by biological influence? More research clearly is required to understand how the adoption process influences subsequent criminality. For example, how does length of time in an orphanage affect an adoptee's future criminal involvement? Do adoption agencies tend to match social characteristics of biological parents with adoptive parents in determining which child should go to what sort of adoptive home? If prospective adoptive parents are routinely informed (as they are in Denmark) about the criminal convictions of biological parents, does this trigger a labeling process or a self-fulfilling prophecy (see *supra*, Chapter 12.3) by which adoptees with such parents are propelled into criminal involvement? Do adoptive parents tend to be more law-abiding than the general population?

Biochemical Imbalances and Crime

Criminologists have also recently examined the influence of endogenous biochemical imbalances on crime. Several studies have described, in a preliminary way, how violent behavior is influenced by certain biochemical factors, including glucose and cholesterol levels (Virkunnen, 1987); carbohydrate intake (Lester, Thatcher, and Monroe-Lord, 1982) and diet in general (Fishbein and Pease, 1988); premenstrual syndrome (Taylor and Dalton, 1983); and testosterone (Schalling, 1987). However, none of these factors has yet been shown to be associated significantly with crime, with the possible exception of testosterone.

Testosterone is the primary androgenic steroid hormone. Recent studies of testosterone in animals and in humans have addressed the relationship between plasma levels and production rates of testosterone on the one hand and aggressive, impulsive, antisocial behavior on the other. The animal research has not shown any direct relationship between testosterone and aggression—although sudden changes in the social rank of monkeys have been found to lead to changes in testosterone levels that, in turn, are sometimes associated with increased fighting (Keverne, Meller, and Eberhart, 1982; Schalling, 1987). In animals, at least, it is presently unclear whether increased testosterone levels are associated with increased aggression only when other, more environmental factors are present.

Testosterone studies of humans, similarly, offer quite mixed findings. A handful of studies have reported a positive association between testosterone and human aggression. For example, Leo Kreuz and Robert Rose (1972) reported that prisoners convicted of violent crimes have higher testosterone levels than those convicted of property offenses. In another study it was found that a group of extremely violent California rapists had significantly higher testosterone levels

In 1978, when former San Francisco Supervisor Dan White was on trial for the shooting deaths of Mayor George Moscone and Supervisor Harvey Milk, the defense attorney claimed that his client's violent behavior was caused by eating too much junk food.

than did nonoffenders, child molesters, and less-violent rapists (Rada, Laws, and Kellner, 1976). But the same study also found no correlation between individual hostility scores of the rapists and their testosterone levels.

Still other studies have found only a very weak or even an insignificant relationship between testosterone and violent criminality. In a recent study, Dan Olweus (1987) correlated plasma testosterone samples and personality profiles of a representative group of healthy Swedish boys, aged 15–17. Initially, Olweus found that the boys' testosterone levels were significantly correlated with their verbal and physical aggression. But on closer inspection he reported that, although quite strong in response to provocation, high levels of testosterone do not lead to unprovoked aggression. Daisy Schalling (1987) reports similar conclusions in her study of 40 male delinquents, aged 14–19, who were residents of a Swedish Borstal School for serious recidivist offenders. She found that high testosterone levels in these boys were associated with high levels of verbal aggression, but not at all with physical aggression.

Intelligence and Crime

In Chapter 10.4, we learned that Lombroso's atavistic, body-type criminals were replaced, during the first quarter of the 20th century, with criminals who inherited feeblemindedness and criminality from their parents. Such concepts as "inferior stock," "mental deficiency," and "imbecility" were major themes in a host of early studies in the U.S. that attempted to trace the evolution of criminality in certain degenerate families (such as Rafter, 1988). During his research on mental defect and imbecility in the U.S., psychologist Henry Goddard (1914) pioneered the use of the Binet-Simon IQ test. Goddard reported that in 16 juvenile reformatories no less than 28 percent (boys in Massachusetts) and as high as 89 percent (girls in Illinois) of juvenile delinquents were mentally defective (IQs less than 75). Interestingly, Goddard warned that "the differences in the percentages are probably due more to the standards used in estimating the defective than to actual differences in numbers" (*ibid.*:8).

Goddard's finding of a link between IQ and criminality was disputed because he had not compared institutionalized criminals with a proper control group. Eventually, Goddard himself repudiated his own conclusion (Wilson and Herrnstein, 1985:152–153; Vold and Bernard, 1986:72–74). With the advent of better measurement techniques in the 1930s (ability to separate intelligence levels associated with criminality, for example, from intelligence levels of criminals who happened to be institutionalized), the percentage of criminals identified as mentally deficient gradually shrank until it neared the percentage of mentally deficient in the general population. Most criminologists therefore assumed, until quite recently, that still better measurement techniques would show intelligence levels of the criminal and the noncriminal to be the same.

However, in recent years the relationship between intelligence and criminality has once again become the subject of heated debate among criminologists. In their widely read book *Crime and Human Nature*, James Q. Wilson and Richard J. Herrnstein (1985:148–172; see also Hirschi and Hindelang, 1977) have argued that there is indeed an heritable link between intelligence and crime. First, they point to considerable research showing that some major aspects of intelligence, as measured by IQ, are inherited. Second, they agree with many recent studies showing that the average IQ of criminals is significantly below the noncriminal population average of 100 (and see Gordon, 1987). Wilson and Herrnstein conclude that, even allowing for the ways in which race and class bias test results, IQ is a fairly good predictor of criminal involvement.

We note that, despite some savage criticisms of their work, Wilson and Herrnstein do not claim that low intelligence is a major *cause* of crime, or even that biological factors are the sole causes of crime. They conclude only that low intelligence is inversely correlated with crime, admitting that the reasons for this correlation are exceedingly complex. Among possible reasons they identify are (*ibid.*:166–172):

▲— Youths with low IQs are unlikely to do well in school. In response to status frustration and academic penalties, and depending on their family and peer relationships, they are likely to be pushed and pulled into asocial behavior (and see A. K. Cohen's explanation of juvenile delinquency, *supra* Chapter 12.1 and Hirschi's control theory, *supra*, Chapter 13.3).

▲— Youths with low IQs are likely to be present-oriented rather than future-oriented. Present-oriented, hedonistic interests are much more conducive to crime than future-oriented interests, which stress deferred gratification in the pursuit of career plans.

▲— Low IQ means a lesser ability to engage in abstract reasoning. If moral reasoning is one form of abstract reasoning, then youths with lower IQs are less able to articulate the difference between right and wrong.

▲— Low IQ is correlated not only with greater involvement in crime but also with more frequent detection. More-intelligent criminals are guided by risks of detection and prosecution, and are naturally drawn to crimes with low clearance rates.

Wilson and Herrnstein's claims about intelligence and crime are vulnerable to the objection that, even if there is a statistical correlation between IQ and crime, this does not mean that low intelligence causes crime. There are at least four reasons that add weight to this objection.

First, it is certainly not true either that all people of low intelligence commit crimes or that no one with high intelligence commits crime. If low intelligence as such were a cause of crime, we could not explain crimes committed by white-collar offenders, by corporate executives, and by politicians.

Second, there is a world of difference between arguing, on the one hand, that low intelligence causes crime and arguing, on the other, that offenses of those with lower intelligence are more likely to be detected. It is quite possible that much of the inverse correlation between intelligence and crime can be explained by the higher detection rates of those with less intelligence.

Third, it is unclear how well any standardized test such as the IQ test can measure intelligence. The Binet-Simon IQ test essentially measures the age-specific ability of children to perform such school-related skills as reading comprehension, general knowledge, analytic and mathematical reasoning, and vocabulary. Critics of the IQ test complain that it is a biased cultural artifact that does not, and cannot, measure intelligence as such. IQ tests are biased, these critics continue, because the abstract and written skills they measure are peculiarly middle-class skills. Intelligence takes many forms (for example, street knowledge, aesthetic and moral skills), not all of which are either practiced or encouraged by the middle class. Thus, as Christopher Jencks complains (1987:36), whether IQ tests measure intelligence rather than academic skills is a political question. Similarly, whether crime is merely correlated with IQ or whether it is caused by it is also a political question.

Fourth, the correlation between IQ and crime might be largely spurious owing to class and racial inequalities in the U.S. Because IQ is quite strongly correlated with both class and race, those who argue that lower IQ is a cause of crime often have been accused of neglecting sociological factors. Thus, members of the working class and the unemployed, both of whom typically score lower on middle-class IQ tests than do members of the middle class, are not arrested more often than other classes because they necessarily commit more crimes but because of their adverse position in the class structure. Moreover, because, in the U.S., socioeconomic status is inversely correlated with race, proponents of the low-intelligence-causes-crime argument come dangerously close to the African Americans-score-lower-because-they-are-African American argument. The truth of this argument, of course, can be tested only in a society that is in fact nondiscriminatory as to race. Yet nowhere in the United States does such a society exist.

In conclusion, it is not possible at this time to claim with any degree of certainty that intelligence, or lack of it, is a cause of criminal behavior. But we note that those who deny this causal relationship are faced with two major empirical problems that remain despite the truth of the four preceding objections (Wilson and Herrnstein, 1985:158–159; Jencks, 1987:37). First, socioeconomic status accounts at most for only 25 percent of the variance in IQ test scores. Second, even when allowing for the confounding influence of class and race, the inverse correlation between IQ and crime is reduced but still strong. As Jencks therefore warns: "The question that ought to be explored is not whether IQ scores predict the statistical likelihood that individuals will engage in murder, rape, robbery, and the like, but why they do so" (1987:37). To his own question, significantly, Jencks provides a well-reasoned sociological answer (*ibid*.:38):

> Adolescents with low IQs commit crimes not because they are inherently more hostile, amoral, or impulsive than their high-IQ classmates, but because both schools and labor markets treat them in ways that make them hostile, amoral, and impulsive. If this is true, the connection between IQ and crime probably varies considerably from one society to another. In societies like our own, youngsters with low IQs cannot do much that others value. This almost inevitably means that they will be treated like dirt and will react accordingly.

Assessment

For the first time in several decades, recognition of biological factors is gaining importance among criminologists, especially among those with training in psychiatry, psychology, or forensic medicine. Debates over the possible influence of biology on criminal behavior are currently the most heated and the most contested in modern criminology. To some criminologists, investigation of biological factors should proceed with the same scientific rigor as investigation of all other factors that might influence criminal behavior. To other criminologists, the claim that biology influences crime is little more than superstitious racism with dangerous implications for the segregation (or worse) of the physically unfit.

In this section we have examined diverse evidence concerning the possible ways in which biology might influence crime. Nowadays, however, there are hardly any criminologists who actually argue that biology exercises its effects independently of social environment. Thus, in recent years there has been a movement away from pure biology toward sociobiology. The basic tendency within this movement is to discard the claim that biology causes crime and to embrace the view that biology is the first stage in a causal sequence leading to crime—a multicausal sequence whose fulfillment depends on the intervention of sociological and psychological factors (see Rowe and Osgood, 1984; Cohen and Machalek, 1988).

Our view is that because crime is a *social* phenomenon, its causes must also be social. Ultimately, all biological explanations of crime confront the great difficulty of separating the effects of genetic causes from those of sociological causes. Nowhere is this difficulty more obvious in criminology than in the analysis of the relationships among gender, race, and social class. To certain of these complicated relationships we turn in Chapter 15.

REVIEW

This chapter examined four influential theories of crime: social learning theory, the labeling perspective, conflict theory, and biocriminology. Each offers a very different view of the processes that culminate in crime.

Social Learning Theory

1. Social learning theory begins with the idea that social behavior is a cognitive process in which personality and environment interact reciprocally. It was pioneered in laboratory settings under the influence of B. F. Skinner's operant conditioning theory, according to which desired behavior can be reinforced by conditioned learning based on rewards and punishments.

2. Some criminologists have argued that whether individuals commit crime depends on their past conditioning history (namely, whether they have been reinforced [or rewarded] for having committed crime). Akers' social learning theory attempted to revise Sutherland's theory of differential association. Its major concepts are (1) differential reinforcement and (2) positive and negative definitions.

3. Social learning theory is a general theory of crime: it attempts to explain all crime.

4. Social learning theory has not (as yet) greatly influenced criminology, partly because it arose at a time when deterministic theories of crime were unfashionable.

CHAPTER 15

CRITICAL CRIMINOLOGY

Preview

Chapter 15 introduces:

☞ radical criminology and its perspectives on crime and social control.
☞ feminist criminology, its criticisms of criminological theory, and its perspectives on crime and social control.

Key Terms

constitutive criminology
left realism
liberal feminism
Marxist feminism
patriarchy

political economy of crime
radical feminism
social control
socialist feminism

Radical criminology and feminist criminology are two perspectives on crime that have gained considerable importance in criminology. In this chapter we introduce the respective theories, concepts, and findings of each perspective.

15.1 ———— RADICAL CRIMINOLOGY

In Chapter 11.3 we outlined Marx and Engels' work on crime. As noted, neither Marx nor Engels devoted much time to analysis of crime; however, several European socialist writers of the late 19th and early 20th centuries did—attempting to apply Marxist theory to an understanding of crime (Greenberg, 1981; Messerschmidt, 1988). Foremost amongst these socialists was Wilhelm Adriaan Bonger, who published *Criminality and Economic Conditions* in 1905. Bonger reasoned that a capitalist economic system promotes egoism at the expense of altruism in all members of society, but that certain people in all social classes (the criminal class) develop a "criminal thought" from such egoism, which eventually leads to crime (*ibid.*:40). All crimes—economic, sexual, political, and pathological—committed both by the economically powerless and the powerful, Bonger argued, were the result of egoism engendered by a capitalist economic system.

Not until some 70 years later was Marxist theory first applied to an understanding of crime in the U.S. Instrumental in the development of this "radical criminology" were a number of articles written throughout the 1970s, such as Herman and Julia Schwendinger's (1975) "Defenders of Order or Guardians of Human Rights?" and (1977) "Social Class and the Definition of Crime," David Gordon's (1971) "Class and the Economics of Crime," Richard Quinney's (1973) "There's a Lot of Us Folks Grateful to the Lone Ranger" and (1973a) "Crime Control in Capitalist Society," Tony Platt's (1974) "Prospects for a Radical Criminology in the United States," and Ray Michalowski and Ed Bolander's (1976) "Repression and Criminal Justice in America." In Britain, Ian Taylor, Paul Walton, and Jock Young (1973), in *The New Criminology*, assembled a devastating critique of mainstream criminology, and then called for a social theory capable of explaining both the wider and immediate origins of the criminal act, as well as the effect of societal reaction on criminal behavior. Although it did not develop an explicit theory of its own, this book prompted theorists in the U.S. to form various perspectives on the political economy of crime during the 1970s and 1980s. In the following section we summarize certain of these positions.

The Political Economy of Crime

In "Toward a Political Economy of Crime," William Chambliss (1975) attempted to apply Marxist theory to an understanding of crime. He concentrated on three areas: the content and operation of criminal law, the consequences of crime for society, and the etiology of criminal behavior. Regarding criminal law, Chambliss argued that acts are defined as criminal "because it is in the interests of the ruling class to so define them" (*ibid.*:152). Chambliss went on to assert that the ruling class is free to commit crimes, whereas the subject classes are punished, and as the gap between these classes widens, the law is used to coerce the subject classes into submission. In this early article, Chambliss saw the law as simply an *instrument* of the ruling class that was used at their uncontested will. The instrumental view of the state asserts that the ruling class (capitalist class) dominates and utilizes the state as a vehicle for maintaining capital accumulation and the preservation of its economic power. The state is seen as an instrument that the ruling class employs to enforce and guarantee the stability of the class structure. Consequently, the institutions of the state are molded in accordance with the goals of the ruling class. The criminal law becomes an instrument that the ruling class uses to promote its interests (for example, working-class harmful behavior [conventional crime] is criminalized but ruling-class harmful behavior [white-collar crime] is not).

Regarding the consequences of crime for society, Chambliss (*ibid.*:152) maintained—following Marx—that crime is actually *functional* for capitalism inasmuch as it reduces surplus labor by providing work for law enforcement, locksmiths, welfare workers, professors of criminology, and a whole host of others who derive a livelihood from the existence of crime. Extending this functional argument, Chambliss (*ibid.*:152) maintained that crime diverts the attention of the lower classes from their exploitation and redirects it "toward other members of their own class rather than toward the capitalist class or the economic system."

Finally, Chambliss discussed the etiology of criminal behavior, contending that both conforming and criminal behavior result from individuals acting rationally in a manner that is compatible with their specific class position. In other words, crime becomes a "reaction to the life conditions of a person's social class" (*ibid.*). Nevertheless, although the type of criminal act varies by class, "class differences in rates of criminal activity are probably negligible" (*ibid.*:166). Ultimately, crime varies according to the political and economic structure of society, and socialist societies have the lowest crime rates because their class struggle is less intense (*ibid.*:153).

In the same year, Steven Spitzer (1975a) devised a Marxist theory of deviance. Assuming that capitalist societies are based on class conflict and that harmony is achieved through dominance of a specific class, Spitzer reasoned that deviants are drawn from groups who create problems for those who rule. Although these groups largely victimize and burden people in their own classes, "their problematic quality ultimately resides in their challenge to the basis and form of class rule" (*ibid.*:640). In other words, populations become problematic for those who rule when they disturb, hinder, or call into question any of the following (*ibid.*:642):

1. capitalist modes of appropriating the product of human labor (such as when the poor "steal" from the rich)

2. social conditions under which capitalist production takes place (for example, those who refuse or are unable to perform wage labor)

3. patterns of distribution and consumption in capitalist society (such as those who use drugs for escape and transcendence rather than sociability and adjustment)

4. the process of socialization for productive and nonproductive roles (including youth who refuse to be schooled or those who deny the validity of family life)

5. ideology that supports the functioning of capitalist society (for example, proponents of alternative forms of social organization)

Spitzer argued that problem populations are created in two ways: *directly*, through fundamental contradictions in the capitalist economy, and *indirectly*, through contradictions in social control institutions. An example of direct creation of a problem population is the inherent production of surplus labor (as technological innovation replaces workers with machines) in capitalist economies. Surplus populations are necessary for capitalism because they help support continued capital accumulation. A surplus population provides a mass labor pool that can be drawn into wage labor when necessary, and that simultaneously keeps wages down by increasing competition for scarce jobs. However, this surplus population is also problematic in that it must be neutralized and controlled (since it may rebel) if capital accumulation and, therefore, profit making are to continue. Thus, members of this group become eligible for processing as deviants.

Spitzer used mass education as an indirect example of the creation of a problem population. The widespread education of youth from all social classes initially was developed to withhold large numbers of young people from the labor market who would later be absorbed into wage labor. Yet education simultaneously provides many youth with critical insights into the oppressive character of capitalism. This ultimately leads to hostilities toward the system and subsequent mobilization against it (for example, by dropouts and radicals). These youth then become eligible for deviant processing.

Spitzer identified two specific and discrete problem populations: *social junk* and *social dynamite*. Social junk embodies those who represent a control cost—the handicapped and mentally ill—but are relatively harmless to society. Their deviant status arises from their failure or inability to participate adequately in the capitalist marketplace. Social dynamite comprises those with the potential to challenge capitalist relations of production and who, therefore, represent a political threat to the capitalist class. An example of social dynamite is the Communist Party.

Finally, Spitzer (*ibid.*:643) maintained a somewhat instrumentalist view of the state, arguing that the institutions of the superstructure—of which the state is part—"originate and are maintained to guarantee the interests of the capitalist class."

In *Class, State and Crime*, Richard Quinney (1977) developed a third model of a political economy of crime. For Quinney (*ibid.*:33–34), the basic question

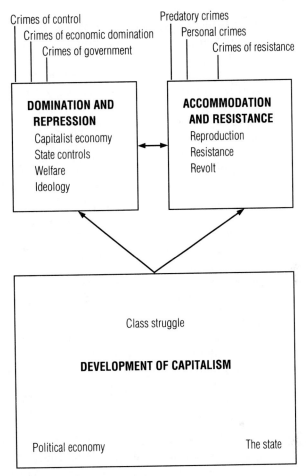

Crimes of control
Crimes of economic domination
Crimes of government

Predatory crimes
Personal crimes
Crimes of resistance

DOMINATION AND REPRESSION

Capitalist economy
State controls
Welfare
Ideology

ACCOMMODATION AND RESISTANCE

Reproduction
Resistance
Revolt

Class struggle

DEVELOPMENT OF CAPITALISM

Political economy   The state

FIGURE   Crime and the Development of Capitalism
15-1   Source: Quinney, 1977, p. 34.

for a Marxist analysis of crime is: "What is the meaning of crime in the development of capitalism?" Answering this, Quinney concentrated his analysis on four major areas. First, to understand crime we must study the development of the capitalist political economy, the forces and relations of production, the capitalist state, and the class struggle between the owners of capital and the working class. Second, we must uncover the systems of domination and repression historically used to benefit the capitalist class. Third, the forms of accommodation and resistance to capitalism by oppressed people must be revealed to understand crime. Finally, the dialectical relationship of accommodation and resistance to the overall conditions of capitalist political economy must be disclosed, since it is there that we find the creation of crimes of domination and crimes of accommodation. Quinney's model is depicted in Figure 15-1.

Quinney (*ibid.*:50–52) identified four types of crimes of domination that result from the reproduction of the capitalist system itself. *Crimes of control* include crimes by the police and FBI, such as misdemeanors, felonies, brutality, illegal surveillance, and violation of civil liberties. *Crimes of government* involve political crime, such as Watergate and CIA assassinations of foreign political leaders. *Crimes of economic domination* consist primarily of corporate crimes ranging from price-fixing to pollution, but also including the close connections between syndicated crime and criminal operations of the state. Finally, *social injuries* are harms not defined as illegal in legal codes, such as the denial of basic human rights resulting from sexism, racism, and economic exploitation.

Crimes of accommodation are acts of adaptation by the lower and working classes in response to oppressive conditions of capitalism and domination by the capitalist class (*ibid.*:54–55). *Predatory crimes* are parasitical in nature, and include such acts as burglary, robbery, and drug dealing. *Personal crimes*—such as murder, assault, and rape—are directed at other members of the lower and working classes, and result from the brutalized conditions of capitalism. Finally, *crimes of resistance* are actions conducted by members of the working class that are specifically directed at the workplace—such as sabotage and machine-breaking. As Quinney (*ibid.*:59) summarizes:

> Crimes of accommodation and resistance thus range from unconscious reactions to exploitation, to conscious acts of survival within the capitalist system, to politically conscious acts of rebellion. These criminal actions, moreover, not only cover the range of meaning but actually evolve or progress from *unconscious reaction* to *political rebellion*. Finally, the crimes may eventually reach the ultimate stage of conscious political action—*revolt*.

Thus, for Quinney, the crimes of domination seem to be the real societal harms, but are not criminalized because they benefit the ruling class. Crimes of accommodation range from simple adaptation to oppressive conditions to conscious political resistance. In fact, for Quinney some crimes and, therefore, criminals, are admirable elements in the overall class struggle.

Quinney (*ibid.*:44–45) also takes an instrumentalist view of the state, arguing that it promotes the interests of the ruling class and "is a device for controlling the exploited class, the class that labors, for the benefit of the ruling class." Quinney further maintains that the "coercive force of the state, embodied in law and legal repression, is the traditional means of maintaining the social and economic order" (*ibid.*:45). Law then "is an instrument of the state that serves the interests of the developing capitalist ruling class" (*ibid.*:45).

These three models of a political economy of crime were developed in the 1970s; in the 1980s, new models emerged. Two in particular—those of Raymond Michalowski (1985) and William Chambliss (1988)—require analysis.

Michalowski unfolds a more enriched Marxist perspective on crime than those developed earlier. He begins by identifying the mode of production as consisting of (1) the elements of production—such as the material base, technology, and division of labor in a society, (2) the relations of production—which include the patterns of ownership and control of capital, the patterns of access to the elements of production, and the patterns of redistribution of what a society produces, and (3) the dominant consciousness of the society. This mode of production shapes both the elements of state law—in particular, what is defined as a crime and what is not—and the characteristics and behavior of individuals. Such individual characteristics as biology, physical characteristics, cognitive and emotional processes, and acquired skills operate within a set of objective relations such as poverty, social class, race, and educational level. It is the combination of these individual characteristics and objective conditions that determines the formation of self and the possibilities of criminal behavior (*ibid.*:29–37).

Michalowski (*ibid.*:37–38) argues further that there are three basic forms of human behavior in U.S. society. *Acts of adaptation* are behaviors of conformity to existing social conditions—such as getting a job or applying for welfare. *Acts of rebellion* involve nonconformist behaviors that threaten the social order—such as acquiring property by illegitimate means (for example, by engaging in theft). As Michalowski (*ibid.*:38) states:

> The individual who decides to steal instead of, or in addition to, working for a living is rebelling against the constraints placed upon the acquisition of property as established by society. Although most acts of rebellion are not undertaken with a view toward social change, genuine acts of revolution would also fall into this category.

Acts of personal and interpersonal maladaptation are illegal acts, but they do not threaten the social order. Drug abuse, domestic violence, and insanity are examples.

The political economy of a society and its mode of production define what acts are adaptive, rebellious, or maladaptive; in "modern state societies it is the institutions of state law that have the additional task of controlling rebellious and maladaptive forms of behavior" (*ibid.*:38). Figure 15-2 depicts Michalowski's political economic model for the study of crime.

Michalowski employs a structuralist theory of the state rather than an instrumentalist theory. As noted, in the instrumentalist version it is simply the presence and domination of the capitalist class in the state that makes it a capitalist state. For structuralists, the state in a capitalist mode of production takes a specifically capitalist form, not because of those who fill decisionmaking positions but because the institution itself reflects capitalist economic relations. That is, the capitalist state is molded to fit and serve the interests of the capitalist economy, regardless of those who fill its offices. State policy then follows a path consistent with the reproduction of the class structure and capitalist economic relations. For Michalowski, state law has developed into a dual system of law in which the capitalist class is essentially free to engage in harmful behavior while pursuing its goal of profit making (regulatory law), whereas harmful behavior by lower- and working-class people is scrupulously repressed (criminal law). Thus it is the

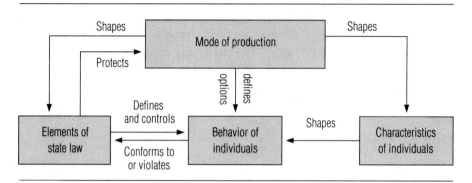

FIGURE   **Michalowski's General Model for the Study of Crime**
15-2   *Source: Michalowski, 1985, p. 22.*

state, shaped by the economic organization of capitalist society, that determines what is and is not a crime.

Finally, William Chambliss (1988a) has recently outlined his structural contradictions theory of crime. Chambliss (*ibid.*:300–309) argues that every historical era and society, while constructing their means of survival, create contradictory forces, dilemmas, and conflicts. Under capitalism, the basic contradiction is between capital and labor: each group has different interests—capitalists want to maintain the status quo and workers want to change it; capitalists want to maintain or increase their share of the surplus and so do workers. This contradiction results in workers demanding better working conditions and higher wages and capitalists resisting their demands. The dilemma for capital, labor, and the state is how to reconcile the conflict inasmuch as the fundamental contradiction is ignored. Resolving the conflict, however, can result either in further conflicts—because the fundamental contradiction persists—or in an additional contradiction (as shown in Figure 15-3).

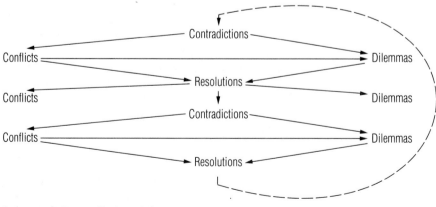

FIGURE   **Structural-Contradictions Theory**
15-3   *Source: Chambliss, 1988, p. 305.*

Chambliss also takes a structuralist position on the state. For Chambliss, the law represents the state's response to various aspects of class struggle in a contradictory capitalist economy. Contradictions create dilemmas and conflicts—which those in state positions attempt to resolve—leaving the contradictions in place. Although Chambliss agrees with instrumentalists that the capitalist class puts pressure on the state to pass laws that serve its interests (winning most of the time), resistance and pressure from other class forces are always present. When resistance leads to open conflict, the state responds through the law. As Chambliss (*ibid.*:122) states:

> The response may be new legislation, new interpretations of old laws, or use of existing laws to repress or ameliorate the conflict. The ruling class will win some and lose some struggles in the face of such conflicts.

Chambliss (*ibid.*:308–309) also identifies two fundamental contradictions in a capitalist political economy that lead to crime. The first is the "wages, profits, and consumption contradiction." If, on the one hand, workers have insufficient money to purchase commodities (because capitalists do not pay them enough in wages), the economy becomes sluggish. If, on the other hand, workers are paid high wages, this cuts into profits, and there is less money for reinvestment. This inherent contradiction of capitalism culminates in crime (*ibid.*:308–309):

> Owners cut corners, violate health and safety regulations, illegally deal in the stock market, and violate securities and exchange regulations; workers steal from employers, supplement their wages by selling illegal drugs, illegally strike and organize, and join illegal political groups. The state sits squarely in the midst of the contradiction: although generally influenced more by owners than workers, it cannot allow the ongoing conflict to disrupt social, political, and economic relations to the point of destroying the existing economic system (capitalism) or the existing political system (democracy). It responds by passing laws to keep workers from disrupting production or stealing property and owners from disregarding the health and safety of workers and consumers. It also passes laws prohibiting certain economic activities that undermine the state's own interests (avoiding taxes by laundering money through overseas banks) or give one group of capitalists an advantage over another (insider trading on the stock market, which disenfranchises those who are not privy to secret corporate information, or forming monopolies). State and government officials work to block efforts by extranational bodies (such as the United Nations) to establish codes of conduct for multinational corporations in developing nations.

In addition, Chambliss (*ibid.*:309) identifies a "wages-labor supply contradiction" as conducive to crime. Capitalism maintains a surplus labor force that helps keep wages down and provides a supply of labor from which capital can draw whenever the demands of workers threaten profits. The demanding workers are let go and fresh labor is brought in. However, this reserve army of labor simultaneously (*ibid.*:309)

> forms an underclass that cannot consume but nonetheless is socialized into a system in which consumption is the necessary condition for happiness. Criminal behavior offers a solution for the underclass: what they cannot earn legitimately they can earn illegitimately.

In sum, the political-economic approach employs Marxist theory to understand the relationship between the political and economic realms of a capitalist society. This approach advances our understanding of why certain behaviors are criminalized by the state while others are not, and how a capitalist economic system itself generates certain *class* patterns of crime.

Left Idealism and Left Realism

As we learned in Chapter 3-1, conventional crime is predominantly an *intra-class* phenomenon. The conventional offender and victim are drawn from those classes—lower and working classes—that radical criminologists tend to represent and reflect in their theorizing. Consequently, several radical criminologists—in particular, Jock Young, John Lea, and Roger Matthews—have attempted to develop a more coherent explanation of conventional crime. In so doing, they have advanced a critique of what they term "left idealism," without identifying by name who the "left idealists" actually are. For example, left idealists allegedly argue that absolute economic deprivation (unemployment) drives people into crime and that the conventional criminal is seen as somewhat of a rebel (Lea and Young, 1984:93–96). Indeed, for some *early* radical criminologists of the 1970s (such as Quinney, discussed earlier), the conventional criminal was depicted as a rebel—and for some radical criminologists, the criminal, rather than the working class, was seen as the vanguard of the revolution (Greenberg, 1981:28). As Jock Young (1986:12) adds, for the left idealist the conventional criminal allegedly

> sees through the inequitable nature of present day society and crime itself in an attempt—however clumsily and ill-thought out—to redress this balance. There is little need to have complex explanations for working-class crime. Its causes are obvious and to blame the poor for their criminality is to blame the victim, to point moral accusations at those whose very actions are a result of their being social casualties. In contrast, the real crime on which we should focus is that of the ruling class: the police, the corporations and the state agencies. This causes real problems for the mass of people, unlike working-class crime which is seen as minor, involving petty theft and occasional violence, of little impact to working-class communities.

Lea and Young (1986:358) also have pointed out that left idealists do not provide any realistic solutions for crime, other than emphasizing "changing the social order."

Thus, left idealists are pictured as adhering to a romantic image of the conventional criminal, making no attempt to understand scientifically the complex nature of conventional working-class crime, focusing almost exclusively on the harms of the "ruling class," and ignoring the development of a coherent program for curbing conventional crime.

Against this, what do *left realists* propose? First, although not denying the harms of the powerful, left realists seem to be preoccupied exclusively with conventional crime. They argue that conventional crime is a real problem for the working class. Rather than viewing crime as the result of absolute deprivation and, therefore, as a form of rebellion, left realists argue that conventional crime is driven by relative deprivation as well as by reactionary, selfish, and individualistic attitudes (Lea and Young, 1984:95–96; Lea and Young, 1986:360). Moreover, conventional crime has a disintegrating and disorganizing effect, pitting the poor against the poor. Rather than helping create a politically conscious community, conventional crime hinders working-class solidarity and thus "the ability to fight back" (*ibid.*:359). As Matthews (1987:373) puts it, crime is not a heralded revolt but "tends to extend the fragmentation of urban life, mimic individualistic and acquisitive values, and limits public space and social and political participation." Because of this disorganizing effect, left realists argue that conventional crime must be examined seriously by radical criminologists. Matthews (*ibid.*:372) goes on:

> The world is always full of surprises. The social reality of crime is inevitably far more complex than available theories. Thus there is a need to engage in a detailed empirical investigation of the object in every case rather than dogmatically reiterate abstract beliefs. Realism demands attention to specificity, as well as an openness to counterfactual examples.

Yet in addition to rejection of the Robin Hood image of the criminal and the need for thoughtful empirical investigations of conventional crime, left realists argue that crime control must also be taken seriously. Rather than ignoring the conventional crime problem—as left idealists allegedly do—left realists argue for a concrete crime control program. Such a program first requires an honest assessment of the state. For left idealists, "the state is the direct instrument of the ruling class" and its ideological and repressive institutions "exist in order to maintain capitalism" (Lea and Young, 1984: 101–102). Reform in such a state is allegedly impossible, and will most likely backfire, turning against the working class. Left realists argue that although the state "represents very largely ruling-class interests," gains can in fact be "wrung out of it; reforms, however difficult to achieve, are possible and, in fact, relate to the state as in essence a site of contradictory interests" (*ibid.*:103). Therefore, the possibility of a concrete crime program does in fact present itself.

Certain elements of this program have been outlined by Lea and Young

(1986:360–363). First, they argue for *demarginalization*. Against marginalizing offenders in prison, left realists propose using such measures as community service orders, victim restitution schemes, and widespread decarceration. Second, left realists advocate *preemptive deterrence* (deterring crime before it is committed) through citizen groups who cooperate with the police, as well as evening youth patrols, such as the Guardian Angels. Third, left realists argue for *minimal use of prisons*. They suggest that prisons, and thus custodial sentences, should be used only in circumstances where there is extreme danger to the community. When prisons are used, they should be organized to maintain as civilized forms of containment as possible. This means placing rehabilitation back on the agenda. As Matthews (1987:394) points out:

> There is thus an urgent need to reaffirm rehabilitation and to investigate forms of incarceration which rather than acting as human warehouses might provide constructive modes of punishment which could ultimately help to reintegrate offenders into social life rather than severing their connections with it.

Fourth, left realists suggest that criminologists *must look realistically at the circumstances of both offender and victim.* Left realists emphasize that people have choices in their lives, yet these choices exist within determinate and variable circumstances. Thus, to "judge an unemployed youth stealing $50 as equal to an accountant fiddling $50 in income tax is invidious" (Lea and Young, 1986:361). At the same time, however, the victim must be considered: $50 stolen from an old-age pensioner is quite different than $50 stolen from a large department store. Moreover, strong intervention is necessary to "recognize that there is this element of choice in crime" and "to accept that it is necessary to counter crime with force, but realistically guided by knowledge of the circumstances involved" (*ibid.*). Fifth, criminologists *must be realistic about policing*. Left realists argue that the "police force" must be transformed into a "police service" accountable to the public. The needs of the community must be the directing energy of police activities. Only if the police are under democratic community control will the public involve itself in crime-control politics. Nevertheless, left realists also seem to demand a more repressive police *force*. As Matthews (1987:396) adds:

> What realist criminology must also take on board is that achieving an adequate level of security for all citizens may only be achievable at a price. That is, it may require levels of policing and surveillance which may in expanding and protecting the rights of some reduce the rights and liberties of others. Thus, although it is important to take rights seriously we cannot frame the problem exclusively in terms of "universal" or "natural" rights.

Finally, according to left realists, criminologists *must be realistic about the problem of crime in the present period.* Because the degree of relative deprivation has continually risen, a situation of considerable discontent exists. Yet, concurrent with this rise of deprivation and discontent, there has been no increase in working-class politics. Consequently, the door is open for a criminal—rather than a political—response in working-class communities. Left realists advocate pursuing "alternative politics that harness the energies of the marginalized," help create a "politics of crime control" that is part of other grass roots movements, and "combat the tendency of a divided and disillusioned public to move to the right" (*ibid.*:363).

In short, what these left realists have essentially accomplished is an attempt to theorize conventional crime realistically while simultaneously developing a "radical law and order" program for curbing such behavior.

Other left realists, such as Michalowski (1983) and Currie (1985), have "given more attention to reconstructing social and economic policies" as well as addressing crime from all directions (Dekeseredy and Schwartz, 1991: 259). For example, Currie calls for the following social/economic changes to reduce crime (cited in *ibid.*:254):

▲— Increased wages for women

▲— Public-supported, community-oriented job creation

▲— Upgrading the quality of work available to disenfranchised people

▲— Intensive job training and supported work designed to help prepare the young and disabled for stable careers

▲— Paid work leaves

Moreover, Dekeseredy and Schwartz (*ibid.*:257) summarize one of Michalowski's strategies for putting a dent in both street and suite crime:

> He suggests that citizen patrols based on democratic principles, and representative of all members of the community, should be organized to prevent both street and suite crime. With regard to the latter, Michalowski contends that citizen patrols could be used to gather information and to study complaints of business crimes. Local citizen groups could use their data to pressure businesses to stop harming the general public, or to initiate legal action against offenders.

Peacemaking and Constitutive Criminology

One of the distinctive products of the leftist concern with "realism" is a renewed attempt to humanize the institutions of criminal justice. This is known as "peacemaking criminology," the eclectic theoretical basis of which lies in a loose mixture of religious humanism and feminism. This combination is most visible in Harold Pepinsky and Richard Quinney's (1991) edited book *Criminology as Peacemaking*. At the beginning of their book Pepinsky and Quinney (*ibid.*:ix) declare that:

> The peacemaking perspective is steadily making its way into criminology. In recent years there have been proposals and programs that foster mediation, conflict resolution, reconciliation, and community. They are part

of an emerging *criminology of peacemaking*, a criminology that seeks to alleviate suffering and thereby reduce crime. This is a criminology that is based necessarily on human transformation in the achievement of peace and justice.

The different authors of the 20 chapters in this book on peacemaking criminology address a wide variety of practical issues that converge on the need to use more humane and more caring approaches to the problem of crime. Though all the authors seem to agree with previous critical criminologists that it is economic, political, and social inequality that fosters crime, the emphasis here is less on the causes of crime than on how to resolve the conflicts of which crime is an expression. The key policies of peacemaking criminology thus involve terms like "responsiveness," "reconciliation," "conflict resolution," "harmony," and "community."

Constitutive criminology is partly an offshoot of peacemaking criminology. It, too, seeks to escape from the alienation, the violence, and the domination that are the business-as-usual of prisons and other criminal justice institutions (De Haan, 1990; Milovanovic and Henry, 1991). But constitutive criminology is also an aspect of a far larger movement outside of criminology known as "postmodernism." At its most abstract level, postmodernism is a reaction—a principled anarchist reaction—to the scientific rationalism and to the positivist certainty of the Enlightenment (Hunt, 1991). It rejects scientific notions of "cause" just as it rejects the idea that "crime" and "criminal law" are simple or fixed categories. Strongly influenced by postmodernism, constitutive criminology is an avowedly political tendency that seeks to get behind or to lay bare the rhetoric, the dogma, and the mystification that goes into public discourse about crime or, in other words, into what constitutes crime.

The chief authors of constitutive criminology are Stuart Henry and Dragan Milovanovic (Henry and Milovanovic, 1994; and see Henry and Milovanovic, 1991). For present purposes, their labors, once stripped of the complex philosophical and linguistic wrappings in which they are packaged, contain two major propositions. First, crime is not what the criminal law says it is. Rather, crime is the ability or the power to impose one's will upon others in any social context whatsoever. Crime is much of what passes for family life, for business practices, and for government activity. Crime, Henry and Milovanovic (1994:8–9) argue,

> is the power to deny others. It is the ultimate form of reification in which those subject to the power of another suffer the pain of being denied their own humanity, the power to make a difference. The victim of crime is thus rendered a non-person, a non-human. The victim is nothing. That is the harm of crime. That is its pain. Crime is the expression of power, the master of power and the handmaiden of pain.

To this radical reformulation of what counts as crime Henry and Milovanovic are keen to add their recommendations for criminal justice policy and practice. These include the abolition of all taken-for-granted assumptions about the "causes" of crime and the "correction" and "treatment" of criminals—the abolition, in other words, of criminology itself. Instead, any human relationship that involves the actual or the potential infliction of pain or suffering must be carefully analyzed in its full structural context, exposed, and restructured in non-harmful ways. Quoting Willem De Haan's (1990:158) brilliant book *The Politics of Redress: Crime, Punishment and Penal Abolition*, Henry and Milovanovic (p. 18) suggest that the process of reconstruction

> (a) . . . includes almost every conceivable reaction to an event—individual, collective, structural, material, or immaterial. (b) It implies that response is mandatory, without pre-defining the event as a crime, an illness, or anything else. (c) It invites analysis of the event before deciding or choosing a proper response. [And] (d) . . . it invokes the consideration of historical and anthropological forms of dispute settlement and conflict resolution for possible cues to rational forms of response.

Radical Perspectives on Social Control

Radical criminologists have also developed revisionist perspectives on the history of social control. In more conventional scholarship, a change in the form of social control is seen as inherently progressive—"from barbarism to enlightenment, from ignorance to expertly guided intervention, from cruelty and vindictiveness to scientific humanism" (Cohen and Scull, 1983:2). Radicals argue, instead, that any form of social control simply corresponds to the political and economic organization of the class society in which it occurs. In capitalist societies, changes in forms of social control actually serve to control the "dangerous classes." Radicals have provided historical accounts of the state, the law, the police, and penal practices; yet space limits our summary to certain works in the latter category only.

Radicals have identified two major transformations in Western penal policies: the first took place from the end of the 18th century to the middle of the 19th century; the second—controversial and still the subject of debate—allegedly occurred from the mid-1960s onward. Regarding the first transformation, radicals have documented the following four changes from the end of the 18th century to the middle of the 19th century (Cohen, 1985:13):

1. The increasing involvement of the state in the business of deviancy control—the eventual development of a centralized, rationalized, and bureaucratic apparatus for the control and punishment of crime and delinquency and the care or cure of other types of deviants.

2. The increasing differentiation and classification of deviant and dependent groups into separate types and categories, each with its own body of "scientific" knowledge and its own recognized and accredited experts—professionals who eventually acquire specialized monopolies.

3. The increased segregation of deviants into "asylums"—penitentiaries, prisons, mental hospitals, reformatories, and other closed, purpose-built institutions. The prison emerges as the dominant instrument for changing undesirable behavior and as the favored form of punishment.

4. The decline of punishment involving the public infliction of physical pain. The mind replaces the body as the object of penal repression, and positivist theories emerge to justify concentrating on the individual offender and not the general offense.

Radicals have documented different aspects of these changes. Consider two works, by Foucault (1977) and by Melossi and Pavarini (1981). Foucault examined the change in France from public forms of punishment—such as whipping, torture, and execution—to private forms of punishment, especially imprisonment. For the first, Foucault discussed the case of Robert François Damiens who attempted in 1757 to murder King Louis XV. Foucault shows through this example how those labeled criminals were often put through a long, anguished death in a theatrical and public spectacle. Some 80 years later, public corporal punishment had disappeared. Incarceration was now the favored punishment and, most importantly, everything inside prison was regulated by time. Thus, in less than a century, one mode of punishment replaced another that was strikingly different: a *public* ceremony that punished the body was superseded by a *private* seclusion that punished the mind. Why did this change occur from punishing the body to punishing the mind? Foucault contends that these different types of punishment reflect the different *power* relations of the time. The public nature of corporal punishment was used to reproduce the sovereign power of the king. All crimes were considered harms to the king, and thus a public ritual demonstrated his sovereign power. Thus for Foucault (*ibid.*:48–49):

> The public execution, however nasty and everyday, belongs to a whole series of great rituals in which power is eclipsed and restored (coronation, entry of the King into a conquered city, the submission of rebellious subjects); over and above the crime that has placed the sovereign in contempt, it deploys before all eyes an invincible force. Its aim is not so much to reestablish a balance as to bring into play, as its extreme point, the dissymmetry between the subject who has dared to violate the law and the all-powerful sovereign who displays his strength. . . . The punishment is carried out in such a way as to give a spectacle not of measure, but of imbalance and excess; in this liturgy of punishment, there must be an emphatic affirmation of power and of its intrinsic superiority.

Imprisonment, however, represented power based not on direct force but on regulation, surveillance, and discipline. By the mid-1800s, Western societies became essentially disciplinary societies, where more and more people were placed in organizations—school, clinic, asylum, prison—whose goal was to create a body of "normals" for adequate participation in the capitalist marketplace. In other words, imprisonment, as the prevalent form of punishment, represented one type of a host of disciplinary institutions that deployed techniques for organizing and training people into normalcy. The extensive use of prison in 19th-century France was not, then, simply the result of clamorous, reform-minded penologists concerned about the nastiness of public torture; rather, it was part of the overall "machinery that assumes responsibility for and places under surveillance" the everyday behavior, identity, activity, and "apparently unimportant gestures" of the masses (*ibid.*:77). For Foucault, the widespread use of incarceration must be understood as a manifestation of the development of broader and new *power* relations. These new power relations are constituted as the explicit control and discipline of *individuals*. Everyday life now entails constant surveillance and judgments of normalcy. In the 19th century, Western capitalist societies developed a "carceral network" of disciplinary institutions whose goal was—and for Foucault continues to be—the control and normalization of the entire social body. Normalizing judgments are found not only in the prison by "social worker judges," but we live in a society of the "teacher-judge," the "doctor-judge," the "educator-judge," and so on. In short, it is with these judges of normalcy (*ibid.*:304)

> that the universal reign of the normative is based; and each individual, wherever he may find himself, subjects to it his body, his gestures, his behavior, his aptitudes, his achievements. The carceral network, in its compact or disseminated forms, with its systems of insertion, distribution, surveillance, observation, has been the greatest support, in modern society, of the normalizing power.

For Foucault, consequently, the prison and incarceration are simply representations of new power relations of the 19th century. Today these social relations continue to be constituted in disciplinary techniques of power, whose goal is the production of normal individuals who are useful to the capitalist marketplace and compliant politically.

In *The Prison and the Factory*, Melossi and Pavarini (1981) follow Foucault's line of reasoning, but develop a more orthodox Marxist understanding of the origins of the prison in Western Europe and in the U.S. They argue that the emergence of the prison corresponded neatly to the development of industrial capitalism. With the growth of the factory system, the prison provided the mechanism for disciplining recalcitrant members of the working class. Prison "has as its basic aim education in discipline and obedience," and is "like a factory producing proletarians, not commodities" (*ibid.*:95, 145). For Melossi and Pavarini, the housing of criminals is only a secondary purpose of prison. Its main function is the reproduction of capitalist social relations; when a factory economy emerged in capitalist societies, penal practices corresponded and developed to serve economic interests.

Incarceration has served as the most prevalent form of punishment throughout the 19th and much of the 20th centuries. However, in the mid-1960s, a second major transformation in penal policies allegedly emerged that supposedly changed each of the four original transformations previously outlined in the following ways (Cohen, 1985:31):

1. *Away from the state:* "decentralization," "deformalization," "decriminalization," "nonintervention"—a call toward divesting the state of certain control functions or at least by-passing them and creating instead innovative agencies which are community-based, less bureaucratic and not directly state-sponsored.

2. *Away from the expert:* "deprofessionalization," "demedicalization," "delegalization," "anti-psychiatry"—a distrust of professionals and experts, and a demystification of their monopolistic claims of competence in classifying and treating various forms of deviance.

3. *Away from the institution:* "deinstitutionalization," "decarceration," "community control"—a lack of faith in traditional, closed institutions and a call for their replacement by non-segregative, "open" measures termed variously "community control," "community treatment," "community corrections," or "community care."

4. *Away from the mind:* "back to justice," "neo-classicism," "behaviorism"— an impatience with ideologies of individualized treatment or rehabilitation based on psychological inner-states models, and a call to reverse the positivist victory and to focus instead on body rather than mind, on act rather than actor.

A well-known work on this alleged new transformation is Andrew Scull's (1977) *Decarceration: Community Treatment and the Deviant.* Scull (*ibid.*:152) argues that this "shift in control styles and practices must be viewed as dependent upon, and a reflection of, more extensive and deep-seated changes in the social organization of advanced capitalist societies." Employing Marx's insights on the reserve army of labor, Scull (*ibid.*:137) argues that since the mid-1960s, advanced capitalist countries—because of technological innovation—have relied less and less on actual human labor to produce societal goods. The result is an expanding surplus population of underemployed and unemployed individuals. Scull notes that the state is then burdened with controlling this growing problem population. However, in the mid-1960s, segregative modes of social control such as the prison became increasingly costly, and a governmental fiscal crisis occurred whereby "state expenditures continuously threatened to outrun available revenue" (*ibid.*:135). Decarceration was the answer to this dilemma, placing convicted criminals in community treatment programs rather than in prison. Decarceration allegedly provided a cheaper alternative to state control of an increasing problem population. As Scull (*ibid.*:121) wrote in 1977: "Decarceration has been taking place on an increasing scale and has been adopted as the most desirable way of dealing with deviance in both England and America."

Stanley Cohen (1985) examined this alleged second transformation of penal policy, and he separates the "words" (rhetoric) of policy from the "deeds" (activity), finding an actual change in penal policy to be illusory. Although decarceration and community control have definitely occurred, they have occurred *in addition* to, rather than as a replacement for, segregative control. Prisons have continued to be used extensively in Britain and the United States. In fact, for Cohen (*ibid.*:37), the entire social control system has expanded:

> The original structures have become stronger; far from any decrease, the reach and intensity of state control have been increased; centralization and bureaucracy remain; professions and experts are proliferating dramatically and society is more dependent on them; informalism has not made the legal system less formal or more just.

A widening of the net has taken place whereby more and more experts, working in a variety of "agencies"—legal and quasi-legal, diversionary and alternative, administrative and professional—are marking out their own territories of jurisdiction, competence and referral" (*ibid.*:86). Once the talk was of typical prisoners, now it is of typical clients. And the primary decisions—who shall be diverted and who shall be inserted—are but instances of the deep structure at work. In short, the disciplinary society—in the sense of Foucault—has greatly expanded.

Finally, Thomas Mathiesen (1974) has argued that contemporary prison in capitalist societies provides an *expurgatory* function. Prison houses a proportion of those who are unproductive in the labor market. It therefore serves the purpose of controlling those who may be, or are, problematic for the smooth functioning of the production system. Thus, prison does not function to *rehabilitate* deviants (indeed, 50–70 percent of inmates are recidivists) nor does it *contain* the dangerous (most prisoners are minor property offenders). Consequently, Mathiesen concludes that the prison is essentially a mechanism for class control and that positive reforms only further legitimate such control. It is necessary therefore to abolish prisons themselves. Following Mathiesen, an abolitionist movement has emerged in Western Europe and North America, arguing for the abolition of prisons as a first step in creating truly democratic forms of social control. For abolitionists, imprisonment is an irrational, inhumane, and ineffective way to control crime, serving instead the interests of the dominant class in a class-stratified society. By abolishing prisons, a "metaphor of punitive thinking" is eradicated, while simultaneously necessitating a movement toward truly democratic and rehabilitative forms of social control (Swaaningen, 1986:19). Although the abolitionist ideology continues to be debated in radical criminological circles (see Bianchi and Swaaningen, 1986; *Contemporary Crises* [1986] 10 [1]), it remains unclear how the support necessary for conducting such a policy could ever emerge in a society like the United States.

Assessment

Radical criminologists, in various forms, have produced sophisticated understandings of crime and social control. Using Marxist social theory, radicals have developed theories that give priority to historical and structural analyses of crime that focus on economic relationships, class struggle, capital accumulation, and the role of the reserve army of labor. In short, radicals have offered a coherent theory of crime and social control.

However, radical criminology is not without its critics. For some, a radical criminology grounded in Marxist theory is seen as actually impossible, inasmuch as crime is not an explicit Marxian concept in the same way mode of production, capital accumulation, and other Marxist terms are (Hirst, 1972; Bankowski, Mungham, and Young, 1977). However, as Greenberg (1981:20–21) points out: "If one starts from the proposition Marxist theory was still incomplete when Marx and Engels died, then it is surely legitimate to extend and develop the theory to deal with new phenomena." Other mainstream criminologists have criticized radical criminology for being unscientific (Turk, 1979), for being moralistic (Klockars, 1979; Toby, 1979), and for being utopian (Nettler, 1978). All these criticisms, however, have been soundly addressed by radicals (Beirne, 1979; Greenberg, 1981:20–25).

The most useful criticisms of radical criminology, therefore, derive from radical criminologists themselves. For example, Spitzer (1980) argues that much of radical criminology is metafunctional. That is, capitalism is theorized "as 'needing' crime in order to justify its oppression of the masses" (*ibid.*:176). Radical criminologists have also identified problems with instrumental outlooks on the state. As noted, this position holds that the ruling class exercises state power directly through manipulation of state policies. Critics have pointed out that neither the state nor the ruling class is monolithic—conflicts of interests exist both within the state and the ruling class, as well as between them (*ibid.*:177; Beirne, 1979; Chambliss and Seidman, 1982:140–144).

Regarding left realists, much of their criticisms of so-called left idealists are now somewhat misplaced. For example, although in the past certain segments of radical criminology clearly romanticized the conventional criminal, this no longer is the case, and does not seem to have been the case for at least the last 15 years (see Balkan, Berger, and Schmidt, 1980; Chambliss, 1988:281). Moreover, most radical criminologists today avoid instrumental versions of the state, adopting some type of structuralist position. Left realists are correct in pointing to deficiencies in radical theories of conventional crime and to the need for radical criminology not only to take this type of crime seriously but also to put together a coherent crime control package, but their solutions to the continued crime-in-the-streets problem have not been received enthusiastically. Stanley Cohen (1986:130–131), for example, states that for left realists

> prisons have to remain; the weak must be given the full protection of the rule of law. The soft parts of the system—welfare, social work, treatment, rehabilitation—instead of being attacked as disguised forms of social control, should be defended in the face of the conservative onslaught on the welfare state. . . . By their overall commitment to "order through law," the left realists have retreated too far from the theoretical gains of twenty years ago. Their regression into the assumptions of

the standard criminal law model of social control—criminalization and punishment—is premature.

Radical criminology has also been criticized for its one-dimensional nature. Radical criminology, it is claimed, attempts to explain all crime in economic terms. This means that other social relations, such as gender and race relations, are at best secondary to class relations. This secondariness has been challenged by feminist criminologists and is discussed in the following section.

Finally, it should be noted that the two most recent versions of radical criminology—peacemaking and constitutive criminology—have not yet generated much discussion by scholars.

Before turning to feminist criminology, we note that not all radical criminologists employ Marxism in their theorizing. Indeed, some—such as anarchists—oppose Marxism and attempt to understand crime and criminalization in terms of power and authoritarian relations. For anarchists, the state—rather than the mode of production—is the source of all social ills, including crime. The most serious social harms are those committed by the state, such as imperialism. Only in a stateless society is crime nonproblematic (Tifft and Sullivan, 1980; Pepinsky, 1978).

15.2   FEMINIST CRIMINOLOGY

During the last century a significant feminist movement has emerged in Western Europe and North America. This feminist movement has made an important impact on the social sciences, including sociology and criminology. Today, many sociologists, and an increasing number of criminologists, identify themselves as feminists. The term *feminist* is commonly and broadly used to refer to all those who consciously maintain that women are discriminated against because of their gender and who seek to end women's resulting subordination through social change.

Although a feminist perspective and, therefore, a feminist criminology take various forms (which we soon discuss), Kathleen Daly and Meda Chesney-Lind (1988:108) recently outlined five core elements of feminist thought that help distinguish feminism from other forms of social theory:

▲__ Gender is not a natural fact but a complex social, historical, and cultural product; it is related to, but not simply derived from, biological sex difference and reproduction capacities.

▲__ Gender and gender relations order social life and social institutions in fundamental ways.

▲__ Gender relations and constructs of masculinity and femininity are not symmetrical but are based on an organizing principle of men's superiority and social- and political-economic dominance over women.

Criminological theory has historically been a male-dominated profession that has ignored or misrepresented women and crime.

▲— Systems of knowledge reflect men's views of the natural and social world; the production of knowledge is gendered.

▲— Women should be at the center of intellectual inquiry, not peripheral, invisible, or appendages to men.

In this section we consider briefly feminist criticisms that criminological theory has embodied only a male point of view. Following this, we turn to the major feminist theoretical perspectives on crime and social control.

Feminist Criticisms of Criminological Theory

Feminist criminologists assert that although suggesting to be general explanations of crime, criminological theory has either *ignored* gender and female crime or *misrepresented* women when female crime is in fact theoretically examined (Heidensohn, 1985:146; Morris, 1987:1–18). This is not a minor difficulty, but a fundamental flaw in criminological theory. We believe Loraine Gelsthorpe and Allison Morris (1988:103) are correct when they state:

Theories are weak if they do not apply to half of the potential criminal population. . . . Theories of crime should be able to take account of both men's and women's behavior and to highlight those factors which operate differently on men and women. Whether or not a particular theory helps us understand women's crime better is of fundamental, not marginal, importance for criminology.

Let us look then at the male bias in some of the influential theories discussed earlier in this book. We begin with those theories that purport to be general theories of crime, yet ignore women and gender.

Robert Merton's theory of anomie argues that U.S. culture socializes all individuals to obtain the culturally desired *goals* of financial success, but does not simultaneously provide everyone with the legitimate *means* necessary for obtaining them (see Chapter 12.3). The consequence is that when the goals have been internalized, yet the approved means are unavailable, the population experiencing this anomic contradiction and, therefore strain, reacts by engaging in antisocial behavior. Merton's theory attempted to comprehend the high rate of conventional crime in lower-class communities. However, Merton made no attempt to determine whether or not his theory applied to gender differences in crime.

Eileen Leonard (1982:57) argues, for example, that by ignoring at least half the population, Merton's theory is inadequate in that it cannot explain the lower crime rate of women who also experience anomic strain. Leonard accepts Merton's notion that social aspirations are learned. She adds, however, that because of gender inequality in U.S. society, men and women experience different socialized goals, which in turn affect their criminality. As Leonard (*ibid.*:58) writes:

> The goal that women are traditionally socialized to desire, above all else, is marriage and a family; the accepted means is to secure the romantic love of a man through courtship. Despite the much discussed emancipation of women, the great majority of them are still taught to find primary fulfillment through marriage and children. Their main concerns revolve around family, husband, children and home. Money and financial success are simply not as vital. This, of course, contrasts with Merton's analysis of economic success as paramount. Women are certainly interested in financial status, but this is largely seen as the responsibility of their husbands.

By revising Merton's theory in terms of gendered goals and means, Leonard argues that women do not experience the level of frustration that men do. Because women can easily achieve their gender-specific, socially approved goals in a legitimate way (marriage and children), they avoid the strain men experience and, therefore, the pressures to engage in crime.

Allison Morris (1987:6) challenges Leonard's thesis, arguing that it is based on stereotypical beliefs rather than on evidence. Reviewing studies on gender differences in motivation to achieve, Morris (*ibid.*:7) concludes that women do in fact strive to achieve in ways that men do. However, because few women actually attain responsible and powerful positions in Western capitalist societies (due to sexist discrimination), gendered stereotypes persist. Thus, if women have the same aspirations as men yet experience more strain (because they do not have the same economic opportunities as men—see Chapter 3.2 for evidence of this assertion), a critical question for anomie theorists remains: "Why is women's recorded crime rate not higher than men's?" (*ibid.*:8). At present, anomie theory—which aspires to be a general explanation of crime—is unable to answer this question.

Similarly, Walter Miller's theory of delinquent gangs (see Chapter 13.1) makes no attempt to deal with gender issues and, as Leonard (1982:134) rightly complains, "simply breaks down when applied to women." Miller assumed that his focal concerns apply both to men and women. Some criminologists argue they do not (*ibid.*); others argue they do (Morris, 1987:5). Either way, Miller fails to account for gender differences in gang participation and crime.

Merton and Miller are only two examples of women's "notable *absence* from most major studies and exclusion from all sociologically based theories" of crime (Heidensohn, 1985:153). Theoretical criminology was constructed by males, is about males, and therefore is not the general explanation of human behavior it claims to be (Leonard, 1982:1–2). Excellent reviews of criminological theory by a number of feminists support this thesis (*ibid.*; Heidensohn, 1985; Morris, 1987). It is impossible for us to review here all criminological theories; accordingly, we do not repeat the reviews but limit ourselves to one additional example, Marxism and radical criminology. Marx and Engels said little about women or crime. As noted, their theoretical concerns focused on economic and class conditions (see Chapter 11.3). Thus, when they did discuss crime, that discussion reflected their theoretical priorities. Specifically, Marx and Engels argued that the circumstances of industrial capitalism demoralized the working class, creating immorality and crime. As Engels (1845:130) stated in *The Conditions of the Working Class in England*:

> Immorality is fostered in every possible way by the conditions of working class life. The worker is poor; life has nothing to offer him; he is deprived of virtually all pleasures. Consequently he does not fear the penalties of the law. Why should he leave the rich man in undisturbed possession of his property? Why should he not take at least a part of this property for himself? What reason has the worker for *not* stealing?

Concentrating on the alleged immorality of the working class, Marx and Engels totally ignored crime committed by women. Though it may be true "that Marx and Engels felt working-class women were also demoralized and brutalized by the day-to-day experiences under industrial capitalism," they in fact "ignored their gender specific brutalization and how this may have contributed to female crime" (Messerschmidt, 1988:384). Moreover, most late 19th- and early 20th-century socialist writers on crime in Western Europe similarly ignored gender and women (*ibid.*:386–391).

Not surprisingly, most contemporary radical criminologists have likewise ignored women and crime. For example, Morris (1987:11) points out that in their book *The New Criminology*, Taylor, Walton, and Young

> argue that only the acceptance of Marxist methods can fill the "blank spots" left by other attempts to construct social theories of deviance. They are unaware of their own "blank spot": women. There is not one word on women in their text and, despite a sharp critique of criminology, they do not notice the relevance or applicability to women of the theories reviewed.

As discussed in this chapter, although radical criminologists differ in the way they analyze crime, they tend to share a commitment to understanding crime solely in terms of class. The best-known theoretical works of radical criminology *completely* ignore gender and women, and most textbooks with this perspective barely consider women and crime at all (Messerschmidt, 1986:7–10).

Consequently, all influential criminological theories—whether mainstream or radical—have ignored gender and women. Throughout the history of criminology, however, "the *presence* of women in a very few seriously distorting stereotyping accounts" has occurred (Heidensohn, 1985:153). In a groundbreaking article, Dorie Klein (1973) examined these accounts. Klein began with Cesare Lombroso (see Chapter 10.3), whose work, clearly discredited today, set the stage for future theorizing about women and crime. In *The Female Offender* (1903) (co-authored with his son-in-law, William Ferrero), Lombroso described women as physically and psychologically passive and as cold and calculating immoral creatures. Women have a limited range of mental possibilities, claimed Lombroso, and although normal women are *feminine*, the female offender is *masculine*. As Klein (*ibid.*:10) points out:

> The anomalies of skull, physiognomy and brain capacity of female criminals, according to Lombroso, more closely approximate that of the man, normal or criminal, than they do those of the normal woman; the female offender often has a "virile cranium" and considerable body hair. Masculinity in women is an anomaly itself, rather than a sign of development, however.

Female crime, like male crime, was biologically predisposed and could be recognized by physical characteristics. Prostitutes were the worst of all female criminals—and, not surprisingly, had the most physical stigmata. Like those of other female criminals, the choices of prostitutes were seen by Lombroso as relating only to the *sexual sphere*. Indeed, women "have no place in any other sphere" than the sexual, according to Lombroso, whereas men are not held "sexually accountable" (*ibid.*:8). In other words, Lombroso's early work on the female offender set the tenor for theorizing about women and crime in two ways: women's criminality is the result of their sexuality and women who commit crimes do so because they resemble men and masculinity.

Klein (*ibid.*:7) analyzed later writings on female crime by such notables as W. I. Thomas, Kingsley Davis, and Otto Pollak who, though not exhibiting the extreme biological determinism of Lombroso, to varying degrees

> rely on those sexual ideologies based on *implicit* assumptions about the physiological and psychological nature of women that are *explicit* in Lombroso's work. Reading the work helps to achieve a better understanding of what kinds of myths have been developed for women in general and for female crime and deviance in particular.

The work of Albert Cohen (1955) is another example of the criminological focus on women's sexuality (see Chapter 13.1). For Cohen, middle-class standards of success are necessarily masculine and, therefore, apply only to males. Boys compete with other boys for economic success and are the rational, aggressive achievers in society; girls' only interest is in developing relationships with boys. As Cohen (*ibid.*:147) states:

> For the adolescent girl as well as for the adult woman, relationships with the opposite sex and those personal qualities which affect the ability to establish such relationships are central in importance. Dating, popularity with boys, pulchritude, "charm," clothes and dancing are preoccupations so central and so obvious that it would be useless pedantry to attempt to document them.

In fact, Cohen argues that the position of girls in society is dependent upon the type of relationship they establish with the opposite sex.

Because of such gender distinctions, there exists a gender difference in delinquency. Lower-class boys tend to turn to the gang because, like the cultural middle-class pattern, the gang characteristically is male. Although Cohen acknowledges there are important differences between middle-class behavior patterns and the delinquent gang, they are similar in their masculine emphasis on achievement, aggressiveness, daring, exploit, active mastery, and pursuit (*ibid.*:139). The delinquent gang is thus inappropriate for girls because it is "irrelevant to the vindication of the girl's status as a girl" and threatening because of its "strongly masculine symbolic function" (*ibid.*:144). For girls, according to Cohen, sexual promiscuity is the most common form of delinquency, simply reflecting their desire to develop relationships with males. When girls are unable to develop what society considers to be satisfactory relationships in appropriate ways (dating and marriage), they experience strain, and react by turning to sexual promiscuity as a short-term solution. As Cohen (*ibid.*:145) states, sexual accessibility

> pays the most immediate and certain dividends by way of male attention, male pursuit, male company, and the wasteful public expenditure of the

male's resources on the female—one of the most socially visible and reassuring evidences of success at the job of being a woman.

Thus, sexual delinquency becomes the solution to the problem of establishing relationships with males.

Cohen's thesis can be criticized for perpetuating the myth that women's identity is found only in the sexual sphere. Eileen Leonard (1982:133) points out her concerns in the following way:

> My major dissatisfaction is that Cohen deals with women in such a stereotypical manner. As frequently occurs, he sexualizes female behavior and refuses to examine given assumptions about women. . . . His analysis is severely limited and obviously the product of an implicit acceptance of the status quo; a white, male, classist interpretation of the sexual activities of women and the "dividends" they pay. Cohen's analysis is characterized as "white" because he ignores varying expectations for behavior among minority groups; "male," because he never considers female attitudes or understandings regarding their behavior; and, "classist," because the standards he imposes are not necessarily shared across class lines.

Cohen ignores gender inequality, why women offend less than men do, and when women do offend, how that behavior is related to relationships with men (*ibid.*).

Perhaps we might excuse Cohen for his thesis because it—like the others we have reviewed—doubtless reflected the dominant gender ideology of his time (the 1950s), but those following Cohen have no such excuse. In fact, it seems that Cohen's thesis has been neither improved upon nor corrected entirely by more contemporary criminologists. As Ngaire Naffine (1987:24) found after reviewing the literature testing and employing Cohen's thesis:

> The conceptual flaw in the research into strain since the 1950s entails the almost total failure of criminologists to examine critically Cohen's original assumptions about men and women. The need to do so has been manifest from the earliest tests of strain which have yielded unexpected results. The depiction of the female as fully absorbed in romantic relationships has proven unhelpful: it does not appear to be a credible explanation of the actions of women. And yet criminologists continue to operate substantially from Cohen's premises, regardless.

In addition to sexuality, simplified misrepresentations of women in terms of their alleged masculinization also persist. Although extreme biological determinism has all but disappeared, a softer version of it persists; women are behaving more like men, and this masculinization causes increases in female crime. In the middle to late 1970s, Freda Adler (1975:15) argued that because of the women's movement, women were becoming more masculine, resulting in an increasing number of women using weapons and "wits to establish themselves as full human beings, as capable of violence and aggression as any man." For Adler (1977:101), because of liberation the "'second sex' had risen" by the mid-1970s, and as gender roles consequently merged, women became increasingly aggressive and violent. In short, "as the gap narrows, the more similar" men and women "look and behave" in terms of both legitimate and illegitimate behavior (*ibid.*:111). However, the evidence does not support Adler's claims. Adler ignores the fact that since 1960 female crimes of violence have increased absolutely but not relative to the rate for males. Research shows that this absolute increase can be attributed to the changing attitudes of those who label females criminal—the public, police, judges, and prosecutors—rather than to the consequences of the women's movement (Box and Hale, 1983; Hindelang, 1979; Chesney-Lind, 1978). As Morris (1987:69) points out: "Social changes in the 1960s led not to changes in criminality among women but to changes *in perceptions* of women and of criminality among women." Thus, though female violent behavior has changed very little in recent decades, the response of the public, police, prosecutors, courts, and juries may well have been affected. Rather than liberation causing more females to be violent, the changing position of women in society affects the attitudes of those who label women criminal.

Studies also indicate that rejection of traditional gender roles and adoption of feminist attitudes both reduce the likelihood that females will engage in crime. For example, in a self-report study of female delinquency, Peggy Giordano and Stephen Cernkovich (1979:477) found no "link between liberated attitudes and actual involvement in delinquency." Rather, they found that "the more 'liberated' the response, the less delinquent" (*ibid.*:477). Similarly, a self-report study by Jennifer James and William Thornton (1980) found that an approval of feminism has little effect on involvement in delinquency. This study also revealed that feminist attitudes actually *inhibit* delinquency, even when females report substantial opportunity and social support for delinquency, or when scant parental supervision takes place (*ibid.*:240).

A more recent example of the liberation-causes-crime perspective is the power-control theory of John Hagan, John Simpson, and A. R. Gillis (1987; see also Hagan, 1989). Hagan *et al.* argue that an instrument-object relationship exists between parents and children. Parents are the instruments of control and children are its objects. However, these power relationships vary by class and by gender. In particular, as women increasingly enter the labor market, they gain "new power in the family" (*ibid.*:791). Thus, Hagan *et al.* identify two family structures based on women's participation in the production system. In *patriarchal* families, the husband/father works outside the home in an authority position while the wife/mother works at home. Patriarchal families "socially reproduce daughters who focus their futures around domestic labor and consumption, as contrasted with sons who are prepared for participation in direct production" (*ibid.*:791). In *egalitarian* families, the wife/mother and husband/father both work in authority positions outside the home. These egalitarian families "socially reproduce daughters who are prepared along with sons to join the production sphere" (*ibid.*:792). Hagan *et al.* (*ibid.*:793) argue that daughters in patriarchal families are taught by parents to avoid risk-taking endeavors, while in egalitarian families both daughters and sons are taught to be more open to risk-taking. It is this combination of the instrument-object relationship and risk-taking that affects delinquency. As Hagan *et al.* (*ibid.*:813) conclude with regard to daughters:

> In our most patriarchal families, in which fathers have authority in the workplace and mothers are not employed outside the home, the instrument-object relationship is most acute; daughters are discouraged from taking risks, and sons are more delinquent than daughters. In more egalitarian kinds of families—for example, those in which mothers and fathers both have authority in the workplace—the instrument-object relationship between parents and daughters is reduced, risk preferences of daughters are more like those of sons, and gender differences in delinquency decline, with average levels of delinquency among daughters increasing.

There are several problems with this theory. First, we cannot simply assume that working in an authority position in the labor market translates into power and authority in the home. Though economic independence for women is a first step toward equality, it does not necessarily guarantee a reduction in *gender* power and authority within the home. For example, David Finkelhor and Kristi Yllö (1985) found in their examination of wife rape that approximately 40 percent of their sample were women victimized by their husbands who used only as much force as necessary to coerce their wives into sex. The victims of this particular type of wife rape were, interestingly, much more likely than other wife rape victims to be educated (more went to college) and middle class. Moreover, 50 percent of the victims held business or professional-level jobs (namely, they worked in authority positions) and were "less likely to have been in relationships based on the traditional roles of husband as decision maker and wife as caretaker" (*ibid.*:45). In other words, this evidence suggests that power-control theory has a simplistic notion of egalitarianism, ignoring the independent role that gender power plays even in so-called egalitarian families.

In addition to the preceding, Meda Chesney-Lind (1989:20) recently pointed out that the power-control theory of female delinquency "is essentially a not-too-subtle variation of the earlier 'liberation' hypothesis. Now, mother's liberation causes daughter's crime." In other words, whereas Adler argued women's liberation caused women to act more like men and to commit crimes, the Hagan *et al.* thesis insists that women who defy their traditional familial roles and work outside the home (act more like men) increase the chance their daughters will become delinquent. Chesney-Lind (*ibid.*) shows, however, that even though over the past decade women's labor force participation rate has increased, during the same time the female delinquency rate (as measured by both self-reports and official statistics) has remained quite stable.

These then are just a few examples of the disregard and misrepresentation of gender and women in criminological theory. However, feminists have not been content simply to provide telling criticisms of conventional criminological theory. They have also developed theoretical perspectives that can be used to explain crime. We turn to these now.

Varieties of Feminist Criminology

As stated earlier, there are several feminist perspectives: each looks at gender relationships in a distinct way, asks different kinds of questions, and therefore explains crime differently. Four major feminist perspectives have been outlined in the feminist literature—liberal, Marxist, radical, and socialist (Jaggar, 1983; Jaggar and Rothenberg, 1984; Donovan, 1985). Recognizing that differences clearly exist *within* each feminist perspective, we outline the core characteristics of each and provide certain examples of their respective application to crime.

As Jaggar and Rothenberg (1984:83–84) point out, *liberal feminism* has its roots in the 18th- and 19th-century social ideals of liberty and equality. Liberty came to be understood as freedom from interference by the state, primarily in the private sphere. The ideal of equality required that (*ibid.*:84)

> each individual should be able to rise in society just as far as his or her talents permit, unhindered by restraints of law or custom. What qualities should count as talents and how they should be rewarded is to be determined by the supply and demand for those talents within a market economy. In order to guarantee that the most genuinely talented individuals are identified, it is necessary to ensure that everyone has an equal opportunity to develop his or her talents. Within the liberal tradition, therefore, equality has come to be construed as equality of opportunity.

Formulation of the ideals of liberty and equality created the conditions that motivated women to demand that these ideals be applied to them as well as to men. From Mary Wollstonecraft's (1792) *A Vindication of the Rights of Women* and John Stuart Mill's (1851) *The Subjection of Women* to *Ms.* magazine and the publications of the National Organization for Women (NOW), the roots of women's subordination, for liberal feminists, are imbedded in the denial to women of civil rights and social opportunities. Liberal feminists argue that women should receive the same rights, and have the same opportunities, as men. Women are oppressed because of gender discrimination, which results in deprivation of the same opportunities and rights that men enjoy. Consequently, women are effectively kept outside the mainstream of society (politics, business, finance, medicine, law, and so forth). If women are kept outside the mainstream of society, liberal feminists argue that this problem can be resolved by letting them in. The liberal feminist program calls for state reform to bring about those changes necessary to promote women's rapid integration into the backbone of society (Messerschmidt, 1986:25–26).

One of the reasons for women's discrimination, according to liberal feminists, is gender role socialization. Liberal feminists argue that conventional family patterns structure masculine and feminine identities. Girls and women, on the one hand, are socialized to be patient, understanding, sensitive, passive, dependent, and nurturant. The female role, liberal feminists continue, centers on functions reflecting such personality traits, specifically in the family (women's identity resides in the domestic sphere) but also in the labor market where women take gender-specific jobs—such as clerical, service, and sales-type jobs. Boys and men, on the other hand, are socialized to be self-confident, independent, bold, responsible, competitive, and aggressive. The male role likewise reflects such traits, as a man is encouraged to find an identity in the public sphere (the workplace), thus providing money and security for "his" family. Because the role and traits associated with femininity are defined as inferior, sexist ideologies arise that hold women to be second-class persons. Accordingly, because of the emphasis on both equality and socialization, liberal feminists have called for policies providing women with equal opportunities (such as the Equal Rights Amendment) and androgynous socialization.

A number of criminologists have used liberal feminist theory to explain the relationships among opportunity, socialization, and crime. Rita Simon (1975), for instance, has argued that until the 1970s women's crime was quite limited because women's opportunities were restricted. With the rise of the second wave of the feminist movement in the 1960s and the subsequent liberated woman of the 1970s, women were provided with more opportunities to act like men. This increased equality in the labor market, Simon alleged, resulted in increased opportunities for women to commit occupationally related crimes, such as embezzlement. However, as noted in the assessment of this section, increased women's crime is found primarily in nonoccupationally related crimes, such as larceny (mostly shoplifting) and fraud.

A more sophisticated formulation of liberal feminist opportunity theory is provided by Josephina Figueira-McDonough (1980), who theorizes that similar levels of strain (resulting from high success aspirations and low legitimate opportunities) lead to similar criminal behavior patterns by both genders if they have equal knowledge of and comparable access to illegitimate means.

Liberal feminists also attempt to explain crime in terms of gender role socialization. In the 1970s several liberal feminist writers emphasized the relationship between gender role and crime. For example, Dale Hoffman-Bustamante (1972) explained how patterns of crime are related to the different role expectations of men and women and thus gender differences in socialization patterns. Ann Oakley (1972:68) was more explicit, contending that "the patterns of male and female crime are tied to cultural patterns of masculinity and femininity, so that the type and the amount of crime committed by each sex express both sex-typed personality and sex-typed social role." Oakley (*ibid.*:72) saw crime as specifically masculine, which therefore helps explain women's lower crime rate:

> Criminality and masculinity are linked because the sorts of acts associated with each have much in common. The demonstration of physical strength, a certain kind of aggressiveness, visible and external "proof" of achievement, whether legal or illegal—these are facets of the ideal male

personality and also of much criminal behavior. Both male and criminal are valued by their peers for these qualities. Thus, the dividing line between what is masculine and what is criminal may at times be a thin one.

Oakley (*ibid*.:70) went on to argue that although crime may be a specific manifestation of masculinity and, therefore, predominantly male:

> The sex difference has narrowed considerably in recent years, suggesting that, as some of the differences between the sex roles are reduced by the conditions of modern life, the deviance of male and female becomes more alike.

This point was later emphasized by Adler (1975) in her book *Sisters In Crime*. As noted earlier, Adler argued that because of the women's movement, by the mid-1970s gender roles had so merged that women became more masculine and, thus, engaged in more violent crime.

Specific types of female crime have also been analyzed by liberal feminists in terms of gender roles. For example, Karen Rosenblum (1975:179) argued that important parallels exist between the attributes of the female gender role and prostitution, so that the latter can be interpreted simply as a consequence and extension of fundamental aspects of the former. Women are defined as sex objects—either of lust or chastity—yet are socialized to be passive sexually and also to use sex as a means to status. Consequently:

> The difference between the utilization of and expectations regarding sexuality is only one of degree. The decision to become a call girl simply requires an exaggeration of one aspect of the situation experienced as a nondeviant woman (*ibid*.:180).

Marxist feminists differ considerably from liberal feminists. Marxist feminists theorize, following Engels (1884), that the class and gender divisions of labor together determine the social position of women and men in any society, but the gender division of labor is seen as resulting from the class division of labor. According to Marxist feminists, as private property evolved, males began to dominate all social institutions. Thus, contemporary Marxist feminists view the capitalist mode of production as the basic organizing mechanism of Western societies, which determines the social relations between classes and genders. Gender and class inequalities result from property relations and the capitalist mode of production. For Marxist feminists, masculine dominance is an ideological manifestation of a class society in which women are primarily dominated by capital and only secondarily by men. The latter form of domination, however, results from the mode of production. Although most Marxist feminists examine masculine dominance and sexism in society, they comprehend the roles of men and women in relation to capital, not in relation to a separate system of masculine power and dominance. Women's labor in the home is analyzed not in terms of how it benefits men but, rather, how it provides profits for the capitalist class (Messerschmidt, 1986:10–11).

An excellent illustration of a Marxist feminist approach to crime is the work of Sheila Balkan, Ron Berger, and Janet Schmidt (1980) in their book *Crime and Deviance in America*. Discussing women's crime, Balkan *et al.* argue that a capitalist mode of production "lays the foundation for a theory of women's criminality" (*ibid.*:211). They go on to state that in order to understand female criminality, we must understand the ideology of sexism and how that ideology legitimates the structure of the family under capitalism. By reason of the needs of a capitalist society—in particular the reproduction of labor power—women's social position has been centered in the family, sexuality, and the home (*ibid.*:215). Sexism, they argue, is an ideological result of capitalist relations that structure women's position and women's crime. Consequently, nonviolent crime by women—such as shoplifting and prostitution—reflects such conditions. Moreover, when women commit violent crimes, such as murder, their victims are usually family members, relatives, or lovers. Women are also less likely to use guns and more likely to use such household implements as kitchen knives as weapons. Thus, women's crime reflects their oppressed position in a capitalist economic system.

Similarly, Julia and Herman Schwendinger's (1983) Marxist feminist analysis of rape contends that the level of male violence in any society is determined primarily by class relations and the mode of production. The Schwendingers argue that societies without commodity production are gender egalitarian, women are deemed equal to men in most aspects of social life, and violence against women is almost nonexistent. When such societies begin to produce for exchange (either voluntarily or imposed by colonial power), men control the production system and women are confined to the home. This new division of labor results in an increase in male authority, a decrease in women's social position, and violence against women. Hence, gender inequality and violence against women become closely tied to and rooted in the mode of production. Indeed, the Schwendingers (*ibid.*:179) conclude that exploitative modes of production in class societies either *produce* or *intensify* gender inequality and violence against women.

Marxist feminists emphasize the structural conditions of a class society (more specifically a capitalist society) as the root cause of masculine dominance, women's special oppression, and thus crime; *radical feminists* see masculine power and privilege as the root cause of all social relations and inequality. For radical feminists, the most important relations in any society are found in *patriarchy* (masculine control of the labor power and sexuality of women); all other relations (such as class) are secondary and derive from male-female relations. In addition to the preceding, radical feminists also assert (Jaggar and Rothenberg, 1984:86):

▲— Women were, historically, the first oppressed group.

▲— Women's oppression is the most widespread, existing in virtually every known society.

▲— Women's oppression is the deepest in that it is the hardest form of oppression to eradicate and cannot be removed by other social changes such as the abolition of class society.

Catharine MacKinnon (1982:515), a prominent radical feminist, adds that in contemporary Western societies the control of women's sexuality by men is central to masculine dominance. Sexuality, the primary social sphere of male power, entails the expropriation of women's sexuality by men, and this expropriation structures men and women as social and sexual beings within society. For MacKinnon, power is maintained over women through compulsory heterosexuality and sexual violence (rape, wife beating, incestuous assault, sexual harassment and pornography).

It follows that when discussing crime, radical feminists concentrate on violence against women. Certain segments of radical feminism emphasize biological determinism in their discussion of crime. For example, writing about rape, Susan Brownmiller (1975:16) argues that "by anatomical fiat—the inescapable construction of their genital organs—the human male was a *natural* predator and the human female served as his *natural* prey" (emphasis added). For Brownmiller, and a number of other radical feminists, gender inequality is the result of the anatomical and biological makeup of men and women. Male anatomy and biology provide men with the apparatus to rape women; by the very nature of their anatomy and biology, women "cannot retaliate in kind" (*ibid.*:14). Women's overall subordination and men's criminality—particularly male violence against females—result from these biological facts. As Brownmiller (*ibid.*:13–14) continues:

> Man's structural capacity to rape and women's corresponding vulnerability are as basic to the physiology of both our sexes as the primal act of sex itself. Had it not been for this accident of biology, an accommodation requiring the locking together of two separate parts, penis into vagina, there would be neither copulation nor rape as we know it.

According to Brownmiller, male human anatomy created a male ideology of rape, which became a weapon in the gender struggle for power. Therefore, rape is "a conscious process of intimidation by which *all* men keep all women in a state of fear" (*ibid.*:14) (emphasis added). For some radical feminists then, rape naturally serves the function of controlling women, and rape and violence are biological acts (Messerschmidt, 1986:160).

Many radical feminists disagree with the extreme biological determinism of Brownmiller, arguing instead that women's victimization at the hands of men results from their social position, rather than biology. For example, Elizabeth Stanko (1985) argues in her book *Intimate Intrusions* that because of masculine dominance and female powerlessness, the "normal" male is physically aggressive and the "normal" female experiences this aggression in the form of sexual violence. For Stanko, violence against women seems to be universal across time and place: "To be a woman—in most societies, in most eras—is to experience physical and/or sexual terrorism at the hands of men" (*ibid.*:9). Thus, male violence is a reflection of the universality of male dominance and the secondary status of women. Moreover, following MacKinnon's position on sexuality, Stanko (*ibid.*:73) argues:

Women learn, often at a very early age, that their sexuality is not their own and that maleness can at any point intrude into it. Sexuality, then, is a form of power, and gender, as socially constructed, embodies it, not the reverse. As such, male sexual and physical prowess takes precedence over female sexual and physical autonomy.

As appendages to men, women are "expected to endure or alternatively have been seen as legitimate, deserving targets of male sexual and physical aggression because that is part of what men *are*. Women, as connected to men, are then violated" (*ibid.*:74). Male violence is customary in patriarchal culture; therefore, it is also customary that women endure it. Thus, this ideology helps maintain male dominance and control over women. As Stanko (*ibid.*:75) concludes: "Forced sexuality for women is 'paradigmatic' of their existence within a social sphere of male power."

In short, radical feminists view the basic structure of social reality as a total system of male domination. This form of domination is constructed by men, enables men to control women's bodies, and thereby trap women as forced sexual slaves (Jaggar, 1983:270).

Finally, *socialist feminism* differs from both Marxist and radical feminism: it prioritizes neither class nor gender. Socialist feminists view both class and gender relations as interacting and co-reproducing each other in society. For socialist feminists, class and gender interact to determine the social organization of society at any particular time in history. To understand class, socialist feminists argue we must recognize how it is structured by gender; conversely, to understand gender requires an examination of how it is structured by class. Consequently, our overall life experiences are shaped by both class and gender relations, and the interaction of these relationships structures crime in society.

An example of a socialist feminist explanation of crime is James Messerschmidt's (1986) book *Capitalism, Patriarchy, and Crime*. Messerschmidt argues that the U.S. is a patriarchal capitalist society, and that the interaction of patriarchy and capitalism patterns the types and seriousness of crime. This interaction creates a powerless group of women and the working and lower classes, and a powerful group of men and the professional-managerial (traditional middle class) and capitalist classes. For Messerschmidt (*ibid.*:42), *power* constituted by *both* gender *and* class is critical to understanding crime:

> It is the powerful (in both the gender and class spheres) who do most of the damage to society, not, as is commonly supposed, the disadvantaged, poor, and subordinate. The interaction of gender and class creates positions of power and powerlessness in the gender/class hierarchy, resulting in different types and degrees of criminality and varying opportunities for engaging in them. Just as the powerful have more legitimate opportunities, so they have more illegitimate opportunities.

Given that men and members of the professional-managerial and capitalist classes have the most power, they have greater opportunities to engage in crime not only more often but also in ways that are more harmful to society. Males of all social classes therefore commit more crime than females, their class position determining the type of crime they may commit (for example, lower- and working-class males have no opportunity to commit corporate crimes, whereas professional- and managerial-class males have no need to resort to conventional crimes). Low female crime rates are understood by Messerschmidt to be related to women's powerless position in the U.S. Their subordinate position relegates women to fewer legitimate as well as fewer illegitimate opportunities, and to fewer resources than men with which to engage in serious forms of crime. Thus, overall, socialist feminists argue that crime is related to the opportunities a gender/class position allows, and they attempt a simultaneous explanation of the gender *and* class patterns of crime.

Feminist Perspectives on Social Control

Feminist scholarship has shown that the *social control* of women occurs in both public and private realms. This control has both ideological and repressive forms. It includes their primary socialization within the family and secondary socialization within, for instance, peer groups, the educational system, and the media. Secondary socialization reinforces ways of acting, thinking, and feeling that are "characteristic" of the female role, of femininity, and of womanhood (Smart and Smart, 1978:2). Much more formal processes of social control occur "through legislation by the State, the implementation of the law, the penal system and the criminal process" (*ibid.*:2). It is to these formal processes—especially the penal system and the criminal process—that feminist criminologists attach the greatest importance (Price and Sokoloff, 1982; Rafter and Stanko, 1982).

A number of feminist scholars have examined discrimination in arrest and criminal processing. They find that young women are far more likely than are young men to be arrested and processed for "status offenses" (behavior that, if engaged in by an adult, would not be considered criminal), such as running away, incorrigibility, and promiscuity (Smart, 1976; Chesney-Lind, 1978; Shacklady-Smith, 1978). Moreover, even though the overwhelming majority of young women are charged with status offenses (rather than criminal offenses), young women are much more likely than are young men to be detained by the state and to be held for longer periods (Messerschmidt, 1987:243). The reason for this discrimination seems to be a gender double standard. As Mary Eaton (1986:25) concludes after a careful review of British and North American literature on juvenile justice processing:

> Adolescent girls who come before the court are more likely than their male counterparts to be questioned about their sexual activity, more likely to have their offenses viewed as an aspect of sexual promiscuity, and more likely to lose their liberty for activities which would not be against the law if committed by an adult.

In other words, feminists argue that the state plays a significant role in the social control of female sexuality.

This state form of social control is not of recent origin. For example, Messerschmidt (1987) shows that during the final quarter of the 19th century, several feminist groups (in the first wave of the feminist movement) were involved in an organized campaign against legalized prostitution. Eventually, the groups joined forces with the conservative social purity movement in an effort to abolish prostitution. This coalition of feminists and conservatives succeeded in raising the age of sexual consent (from as low as 10, in some states, to 18) for the purpose of "protecting" young women from prostitution. Nevertheless, by the early part of the 20th century, when many female adolescents were in open rebellion against rigid Victorian sexual standards, age-of-consent laws had the effect of creating a new youthful offender, the female sex delinquent. Females, as opposed to males, were much more likely to be brought before the court for their real or alleged sexuality. And "immorality" (defined as admitting to or caught in the act of sexual intercourse, or showing through behavior that one had had intercourse in the past or most likely would in the future) came to be the most frequent offense for which young women were sentenced to reformatories.

In addition to identifying the relationship between criminal processing and social control of female sexuality, feminist criminologists also challenge the chivalry theory of Otto Pollak (1961), who argued that women receive preferential treatment from males in the criminal justice system. Studies comparing male and female offenders reveal that women do not receive special treatment because of gender, that women who commit "masculine" crimes tend to receive harsher punitive treatment than other women offenders, and that married female offenders (and those who are economically dependent on a man) receive less harsh punitive treatment than other women (Chesney-Lind, 1978; Kruttschnitt, 1982; Nagel, 1981). Thus, the preferential treatment is not women over men, but traditional women over nontraditional women. This research shows how the judicial system punishes women who deviate from their predetermined roles.

Feminist scholars have also examined how gender inequality is reinforced through judicial processing. Mary Eaton's (1986) *Justice for Women? Family, Court and Social Control* illustrates this point. Eaton shows how the traditional nuclear family model—husband full time in the labor market, wife full time at home—dominates discourse within the court system. Eaton found that women tend to be viewed by the court system in precisely the same way as other institutions—such as the school system, the workplace, and the mass media—envisage them: subordinate family members who are chiefly home-centered. Courts of law use and endorse this model, thereby contributing to reproduction of gender inequality and inferior perception of women.

Eaton's work is important because it demonstrates that reproduction of the subordinate status of women is found not only in sentencing, but also in the routine bureaucratic processes of the courts themselves. Focusing on the social interactions of courtroom judges, lawyers, probation officers, and defendants, Eaton reports that by showing they have acted "appropriately" as members of

Conditions in women's prisons today are poor, and rehabilitation programs show little or no imagination.

a traditional nuclear family, men and women defendants evidence responsibility, respectability, and a noncriminal identity, thereby receiving preferential treatment. By reinforcing the traditional nuclear family model, courts simultaneously encourage and sustain the subordinate status of women. As Eaton (*ibid.*:56) further points out, this effect does not require discrimination:

> Indeed, the use of the same model of the family in pleas for *both* men *and* women enhances the effectiveness of familial ideology. In its very *lack* of discrimination this familiar rhetoric reinforces the subordination of women.

Feminist criminologists have also examined the history of women's prisons. For example, Nicole Hahn Rafter's (1985) *Partial Justice: Women in State Prisons, 1800–1935* analyzes the origin and development of women's prisons and reformatories. Rafter shows how these two different types of institutions developed over time. Prior to the late 1800s, custodial female prisons, as a part of male prisons, were the prevalent form of institutionalizing female offenders. Run by men, these prisons employed male guards only, they provided inferior care compared to the care provided males, and the female inmates were often victims of physical and sexual violence. In the late 1800s, the Womens Prison Movement—consisting of some of the same women involved in the antiprostitution campaign—began to demand reforms for women that, they argued, would better suit their "needs." These demands led to female reformatories administered by women and organized on a traditional nuclear family model, in which women inmates were treated as children and trained in the virtuousness and incorruptibility of domestic labor. Although these institutions removed male sexual violence and abusive male control, often the women were incarcerated for longer periods than in prisons, and for crimes—such as "immorality"—that did not apply to men. Coupled with strict control and resolute discipline, women's reformatories, Rafter argues, were no less oppressive than prisons. The result, however, was a mechanism that enhanced the social control of women and reproduced their subordinate status.

Reformatories for women were discontinued after the mid-1930s, but the oppressive conditions inside female prisons remained. Rafter and others (see Chesney-Lind, 1986:93–95 for a review) show that women's prisons today are inferior in comparison to men's (in terms of rehabilitation programs, for example) and that women continue to be trained for such domestic and "feminine" labor as secretarial work and hairstyling.

Assessment

Feminist criminology, though relatively new, has made significant contributions to the field of criminology and will continue to flourish in the future. Its criticisms of the gender bias in criminological theory are of major importance, and must be taken seriously. Moreover, developments in feminist theory and work on gender and social control add new dimensions to the subject. Unfortunately, as Daly and Chesney-Lind (1988:102) point out: "The field remains essentially untouched" by such developments and, therefore, the "time has come for criminologists to step into the world of feminist thought and for feminist scholars to move more boldly into all areas of criminology." We wholeheartedly support this view.

Given that feminist criminology is a very recent phenomenon, it has not been the subject of much commentary. Most concerns, when raised, have centered on the feminist theories used to explain crime. For example, liberal feminism has been criticized for its inability to

> explain the emergence of gender inequality, nor can it account, other than by analogy, for effects of race and class stratification on the conditions of women's lives. Its analysis for change tends to be limited to issues of equal opportunity and individual choice (Andersen, 1988:318).

Moreover, liberal feminist positions on crime have been criticized as well. For instance, Rita Simon's position that the women's movement has increased women's opportunities in the labor market and that this explains their increasing involvement in property crimes ignores the fact that the sharpest increases in property crimes are found in *nonoccupational* theft, such as larceny (mostly shoplifting) and minor fraud (such as check and welfare fraud) (Steffensmeier,

1981). Moreover, most female property offenders are adolescents with little or no contact with the labor market (Miller, 1983:60).

The liberal feminist emphasis on gender role socialization has also been criticized. Smart (1976:69) has argued that liberal feminism fails to place the discussion of gender roles "within a structural explanation of the social origin of those roles." In other words, liberal feminists do not account historically, socially, and economically for women's subordinate position in the gender division of labor and, therefore, do not explain the broader reasons for the current patterns of socialization. Smart also criticizes role theory for not discussing female motivation or intent. As she (*ibid.*:69) points out: "Role theory does not explain why, even though women are socialized into primarily conforming patterns of behavior, a considerable number engage in crime."

Both Marxist feminism and radical feminism have been criticized for being reductionist. Marxist feminists have been faulted for reducing all social phenomena—including male *and* female crime—to economic conditions, and for being unable to explain gender divisions and power relations between men and women. Radical feminist theory has been criticized for its view that social classes are simply an epiphenomenon of gender inequality. Moreover, a major problem with radical feminist theory is that it assumes universal female subordination. Yet anthropological research shows that in many gathering and hunting societies gender relations were quite equal, and men did not control the labor power and sexuality of women (Reiter, 1975; Shostak, 1983). Radical feminists have also been criticized for explaining male violence against women in biological terms or as simply a reflection of masculine power and dominance. Finally, the term *patriarchy*, which both radical and socialist feminists use to label masculine dominance, has been criticized for its timeless characterization of masculine power and prestige. In other words, neither radical nor socialist feminists have adequately accounted for historical changes in, and the various forms of, patriarchy.

REVIEW

This chapter outlined two important contemporary perspectives on crime: radical criminology and feminist criminology.

Radical Criminology

1. Although Marx and Engels devoted little time to the analysis of crime, several European socialist writers—such as Wilhelm Adriaan Bonger—of the late 19th and early 20th centuries did, attempting to apply Marxist theory to an understanding of crime.

2. It was not until the 1970s that a *radical criminology* emerged in the United States.

3. Since the 1970s, radical criminology has developed a more theoretically coherent political-economic approach to crime.

4. This political-economic approach employs Marxist theory to understand (a) why some behavior is criminalized and other behavior is not and (b) how a capitalist economic system generates class patterns of crime.

5. Some radical criminologists have developed a *left realist* approach to crime. They attempt to fashion empirical investigations of conventional crime, argue that crime control must be taken seriously, and have developed a *radical law-and-order* program for curbing conventional crime.

6. The newest attempts at radical theorizing are peacemaking and constitutive criminology.

7. Radical criminology has also compiled a revised history of social control, identifying two major transformations in Western penal policies: the first took place between the end of the 18th century and the middle of the 19th century; the second, which is controversial and currently being debated, allegedly occurred from the mid-1960s onward.

Feminist Criminology

1. Feminist criminologists have provided important criticisms of criminological theory.

2. Feminists have demonstrated that in attempting to offer a general explanation of crime, criminological theory has either ignored gender and female crime or misrepresented women when female crime is examined.

3. Feminists have developed four major perspectives—liberal, Marxist, radical, and socialist—that have been used to explain crime.

4. Each feminist perspective looks at gender relationships in distinct ways, asks different questions, and explains crime differently.

5. Feminist scholarship has shown that social control of women occurs in numerous ways.

6. Feminist criminologists have concentrated on the criminal process and penal system as aspects of this social control.

QUESTIONS FOR CLASS DISCUSSION

1. How does the political-economic approach to crime compare with some of the other theories discussed in this book?

2. Are left realists correct to argue that radical criminologists have ignored conventional crime? Discuss.

3. Choose several crimes—such as corporate and syndicated crime—and explain how each feminist perspective would explain them.

RECOMMENDED READINGS

Carlen, Pat (1988). *Women, Crime and Poverty*. Philadelphia: Open University Press. This book provides a discussion of the class and gender conditions affecting women's crime in England today.

Cohen, Stanley (1985). *Visions of Social Control*. Cambridge: Polity Press. One of the most important criminology books of the decade because of its comprehensive analysis of the so-called "second transformation" in Western penal policies.

Daly, Kathleen and Meda Chesney-Lind (1988). "Feminism and Criminology." *Justice Quarterly* 5(4):101–143. This article sketches the major elements of feminist thought and shows the relevance and importance of feminism for criminology.

Gelsthorpe, Loraine and Allison Morris (eds) (1990). *Feminist Perspectives in Criminology*. Philadelphia: Open University Press. A book of readings on differing feminist perspectives in criminology.

Klein, Dorie (1973). "The Etiology of Female Crime: A Review of the Literature." *Issues in Criminology* 8:3–30. The definitive examination of criminological accounts of women and crime by male scholars.

Lea, John and Jock Young (1984). *What Is to Be Done About Law and Order?* New York: Penguin. This book contains the major arguments advanced by left realists.

Messerschmidt, James (1986). *Capitalism, Patriarchy, and Crime: Toward a Socialist Feminist Criminology*. Totowa, NJ: Rowman and Littlefield. A socialist feminist view of crime, and what to do about it.

Michalowski, Raymond (1985). *Order, Law and Crime*. New York: Random House. A first-rate political economic analysis of crime and criminalization.

Rafter, Nicole Hahn (1985). *Partial Justice: Women in State Prisons, 1800–1935*. Boston: Northeastern University Press. The best book on the history of women's prisons in the United States.

Schwendinger, Julia and Herman Schwendinger (1983). *Rape and Inequality*. Beverly Hills, CA: Sage. An example of how Marxist feminists analyze one particular crime, rape.

Stanko, Elizabeth (1985). *Intimate Intrusions: Women's Experience of Male Violence*. Boston: Routledge & Kegan Paul. This book provides a radical feminist analysis of male violence against women.

CHAPTER 16

COMPARATIVE CRIMINOLOGY

Preview

Chapter 16 introduces:

    ☞ the importance of comparative criminology to the understanding
    of crime in the United States.
    ☞ recent developments in comparative criminology, its key concepts,
    and sources of data.

☞ the difficult conceptual problems facing comparative criminology, especially methodological and epistemological issues.

☞ cross-national generalizations about crime and crime rates.

☞ the punitive nature of criminal justice in the United States when viewed in comparative perspective.

Key Terms

epistemological relativism   modernization thesis
ethnocentrism   systematic comparative
methodological relativism   criminology

Much of the information in this book has been illustrated through historical and comparative studies. We are now concerned, however, in a more rigorous and explicit way, with comparing crime rates and penal policies of the U.S. with those of other countries. In this final chapter we introduce certain major findings of recent comparative studies of crime.

16.1 ———— COMPARATIVE CRIMINOLOGY: AN INTRODUCTION

Only rarely do textbooks explicitly stress the importance of *comparative* criminology; yet at least two reasons dictate its importance. First, since the 1930s the vast majority of theories regarding the causes of crime have been fashioned in the cultural context of U.S. society. Few such theories have been tested against the criminological evidence of other countries. In exactly the same way that scientific theories must be scrutinized under as diverse conditions as possible, so too must theories regarding the causes of crime. Undertaken in a sensitive manner, comparative analysis can remedy what sociologists term criminological *ethnocentrism*, namely, the view that criminological concepts and generalizations about a particular society necessarily apply to crime in all other parts of the globe. Second, to understand why penal policies in the United States have continually failed to control crime, we must learn from the experience of countries with more successful policies. One reason why the U.S. has experienced such high crime rates is that, in attempting to apply penal policies to crime, policymakers have relied on limited parochial theories regarding the causes of crime.

We begin by noting certain official crime data regarding cross-national rates of violence. According to 1992 United Nations data, the U.S. clearly has the

TABLE 16-1 Rates of Homicide and Injury Purposely Inflicted by Other Persons, 1986–1990 (per 100,000 population by country)

COUNTRY	RATE	YEAR
Colombia	49.0	1986
El Salvador	40.4	1984
Mexico	19.9	1986
U.S.A.	8.9	1988
Costa Rica	4.0	1988
Finland	3.2	1989
Australia	2.4	1988
Canada	2.1	1989
Italy	1.9	1988
New Zealand	1.8	1988
Scotland	1.7	1990
Sweden	1.5	1989
France	1.1	1989
The Netherlands	1.0	1989
West Germany	1.0	1990
Ireland	0.6	1989
Japan	0.6	1990
England and Wales	0.5	1990

Source: United Nations, 1992, pp. 438–459.

highest rate of violent crime among industrialized nations. From the data in Table 16-1 we see, in comparative terms, the extent of homicide and serious personal injury in the U.S. Among developed countries the chance of being murdered, or suffering some other serious injury, is 4.2 times greater in the U.S. than in Canada, 3.7 times greater than in Australia, 6.0 times greater than in Sweden, 8.9 times greater than in the Netherlands, and 15 times greater than in Ireland, Japan, and England and Wales. These differences are astonishing. Statistical data for property crimes are similarly alarming. Police-generated data tell us that the chance of having property stolen in the U.S. is 17 times greater than in France, 9 times greater than in Australia, more than 3 times greater than in Italy or Ireland, and 20 percent greater than in England and Wales (Archer and Gartner, 1984).

These figures force us to raise a number of difficult questions. Is there actually more crime in the U.S. than in other countries? If indeed there is more crime in the U.S. than in other countries, why is this so? How do we draw valid comparisons between crime rates in the U.S. and those in other parts of the world? Such questions have no simple answers. We learned in Chapter 2 how difficult it is to measure crime rates in the U.S.; we will learn here that it is even more difficult to make reliable comparisons between U.S. crime rates and those elsewhere. Toward the end of the chapter we shall appreciate the value of comparative criminology in understanding the apparent failure of penal policies in the U.S. We begin with a brief sketch of the development of comparative criminology, its key concepts, and chief sources of data.

16.2 _____ CONCEPTS AND DATA IN COMPARATIVE CRIMINOLOGY

Although comparative criminology has a long and checkered history, as a disciplined and rigorous study it is of very recent origin. In this section we outline the development of a specific type of comparative criminology, the goal of which is to establish cross-cultural generalizations regarding crime. This approach we term *systematic comparative criminology*, which means *the systematic comparison of crime in two or more cultures using the same set of criteria*. As we shall see, behind this simple definition lurk some difficult issues.

The Development of Systematic Comparative Criminology

As far back as the late 18th century, many Enlightenment writers were eager to discuss aspects of crime and criminal law in cultures other than their own, including philosophers Montesquieu and Hegel, and economists Jeremy Bentham and Adam Smith. Yet no Enlightenment figures pursued the comparative study of crime in a rigorous and systematic way. Instead, Enlightenment discussions of crime in different cultures were usually intended to illustrate, and were therefore secondary to, traditional inquiries in jurisprudence, theology, social philosophy, and even prison architecture. This inadequacy also extended to the writings of certain 19th-century theorists discussed earlier (see Chapters 10 and 11), such as Quetelet, Lombroso, Engels, Ferri, and Tarde, and to the flourishing schools of British and U.S. anthropology of the 1930s and 1940s.

Little research was conducted in comparative criminology even as recently as the 1950s and 1960s. Between 1950 and 1963, few journal articles addressed the broad area of conformity and deviance, and only a minority of this fraction systematically compared the phenomena of crime in two or more cultures (Marsh, 1967:449–453). In their investigations of crime, criminologists of this era rarely ventured far from home and, when they did, tended to do so in the accessible countries of Western Europe. When attention did turn to non-Western cultures, it was highly selective in focus and limited to India, China, Japan, Israel, South Africa, and the U.S.S.R. (Miracle, 1981).

It is instructive to consider the major comparative texts of the 1960s. Hermann Mannheim's (1965) *Comparative Criminology*, for example, referred extensively to various cultures around the world, but nowhere did it undertake a systematic comparative criminology. Criminologists often regard Wolfgang and Ferracuti's (1967) *The Subculture of Violence* as a comparative text, yet only three of its 400 pages contain the systematic comparison of two or more cultures, and another nine pages are insular descriptions of aggressive subcultures in seven countries. Similarly, Cavan and Cavan's (1968) *Delinquency and Crime: Cross-Cultural Perspectives* contains isolated case studies of 14 societies. All three books, therefore, primarily comprise studies of cultures in isolation. But single-culture studies ("We do it this way, they do it that way.") do not provide the foundation for an adequate comparative criminology.

Comparative criminology must be clearly distinguished from the simple extension of the concepts of any given national criminology to other cultures. The protocols of disciplined, cross-cultural study differ from those of the intra-cultural analysis of our own society. Although the tradition of *single-culture* studies continues (Ferracuti and Wolfgang, 1983; Johnson, 1983; Hartjen and Priyadarsini, 1984), some of the gaps and cultural biases are disappearing. In the last few years, cross-cultural studies have begun to supply an important perspective to criminology in the U.S. This progress is evident in the increasing number of books that explicitly compare crime in two or more cultures (Black, 1976; Gurr, Grabosky, and Hula, 1977; Clinard, 1978; Holyst, 1979; Newman, 1980; Shelley, 1981, 1981a; Sumner, 1982; Adler, 1983; Johnson and Barak-Glantz, 1983; Archer and Gartner, 1984; Los, 1988). In addition, certain researchers have begun to identify the extent of transnational crimes—crimes committed by one country against another or by transnational corporations against Third World countries in particular (see Chapter 7.2 and Sumner, 1982a; Cohen, 1983; Messerschmidt, 1986; Michalowski and Kramer, 1987).

We now attempt to organize certain of the guiding principles on which many of the foregoing studies have been based. How should comparative criminology proceed? What crimes can be compared cross-culturally? How should comparative generalizations regarding crime be tested?

Constructing Cross-National Generalizations about Crime

Recent studies provide only broad procedural guidelines for constructing comparative generalizations regarding crime. Clinard and Abbott (1973:2) offered this procedural advice:

> The goal of a comparative criminology should be to develop concepts and generalizations at a level that distinguishes between universals applicable to all societies and unique characteristics representative of one or a small set of societies. . . . Research should proceed . . . first in a single culture at one point in time . . . second in societies generally alike . . . and third in completely dissimilar societies.

In other words, comparative criminology must proceed in three stages. Any generalization must be tested (1) in one culture at a single point in time, (2) across two cultures that share some common sociological features—such as a similar level of technological development or a common type of political culture, and (3) across cultures that are completely dissimilar. Because this advice follows the course often used for testing generalizations in the natural sciences, it has much to recommend it. Clearly it is easier to generalize about the United States and England, for example, than about the United States and Japan.

But the third stage of testing is very difficult to conduct. What criteria allow us to identify cultures that are completely dissimilar? Such criteria are increasingly rare in the modern world, whose outermost reaches have been penetrated by the routine operations of transnational corporations and the common culture of commercialism. Even with such criteria, the third level of verification is unlikely to occur: a society sufficiently different to offer meaningful counterexamples normally has no examples of the original phenomenon (MacIntyre, 1971:266). Without such examples, it follows that we cannot hope to find counterexamples.

Assume that what Clinard and Abbott actually meant was not cultures completely dissimilar, but cultures as different as possible. What sociological properties would such cultures have? No doubt these properties would include major differences in religious or scientific beliefs, economic systems, political structures, and the degree of technological development. The greater the difference between any two cultures along such axes, one presumes, the more entitled we are to term them "dissimilar." But this is not without difficulty. The more two cultures differ, the less likely it is that they have common items to compare, and the less likely it is that verifiable generalizations can be made about them. This difficulty is precisely why DeFleur (1969)—finding great structural differences between the lower social strata of Cordoba (Argentina) and U.S. cities—was forced to reject the comparative explanatory power of Cohen's (1955) concept of reaction formation when applied to juvenile delinquency (see Chapter 13.1). This is also the reason why we reject a study (cited in Robertson and Taylor, 1973:38) that attempted to apply the findings of urban overcrowding theory in the U.S. to delinquency rates in Calcutta (India). A disquieting factor here—one never part of any theory deduced from U.S. data—is that not only are the houses in Calcutta overcrowded with residents, the pavements are also. Accordingly, Lois DeFleur (1969:38–39) sensibly warns that in the absence of

> accumulated research findings on cities such as Cordoba, their characteristics as social systems cannot be adequately understood in some convenient *a priori* sense. . . . The immediate task before us is to develop specific theories which are both consistent with and relevant to particular sociocultural systems.

Given the dearth of empirical comparative studies of crime, DeFleur's warning means there are as yet no verifiable generalizations that can be made about cultures whose social structures are very different from one another.[1] Comparisons between very similar countries are all that seems legitimate at the moment. We now outline the cross-national data available for this task.

---

[1] There must be a minimum of five formal rules for the construction of cross-cultural generalizations regarding crime (Beirne, 1983:34–35):

1. Crime in different cultures can be compared only if the definition and meaning of criminal behavior in these cultures is the same.
2. An event p (e.g., urbanization) is not the cause of rising crime rates if it occurs when rising crime rates do not occur.
3. p is not the cause of rising crime rates if p does not occur when rising crime rates do occur.
4. p is not necessarily the cause of rising crime rates if one or more other variables (a, or a, b . . . n) are present in the same circumstances as p.
5. For the generalization "p causes rising crime rates" to be intelligible, it must be explained by a theory.

Cross-National Crime Data

One of the greatest obstacles to comparative criminology is the lack of reliable cross-national data. Most existing data ignore national differences in the legal definitions of crime as well as the variety of ways in which crimes are reported by the public and accepted and recorded by the police. These problems plague the data of Interpol, the World Health Organization, the World Crime Survey, and Amnesty International. Accordingly, much of these data are inadequate for rigorous comparisons.

Scholars acknowledge that the best available data are provided by the United Nations, and by Archer and Gartner (1984) in their *Comparative Crime Data File*. We examine each in turn.

United Nations   The United Nations has collected and analyzed comparative statistical data on crime since 1946. Although the UN's original concern was limited to a rather simplistic notion of the prevention of crime and the treatment of offenders, it now adopts a much broader policy toward crime. This larger view is clearly stated in *Article 55* of the *United Nations Charter* (United Nations, 1983:iii):

> With a view to the creation of conditions of stability and well-being which are necessary for peaceful and friendly relations among nations based on respect for the principle of equal rights and self-determination of peoples, the United Nations shall promote:
> (a) higher standards of living, full employment, and conditions of economic and social progress and development;
> (b) solutions of international economic, social, health, and related problems; and international cultural and educational cooperation; and
> (c) universal respect for, and observance of, human rights and fundamental freedoms for all without distinction as to race, sex, language or religion.

This extension of UN scope to include human rights largely resulted from the exposure of Nazi atrocities at the end of World War II. The perspective was first extended to war crimes and genocide, and then to widespread use of cruel, inhumane, or degrading treatment of political dissidents. It now includes violation of human rights, political and economic abuses of colonial and institutional terrorism, and crime resulting from abuses of economic and political power by transnational enterprises (López-Rey, 1985:6). The complex organizational machinery of UN criminal policy (based in Geneva, Vienna, and New York City) includes the General Assembly, the Secretariat, the International Court of Justice, the Committee on Crime Prevention and Control, the Commission for Social Development, and various specialist bodies such as the Crime Prevention and Criminal Justice Branch, the Commission of Human Rights, and the Fund for Drug Abuse Control.

The UN has wrestled often with the need to provide adequate sets of international criminal statistics, but has never succeeded. It has tried to collect and disseminate data in two ways. First, since 1955, UN congresses on crime prevention—during which researchers report on crime in their own countries—have been held every five years. Some of these reports appear in the UN publication *Crime Prevention and Criminal Justice*, and include such diverse topics as human rights, capital punishment, and torture; prison labor, aftercare, parole, and recidivism; economic development, crime, and colonialism; juvenile delinquency; and ethical standards in criminal justice.

Many UN reports contain data on crime rates, but few provide useful data for comparative criminology: the vast majority concern data in only one country. Strictly, then, they are not even comparative in nature. Second, the UN publishes in its annual *Demographic Yearbook* a limited amount of data concerning rates of homicide and personal injury in selected countries. These data almost entirely omit African and Asian countries, whose inhabitants represent two-thirds of the world's population. Moreover, the *Yearbook*'s homicide data are calculated from each country's unique system of national crime statistics, each of which defines homicide differently. The *Yearbook*'s homicide rates are thus of dubious value for comparative criminology.

It is difficult to understand why the UN has not managed to do a better job concerning data collection on crime. Because crime data are politically sensitive materials, perhaps the UN is reluctant to publish them for fear of embarrassing some of its members. Whatever the reason for their inadequacies, we agree with a Chair of the UN Committee on Crime Prevention and Control that UN data do not permit one to estimate, comparatively, the extent of crime (López-Rey, 1985:131; but see Kalish, 1988).

Comparative Crime Data File   The most ambitious set of data is provided by Dane Archer and Rosemary Gartner's (1984:171–328) *Comparative Crime Data File (CCDF)*. The *CCDF* appears to offer several advantages over UN data. Most impressively, the *CCDF* is as comprehensive in its scope as is currently possible. After lengthy correspondence with national and metropolitan governments throughout the world, and after a search of existing statistical documents of many national and international agencies, Archer and Gartner managed to obtain crime data on 110 countries and 44 large cities. The *CCDF* also:

▲— lists both the raw number of offenses and the offense rate (per 100,000) for murder, manslaughter, homicide, rape, assault, robbery, and theft. It tabulates the data under the legal labels with which they arrive, adding explanatory footnotes where appropriate

▲— lists categories for offenses known and convictions

▲— combines multiple definitions of the same event into a single entry (such as murder)

In preparing the *CCDF*, the authors (*ibid.*:22–28) sensitively identified several key methodological problems in translating national crime data into a comprehensive international data set. Because these problems apply to any attempt to construct comparable transnational crime data, they are worth summarizing:

▲— Different countries record offenses in different ways. For example, some countries use a single national item termed "murder and manslaughter," whereas others distinguish between them. The *CCDF* tabulates the data under the label with which it arrives, with explanatory footnotes when appropriate.

▲— Some homicide data are based on offenses known to the police, others on convictions. The *CCDF* lists both categories.

▲— Some countries' definitions of homicide are unique (such as Scotland: culpable homicide).

▲— Some countries' definitions of homicide have several subdivisions (for example, France: *meurtre*, *assassinat*, *parricide*, and *empoisonnement*). The *CCDF* combines these into a single entry (murder).

▲— For certain countries with small populations (such as New Zealand, where homicides from 1946–1947 increased from two to four), a modest change in the number of offenses produces a dramatic change in the crime rate. The *CCDF* usefully lists both the raw number of offenses and the offense rate.

▲— The size of a country's population cannot always be estimated accurately, especially if censuses are undertaken only every 10 years and with varying degrees of thoroughness.

▲— Methods for measuring crime rates sometimes change. Until 1926, for example, Finland based its crime statistics on convictions; after 1927 it changed its base to offenses known to the police.

▲— Political events can create problems with longitudinal analyses of crime rates. It is almost impossible to study "Germany's" changing crime rates from 1900 to the present, for example, because in 1946 Germany was divided into the Federal Republic of Germany and the German Democratic Republic. Prior to the political reunification of Germany in 1989–1990, each country had its own legal system with wide variations in definitions of crimes.

▲— There is variation in the quality of crime data collected and published by different countries. Certain countries, such as those in central Africa, do not even collect crime statistics. Other countries, such as the former Soviet Union, did not freely publish their crime statistics because they had been regarded as classified data.

Victimization Surveys

As discussed in Chapter 2.1, victimization surveys offer a more reliable indicator of crime trends in the U.S. than do police-based statistics such as the *Uniform*

Crime Reports (*UCR*). Besides the *National Crime Victimization Survey* in the United States (see Chapter 2.1), national victimization surveys also have been conducted in Canada, Holland, West Germany, Britain, Ireland, and Switzerland. At first glance, the growth of these surveys offers a good source of information on comparative crime trends. Common sense tells us that if victims of crime are more willing to report their victimization to survey interviewers than to police officers, then victimization surveys reveal more about the incidence of crime than do police statistics.

Yet, victimization surveys have their own peculiar methodological limitations that complicate their use in comparative analysis. Most surveys outside the U.S., for example, have been very small. Are these small samples as representative of the levels of victimization of their national populations as the large samples in the U.S. *National Crime Victimization Survey*? In some countries (such as the U.S.), victimization rates are calculated with households as the data base; in other countries (for instance, Holland), rates are based on *per-capita* victimizations. This difference casts some doubt on the validity of comparative studies of victimization. Because household size tends to decline with affluence, different data bases tend to obscure differences in the opportunity for crime that arise from variations in population size and household composition (for burglary see Breen and Rottman, 1985:56–57). Further problems arise from the wording of survey questions—these reflect legal definitions of crime, which vary from one country to another. Thus, in their analysis of U.S., Irish, and Dutch victimization surveys, Breen and Rottman (1985:67) concluded that comparisons based on U.S. and Irish surveys were accurate only for burglary and vehicle thefts, and that comparisons based on Dutch surveys were even more approximate in nature.

Some of these problems appear to have been overcome in the *1992 International Crime Survey* (Van Dijk and Mayhew, 1993; and see Beirne and Perry, 1994). The *1992 International Crime Survey* (*ICS*) expands upon the efforts of an earlier *ICS* survey conducted in 1989. The 1992 *ICS* combines the findings of both surveys, reporting the results from 20 countries. Eight of these countries took part in both sweeps (Australia, Belgium, Canada, England/Wales, Finland, the Netherlands, the United States, and Japan); another seven in 1989 (West Germany, France, Northern Ireland, Norway, Scotland, Spain, and Switzerland); and another five in 1992 (Italy, New Zealand, Sweden, Czechoslovakia [now the Czech Republic and the Slovak Republic] and Poland).[1]

Though there is little new in the format and methodology of the survey itself, the *ICS* is unique in its consistent attempt to apply standardized questionnaires, sampling methods, and data analyses to a large number of countries. In each country, 500–2,500 subjects (in West Germany, the exception, data were collected from over 5,200 subjects) were selected by random digit dialing telephone

---

[1] The 1992 *ICS* includes findings from Czechoslovakia, Japan, and Poland even though the survey methodology for these countries differed—in unspecified ways—from that for the other 17 countries.

interviews for a total of just over 55,000 respondents. Subjects were questioned about 11 main forms of "ordinary" victimization, divided into "household property crimes" and "personal crimes." The former included theft of, theft from, and vandalism to cars; theft of motorcycles; theft of bicycles; burglary with entry; attempted burglary; and, only in 1992, break-ins to outbuildings. The latter included robbery; theft of personal property, pickpocketing, and noncontact personal thefts; sexual incidents, sexual assaults, and offensive sexual behavior; and assaults/threats, assaults with force, and threats without force. If the subjects indicated that they had been victimized, more detailed questions then were asked about the event(s). Subjects also were asked a number of questions reflecting fear of crime, attitudes toward police, etc. Prior to presentation in the *ICS* report (with the exception of Poland, Czechoslovakia, and Japan), interview data were weighted for gender, regional population distribution, age, and household composition, so as to make the samples as representative as possible of actual national populations aged 16 or more.

ICS data reveal that, for countries participating in both the 1989 and 1992 surveys, the overall victimization rates (for 11 crimes) were highest (27.5–30.0 percent) in New Zealand, the Netherlands, Australia, Canada, and the U.S. (p. 26). In terms of specific forms of victimization—both personal and property— the U.S. is consistently among the five highest nations. However, with the exception of attempted burglary, it is not the industrial world's leader. New Zealand and Australia vie for this dubious title. Both countries exhibited relatively high rates of victimization with respect to property crimes like car theft (2.7 percent) and attempted burglary (Australia 2.8 percent, New Zealand 2.5 percent). Canada, too, is positioned quite prominently among high-crime nations and is a high-risk nation in terms of theft from, and vandalism of, cars; burglary; personal theft; sexual incidents and assaults; and assault with threat and assault with force.

While the five countries above displayed high rates of both property and personal crimes, in other countries the situation is more mixed. Thus, England and Wales rank middle to low in terms of victimization rates for violence (such as sexual assault 0.3 percent, assault with force 1.1 percent), but very high in terms of victimization rates for property, such as theft of cars and theft from cars (2.8 percent and 7.1 percent, respectively) and vandalism of cars (8.7 percent). Two former socialist countries, Czechoslovakia and Poland (Warsaw), score low for theft of and from cars—pure conjecture without data on car ownership rates!—though Czechoslovakia has the highest rate of burglary (4.3 percent). Moreover, both Czechoslovakia and Poland report high victimization rates for violence; Poland stands at or near the top of the list for robbery (1.9 percent), sexual assault (2.0 percent), and assault with threat (4.0 percent), as does Czechoslovakia for sexual assault (2.4 percent).

The most striking observation, and confirmation of existing police-based data, is that Switzerland (15.0–17.4 percent) and Japan (under 12.4 percent) are among the nations with the lowest overall victimization rates; also at low levels are Norway (15.0–17.4 percent) and Northern Ireland (12.5–14.9 percent).

According to the *ICS*, not one Swiss resident was the victim of car theft, only 0.1 percent of Japanese subjects had been victims of robbery, and 0.2 percent of respondents in Japan and Switzerland report attempted burglary. Contrast these data with the highest reported figures: a 2.8 percent car theft rate in England and Wales; a 2.9 percent robbery rate in Spain; and a 4.6 percent attempted burglary rate in the U.S. In terms of relative risk, then, Switzerland and Japan appear to be the safest of the nations surveyed.

The *ICS* also contains interesting data about the overall prevalence rates of victimization (pp. 34–35). Here, one of the most striking findings is that, of the countries (excluding Japan) that participated in both the 1989 and 1992 surveys, the U.S. does not have the highest overall victimization rates. For these years, the overall prevalence of victimization (the proportion of persons victimized once or more in one year) was estimated to be 26.1 percent for the U.S., compared with the Netherlands' 31.3 percent, England and Wales' 30.2 percent, and Australia's 28.6 percent. In terms of percentage changes between 1989 and 1992, only the U.S. shows a decline in victimization rates! In the U.S. the overall prevalence of victimization actually decreased during this time by 13 percent; in contrast, that of England and Wales, for example, increased by 56 percent. However, in relative terms, these increases are extreme given that the rate for the Netherlands increased by only 17 percent, Belgium by 9 percent, Australia by 3 percent, and Canada by 1 percent.

Interesting as the *ICS* data are, it must be stressed that they cannot be accepted at face value. As we already know (see Chapter 2.1), peculiar methodological problems are associated with all victimization surveys. Thus, there is no reason to suppose that the rate of underreporting to survey interviewers is the same in each country. Quite the contrary. Consider, for example, the finding that the prevalence of victimization was 26.1 percent in the U.S., compared with 31.3 percent in the Netherlands. Does the surprisingly high figure in the Netherlands derive from the fact that more persons are victimized there? Or are the Dutch simply more likely to report victimization? We believe that it is very likely that, when compared with the U.S. rate, the Dutch victimization rate is greatly exaggerated because the population is more sensitive to violence and far more likely to report it.

We therefore have good reason to be cautious about the present usefulness of victimization surveys in comparative criminology. But let us now explore various comparative generalizations about crime in the wider context of certain analytical problems that apply to all comparative studies. These problems derive from a set of issues associated with what sociologists term "cultural relativism."

16.3 ——— CULTURAL RELATIVISM AND COMPARATIVE CRIMINOLOGY

Cultural relativism has two forms: epistemological and methodological (Beirne, 1983a:377–385). *Epistemological relativism* involves the extraordinary claim that one can understand another culture only through the prism of one's own culturally determined system of values. It implies the impossibility of meaningful comparative generalizations, therefore, other than comparison that stems from ethnocentrism. Thus, if *our* concepts of crime differ from those of another culture, it is meaningless to say that an action does or does not seem criminal to the other culture in our terms. Although this conclusion has some logical and philosophical merit, it is so pessimistic that for practical purposes it can only be noted and then—not entirely with satisfaction—ignored. *Methodological relativism* is a strategy that operates as a sensitizing device to variation in the definition and meaning of crime in other cultures. It is a slogan system requiring the criminologist to "maximize his understanding of alien cultures by honest-to-God fieldwork, moral charity, intellectual humility and a determination of the taken-for-granted assumptions of both his own and others' cultural milieu" (Dixon, 1977:76). Methodological relativism, therefore, operates as a warning to potential comparativists regarding certain methodological difficulties peculiar to comparative analysis.

The difficult issues of relativism can be better understood by examining the methods and findings of a classic case study in the literature of comparative anthropology: Julia Brown's (1952) comparative study of deviations from sexual mores.

A Case Study of Comparative Sexual Deviance

In her study, Brown (1952) proposed that every known society has a range of approved sexual practices and another range of practices subject to taboo. Those members of a society who faithfully follow the approved sexual customs are rewarded; those who deviate from such customs are punished. Brown (*ibid.*:135) focused on the following three problems: (a) the relative frequency with which specific types of sexual practices are considered deviant by different societies, where frequency is defined as the percentage of societies that forbids such practices; (b) the relative severity with which various deviant sexual practices are punished; and (c) the degree of correlation between the frequency and the severity of punishments. Addressing the first two problems, Brown analyzed data in the Human Relations Area File,[2] gleaning information about the sexual practices punished by 110 societies in Africa, North America, South America, Eurasia, and Oceania (*ibid.*:135–136). Brown's findings are summarized in Table 16-2.

---

[2] The Human Relations Area File was sponsored in 1937 by anthropologist George Murdock and others at Yale University's Institute of Human Relations. It is now a massive ethnographic data bank available at more than 200 universities in the U.S. and worldwide. Five sorts of data inadequacy in the HRAF are listed by Robert Marsh (1967:262–267): it may lack data for particular research problems; its coverage varies greatly from one society to another; its relative coverage of different practices within societies varies greatly; some of its sources are of inferior quality; and the comparability of some of its key definitions is questionable.

TABLE
16-2

Percentages of Societies Punishing Specific Sexual Practices

NUMBER OF SOCIETIES	% PUNISHING	PRACTICE AND PERSON PUNISHED
54	100	Incest
82	100	Abduction of married woman
84	99	Rape of married woman
55	95	Rape of unmarried woman
43	95	Sex during post-partum period
15	93	Bestiality by adult
73	92	Sex during menstruation
88	89	Adultery (paramour punished)
93	87	Adultery (wife punished)
22	86	Sex during lactation period
57	86	Infidelity of fiancée
52	85	Seduction of another man's fiancée
74	85	Illegitimate impregnation (woman punished)
62	84	Illegitimate impregnation (man punished)
30	77	Seduction of prenubile girl (man punished)
44	68	Male homosexuality
49	67	Sex during pregnancy
16	44	Masturbation
97	44	Premarital relations (woman punished)
93	41	Premarital relations (man punished)
12	33	Female homosexuality
67	10	Sex with one's betrothed

Source: Brown, 1952, p. 138, abridged.

Brown next determined a punishment scale for deviant sexual practices. Her scale of ratings was based on a combination of the percentage of societies that forbade a specific practice and the intensity (mild, moderate, severe, very severe) of the punishment inflicted for each sexual deviation. The scale is summarized in Table 16-3.

Tables 16-2 and 16-3 contain at least two important findings. Examining the data in Table 16-2, we learn that the sexual practices most often forbidden in Brown's sample are incest, abduction, and rape. Those practices least often forbidden are premarital affairs and intercourse with one's fiancée. Second, from Table 16-3 and from a series of correlational analyses, Brown inferred that the more often a given sexual practice is forbidden, the more severely and the more often is it punished. Assuming that severity of punishment reflects the seriousness of an offense, as Brown (*ibid.*:138) did, we can infer that incest, abduction, and rape are generally viewed as the most serious offenses. However, Brown went beyond this inference to argue:

> The fact that these correlations exist is of interest since it tends to support the view that there may be generalized attitudes of permissiveness and punitiveness toward sexual activity (*ibid.*:139).

How justified was Brown in her finding that different cultures have common attitudes toward sexual deviation? There are at least two problems with the

TABLE
16-3

Mean Severity Values of Specific Punishments

MEAN SEVERITY VALUE	SPECIFIC PUNISHMENT
1.0	Small fine
1.2	Fistfight
1.4	Quarreling within family
1.5	Parental reproof
1.8	Beating by family member
2.1	Duel
2.2	Public ridicule and disgrace
2.2	Enforced marriage
2.2	Illness
2.2	Bad luck
2.3	Danger to near kin
2.4	Ceremonial penance
2.4	Lowered bride-price
2.4	Knifing
2.5	Temporary exile
2.5	Humiliation at wedding
2.5	Heavy fine
2.5	Enslavement of relative
2.5	Divorce, and return of bride-price
2.5	Public flogging
2.6	Difficulty in acquiring a husband
2.6	Failure of hunting or fishing
2.6	Desertion of spouse
2.7	Puniness of offspring, injury to child
2.9	Divorce with disgrace, no remarriage allowed
2.9	Facial mutilation
2.9	Multiple mutilation
2.9	Madness
3.0	Spearing of legs
3.1	Repudiation of bride by groom
3.1	Sorcery to injure or kill
3.3	Loss of virility
3.4	Public raping
3.4	Enslavement
3.4	Destruction of major property
3.5	Barrenness
3.6	Permanent exile
3.7	Life imprisonment
3.7	Torture, possibly resulting in death
3.7	Enforced suicide
3.9	Death

Source: Brown, 1952, p. 137, abridged.

method Brown used to arrive at this generalization. One problem refers to the definition of certain behavior as criminal, the other to the seriousness attached to such behavior.

Brown's assumption that all 110 societies criminalize sexual practices similarly is most implausible. Consider incest. It is true that anthropologists have not discovered any place, past or present, where incest is tolerated in an entire society (Slater, 1959; Hughes, 1964). But there are documented cases where some cultures regard incest—however defined—as a necessary and obligatory social practice. For example, what we regard as incest seems to have been obligatory for members of royal families in Inca Peru and Hawaii, and in ancient Egypt, where Cleopatra was the offspring of a brother-sister union (Guttmacher, 1951:16). Moreover, because they had already been completely familiar *in utero*, fraternal twins of the opposite sex in Bali have been permitted to marry. According to Mayer (1953:31), the Gusii of southwestern Kenya will not proclaim it a sexual taboo, if, during the ceremony of "taking by stealth," sexual intercourse occurs between kin as close as brother and sister.

How do such counterexamples affect Brown's generalization about sexual practices in similar *simple* societies? (We do not agree with Brown's characterization of technologically undeveloped societies as "simple" because in many ways, especially in the realm of certain social relationships, such societies are actually quite *advanced*). As formulated—there are "generalized attitudes of permissiveness or punitiveness toward sexual activity"—Brown's generalization can be neither falsified nor confirmed by counterexamples. It cannot clearly be falsified because conditional clauses (of the sort "No society exerts incest taboos during the rainy season") could in principle account for any number of counter-factual cases. This limitation is shared by all scientific and sociological attempts to generalize.

Additionally, Brown's generalization cannot be confirmed. One of the necessary criteria for an intelligible generalization is that there must be an identity between the practices within its scope. But there is no way of knowing from Brown's research, or from much data lodged in the Human Relations Area File, whether the sexual practices defined as incestuous are the same practices in the societies observed: Are they perhaps seen as similar only by the observer's own methodology? The sexual practices defined as incestuous by the Western observer inclined to generalizations, by the Sambia tribe in the highlands of New Guinea, and by travelers in North America may in fact all be quite different.

The problem of the identity of social practices is probably acute, therefore, for comparisons between *simple* societies. There is good reason to suppose that the problem is even more acute for comparisons between *simple* and modern societies, and even for comparisons between modern societies with similar legal cultures and traditions. Suppose, for example, that we wished to compare incest rates between England and the U.S. (see further Hughes, 1964). Under the *Sexual Offenses Act* of 1956, it is an offense for a male in England to have sexual intercourse with a female whom he knows to be his granddaughter, daughter, sister, or mother. But in the U.S., statutory incest refers to an additional range of behavior not prohibited by English law: sexual relations between males and their grandmothers, nieces, and aunts. Moreover, marriage between first cousins is not an uncommon practice in England; in the U.S. it is illegal in nearly half the states.

A second difficulty with Brown's generalization is the assumption that a rank order of punishment can be applied meaningfully across cultures. How items are entered in cross-cultural rankings in part depends on the values of those doing the ranking. How is an objective order of punishment to be devised? And by whom? Brown devised her rank order on the advice of "judges conversant with anthropological phenomena" (*ibid.*:137). Yet consider the item "death" as the most serious punishment in her scale. There are many cases recorded (in the Homeric myths, the Icelandic sagas, and others) where banishment or permanent exile is seen as far more serious a punishment than death. Moreover, in some modern cultures (for example, among the top levels of the Japanese military) enforced suicide is not even a punishment but an honorable recourse to defeat in war. In some cultures (for instance, in England among men of gentle birth and fashion until 1850: Andrew, 1980), a duel is not a punishment (as in Brown's scale) but the normal form of asserting honor or reputation following insult.

Return to the idea of exile to illustrate another point. Exactly how much of a punishment is exile? The *effect* of exile partly determines the answer to this question. Exile is culturally and subjectively variable; for example, to an Orpheus exiled to the Greek underworld Hades, to Alexander Solzhenitsyn exiled from Russia to Vermont, and to Yasser Arafat exiled from his Palestinian homeland, expulsion certainly has very different effects. The seriousness of expulsion depends partly "on how easy it is to attach oneself to another community and to what extent one is a second-class citizen in that community" (Moore, 1978:124): does the exile become a refugee, a hero, an outlaw, or a welfare immigrant? The number of such complicating items can of course be multiplied greatly. But their message is a simple one: the severity of punishment attached to practices in a given society cannot simply be wrenched from its specific cultural context and artificially inserted into a rank order. Following the claims of epistemological relativism, we must initially understand punishment in its own cultural milieu, within its own system of meaning.

Let us summarize the discussion so far. The aim of comparative criminology is the construction of cross-cultural generalizations on crime. Three initial problems confront comparativists. The first is variation in the type of society. At present it seems that only societies with common sociological and structural features are appropriate as units of comparison, which sharply curtails the range of societies for which generalizations legitimately can be made. The second problem concerns cultural variation in the definition of illegal practices. If legal definitions differ, what range of behavior is actually compared? Finally, there is cultural variation in the meaning of the seriousness of crime. If an offense is regarded with different degrees of seriousness in different countries, then it is quite possibly meaningless to compare the rates of that offense in different countries.

How, then, should the comparative criminologist proceed? Do cross-cultural generalizations on crime necessarily ignore cultural density? Consider now one attempt to resolve these questions.

Toward Uniform Cross-National Crime Statistics?

One of the most influential strategies of methodological relativism in criminology has been suggested by Marvin Wolfgang (1967). The major comparative problem identified by Wolfgang is the adequacy and reliability of international criminal statistics. He correctly notes that statistical data produced by agents such as Interpol are based on an unwarranted assumption: that such crimes as homicide, robbery, and rape, for example, are regarded with the same degree of seriousness by all countries. This error is aggravated by wide cultural variation in legal definitions of crime, and by differing attitudes toward the sanctity of life and property.

Wolfgang makes several proposals to remedy this situation. The first relates to such official administrative policies as police efficiency; quality of criminal records; and discrepancies among countries for reported crimes, trials, and convictions. According to Wolfgang (1967:66), national police data must be standardized. These data could easily be made more reliable because "a team of experts from an international organization could, like the field representatives of the Department of Justice in the United States, help individual countries to set up and promote reliable reporting systems" (*ibid.*).

Wolfgang's second proposal is even more unconventional: the elimination of legal definitions of crime for purposes of comparative measurement of crime rates. The legal components of homicide, robbery, rape, and so forth would be replaced by requests for information about the type and extent of physical injury in violent crimes and/or the monetary value of property stolen or damaged. Thereby, Wolfgang argues, specific legal definitions of crime in national data would be eliminated but cultural integrity maintained.

Finally, Wolfgang proposes the use of a *psychophysical* weighting scale. A weighted crime for each participating country could thus be had by obtaining for each country the sum of the frequency of each measured crime, multiplying by its weight, and then dividing by a constant population unit.

Would such a scale really permit a comparativist to assess the relative seriousness of crimes in different countries? We think not. Wolfgang's strategy has two serious difficulties. The first concerns the proper subject matter of criminology; the second returns us to the problem of cultural variation in the meaning of crime.

Wolfgang's major proposal for comparative research is the elimination of legal definitions of crime. Behind this proposal lurks what should be the central theoretical problem of criminology as a discipline: if criminological generalizations are based solely on legal definitions, then criminology depends exclusively on the values enshrined in criminal law (see Chapter 1.2). But no credible criminologist enjoys the license to study solely the practices prohibited by criminal law.

Assume the primary goal of criminology is the construction of sociological generalizations regarding the distribution and causes of antisocial practices. Some, but not all, of such practices will be forbidden by criminal law. If this is true, then the unqualified acceptance of legal definitions of crime makes criminology a parasitic affair at the very outset. If legal definitions of crime are eliminated from comparative criminology, much of what is most interesting and important about different cultures—why certain cultures define certain practices and not others as illegal, cultural variation in notions of right and justice, and different penal practices, to mention but a few—is wished away by fiat. Wolfgang's strategy is not unlike that of students of religious practices who, in attempting to compare the extent of religious sentiments in different cultures, base their analyses exclusively on official statistics of baptisms, church attendance, and marriages. Perhaps such practices aid in understanding what people do, but not necessarily why people do them or what they mean. Indeed, replacement of legal definitions of crime by such neutral indicators as assessment of bodily and monetary damages provided by lawful national authorities still results in a criminology based on definitions of criminal justice agencies. By no stretch of sociological imagination can such indicators be termed neutral. Additionally, if the legal definition of crime is abandoned entirely as the initial object of study, we risk describing social practices and relations not as they in fact are, but only as we would like them to be.

Wolfgang's strategy is vulnerable to a second objection: the actual comparability of meanings and values imbedded in different cultures, which applies even when two cultures define the same range of behavior as illegal. Philosophically, it is quite difficult to understand the relationship between one's reason for acting and the act itself. Consider why one's reason for acting in a certain way cannot be understood independently of the act itself, and probably rightly so.

In his brilliant book *Suicide*, Émile Durkheim (1897:66) defined the physical act of suicide as "death which results directly or indirectly from a positive or negative act of the victim himself, which he knows will produce this result." Note that Durkheim specifically excluded from his definition one's reason, motive, or intention. Durkheim did this for two reasons. First, he thought that subjective states do not lend themselves to precise scientific measurement. Second, Durkheim believed that the act of suicide can be preceded by an infinity of subjective states that do not lend themselves to generalization. What appears to be the supremely private act—suicide—can be explained properly, therefore, only by denying the relevance of subjective states. But is such an explanation complete? Durkheim argued in *Suicide* that the act of suicide, and the differing rates of suicide in different cultures, can be explained properly by social and moral bonds that are either too weak or too strong. Such bonds affect the general climate of moral and psychological health. At a certain level of intensity, certain suicide-prone persons (for example, the young, the elderly, the divorced) respond to adverse social conditions by killing themselves.

But Durkheim's explanation of suicide is itself incomplete. How can we explain the fact that when faced with an apparently true generalization—"Other things being equal, more Protestants than Catholics kill themselves in response to the same set of circumstances (e.g., the Wall Street crash of 1929)"—some Protestants kill themselves (or kill others) and some do not? Answering this important question, Russell Keat and John Urry (1975:163; and see Lukes, 1973:191–225) stress that we must

> examine the subjective states of the people involved, their beliefs, values, purposes, emotions, and so on. In other words, we would have to analyze those circumstances from the agent's viewpoint, since it is the way they are interpreted that partly determines the agent's action."

What one person, or group of persons, subjectively regards as a sufficient set of circumstances warranting suicide now becomes an important part of any generalization regarding social conditions and suicide rates. Clearly, these circumstances are more difficult to grasp, and therefore more difficult to compare, at the level of cross-cultural analysis. Attitudes toward death and, indeed, what actually counts as death and life, vary across cultures; they mean different things.

16.4 _____ COMPARATIVE GENERALIZATIONS REGARDING CRIME

In this section we examine the strengths and weaknesses of certain recent generalizations in comparative criminology.

The Modernization (or Convergence) Thesis

Since the early 1960s, sociologists have often argued that the mere fact of technological development produces common effects that tend, irrespective of different or even antagonistic political systems, to make all societies increasingly similar (for example, Bell, 1961; Kerr, 1962). In this scenario, technology itself is seen as a factor that inevitably determines that all modern societies eventually converge to a common industrial model. This industrial model, also termed the *modernization theory*, has eight characteristics (Lane, 1970:184–185):

1. Populations grow rapidly, family size falls, women are emancipated, relationships between spouses become more equal.
2. Knowledge, wealth, political power, and human rights become more available to the entire population.
3. The division of labor is highly developed, and education and occupation determine individual positions in the social hierarchy.
4. Ideological differences are minimized and a premium is placed on hard work and economic productivity.
5. Legal systems apply a more-or-less common law to individuals of all social ranks.
6. Although political ideologies can be quite different, the central government organizes all of society.
7. Human relationships tend to be specific and achievement-oriented rather than diffuse and ascribed.
8. Large-scale urbanism ensures that social relationships are impersonal, superficial, and differentiated.

The industrial convergence theory has exerted great influence on recent comparative criminology (see, for example, Shelley, 1981). Yet one of the basic problems with existing modernization theory is that there is a wide range of crime rates—both interpersonal and property—among modern societies. Moreover, crime patterns in the Third World are not likely to repeat patterns of criminality in the more technologically advanced nations of the world. Criminality in the Third World is not simply a replay of the histories of more modernized nations. Indeed, many crimes committed in Third World countries actually originate in the First World, in the form of transnational crime (see Chapter 7.2).

Consider certain recent examples of transnational crimes. The widely criticized $1 billion powdered baby-milk sales throughout the Third World by Swiss-based Nestlé is an example of transnational corporate crime committed by a corporation outside the U.S. Medical evidence shows that bottle-fed infants, especially in poverty-stricken slums and rural areas of the Third World, are much more likely than breast-fed infants to succumb to disease, poor diets, and malnutrition (*New Statesman*, November 23, 1984). It is commonly accepted that breast milk is superior to manufactured milk, and that illiteracy, inadequate refrigeration, and lack of clean water amplify the problems associated with milk substitutes. According to a 1979 World Health Organization study (cited in Baker, 1985:182), annually as many as 10 million serious cases of malnutrition or illness may result from the improper use of infant formula or bottles, and that 10 percent of these babies die. However, despite this recognition, Nestlé has consistently violated World Health codes by over-supplying hospitals with free milk powder, improperly labeling tins of milk powder, and providing hospital staff with expensive gifts in the hope that pregnant mothers are directed to buy milk powder.[3]

Moreover, the worst industrial accident of record occurred when toxic gas leaked from a Union Carbide insecticide plant early on the morning of December 3, 1984, in the central Indian town of Bhopal (see Chapter 7.2). The fumes from the gas killed more than 3,500 Indians and injured 200,000 others, leaving many with chronic lung and psychological problems (*The New York Times*, February 15, 1989). According to *The New York Times* (December 4, 1989):

> Witnesses said thousands of people had been taken to hospitals gasping for breath, many frothing at the mouth, their eyes inflamed. The streets were littered with the corpses of dogs, cats, water buffalo, cows and birds killed by the gas, methyl isocyanate, which is widely used in the preparation of insecticides. Doctors from neighboring towns and the Indian Army were rushed to the city of 900,000, where hospitals were said to be overflowing with the injured. Most of the victims were children

---

[3] In 1984, Nestlé agreed, after worldwide protests and a consumer boycott, to modify its aggressive marketing techniques promising, for example, to promote breast feeding as superior to formula and to warn of the hazards of misuse through graphic labels that can be understood by people who cannot read (see *Time*, February 6, 1984).

Lowry's "Industrial Landscape" (1955) conveys all the bleakness of the industrial scene, which the artist himself described as that "apocalypse of grime."

and old people who were overwhelmed by the gas and suffocated, Indian press reports said.

It is likely that tragedies such as that of Bhopal will occur more frequently in future years. Dr. Jan Huismans, director of the International Register for Potentially Toxic Chemicals, a UN organization, recently warned: "We have received information on planned exports of millions of metric tons of hazardous waste from European and U.S. companies to Third World countries such as Guinea Bissau, the Congo, Benin, Ethiopia, Peru, Argentina and Venezuela" (Shabecoff, 1988). Even if Third World tragedies such as Bhopal are condemned by the international community, there is as yet no effective international enforcement or adjudicatory machinery with which to halt it.[4] Only in February 1989

---

[4] In the First World, examples of nonenforcement include the condemnation by the World Court in the Hague of the U.S. government's mining of Nicaraguan harbors and the British government's use of secret (Diplock) courts in Northern Ireland for trying members of the Irish Republican Army.

did Union Carbide agree to pay $470 million of the $3 billion in damages sought by the Indian government (*The New York Times*, February 15, 1989). In response to this uncertain and dangerous climate, the Organization of African Unity has condemned toxic dumping as "a crime against Africa and African people," and the Nigerian government has indicated that those found guilty by its courts of importing waste materials might face the firing squad (Shabecoff, 1988).

In his book *Crime, Justice and Underdevelopment* Colin Sumner (1982) expresses justifiable hostility toward modernization as the variable in accounting for patterns of crime in the Third World. He stresses that it is the more advanced, colonial countries that cause much crime in dependent, colonized countries: "The penetration of capital into the Third World most definitely does not mean the 'healthy' development of capitalist production with an industrial base, diversified products, cheap luxury goods, mass output . . ." (*ibid.*:24). The crimes of imperial countries against their colonies are legion. In Africa, for example, the military forces of the British and French governments ultimately supported the slave trade, largely created prostitution in the mid-19th century, brought with them alien fatal diseases unknown to native populations, and pillaged the raw materials of occupied territories.

The best explanation of transnational crimes, both corporate and political, committed against the Third World (see Chapters 7.2 and 9.3) is provided not by modernization theory but by *underdevelopment theory*. André Gunder Frank (1971), for example, has argued that underdevelopment in the Third World actually results from a global system entailing the political and economic control of underdeveloped societies by developed ones. According to this theory, the wealth of developed societies—such as the U.S. and the nations of Western Europe—results from colonial exploitation of much of Africa, Asia, and Central and Latin America. Through military and political domination, the developed societies have monopolized and controlled the international trade market. Through such monopoly and control, the interests of developed societies have been served while those of the Third World have been restricted.

The strength of underdevelopment theory is its concentration on history. It shows, for example, that modernization itself is dependent on political and economic power within an interacting global capitalist system. In other words, we cannot understand patterns of crime in comparative perspective if we view societies in isolation from one another.

Urbanization and Homicide

Another example of existing comparative generalizations on crime derives from an additional aspect of the modernization thesis. As discussed often in this book, criminologists believe urbanism is a bedrock cause of the growth of impersonal, violent, and predatory crime. In the U.S. this causal relationship is clearly documented by cross-sectional data in the *UCR*. Recall two points made in Chapter 4.1. First, there is a strong positive correlation between city size and homicide rates[5]: the larger the city population, the higher the homicide rate. Second, rural areas tend to have higher homicide rates than very small cities.

For comparative criminology, then, two important questions await answers. Does the same correlation between city size and homicide rates also exist in countries other than the U.S.? Do rural areas of other countries also have higher homicide rates than their very small cities? Archer and Gartner (1984:98–117) have considered these questions, and draw four conclusions:

1. The absolute size of a city does not correspond directly with its homicide rate. In other words, cities around the world with a population between 500,000–999,999 do not have a homicide rate of (or even near, in many cases) 18 per 100,000. Comparatively, cities of the same size show great variation in their homicide rates.

2. The finding in No. 1 suggests "the intriguing possibility that large cities have homicide rates which are unusually high *only in terms of the overall homicide rates of their societies*" (*ibid.*:107). For variations in homicide rates, therefore, it is not absolute city size that is important but size of a city relative to its national population (see Table 16-4). Extending their analysis, Archer and Gartner (*ibid.*:105–108) report that of the primary cities of 23 countries, 17 have homicide rates higher than their national homicide average. Five of six exceptions to this tendency were Third World countries; the sixth was Tokyo, the primary city of Japan.

3. These five exceptions, in turn, suggest that the factors which produce high homicide rates in large cities of developed countries are not present, or are not present in the same circumstances, in large cities of underdeveloped countries. As Archer and Gartner (*ibid.*:108) hypothesize:

   It might be that primary cities weaken kinship and community ties in developed societies but not in developing societies. Perhaps developing societies have lower rates of mobility, or perhaps people moving to cities in developing societies move with their families rather than alone. Developed societies might also have greater controls over rural homicides— for example, decentralized law enforcement, which reduces blood feuds, marauding gangs, etc.

4. A city's homicide rate does not necessarily increase as its population expands. Longitudinal data (Archer and Gartner, 1984:108–114) reveal that of 34 international primary cities, the homicide rates of 17 have declined with city growth and those of 17 have increased. Thus, at

---

[5] So strong is this correlation that in 1986, for example, the *UCR* reveals only one exception to it. This exception occurred in cities with a population of 250,000–499,000, which reported slightly higher homicide rates than cities with a population of 500,000–999,000. For whatever reason, this was almost certainly a one-year statistical aberration. Longitudinal data show decisively (Archer and Gartner, 1984:104) that the relationship between city size and homicide rates over time is strong and monotonic.

TABLE 16-4 **Primary-City and National Homicide Rates—A Cross-Sectional Comparison**

CITY HOMICIDE RATE LOWER THAN NATIONAL AVERAGE (N = 6)	HOMICIDE RATE	CITY HOMICIDE RATE HIGHER THAN NATIONAL AVERAGE	HOMICIDE RATE
1. Guyana (1966–1970)	6.18	1. Australia (1966–1970)	1.28
Georgetown	5.21	*Sydney*	1.57
2. Japan (1966–1970)	2.23	2. Austria (1966–1970)	0.73
Tokyo	1.78	*Vienna*	0.89
3. Kenya (1964–1968)	5.67	3. Belgium (1965–1969)	0.29
Nairobi	5.27	*Brussels*	0.45
4. Panama (1966–1970)	11.07	4. Finland (1966–1970)	0.35
Panama City	4.96	*Helsinki*	0.65
5. Sri Lanka (1966–1970)	6.09	5. France (1966–1970)	0.45
Colombo City	5.59	*Paris*	0.61
6. Turkey (1966–1970)	9.65	6. India (1966–1970)	2.72
Istanbul	4.84	*Bombay*	2.85
		7. Ireland (1966–1970)	0.34
		Dublin	0.35
		8. Mexico (1962, '66, '67, and 1972)	13.24
		Mexico City	13.34
		9. Netherlands (1966–1970)	0.50
		Amsterdam	1.23
		10. New Zealand (1966–1970)	0.16
		Wellington	2.32
		11. Northern Ireland (1964–1968)	0.20
		Belfast	0.35
		12. Philippines (1966–1970)	7.98
		Manila	23.86
		13. Rhodesia (1966–1970)	5.33
		Salisbury	7.20
		14. Scotland (1966–1970)	0.78
		Glasgow	1.56
		15. Spain (1964–1968)	0.49
		Madrid	0.56
		16. Sudan (1961–1964 and 1968)	5.67
		Khartoum	30.25
		17. Trinidad & Tobago (1966–1970)	14.00
		Port-of-Spain	15.31

Source: Archer and Gartner, 1984, p. 106.

present there is no discernible correlation between city growth and homicide rates.

The foregoing conclusion is reinforced by a cross-national study of homicide rates in 34 countries by Steven Messner (1980). Although Messner's study relied on inadequate Interpol data, his findings regarding the cross-national correlates of murder are nevertheless quite interesting. Messner reports that, when controlling for variations in countries' Gross National Product, population size, population density, and degree of urbanization, high homicide rates tend to be accompanied by high levels of income inequality. Messner (*ibid.*:194) concludes that countries with high murder rates tend to be those in which popular expectations of how income should be distributed are incompatible with how income actually is distributed. The discrepancy, he (Messner, 1980:194) continues,

> between socially induced expectations concerning income distribution and actual patterns of distribution undermines general respect for social rules and regulations. This breakdown in the normative order is ... reflected in the high murder rates of industrial nations with high levels of income inequality.

Countries with Low Crime Rates: Switzerland, Japan, and Ireland

One of the most interesting sets of questions for comparative criminology concerns the nature of countries with low crime rates. Why do some countries consistently have low crime rates? What, if anything, do these countries have in common? What can we learn from their experience?

Switzerland   According to the best-selling guidebook on Switzerland: "It is remarkable, but true, that there is almost no crime in Switzerland" (quoted in Balvig, 1988:11).

Switzerland is a highly affluent, urbanized, and industrialized European country. Although it has one of the highest rates of firearm ownership in the world, nevertheless, as Marshall Clinard (1978:1) notes in his book *Cities With Little Crime*, Switzerland appears to be an exception to the general rule that a high crime rate accompanies high levels of affluence, industrialization, and urbanization. Using conventional data (crimes reported to the police and conviction statistics on crimes against persons, property, and morals), Clinard suggests that the Swiss crime rate either remained fairly constant or actually declined between 1960 and 1971. He supports this finding with other data collected in 1973—parliamentary debates in Zurich, media crime reports, and the deductible/premium ratios of crime insurance policies.

At several points in his book, Clinard compares crime in Switzerland with crime in other so-called advanced countries. Both Switzerland and Sweden, for example, share certain features. Both are democracies with roughly similar demographic profiles, and both have large foreign-worker populations and strong currencies. In addition, both countries have avoided war for 150 years. Yet crime, especially violent crime, is generally regarded as a far more serious social problem in Sweden than in Switzerland. Why, then, is the Swiss crime rate so much lower than the Swedish crime rate? Clinard explains their different crime rates in terms of different aspects of Swiss and Swedish society. In particular, he (*ibid.*:152–155) points to the decentralization of the Swiss political system and its encouragement of private enterprise, and to the centralization of Swedish political and economic life, and its extensive social welfare programs that dull individual responsibility. Small is beautiful! Although we disagree with Clinard's explanation—we offer an alternative explanation forthwith—it is worth itemizing certain of Clinard's policy recommendations for the U.S. that stem from his study (*ibid.*:155–158):

1. Switzerland's lower crime rate cannot be explained by individualistic personality differences.

2. The pronounced differences in the extent of crime in Switzerland and Sweden indicate that common crimes in these two highly affluent countries cannot be explained by economic disadvantages or poverty.

3. Slum areas, which accompanied Swedish but not Swiss industrialization, can and should be controlled by the dispersal of industry and the restricting of city size to a maximum of 250,000–500,000.[6]

4. The prevention of crime can be encouraged by greater political decentralization and by increased citizen responsibility for obedience to laws and crime control.

5. Youth and adults should be integrated into common pursuits and activities.

6. Greater use should be made of such noncustodial sanctions as citations rather than arrests and suspended sentences rather than incarceration.

7. Guns and other lethal weapons should be rigidly controlled.

In his book *The Snow-White Image*, Danish criminologist Flemming Balvig (1988) argues that Clinard's account of the low Swiss crime rate needs serious revision. Balvig suggests that because Clinard was not a Swiss (or even a European) criminologist, he was therefore not privy to information that the reticent Swiss prefer to keep to themselves. Balvig argues: "*The basic image of Swiss society encourages or perhaps even compels a view of Switzerland as a land of little crime and of most Swiss as law abiding*" (*ibid.*:105). To an American such as Clinard, whose native country has experienced extremely high rates of violent crime for nearly three decades, it is not at all surprising that Switzerland should be perceived as a country with relatively low crime rates (*ibid.*:18).

Various changes have occurred since Clinard's study of 1973. Although Swiss common crime rates remain relatively low, they are in fact rising. According to two victimization surveys, for example, in 1984 almost 9 percent of the inhabitants of French-speaking regions of Switzerland claimed to have been victims of simple theft (excluding break-ins and thefts of means of transportation) (*ibid.*:51). Yet such figures tend to be absent from police statistics, Balvig argues, simply because Swiss police are inclined to omit them! Such practices were

---

[6] Clinard's argument that in Sweden in the late 1970s slum conditions existed in urban areas is without foundation. In fact, as O'Kelly and Carney (1986:184) recently recorded in their historical sketch of economic and class conditions in Sweden: "Urban slums and massive urban poverty were averted early by Sweden's acceptance of rational social planning." Late industrialization and more than 50 years of social democratic rule have *completely* abolished slum conditions in Sweden.

invisible to Clinard. Balvig writes: "The Swiss police are to an unusual degree still keeping crime figures down by bypassing many crime reports either by not recording them on paper or by not counting them in their compilation of crime figures" (*ibid.*:46–57).

Moreover, the high levels of Swiss corporate crime, which Clinard himself reported in 1973, are confirmed in Balvig's study. In recent years, he reports, some Swiss banks have even been suspected of basing their financial operations on Italian Mafia money derived, in part, from drug trafficking. "There is," Balvig writes, "a constant stream of trials being conducted [in Switzerland] involving colossal sums of money" (*ibid.*:69). Although no precise figures are available, it is difficult to imagine that Switzerland is not one of the great centers of financial corruption in the world. Switzerland has acquired its position as an international financial center partly because it has almost no control on money laundering and innumerable bank secrecy laws. In one recent case, two Lebanese brothers used Swiss banks to launder as much as $1.3 billion in drug money from the U.S., Colombia, Turkey, and elsewhere (*New York Times*, April 4, 1989).

Balvig's overall depiction of Switzerland is nonetheless that of a country with much lower rates of violent crime than the U.S. However, this is not because the Swiss are somehow naturally less violent. As Balvig remarks: "A country should not be judged on the basis of its level of crime alone, but also on its manner of controlling crime" (*ibid.*:58). In Switzerland, control of the small underclass population seems to have been perfected to a fine art. The punitive and nonpunitive sides of Swiss crime control have been combined into a highly effective system that coordinates control of the bottom echelons of Swiss society, the family, education, and the labor market. At the same time, resources devoted to fighting corporate crime are relatively small, and the vigor with which corporate criminals are prosecuted relatively weak (*ibid.*:58–71).

Japan For much of the 20th century Japan has had persistently low, stable, and occasionally declining crime rates. "This phenomenon [is] all the more remarkable," comments Elliott Currie (1985:46), "because the Japanese have generally minimized the use of formal criminal-justice sanctions in fighting crime." When criminologists attempt to explain Japanese crime rates, they usually refer to the strong elements of social control in Japanese life. For example, Freda Adler (1983:123; and see Bayley, 1976) writes that in Japan "[r]egulation and control characterize daily life, where the individual is strongly committed to the group." Such control, this explanation continues, is manifest in certain vital areas: the patriarchal nature of the family, the quality of formal education, the power of religion, and the surrogate family provided by businesses in urbanized areas. In such ways Japanese life is controlled to such an extent that, to many citizens, crime and deviance are actually unthinkable. These ordered features of Japanese life are themselves supplemented by an efficient police force that has an excellent rapport with the Japanese public (Bayley, 1976a).

Before arguing the relevance of the Japanese experience to understanding crime in the United States, we note our disagreement with the foregoing explanations. The Japanese experience correctly reflects the fact that high crime rates are by no means an inevitable feature of modernized societies. However, we believe that explanations of low Japanese crime rates inappropriately focus on the element of control in Japanese life. Two decades of failed get-tough conservative crime policies in the U.S. should tell us that *control*, as such, explains neither low nor high crime rates. In Japan's case the emphasis on control neglects, as Currie (1985:46–47) stresses, the ways in which Japanese society is more *supportive* of its citizenry than is the U.S. in terms of providing social and welfare services. In the control explanation (*ibid.*:46):

> Nothing is said about the far narrower spread of income inequality in Japan, or the relative absence of a severely deprived and marginal "underclass" which in turn partly reflects a conscious and generally effective (if sometimes overstated) full-employment policy and a range of deliberate efforts to integrate Japanese workers into a stable, enduring connection with a workplace.

Ireland   Throughout the 1950s and early 1960s, the Republic of Ireland had exceptionally low and stable crime rates. However, by 1975 there were five times as many recorded "shopbreakings," six times as many "housebreakings," and 29 times as many robberies as had been recorded in 1951. A substantial increase was also recorded for offenses against the person, with indictable assaults rising seven times over the same 25 years (Rottman, 1980:3–4). In the 1950s the average annual number of homicides was 7.2, in the 1960s 10.1, and 20.8 during 1970–1975. By 1987 the number of homicides had risen to 29 (Report of Gardai Commissioner, 1988).

An explanation for such dramatic changes suggests that Ireland both conforms to major strands of the modernization thesis and yet differs from it in significant ways. During the 1940s the rapid decline of Irish agriculture—which was not relieved but exacerbated by intensive industrialization during the early 1960s—created serious unemployment among the Irish working class. This, in turn, led to enormous intrafamilial conflict and other forms of dislocation, such as emigration. Rottman (1980:117–140) has analyzed the changing Irish homicide patterns immediately after these two great upheavals. He shows that the two decades were separated by the diminishing importance of family homicide, an increasing proportion of homicides involving strangers, and a greater incidence of homicides in which females kill males. In these respects Ireland appears to conform to the modernization thesis.

But in other respects Ireland contradicts the modernization thesis. For example, after the industrialization of the 1960s, crime rates did not increase more in urban areas than in rural areas: the increase was diffuse rather than concentrated in cities (Rottman, 1980:116). Again, even though we are dealing with a small number of homicides, the rising percentage of males murdered by women—a 41.3 percent increase between the 1950s and the 1970s—is probably not typical of other modernized countries. Moreover, even after the 1960s surge of industrialization, Ireland still had atypically low crime rates: according to official *gardai* (police) statistics, Ireland's homicide rate between 1979 and 1983 was 15 times lower than that of the U.S. (see Table 16-1). Finally, Irish rates of violent crime may actually have been declining since 1986. As three Irish sociologists (Tomlinson, Varley, and McCullagh, 1988:14) have remarked concerning recent perceptions of crime in Ireland:

> We have been encouraged to worry about a surge in crime, the appearance of which may have more to do with the growth of private insurance policies (and the need to report break-ins to the police before making a claim), than with any dramatic increase in criminal activity as such.

It is fair to say, therefore, that Ireland is a real exception to the view that rising crime rates accompany modernization. Although there is as yet no sustained explanation of Ireland's persistently low crime rates, we note especially the powerful influence of Roman Catholicism in government, education, and family. An additional factor is undoubtedly the relationship between the Irish citizenry and the Gardai, the Irish police force. According to the *Irish Value Survey* (Fogarty, 1983:157), 86 percent of the Irish population has "a great deal" or "quite a lot" of confidence in the Irish police—more confidence, in fact, than in any other Irish institution. Moreover, similar levels of confidence in the police are exhibited by a remarkable 84.5 percent of Irish skilled and unskilled manual workers (*ibid.*:169).

One of the few attempts to identify common features among countries with low crime rates is Freda Adler's (1983) book *Nations Not Obsessed With Crime.* Adler isolated five diverse "regions" in the world (European capitalist, European socialist, Latin America, Islam, and Asia), and then selected from each region a pair of countries (respectively: Switzerland/Eire, Bulgaria/German Democratic Republic, Costa Rica/Peru, Algeria/Saudi Arabia, and Japan/Nepal) with the lowest, or among the lowest, crime rates in its region. Adler's strategy was twofold. First, she attempted to determine for each such country the statistical correlations existing between their arrest rates per 100,000 population (as a reasonable index of crime rates) and 47 socioeconomic variables. These variables included such factors as age and occupational structures, national income, education, and patterns of consumer expenditure. Adler inferred from her statistical analysis that these 10 countries had no truly significant socioeconomic or cultural factors in common. Even after analyzing the variables by comparing each of the low crime rate countries with the mean of its region, no specific common factors emerged. However, Adler (*ibid.*:10) managed to identify various broad trends among the 10 countries:

> Most low crime countries have in common lower than average population densities, lower than average urban populations . . . lower than average population numbers which are economically active, a lower than

average number of radio receivers and telephones, a higher than average population in agriculture . . . and a higher than average crude death rate.

However, the broad sociocultural differences among these countries are quite startling. The 10 countries have a variety of state structures, including people's republic, military government, parliamentary democracy, popular democracy, absolute monarchy, and constitutional monarchy. Their economies range from subsistence agriculture (Nepal, Peru) to extensive industrialization (GDR, Switzerland, Japan). Some have urbanized slowly (Ireland, Switzerland), others quickly (Saudi Arabia, Japan). In some (Peru), unemployment rates are high; in others (GDR, Bulgaria, Japan, Switzerland) they are low. Some of the countries contain homogeneous populations, others heterogeneous. As Adler concludes: "These countries represent a broad spectrum of socioeconomic and politico-cultural systems" (*ibid.*:130).

Adler's second, qualitative strategy was an analysis of the formal and informal mechanisms of social control in each of the 10 countries. At first glance, Adler suggests (*ibid.*:124–126), there is variety in their systems of law, politics, and criminal justice. Each has differing levels of success in solving reported crimes, ranging from high (Japan, Saudi Arabia) to low ("probably among some of the countries whose figures are not available") (*ibid.*:125). It is difficult to measure their actual support for human rights. Five countries retain the use of capital punishment; although, with the exception of Japan, executions are quite rare.

Nevertheless, Adler does find a common aspect among countries with low crime rates: the element of popular involvement in, or popularity of, the criminal justice system. Six of the 10 countries—four highly industrialized (Japan, Switzerland, Bulgaria, and the GDR) and two underdeveloped (Nepal and Peru)—are "marked by an extraordinarily high degree of popular participation in crime control" (*ibid.*:128). Moreover, Saudi Arabia, Algeria, and Ireland have succeeded, despite foreign intervention, in maintaining the integrity of their indigenous systems of social control. Costa Rica (which has no standing army) has fostered local self-government and is actively popularizing its criminal justice system.

A second common factor is that all 10 countries seem to have strong elements of social control outside the criminal justice system. According to Adler, these elements do not exercise control by formal constraint; rather, "they transmit and maintain values by providing for a sharing of norms and by ensuring cohesiveness" (*ibid.*:130). First and foremost, her argument continues, is survival of the power of the family, even during modernization. In each case the family remains a closely woven unit that exerts a powerful influence on its members, often patriarchal in nature. In societies where employment levels are high—with women comprising a large segment of the labor force—strong efforts have been made to provide for children during work hours in day-care facilities and kindergartens. The retention of traditional family values is itself reinforced by a second system of control: religious, moral, or secular values. In all 10 countries—be they Islamic, Christian, or socialist—such values exhort the citizenry to act for the common good; they "solidify the moral obligations of the community to reaffirm in common their common sentiments" (*ibid.*:132).

There is much of value in Adler's analysis. Quite remarkably, hers is the only study to date that addresses the immensely important question of what distinguishes countries with, respectively, high and low crime rates.

However, we note two difficulties with Adler's analysis. First, her study is so brief that she avoids all thorny methodological and relativist problems of comparative research. Indeed, Adler condenses her observations on each country's demography, history, law, economy, family, and polity into a mere eight pages. It is quite likely that, on closer inspection, countries with low rates of crime will be found to have large structural differences. Second, when examining countries whose native tongue is not English, Adler is forced to rely either on statements by government officials or on secondary English-language commentaries. Interviewing government officials about such things as the popularity of the criminal justice system, for example, is not a very reliable way to gather objective information on other cultures. And, reliant on secondary sources, she is necessarily unable to determine either the accuracy of their analyses or the range of opinions they reflect.

16.5 ——— U.S. CRIME IN COMPARATIVE PERSPECTIVE

Our chief focus in this chapter has been to introduce various theoretical and methodological issues of central importance to comparative criminology. We have examined certain of the major issues involved in actually doing comparative studies, and have outlined some of the most common comparative generalizations on crime.

Students often ask: "*Why* does the U.S. have one of the highest crime rates in the world?" Because we stress how difficult it is to offer plausible answers to questions such as this, our only answer is that "We really don't know." However, if pressed to respond with a simple answer to this question, we would reply that at least five factors distinguish the social structure of the U.S. from other "comparable societies," and that these factors contribute to its high crime rate:

1. The U.S. has had one of the highest rates of structural unemployment since 1945.

2. The U.S. has the largest underclass of persons economically, socially, and politically discriminated against because of race and ethnic background.

3. The U.S. has inferior support systems of welfare, social security, health, and education.

4. The extreme commercialism of U.S. capitalism provides incentives and motivations to circumvent acceptable (namely, legal) means of achievement.

5. The U.S. criminal justice system is one of the most punitive control mechanisms in the world.

We conclude this chapter with a brief outline of No. 5, reviewing comparative evidence on the relationship between punitive penal policies and crime rates in the U.S.

Punitive Penal Policies

In the early part of this chapter we cited data on the comparatively high rates of personal and property crimes in the U.S. These data have been explained in numerous ways, but in recent times criminologists have tended to focus on the general climate of tolerance and permissiveness in the U.S. (whose roots go back to the turbulent liberalism of the 1960s). It was not accidental, this explanation continues, that the turbulence and permissiveness of the 1960s coincided with unprecedented increases in the rates of violent crime. This *permissiveness* has become a favorite target of conservatives, and as an explanation of crime it surfaces in two major forms.

Both explanations of permissiveness focus on the consequences of the apparent weakening of *social control* in U.S. society. One explanation focuses on weakened control in such crucial socializing agencies as families, schools, and neighborhoods. For some, therefore, the rise of permissiveness derives from liberal or weak-minded child-rearing practices within families (for example Hirschi, 1983) that are, in their turn, paralleled and reinforced by lax discipline in high schools (including Toby, 1983). The other explanation refers to the loss of control, or the lack of punitiveness, in the criminal justice system and, specifically, to the mild or lax punishment apparently meted out to convicted criminals (van den Haag, 1975; von Hirsch, 1976).

We firmly reject the foregoing explanations because the evidence simply does not support them.

Regarding the first explanation, it is very difficult to support the argument that U.S. society has somehow become more *permissive* (and, what, precisely does this vague term mean?) in its child-rearing practices since the 1960s. Take only the example of corporal punishment of children. In Chapter 4.2 we outlined the extraordinary amount of child abuse in the U.S., notwithstanding the positive relationship demonstrated between the development of aggression in children and the use of corporal punishment (Solheim, 1982:153; Straus, 1991). For us the corporal punishment of children *is* a form of child abuse. About 75 percent of the U.S. public believes that physical punishment of children is acceptable behavior, and as many as 98 percent of parents in the U.S. sometimes "spank" their children (Solheim, 1982:151). These figures contrast with Sweden, where the belief is held by only about 25 percent (*ibid.*). Yet, as Currie (1985:42) points out:

> In Sweden, where corporal punishment was outlawed in 1979, even when inflicted by parents, rates of serious violent crime are much lower than in Finland, where corporal punishment is more widely accepted. But the Finns are less violent than we Americans, whose support for

punishment is among the highest in the industrial world. Even higher rates of criminal violence are found in some Caribbean countries, where corporal punishment—especially in low-income families—is applied on a scale and with a severity that might shock even Americans.

Evidence is also easy to provide against the argument that the U.S. criminal justice system is insufficiently firm with its target populations. Indeed, the U.S. and Turkey are the only Western countries that retain and use the death penalty! Comparative evidence consistently reveals that the U.S. incarcerates a greater proportion of its population than other Western countries. In 1977 the incarceration rate in federal and state prisons in the U.S. was 208 per 100,000. This figure does not include the 274,000 inmates of local jails in the U.S. (Bureau of Justice Statistics, 1986). At the opposite extreme, according to Doleschal and Newton (1981; and see Currie, 1985:Ch. 3), the Dutch rate was about 22 per 100,000. In between these extremes lay most of the rest of the world's industrial societies, many clustered toward the lower end of the scale: Japan/44, Norway/45, Sweden/40, West Germany/60, Denmark/54, France/56, and Great Britain/84.[7]

Moreover, the gap between the U.S. incarceration rate and those of other countries may well be increasing. According to the longitudinal data in Figure 16-1, the U.S. incarceration rate has grown consistently since 1925, with reductions occurring only during World War II and the Vietnam era. During the entire period 1925–1985, the average annual growth rate of the prison population was 2.8 percent (Bureau of Justice Statistics, 1986a). By 1992 the U.S. incarceration rate was the highest ever recorded, as was the number (more than 883,593) of inmates (Bureau of Justice Statistics, 1993).

According to a survey conducted for the Bureau of Justice Statistics (cited in *Criminal Justice Newsletter*, December 1, 1987), public opinion in the U.S. strongly favors prison sentences even longer than those currently meted out. For example, for rapes without additional injury to the victim, 94 percent favored a prison term, and the average recommended sentence was more than 15 years. The public preference for assault was 3.6–7.7 years, as opposed to current actual time served of, on average, 2.4 years. These strong preferences for punitive policies are, arguably, among the most intense in the world.

We suggest that there is no evidence that the punitive nature of U.S. penal sanctions reduces the crime rate significantly. On the contrary: punitive penal policies are a violent part of the very problem they are apparently designed to solve. Instead of pursuing ever-harsher penal policies, we should pursue reductions in the crime rate through social policies applied to the class structure itself. Certain societies in western Europe have reported great success with a host of practical social policies; in conclusion, we can do no better than to recommend Currie's (1985:275–276) summary of them:

---

[7] There is some evidence (e.g., Bureau of Justice Statistics, 1987) to show that the discrepancy between the U.S. and other countries diminishes when incarceration rates are put in the context of different conviction rates.

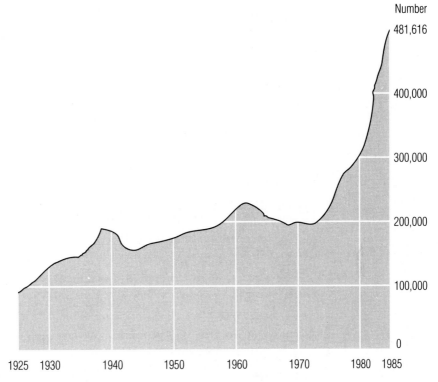

Number

481,616

400,000

300,000

200,000

100,000

0

1925 1930   1940   1950   1960   1970   1980 1985

FIGURE   **U.S. State and Federal Prisoners, 1925–1985**[1]

16-1   [1] Prior to 1977, prisoner reports were based on the custody population. Beginning in 1977, focus is on the jurisdiction population.

Source: Bureau of Justice Statistics, State and Federal Prisoners, 1925–1985, *U.S. Department of Justice, Report NCJ-102494, p. 1.*

▲— exploration and development of intensive rehabilitation programs for youthful offenders, preferably in the local community or in a supportive institutional milieu

▲— community-based, comprehensive family support programs, emphasizing local participation and respect for cultural diversity

▲— improved family planning services and support for teenage parents

▲— paid work leaves and more accessible childcare for parents with young children, to ease the conflicts between child rearing and work

▲— high-quality early-education programs for disadvantaged children

▲— expanded community dispute-resolution programs

▲— comprehensive, locally based services for domestic violence victims

▲— intensive job training, perhaps modeled along the lines of supported work, designed to prepare the young and the displaced for stable careers

▲— strong support for equity in pay and working conditions, aimed at upgrading the quality of low-paying jobs

▲— substantial *permanent* public or public-private job creation in local communities, at wages sufficient to support a family breadwinner, especially in such areas of clear and pressing social need as public safety, rehabilitation, childcare, and family support

▲— universal—and generous—income support for families headed by individuals outside the paid labor force

REVIEW

Chapter 16 teaches the importance of testing theories under as diverse conditions as possible and, therefore, the crucial role of comparative studies for the theoretical development of criminology in the U.S. The major task of this chapter has been to outline the key concepts, data, and findings of comparative criminology.

Concepts and Data in Comparative Criminology

1. Until very recently there was no systematic comparative criminology in the sense of analyses that systematically compare crime in two or more cultures. The ideal goal of comparative criminology is to test generalizations regarding crime in three stages: (1) in similar societies, (2) in societies largely similar but different in some respects, and (3) in societies as different as they possibly can be. This goal is unlikely to be met.

2. There are various sources of cross-national crime data, including those of the United Nations and other international agencies, the Comparative Crime Data File, and victimization surveys. For comparative purposes, using these sources entails the difficulty that societies both define certain practices as crimes in different ways and also differ in the degree of seriousness that they attach to them.

Cultural Relativism and Comparative Criminology

1. We explored the foregoing difficulty in the context of a set of issues raised by cultural relativism. Epistemological relativism—which we were forced to recognize but then ignore—holds that because one can never understand the beliefs of cultures different from our own, we cannot therefore compare our culture with such cultures. Methodological relativism is a strategy for comparing different cultures that, at the same time, attempts to respect the facts of cultural diversity.

2. The precise difficulties presented by cultural relativism were illustrated by Brown's (1952) classic study of sexual deviance.

3. We examined Wolfgang's (1967) methodological strategy to reformulate crime statistics in order to overcome the difficulties raised by Brown's

attempt to construct cross-national generalizations regarding sexual deviance.

Comparative Generalizations about Crime

1. In this section several cross-national generalizations regarding crime were outlined. Each has its own respective merits, and its own conceptual and relativist problems.

2. The crime and modernization thesis suggests that generalizations can be made about the way in which industrialization and urbanization affect crime rates in all societies. The major problems with generalizations derived from this thesis are that (1) they ignore relativist issues regarding differences in legal definitions of crime; (2) they are often contradicted by empirical evidence; (3) they wrongly assume that criminality in Third World societies is a replay of the history of criminality in technologically advanced societies, and (4) they often ignore the repressive colonial influence of First World countries and transnational corporations on the patterns of crime in the Third World.

3. We examined, and were largely unable to dispute, the generalization that homicide rates are likely to be higher in societies with high degrees of social and economic inequality. The correlation between homicide rates and urbanization, however, was determined to be problematic.

4. Little research has been completed on the sociological nature of societies with low crime rates. We outlined the available research and applied it especially to the cases of Switzerland, Japan, and Ireland; and could offer only provisional answers.

U.S. Crime in Comparative Perspective

1. There are many reasons why we believe the U.S. has one of the highest crime rates in the world. Our reasons, as with those of other criminologists, remain tentative and as yet unsubstantiated.

2. One of the many reasons in No. 1. is that U.S. society, including its criminal justice system, is one of the most punitive in the world. Punitive penal policies are a violent part of the very problem they are apparently designed to solve.

3. To address the causes of high rates of crime, one must look beyond penal policies to fundamental changes in society itself.

QUESTIONS FOR CLASS DISCUSSION

1. In the fifth century B.C., Greek historian Herodotus (quoted in Feyerabend, 1987:42) recorded the following story:

When Darius was king of Persia, he summoned the Greeks who happened to be present at his court, and asked them what they would take to eat the dead bodies of their fathers. They replied they would not do it for any money in the world. Later, in the presence of the Greeks, and through an interpreter, so that they could understand what was said, he asked some Indians, of the tribe called Callatiae, who do in fact eat their parents' dead bodies, what they would take to burn them. They uttered a cry of horror and forbade him to mention such a dreadful thing.

What does this story tell us about the problem of cultural relativism?

2. Do crime rates in the Third World tend to repeat the patterns of recorded crime in countries such as the U.S.?

3. What lessons, if any, can U.S. policymakers derive from the incidence of crime in other countries?

4. In the rural communities of 19th-century Russia, *samosud* (self-judgment) was an important and widely practiced type of justice that bypassed the formal criminal justice system. During *samosud*, aggrieved peasants took justice into their own hands. Consider, when you have read the following description of *samosud* (reported in Frierson, 1987:67), whether any aspects of it can be applied fruitfully to crime and punishment in the U.S.

Vodka played a frequent role in community sentencing. The guilty party often had to buy liquor for the whole village after returning any stolen goods and enduring a group beating or shaming. The Bolkhovskii district, Orel province, was the setting for an incident of *samosud* in the summer of 1898 that combined all three punishments of beating, shaming, and demanding vodka. In the village of Padimlo, a posse of peasants broke into the house of a suspected thief and found the stolen goods in his storehouse. The thief fell to his knees and begged mercy of the crowd. They agreed to forgive him in exchange for two bottles of vodka. He produced the vodka, which they proceeded to drink. Suddenly an old man began to heckle and rebuke the thief for bringing shame to their village, which would now have the reputation of being a place where neighbors stole from each other. This caught the attention of the other men, who began to beat him. The thief managed to break free and run away, leaving the posse in drunken, staggering pursuit. When they realized they had lost him, they drank up the rest of the vodka before heading back to his house. There they surrounded the dwelling, some even crawled up on the roof, and called him out to meet them. When he did so, they tied a sack of wheat around his neck and paraded him through the village. The community then demanded more vodka, threatening to turn him in to the land captain if he refused. His son ran to the tavern for another bottle. The thief finally earned his release by swearing never to steal from his neighbors again and by eating earth to seal the oath.

5. Why are the rates of violent crime in the U.S. so high in comparison with other modern industrialized countries?

RECOMMENDED READINGS

Beirne, Piers and Joan Hill (1991). *Comparative Criminology: An Annotated Bibliography*. New York: Greenwood Press. Provides students and researchers with a list of 500 annotated references in comparative criminology.

Currie, Elliott (1985). *Confronting Crime: An American Challenge*. New York: Pantheon Books. Although its use of crime statistics is somewhat crude, this is nevertheless a brilliant book whose focus is violence, punishment, and government policies in the United States. This focus is sharpened through numerous cross-national comparisons.

Robertson, Roland and Laurie Taylor (1973). *Deviance, Crime and SocioLegal Control*. London: Martin Robertson. Contains original discussion on the importance of differences in cross-cultural meanings for comparative criminology, but has been sadly neglected in the United States.

Skocpol, Theda and Margaret Somers (1980). "The uses of comparative history in macrosocial inquiry." *Comparative Studies in Society and History*, 22:174–197. An excellent account of the interplay between different methods of historical inquiry.

REFERENCES

Authors' Note: Certain references have two publication dates. The first refers to the original date of publication, the second to the edition used here and to which page citations in the text refer.

A

Abadinsky, Howard. 1983. *The Criminal Elite: Professional and Organized Crime.* Westport, Conn.: Greenwood.

———. 1989. *Drug Abuse: An Introduction.* Chicago: Nelson-Hall.

Abt, Vicki, and Douglas J. McDowell. 1987. "Does the Press Cover Gambling Issues Poorly?" *Social Science Research* 71(3): 193–97.

Abt, Vicki, James F. Smith, and Eugene Martin Christiansen, 1985. *The Business of Risk: Commercial Gambling in Mainstream America.* Lawrence, Kans.: University of Kansas Press.

Adler, Freda. 1975. *Sisters in Crime: The Rise of the New Female Offender.* New York: McGraw-Hill.

———. 1977. "The Interaction Between Women's Emancipation and Female Criminality: A Cross-Cultural Perspective." *International Journal of Criminology and Penology* 5(1):101–112.

———. 1983. *Nations Not Obsessed with Crime.* Littleton, Colo.: Fred B. Rothman.

Adler, Jeffrey S. 1989. "A Historical Analysis of the Law of Vagrancy." *Criminology* 27(2):209–29.

Ageton, Suzanne. 1983. "The Dynamics of Female Delinquency, 1976–1980." *Criminology* 21(4):555–84.

Ageton, Suzanne, and Delbert S. Elliott. 1974. "The Effects of Legal Processing on Self-Concept." *Social Problems* 22(1):87–100.

Agnew, Robert. 1985. "Social Control Theory and Delinquency: A Longitudinal Test." *Criminology* 23(1):47–61.

Akers, Ronald L. 1973. *Deviant Behavior.* Belmont, Calif.: Wadsworth.

Akers, Ronald L., Marvin D. Krohn, Lonn Lanza-Kaduce, and Marcia Radosevich. 1979. "Social Learning and Deviant Behavior: A Specific Test of a General Theory." *American Sociological Review* 44(4):636–55.

Albanese, Jay. 1985. *Organized Crime in America.* Cincinnati: Anderson.

Albanese, Jay S., and Robert D. Pursley. 1993. *Crime in America: Some Existing and Emerging Issues.* Englewood Cliffs, N.J.: Prentice-Hall.

Albini, Joseph L. 1971. *The American Mafia: Genesis of a Legend.* New York: Appleton-Century-Crofts.

Alexander, Herbert E. 1985. "Organized Crime and Politics." In *The Politics and Economics of Organized Crime*, ed. Herbert E. Alexander and Gerald E. Caiden, 89–98. Lexington, Mass.: Lexington Books.

Allen, Donald M. 1980. "Young Male Prostitutes: A Psychosocial Study." *Archives of Sexual Behavior* 9(5):399–426.

Altheide, David L., Patricia A. Adler, Peter Adler, and Duane A. Altheide. 1978. "The Social Meanings of Employee Theft." In *Crime at the Top*, ed. John Johnson and Jack Douglas, 90–124. New York: Lippincott.

Amir, Menachim. 1967. "Victim-Precipitated Forcible Rape." *Journal of Criminal Law, Criminology, and Police Science* 58(4):493–502.

———. 1971. *Patterns in Forcible Rape.* Chicago: University of Chicago Press.

Andersen, Margaret L. 1993. *Thinking about Women: Sociological Perspectives on Sex and Gender.* New York: Macmillan.

Anderson, Scott, and Jon Lee Anderson. 1986. *Inside the League.* New York: Dodd, Mead and Company.

Andrew, D. T. 1980. "The Code of Honour and Its Critics: The Opposition to Duelling in England, 1700–1850." *Social History* 5:409–34.

Archer, Dane, and Rosemary Gartner. 1984. *Violence and Crime in Cross-National Perspective.* New Haven: Yale University Press.

Asinoff, Robert. 1985. "India Accident Raises Questions of Corporate Responsibility." *In These Times* (Dec. 19–Jan. 8):10.

B

Bachand, Donald J., and George A. Chressanthis. 1988. "Property Crime and the Elderly Offender: A Theoretical and Empirical Analysis, 1964–1984." In *Older Offenders*, ed. Belinda McCarthy and Robert Longworthy, 76–103. New York: Praeger.

Bailey, William C., and Ruth D. Peterson. 1987. "Police Killings and Capital Punishment: The Post-Furman Period." *Criminology* 25(1):1–25.

Baker, Michael, and Alan F. Westin. 1987. *Employer Perceptions of Workplace Crime.* Washington, D.C.: U.S. Department of Justice.

Baker, James C. 1985. "The International Infant Formula Controversy: A Dilemma in Corporate Social

Responsibility." *Journal of Business Ethics* 4(3):181–90.

Balbus, Isaac D. 1973. *The Dialectics of Legal Repression.* New York: Russell Sage.

Balkan, Sheila, Ronald Berger, and Janet Schmidt. 1980. *Crime and Deviance in America: A Critical Approach.* Monterey, Calif.: Wadsworth.

Ball, John, Lawrence Rosen, John Flueck, and David N. Nurco. 1981. "The Criminality of Heroin Addicts: When Addicted and When Off Opiates." In *The Drugs-Crime Connection*, ed. James Inciardi, 39–65. Beverly Hills: Sage.

Ball, Richard A. 1966. "An Empirical Exploration of Neutralization Theory." *Criminology* 4(2):22–32.

Balvig, Flemming. 1988. *The Snow-White Image: The Hidden Reality of Crime in Switzerland.* Translated by Karen Leander. Oslo: Norwegian University Press.

Bandura, Albert. 1973. *Aggression: A Social Learning Analysis.* Englewood Cliffs, N.J.: Prentice-Hall.

Bankowski, Zenon, Geoff Mungham, and Peter Young. 1977. "Radical Criminology or Radical Criminologist?" *Contemporary Crises* 1(1):37–51.

Barak, Gregg. 1988. "Newsmaking Criminology: Reflections on the Media, Intellectuals, and Crime," *Justice Quarterly*, 5(4):565–587.

Barron, James. 1987. "Father, Son Arrested in Md. in Check Probe." *Washington Post* (Oct. 22):A10.

Barry, Kathleen. 1979. *Female Sexual Slavery.* Englewood Cliffs, N.J.: Prentice-Hall.

Bart, Pauline B., and P. H. O'Brien. 1985. *Stopping Rape: Successful Survival Strategies.* New York: Pergamon Press.

Baumer, Terry L., and Dennis P. Rosenbaum. 1984. *Combating Retail Theft: Programs and Strategies.* Boston: Butterworth.

Bayley, David H. 1976. "Learning about Crime: The Japanese Experience." *Public Interest* 44 (Summer):55–68.

———. 1976a. *Forces of Order: Police Behavior in Japan and the United States.* Berkeley: University of California Press.

Beaty, Jonathan, and S. C. Gwynne (1991). "The Dirtiest Bank of All," *Time* (July 29):42–47.

Beccaria, Cesare. 1764, 1963. *On Crimes and Punishments.* Translated by Henry Paolucci. Indianapolis: Bobbs-Merrill.

Becker, Howard S. 1963. *Outsiders: Studies in the Sociology of Deviance.* New York: Free Press.

Bedau, Hugo Adam. 1974. "A Philosopher's View: Are There Really 'Crimes without Victims'?" In *Victimless Crimes: Two Sides of a Controversy*, ed. Edwin Schur and Hugo Adam Bedau, 55–105. Englewood Cliffs, N.J.: Prentice-Hall.

Beirne, Piers. 1983. "Generalization and Its Discontents: The Comparative Study of Crime." In *Comparative Criminology*, ed. Israel Barak-Glantz and Elmer Johnson, 19–38. Beverly Hills: Sage.

———. 1983a. "Cultural Relativism and Comparative Criminology." *Contemporary Crises* 7:371–91.

———. 1987. "Adolphe Quetelet and the Origins of Positivist Criminology." *American Journal of Sociology* 92(5):1140–69.

———. 1987a. "Between Classicism and Positivism: Crime and Penalty in the Writings of Gabriel Tarde." *Criminology* 25(4):785–819.

———. 1988. "Heredity versus Environment: A Reconsideration of Charles Goring's *The English Convict* (1913)." *British Journal of Criminology* 28(3):315–39.

———. 1993. *Inventing Criminology: Essays on the Rise of 'Homo Criminalis'.* Albany, N.Y.: State University of New York Press.

———. 1994. "The Law is an Ass: Reading E. P. Evans' *The Medieval Prosecution and Capital Punishment of Animals.*" *Society & Animals* 2(1): 27–46.

Beirne, Piers, and Alan Hunt. 1989. "Law and the Constitution of Soviet Society: The Case of Comrade Lenin." *Law & Society Review* 22(3):575–614.

Beirne, Piers, and Barbara Perry 1994. "Criminal Victimization in the Industrialized World." *Crime, Law and Social Change*, forthcoming.

Bell, Daniel. 1961. *The End of Ideology.* New York: Collier.

Bell, Laurie, ed. 1987. *Good Girls/Bad Girls: Feminists and Sex Trade Workers Face to Face.* Seattle: The Seal Press.

Bell, Raymond. 1976. "Moral Views on Gambling Promulgated by Major American Religious Bodies." In *Gambling in America*, Commission on the Review of the National Policy Toward Gambling, 161–239. Washington, D.C.: U.S. Government Printing Office.

Bellis, David J. 1981. *Heroin and Politicians: The Failure of Public Policy to Control Addiction in America.* Westport, Conn.: Greenwood.

Bennett, James. 1981. *Oral History and Delinquency: The Rhetoric of Criminology.* Chicago: University of Chicago Press.

Bennett, Trevor, and Richard Wright. 1984. *Burglars on Burglary.* Brookfield, Vt.: Gower.

Benson, Donna J., and Gregg E. Thompson. 1982. "Sexual Harassment on a University Campus: The Confluence of Authority Relation, Sexual Interest, and Gender Stratification." *Social Problems* 29(3):236–51.

Benson, George C. S. 1978. *Political Corruption in America*. Lexington, Mass.: Lexington Books.

Bentham, Jeremy. 1780, 1973. *An Introduction to the Principles of Morals and Legislation*. New York: Hafner Press.

———. 1787, 1971. *Panopticon: or, The Inspection-House*. 3 Vols. Dublin; London: reprinted and sold by T. Payne.

Bequai, August. 1978. *White-Collar Crime: A 20th-Century Crisis*. Lexington, Mass.: Lexington Books.

Berman, Daniel. 1978. *Death on the Job*. New York: Monthly Review Press.

Bernard, Thomas J. 1983. *The Consensus-Conflict Debate: Form and Content in Social Theories*. New York: Columbia University Press.

———. 1987. "Structure and Control: Reconsidering Hirschi's Concept of Commitment." *Justice Quarterly* 4(3):409–24.

Berrill, Kevin T. 1992. "Anti-Gay Violence and Victimization in the United States: An Overview." In *Hate Crimes: Confronting Violence Against Lesbians and Gay Men*, eds. Gregory M. Herek and Kevin T. Berrill, 19–45. Newbury Park, Calif.: Sage.

Bianchi, Herman, and Rene Van Swaaningen, eds. 1986. *Abolitionism: Towards a Nonrepressive Approach to Crime*. Amsterdam: Free University Press.

Biderman, Albert D., Louise Johnson, Jennie McIntyre, and Adrianne Weir. 1967. *Report on a Pilot Study in the District of Columbia on Victimization and Attitudes to Law Enforcement*. U.S. President's Commission on Law Enforcement and Administration of Justice, Field Surveys 1. Washington, D.C.: U.S. Government Printing Office.

Black, Donald. 1970. "Production of Crime Rates." *American Sociological Review* 35(4):733–48.

———. 1976. *The Behavior of Law*. New York: Academic Press.

———. 1989. *Sociological Justice*. New York: Oxford University Press.

Black, George. 1981. *Triumph of the People: The Sandinistas' Revolution in Nicaragua*. London: Zed Press.

Blau, Judith R., and Peter M. Blau. 1982. "The Cost of Inequality: Metropolitan Structure and Violent Crime." *American Sociological Review* 47(1):114–29.

Block, Alan. 1977. "Aw—Your Mother's in the Mafia: Women Criminals in Progressive New York." *Contemporary Crises* 1(1):5–22.

———. 1979. "The Snowman Cometh: Coke in Progressive New York." *Criminology* 17(1):75–99.

———. 1980. "Searching for Women in Organized Crime." In *Women, Crime, and Justice*, ed. Susan K. Datesman and Frank R. Scarpitti, 192–213. New York: Oxford University Press.

———. 1983. *East Side—West Side: Organizing Crime in New York, 1930–1950*. New Brunswick, N.J.: Transaction.

Block, Alan A. ed. 1991. *The Business of Crime: A Documentary Study of Organized Crime in the American Economy*. Boulder: Westview Press.

Block, Alan, and Thomas Bernard. 1988. "Crime in the Waste Oil Industry." *Deviant Behavior* 9:113–29.

Block, Alan, and William J. Chambliss. 1981. *Organizing Crime*. New York: Elsevier.

Block, Alan, and Frank Scarpitti. 1985. *Poisoning for Profit*. New York: William Morrow.

Block, Maggie, Rosa Bernstein, Penny Ciancanelli, Gay Ferguson, Alan Howard, Kathy Huenemann, Marta Sanchez, Bob Seltzer, Julio Velazquez, and Sol Yurick. 1972. "Nixon and Organized Crime." *North American Congress on Latin America (NACLA)* 6:3–17.

Blok, Anton. 1974. *The Mafia of a Sicilian Village, 1860–1960*. New York: Harper and Row.

Blumer, Herbert. 1971. "Social Problems as Collective Behavior." *Social Problems* 18(3):298–306.

Blundell, William E. 1976. "Equity Funding: 'I Did It for the Jollies.'" In *Swindled*, ed. Donald Moffit, 31–44. Princeton: Dow Jones Books.

Boggs, Sarah L. 1966. "Urban Crime Patterns." *American Sociological Review* 30(6):899–908.

Bohman, Michael C., Robert Cloninger, Soren Sigvardsson, and Anne-Liis von Knorring. 1982. "Predisposition to Petty Criminality in Swedish Adoptees." *Archives of General Psychiatry* 39(11):1233–41.

Boostrom, Ronald L. 1974. "The Personalization of Evil: The Emergence of American Criminology, 1865–1910." Unpublished Ph.D. dissertation, University of California, Berkeley.

Bordua, David J. 1961. "Delinquent Subcultures: Sociological Interpretations of Gang Delinquency." *Annals of the American Academy of Political and Social Science* 338(61):119–36.

Boston Herald. 1988. "7 Cops Guilty in Racketeering Case." (Sept. 4):10.

Boudreau, John F., Quon Y. Kwan, William F. Faragher, and Genevieve C. Denault. 1977. *Arson and Arson Investigation*. Washington, D.C.: U.S. Government Printing Office.

Box, Steven. 1983. *Power and Mystification*. New York: Tavistock.

———. 1987. *Recession, Crime and Punishment*. London: Macmillan.

Box, Steven, and Chris Hale. 1983. "Liberation and Female Criminality in England and Wales Revisited." *British Journal of Criminology* 22(3):35–49.

Brady, James P. 1983. "Arson, Urban Economy, and

Organized Crime: The Case of Boston." *Social Problems* 31(1):1–27.

Braithwaite, John. 1979. "Transnational Corporations and Corruption: Towards Some International Solutions." *International Journal of the Sociology of Law* 7(2):125–42.

———. 1979a. *Inequality, Crime, and Public Policy*. Boston: Routledge & Kegan Paul.

———. 1981. "The Myth of Social Class and Criminality Reconsidered." *American Sociological Review* 46(1):36–57.

———. 1984. *Corporate Crime in the Pharmaceutical Industry*. Boston: Routledge & Kegan Paul.

Brake, Mike, 1980. *The Sociology of Youth Culture and Youth Subcultures*. Boston: Routledge & Kegan Paul.

Branfman, Frank. 1978. "South Vietnam's Police and Prison System: The U.S. Connection." In *Uncloaking the CIA*, ed. Howard Frazier, 110–27. New York: Free Press.

Brantingham, Paul, and Patricia Brantingham. 1984. *Patterns in Crime*. New York: Macmillan.

Bray, Howard. 1980. *Pillars of the Post*. New York: W. W. Norton.

Breacher, Edward M. 1972. *Licit and Illicit Drugs*. Boston: Little, Brown.

Brecher, Jeremy. 1980. *Strike!* Boston: South End Press.

Breen, Richard, and David B. Rottman. 1985. *Crime Victimisation in the Republic of Ireland*. Dublin: The Economic and Social Research Institute, paper no. 121.

Breines, Wini, and Linda Gordon. 1983. "The New Scholarship on Family Violence." *Signs* 8(3):490–531.

Brenner, M. Harvey. 1976. *Estimating the Social Costs of National Economic Policy*. Joint Economic Committee of the U.S. Congress. Washington, D.C.: U.S. Government Printing Office.

Briar, Scott, and Irving Piliavin. 1965. "Delinquency, Situational Inducements, and Commitment to Conformity." *Social Problems* 13(1):35–45.

Brody, Jane. 1983. "Study Finds Much Heart Bypass Surgery Can Be Put Off or Avoided." *New York Times* (Oct. 27):A28.

Brody, Reed. 1985. *Contra Terror in Nicaragua: Report of a Fact-finding Mission, September 1984–January 1985*. Boston: South End Press.

Brown, Julia S. 1952. "A Comparative Study of Deviations from Sexual Mores." *American Sociological Review* 17(2):135–46.

Browne, Angela. 1987. *When Battered Women Kill*. New York: The Free Press.

Brownmiller, Susan. 1975. *Against Our Will: Men, Women, and Rape*. New York: Simon and Schuster.

Buder, Leonard, 1986. "In Partial Verdict, U.S. Jury Finds 6 Radicals Guilty of 2 Bombings." *New York Times* (Mar. 5):B3.

Buikhuisen, Wouter, and Fokke P. H. Dijksterhuis. 1971. "Delinquency and Stigmatisation." *British Journal of Criminology* 11(2):185–87.

Buitrago, Ann Mari. 1988. "Report on CISPES Files Maintained by FBI Headquarters and Released under the Freedom of Information Act." Fund for Open Information and Accountability, Inc. New York.

Bulmer, Martin. 1984. *The Chicago School of Sociology: Institutionalization, Diversity, and the Rise of Sociological Research*. Chicago: University of Chicago Press.

Bureau of Justice Statistics. 1984. *Bank Robbery*. U.S. Department of Justice, Report NCJ-94463.

———. 1985. *The Crime of Rape*. U.S. Department of Justice, Report NCJ-96777.

———. 1986. *Jail Inmates, 1986*. U.S. Department of Justice, Report NCJ-107123.

———. 1986a. *State and Federal Prisoners, 1925–1985*. U.S. Department of Justice, Report NCJ-102494.

———. 1987. *Violent Crime Trends*. U.S. Department of Justice, Report NCJ-107217.

———. 1987a. *Imprisonment in Four Countries*. U.S. Department of Justice, Report NCJ-103967.

———. 1988. *Prisoners in 1987*. U.S. Department of Justice, Report NCJ-110331.

———. 1988. "Proceedings of the Third Workshop on Law and Justice Statistics." U.S. Department of Justice, Report NCJ-112230.

———. 1988a. "Criminal Victimization 1987." U.S. Department of Justice, Report NCJ-113587.

———. 1988b. "Lifetime Likelihood of Victimization." U.S. Department of Justice, Report NCJ-104274.

———. 1988c. "Households Touched by Crime, 1987." U.S. Department of Justice, Report NCJ-111240.

———. 1989. "New Directions for the National Crime Survey." U.S. Department of Justice, Report NCJ-115571.

———. 1989a. "BJS Data Report, 1988." U.S. Department of Justice, Report NCJ-116262.

———. 1993a. *Highlights from 20 Years of Surveying Crime Victims*. Washington, D.C.: Department of Justice.

———. 1993b. *Prisoners in 1992*. U.S. Department of Justice, Report NCJ-141874.

Burgess, Ann W., and Linda L. Holmstrom. 1983. *The Victim of Rape*. New Brunswick, N.J.: Transaction Books.

Burgess, E. W. 1925. "The Growth of the City: An Introduction to a Research Project." In *The City*, ed. Robert E. Park and E. W. Burgess, 47–62. Chicago: University of Chicago Press.

Burgess, Robert L., and Ronald L. Akers. 1966. "A Differential Association—Reinforcement Theory of Criminal Behavior." *Social Problems* 14(2):128–47.

Bursik, Robert J. 1984. "Urban Dynamics and Ecological Studies of Delinquency." *Social Forces* 63(2):393–413.

Burstyn, Varda, 1983. "Masculine Dominance and the State." In *The Socialist Register*, ed. Ralph Miliband and John Saville, 45–89. London: The Merlin Press.

———. 1984. "Anatomy of a Moral Panic." *Fuse* (Summer):29–38.

———. 1985. "Beyond Despair: Positive Strategies." In *Women against Censorship*, ed. Varda Burstyn, 152–80. Toronto: Douglas and McIntyre.

Business Week. 1989. "America's Gambling Fever." Apr. 24:112–20.

Butler, Sandra. 1979. *Conspiracy of Silence: The Trauma of Incest.* San Francisco: New Glide Publications.

Bynum, Timothy. 1987. "Controversies in the Study of Organized Crime." In *Organized Crime in America: Concepts and Controversies*, ed. Timothy Bynum, 3–11. Monsey, N.Y.: Willow Tree Press.

Byrne, James M., and Robert J. Sampson, eds. 1986. *The Social Ecology of Crime.* New York: Springer-Verlag.

C

Cadoret, Remi J. 1978. "Psychopathy in Adopted-Away Offspring of Biological Parents with Antisocial Behavior." *Archives of General Psychiatry* 35:176–84.

Cahill, Tom A. 1985. "Rape behind Bars." *The Progressive* (Nov.):12–21.

Calonius, Erik, with Tom Morganthau. 1987. "The Secret Warriors Tell Their Story." *Newsweek* (Feb. 9):26–28.

Calvin, Allen D. 1981. "Unemployment among Black Youths, Demographics, and Crime." *Crime and Delinquency* 27 (Apr.):234–44.

Calavita, Kitty, and Henry N. Pontell. 1990. " 'Heads I Win, Tails You Lose': Deregulation, Crime, and Crisis in the Savings and Loan Industry." *Crime and Delinquency* 36(3):309–41.

Cameron, Mary Owen. 1964. *The Booster and the Snitch.* New York: Free Press.

Caminer, Brian F. 1985. "Credit Card Fraud: The Neglected Crime." *Journal of Criminal Law and Criminology* 76 (Fall):746–63.

Campbell, Anne. 1984. *The Girls in the Gang: A Report from New York City.* London: Basil Blackwell.

Carlen, Pat. 1988. *Women, Crime and Poverty.* Philadelphia: Open University Press.

Carroll, Leo, and Pamela Irving Jackson. 1983. "Inequality, Opportunity, and Crime Rates in Central Cites." *Criminology* 21(2):170–94.

Carson, W. G. 1979. "The Conventionalization of Early Factory Crime." *International Journal of the Sociology of Law* 7(1):37–60.

Casper, Barry M., and Paul D. Wellstone 1981. *Powerline: The First Battle of America's Energy War.* Boston: University of Massachusetts Press.

Castleman, Barry. 1979. "The Export of Hazardous Factories to Developing Nations." *International Journal of Health Services* 9(4):569–606.

Castro, Janice. 1988. "The Cash Cleaners." *Time* (Oct. 24):65–66.

Cates, Willard, Jack C. Smith, Roger W. Rochet, and David Grimes. 1982. "Morality from Abortion and Childbirth: Are the Statistics Biased?" *Journal of the American Medical Association* 248(2):192–96.

Cavan, Ruth Shonle, and Jordan True Cavan. 1968. *Delinquency and Crime: Cross-Cultural Perspectives.* Philadelphia: J. J. Lippincott.

Center for Constitutional Rights. 1988. "Political Spying and the Central America Movement." *Movement Support Network News* 4:1–3.

Cernkovich, Stephen A. 1978. "Evaluating Two Models of Delinquency Causation." *Criminology* 16(3):335–52.

Cernkovich, Stephen A., and Peggy G. Giordano. 1979. "A Comparative Analysis of Male and Female Delinquency." *Sociological Quarterly* 20(2):131–45.

———. 1987. "Family Relationships and Delinquency." *Sociological Quarterly* 20(2):131–45.

Chambliss, William J. 1964. "A Sociological Analysis of the Law of Vagrancy." *Social Problems* 12(1):67–77.

———. 1975. "Toward a Political Economy of Crime." *Theory and Society* 2(Summer):149–70.

———. 1976. "Functional and Conflict Theories of Crime." In *Whose Law? What Order?*, ed. William J. Chambliss and Milton Mankoff, 1–28. New York: John Wiley.

———. 1988. *On the Take: From Petty Crooks to Presidents.* Bloomington, Ind.: Indiana University Press.

———. 1988a. *Exploring Criminology.* New York: Macmillan.

Chambliss, William J., and Robert B. Seidman. 1971. *Law, Order, and Power.* Reading, Mass.: Addison-Wesley.

Chapin, Bradley. 1983. *Criminal Justice in Colonial America, 1606–1660.* Athens, Ga.: University of Georgia Press.

Chemerinsky, Erwin. 1981. "Fraud and Corruption against the Government: A Proposed Statute to Establish a Taxpayer Remedy." *Journal of Criminal Law and Criminology* 72(4):1482–99.

Chesney-Lind, Meda. 1978. "Chivalry Reexamined: Women and the Criminal Justice System." In *Women, Crime, and the Criminal Justice System*, ed.

Lee Bowker 335–66. Lexington, Mass.: Lexington Books.

———. 1986. "Women and Crime: The Female Offender." *Signs* 12(1):78–96.

———. 1989. "Girl's Crime and Woman's Place: Toward a Feminist Model of Female Delinquency." *Crime and Delinquency* 35(1):5–29.

Chesney-Lind, Meda, and Noelie Rodriguez. 1983. "Women under Lock and Key: A View Inside." *The Prison Journal* 63(Summer/Autumn):47–65.

Chevalier, Louis. 1973. *Laboring Classes and Dangerous Classes in Paris during the First Half of the Nineteenth Century.* Translated by Frank Jellinek, Princeton: Princeton University Press.

Chicago Tribune. 1993. "2 ex-Chicago Heights officers get 30 years" (Feb. 26):3.

Chiricos, Theodore G., and Gordon P. Waldo. 1975. "Socioeconomic Status and Criminal Sentencing." *American Sociological Review* 40(6):753–72.

Chomsky, Noam. 1985. *Turning the Tide: U.S. Intervention in Central America and the Struggle for Peace.* Boston: South End Press.

Chomsky, Noam, and Edward S. Herman. 1977. "The United States versus Human Rights in the Third World." *Monthly Review* 29 (July–Aug.):22–45.

———. 1979. *The Washington Connection and Third World Fascism.* Boston: South End Press.

Christiansen, Karl O. 1977. "A Preliminary Study of Criminality among Twins." In *Biosocial Bases of Criminal Behavior,* ed. Sarnoff A. Mednick and Karl O. Christiansen, 89–108. New York: Gardner.

———. 1977a. "A Review of Studies of Criminality among Twins." In *Biosocial Bases of Criminal Behavior,* ed. Sarnoff A. Mednick and Karl O. Christiansen, 45–88. New York: Gardner.

Chunn, Dorothy E., and Shelley A. M. Gavigan. 1988. "Social Control: Analytical Tool or Analytical Quagmire?" *Contemporary Crises* 12(2):107–24.

Church Committee. 1975. Select Committee to Study Governmental Operations with Respect to Intelligence Activities. *Alleged Assassination Plots Involving Foreign Leaders.* Washington, D.C.: U.S. Government Printing Office.

———. 1976. Select Committee to Study Governmental Operations. *Intelligence Activities and the Rights of Americans.* Washington, D.C.: U.S. Government Printing Office.

Churchill, Ward, and Jim Vander Wall. 1988. *Agents of Repression.* Boston: South End Press.

Cicourel, Aaron V. 1968. *The Social Organization of Juvenile Justice.* New York: John Wiley.

Clark, Lorenne, and Debra Lewis. 1977. *Rape: The Price of Coercive Sexuality.* Toronto: Women's Press.

Clark, Terry N. 1969. *Gabriel Tarde on Communication and Social Influence.* Chicago: University of Chicago Press.

Clarke, Oscar W., John Glasson, Alison M. August, John A. Barrasso, Charles H. Epps, Robert McQuillan, Victoria N. Ruff, Charles W. Plows, George T. Wilkins, and David Orentticher. 1993. "Mandatory Parental Consent to Abortion." *Journal of the American Medical Association* 269(1):81–86.

Claybrook, Joan. 1984. *Retreat from Safety.* New York: Pantheon.

———. 1986. "White-Collar Crime." *Trial* Apr.:35–36.

Clinard, Marshall B. 1952. *The Black Market: A Study of White-Collar Crime.* New York:Rinehart.

———. 1964. "The Theoretical Implications of Anomie and Deviant Behavior." In *Anomie and Deviant Behavior,* ed. M. Clinard, 1–56. New York: Free Press.

———. 1974. *Sociology of Deviant Behavior.* New York: Holt, Rinehart and Winston.

———. 1978. "Comparative Crime Victimization Surveys: Some Problems and Results." *International Journal of Criminology and Penology* 6(3):221–31.

———. 1978a. *Cities with Little Crime: The Case of Switzerland.* Cambridge: Cambridge University Press.

Clinard, Marshall B., and Daniel J. Abbott. 1973. *Crime in Developing Countries: A Comparative Perspective.* New York: John Wiley.

Clinard, Marshall B., and Richard Quinney. 1973. *Criminal Behavior Systems.* New York: Holt, Rinehart and Winston.

Clinard, Marshall B., and Peter C. Yeager. 1980. *Corporate Crime.* New York: Free Press.

Cloward, Richard A., and Lloyd E. Ohlin. 1960. *Delinquency and Opportunity: A Theory of Delinquent Gangs.* New York: Free Press.

Cockburn, Leslie. 1987. *Out of Control.* New York: Atlantic Monthly Press.

Cohen, Albert K. 1955. *Delinquent Boys: The Culture of the Gang.* New York: Free Press.

———. 1965. "The Sociology of the Deviant Act: Anomie Theory and Beyond." *American Sociological Review* 30(1):5–14.

Cohen, Bernard. 1980. *Deviant Street Networks: Prostitution in New York.* Lexington, Mass.: Lexington Books.

Cohen, Lawrence E., and Kenneth Land. 1987. "Age Structure and Crime: Symmetry versus Asymmetry and the Projection of Crime Rates Through the 1990s." *American Sociological Review* 52(2):170–83.

Cohen, Lawrence E., and Richard Machalek. 1988. "A General Theory of Expropriative Crime: An Evolutionary Ecological Approach." *American Journal of Sociology* 94(3):465–501.

Cohen, Stanley. 1972, 1980. *Folk Devils and Moral Panics: The Creation of the Mods and Rockers.* New York: St. Martin's Press.

———. 1982. "Western Crime Control Models in the Third World." *Research in Law, Deviance, and Social Control* 4:85–119.

———. 1985. *Visions of Social Control.* Cambridge: Polity Press.

———. 1986. "Community Control: To Demystify or to Reaffirm?" In *Abolitionism: Towards a Non-Repressive Approach to Crime,* ed. Herman Bianchi and Rene Van Swaaningen, 127–32. Amsterdam: Free University Press.

———. 1988. "The Object of Criminology: Reflections on the New Criminalization." In *Against Criminology,* Stanley Cohen, 235–76. New Brunswick N.J.: Transaction.

Cohen, Stanley, and Andrew Scull. 1983. "Social Control in History and Sociology." In *Social Control and the State,* ed. Stanley Cohen and Andrew Scull, 1–14. Oxford: Martin Robertson.

Cole, Susan. 1987. "Sexual Politics: Contradictions and Explosions." In *Good Girls/Bad Girls: Feminists and Sex Trade Workers Face to Face,* ed. Laurie Bell, 33–36. Seattle: The Seal Press.

Coleman, James. 1989. *The Criminal Elite.* New York: St. Martin's Press.

Collins, James J., Robert L. Hubbard, and J. Valley Rachal. 1985. "Expensive Drug Use and Illegal Income: A Test of Explanatory Hypotheses." *Criminology* 23(4):743–64.

Comer, Michael J. 1985. *Corporate Fraud.* London: McGraw-Hill.

Commission. 1970. *The Report of the Commission on Obscenity and Pornography.* Washington, D.C.: U.S. Government Printing Office.

Commission on the Review of the National Policy Toward Gambling. 1976. *Gambling in America, Final Report.* Washington, D.C.: U.S. Government Printing Office.

Conger, Rand D. 1978. "From Social Learning to Criminal Behavior." In *Crime, Law, and Sanctions,* ed. Marvin D. Krohn and Ronald L. Akers, 91–104. Beverly Hills, Calif.: Sage.

Congressional Quarterly. 1988. "Record Number of Women, Blacks in Congress." 46 (Nov. 12):3293–95.

Conklin, John. 1972. *Robbery and the Criminal Justice System.* New York: Lippincott.

———. 1977. *Illegal but Not Criminal.* Englewood Cliffs, N.J.: Prentice-Hall.

Conway, Lucian G., and Joe A. Cox. 1987. "Internal Business Shrinkage." *Baylor Business Review* (Summer):8–11.

Cook, Philip J. 1983. *Robbery in the United States: An Analysis of Recent Trends.* Washington, D.C.: U.S. Department of Justice.

———. 1986. "The Relationship between Victim Resistance and Injury in Noncommercial Robbery." *Journal of Legal Studies* 15(2):405–16.

Cook, Philip J., and Gary A. Zarkin. 1985. "Crime and the Business Cycle." *Journal of Legal Studies* 14(1):115–28.

Cooke, Cynthia W., and Susan Dworkin. 1981. "Tough Talk about Unnecessary Surgery." *Ms.* 10(4):42–44.

Cooley, Charles H. 1930. *Sociological Theory and Social Research.* New York: Henry Holt.

Corn, David. 1988. "Bush's CIA: The Same Old Dirty Tricks." *The Nation* (Aug. 27–Sept. 3):157–60.

Crawford, Susan. 1993. "A Wink Here, a Leer There: It's Costly." *The New York Times* (March 28):17.

Cressey, Donald. 1969. *Theft of the Nation.* New York: Harper and Row.

———. 1971. *Other People's Money.* New York: Free Press.

Crites, Laura, ed. 1976. *The Female Offender.* Lexington, Mass.: Lexington Books.

Crowe, Raymond R. 1975. "An Adoptive Study of Psychopathy: Preliminary Results from Arrest Records and Psychiatric Hospital Records." In *Genetic Research in Psychiatry,* ed. Ronald R. Fieve, David Rosenthal, and Henry Brill, 95–103. Baltimore, Md.: Johns Hopkins University Press.

Cullen, Francis, William J. Maakestad, and Gray Cavender. 1987. *Corporate Crime Under Attack.* Cincinnati: Anderson.

Cullen, Francis, John Wozniak, and James Frank. 1985. "The Rise of the Elderly Offender: Will a New Criminal Be Invented?" *Crime and Social Justice* 23:151–65.

Curran, Debra. 1984. "Characteristics of the Elderly Shoplifter and the Effect of Sanctions on Recidivism." In *Elderly Criminals,* ed. William Wilbanks and Paul Kim, 123–37. New York: University Press of America.

Current Population Reports. 1988. *Projections of the Population of the U.S. by Age, Sex, and Race: 1983 to 2080.* Washington, D.C.: U.S. Government Printing Office.

Currie, Elliot. 1985. *Confronting Crime: An American Challenge.* New York: Pantheon.

Currie, Elliot. 1993. *Reckoning: Drugs, the Cities, and the American Future.* New York: Hill and Wang.

Currie, Elliot, and Jerome H. Skolnick. 1984. *America's Problems: Social Issues and Public Policy.* Boston: Little, Brown.

Curtis, Lynn A. 1974. "Victim Precipitation and Violent Crime." *Social Problems* 21(4):594–605.

D

Dahrendorf, Ralf. 1959. *Class and Class Conflict in an Industrial Society.* London: Routledge & Kegan Paul.

Daly, Kathleen. 1989. "Gender and Varieties of White-Collar Crime." *Criminology* 27(4):769–93.

Daly, Kathleen, and Meda Chesney-Lind. 1988. "Feminism and Criminology." *Justice Quarterly* 5(4):101–43.

Davis, Nanette J. 1980. *Sociological Constructions of Deviance.* Dubuque, Iowa: Wm. C. Brown.

———. 1988. "Battered Women: Implications for Social Control." *Contemporary Crises* 12(4):345–72.

DeFleur, Lois. 1969. "Alternative Strategies for the Development of Delinquency Theories Applicable to Other Cultures." *Social Problems* 17(2):30–39.

DeFleur, Melvin L., and Richard Quinney. 1966. "A Reformulation of Sutherland's Differential Association Theory and a Strategy for Empirical Verification." *Journal of Research in Crime and Delinquency* 3(1):1–22.

DeFronzo, James. 1983. "Economic Assistance to Impoverished Americans." *Criminology* 21(1):119–36.

DeGeorge, Gail. 1987. "A Wave of Embezzlements Hits Banking." *Business Week* (May 18):49.

De Haan, Willem. 1990. *The Politics of Redress: Crime, Punishment and Penal Abolition.* Boston: Unwin Hyman.

Dekesedevy, Walter S., and Ronald Hinch. 1991. *Woman Abuse: Sociological Perspectives.* Lewiston, NY: Thompson Educational Publishers.

Dekesedevy, Walter S., and Martin D. Schwartz. 1991. "British and U.S. Realism: A Critical Comparison." *International Journal of Offender Therapy and Comparative Criminology* 35(3):248–262.

Department of Justice, Bureau of Justice Statistics. 1987. *Criminal Victimization in the U.S. 1985.* Washington, D.C.: U.S. Government Printing Office.

Department of Justice. 1988. *United States Secret Service Investigative Activity.* Washington, D.C.: Treasury Department.

Department of Labor. 1988. *Labor Force Statistics Derived from the Current Population Survey, 1948–1987.* Washington, D.C.: U.S. Government Printing Office.

Diamond, Stanley. 1973. "The Rule of Law versus the Order of Custom." In *The Social Organization of Law,* ed. Donald Black and Maureen Mileski, 318–34. New York: Seminar Press.

Dinges, John, and Saul Landau. 1980. *Assassination on Embassy Row.* New York: Pantheon Books.

Dirks, Raymond L., and Leonard Gross. 1974. *The Great Wall Street Scandal.* New York: McGraw-Hill.

Ditton, Jason. 1977. "Perks, Pilferage, and the Fiddle: The Historical Structure of Invisible Wages." *Theory and Society* 4:39–71.

———. 1977a. *Part-Time Crime.* New York: Macmillan.

———. 1979. *Controlology.* London: Macmillan.

Dixon, Keith. 1977. "Is Cultural Relativism Self-Refuting?" *British Journal of Sociology* 28(1):75–88.

Dobash, R. Emerson, and Russell P. Dobash. 1979. *Violence against Wives.* New York: Free Press.

Doleschal, Eugene, and Anne Newton. 1981. *International Rates of Imprisonment.* Hackensack, N.J.: National Council on Crime and Delinquency.

Domhoff, G. William. 1967. *Who Rules America?* Englewood Cliffs, N.J.: Prentice-Hall.

Donnerstein, Edward, and Daniel B. Linz. 1986. "The Question of Pornography." *Psychology Today* (Dec.):56–59.

Donovan, Josephine. 1985. *Feminist Theory.* New York: Ungar.

Douglas, Jack D. 1977. "Watergate: Harbinger of the American Prince." In *Official Deviance,* ed. Jack D. Douglas and John M. Johnson, 112–20. New York: Lippincott.

Douglas, Jack D., and Paul K. Rasmussen, with Carol Ann Flanagan. 1977. *The Nude Beach.* Beverly Hills: Sage.

Dowie, Mark. 1977. "Pinto Madness." *Mother Jones* 2(7):18–19, 32.

———. 1979. "The Corporate Crime of the Century." *Mother Jones* 4(9):23–25, 37.

———. 1987. "The Dumping of Hazardous Products on Foreign Markets." In *Corporate Violence,* ed. Stuart Hills, 47–58. Totowa, N.J.: Rowman and Littlefield.

Dubowitz, Howard, Maureen Black, Raymond H. Starr, Jr., and Susan Zuravin. 1993. "A Conceptual Definition of Child Neglect." *Criminal Justice & Behavior* 20(1):8–26.

Duesterberg, Thomas J. 1979. "Criminology and the Social Order in Nineteenth-Century France." Ph.D. dissertation, Indiana University.

Duggan, Lisa, Nan Hunter, and Carol S. Vance. 1985. "False Promises: Feminist Anti-Pornography Legislation in the U.S." In *Women against Censorship,* ed. Varda Burstyn, 130–51. Toronto: Douglas and McIntyre.

Dumm, Thomas L. 1987. *Democracy and Punishment: Disciplinary Origins of the United States.* Madison: University of Wisconsin Press.

Durkheim, Émile. 1893, 1984. *The Division of Labor in Society.* Translated by W. D. Halls. New York: Free Press.

———. 1894, 1982. *The Rules of Sociological Method.* Translated by W. D. Halls. London: Macmillan.

———. 1897, 1951. *Suicide: A Study in Sociology.* Translated by J. A. Spaulding and G. Simpson. New York: Free Press.

———. 1900, 1958. *Professional Ethics and Civil Morals.* Translated by Cornelia Brookfield. Glencoe, Ill.: Free Press.

———. 1901, 1983. "Two Laws of Penal Evolution." In *Durkheim and the Law,* ed. Steven Lukes and Andrew Scull, 102–32. Translated by T. Anthony Jones and Andrew Scull. New York: St. Martin's Press.

———. 1912, 1948. *The Elementary Forms of Religious Life.* Translated by Joseph W. Swain. Glencoe, Ill.: Free Press.

Duster, Troy. 1987. "Crime, Youth Unemployment, and the Black Underclass." *Crime and Delinquency* 33(2):300–16.

Dwyer, Lynn E. 1983. "Structure and Strategy in the Antinuclear Movement." In *Social Movements of the Sixties and Seventies,* ed. Jo Freeman, 148–61. New York: Longman.

Dye, Nancy Schrom. 1980. "History of Childbirth in America." *Signs,* 6(1):97–108.

E

Eadington, William R., and James H. Frey. 1984. "Preface." *The Annals of the American Academy of Political and Social Science* (July):9–11.

Eaton, Mary. 1986. *Justice for Women? Family, Court, and Social Control.* Philadelphia: Open University Press.

Eddy, Paul, Hugo Sabogal, and Sara Walden. 1988. *The Cocaine Wars.* New York: W. W. Norton.

Edwards, Anne. 1988. *Regulation and Repression.* Sydney: Allen & Unwin.

Ehrenreich, Barbara. 1988. "Drug Frenzy," *Ms.* (Nov.):20–21.

Ehrenreich, Barbara, and Deidre English. 1973. *Witches, Midwives, and Nurses: A History of Women Healers.* Old Westbury, N.Y.: The Feminist Press.

Einstadter, Werner. 1969. "The Social Organization of Armed Robbery." *Social Problems* 17(1):64–83.

Einstein, Zillah R. 1988. *The Female Body and the Law.* Berkeley: University of California Press.

Elliott, Delbert S., and Suzanne S. Ageton. 1980. "Reconciling Race and Class Differences in Self-Reported and Official Estimates of Delinquency." *American Sociological Review* 45(1):95–110.

Elliott, Delbert S., and David Huizinga. 1983. "Social Class and Delinquent Behavior in a National Youth Panel: 1976–1980." *Criminology* 21(2):149–77.

Emerson, Steven. 1988. *Secret Warriors: Inside the Covert Military Operations of the Reagan Era.* New York: G. P. Putnam's Sons.

Engels, Friedrich. 1843, 1975. "Outlines of a Critique of Political Economy." In *Karl Marx/Frederick Engels: Collected Works,* Vol. 3, 419–43. New York: International Publishers.

———. 1845, 1975. *The Condition of the Working Class in England.* In *Karl Marx/Frederick Engels: Collected Works,* Vol. 4., 295–583. New York: International Publishers.

———. 1884, 1970. *The Origin of the Family, Private Property, and the State.* In *Karl Marx and Frederick Engels: Selected Works,* Vol. 3., 191–334. Moscow: Progress Publishers.

———. 1885, 1975. *Anti-Dühring.* London: Lawrence & Wishart.

———. 1886, 1970. "Ludwig Feuerbach and the End of Classical German Philosophy." In *Karl Marx and Frederick Engels: Selected Works,* Vol. 3., 337–76. Moscow: Progress Publishers.

———. 1888, 1970. "The Role of Force in History." In *Karl Marx and Frederick Engels: Selected Works,* Vol. 3., 377–428. Moscow: Progress Publishers.

———. 1893, 1970. "Letter to F. Mehring in Berlin." In *Karl Marx and Frederick Engels: Selected Works,* Vol. 3., 495–99. Moscow: Progress Publishers.

Epstein, Samuel. 1978. *The Politics of Cancer.* San Francisco: Sierra Club Books.

Ericson, Richard V., Patricia M. Baranek, and Janet B. L. Chan. 1980. *Visualizing Deviance.* Toronto: University of Toronto Press.

———. 1989. *Negotiating Control: A Study of News Sources.* Toronto, Ontario: University of Toronto Press.

Erikson, Kai T. 1966. *Wayward Puritans: A Study in the Sociology of Deviance.* New York: John Wiley.

Erskine, Hazel. 1972. "The Polls: Gun Control." *Public Opinion Quarterly* 36(3):455–69.

Evans, Ernest. 1983. "The Use of Terrorism by American Social Movements." In *Social Movements of the Sixties and Seventies,* ed. Jo Freeman, 252–61. New York: Longman.

F

Faris, Robert E. L. 1967, 1970. *Chicago Sociology, 1920–1932.* Chicago: University of Chicago Press.

Farley, Lin. 1978. *Sexual Shakedown.* New York: Warner Books.

Farley, Reynolds. 1980. "Homicide Trends in the United States." *Demography* 17(2):177–88.

Farrell, Kathleen L., and John A. Ferrara. 1985. *Shoplifting.* New York: Praeger.

Farrington, David P. 1987. "Implications of Biological Findings for Criminological Research." In *The Causes of Crime: New Biological Approaches,* ed. Sarnoff A. Mednick, Terrie Moffitt, and Susan A. Stack, 42–64. Cambridge: Cambridge University Press.

Faulk, M. 1977. "Men Who Assault Their Wives." In *Battered Women: A Psycho-Sociological Study of Domestic Violence,* ed. Maria Roy, 119–26. New York: Van Nostrand Reinhold.

Federal Bureau of Investigation. 1988. *Uniform Crime*

Reports. Washington, D.C.: U.S. Government Printing Office.

Federal Bureau of Investigation. 1992. *Uniform Crime Reporting Handbook: NIBRS Edition.* Washington, D.C.: U.S. Government Printing Office.

Feiden, Doug. 1979. "The Great Getaway: The Inside Story of the Lufthansa Robbery." *New York* (June 4):37–42.

Feinberg, Gary. 1984. "A Profile of the Elderly Shoplifter." In *Elderly Criminals,* ed. Evelyn Newman, Donald Newman, and Mindy Gewirtz, 35–50. Cambridge: Oelgeschlager, Gunn and Hain.

Felson, Richard, and Henry J. Steadman. 1983. "Situational Factors in Disputes Leading to Criminal Violence." *Criminology* 21(1):59–74.

Ferdinand, Theodore N. 1967. "The Criminal Patterns of Boston Since 1849." *American Journal of Sociology* 73(1):84–99.

Ferguson, Ann. 1984. "Sex War: The Debate between Radical and Libertarian Feminists." *Signs* 10(1): 106–12.

Ferracuti, Franco, and Marvin E. Wolfgang, eds. 1983. *Criminological Diagnosis: An International Perspective.* 2 Vols. Lexington, Mass.: Lexington Books.

Feyerabend, Paul. 1987. *Farewell to Reason.* London: Verso.

Feyerherm, William. 1981. "Measuring Gender Differences in Delinquency: Self Reports versus Police Contact." In *Comparing Female and Male Offenders,* ed. Marguerite Q. Warren, 46–54. Beverly Hills: Sage.

Figueira-McDonough, Josephina, William H. Barton, and Rosemary C. Sarri. 1981. "Normal Deviance: Gender Similarities in Adolescent Subcultures." In *Comparing Female and Male Offenders,* ed. Marguerite Q. Warren, 17–45. Beverly Hills: Sage.

Figueira-McDonough, Josephina, with Elaine Selo. 1980. "A Reformulation of the Equal Opportunity Explanation of Female Delinquency." *Crime and Delinquency* 26(3):333–43.

Fink, Arthur E. 1938. *Causes of Crime: Biological Theories in the United States 1800–1915.* Philadelphia: University of Pennsylvania Press.

Finkelhor, David. 1979. *Sexually Victimized Children.* New York: Free Press.

Finkelhor, David, and Kersti Yllö. 1985. *License to Rape: Sexual Abuse of Wives.* New York: Holt, Rinehart and Winston.

Fishbein, Diana, and Susan Pease. 1988. "The Effects of Diet on Behavior." *Research in Corrections* 1(2):1–47.

Fisher, Joseph C. 1976. "Homicide in Detroit: The Role of Firearms." *Criminology* 14(Nov.):387–400.

Fishman, Mark. 1978. "Crime Waves as Ideology." *Social Problems* 25(5):53–543.

Flanagan, William G., and Brigid McMenamin. 1992. "Why Cybercrooks Love Cellular." *Forbes* (December 21):189.

Fogarty, Michael, ed. 1984. *Irish Values and Attitudes: Report of the European Value Systems Survey.* Dublin: Dominican Publications.

Foucault, Michel. 1979. *Discipline & Punish: The Birth of the Prison.* Translated by Alan Sheridan. New York: Vintage Books.

———. 1980. *Power/Knowledge: Selected Interviews and Other Writings, 1972–1977.* Translated by Colin Gordon *et al.* New York: Pantheon.

Frank, André Gunder. 1971. *Sociology of Development and the Underdevelopment of Sociology.* London: Pluto Press.

Frank, Nancy K. 1985. *Crimes against Worker Health and Safety.* San Francisco: Sierra Club Books.

Frank, Nancy K., and Michael J. Lynch. 1992. *Corporate Crime, Corporate Violence.* Albany, NY: Harrow and Heston.

Frappier, John. 1984. "Above the Law: Violations of International Law by the U.S. Government from Truman to Reagan." *Crime and Social Justice* 21/22:1–36.

Freedman, Estelle. 1981. *Their Sisters' Keepers.* Ann Arbor, Mich.: University of Michigan Press.

Frégier, H. A. 1840. *Des classes dangereuses de la population dans les grandes villes, et des moyens de les rendre meilleurs.* 2 Vols. Paris: Baillière.

Friedman, Robert I. 1984. "Senator Paul Laxalt, the Man Who Runs the Reagan Campaign." *Mother Jones* 9(7):32–39.

Frierson, Cathy. 1987. "Crime and Punishment in the Russian Village: Rural Concepts of Criminality at the End of the Nineteenth Century." *Slavic Review* 46(1):55–69.

Fuller, Lon L. 1949. "The Case of the Speluncean Explorers." *Harvard Law Review* 62(4):616–45.

G

Galliher, John F. 1980. "The Study of the Social Origins of Criminal Law: An Inventory of Research Findings." *Research in Law and Sociology* 3:301, 319.

Galliher, John F., and John R. Cross. 1983. *Morals Legislation without Morality: the Case of Nevada.* New Brunswick, N.J.: Rutgers University Press.

Gallup, George Jr. 1993. *The Gallup Poll: Public Opinion 1992.* Wilmington, Del.: Scholarly Resources.

Galton, Francis. 1869. *Hereditary Genius.* London: Macmillan.

———. 1889. *Natural Inheritance.* London: Macmillan.

Gardiner, John. 1970. *The Politics of Corruption: Organized Crime in an American City.* New York: Russell Sage.

Garfinkel, Harold. 1956. "Conditions of Successful Degradation Ceremonies." *American Journal of Sociology* 61(5):420–24.

Garitty, Michael. 1980. "The U.S. Colonial Empire Is As Close as the Nearest Reservation." In *Trilateralism: The Trilateral Commission and Elite Planning for World Management*, ed. Holly Sklar, 238–688. Boston: South End Press.

Garland, David. 1983. "Durkheim's Theory of Punishment: A Critique." In *The Power to Punish*, ed. David Garland and Peter Young, 37–61. London: Heinemann Educational Books.

———. 1985. *Punishment and Welfare: A History of Penal Strategies.* Aldershot, Hants: Gower.

Garofalo, James. 1981. "Crime and the Mass Media: A Selective Review of Research." *Journal of Research in Crime and Delinquency* 18(2):319–50.

Garrow, David. 1981. *The FBI and Martin Luther King Jr.* New York: Penguin.

Gaylord, Mark S., and John F. Galliher. 1988. *The Criminology of Edwin Sutherland.* New Brunswick, N.J.: Transaction Books.

Geis, Gilbert. 1979. *Not the Law's Business: An Examination of Homosexuality, Abortion, Prostitution, Narcotics, and Gambling in the United States.* New York: Schocken Books.

Geis, Gilbert, and Colin Goff. 1983. "Introduction." In *White Collar Crime: the Uncut Version*, Edwin H. Sutherland, ix–xxxiii. New Haven: Yale University Press.

Geis, Gilbert, Henry N. Pontell, and Paul D. Jesilow. 1988. "Medicaid Fraud." In *Controversial Issues in Crime and Justice*, ed. Joseph Scott and Travis Hirschi, 17–39. Beverly Hills: Sage.

Geis, Gilbert, Paul D. Jesilow, Henry N. Pontell, and Mary Jane O'Brien. 1985. "Fraud and Abuse by Psychiatrists against Government Medical Benefit Programs." *American Journal of Psychiatry* 142 (Feb.):231–34.

Gelles, Richard J. 1977. "Power, Sex, and Violence: The Case of Marital Rape." *The Family Coordinator* 26(4):339–47.

———. 1979. "The Truth about Husband Abuse." *Ms.* 7 (Oct.):65–66.

Gelsthorpe, Loraine, and Allison Morris. 1988. "Feminism and Criminology in Britain." *British Journal of Criminology* 28(2):93–110.

General Accounting Office. 1988. *Controlling Drug Abuse: A Status Report.* Washington, D.C.: GAO/GGD.

Gibbons, Don C. 1979. *The Criminological Enterprise: Theories and Perspectives.* Englewood Cliffs, N.J.: Prentice-Hall.

Gil, David G., ed. 1979. *Child Abuse and Violence.* New York: AMS Press.

Giordano, Peggy C., and Stephen A. Cernkovich. 1979. "On Complicating the Relationship between Liberation and Delinquency." *Social Problems* 26(4):467–81.

Glaser, Daniel. 1956. "Criminality Theories and Behavioral Images." *American Journal of Sociology* 61(4):433–44.

———. 1960. "Differential Association and Criminological Prediction." *Social Problems* 8(1):6–14.

———. 1970. *Crime in the City.* New York: Harper and Row.

Glen, Kristin B. 1986. "Understanding the Abortion Debate: A Legal, Constitutional, and Political Framework." *Socialist Review* 16(5):51–69.

Glueck, Sheldon, and Eleanor Glueck. 1950. *Unraveling Juvenile Delinquency.* New York: The Commonwealth Fund.

———. 1956. *Physique and Delinquency.* New York: Harper.

Goddard, Henry H. 1914. *Feeble-Mindedness, Its Causes and Consequences.* New York: Macmillan.

Goetting, Ann. 1983. "The Elderly in Prison: Issues and Perspectives." *Journal of Research in Crime and Delinquency* 20(3):291–309.

Goff, Colin H., and Charles E. Reasons. 1986. "Organizational Crimes against Employees, Consumers, and the Public." In *The Political Economy of Crime*, ed. Brian D. Maclean, 204–31. Scarborough, Ontario: Prentice-Hall Canada.

Goffman, Erving. 1961. *Asylums.* New York: Anchor Books.

———. 1963. *Stigma.* Englewood Cliffs, N.J.: Prentice-Hall.

———. 1967. *Interaction Ritual: Essays on Face-to-Face Behavior.* Garden City, N.J.: Doubleday.

Gold, Martin. 1963. *Status Forces in Delinquent Boys.* Ann Arbor, Mich.: Institute for Social Research.

Goldstein, Leslie Friedman. 1988. *The Constitutional Rights of Women.* Madison, Wis.: University of Wisconsin Press.

Good, David H., and Maureen A. Pirog-Good. 1987. "A Simultaneous Probit Model of Crime and Employment for Black and White Teenage Males." *The Review of Black Political Economy* 16(1–2):109–27.

Goode, Erich. 1984. *Drugs in American Society.* New York: Alfred A. Knopf.

Goodman, Ellen. 1993. "Sex, Power and the Establishment." *Boston Globe* (April 29):15.

Gordon, Linda. 1976. *Woman's Body, Woman's Right: A Social History of Birth Control in America.* New York: Grossman.

———. 1981. "The Long Struggle for Reproductive Rights." *Radical America* 15 (1/2):75–88.

Gordon, Michael R. 1993. "Pentagon Report Tells of

Aviators' 'Debauchery.'" *The New York Times* (April 24):1,9.

Gordon, Robert A. 1987. "SES versus IQ in the Race—IQ—Delinquency Model." *International Journal of Sociology and Social Policy* 7(3):30–96.

Goring, Charles. 1913. *The English Convict: A Statistical Study.* London: H.M.S.O.

Graber, Doris A. 1980. *Crime News and the Public.* New York: Praeger.

Graham, Hugh Davis, and Ted Robert Gurr. 1969. *The History of Violence in America.* New York: Bantam.

Graham, James M. 1975. "Amphetamine Politics on Capitol Hill." In *Whose Law? What Order? A Conflict Approach to Criminology,* ed. William J. Chambliss and Milton Mankoff, 107–22. New York: John Wiley.

Gramsci, Antonio. 1926, 1978. "Some Aspects of the Southern Question." In *Gramsci: Selections from Political Writings,* translated by Quintin Hoare, 441–62. New York: International Publishers.

Gravley, Eric. 1988. "Building the Case against America's Narcotic Jihad." *In These Times* (Dec. 14–20):3, 10.

Green, Edward. 1970. "Race, Social Status, and Criminal Arrest." *American Sociological Review* 35(3):476–90.

Green, Gary S. 1987. "Citizen Gun Ownership and Criminal Deterrence: Theory, Research, and Policy." *Criminology* 25(2):63–81.

Green, Mark, Beverly C. Moore, and Bruce Wasserstein. 1972. *The Closed Enterprise System.* New York: Bantam Books.

Green, Mark, and John Francis Berry. 1985. *The Challenge of Hidden Profits.* New York: William Morrow and Co.

———. 1985a. "White-Collar Crime Is Big Business: Corporate Crime 1." *The Nation* (June 8):705–06.

Greenberg, David F. 1977. "Delinquency and the Age Structure of Society." *Contemporary Crises* 1(2):189–224.

———, ed. 1981. *Crime and Capitalism: Readings in Marxist Criminology.* Palo Alto, Calif.: Mayfield.

———. 1983. "Crime and Age." In *Encyclopedia of Crime and Justice,* Vol. 1., ed. Sanford Kadish, 30–35. New York: Macmillan.

———. 1985. "Age, Crime, and Social Explanation." *American Journal of Sociology* 91(1):1–21.

———. 1988. *The Construction of Homosexuality.* Chicago: University of Chicago Press.

Greenberg, David, Douglas Wolf, and Jennifer Pfiester. 1986. *Using Computers to Combat Welfare Fraud.* Westport, Conn.: Greenwood Press.

Greer, Germaine. 1973. "Seduction is a Four-Letter Word." *Playboy* (Jan.):12–13.

Griffin, Susan. 1971. "Rape: The All-American Crime." *Ramparts* (Sept.):26–35.

Gropper, Bernard A. 1985. "Probing the Links between Drugs and Crime." *National Institute of Justice: Research in Brief.* Washington, D.C.: U.S. Department of Justice.

Gross, Jane. 1989. "Epidemics from Urban Hospitals: Wounds from Assault Rifles." *New York Times* (Feb. 21):A1.

Groth, A. Nicholas, and Jean Birnbaum. 1979. *Men Who Rape.* New York: Plenum.

Guarasci, Richard. 1987. "Death by Cotton Dust." In *Corporate Violence,* ed. Stuart Hills, 76–92. Totowa, N.J.: Rowman and Littlefield.

Guillot, Ellen Elizabeth. 1943. "Social Factors in Crime as Explained by American Writers of the Civil War and Post Civil War Period." Unpublished Ph.D. dissertation, University of Pennsylvania.

Gurr, Ted Robert, Peter N. Grabosky, and Richard C. Hula. 1977. *The Politics of Crime and Conflict.* Beverly Hills: Sage.

Gusfield, Joseph R. 1963. *Symbolic Crusade.* Urbana, Ill.: University of Illinois Press.

Gutman, Roy. 1988. *Banana Diplomacy: The Making of American Foreign Policy in Nicaragua, 1981–1987.* New York: Simon and Schuster.

Guttmacher, Manfred Schanfarber. 1951. *Sex Offenses.* New York: W. W. Norton.

H

Hacker, Andrew. 1988. "Black Crime, White Racism." *New York Review of Books* 35(3):36–41.

Hagan, John. 1974. "Extra-Legal Attributes and Criminal Sentencing: An Assessment of a Sociological Viewpoint." *Law & Society Review* 8(3):357–83.

———. 1980. "The Legislation of Crime and Delinquency: A Review of Theory, Method, and Research." *Law & Society Review* 14(3):603–28.

Hagan, John, John H. Simpson, and A. R. Gillis. 1979. "The Sexual Stratification of Social Control: A Gender-Based Perspective on Crime and Delinquency." *British Journal of Sociology* 30(1):25–38.

———. 1987. "Class in the Household: A Power-Control Theory of Gender and Delinquency." *American Journal of Sociology* 92(4):788–816.

Hall, Jerome. 1952. *Theft, Law, and Society.* New York: Bobbs-Merrill.

———. 1969. "Theft, Law, and Society: The Carrier's Case." In *Crime and the Legal Process,* ed. William J. Chambliss, 32–51. New York: McGraw-Hill.

Hall, Stuart, Chas Critcher, Tony Jefferson, John Clarke, and Brian Roberts. 1978. *Policing the Crisis: Mugging, the State, and Law and Order.* London: Macmillan.

Hall, Stuart, and Tony Jefferson, eds. 1976. *Resistance through Rituals.* London: Macmillan.

Haller, Mark. 1976. "Bootleggers and American Gambling, 1920–1950." In *Gambling in America*, Commission on Review of National Policy toward Gambling, 102–43. Washington, D.C.: U.S. Government Printing Office.

Halpern, Sue. 1990. "Teen-Abortion Laws turn Trauma to Tragedy." *Rolling Stone* (August 9):43, 44, 72.

Hamilton, Lee H. 1993. "Case Closed." *The New York Times* (Jan. 24):17.

Hamlin, John E. 1988. "The Misplaced Role of Rational Choice in Neutralization Theory." *Criminology* 26(3):425–38.

Hamm, Mark S. 1993. *American Skinheads: The Criminology and Control of Hate Crime*. Westport, Conn.: Praeger.

Haran, James F., and John M. Martin. 1977. "The Imprisonment of Bank Robbers: The Issue of Deterrence." *Federal Probation* 41(3):29–36.

———. 1984. "The Armed Urban Bank Robber: A Profile." *Federal Probation* 48(4):47–53.

Harlow, Caroline Wolf. 1987. *Robbery Victims*. Washington, D.C.: U.S. Department of Justice.

Harries, Keith D. 1974. *The Geography of Crime and Justice*. New York: McGraw-Hill.

Hart, Barbara. 1986. "Lesbian Battering: An Examination." In *Naming the Violence: Speaking Out About Lesbian Violence*, ed. Kerry Lobel, 173–89. Seattle: Seal Press.

Hartjen, Clayton A., and S. Priyadarsini. 1984. *Delinquency in India: A Comparative Perspective*. New Brunswick, N.J.: Rutgers University Press.

Hartung, Frank E. 1950. "White-Collar Offenses in the Wholesale Meat Industry in Detroit." *American Journal of Sociology* 56(1):25–34.

Hay, Douglas. 1975. "Property, Authority and the Criminal Law." In *Albion's Fatal Tree*, Douglas Hay, Peter Linebaugh, John G. Rule, E. P. Thompson, and Cal Winslow. 17–63. New York: Pantheon.

Heidensohn, Frances. 1985. *Women and Crime: The Life of the Female Offender*. New York: New York University Press.

Helmer, John. 1975. *Drugs and Minority Oppression*. New York: Seabury Press.

Henderson, Charles Richmond. 1893. *Introduction to the Study of the Dependent, Defective, and Delinquent Classes*. Boston: D.C. Heath.

Henry, Stuart. 1976. "The Other Side of the Fence." *Sociological Review* 24(Nov.):793–806.

———. 1977. "On the Fence." *British Journal of Law and Society* 4(1):124–33.

———. 1978. *The Hidden Economy*. London: Martin Robertson.

———, ed. 1981. *Can I Have It in Cash?* London: Astragal Books.

———. 1987. "The Political Economy of Informal Economies." *Annals of the American Academy of Political and Social Science* 493(Sept.):137–53.

Henry, Stuart, and Gerald Mars. 1978. "Crime at Work: The Social Construction of Amateur Property Theft." *Sociology* 12(2):245–63.

Henry, Stuart, and Dragan Milovanovic. 1991. "Constitutive Criminology: the Maturation of Critical Criminology," *Criminology*, 29:293–315.

Henry, Stuart, and Dragan Milovanovic. 1994. "The Constitution of Constitutive Criminology: A Postmodern Approach to Criminological Theory." Forthcoming in David Nelken, ed. *The Futures of Criminology*. London: Sage.

Henshaw, Stanley K. 1987. "Characteristics of U.S. Women Having Abortions, 1982–1983." *Family Planning Perspectives* 19(1):5–13.

Hepburn, John. 1977. "Testing Alternative Models of Delinquency Causation." *Journal of Criminal Law and Criminology* 67(4):450–60.

Herbert, David. 1982. *The Geography of Urban Crime*. London: Longman.

Herman, Edward. 1982. *The Real Terror Network*. Boston: South End Press.

Herman, Ellen. 1984. "Introduction." In *Not an Easy Choice*, Kathleen McDonnell, i–xv. Boston: South End Press.

Herman, Judith. 1981. *Father-Daughter Incest*. Cambridge, Mass.: Harvard University Press.

Herman, Judith, and Lisa Hirschman. 1977. "Father-Daughter Incest." *Signs* 2(4): 735–56.

Herrnstein, Richard J. 1983. "Some Criminogenic Traits of Offenders." In *Crime and Public Policy*, ed. James Q. Wilson, 31–49. San Francisco: Institute for Contemporary Studies.

Hess, Henner. 1973. *Mafia and Mafioso: The Structure of Power*, Lexington, Mass.: D.C. Heath.

Hills, Stuart, ed. 1987. *Corporate Violence*. Totowa, N.J.: Rowman and Littlefield.

Hills, Stuart L., and Ron Santiago. 1992. *Tragic Magic: The Life and Crimes of a Heroin Addict*. Chicago: Nelson-Hall.

Hinckle, Warren, and William Turner. 1981. *The Fish is Red—The Story of the Secret War against Castro*. New York: Harper and Row.

Hindelang, Michael J. 1970. "The Commitment of Delinquents to their Misdeeds: Do Delinquents Drift?" *Social Problems* 17(4):502–09.

———. 1973. "Causes of Delinquency: A Partial Replication and Extension." *Social Problems* 20(4):471–87.

———. 1974. "Moral Evaluations of Illegal Behaviors." *Social Problems* 21(3):370–85.

———. 1979. "Sex Differences in Criminal Activity." *Social Problems* 27(2):143–56.

———. 1981. "Variations in Sex-Race-Age-Specific Incidence Rates of Offending." *American Sociological Review* 46(4):461–74.

Hindelang, Michael J., Travis Hirschi, and Joseph Weis. 1979. "Correlates of Delinquency: The Illusion of Discrepancy between Self-Report and Official Measures." *American Sociological Review* 44(6):995–1014.

Hindess, Barry. 1973. *The Use of Official Statistics in Sociology.* London: Macmillan.

Hirschi, Travis. 1969. *Causes of Delinquency.* Berkeley: University of California Press.

———. 1983. "Crime and the Family." In *Crime and Public Policy*, ed. James Q. Wilson, 53–68. San Francisco: Institute for Contemporary Studies.

Hirschi, Travis, and Michael Gottfredson. 1983. "Age and the Explanation of Crime." *American Journal of Sociology* 89(3):552–84.

Hirschi, Travis, and Michael J. Hindelang. 1977. "Intelligence and Delinquency: A Revisionist Review." *American Sociological Review* 42(4):571–87.

Hirst, Paul Q. 1972. "Marx and Engels on Law, Crime, and Morality." *Economy and Society* 1(Feb.):28–56.

Hite, Shere. 1976. *The Hite Report on Female Sexuality.* New York: Knopf.

Hobsbawn, Eric. 1959. *Primitive Rebels.* New York: W. W. Norton.

Hoffman, Abbie, and Jonathan Silvers. 1980. "An Election Held Hostage." *Playboy* 35(10):73–74.

Hoffman, David. 1986. "Aide to Bush Opened Doors for Guerrilla War Expert." *The Washington Post* (Oct. 24):A1, A20.

Hoffman-Bustamante, Dale. 1973. "The Nature of Female Criminality." *Issues in Criminology* 8(2):117–32.

Hofstadter, Richard, and Michael Wallace. 1970. *Violence: A Documentary History.* New York: Knopf.

Hollinger, Richard C., and John P. Clark. 1983. *Theft by Employees.* Lexington, Mass.: Lexington Books.

Holmes, Ronald M., and James E. DeBurger. 1985. "Profiles in Terror: The Serial Murderer." *Federal Probation* 49(3):29–34.

———. 1988. *Serial Murder.* Beverly Hills: Sage.

Holmstrom, Lynda L., and Ann Burgess. 1980. "Sexual Behavior of Assailants During Reported Rape." *Archives of Sexual Behavior* 9(3):34–45.

———. 1983. *The Victim of Rape.* New Brunswick, N.J.: Transaction Books.

Holyst, Bruno. 1979. *Comparative Criminology.* Lexington, Mass.: Lexington Books.

Henegger, Barbara. 1989. *October Surprise.* New York: Tudor Publishing Co.

Hooton, Ernest Albert. 1939. *Crime and the Man.* Cambridge, Mass.: Harvard University Press.

Hopkins, Elaine. 1988. "A Matter of Conscience for a G-Man." *The Progressive* 52:14.

Howe, Laura K. 1977. *Pink-Collar Ghetto.* New York: G. P. Putnam.

Hughes, Graham. 1964. "The Crime of Incest." *Journal of Criminal Law, Criminology, and Police Science* 55(3):322–36.

Huizinga, David, and Delbert S. Elliott. 1987. "Juvenile Offenders: Prevalence, Offender Incidence, and Arrest Rates by Race." *Crime and Delinquency* 33(2):206–23.

Humphreys, Laud. 1970. *Tearoom Trade: Impersonal Sex in Public Places.* Chicago: Aldine.

Humphries, Drew. 1981. "Serious Crime, News Coverage, and Ideology." *Crime & Delinquency* 27(2):191–205.

Hunt, Alan. 1978. *The Sociological Movement in Law.* London: Macmillan.

Hunt, Alan. 1991. "Postmodernism and Critical Criminology." Pp. 79–85 in Brian D. MacLean and Dragan Milovanovic, eds. 1991. *New Directions in Critical Criminology.* Vancouver: The Collective Press.

Hunt, Morton. 1979. "Legal Rape." *Family Circle* 92(1):24, 37–38, 125.

Hymowitz, Carol, and Timothy D. Schellhardt. 1986. "The Glass Ceiling." *The Wall Street Journal* (March 24):1D,4D–5D.

I

Ignatius, David. 1986. "The Contrapreneurs: Skirting Congress and the Law for Years." *The Washington Post* (Dec. 7):D1, D2.

Inciardi, James A. 1975. *Careers in Crime.* Chicago: Rand McNally.

———. 1986. *The War on Drugs: Heroin, Cocaine, Crime, and Public Policy.* Palo Alto, Calif.: Mayfield.

Ingrassia, Michele. 1993. "Abused and Confused." *Newsweek* (Oct. 25):57–58.

Island, David, and Patrick Letellier, eds. 1991. *Men Who Beat the Men Who Love Them: Battered Gay Men and Domestic Violence.* New York: Harrington Park Press.

J

Jackall, Robert. 1980. "Crime in the Suites." *Contemporary Sociology* 9:357–58.

Jackson, Bruce. 1964. *A Thief's Primer.* New York: Macmillan.

Jacobs, David. 1981. "Inequality and Economic Crime." *Sociology and Social Research* 66(1):12–28.

Jacobs, David, and David Britt. 1979. "Inequality and Police Use of Deadly Force: An Empirical Assessment of a Conflict Hypothesis." *Social Problems* 26(4):403–12.

Jacobs, Patricia, Muriel Brunton, and Marie M. Melville.

1965. "Aggressive Behaviour, Mental Subnormality, and the XYY Male." *Nature* 208:1351–52.

Jacobson, Michael. 1985. *The Enigmatic Crime: A Study of Arson*. Unpublished Ph.D. dissertation, City University of New York.

Jacobson, Michael, and Philip Kasinitz. 1986. "Burning the Bronx for Profit." *The Nation* (Nov. 15):512–15.

Jaggar, Alison M. 1983. *Feminist Politics and Human Nature*. Totowa, N.J.: Rowman and Allanheld.

Jaggar, Alison M., and Paula Rothenberg, eds. 1984. *Feminist Frameworks*. New York: McGraw-Hill.

James, Jennifer. 1982. "The Prostitute as Victim." In *The Criminal Justice System and Women*, ed. Barbara Raffel Price and Natalie J. Sokoloff, 291–315. New York: Clark Boardman.

James, Jennifer, and William Thornton. 1980. "Women's Liberation and the Female Delinquent." *Journal of Research in Crime and Delinquency* 17(3):230–44.

Jaspan, Norman. 1974. *Mind Your Own Business*. Englewood Cliffs, N.J.: Prentice-Hall.

Jeffery, Clarence Ray. 1965. "Criminal Behavior and Learning Theory." *Journal of Criminal Law, Criminology, and Police Science* 56(3):294–300.

———, ed. 1979. *Biology and Crime*. Beverly Hills: Sage.

Jencks, Christopher. 1987. "Genes and Crime." *New York Times Review of Books* (Feb. 12):33–34.

Jenkins, Philip. 1984. "Varieties of Enlightenment Criminology." *British Journal of Criminology* 24(2):112–30.

———. 1988. "Myth and Murder: The Serial Killer Panic of 1983–1985." *Criminal Justice Research Bulletin* 3(11):1–7.

Jensen, Gary F. 1972. "Delinquency and Adolescent Self-Conceptions: a Study of the Personal Relevance of Infraction." *Social Problems* 20(1)84–102.

Jesilow, Paul D., Henry N. Pontell, and Gilbert Geis. 1985. "Medical Criminals: Physicians and White-Collar Offenses." *Justice Quarterly* 2(2):149–65.

Jesilow, Paul, Henry N. Pontell, and Gilbert Geis. 1993. *Prescription for Profit: How Doctors Defraud Medicaid*. Berkeley: University of California Press.

Jessop, Bob. 1982. *The Capitalist State: Marxist Theories and Methods*. Oxford: Martin Robertson.

Joe, Tom. 1987. "Economic Inequality: The Picture in Black and White." *Crime and Delinquency* 33(2):287–99.

Johansen, Bruce, and Roberto Maestas. 1979. *Wasichu: The Continuing Indian Wars*. New York: Monthly Review Press.

Johnson, Allan Griswold. 1980. "On the Prevalence of Rape in the United States." *Signs* 6(1):136–46.

Johnson, Elmer H., ed. 1983. *International Handbook of Contemporary Developments in Criminology*. 2 Vols. Westport, Conn.: Greenwood.

Johnson, Elmer H., and Israel L. Barak-Glantz, eds. 1983. *Comparative Criminology*. Beverly Hills, Calif.: Sage.

Johnson, Lloyd, Patrick O'Malley, and Jerald Baldwin. 1992. *Smoking, Drinking and Illicit Drug Use Among American Secondary School Students, College Students, and Young Adults, 1975–91*. Washington, D.C.: National Institute on Drug Abuse.

Judis, John. 1988. "The Big Sleazy: A New Era of Government Corruption." *In These Times* (July 20–Aug. 2):7.

Jurik, Nancy, and Peter Gregware. 1992. "A Method for Murder: The Study of Homicides by Women." *Perspectives on Social Problems* 4:179–201.

K

Kalish, Carol B. 1988. "International Crime Rates." *Bureau of Justice Statistics*. U.S. Department of Justice, NCJ-110776.

Kallis, M. Jeffery, and Dinoo J. Vanier. 1985. "Consumer Shoplifting: Orientations and Deterrents." *Journal of Criminal Justice* 13(4):459–73.

Kania, Richard R., and Ruth E. Tanham. 1987. "Rise and Fall of Television Crime." Unpublished paper presented at the American Society of Criminology annual meetings, Montreal.

Katz, Jack. 1988. *Seductions of Crime*. New York: Basic Books.

Keat, Russell, and John Urry. 1975. *Social Theory as Science*. London: Routledge & Kegan Paul.

Kefauver Committee. 1951. *Special Committee to Investigate Organized Crime in Interstate Commerce*. Washington, D.C.: U.S. Government Printing Office.

Kellor, Frances A. 1899. "Psychological and Environmental Study of Women Criminals." *American Journal of Sociology* 5(4):527–43, and 5(5):671–82.

———. 1901. *Experimental Sociology. Delinquents*. New York: Macmillan.

Kelly, Orr, and Ted Gest. 1982. "Reagan Revolution Takes Firm Hold at Justice." *U.S. News and World Report* (Apr. 26):24–26.

Kennedy, Leslie W., Robert A. Silverman, and David R. Forde. 1991. "Homicide in Urban Canada: Testing the Impact of Economic Inequality and Social Disorganization," *Canadian Journal of Sociology*, 16(4):397–410.

Kerr, Clark, John T. Dunlop, Frederick H. Harbison, and Charles A. Myers. 1962. *Industrialism and Industrial Man*. London: Heinemann.

Keverne, E. B., R. E. Meller, and J. A. Eberhart. 1982.

"Social Influences on Behavior and Neuroendocrine Responsiveness in Talapoin Monkeys." *Scandinavian Journal of Psychology* 1:37–47.

Kilpatrick, Dean G., Patricia A. Riesnick, and Lois J. Veronin. 1981. "Effects of a Rape Experience: A Longitudinal Study." *Journal of Social Issues* 37(4):105–22.

Kimmel, Michael S. 1993. "Does Pornography Cause Rape?" *Violence Update* 3(10):1–8.

King, Harry, and William J. Chambliss. 1984. *Harry King: A Professional Thief's Journey*. New York: John Wiley.

Kitsuse, John I., and Aaron V. Cicourel. 1963. "A Note on the Uses of Official Statistics." *Social Problems* 11(2):131–39.

Kitsuse, John I., and David C. Dietrick. 1959. "Delinquent Boys: A Critique." *American Sociological Review* 24(2):208–15.

Klanwatch. 1989. *Intelligence Report: Special Report on Hate Crime in 1988*. Montgomery, Ala.: Southern Poverty Law Center.

Klein, Dorie. 1973. "The Etiology of Female Crime: A Review of the Literature." *Issues in Criminology* 8(2):3–30.

———. 1979. "Can This Marriage Be Saved? Battery and Sheltering." *Crime and Social Justice* 12 (Winter):19–33.

Klemke, Lloyd W. 1992. *The Sociology of Shoplifting: Boosters and Snitches Today*. Westport, Conn.: Praeger.

Klockars, Carl B. 1974. *The Professional Fence*. New York: Free Press.

———. 1979. "The Contemporary Crises of Marxist Criminology." *Criminology* 16(3):477–515.

Knapp Commission. 1972. *Knapp Commission Report on Police Corruption*. New York: Braziller.

Knickerbocker, Brad. 1990. "Reports of Racial Violence Grow." *Christian Science Monitor* (Oct. 5):6.

Kobrin, Solomon. 1951. "The Conflict of Values in Delinquent Areas." *American Sociological Review* 16(5):653–61.

Kolko, Gabriel. 1962. *Wealth and Power in America*. New York: Praeger.

Kornhauser, Ruth Rosner. 1978. *Social Sources of Delinquency*. Chicago: University of Chicago Press.

Kreuz, Leo E., and Robert M. Rose. 1972. "Assessment of Aggressive Behavior and Plasma Testosterone in a Young Criminal Population." *Psychosomatic Medicine* 34(4):321–32.

Krohn, Marvin D., and James L. Massey. 1980. "Social Control and Delinquent Behavior: An Examination of the Elements of the Social Bond." *Sociological Quarterly* 21(4):529–44.

Krohn, Marvin D., Lonn Lanza-Kaduce, and Ronald L. Akers. 1984. "Community Context and Theories of Deviant Behavior: An Examination of Social Learning and Social Bonding Theories." *Sociological Quarterly* 25(3):353–71.

Kruger, Henrik. 1980. *The Great Heroin Coup*. Boston: South End Press.

Kruttschnitt, Candace. 1982. "Women, Crime, and Dependency." *Criminology* 9(4):495–513.

Kunstler, William. 1978. "FBI Letters: Writers of the Purple Rage." *The Nation* (Dec. 30):721–22.

Kunze, Michael. 1987. *Highroad to the Stake*. Translated by William E. Yuill. Chicago: University of Chicago Press.

Kurtz, Howard. 1988. "E. F. Hutton to Plead Guilty." *Washington Post* (Apr. 2):A3.

Kwitny, Jonathan. 1987. *The Crimes of Patriots: A True Tale of Dope, Dirty Money, and the CIA*. New York: Norton

L

Lafleur, Laurence J. 1973. "Introduction." In *The Principles of Morals and Legislation*, Jeremy Bentham, vii–xv. New York: Hafner.

Lagrange, Randy L., and Kenneth F. Ferraro. 1989. "Assessing Age and Gender Differences in Perceived Risk and Fear of Crime," *Criminology*, 27(4):697–719.

Lamour, Catherine, and Michael R. Lamberti. 1974. *The International Connection: Opium from Growers to Pushers*. New York: Pantheon Books.

Lander, Bernard. 1954. *Towards an Understanding of Juvenile Delinquency*. New York: Columbia University Press.

Lane, David. 1970. *Politics and Society in the USSR*. London: Weidenfeld and Nicolson.

Lane, Roger. 1979. *Violent Death in the City: Suicide, Accident, and Murder in Nineteenth-Century Philadelphia*. Cambridge, Mass.: Harvard University Press.

Lanza-Kaduce, Lonn. 1980. "Deviance among Professionals: The Case of Unnecessary Surgery." *Deviant Behavior* 1:333–59.

Laub, John H. 1983. *Criminology in the Making: An Oral History*. Boston: Northeastern University Press.

Laub, John H., and M. Joan McDermott. 1985. "An Analysis of Serious Crime by Young Black Women." *Criminology* 23(1):81–98.

Laub, John H., and Robert J. Sampson. 1988. "Unraveling Families and Delinquency: A Reanalysis of the Glueck's Data." *Criminology* 26(3):355–80.

Lea, John, and Jock Young. 1984. *What is to Be Done about Law and Order?* New York: Penguin.

———. 1986. "A Realistic Approach to Law and Order." In *The Political Economy of Crime: Readings for a Critical Criminology*, ed. Brian MacLean, 358–64. Englewood Cliffs, N.J.: Prentice-Hall.

Lebolt, Scot A., David A. Grimes, and Willard Cates. 1982. "Mortality from Abortion and Childbirth: Are the Populations Comparable?" *Journal of the American Medical Association* 248(2):188–91.

Lederer, Laura, ed. 1980. *Take Back the Night: Women on Pornography*. New York: William Morrow.

Lemert, Edwin M. 1951. *Social Pathology: A Systematic Approach to the Theory of Sociopathic Behavior*. New York: McGraw-Hill.

———. 1967. *Human Deviance, Social Problems, and Social Control*. Englewood Cliffs, N.J.: Prentice-Hall.

Lens, Sidney. 1973. *The Labor Wars: From the Molly Maguires to the Sitdowns*. New York: Doubleday.

Leonard, Eileen B. 1982. *Women, Crime, and Society: A Critique of Criminology Theory*. New York: Longman.

Lester, M. L., R. W. Thatcher, and L. Monroe-Lord. 1982. "Refined Carbohydrate Intake, Hair Cadmium Levels and Cognitive Functioning in Children." *Journal of Nutrition and Behavior* 1:1–14.

Levi, Ken. 1981. "Becoming a Hit Man: Neutralization in a Very Deviant Career." *Urban Life* 10(Apr.):47–63.

Levi-Strauss, Claude. 1971. "The Family." In *The Family in Transition: Rethinking Marriage, Child Rearing and Family Organization*, ed. Arlene S. Skolnick and Jerome H. Skolnick, 50–72. Boston: Little, Brown.

Levin, Jack, and James A. Fox. 1988. *Elementary Statistics in Social Research*. New York: Harper & Row.

Levin, Jack, and Jack McDevitt. 1993. *Hate Crimes: The Rising Tide of Bigotry and Bloodshed*. New York: Plenum Press.

Lewis, Diane. 1981. "Black Women Offenders and Criminal Justice: Some Theoretical Considerations." In *Comparing Female and Male Offenders*, ed. Marguerite Q. Warren, 89–105. Beverly Hills: Sage.

Liebert, Robert M., and Joyce Sprafkin. 1988. *The Early Window: Effects of Television on Children and Youth*. New York: Pergamon.

Lifschultz, Lawrence. 1988. "Inside the Kingdom of Heroin." *The Nation* (Nov. 14):477, 492–96.

Lindesmith, Alfred R. 1947. *Opiate Addiction*. Bloomington, Ind.: Principia Press.

Linebaugh, Peter. 1976. "Karl Marx, The Theft of Wood and Working Class Composition." *Crime and Social Justice* 6(Fall/Winter):5–16.

Link, Bruce G., Francis T. Cullen, James Frank, and John F. Wozniak. 1987. "The Social Rejection of Former Mental Patients: Understanding Why Labels Matter." *American Journal of Sociology* 92(6):1461–1500.

Lizotte, Alan J. 1978. "Extra-Legal Factors in Chicago's Criminal Courts: Testing the Conflict Model of Criminal Justice." *Social Problems* 25(5):564–80.

Lobel, Kerry. 1986. "Introduction." In *Naming the Violence: Speaking Out About Lesbian Battering*, ed. Kerry Lobel, 1–8. Seattle: Seal Press.

Loftin, Colin, and Robert H. Hill. 1974. "Regional Subculture and Homicide: An Examination of the Gastil-Hackney Thesis." *American Sociological Review* 39(5):714–24.

Lombroso, Cesare. 1876. *L'Uomo delinquente* (Criminal Man). Milan: Hoepli.

———. 1902, 1918. *Crime: Its Causes and Remedies*. Translated by Henry P. Horton. Boston: Little, Brown.

Lombroso, Cesare, and William Ferrero. 1893, 1895. *The Female Offender*. London: T. Fisher Unwin.

López-Rey, Manuel. 1985. *A Guide to United Nations Criminal Policy*. Aldershot, Hants: Gower.

Los, Maria. 1983. "Economic Crimes in Communist Countries." In *Comparative Criminology*, ed. Israel Barak-Glantz and Elmer H. Johnson, 39–57. Beverly Hills: Sage.

Lott, Bernice, Mary E. Reilly, and Dale R. Howard. 1982. "Sexual Assault and Harassment: A Campus Community Case Study." *Signs* 8(Winter):296–319.

Lowman, John, Robert J. Menzies, and T. S. Palys, eds. 1987. *Transcarceration: Essays in the Sociology of Social Control*. Aldershot: Gower.

Luckenbill, David F. 1977. "Criminal Homicide as a Situated Transaction." *Social Problems* 25(2):176–86.

———. 1981. "Generating Compliance: The Case of Robbery." *Urban Life* 10(1):25–46.

———. 1982. "Compliance under Threat of Severe Punishment." *Social Forces* 60(3):811–25.

———. 1986. "Deviant Career Mobility: The Case of Male Prostitutes." *Social Problems* 33(4):283–96.

Lukes, Steven. 1973. *Emile Durkheim: His Life and Work*. London: Penguin.

Lynd, Robert S. 1939. *Knowledge for What?* Princeton: Princeton University Press.

M

Maas, Peter. 1986. *Manhunt*. New York: Random House.

MacKinnon, Catharine A. 1979. *Sexual Harassment of Working Women*. New Haven, Conn.: Yale University Press.

———. 1982. "Feminism, Marxism, Method, and the State: An Agenda for Theory." *Signs* 7(3):515–44.

———. 1984. "Not a Moral Issue." *Yale Law and Policy Review* 2(2):321–45.

———. 1986. "Pornography and Sex Discrimination." *Law and Inequality* 4(1): 38–49.

MacIntyre, Alasdair. 1971. "Is a Science of Comparative Politics Possible?" In *Against the Self-Images of the Age*, MacIntyre, 260–79. London: Duckworth.

———. 1981. *After Virtue*. Notre Dame: University of Notre Dame Press.

Maier, Pauline. 1972. *From Resistance to Revolution: Colonial Radicals and the Development of American Opposition to Britain, 1765–1776*. New York: Knopf.

Mannheim, Herman. 1965. *Comparative Criminology*. 2 Vols. London: Routledge & Kegan Paul.

Manning, Peter K. 1975. "Deviance and Dogma: Some Comments on the Labelling Perspective." *British Journal of Criminology* 15(1):1–20.

Marable, Manning. 1983. *How Capitalism Underdeveloped Black America*. Boston: South End Press.

Marcuse, Herbert. 1964. *One Dimensional Man*. Boston: Beacon Press.

Mars, Gerald. 1983. *Cheats at Work*. Boston: Unwin.

Marsh, Robert M. 1967. *Comparative Sociology*. New York: Harcourt Brace & World.

Marshall, Johnathan, Peter Dale Scott, and Jane Hunter. 1987. *The Iran-Contra Connection*. Boston: South End Press.

Martin, Del. 1982. "Battered Women: Society's Problem." In *The Criminal Justice System and Women*, ed. Barbara Raffel Price and Natalie J. Sokoloff, 263–90. New York: Clark Boardman.

Marx, Gary T. 1981. "Ironies of Social Control: Authorities as Contributors to Deviance through Escalation, Non-Enforcement, and Covert Facilitation." *Social Problems* 28(3):221–46.

Marx, Karl. 1842, 1975. "Comments on the Latest Prussian Censorship Instruction." In *Marx/Engels Collected Works*, Vol. 1, 109–31. London: Lawrence & Wishart.

———. 1842a, 1975. "Proceedings of the Sixth Rhine Province Assembly. Debates on the Law on Thefts of Wood." In *Karl Marx/Frederick Engels: Collected Works*, Vol. 1, 224–63. London: Lawrence & Wishart.

———. 1852, 1969. "The Eighteenth Brumaire of Louis Bonaparte." In *Karl Marx and Frederick Engels: Selected Works*, Vol. 1, 398–487. Moscow: Progress Publishers.

———. 1853, 1956. "Capital Punishment." In *Karl Marx: Selected Writings in Sociology and Social Philosophy*, ed. T. B. Bottomore and Maximilian Rubel, 228–30. New York: McGraw-Hill.

———. 1857–1858, 1973. *Grundrisse: Introduction to the Critique of Political Economy*. Translated and introduced by Martin Nicolaus. New York: Vintage.

———. 1859, 1969. "Preface to *A Contribution to the Critique of Political Economy*." In *Karl Marx and Frederick Engels: Selected Works*, Vol. 1, 502–06. Moscow: Progress Publishers.

———. 1859a. "Population, Crime, and Pauperism." *New York Daily Tribune* (Sept. 16).

———. 1868, 1967. *Capital*. 3 Vols. New York: International Publishers.

———. 1871, 1969. "The Civil War in France." In *Karl Marx and Frederick Engels: Selected Works*, Vol. 2, 190–244. Moscow: Progress Publishers.

Marx, Karl, and Friedrich Engels. 1845, 1976. *The German Ideology*. Moscow: Progress Publishers.

———. 1845a, 1975. *The Holy Family*. In *Karl Marx and Frederick Engels: Collected Works*, Vol. 4, 9–211. New York: International Publishers.

———. 1848, 1969. "The Communist Manifesto." In *Karl Marx and Frederick Engels: Selected Works*, Vol. 1, 108–37. Moscow: Progress Publishers.

Mathiesen, Thomas. 1974. *The Politics of Abolition*. Oslo: Universitetsforlaget.

Matsueda, Ross L. 1988. "The Current State of Differential Association Theory." *Crime & Delinquency* 34(3):277–306.

Mattelart, Armand. 1983. *Transnationals and the Third World*. South Hadley, Mass.: Bergin and Garvey.

Mattera, Philip. 1985. *Off the Books*. New York: St. Martin's Press.

Matthews, Roger. 1987. "Taking Realist Criminology Seriously." *Contemporary Crises* 11(4):371–401.

Matza, David. 1964. *Delinquency and Drift*. New York: John Wiley.

———. 1969. *Becoming Deviant*. Englewood Cliffs, N.J.: Prentice-Hall.

Matza, David, and Gresham M. Sykes. 1961. "Juvenile Delinquency and Subterranean Values." *American Sociological Review* 26(5):712–19.

Mayer P. 1953. "Gusii Initiation Ceremonies." *Journal of the Royal Anthropological Institute* 83:9–36.

McCaghy, Charles H., Peggy C. Giordano, and Trudy Knicely Henson. 1977. "Auto Theft: Offender and Offense Characteristics." *Criminology* 15(3):367–85.

McCarthy, Belinda, and Robert Langworthy. 1988. *Older Offenders*. New York: Praeger.

McClennan Committee. 1963. Hearings before the Permanent Subcommittee on Investigations. *Organized Crime and Illicit Traffic in Narcotics*. Washington, D.C.: U.S. Government Printing Office.

McClintock, F. H., and Evelyn Gibson. 1961. *Robbery in London*. London: Macmillan.

McClintock, Michael. 1985. *The American Connection:*

State Terror and Popular Resistance in Guatemala. London: Zed Books.

McCormack, Thelma. 1985. "Making Sense of Research on Pornography." In *Women against Censorship*, ed. Varda Burstyn, 181–205. Toronto: Douglas and McIntyre.

McCoy, Alfred. 1972. *The Politics of Heroin in Southeast Asia.* New York: Harper and Row.

McCoy, Charles. 1987. "Financial Fraud: Theories behind Nationwide Surge in Bank Swindles." *Wall Street Journal* (Oct. 2):23.

McDevitt, Jack. 1989. "The Study of the Implementation of the Massachusetts Civil Rights Act." Unpublished paper.

McGlothlin, William H., M. Douglas Anglin, and Bruce D. Wilson. 1978. "Narcotic Addiction and Crime." *Criminology* 16(3):293–315.

McIntosh, Mary. 1973. "The Growth of Racketeering." *Economy and Society* 2(1):35–69.

———. 1976. "Thieves and Fences: Market and Power in Professional Crime." *British Journal of Criminology* 16(3):257–66.

McLennan, Barbara N. 1970. *Crime in Urban Society.* New York: Dunellen.

Medea, Andrea, and Kathleen Thompson. 1874. *Against Rape.* New York: Farrar, Straus, and Giroux.

Mednick, Sarnoff A., Vicki Pollock, Jan Volavka, and William F. Gabrielli Jr. 1982. "Biology and Violence." In *Criminal Violence*, ed. Marvin E. Wolfgang and Neil Alan Weiner, 21–80. Beverly Hills: Sage.

Mednick, Sarnoff A., William F. Gabrielli Jr., and Barry Hutchings. 1987. "Genetic Factors in the Etiology of Criminal Behavior." In *The Causes of Crime: New Biological Approaches*, ed. Sarnoff A. Mednick, Terrie Moffitt, and Susan A. Stack, 74–91. Cambridge: Cambridge University Press.

Meese Commission. 1986. Attorney General's Commission on Pornography. *Final Report.* Washington, D.C.: U.S. Department of Justice.

Meier, Robert F. 1983. "Shoplifting." In *Encyclopedia of Crime and Justice*, Vol. 4, ed. Sanford H. Kadish, 1497–1500. New York: Free Press.

Melossi, Dario, and Massimo Pavarini. 1981. *The Prison and the Factory: Origins of the Penitentiary System.* Totowa, N.J.: Barnes and Noble.

Merton, Robert K. 1938, 1969. "Social Structure and Anomie." In *Delinquency, Crime, and Social Process*, ed. Donald R. Cressey and David A. Ward, 254–84. New York: Harper and Row.

Messerschmidt, James W. 1986. *The Trial of Leonard Peltier.* Boston: South End Press.

———. 1986a. *Capitalism, Patriarchy, and Crime: Toward a Socialist Feminist Criminology.* Totowa, N.J.: Rowman and Littlefield.

———. 1987. "Feminism, Criminology, and the Rise of the Female Sex 'Delinquent,' 1880–1930." *Contemporary Crises* 11(3):243–63.

———. 1988. "From Marx to Bonger: Socialist Writings on Women, Gender and Crime." *Sociological Inquiry* 58(4):378–92.

———. 1993. *Masculinities and Crime: Critique and Reconceptualization of Theory.* Lanham, MD: Rowman and Littlefield.

Messner, Steven F. 1980. "Income Inequality and Murder Rates." *Comparative Social Research* 3:185–98.

Messner, Steven, and Kenneth Tardiff. 1985. "The Social Ecology of Urban Homicide: An Application of the Routine Activities Approach." *Criminology* 23(2):241–67.

Michael, Jerome, and Mortimer J. Adler. 1933, 1971. *Crime, Law, and Social Science.* Montclair, N.J.: Patterson Smith.

Michalowski, Raymond J. 1983. "Crime Control in the 1980s: A Progressive Agenda." *Crime and Social Justice* 19 (Summer):13–23.

Michalowski, Raymond J. 1985. *Order, Law, and Crime.* New York: Random House.

Michalowski, Raymond J., and Ed Bolander. 1976. "Repression and Criminal Justice in Capitalist America." *Sociological Inquiry* 46(2):99–110.

Michalowski, Raymond J., and Ronald C. Kramer. 1987. "The Space Between Laws: The Problem of Corporate Crime in a Transnational Context." *Social Problems* 34(1):34–53.

Mieczkowski, Thomas. 1986. "Geeking Up and Throwing Down: Heroin Street Life in Detroit." *Criminology* 24(4):645–66.

Mill, John Stuart. 1851, 1970. *The Subjection of Women.* New York: Source Book Press.

Miller, Eleanor. 1983. "International Trends in the Study of Female Criminality: An Essay Review." *Contemporary Crises* 7(1):59–70.

———. 1986. *Street Women.* Philadelphia: Temple University Press.

Miller, Walter B. 1958. "Lower Class Culture as a Generating Milieu of Gang Delinquency." *Journal of Social Issues*, 14(3):5–19.

Mills, C. Wright. 1956. *The Power Elite.* New York: Oxford University Press.

Milovanovic, Dragan, and Stuart Henry. 1991. "Constitutive Penology," *Social Justice* 18(3):204–224.

Mintz, Morton. 1985. "At Any Cost: Corporate Greed, Women, and the Dalkon Shield." *The Progressive* (Nov.):20–25.

———. 1986. "A Crime against Women: A. H. Robbins

and the Dalkon Shield." *Multinational Monitor* (Jan. 15):1–7.

Miracle, Andrew. 1981. "Cross-Cultural Research and the Role of Anthropology in Criminal Justice." *Journal of Criminal Justice* 9(5):383–88.

Mohr, James C. 1978. *Abortion in America*. New York: Oxford University Press.

Mokhiber, Russell. 1988. *Corporate Crime and Violence*. San Francisco: Sierra Club.

Moore, Mark. 1977. *Buy and Bust*. Lexington, Mass.: Lexington Books.

Moore, Sally Falk. 1978. *Law as Process*. London: Routledge & Kegan Paul.

Moore, Thomas. 1988. "The Black-on-Black Crime Plague." *U.S. News and World Report* (Aug. 22)49–55.

Moore, William. 1974. *The Kefauver Committee and the Politics of Crime, 1950–1952*. Columbia, Mo.: University of Missouri Press.

Morgan, Robin. 1980. "Theory and Practice: Pornography and Rape." In *Take Back the Night: Women on Pornography*, ed. Laura Lederer, 134–47. New York: William Morrow.

Morris, Allison. 1987. *Women, Crime, and Criminal Justice*. New York: Basil Blackwell.

Moyers, Bill. 1988. *The Secret Government: The Constitution in Crisis*. Washington, D.C.: Seven Locks Press.

Mueller, John H., Karl Schuessler, and Herbert Costner. 1970. *Statistical Reasoning in Sociology*. Boston: Houghton Mifflin.

Mulvihill, Donald J., H. H. Tumin, and Lynn A. Curtis. 1969. *Crimes of Violence: A Staff Report Submitted to the National Commission on the Causes and Prevention of Violence*. Washington, D.C.: U.S. Government Printing Office.

Mungham, Geoff, and Geoff Pearson. 1976. *Working-Class Youth Culture*. London: Routledge & Kegan Paul.

Murphy, Daniel. 1986. *Customers and Thieves: An Ethnography of Shoplifting*. Brookfield, Vt.: Gower.

Murray, John. 1986. "Marijuana's Effects on Human Cognitive Functions, Psychomotor Functions, and Personality." *Journal of General Psychology* 113(1):23–55.

Musto, David F. 1973. *The American Disease: Origins of Narcotic Control*. New Haven, Conn.: Yale University Press.

Myers, Martha A. 1988. "Social Background and the Sentencing Behavior of Judges." *Criminology* 26(4):649–75.

N

Naffine, Ngaire. 1987. *Female Crime: The Construction of Women in Criminology*. Boston: Allen and Unwin.

Nagel, Ilene. 1981. "Sex Differences in the Processing of Criminal Defendants." In *Women and Crime*, ed. Allison Morris, 44–62. Cambridge: Cambridge University Press.

Nagi, Saad Z. 1975. "Child Abuse and Neglect Programs: A National Overview." *Children Today* 4(May–June):13–17.

Nash, Nathaniel. 1985. "Capitalist Punishment." *The New Republic* (May 27):5–6.

National Advisory Commission on Criminal Justice Standards and Goals. 1973. *A National Strategy to Reduce Crime*. Washington, D.C.: U.S. Government Printing Office.

National Center on Child Abuse and Neglect. 1993. "National Child Abuse and Neglect Data System: Working Paper 2." Washington, D.C.: U.S. Department of Health and Human Services.

National Coalition for Jail Reform. 1986. "Jail Is the Wrong Place to Be for Public Inebriates." Washington, D.C.: National Coalition for Jail Reform.

National Commission on the Causes and Prevention of Violence. 1970. *Final Report. To Establish Justice, To Insure Domestic Tranquility*. New York: Bantam Books.

National Crime Survey. 1987. *Criminal Victimization in the U.S., 1985*. Washington, D.C.: U.S. Department of Justice.

National Institute of Law Enforcement and Criminal Justice. 1980. *Arson Prevention and Control*. Washington, D.C.: U.S. Department of Justice.

National Institute on Drug Abuse. 1987. *National Trends in Drug Use and Related Factors among American High School Students and Young Adults, 1975–1986*. Washington, D.C.: U.S. Government Printing Office.

Nelli, Humbert S. 1981. *The Business of Crime*. Chicago: University of Chicago Press.

———. 1987. "A Brief History of American Syndicate Crime." In *Organized Crime in America: Concepts and Controversies*, ed. Timothy S. Bynum, 15–29. Monsey, New York: Willow Tree Press.

Nelson, Steve, and Menachem Amir. 1975. In *Victimology: A New Focus*, Vol. V, ed. Israel Drapkin and Emilio Viano, 47–64. Lexington, Mass.: Lexington Books.

Nettler, Gwynn. 1978. *Explaining Crime*. New York: McGraw-Hill.

Newman, Evelyn, Donald Newman, and Mindy Gewirtz. 1984. *Elderly Criminals*. Cambridge: Delgeschlarger, Gunn, and Hain.

Newman, Graeme R., ed. 1980. *Crime and Deviance: A Comparative Perspective*. Beverly Hills: Sage.

Newman, Oscar. 1973. *Defensible Space: Crime Prevention through Urban Design*. London: Macmillan.

Newton, George D., and Frank E. Zimring. 1969. *Firearms and Violence in American Life*. Washington, D.C.: U.S. Government Printing Office.

New York Times. 1984. "Professional Blamed for Vehicle Theft Rise." (Nov. 26):A13.

———. 1986. "Toledo Abortion Clinic Damaged in Arson Fire." (Jan. 1):6.

———. 1987. "Florida Bank Indictments." (May 2):39.

———. 1987a. "Boesky and Levine Snared in Inquiry." (Jan. 2):D2.

———. 1988a. "Baltimore Policeman Is Held in Sales of Heroin by Phone." (Jan. 3): A31.

———. 1988b. "Policewoman Seized by U.S. Drug Agents in Big Heroin Raid." (Mar. 3):B5.

———. 1993. "U.S. Inquiry into Trading." (June 26):A39.

———. 1993a. "Ex-Officer Guilty in Sale of Information to Gotti." (February 28):A46.

Nielsen, J. 1971. "Prevalence and a 2 Years Incidence of Chromosome Abnormalities among All Males in a Forensic Psychiatric Clinic." *British Journal of Psychiatry* 119:503–12.

Nye, F. Ivan. 1958. *Family Relationships and Delinquent Behavior*. New York: John Wiley.

Nye, Robert. 1982. "Heredity, Pathology and Psychoneurosis in Durkheim's Early Work." *Knowledge and Society* 4:103–42.

O

Oakley, Ann. 1972. *Sex, Gender, and Society*. New York: Harper and Row.

Oberdorfer, Don, and Patrick E. Tyler. 1983. "U.S. Backed Nicaraguan Rebel Army Swells to 7,000 Men." *The Washington Post* (May 8):A1, A10, A11.

Oberschall, Anthony. 1972. "The Institutionalization of American Sociology." In *The Establishment of Empirical Sociology: Studies in Continuity, Discontinuity, and Institutionalization*, ed. A. Oberschall, 187–251. New York: Harper and Row.

O'Kelly, Charlotte G., and Larry S. Carney. 1986. *Women and Men in Society*. Belmont, Calif.: Wadsworth.

O'Neil, William L. 1969. *The Woman Movement: Feminism in the United States*. New York: Barnes and Noble.

Ortega, Suzanne T., and Jessie L. Myles. 1987. "Race and Gender Effects on Fear of Crime: An Interactive Model with Age." *Criminology* 25(1):133–52.

Ortiz, Roxanne Dunbar. 1977. *The Great Sioux Nation*. Berkeley: Moon Books.

P

Paolucci, Henry. 1963. "Translator's Introduction." In *On Crime and Punishments*, Cesare Beccaria (1764), ix–xxiii. Indianapolis: Bobbs-Merrill.

Parenti, Michael. 1983. *Democracy for the Few*. New York: St. Martin's.

Park, Robert E. 1915. "The City: Suggestions for the Investigation of Human Behavior in the City." *American Journal of Sociology* 20(5):577–612.

Parker, Donn B. 1976. *Crime By Computer*. New York: Charles Scribner.

Parmalee, Maurice. 1918. *Criminology*. New York: Macmillan.

Pear, Robert. 1980. "Sexual Harassment at Work Outlawed." *New York Times* (Apr. 12):1, 20.

Pearce, Frank. 1976. *Crimes of the Powerful*. London: Pluto Press.

Pearson, Geoffrey, and John Twohig. 1976. "Ethnography through the Looking-Glass." In *Resistance Through Rituals: Youth Subcultures in Post-War Britain*, ed. Stuart Hall and Tony Jefferson, 119–25. London: Hutchinson.

Pearson, Karl. 1919. "Charles Goring and His Contribution to Criminology." In Goring (1919), abridged version, Goring (1913), xv–xx.

Pelton, Leroy H., ed. 1981. *The Social Context of Child Abuse and Neglect*. New York: Human Sciences.

Pepinsky, Harold E. 1978. "Communist Anarchism As an Alternative to the Rule of Criminal Law." *Contemporary Crises* 2(3):315–34.

Pepinsky, Harold E., and Richard Quinney, eds. 1991. *Criminology as Peacemaking*. Bloomington, Ind.: Indiana University Press.

Perrot, Michelle. 1975. "Délinquance et système pénitentaire en France au XIXe siècle." *Annales: Economies, société, civilisations* 30(1):67–91.

Petchesky, Rosalind Pollack. 1984. *Abortion and Woman's Choice: The State, Sexuality, and Reproductive Freedom*. Boston: Notheastern University Press.

Petit, Jacques G. 1984. "The Birth and Reform of Prisons in France." In *The Emergence of Carceral Institutions: Prisons, Galleys, and Lunatic Asylums, 1550–1900*, ed. Pieter Spierenburg, 125–47. Rotterdam: Erasmus University.

Pfohl, Stephen. 1984. "The Discovery of Child Abuse." In *Deviant Behavior*, ed. Delos Kelly, 45–65. New York: St. Martin's.

———. 1985. *Images of Deviance & Social Control*. New York: McGraw-Hill.

Pfost, Donald. 1987. "Reagan's Nicaraguan Policy: A Case Study of Political Deviance and Crime." *Crime and Social Justice* 27/28:66–87.

Phillips, Llad, and Harold Votey. 1987. "Rational Choice Models of Crimes by Youth." *The Review of Black Political Economy* 16(1–2):129–87.

Pizzo, Stephen, Mary Fricker, and Paul Muolo. 1989. *Inside Job: The Looting of America's Savings and Loans*. New York: McGraw-Hill.

Platt, Tony. 1974. "Prospects for a Radical Criminology in the United States." *Crime and Social Justice* 1(Spring/Summer):2–10.

Platt, Tony, and Paul Takagi. 1979. "Biosocial Criminology: A Critique." *Crime and Social Justice* 11(Spring/Summer):5–13.

Pleck, Elizabeth, Joseph H. Pleck, Miriam Grossman, and Pauline B. Bart. 1977–78. "The Battered Data Syndrome: A Reply to Steinmetz." *Victimology* 2(3–4):680–83.

Polk, Kenneth, and William Schafer. 1972. *Schools and Delinquency*. Englewood Cliffs, N.J.: Prentice-Hall.

Pollak, Otto. 1961. *The Criminality of Women*. Philadelphia: University of Pennsylvania Press.

Pollock, John Crothers, and Arney Ellen Rosenblatt. 1984. "Fear of Crime: Sources and Responses." In *Criminal Justice*, ed. John J. Sullivan and Joseph L. Victor, 34–36. Guildford, Conn.: Dushkin Publishing.

Polsky, Ned. 1967. *Hustlers, Beats, and Others*. Chicago: Aldine.

Porterfield, Austin L. 1943. "Delinquency and Its Outcome in Court and College." *American Journal of Sociology* 49(3):199–208.

Portland Press Herald. 1993. "Health Firm Fined $61 Million for Selling Faulty Heart Catheters." (Oct. 16):1, 6.

Powell, Elwin H. 1966. "Crime as a Function of Anomie." *Journal of Criminal Law, Criminology, and Police Science* 57(2):161–71.

Prados, John. 1986. *Presidents' Secret Wars*. New York: William Morrow.

Prescott, Suzanne, and Carolyn Letko. 1977. "Battered Women: A Social Psychological Perspective." In *Battered Women*, ed. Maria Roy, 72–96. New York: Van Nostrand Reinhold.

President's Commission on Law Enforcement and the Administration of Justice. 1967. *The Challenge of Crime in a Free Society*. Washington, D.C.: U.S. Government Printing Office.

———. 1967a. *Task Force Report: Organized Crime*. Washington, D.C.: U.S. Government Printing Office.

President's Commission on Organized Crime. 1984. *The Cash Connection: Organized Crime, Financial Institutions, and Money Laundering*. Washington, D.C.: U.S. Government Printing Office.

———. 1986. *The Impact: Organized Crime Today*. U.S. Government Printing Office.

———. 1986a. *The Edge: Organized Crime, Business, and Labor Unions*. Washington, D.C.: U.S. Government Printing Office.

Price, Barbara Raffel, and Natalie Sokoloff, ed. 1982.

The Criminal Justice System and Women. New York: Clark Boardman.

Pyatt, Rudolph A. 1987. "Shoplifting's Pinch." *Washington Post* (Oct. 13):E1, E5.

Q

Quetelet, Adolphe. 1831, 1984. *Research on the Propensity for Crime at Different Ages*. Translated by Sawyer Sylvester. Cincinnati: Anderson

———. 1842. *A Treatise on Man*. Translated by R. Knox and T. Smibert. Edinburgh: Chambers.

———. 1848. *Du système social et des lois qui le régissent*. Paris: Guillaumin.

———. 1826. "Mémoire sur les lois des naissances et de la mortalité à Bruxelles." *Nouveaux mémoires de l'académie royale des sciences et belles-lettres de Bruxelles* 3:495–512.

Quinney, Richard. 1970. *The Social Reality of Crime*. Boston: Little, Brown.

———. 1973. "There's a Lot of Us Folks Grateful to the Lone Ranger: Some Notes on the Rise and Fall of American Criminology." *Insurgent Sociologist* 4(Fall):56–64.

———. 1973a. "Crime Control in Capitalist Society: A Critical Philosophy of Legal Order." *Issues in Criminology* 8(Spring):75–79.

———. 1977. *Class, State, & Crime*. New York: Longman.

Quinney, Richard, and John Wildeman. 1977. *The Problem of Crime*. New York: Harper and Row.

R

Rada, Richard T., D. R. Laws, and Robert Kellner. 1976. "Plasma Testosterone Levels in the Rapist." *Psychosomatic Medicine* 38(4):257–68.

Rafter, Nicole Hahn. 1985. *Partial Justice: Women in State Prisons, 1800–1935*. Boston: Northeastern University Press.

———. ed. 1988. *White Trash: The Eugenic Family Studies, 1877–1919*. Boston, Mass.: Northeastern University Press.

Rafter, Nicole Hahn. 1992. "Criminal Anthropology in the United States," *Criminology* 30(4):525–545.

Rafter, Nicole Hahn, and Elizabeth A. Stanko, eds. 1982. *Judge, Lawyer, Victim, Thief*. Boston: Northeastern University Press.

Ranelagh, John. 1987. *The Agency: The Rise and Decline of the CIA*. New York: Simon and Schuster.

Ratner, R. S., and John L. McMullan, eds. 1987. *Criminal Justice Politics in Canada*. Vancouver: University of British Columbia Press.

Rausch, Sharla. 1983. "Court Processing versus Diversion of Status Offenders: A Test of Deterrence and

Labeling Theories." *Journal of Research in Crime and Delinquency* 20(1):39–54.

Ray, Joann. 1987. "Every Twelfth Shopper: Who Shoplifts and Why?" *Social Casework* 68(4):234–39.

Ray, Oakley. 1983. *Drugs, Society, and Human Behavior.* St. Louis: C. V. Mosley.

Reasons, Charles. 1974. "The Politics of Drugs: An Inquiry in the Sociology of Social Problems." *Sociological Quarterly* 15(381):404.

Reckless, Walter C. 1940. *Criminal Behavior.* New York: McGraw-Hill.

———. 1961. *The Crime Problem.* New York: Appleton-Century-Crofts.

Reckless, Walter C., Simon Dinitz, and Ellen Murray. 1956. "Self-Concept as an Insulator against Delinquency." *American Sociological Review* 21(6):744–46.

Redburn, F. Stevens, and Terry E. Buss. 1986. *Responding to America's Homeless: Public Policy Alternatives.* New York: Praeger.

Redhead, Steve. 1987. *Sing When You're Winning: The Last Football Book.* Manchester: Manchester University Press.

Redl, Fritz, and David Wineman. 1951. *Children Who Hate.* Chicago: Free Press of Glencoe.

Reiman, Jeffrey. 1984. *The Rich Get Richer and the Poor Get Prison.* New York: John Wiley.

Reisner, Marc. 1991. *Game Wars: The Undercover Pursuit of Wildlife Poachers.* New York: Viking.

Reiss, Albert J., and Michael Tonry, eds. 1986. *Communities and Crime.* Chicago: University of Chicago Press.

Reiss, Albert J. Jr. 1951. "Delinquency As the Failure of Personal and Social Controls." *American Sociological Review* 16(2):196–207.

Reiter, Rayna. 1975. *Toward an Anthropology of Women.* New York: Monthly Review Press.

Renzetti, Claire M. 1992. *Violent Betrayal: Partner Abuse in Lesbian Relationships.* Newbury Park, Calif.: Sage.

Reuter, Peter. 1983. *Disorganized Crime.* Cambridge, Mass.: MIT Press.

Reuter, Peter, and Jonathan B. Rubinstein. 1978. "Fact, Fancy, and Organized Crime." *Public Interest* 53 (Fall):45–67.

Rich, Spencer. 1988. "HHS Says '86 Welfare Errors Cost $1.1 Billion." *Washington Post* (Apr. 30):A15.

Riedel, Marc, and Margaret A. Zahn. 1985. *The Nature and Patterns of American Homicide.* Washington, D.C.: U.S. Government Printing Office.

Ritchie, Robert C. 1986. *Captain Kidd and the War against the Pirates.* Cambridge, Mass.: Harvard University Press.

Rivera, Beverly, and Cathy Spatz Widom. 1990. "Childhood Victimization and Violent Offending." *Violence and Victims* 5(1):19–35.

Robin, Gerald D. 1963. "Patterns of Department Store Shoplifting." *Crime and Delinquency* 9(2):163–72.

Roby, Pamela A. 1969. "Politics and Criminal Law: Revision of the New York State Penal Law on Prostitution." *Social Problems* 17(1):83–109.

Rosecrance, John. 1988. *Gambling without Guilt: The Legitimization of an American Pastime.* Pacific Grove, Calif.: Brooks/Cole.

Rosen, Ruth. 1982. *The Lost Sisterhood: Prostitution in America, 1900–1918.* Baltimore: Johns Hopkins University Press.

Rosenblum, Karen. 1975. "Female Deviance and the Female Sex Role: A Preliminary Investigation." *British Journal of Sociology* 25(2):169–85.

Ross, H. Laurence. 1982. *Deterring the Drinking Driver.* Lexington, Mass.: Lexington Books.

Rossi, Peter, James D. Wright, Gene A. Fisher, and Georgianna Willis. 1987. "The Urban Homeless: Estimating Composition and Size." *Science* 235:1336–41.

Rothman, David. 1971. *The Discovery of the Asylum: Social Order and Disorder in the New Republic.* Boston: Little, Brown.

Rowan, Roy. 1986. "Biggest Mafia Bosses." *Fortune* (Nov. 10):24–38.

Rowe, David C., and D. Wayne Osgood. 1984. "Heredity and Sociological Theories of Delinquency: A Reconsideration." *American Sociological Review* 49(4):526–40.

Rowe, James L. 1986. "Americans Abroad Said to Evade Taxes." *Washington Post* (Aug. 13):G1.

Rubenstein, Richard. 1970. *Rebels in Eden: Mass Political Violence in the U.S.* Boston: Little, Brown.

Rubin, Gayle. 1984. "Thinking Sex: Notes for a Radical Theory of the Politics of Sexuality." In *Pleasure and Danger: Exploring Female Sexuality,* ed. Carol S. Vance, 267–319. Boston: Routledge & Kegan Paul.

Russell, Diana E. H. 1975. *The Politics of Rape.* New York: Stein and Day.

———. 1982. *Rape in Marriage.* New York: Macmillan.

———. 1984. *Sexual Exploitation.* Beverly Hills: Sage.

———. 1986. *The Secret Trauma: Incest in the Lives of Girls and Women.* New York: Basic Books.

Russell, Dick. 1988. "Welcome to Dioxinville, Arkansas." *In These Times* (Mar. 9–15): 8–13.

S

Sabo, Donald. 1992. "Understanding Men in Prison: The Relevance of Gender Studies." *Men's Studies Review* 9(1):4–9.

Saleilles, Raymond. 1898, 1911. *The Individualization of Punishment.* Translated by Rachel Szold Jastrow. Boston: Little, Brown.

Sampson, Robert J. 1987. "Urban Black Violence: The

Effect of Male Joblessness and Family Disruption." *American Journal of Sociology* 93(2):348–82.

Sanday, Peggy. 1981. "The Socio-Cultural Context of Rape: A Cross-Cultural Study." *Journal of Social Issues* 37(1):5–27.

Sanders, William B. 1980. *Rape and Women's Identity.* Beverly Hills: Sage.

Sasuly, Richard. 1982. *Bookies and Bettors.* New York: Holt, Rinehart and Winston.

Scacco, Anthony M. 1982. *Male Rape: A Casebook of Sexual Aggressions.* New York: AMS Press.

Scarpitti, Frank R., and Alan Block. 1987. "America's Toxic Waste Racket: Dimensions of the Environmental Crisis." In *Organized Crime in America: Concepts and Controversies,* ed. Timothy S. Bynum, 115–28. Monsey, N.Y.: Willow Tree Press.

Schalling, Daisy. 1987. "Personality Correlates of Plasma Testosterone Levels in Young Delinquents: An Example of Person-Situation Interaction?" In *The Causes of Crime: New Biological Approaches,* ed. Sarnoff A. Mednick, Terrie Moffitt, and Susan A. Stack, 283–91. Cambridge: Cambridge University Press.

Schechter, Susan. 1982. *Women and Male Violence.* Boston: South End Press.

Scheffer, David J. 1987. "U.S. Law and the Iran-Contra Affair." *The American Journal of International Law* 81(3):696–723.

Scherschel, Patricia M. 1983. "Credit Card Ripoffs: A Spreading Epidemic." *U.S. News and World Report* (Oct. 3):78–79.

———. 1987. "How to Avoid an IRS Audit." *U.S. News and World Report* (Mar. 2):63.

Schlossman, Steven, and Michael Sedlak. 1983. "The Chicago Area Project Revisited." *Crime & Delinquency* 29(3):398–462.

Schmalz, Jeffrey. 1988. "Bank Indicted by U.S. for Money Laundering Case." *New York Times* (Oct. 12):A56.

Schmidhauser, John R. 1959. "The Justices of the Supreme Court: A Collective Portrait." *Midwest Journal of Political Science* 3:2–37, 40–9.

Schrag, Clarence. 1962. "Delinquency and Opportunity: Analysis of a Theory." *Sociology and Social Research* 46(2):167–75.

Schrager, Laura Shill, and James F. Short. 1978. "Toward a Sociology of Organizational Crime." *Social Problems* 25(4):407–19.

Schuessler, Karl, ed. 1973. "Introduction." In *Edwin H. Sutherland on Analyzing Crime,* ix–xxxvi. Chicago: University of Chicago Press.

Schur, Edwin M. 1968. *Law and Society: A Sociological View.* New York: Random House.

———. 1974. "A Sociologist's View: The Case for Abolition." In *Victimless Crimes: Two Sides of a Controversy,* Edwin M. Schur and Hugo Adam Bedau, 3–52. Englewood Cliffs, N.J.: Prentice-Hall.

———. 1979. *Interpreting Deviance: A Sociological View.* New York: Harper and Row.

———. 1984. *Labeling Women Deviant: Gender, Stigma, and Social Control.* New York: Random House.

———. 1988. *The Americanization of Sex.* Philadelphia: Temple University Press.

Schwartz, Richard D., and Jerome C. Miller. 1964. "Legal Evolution and Societal Complexity." *American Journal of Sociology* 70(2):159–69.

Schwartz, Richard D., and Jerome H. Skolnick. 1964. "Two Studies of Legal Stigma." In *The Other Side,* ed. Howard S. Becker, 103–17. New York: Free Press.

Schwendinger, Herman, and Julia Schwendinger. 1974. *The Sociologists of the Chair: A Radical Analysis of the Formative Years of North American Sociology (1883–1922).* New York: Basic Books.

———. 1975. "Defenders of Order or Guardians of Human Rights?" In *Critical Criminology,* ed. Ian Taylor, Paul Walton, and Jock Young, 113–46. London: Routledge & Kegan Paul.

———. 1977. "Social Class and the Definition of Crime." *Crime and Social Justice* 7(Spring/Summer):4–13.

———. 1985. *Adolescent Subcultures and Delinquency.* New York: Praeger.

Schwendinger, Julia, and Herman Schwendinger. 1971. "Sociology's Founding Fathers: Sexists to the Man." *Journal of Marriage and the Family* 33(4):783–99.

———. 1983. *Rape and Inequality.* Beverly Hills: Sage.

Sciolino, Elaine. 1988. "Fighting Narcotics: U.S. Is Urged to Shift Tactics." *New York Times* (Apr. 10):A1, A10.

Skocpol, Theda, and Margaret Somers. 1980. "The Uses of Comparative History in Macrosocial Inquiry." *Comparative Studies in Society and History* 22(2):174–97.

Scott, Valerie, Peggy Miller, and Ryan Hotchkiss. 1987. "Realistic Feminists." In *Good Girls/Bad Girls: Feminists and Sex Trade Workers Face to Face,* ed. Laurie Bell, 204–17. Seattle: The Seal Press.

Scott, Walter. 1988. "Personality Parade." *Parade Magazine* (Oct. 30):2.

Scull, Andrew. 1977. *Decarceration: Community Treatment and the Deviant—A Radical View.* Englewood Cliffs, N.J.: Prentice-Hall.

Scully, Diana. 1980. "How Residents Learn to Talk You into Unnecessary Surgery." *Ms.* 8(11):89–93.

———. 1980a. *Men Who Control Women's Health.* Boston: Houghton Mifflin.

Seager, Jodi. 1993. *Earth Follies: Coming to Feminist Terms with the Global Environmental Crisis.* New York: Routledge.

Sellin, Thorsten. 1938. *Culture Conflict and Crime.* New York: Social Science Research Council.

Shabecoff, Philip. 1988. "Irate and Afraid, Poor Nations Fight Efforts to Use Them as Toxic Dumps." *New York Times* (July 5):C4.

Shacklady-Smith, Leslie. 1978. "Sexist Assumptions and Female Delinquency: An Empirical Investigation." In *Women, Sexuality, and Social Control*, ed. Carol Smart and Barry Smart, 74–86. Boston: Routledge & Kegan Paul.

Shavelson, Lonny. 1988. "Tales of Troubled Waters." *Hippocrates* (Mar./Apr.):70–77.

Shaw, Clifford R. 1930. *The Jack-Roller: A Delinquent Boy's Own Story*. Chicago: University of Chicago Press.

Shaw, Clifford R., and Henry D. McKay. 1942, 1969. *Juvenile Delinquency and Urban Areas*. Chicago: University of Chicago Press.

Shaw, Clifford R., *et al.* 1929. *Delinquency Areas: A Study of the Geographic Distribution of School Truants, Juvenile Delinquents, and Adult Offenders in Chicago*. Chicago: University of Chicago Press.

Shaw, Clifford, Henry D. McKay, and James F. McDonald. 1938. *Brothers in Crime*. Chicago: University of Chicago Press.

Sheehan, Daniel. 1988. *Inside the Shadow Government*. Washington, D.C.: The Christic Institute.

Sheley, Joseph F., and Cindy D. Ashkins. 1981. "Crime, Crime News, and Crime Views." *Public Opinion Quarterly* 45(4):492–506.

Shelley, Louise I. 1981. *Crime and Modernization: The Impact of Industrialization and Modernization on Crime*. Carbondale: Southern Illinois University Press.

———, ed. 1981a. *Readings in Comparative Criminology*. Carbondale: Southern Illinois University Press.

Shenon, Philip. 1988. "Noriega Indicted by U.S. for Links to Illegal Drugs." *New York Times* (Feb. 6):A1, A5.

———. 1988a. "Enemy Within: Drug Money Is Corrupting the Enforcers." *New York Times* (Apr. 11):A1, A12.

———. 1988b. "McFarlane Admits Withholding Data on Aid to Contras." *New York Times* (Mar. 12):A1, A6.

———. 1988c. "North, Poindexter, and Two Others Indicted." *New York Times* (Mar. 17):A1, D27.

Sherman, Janet Schmidt, Jon Christensen, and Joel Henderson. 1982. "Reorganized Crime: The Creation of the Uniform Crime Reports." *Research in Law, Deviance and Social Control*. 4:3–52.

Shoemaker, Donald J. 1984. *Theories of Delinquency*. New York: Oxford University Press.

Short, James F. 1957. "Differential Association and Delinquency." *Social Problems* 4(3):233–39.

———. 1958. "Differential Association with Delinquent Friends and Delinquent Behavior." *Pacific Sociological Review* 1(1):20–25.

———. 1962. "Gang Delinquency and Anomie." In *Anomie and Deviant Behavior*, ed. Marshall B. Clinard, 98–127. New York: Free Press.

———. 1969. "Introduction to the Revised Edition." In *Juvenile Delinquency and Urban Areas*, Clifford R. Shaw and Henry D. McKay, xxv–liv. Chicago: University of Chicago Press.

Short, James F., and Fred L. Strodtbeck. 1965. *Group Process and Gang Delinquency*. Chicago: University of Chicago Press.

Shostak, Marjorie. 1983. *Nisa: The Life and Words of a !Kung Woman*. New York: Vintage Books.

Shover, Neal. 1972. "Structures and Careers in Burglary." *The Journal of Criminal Law, Criminology, and Police Science* 64(4):540–49.

Shuchman, Miriam. 1981. "Victims of Rape: Where Can They Turn?" *The Progressive* (July):27–30.

Sick, Gary. 1991. *October Surprise: America's Hostages in Iran and the Election of Ronald Reagan*. New York: Times Books.

———. 1993. "Missing Link." *The New York Times* (Jan. 24):17.

Sidel, Ruth. 1987. *Women and Children Last*. New York: Penguin.

Silverman, Daniel, and Sharon L. McCombie. 1980. "Counseling the Mates and Families of Rape Victims." In *Rape Crisis Intervention Handbook*, ed. Sharon L. McCombie, 173–81. New York: Plenum Press.

Simon, Carl P., and Ann D. Witte. 1982. *Beating the System: The Underground Economy*. Boston: Auburn House Publishing.

Simon, David R., and D. Stanley Eitzen. 1986. *Elite Deviance*. Boston, Mass.: Allyn and Bacon.

Simon, Rita. 1975. *Women and Crime*. Lexington, Mass.: D.C. Heath.

Simpson, A. W. Brian. 1984. *Cannibalism and the Common Law*. Chicago: University of Chicago Press.

Simpson, Sally. 1986. "The Decomposition of Antitrust: Testing a Multi-Level Longitudinal Model of Profit-Squeeze." *American Sociological Review* 51(6):859–75.

———. 1987. "Cycles of Illegality: Antitrust Violations in Corporate America." *Social Forces* 65 (June):943–63.

Singleton, Royce Jr., Bruce C. Straits, Margaret M. Straits, and Ronald J. McAllister. 1988. *Approaches to Social Research*. New York: Oxford University Press.

Skinner, B. F. 1953. *Science and Human Behavior*. New York: Macmillan.

Sklar, Holly, and Robert Lawrence. 1981. *Who's Who in the Reagan Administration*. Boston: South End Press.

Skolnick, Jerome. 1969. *The Politics of Protest*. New York: Ballantine Books.

Slater, M. K. 1959. "Ecological Factors in the Origin of Incest." *American Anthropologist*, 61:1041–58.

Smart, Carol. 1976. *Women, Crime, and Criminology: A Feminist Critique*. Boston: Routledge & Kegan Paul.

———. 1979. "The New Female Offender: Reality or Myth?" *British Journal of Criminology* 19(1):50–59.

Smart, Carol, and Barry Smart, eds. 1978. *Women, Sexuality, and Social Control*. Boston: Routledge & Kegan Paul.

Smith, Douglas, and Christy A. Visher. 1980. "Sex and Involvement in Deviance/Crime: A Quantitative Review of the Empirical Literature." *American Sociological Review* 45(4):691–701.

Smith, Dwight. 1976. *The Mafia Mystique*. New York: Basic Books.

Smith, James F., and Vicki Abt. 1984. "Gambling as Play." *The Annals of the American Academy of Political and Social Science* (July):122–32.

Smith, Lynn Newhart, and Gary D. Hill. 1991. "Victimization and Fear of Crime," *Criminal Justice and Behavior* 18(2):217–239.

Snell, John E., Richard J. Rosenwald, and Ames Robey. 1964. "The Wifebeater's Wife: A Study of Family Interaction." *Archives of General Psychiatry* 11(Aug.):107–12.

Snodgrass, Jon. 1973. "The Criminologist and His Criminal: The Case of Edwin H. Sutherland and Broadway Jones." *Issues in Criminology* 8(1):1–17.

———. 1976. "Clifford R. Shaw and Henry D. McKay: Chicago Criminologists." *British Journal of Criminology* 16(1):1–19.

Sokoloff, Natalie. 1980. *Between Money and Love*. New York: Praeger.

Solheim, Joan Senzek. 1982. "A Cross-Cultural Examination of Use of Corporal Punishment on Children: A Focus on Sweden and the U.S." *Child Abuse and Neglect* 6:147–54.

Sowell, Thomas. 1988. "Let's Just Say No to Anti-Drug Laws." *The Boston Herald* (Aug. 20):19.

Sparks, Richard F. 1981. "Surveys of Victimization—An Optimistic Assessment." *Crime and Justice: An Annual Review of Research* 3:1–60.

Spector, Malcolm. 1981. "Beyond Crime: Seven Methods to Control Troublesome Rascals." In *Law and Deviance*, ed. H. Laurence Ross, 127–57. Beverly Hills: Sage.

———. 1975a. "Toward a Marxian Theory of Deviance." *Social Problems* 22(5):638–51.

———. 1980. "Left-Wing Criminology—An Infantile Disorder." In *Radical Criminology: The Coming Crises*, ed. James A. Inciardi, 169–90. Beverly Hills: Sage.

Spolar, Chris. 1985. "$1 Billion Waste Uncovered in Medicare." *50 Plus* (Nov.): 11–12.

Staats, Gregory R. 1977. "Changing Conceptualizations of Professional Criminals: Implications for Criminology Theory." *Criminology* 15(1):49–65.

Stack, Steven, and Mary Jeanne Kanavy. 1983. "The Effect of Religion on Forcible Rape: A Structural Analysis." *Journal for the Scientific Study of Religion* 22(1):67–74.

Stanko, Elizabeth. 1985. *Intimate Intrusions: Women's Experience of Male Violence*. Boston: Routledge & Kegan Paul.

Stanton, Duncan. 1976. "Drugs, Vietnam, and the Vietnam Veteran: An Overview." *American Journal of Drugs and Alcohol Abuse* 3:557–70.

Staples, Robert. 1987. "Black Male Genocide: A Final Solution to the Race Problem in America." *Black Scholar* 18 (May/June):2–11.

Statistical Abstract of the U.S. 1992. Washington, D.C.: U.S. Government Printing Office.

Stead, Philip John. 1983. *The Police of France*. London: Macmillan.

Steffensmeier, Darrell J. 1981. "Crime and the Contemporary Woman: An Analysis of Changing Levels of Female Property Crimes, 1960–1975." In *Women and Crime in America*, ed. Lee Bowker, 39–59. New York: Macmillan.

———. 1983. "Organization Properties and Sex Segregation in the Underworld: Building a Sociological Theory of Sex Differences in Crime." *Social Forces* 61(4):1010–32.

———. 1986. *The Fence: In the Shadow of Two Worlds*. Totowa, N.J.: Rowman & Littlefield.

Steffensmeier, Darrell J., Emilie Andersen Allan, Miles D. Harer, and Cathy Streifel. 1989. "Age and the Distribution of Crime." *American Journal of Sociology* 94(4):803–31.

Steinmetz, Susan. 1977–1978. "The Battered Husband Syndrome." *Victimology* 2(3–4):499–509.

Sterngold, James. 1987. "Tangled Trail Ends Today for Levine." *New York Times* (Feb. 20):D1, D4.

Stevenson, Richard W. 1987. "$44 Million Embezzling Is Charged." *New York Times* (Feb. 20):D1, D4.

Stinchcombe, Arthur. 1963. "Institutions of Privacy in the Determination of Police Administrative Practice." *American Journal of Sociology* 69(2):150–60.

———. 1964. *Rebellion in a High School*. Chicago: Quadrangle.

St. James, Margo. 1987. "The Reclamation of Whores." In *Good Girls/Bad Girls: Feminists and Sex Trade Workers Face to Face*, ed. Laurie Bell, 81–87. Seattle: The Seal Press.

Straus, Murray A. 1977–1978. "Wife Beating: How Common and Why?" *Victimology* 2(3–4):443–57.

Straus, Murray A., and Richard J. Gelles. 1988. "How Violent Are American Families? Estimates from the National Family Violence Resurvey and Other

Studies." In *Family Abuse and Its Consequences: New Directions in Research*, eds. Gerald T. Hotaling, David Finkelhor, John T. Kirkpatrick, and Murray Straus, 14–36. Newbury Park, Calif.: Sage.

Straus, Murray A., Richard J. Gelles, and Susan Steinmetz. 1980. *Behind Closed Doors*. New York: Doubleday.

Sumner, Colin. 1982. "Crime, Justice and Underdevelopment: Beyond Modernisation Theory." In *Crime, Justice and Underdevelopment*, ed. Colin Sumner, 1–39. London: Heinemann.

Surette, Ray, ed. 1984. *Justice and the Media*. Springfield, Ill.: Charles C. Thomas.

Surette, Ray. 1992. *Media, Crime, and Criminal Justice*. Pacific Grove, Calif.: Brooks/Cole.

Sutherland, Edwin H. 1924, 1947. *Criminology*. Philadelphia: J. B. Lippincott.

———. 1937. *The Professional Thief: By a Professional Thief*. Chicago: University of Chicago Press.

———. 1942, 1956. "Development of the Theory." In *The Sutherland Papers*, ed. Albert Cohen, Alfred Lindesmith, and Karl Schuessler, 13–29. Bloomington: Indiana University Press.

———. 1949, 1983. *White Collar Crime*. New Haven, Conn.: Yale University Press.

Sutherland, Edwin H., and Donald R. Cressey. 1970. *Criminology*. Philadelphia: L. B. Lippincott.

Swaaningen, Rene Van. 1986. "What is Abolitionism?" In *Abolitionism: Towards a Non-Repressive Approach to Crime*, ed. Herman Bianchi and Rene Van Swaaningen, 9–21. Amsterdam: Free University Press.

Swigert, Virginia. 1984. "Public-Order Crime." In *Major Forms of Crime*, ed. Robert Meier, 95–117. Beverly Hills: Sage.

Sykes, Gresham M., and David Matza. 1957. "Techniques of Neutralization: A Theory of Delinquency." *American Sociological Review* 22(6):664–70.

T

Tallmer, Matt. 1987. "Chemical Dumping as a Corporate Way of Life." In *Corporate Violence*, ed. Stuart Hills, 111–20. Totowa, N.J.: Rowman & Littlefield.

Tannenbaum, Frank. 1938. *Crime and the Community*. Boston: Ginn.

Tappan, Paul W. 1947. "Who Is the Criminal?" *American Sociological Review* 12(1):96–102.

Tarde, Gabriel. 1884. "What Is a Society?" *Revue philosophique* 18:501.

———. 1886. "Problèmes de penalité." In *La criminalité comparée*, Tarde, 122–211. Paris: Alcan.

———. 1886a, 1902. *La criminalité comparée*. Paris: Alcan.

———. 1890, 1903. *The Laws of Imitation*. Translated by E. Parsons. New York: Henry Holt.

———. 1890a, 1912. *Penal Philosophy*. Translated by R. Howell. Boston: Little, Brown.

———. 1892. "The Crimes of Crowds." *Archives de l'Anthropologie criminelle* 7:353–86.

———. 1893. "Crowds, Sects, and Crime." *Revue des deux mondes* 120:349–87.

———. 1902. *La criminalité comparée*. Paris: Felix Alcan.

Taylor, Ian, Paul Walton, and Jock Young. 1973. *The New Criminology*. London: Routledge & Kegan Paul.

Taylor, Ian. 1983. *Crime, Capitalism, and Community: Three Essays in Socialist Criminology*. Toronto: Butterworths.

Taylor, Laurie. 1984. *In the Underworld*. Oxford: Basil Blackwell.

Taylor, Lawrence, and Katharina Dalton. 1983. "Premenstrual Syndrome: A New Criminal Defense?" *California Western Law Review*, 19:269–87.

Thomas, William I., and Florian Znaniecki. 1918–1920. *The Polish Peasant in Europe and America*. Chicago: University of Chicago Press.

Thomas, William I. 1923. *The Unadjusted Girl: With Cases and Standpoint for Behavior Analysis*. Boston: Little, Brown.

Thornberry, Terence P. 1973. "Race, Socio-Economic Status, and Sentencing in the Juvenile Justice System." *Journal of Criminal Law, Criminology and Police Science* 64(1):90–98.

Thornberry, Terence, and R. L. Christenson. 1984. "Unemployment and Criminal Involvement: An Investigation of Reciprocal Causal Structures." *American Sociological Review* 49(3):398–411.

Thornberry, Terence, and Margaret Farnworth. 1982. "Social Correlates of Criminal Involvement: Further Evidence on the Relationship between Social Status and Criminal Behavior." *American Sociological Review* 47(4):505–18.

Thrasher, Frederic Milton. 1927. *The Gang: A Study of 1,313 Gangs in Chicago*. Chicago: University of Chicago Press.

Tietze, Christopher. 1981. *Induced Abortion: A World View*. New York: Population Council.

Tifft, Larry, and Dennis Sullivan. 1980. *The Struggle to Be Human: Crime, Criminology, and Anarchism*. Orkney, U.K.: Cienfuegos Press.

Time. 1983. "Wife Beating: The Silent Crime." (Sept. 5):23.

Tittle, Charles R. 1975. "Labeling and Crime: An Empirical Evaluation." In *The Labeling of Deviance*, ed. Walter R. Gove, 241–63. Beverly Hills: Sage.

Tittle, Charles R., Wayne J. Villemez, and Douglas A. Smith. 1978. "The Myth of Social Class and Criminality: An Empirical Assessment of the Empirical Evidence." *ASR* 43:643–656.

Toby, Jackson. 1957. "Social Disorganization and Stake

in Conformity: Complementary Factors in the Predatory Behavior of Hoodlums." *Journal of Criminal Law, Criminology and Police Science* 48(1):12–17.

———. 1979. "The New Criminology Is the Old Sentimentality." *Criminology* 16(3):516–26.

———. 1983. "Crime in the Schools." In *Crime and Public Policy*, ed. James Q. Wilson, 69–88. San Francisco: Institute for Contemporary Studies.

Tombs, Robert. 1980. "Crime and the Security of the State: The Dangerous Classes and Insurrection in Nineteenth-Century Paris." In *Crime and the Law: the Social History of Crime in Western Europe since 1500*, ed. V.A.C. Gatrell, Bruce Lenman, and Geoffrey Parker, 214–37. London: Europa.

Tomlinson, Mike, Tony Varley, and Ciaran McCullagh. 1988. "Introduction." In *Whose Law and Order? Aspects of Crime and Social Control in Irish Society*, ed. Mike Tomlinson *et al.*, 9–20. Belfast: Sociological Association of Ireland.

Tremblay, Pierre. 1986. "Designing Crime: The Short Life Expectancy and the Workings of a Recent Wave of Credit Card Bank Frauds." *British Journal of Criminology* 26(3):234–53.

Turk, Austin. 1969. *Criminality and Legal Order*. Chicago: Rand McNally.

———. 1979. "Analyzing Official Deviance: For a Nonpartisan Conflict Analysis in Criminology." *Criminology* 16(3):459–76.

———. 1982. *Political Criminality: The Defiance and Defense of Authority*. Beverly Hills: Sage.

Tushnet, Mark. 1988. *Central America and the Law: The Constitution, Civil Liberties, and the Courts*. Boston: South End Press.

U

United Nations. 1983. *Human Rights: A Compilation of International Instruments*. New York: United Nations, publication E.83.XIV.1.

———. 1986. *Demographic Yearbook, 1984*. New York: United Nations, Department of International Economic and Social Affairs, Statistical Office.

U.S. House of Representatives, Subcommittee on Crime. 1980. *Increasing Violence Against Minorities*. Washington, D.C.: U.S. Government Printing Office.

U.S. Senate, Subcommittee on Terrorism, Narcotics, and International Operations. 1989. *Drugs, Law Enforcement, and Foreign Policy*. Washington, D.C.: U.S. Government Printing Office.

Useem, Michael. 1984. *The Inner Circle*. New York: Oxford University Press.

V

Valukas, Anton R., and Ira Raphaelson. 1988. "Judicial Corruption." In *Prosecution of Public Corruption Cases*, ed. U.S. Department of Justice, 1–15. Washington, D.C.: Department of Justice.

Vance, Carol S. 1986. "The Meese Commission on the Road." *The Nation* (Aug. 2/9):65, 76–82.

van den Haag, Ernest. 1969. "Is Pornography a Cause of Crime?" In *The Norton Reader*, ed. Arthur M. Eastman, 838–45. New York: W. W. Norton.

———. 1975. *Punishing Criminals: Concerning a Very Old and Painful Question*. New York: Basic Books.

Van Dijk, Jan J. M., and Patricia Mayhew. 1993. *Criminal Victimization in the Industrialized World: Key Findings of the 1989 and 1992 International Crime Surveys*. Pp. 1–49 in *Understanding Crime: Experiences of Crime and Crime Control*. Rome: United Nations, publication 49.

Vaz, Edmund W., ed. 1967. *Middle-Class Juvenile Delinquency*. New York: Harper and Row.

Virkkunen, Matti. 1987. "Metabolic Dysfunctions among Habitually Violent Offenders: Reactive Hypoglycemia and Cholesterol Levels." In *The Causes of Crime: New Biological Approaches*, ed. Sarnoff A. Mednick, Terrie Moffitt, and Susan A. Stack, 292–311. Cambridge: Cambridge University Press.

Viscusi, W. Kip. 1986. "Market Incentives for Criminal Behavior." In *The Black Youth Employment Crisis*, ed. Richard B. Freeman and Harry J. Holzer, 301–46. Chicago: The University of Chicago Press.

Vold, George B. 1958. *Theoretical Criminology*. New York: Oxford University Press.

Vold, George B., and Thomas J. Bernard. 1986. *Theoretical Criminology*. New York: Oxford University Press.

von Hirsch, Andrew. 1976. *Doing Justice: The Choice of Punishments*. New York: Hill and Wang.

Voorhis, Patricia Van, Francis T. Cullen, Richard A. Mathers, and Connie Chenoweth Garner. 1988. "The Impact of Family Structure and Quality on Delinquency: A Comparative Assessment of Structural and Functional Factors." *Criminology* 26(2):235–61.

Voss, Harwin L. 1964. "Differential Association and Reported Delinquent Behavior: a Replication." *Social Problems* 12(1):78–85.

W

Waldman, Michael. 1990. *Who Robbed America?* New York: Random House.

Walker, Lenore E. 1978. "Treatment Alternatives for Battered Women." In *The Victimization of Women*, ed. Jane R. Chapman and Margaret Gates, 143–47. Beverly Hills: Sage Publications.

———. 1979. *The Battered Woman*. New York: Harper and Row.

Walker, Samuel. 1980. *Popular Justice: A History of American Criminal Justice*. New York: Oxford University Press.

————. 1989. *Sense and Nonsense about Crime: A Policy Guide.* Monterey, Calif.: Brooks/Cole.

Wall Street Journal. 1987. "Judge Pleads Guilty in Corruption Probe." (Jan. 22):10.

————. 1992a. "Baxter Made Cut-Rate Deal with Syria to Escape Blacklist, U.S. Probe Finds." (Dec. 22):A3.

————. 1992b. "Foreign Job Bid by Southern Co. Probed by SEC." (Feb. 6):A4.

————. 1993a. "Justice Department Probing for Possible Law Violations." (May 20):A7.

————. 1993b. "Two are Convicted of Insider Trading by Houston Jury." (June 7):B8J.

Walsh, Dermot. 1986. *Heavy Business: Commercial Burglary and Robbery.* Boston: Routledge & Kegan Paul.

Walsh, Dermot, and Adrian Poole. 1983. *A Dictionary of Criminology.* Boston: Routledge & Kegan Paul.

Walsh, Marilyn E. 1977. *The Fence.* Westport, Conn.: Greenwood Press.

Warr, Mark. 1985. "Fear of Rape among Urban Women." *Social Problems* 32(3):238–50.

Washington, James Melvin, ed. 1986. *A Testament of Hope: The Essential Writings of Martin Luther King, Jr.* New York: Harper and Row.

Weber, Max. 1924, 1978. *Economy and Society,* ed. Guenther Roth and Claus Wittich. Translated by Ephraim Fischoff *et al.* 2 Vols. Berkeley: University of California Press.

Webster, Paula. 1981. "Pornography and Pleasure." *Heresies* 3(1):48–51.

Weis, Joseph G. 1976. "Liberation and Crime: The Invention of the New Female Criminal." *Crime and Social Justice* 6(Fall):17–27.

Weld, William F. 1988. "Introduction: Why Public Corruption is not a Victimless Crime." *Prosecution of Public Corruption Cases,* ed. U.S. Department of Justice, i–v. Washington, D.C.: Department of Justice.

Weldon, W. F. R. 1894–1895. "An Attempt to Measure the Death-Rate Due to the Selective Destruction of Carcinus Moenas with Respect to a Particular Dimension." *Proceedings of the Royal Society of London* 57:360–82.

Wells, L. Edward, and Joseph H. Rankin. 1988. "Direct Parental Controls and Delinquency." *Criminology* 26(2):263–85.

West, Donald J., and Buz de Villiers. 1993. *Male Prostitution.* New York: Harrington Park Press.

Weyler, Rex. 1982. *Blood of the Land.* New York: Everest House.

Wheeler, Linda. 1986. "Auto Thefts in Region Soar: Professionals, Youths Blamed." *Washington Post* (Aug. 15):A1.

Whyte, William Foote. 1943. *Streetcorner Society.* Chicago: University of Chicago Press.

Widom, Cathy Spatz. 1989. "Child Abuse, Neglect, and Violent Criminal Behavior." *Criminology* 17(2):251–71.

Wilbanks, William, and Paul Kim. 1984. *Elderly Criminals.* New York: University Press of America.

Wilkins, Leslie T. 1964. *Social Deviance: Social Policy, Action, and Research.* London: Tavistock.

Williams, Linda S. 1984. "The Classic Rape: When Do Victims Report?" *Social Problems* 31(4):459–67.

Willis, Paul. 1978. *Profane Culture.* Boston: Routledge & Kegan Paul.

Wilson, James Q. 1985. *Thinking About Crime.* New York: Vintage.

Wilson, James Q., and Richard J. Herrnstein. 1985. *Crime & Human Nature.* New York: Simon and Schuster.

Wise, David. 1976. *The American Police State.* New York: Random House.

Witkin, Herman A., Sarnoff A. Mednick, Fini Schulsinger, Eskild Bakkestrom, Karl O. Christiansen, Donald R. Goodenough, Kurt Hirschhorn, Claes Lundsteen, David R. Owen, John Philip, Donald B. Rubin, and Martha Stocking. 1976, 1977. "XYY and XXY Men: Criminality and Aggression." In *Biosocial Bases of Criminal Behavior,* ed. Sarnoff A. Mednick and Karl O. Christiansen, 165–87. New York: Gardner.

Wolf, Douglas, and David Greenberg. 1986. "The Dynamics of Welfare Fraud." *Journal of Human Resources* 21(4):437–55.

Wolfe, David A. 1985. "Child-Abusive Parents: An Empirical Review and Analysis." *Psychological Bulletin* 97(3):462–82.

Wolfgang, Marvin E. 1958. *Patterns in Criminal Homicide.* Philadelphia: University of Pennsylvania Press.

————. 1967. "International Criminal Statistics: A Proposal." *Journal of Criminal Law, Criminology, and Police Science* 58(1):65–69.

————. 1968. "Urban Crime." In *The Metropolitan Enigma,* ed. James Q. Wilson, 245–81. Cambridge, Mass.: Harvard University Press.

Wolfgang, Marvin E., and Franco Ferracuti. 1967. *The Subculture of Violence.* London: Tavistock.

Wollstonecraft, Mary. 1792, 1975. *A Vindication of the Rights of Women.* New York: W. W. Norton.

Wolock, Isabel, and Bernard Horowitz. 1984. "Child Maltreatment as a Social Problem: The Neglect of Neglect." *American Journal of Orthopsychiatry* 54(4):530–34.

Won, George, and George Yamamoto. 1968. "Social Structure and Deviant Behavior: A Study of Shoplifting." *Sociology and Social Research* 53(1):44–55.

Woodward, Bob. 1988. *Veil: The Secret Wars of the CIA. 1981–1987.* New York: Simon and Schuster.

Wright, James D., and Linda L. Marston. 1975. "The

Ownership of the Means of Destruction: Weapons in the U.S." *Social Problems* 23(1):93–106.

Wright, James, Peter H. Rossi, and Kathleen Daly. 1983. *Under the Gun: Weapons, Crime, and Violence in America.* New York: Aldine.

Wyden, Peter. 1979. *Bay of Pigs: The Untold Story.* New York: Simon and Schuster.

Y

Yablonsky, Lewis. 1962. *The Violent Gang.* New York: Macmillan.

Yin, Peter. 1985. *Victimization and the Aged.* Springfield, Ill.: Charles C. Thomas.

Yorke, Jeffery. 1987. "Father, Son Arrested in Md. in Check Probe." *Washington Post* (Oct. 22):A18.

Young, Gary. 1978. "Justice and Capitalist Production: Marx and Bourgeois Ideology." *Canadian Journal of Philosophy* 8(3):421–55.

Young, Jock. 1971. "The Role of the Police as Amplifiers of Deviancy, Negotiators of Reality and Translators of Fantasy." In *Images of Deviance*, ed. Stanley Cohen, 27–61. Harmondsworth: Penguin.

———. 1986. "The Failure of Criminology: The Need for a Radical Realism." In *Confronting Crime*, ed. Roger Matthews and Jock Young, 4–30. Beverly Hills: Sage.

Young, Vernetta D. 1980. "Women, Race, and Crime." *Criminology* 18(1):26–34.

Z

Zietz, Dorothy. 1981. *Women Who Embezzle or Defraud: A Study of Convicted Felons.* New York: Praeger.

Zimring, Franklin E., and James Zuehl. 1986. "Victim Injury and Death in Urban Robbery: A Chicago Study." *Journal of Legal Studies* 15(1):1–40.

GLOSSARY

A

abortion The removal of an embryo or fetus from the uterus to end a pregnancy, which became a constitutional right in the 1973 Supreme Court decision of Roe v. Wade. (p. 193)

age discrimination In U.S. society, it is most pronounced for youth but also affects the elderly; unequal generational divisions between young and old are prevalent, and social behavior—including crime—is linked to the aging process. (p. 89)

aggravated assault An unlawful attack by one person upon another for the purpose of inflicting severe or aggravated bodily injury. (p. 112)

amateur property crime The activities of offenders who engage in crime when the opportunity arises, who do not extensively plan their theft or always think of themselves as criminals, and who usually do not specialize in one type of property crime. (p. 144)

analogous social injury Legally permissible acts that cause social harm. (p. 17)

anomie A condition of normlessness; a breakdown in the social order. A concept favored by Merton in his explanation of the high rate of crime and deviance in the United States. (p. 417–422)

arson The willful or malicious burning of a house, public building, motor vehicle, aircraft, or other property of another. (p. 163)

automobile theft The unlawful taking of, or attempting to take, an automobile (p. 156)

B

battering Slapping, shoving, pushing, and other violent acts that result in injury to the victim; typically occurs for years. (p. 126)

biochemical imbalances The alleged influence of glucose and cholesterol levels, carbohydrate intake, premenstrual syndrome, and testosterone on criminal behavior. (p. 511)

bookmaking Organized illegal betting on horse racing and other sporting events. (p. 265)

born criminality Cesare Lombroso's theory that physical attributes are associated with, or even cause, criminal behavior. (p. 348)

burglary The unlawful entry into a house, business, or other structure, with the intent to commit a felony. (p. 150)

C

carjacking The use of direct physical force to steal a motor vehicle from a driver. (p. 158)

check fraud Deliberate deception for personal gain by the use of a counterfeit or forged check. (p. 167)

Chicago school of criminology Part of the post-Progressive Era social science movement that evolved at the University of Chicago between 1915 and the early 1940s. (p. 401)

child abuse Those intentional acts of a parent or guardian that result, or are likely to result, in physical, mental, or emotional injury or impairment of a child. (p. 132).

child neglect Injury or impairment resulting from a parent or guardian's inattention to a child's basic needs for health, nutrition, shelter, education, supervision, affection, and protection. (p. 132)

civil disobedience A nonviolent action against the state or a refusal to obey certain laws considered unjust. (p. 290)

class (or social class) A group of people who share the same position in the same production system. (p. 60)

classical criminology Part of the humanist reaction during the Enlightenment to the barbarities and inequities characteristic of feudal systems of justice. It was popularized by classical theorists Cesare Beccaria and Jeremy Bentham. (p. 332)

collective embezzlement Siphoning funds from a savings and loan institution for personal gain, at the expense of the institution and with the implicit or explicit sanction of its management. (p. 224)

communism   A theory advocating the elimination of private property. It's proponents tentatively believed that with the abolition of private property and with the disappearance of the class nature of the state, crime would almost disappear under communism. (p. 389)

complaintless crimes   Public-order crimes in which those directly involved do not feel harmed or victimized and so do not report the behavior to police. (p. 179)

concept   An idea that describes a property of an empirical datum or a relation among empirical data. It is usually a smaller part of a theory that is used to generate hypotheses. (p. 37)

conduct norm   A rule of behavior that embodies the values of some powerful group in society. (p. 16)

constitutive criminology   Partly an offshoot of peacemaking criminology and postmodernism, it is a political tendency that seeks to lay bare the rhetoric, the dogma, and the mystification that goes into public discourse about crime. (p. 534)

containment   A theory suggesting that variation in the crime rates of different social groups is caused by variations in the ability to contain norm-violating behavior in the face of social change and cultural conflict. (p. 458)

control   A theory arguing that to find the factors leading to delinquency one must look for the causes of conformity; that delinquency turns out to be merely an absence of the causes of conformity. (p. 460)

corporate crimes   Illegal or socially injurious acts of intent or indifference that are committed to further corporate goals, and that physically and/or economically harm individuals in the U.S. and/or abroad. (p. 217)

corporate theft   Differs from other forms of theft in that it does not entail face-to-face confrontation and it is not always easily apparent that a theft has occurred. (p. 237)

corporate violence   Acts of violence committed by corporations against workers, consumers, or the public. (p. 230)

corrupt campaign practices   Various forms of illegal or unethical behaviors used to obtain political office, ultimately for the purpose of influencing state policy. (p. 294)

credit card fraud   The use of stolen credit cards to purchase goods. (p. 169)

crime   In criminal law, crime is an action or omission prohibited by law that is voluntary and that coincides with a defendant's mental state. This book uses an eclectic and more sociological approach to crime, however, which sees it as a dynamic outcome of litigation between the state and the social relations embedded in gender, race, age, and class. Crime can be seen as a violation of conduct nroms, as social harm or analogous social injury, as a violation of human rights, and as a form of deviance. (p. 11–22)

crime rate   The prevalence of crime relative to the population. (p. 36)

criminal corporations   Corporations deliberately set up, managed, or taken over for the exclusive purpose of conducting criminal activity. (p. 217)

criminal justice system   Elaborate system used to deal with those who violate criminal laws. (p. 11)

criminal law   Rules enacted by legislatures or from judicial decisions that protect members of the public from state definitions of wrongdoing. (p. 11)

criminal syndicate   An association, which can include business people, police, politicians, and criminals, formed to conduct specific illegal enterprises for profit. (p. 262)

criminalization   The process whereby criminal law is selectively applied to social behavior. It involves the enactment of legislation that outlaws certain types of behavior and provides for surveillance and policing of that behavior and, if detected, punishment. (p. 24, 497)

D

dangerous classes   A derogatory 19th-century term applied by law-abiding citizens to describe those members of the working classes, the unemployed, and the unemployable who seemed to pose a threat to law and order. (p. 342)

deceptive advertising   Occurs when advertisements are misleading in a material respect; advertisers can make false statements so long as they are not deceptive. (p. 237)

decriminalization   The removal of criminal prohibitions for certain behaviors while still regulating them. (p. 191)

deviance   Any social behavior or social characteristic that departs from the conventional norms and standards of a community or society and for which the deviant is sanctioned. (p. 20)

differential association   A theory that attempts to explain both the process by which a person learns to engage in crime and also the content of what is learned. (pp. 423, 424)

drift   The lack of commitment to either the subculture of delinquency or conventional culture. (p. 453)

E

election fraud   A form of state corruption that includes illegal voting, false voter registration, and stuffing ballot boxes. (p. 294)

embezzlement   The taking of money from the workplace for one's personal use. (p. 222)

employee theft   Stealing merchandise or job-related items from the workplace. (p. 219)

Enlightenment   Philosophical and humanistic movement of the 18th century professing that reason and experience, rather than faith and superstition, must replace the excesses and corruption of feudal societies. It opposed cruel and inhumane punishments and disagreed with the prevailing views of the time of the relation between crime and punishment. (p. 330)

epistemological relativism   Involves the extraordinary claim that one can understand another culture only through the prism of one's own culturally determined system of values. (p. 574)

ethnocentrism   The view that criminological concepts and generalizations about a particular society necessarily apply to crime everywhere. (p. 564)

F

fencing   Buying, selling, or dealing in stolen goods. (p. 158)

financial fraud   A form of fraud that serves the interests of the corporation. (p. 238)

G

gender   Historically and culturally developed patterns of behavior by, and relationships between, males and females. (p. 71)

genes   Have been linked to crime in studies of the XYY chromosome, of twins, and of adoptees. (p. 504)

H

hate crimes   Violence perpetrated on persons because of their race, ethnicity, or sexual orientation. (p. 112)

human rights   Natural and inalienable rights accorded to all human beings, such as the right to life, liberty, and happiness. They also may include rights essential to a dignified human existence, such as freedom of movement, free speech, a good education, employment, and so on. (p. 18)

I

ideology   Any set of structured beliefs, values, and ideas that can both reflect social reality and simultaneously distort it. (p. 384)

imitation   Gabriel Tarde reasoned that crime was influenced by the processes of imitation, and that thereby people are socialized into criminality. (p. 367)

incestuous assault   Sexual contact that an adult family member imposes on a child who is unable to alter or understand the adult's behavior, often because of his/her powerlessness in the family and because of his/her early stage of psychological development. (p. 133)

insider trading   Occurs when information unavailable to the public is used to gain an advantage over others in the buying and selling of stock. (p. 229)

IQ (intelligence quotient)   A cultural measure of the abilities of children in reading, comprehension, general knowledge, analytic and mathematical reasoning, and vocabulary. (p. 513)

international law   Various treaties, agreements, customary law principles, and general legal principles that serve to judge the actions and behavior of nation states assenting to them. (p. 304)

interpersonal coercion   Occurs when a woman has sex with her husband or employer in the face of nonviolent threats. (p. 117)

L

labeling   A perspective suggesting that crime and deviance exist in the eye of the beholder. (pp. 477, 481)

labor racketeering   The infiltration, domination, and use of a union for personal benefit by illegal, violent, and fraudulent means. (p. 275)

larceny   The unlawful taking of property from the possession of someone other than one's employer. (p. 152)

left idealism   A type of critical criminology that focuses almost exclusively on the harms of the ruling class, and that ignores the development of a coherent program for curbing conventional crime. (p. 530)

left realism   The view that conventional crime is driven by relative deprivation and by reactionary, selfish, and individualistic attitudes. (p. 531)

legalization   Complete removal of all criminal sanctions for certain behaviors without subsequent regulation. (p. 191)

liberal feminism   Views women's subordinate status in society as stemming from socialization processes and unequal opportunities and rights for women. (p. 550–551)

loan sharking   Financial loans at extremely high interest rates with rapid repayment required and violence as a potential sanction for nonpayment. (p. 270)

lottery   A game in which chances to share in the distribution of prizes are determined by lot or drawing. (p. 182)

M

mafia   A method or system of patron-client relationships; in Sicily it was a system dependent upon patronage and the ability of a "man of respect" to utilize violence when necessary. (p. 251)

manslaughter   The killing of another person through gross negligence or without specific intent. (p. 106)

Marxist feminism   Theorizes that class and gender divisions of labor together determine the social position of women and men in any society, but the gender division of labor derives from the class division of labor. (p. 552–553)

methodological relativism   A strategy that operates as a sensitizing device to variation in the definition and meaning of crime in other cultures. It serves as a warning to potential comparativists regarding certain methodological difficulties peculiar to comparative analysis. (p. 575)

methodology   Techniques of measurement used to collect and manipulate empirical data. (p. 37)

middle-class measuring rod   Prevailing middle-class standards by which, in A. K. Cohen's theory of the origin of delinquent gangs, all children are evaluated. (p. 440)

mode of production   A Marxist concept denoting the means of production and the social relations of production. (p. 382)

modernization thesis   The view that technological development produces common effects that tend to make all societies increasingly similar, irrespective of different or even antagonistic political systems. (p. 582)

money laundering   The process by which one conceals the existence, illegal source, or illegal application of income, and then disguises that income to make it appear legitimate. (p. 273)

motor vehicle theft   Is the unlawful taking or attempting to take a motor vehicle such as an automobile, van, truck or motorcycle. (p. 156)

murder   The willful killing of one human being by another, usually with premeditation. (p. 106)

N

neoclassical criminology   Doctrinal and procedural compromise between classicism and positivism, devised roughly between 1880 and 1920, that has become the basis of criminal responsibility and punishment in most Western societies. (pp. 357, 358)

numbers   An illegal form of lottery in which the customer (or bettor) places a bet by choosing three numbers between 000 and 999. (p. 264)

O

occupational crime   Crimes committed by individuals in the course of their occupations for direct personal gain. (p. 217)

occupational fraud   A deliberate workplace deception practiced for personal financial gain. (p. 218)

occupational theft   Stems from an abuse of trust between employee and employer and includes employee theft and embezzlement. (p. 218)

official crime data   Data collected by the government and its official agencies. (p. 32)

P

pari-mutuel betting   Gambling on horse races and greyhound races at a track or at off-track locations. (p. 184)

patriarchy   Male control of the labor power and sexuality of women. (p. 548)

physician fraud   A type of occupational fraud that involves writing pharmaceutical prescriptions, performing unnecessary surgical procedures, or over-treating Medicaid and Medicare patients. (p. 225)

political bribery   The acceptance of money or property to state officials in return for favors. (p. 292)

political crime   Includes crimes against the state (violations of law for the purpose of modifying or changing social conditions) and crimes by the state, both domestic (violations of law and unethical acts by state officials and agencies whose victimization occurs inside the United States) and international (violations of domestic and international law by state officials or agencies whose victimization occurs outside the United States). (p. 286)

political economy of crime   An attempt to apply Marxist theory to an understanding of crime, whereby it is argued that the ruling class defines certain acts as criminal when it is in its best interest to do so. (p. 522)

political kickbacks   The illegal or unethical use of state authority for personal or political gain. (p. 294)

positivism   The belief that crime can be observed directly by using the procedures and explanatory logic of the natural sciences. (p. 30)

positivist criminology   The second great theoretical movement in modern criminology, its method of analysis is based on the collection of observable scientific facts, and its aim is to uncover, to explain, and to predict the ways in which observable facts occur in uniform patterns. (p. 340)

price-fixing   Violates antitrust laws through collusion to ensure profits above those that would be produced in a competitive industry. (p. 239)

primary deviance   An original act of crime or deviance that may derive from a wide variety of social, cultural, psychological, and physiological events. (p. 480)

professional property crime   The activities of offenders who carefully plan and execute their crimes, who use sophisticated techniques and skills, who are committed to crime as a life-style, and who tend to specialize in one form of property crime. (p. 144)

property crime   The unlawful damage to, or taking of, the property of another, regardless of whether the threat or actual use of physical violence occurs. (p. 97, 144)

prostitution   The consensual grant of nonmonogamous sexual services to clients for payment. (p. 201)

R

racial inequality   The assumption that genetic differences in skin color acquire social significance when used to justify unequal treatment of one race by another; one race (white) uses skin color to legitimate domination and control of other races. (p. 81)

radical feminism   Sees masculine power and privilege as the root of all social relations in any society; all other relations (such as class) are secondary and derive from gender relations. (p. 554)

rape   As traditionally defined in the criminal law, the carnal knowledge of a female forcibly and against her will, though an expanded definition is used in this book. (p. 115)

reaction formation   A process of adjustment in which the academic success typically denied working-class boys is contemptuously redefined as "sissy" and street knowledge is regarded as superior. (p. 441)

repressive and restitutive law   Two forms of legal sanctions that correspond in Durkheim's work to the two forms of social solidarity: repressive sanctions and restitutive sanctions. (p. 372)

robbery   The unlawful taking, or attempting to take, something of value from another person or persons by using violence or the threat of violence. (p. 144)

S

secondary deviance   Society's reaction to some of those who engage in primary deviance, often causing them to accept their identity as a deviant. (p. 480)

sexual harassment   Occurs when the submission to or rejection of sexual advances affects one's employment, or when it affects an individual's work performance by creating an environment that is intimidating, hostile and offensive. (p. 135)

shoplifting   A type of larceny that entails the theft of property from a retail store by "customers." (p. 153)

social classes   Largely occupational groupings whose life chances and consciousness are determined chiefly by their economic position within a given mode of production. (p. 383)

social coercion   Occurs when women feel they should have sex with their husbands even if they do not want to because of social pressures—their wifely "duty." (p. 117)

social control   Occurring in both public and private realms, this control has ideological and repressive forms, including primary socialization within the family and secondary socialization within peer groups, the educational system, and the media. (p. 556)

social disorganization   A lack of fit between culturally prescribed aspirations and socially structured avenues for achieving them. (p. 417)

social ecology   A type of research that examines different geographical areas of cities, communities, and neighborhoods and the area concentrations, regularities, and patterns of social life in such fields as work/leisure, health/sickness, and conformity/deviance. (p. 401)

social inequality   The fact that critical aspects of life—such as economic benefits, life chances, social privileges and political power—are unequally distributed in U.S. society. (p. 63)

social mechanics   A 19th-century discourse based on the belief that the same law-like regularity existing in the heavens and the world of nature also exists in society. (p. 344)

social position   One's individual location in society based on such social characteristics as class, gender, race, and age. (p. 59)

social problem   A social condition that is perceived as having some harmful effects; opinions about whether a condition is a social problem vary among groups and depend upon how and by whom the condition is defined and perceived in society. (p. 5)

social solidarity   Social order that is abstract and internal to consciousness and that is observable via other more visible aspects of social life. (p. 371)

socialist feminism   Argues that the relationship of class and gender structures crime in society. (p. 555)

societal reaction   Part of the process of deviance by which society labels primary deviants, thus giving them an identity that leads them to act in expected ways, causing secondary deviance. (p. 480)

sociological problem   A sociological explanation of how patterns of crime arise from the interplay of political, economic, social, and ideological structures in society. (p. 21)

statistics   A set of techniques for the reduction of quantitative data to a limited number of more convenient and easily communicated descriptive terms. (p. 30)

status frustration   Lack of status in middle-class life, which causes negative feelings and the search for status in delinquent subcultures. (p. 441)

stigma   A sign of disgrace imposed on an individual. (p. 485)

subculture   Applied by Cohen to the study of delinquency, it is a set of beliefs, values, codes, tastes, and prejudices that differ in some way from the main or dominant culture. (p. 439)

systematic comparative criminology   The systematic comparison of crime in two or more cultures using the same set of criteria. (p. 566)

T

tax fraud   Defrauding the government by cheating on one's income tax return. (p. 171)

techniques of neutralization   The process by which potential delinquents are freed from conventional social and moral controls and because of which they are then able to engage in delinquency. (p. 453)

the state   The central political institution of a given society, whose major apparatuses are the government, the legal system, the military, and a variety of public bureaucracies. (p. 23)

theories   Sets of assumptions, mediated by concepts, that guide the interpretation of data and that try to explain both regularities and irregularities in data. (p. 55)

U

unofficial crime data   Nongovernmental data usually collected by private or independent agencies and researchers. (p. 48)

utilitarianism   The doctrine of free will that held that all men rationally and freely chose to engage in the social contract, and that those who challenged this contract, broke its rules, or pursued harmful pleasures or wickedness were liable to be punished. (p. 332)

V

victim precipitation   Cited as a defense to a crime when the victim is said to be a direct, positive precipitator in the crime. (p. 111)

victimization surveys   Surveys of representative samples of a general population in an attempt to discern what crimes have been experienced in a given period. (p. 44)

victimless crimes   Created when we attempt to ban the exchange between willing partners of strongly desired goods and services through criminal legislation. (p. 179)

W

wife rape   Differs from rape in that women are raped only by a husband or ex-husband. (p. 124)

white-collar crime   Term coined by Sutherland to describe a crime committed by a person of respectability and high social status in the course of his occupation. It typically takes an economic form and is stimulated by economic cycles. (pp. 429–431)

TEXT CREDITS

Chapter 10

From *Discipline and Punish: The Birth of the Prison*, by Michel Foucault, translated by Alan Sheridan. Copyright © 1977 by Alan Sheridan. Reprinted by permission of Pantheon Books, a division of Random House, Inc.

Reprinted with permission of Macmillan Publishing Company from *Of Crimes and Punishments* by Cesare Beccaria. Copyright © 1985 by Macmillan Publishing Company; copyright © 1963.

Chapter 11

Reprinted with permission of The Free Press, a division of Macmillan, Inc., from Emile Durkheim, *The Division of Labor in Society*, translated by W. D. Halls. Translation, copyright © 1984 by Higher and Further Education Division Macmillan Publishers Ltd. Copyright © 1984 by The Free Press.

Reprinted with permission of International Publishers Co., Inc., New York, from "The Condition of the Working Class in England," *Collected Works*, Vol. 4 by Karl Marx/Friedrich Engels.

Chapter 12

Shaw & McKay, *Juvenile Delinquency and Urban Areas (1942)*, © 1942, 1969 by the University of Chicago. All rights reserved.

Chapter 13

From *Visions of Social Control* by Stanley Cohen, Cambridge: Polity Press, 1985. Reprinted by permission of the publisher.

PHOTO CREDITS

Part One Opener

Paul Conklin/Monkmeyer.

Chapter 1

Page **4**, copyright R. Shefke; page **6**, Claudio Edinger/Gamma Liaison; page **10**, Stock Montage; page **19**, Chris Schwarz/Tony Stone Images.

Chapter 3

Page **65**, Larry Lambert/Picture Group; page **67**, Dan Ogust/The Image Works; page **75**, Spencer Grant/ Monkmeyer; page **83**, Rick Smolan/Stock Boston; page **88**, copyright Bill Stanton/International Stock Photo; page **96**, Mimi Cotter/International Stock Photo.

Part Two Opener

Mimi Forsyth/Monkmeyer.

Chapter 4

Page **108**, UPI/Bettmann Newsphotos; page **110**, Reuters/Bettmann; page **114**, Leonard Freed/Magnum; page **123**, Rhoda Sidney/Monkmeyer; page **128**, Roy Morsch/The Stock Market; page **132**, copyright 1989 Grant Le Duc/Monkmeyer; page **137**, Wide World Photos.

Chapter 5

Page **154**, Kagan/Monkmeyer; page **159**, Christopher Volker/Gamma Liaison; page **165**, Laima Druskis/ Stock Boston.

Chapter 6

Page **183**, copyright Scott Thode/International Stock Photo; page **189**, Tom Grill/Comstock; page **194**, UPI/Bettmann Newsphotos; page **207**, Wide World Photos.

Chapter 7

Page **227**, Scott Thode/International Stock Photo; page **235**, Spencer Grant/Monkmeyer; page **244**, copyright Ragher Rai/Magnum.

Chapter 8

Page **254**, Bettmann Archive; page **267**, Eugene Richards/Magnum; page **271**, Ryan Williams/International Stock Photo.

Chapter 9

Page **287**, Bettmann Archive; page **299**, Bettmann Archive; page **301**, UPI/Bettmann; page **322** (top three), UPI/Bettmann Newsphotos; photo **322** (bottom), Wide World Photos.

Part Three Opener

The Bettmann Archive.

Chapter 10

Page **331**, Culver Pictures; page **33**, Bettmann Archive; page **349**, Bettmann Archive.

Chapter 11

Page **366**, G. Sirot/P. Ziolo; page **370**, Presses Universitaires de France; page **381**, Brown Brothers; page **388**, Harcourt Brace Collection.

Chapter 12

Page **400**, Granger Collection.

Chapter 13

Page **442**, Steve Starr/Stock Boston.

Chapter 14

Page **488**, David Hitch/Courtesy Worcester Telegram Gazette; page **492**, Bettmann; page **512**, Harcourt Brace Collection.

Chapter 15

Page **542**, John Storey/Wide World Photos; page **558**, Peter Tenzer Studio/International Stock Photo.

Chapter 16

Page **584**, The Tate Gallery London.

FIGURE AND TABLE CREDITS

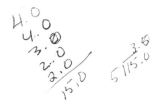

Chapter 1

Figure 1–1: U.S. Government Printing Office; **Table 1–1:** From *The Behavior of Law* by Donald Black. Published by Academic Press, Inc.

Chapter 2

Figures 2–4 through 2–6: U.S. Government Printing Office; **Figure 2–7:** From "Reconciling Race and Class Differences in Self-Reported and Official Estimates of Delinquency" by Delbert Elliott and Susan Ageton. *American Sociological Review*, Vol. 45, 1980, Appendix A, pp. 108–09. Reprinted by permission of the American Sociological Association.

Chapter 3

Tables 3–1 through 3–8: U.S. Government Printing Office.

Chapter 4

Table 4–1: Diana E. H. Russell, *Sexual Exploitation: Rape, Child Sexual Abuse, and Workplace Harassment* (Sage Publications, Beverly Hills, 1984), p. 61. Reprinted by permission of Sage Publications, Inc.; **Table 4–2:** U.S. Government Printing Office.

Chapter 5

Table 5–1 and Figure 5–1: U.S. Government Printing Office.

Chapter 6

Table 6–1: From *Gambling Without Guilt*, by J. Rosecrance, pp. 4–5. Copyright © 1988 by Wadsworth, Inc. Reprinted by permission of the publisher, Brooks/Cole Publishing Company, Pacific Grove, California, a division of Wadsworth, Inc.; **Table 6–2:** General Accounting Office, 1988:5; **Figure 6–1:** From "Thinking Sex: Notes for a Radical Theory of the Politics of Sexuality" by Gayle Rubin in *Pleasure and Danger: Exploring Female Sexuality*, ed. Carol S. Vance, 267–319. Boston: Routledge & Kegan Paul.

Chapter 8

Figure 8–1: From *On the Take: From Petty Crooks to Presidents* by William J. Chambliss, 1988. Bloomington, IN: Indiana University Press; **Figures 8–2 through 8–4:** General Accounting Office.

Chapter 9

Figure 9–1: From *Blood of the Land* by Rex Wayler, 1982. New York: Everest House; **Figure 9–2:** From *The Politics of Heroin in Southeast Asia* by Alfred McCoy. New York: Harper & Row; **Figure 9–3:** From "Inside the Kingdom of Heroin" by Lawrence Lifschultz in *The Nation* (Nov. 14):477, 492–96; **Figures 9–4 and 9–5:** General Accounting Office, 1988.

Chapter 10

Table 10–2: From *Research on the Propensity for Crime at Different Ages* by Adolphe Quetelet, 1984, Anderson Publishing Co. Reprinted with permission of the publisher.

Chapter 12

Figures 12–1 through 12–3: From *Juvenile Delinquency and Urban Areas* by Clifford R. Shaw. Chicago: University of Chicago Press. **Table 12–1:** From "Social Structure and Anomie" by Robert Merton in *Delinquency, Crime, and Social Process*, ed. Donald R. Cressey and David A. Ward, 1938, 1969, 254–84. New York: Harper & Row.

Chapter 13

Table 13–1: From *Delinquency and Opportunity: A Theory of Delinquent Gangs*, by Richard A. Cloward and Lloyd E. Ohlin, 1960. New York: Free Press.

Chapter 14

Figure 14–1: From "The Role of Police as Amplifiers of Deviancy, Negotiators of Reality and Translators of Fantasy." In *Images of Deviance*, ed. Stanley Cohen, 27–61. Harmondsworth: Penguin. **Figure 14–2:** From *Politics and Society in the USSR* by David Lane. London: Weidenfeld and Nicholson; **Figure 14–3:** Richard Quinney.

Chapter 15

Table 15–1: From "A Review of Studies of Criminality Among Twins" by Karl O. Christiansen. In *Biosocial Bases of Criminal Behavior*, 1977, ed. Sarnoff A. Mednick and Karl O. Christiansen. Reprinted by permission of Gardner Press, Inc.; **Table 15–2 and Figure 15–1:** From "Genetic Factors in the Etiology of Criminal Behavior" by Sarnoff A. Mednick, William F. Gabrielli Jr., and Barry Hutchings. In *The Causes of Crime: New Biological Approaches*, 1987, ed. Sarnoff A. Mednick, Terrie Moffitt, and Susan A. Stack, pp. 74–91. Cambridge: Cambridge University Press. Reprinted by permission of the publisher; **Figure 15–3:** Richard Quinney; **Figure 15–4:** From *Order, Law and Crime* by Raymond J. Michalowski, 1985, p. 22. New York: Random House; **Figure 15–5:** From *On the Take: From Petty Crooks to Presidents* by William J. Chambliss, 1988. Bloomington, IN: Indiana University Press.

Chapter 16

Tables 16–1 through 16–3: From "A Comparative Study of Deviations from Sexual Mores" by Julia S. Brown, 1952. *American Sociological Review*, 17(2): pp. 135–46; **Table 16–4:** From *Violence and Crime in Cross-National Perspective* by Dane Archer and Rosemary Gertner. Copyright 1984 by Yale University Press. Reprinted by permission of the publisher; **Figure 16–1:** U.S. Department of Justice.

SUBJECT INDEX

See Author Index for names of persons who are authors. Persons who are not authors are included in this index. Geographical areas are included only when they are discussed in a substantive manner.

Author Index

See Subject Index for names of persons who are not authors.